Footprint

The travel guide

Bali

Handbook with Lombok and the Eastern Isles

Liz Capaldi, Joshua Eliot,
Jane Bickersteth and Jasmine Saville

*As I said this morning to Charlie
There is far too much music in Bali,
And although as a place it's entrancing,
There is also a thought too much dancing.
It appears that each Balinese native,
From the womb to the tomb is creative,
And although the results are quite clever,
There is too much artistic endeavour.*

A poem to Charlie Chaplin by Noel Coward

Bali Handbook
First edition
© Footprint Handbooks Ltd 2000

Published by Footprint Handbooks
6 Riverside Court
Lower Bristol Road
Bath BA2 3DZ. England
T +44 (0)1225 469141
F +44 (0)1225 469461
Email discover@footprintbooks.com
Web www.footprintbooks.com

ISBN 1 900949 73 3
CIP DATA: A catalogue record for this
book is available from the British Library.

In USA, published by
NTC/Contemporary Publishing Group
4255 West Touhy Avenue, Lincolnwood
(Chicago), Illinois 60712-1975, USA
T 847 679 5500 F 847 679 24941
Email NTCPUB2@AOL.COM

ISBN 0-658-01454-4
Library of Congress Catalog Card
Number: 00-132907

Credits

Series editors
Patrick Dawson and Rachel Fielding

Editorial
Editor: Sarah Thorowgood
Maps: Sarah Sorensen

Production
Typesetting: Emma Bryers, Leona Bailey
Maps: Kevin Feeney (colour),
Robert Lunn, Claire Benison, Alasdair
Dawson, Angus Dawson
Front cover: Camilla Ford

Design
Mytton Williams

Photography
Front cover: Art Directors and Trip.
Back cover: Impact Photos.
Inside colour section: Impact Photos,
Art Directors and Trip, Pictures Colour
Library, Eye Ubiquitous, Robert Harding.

Print
Manufactured in Italy by LEGOPRINT

Bali & the Eastern Isles

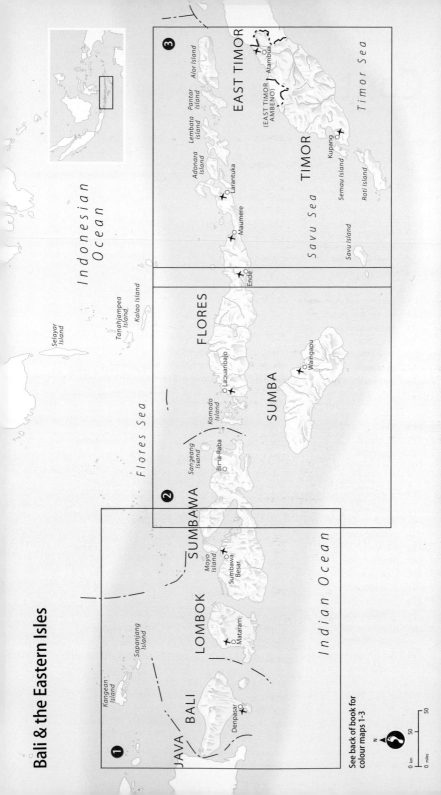

See back of book for colour maps 1–3

Contents

1

3 A foot in the door

2

11 Essentials
13 Planning your trip
19 Before you travel
24 Getting there
25 Touching down
31 Where to stay
34 Getting around
42 Keeping in touch
43 Food and drink
48 Shopping
50 Holidays and festivals
52 Health
60 Further reading

3

69 Bali
72 Denpasar
78 South Bali
109 Nusa Penida and
     Nusa Lembongan
113 The Bukit Peninsula
     and Nusa Dua
128 North and east from
     Denpasar
130 Ubud
147 North of Ubud
149 Gianyar to Mount Batur
     via Bangli
158 Pura Besakih and
     Mount Agung
161 East Bali and Regency of
     Kerangasem
189 North from Denpasar to
     Lake Bratan

195 North Coast,
     Buleleng Regency
198 Singaraja
201 West of Singaraja
217 The West
224 Background
224 History
228 Land and environment
231 Art and architecture
235 Culture
249 Modern Bali

4

255 West Nusa Tenggara:
     Lombok and
     Sumbawa
258 Lombok
258 Ins and outs
263 Ampenan – Mataram –
     Cakranegara
270 Lombok's west coast
276 The Gilis
286 Northwest coast and
     Mount Rinjani
289 Central Lombok and
     the West
293 East Lombok
294 South Lombok and the
     south coast
300 Background
305 Sumbawa
306 Alas
307 Taliwang
307 Maluk
308 Sumbawa Besar
311 Moyo Island
312 Mount Tambora
313 Sumbawa Besar to
     Bima-Raba
313 Dompu
314 Hu'u
314 Bima-Raba
318 Sape

5

319 East Nusa Tenggara
322 Ins and outs
324 Komodo
329 Flores
332 Labuanbajo to Ende
347 Ende to Larantuka
358 Lembata
361 Alor
365 Sumba
383 West Timor
395 Roti (Rote)
398 Savu (Sabu)

6

399 Background
402 History
410 Modern Indonesia

7

427 Footnotes
429 Indonesian words
     and phrases
432 Glossary
435 Index
438 Shorts
439 Maps

Inside front cover
Hotels and restaurant
           price guide
Dialling codes
Useful websites

Inside back cover
Map symbols
Weights and measures

Right: two of Mount Kelimutu's three multi-coloured crater lakes on the island of Flores. In local folklore they are the resting places for souls called by Mutu. Today they entice scores of visitors to climb to 1,640 metres and watch the sun rise.

A foot in the door

4

Right: the Kecak or Monkey Dance, one of Bali's more popular dance dramas where a central figure is coaxed into a trance and communicates with the gods or the ancestors. *Below*: the interior highland village of Ubud is a popular place to stay away from the bustle of Bali's coast. Here a festival enlivens a temple in the Monkey Forest.

Above: Komodo Island and its eponymous dragons are one of the highlights of a journey through the Eastern Isles. Very occasionally the dragons show a taste for the odd human. *Right*: the Gilis off the coast of Lombok are a popular retreat for weary backpackers. Here cheap accommodation and an idyllic setting cause many to stay for days more than they originally planned.

Highlights

Bali can be as tourist-ridden or as unspoilt as you desire. Some of the most luxurious **Bali** and elegant hotels in the world, where guests may spend an average Indonesian's yearly income over a weekend are balanced by small inexpensive guest houses perched on the beach or tucked away and surrounded by nature in the jungle. The fact is that since Bali's first, early years as a tourist destination at the beginning of the 20th century, visitors have been entranced by this incomparably beautiful island with its spectacular, mountainous interior, its crafted landscapes of rice fields and villages, and its vibrant culture.

On the Island of the Gods, appropriately, the sacred is to be found in every village. Temples, festivals, dance and music mark the passage of time, and the life-stages of every woman and man. Each village has its gamelan orchestra and dance troupe and interested visitors are welcome. Bali also has spectacularly situated temples such as Besakih, the mother temple, on the slopes of the sacred volcano Gunung Agung.

The main beach resorts on Bali are in the south: crowded Kuta, popular with Australians and young surfers; upmarket Nusa Dua where you are sure to be pampered; Jimbaran with the best location; and Sanur. Newer, smaller, perhaps more attractive resorts include Amed and Tulamben on the east coast, and Pemuteran on the northwest coast, all of which have good diving and snorkelling, and the sparsely developed beach area stretching north from Seminyak to Canggu.

After the rigours of the beach, hire a car to explore the back roads, and stop to wander around small, pretty, flower-filled villages away from the main tourist centres. There are panoramic drives and spectacular hikes in the central volcanic mountain chain. The Bali Barat National Park, at the western end of the island, with its natural vegetation of savannah, rainforest and coastal mangrove swamps, supports over 150 bird species and other wildlife.

Lombok is like Bali – but different. It is physically dominated by Gunung Rinjani, one **The Eastern** of Indonesia's highest and most beautiful mountains. It also has its beaches: **Isles: from west** well-developed Senggigi which becomes more attractive and less-developed the **to east** further north you go; Kuta in the south surrounded by miles of deserted beaches; and the Gili Islands, a haven for those with sore muscles and aching minds. Lombok is also less developed and less visited than Bali, an attraction in itself.

People tend to bus through **Sumbawa** scarcely taking the time to knock the dust from their shoes. Pulau Moyo Nature Reserve, off the north west coast, has beautiful coral reefs, turtles and other wild animals while Bima, at the eastern end of the island, is the capital of a sultanate fallen on hard times. The reason why people tend to skip Sumbawa is their hurry to get to **Komodo** – home of the famous Komodo dragon.

Flores is a popular island on the overland backpackers' trail to Australia. Kelimutu is the great attraction, a volcano which visitors climb in darkness so they can be at the summit at day break, to watch the sunrise illuminate the extinct volcano's three crater lakes of differing colours. Maumere is an established dive centre while Larantuka, at the far eastern end of the island, still reflects its short period under Portuguese tutelage.

Sumba, the 'Island of Spirits', is a gem, and except at the time of its famous Pasola, a thrilling, ritual battle fought by men on horseback, there are few travellers and Sumba's indigenous culture remains very much intact. There are fascinating customs, ceremonies and artefacts including extraordinary funerals, unique architecture, stone megaliths and to top it all the island is ringed with deserted, sandy beaches and surfers' waves.

The adventurous traveller will no doubt want to hop among the small islands which make up the **Solor** and **Alor** archipelagos east of Flores, and **Roti** and **Sabu** which lie between Sumba and Timor. Today, these beautiful islands are still imbued with traditional culture: apparently head-hunting was still practised here in the 1950s.

The ring of fire

Bali, and the islands that stretch eastwards to Timor are, collectively, lands of stunning scenic beauty with their mist shrouded mountain peaks, shimmering green rice terraces, untouched tropical islands, sparkling blue seas and coral reefs, and smouldering volcanoes. For sheer geographical and zoological diversity, Bali and the Eastern Islands are hard to beat. The great Victorian naturalist Alfred Russel Wallace noted the remarkable natural changes that characterize this fragmented region when he travelled through the islands in the mid-19th century. These are paralleled by equally pronounced cultural transformations. It may have been said before, but here there is something for everyone.

Bali and Lombok offer some of the world's most sophisticated resorts where you can be pampered in a luxury spa, pursue sporting activities from the normal to the extreme, or indulge in fine dining. But for those in search of adventure, there are countless opportunities to venture far off the beaten track visiting remote traditional villages, or island hopping to unspoilt destinations. While you might find yourself the only foreigner in some remote place, it is relatively easy to travel around using local transport, which could be anything from a horse drawn carriage or traditional fishing boat to a modern minibus or a ferry.

Geological inheritance Bali and the islands of Nusa Tenggara lie on the boundary of two tectonic plates, part of the Pacific 'Ring of Fire'. The collision of these two plates has created a volcanic arc of islands running down from Sumatra through Java, Bali, Lombok, Sumbawa, and Flores through to Alor. The black beaches of Bali, the three-coloured crater lakes of Kelimutu, and the more than 400 volcanoes that mark Indonesia's Ring of Fire, are all part of this geological inheritance. For the Balinese, volcanoes are life-giving and life-taking. Perhaps the most devastating eruption in recent human history occurred here. Not the well-known obliteration of Krakatoa in 1883, but the far more devastating eruption of Tambora on the island of Sumbawa on 5th July 1815. The southern arc of islands in Nusa Tenggara, including Sumba, Savu, Roti and Timor, has no volcanoes.

Wallace's line The treacherous Lombok strait, the deepest strip of water in the archipelago and a passage-way for nuclear submarines, marks the divide between two zoogeographic worlds, the Asian and the Australasian. Even non-naturalists should feel a frisson of excitement as they cross Wallace's line and the lush vegetation of Bali, with its monkeys (and, formerly, tigers) gives way to a savannah landscape of parrots, cockatoos – and dragons.

On the lava-beaten track If strenuous activity is what makes a holiday for you, then there are volcanoes to climb, reefs to explore, rivers to raft and waves to catch. One of the more arduous and popular climbs is Gunung Rinjani, the hauntingly beautiful volcano that dominates the landscape of Lombok. At 3726 metres this is the second highest mountain in Indonesia and takes three to five days to climb. Many of the islands, notably Lombok, Bali, Sumba, Sumbawa, Roti and Savu provide excellent surfing, some of it world-class. Western owned and run diving operations ensure high safety standards for divers and water sports from snorkelling to dolphin watching are also possible. Bali offers white water rafting, there are guided nature walks and bird watching, and cycling tours are becoming increasingly popular whether short outings along country lanes or month-long tours through the islands. A final bonus is the Indonesian people; friendly and generous by nature, they will add delight to your travels particularly as you venture off the beaten track.

Left: Bali is one of the world's most beautiful islands. A large element of this beauty lies in the engineered landscapes of the uplands where centuries of human activity have reworked the slopes into a patchwork of terraced rice fields.
Below: Gunung Agung, Bali's sacred mountain, the giver and taker of life, rises to 3,140 metres.

Above: Senggigi is Lombok's premier beach resort. With a well-developed tourist infrastructure it attracts tourists who want something a little different from better-known Bali. **Left**: travel in the Eastern Isles may not always be rapid or restful, but it is usually relatively colourful.

Sacred ceremonies and sumptuous celebrations

This is also a land touched by magic, where deeply rooted, animist beliefs still influence daily life. Bali's countless sacred ceremonies, joyous colourful processions, elaborate wayside offerings, and the songs, dances and music that infuse day-to-day existence make this an island where religion is the breath of life. There are thousands of temples on Bali, some of them dramatically situated on rocky promontories overlooking the sea, or set high up on sacred mountains.

Nature, culture and economy

Bali and the Eastern Islands cover just a small slice of Indonesia, the world's greatest archipelagic nation. But even here nature, culture and economy have combined in unexpected ways. The bronze Moko drums of Alor, traditionally used as unlikely units of currency, have their parallels in the Dongson drums of northern Vietnam, thousands of miles to the north. Historically, Timor was renowned for its aromatic sandalwood groves that once made this barren island a target for Chinese traders and Portuguese adventurers. Whilst Sumba's *pasola* festival, where massed teams of horsemen engage in ritual combat, is timed to coincide with the arrival of a marine worm.

Cultural cradle

Hinduism arrived in Indonesia with Indian merchants long before the earliest known records of its existence in the region, perhaps as early as the 3rd century. By the 14th century Islam was in the ascendancy forcing the great Hindu Majapahit dynasty to flee Java for the sanctuary of Bali along with the intelligentsia, priests and leading exponents of the arts. This mass exodus of talent lay the foundations for Bali's extraordinarily vibrant artistic tradition. Daily performances of dance and gamelan music are a religious offering to the gods but also offer the visitor an insight into Balinese art and culture.

Christian traders and invaders

The cultural mix of Nusa Tenggara was enriched by successive waves of traders and invaders from the Javanese and the Chinese in the early centuries of the Christian era, to the Portuguese in the 16th century, followed within one century by the Dutch. The legacy of the Portuguese is reflected most clearly in eastern Flores and the islands of Solor and Alor, which support the largest Catholic populations in Indonesia. Larantuka, the main port for eastern Flores, puts on sumptuous celebrations and processions each Easter week. Dutch Protestant missionaries had limited success in Eastern Indonesia, neither being able to convert great numbers of Muslims or Catholics, nor even the animists of the islands.

Design originals

While the people of the islands of the East may have absorbed Islam, Hinduism and Christianity to varying extents, they have not snuffed out their traditional arts and cultures. In cloth, music and architecture traditional life is alive and well. The distinctive ikat cloths of Sumba, Savu, Rote, Alor and Timor are sought after by collectors and museums. The Sasaks of Lombok who, while they may be putative Muslims, have clung tenaciously to their traditional language, dress and customs. And the tall, thatched, conical ancestral houses of Sumba are without parallel in Indonesia.

Left: *a temple festival on Bali. There can be few – if any – islands of comparable size that have as many festivals as Bali does. With 20,000 temples, each staging a festival every 210 days (according to the local calendar), they are difficult to avoid.*

Essentials

2

12

Essentials

13	**Planning your trip**		**31**	**Where to stay**
13	Where to go		**34**	**Getting around**
16	When to go		**34**	Air
18	Finding out more		**35**	Train
18	Language		**35**	Bus
19	**Before you travel**		**37**	Bicycling
19	Entry requirements		**38**	Car hire and road transport
19	Vaccinations		**39**	Other local transport
22	Money		**42**	**Keeping in touch**
24	**Getting there**		**42**	Communications
24	Air		**42**	Media
25	Road		**43**	**Food and drink**
25	Boat		**48**	**Shopping**
25	**Touching down**		**50**	**Holidays and festivals**
25	Airport information		**52**	**Health**
25	Airport tax		**60**	**Further reading**
25	Tourist information		**65**	The Internet
27	Rules, customs and etiquette			
30	Safety			

Planning your trip

Where to go

Java may be Indonesia's political and economic heartland and Sumatra may be the country's largest island, but Bali is the honeypot that attracts more tourists than any other island in this massive, sprawling archipelago. There are more hotels, restaurants, guesthouses and tour companies on Bali alone than in all the other places covered in this book put together. However, for those with the time and the inclination to venture further east, along the ribbon of islands that dot the tropical seas from Bali to Timor, there are great enticements. Each island has its own physical and cultural character, from the three-colour lakes of Keli Mutu on Flores to the giant dragons of Komodo. Travel may not always be terribly comfortable or fast, but at least it is usually easy.

Compared with **roads** in the west, those in Indonesia are poor. Even in Bali, one of Indonesia's most developed and richest islands, roads are narrow, winding and slow. Over much of the rest of the eastern islands from Lombok east to Timor all-weather roads only link the more important centres. In the wet season even these may be periodically impassable due to flooding, subsidence and landslips. However due to the size (small) and shape (generally, long) of these islands, there are no great expanses of inaccessible land as there are, for instance, on Kalimantan and West Papua.

That, so to speak, is the bad news (or the good news, depending on one's viewpoint). The good news is that many of the horror stories of the past, when bus passengers were regularly stranded for days in towns that they would now wish to forget are, to a large extent, history.

A second factor to bear in mind is the challenge of travelling between the smaller islands of the Eastern Isles where there may be just one **ferry** a day between some islands, sometimes just one a week. **Flying**, though in theory a much faster alternative, has its own problems. It is often impossible to book flights between the more out of the way spots, and even a booked seat may magically disappear if a VIP (and there are an awful lot of VIPs in Indonesia) should suddenly decide to make the journey. So, make sure that you leave enough time to get back to Bali for your return flight and don't assume that you can hop on the first flight.

Bali Bali has slow but abundant year-round public transport. Because distances are comparatively short on Bali, the fact that the minivans often travel slowly doesn't really matter. Denpasar, Bali's capital, is serviced by more international airlines than any other city in the country other than Jakarta. Traffic jams, caused by slow moving trucks, are a persistent feature along the main arterial roads in the south of the island. If travelling to catch a flight make sure you allow plenty of time.

Lombok Transport on Lombok is comparatively good and roads are reasonable. There are daily ferry connections with Bali and also east with Sumbawa. There are also frequent air connections with Bali and rather less frequent flights to other destinations in the eastern islands.

East Nusa Tenggara As you travel east from Lombok road conditions tend to deteriorate, although the main highway rarely – except after torrential storms or an earthquake! – descends into impassability. Ferries link the main islands, usually daily, although smaller islands off the main east-west route may be served less frequently. There are air services to most islands but these are often over-booked, unbooked and multi-booked without apparently any consideration to the number of seats on the aircraft. There are international air connections between Kupang and Darwin.

Transport & travelling
NB Below is only a selection of places of interest & is not by any means exhaustive. It is designed to assist in planning a trip to these eastern islands of Indonesia

Essentials

Timetabling a visit	Some people come to Indonesia and hole up on Bali for the full extent of their stay. It really is an island packed full of things to do: from white-water rafting to meditation and dolphin watching. Because distances are short and communications good, many people from the region (Singapore, for example) come here for long weekends. However, for those who want to explore the islands to the east, a little more attention needs to be paid to timetabling a visit – and especially those who want to work their way through all the islands of Nusa Tenggara. Some may find that that even two months – the length of a visitor's visa – is not enough time to experience all the islands, except briefly. Remember when travelling through the islands that overland transport is slow, ferries don't travel every day, and flights are often full or intermittent. So err on the side of caution when working out how long it will take getting from A to B.
Wildlife, national parks & botanical gardens	**Bali** Visit the north coast for dolphin watching and the **Bali Barat National Park** in the west. Botanical gardens at **Bedugul**. **East Nusa Tenggara Komodo**: home of the magnificent dragon, which can also be seen on the neighbouring island of Rinca. These amazing creatures are best seen in the wild on a nature walk, rather than in the corral. There is good diving in the Komodo National Park area, good amenities, although accommodation in the PHPA huts is fairly basic. **Sumbawa**: Pulao Moyo Nature Reserve - this island is a protected habitat with abundant wildlife and beautiful offshore coral reefs, excellent for diving and snorkelling.
Hill stations	**Ubud** on Bali is the most sophisticated and foreigner-centric hill resort in Indonesia.
Trekking & natural features	**Bali** The volcanoes of **Mount Batur** and **Mount Agung**, upland **Lake Bratan**, and the iridescent terraced **paddy fields** of the south and east – all well trodden by countless tourists. **Lombok and Sumbawa** Climb **Mount Rinjani**, a three day climb, for its views (when clear), crater and crater lake, one of the most rewarding and spectacular climbs in the country; the areas round the villages of **Senaru** and **Batu Koq**, and **Tetebatu** are good for hiking. **Mount Tambora**, a volcano that changed the world's climate, on Sumbawa is less commonly climbed – and very hot! **East Nusa Tenggara** Climb **Mount Kelimutu** on Flores and see its three-coloured crater lakes.
Beaches & coastal idylls	**Bali** The island has a succession of beach resorts – frenetic **Kuta**, ersatz **Nusa Dua**, long-established **Sanur**, pleasant **Candi Dasa** and **Lovina Beach**, plus other smaller, quieter, newer places such as **Amed** and **Tulamben** on the east coast and **Pemuteran** on the northwest coast. **Lombok Senggigi** is the most developed beach area with plenty of nightlife. Going up the coast the beaches become increasingly deserted with one or two very elegant resorts including the Oberoi Resort north of Bangsal. The south coast beaches are less developed; **Kuta** has a spectacular setting and good accommodation. For an island getaway go to the **Gili Islands**; **Gili Trawangan** has gained a reputation as the party island, **Gili Meno** and **Gili Air** are quieter. **Sumbawa** has no beach resorts as such. Beach accommodation is available at the areas made popular by surfers, primarily at **Hu'u** (see surfing). **East Nusa Tenggara** There is a nascent beach resort developing round **Labuhan Bajo** on the west coast of Flores, with some accommodation on offshore islands, good diving and snorkelling, fantastic sunsets. Modest beaches and islands near **Kupang** in West Timor.
Diving	**Bali** Lots of dive outfits and some reasonable dive sites but better for beginners than for the cognoscenti.

Lombok Well-organized, reliable operators based at **Senggigi** and the **Gili Islands**.
Sumbawa Good snorkelling and diving off **Moyo** Island, Sumbawa.
East Nusa Tenggara Diving near **Maumere** in Flores, now much recovered from the earthquake of December 1992. Outstanding coral reefs off the island of Alor, one of the best dive sites in Indonesia. No dive companies currently operate on the island; arrange a trip in Kupang with Pitoby Watersports.

Bali The most popular surfing in Indonesia with some good breaks but a tendency to become over-crowded at peak times of year; rafting on the Ayung River. **Surfing & rafting**
Lombok Surfing is not as good as Bali but both **Gili Air** and **Desert Point** off Bangko Bangko can be excellent. The south coast is more reliable: **Kuta** and **Tanjung Aan**, or further west, **Selong Blanak** and **Blongas**; going east **Awang Bay** and **Gumbang Bay**.
Sumbawa Modest surfing at **Taliwang** and **Maluk** on Sumbawa, better at **Hu'u**, also on Sumbawa.

Bali Bali's most notable **temples** are Besakih, Uluwatu and Tanah Lot; other historical sites include the **caves** of Goa Gajah and ancient **stone carvings** of Yeh Pulu, the **burial chambers** of Gunung Kawi; murals in the **Kerta Ghosa**, Hall of Justice, in Klungkung and the **royal bathing pools** of Tirtagangga. **Bali Tenganan** is the village home of Bali's 'original' inhabitants. **Historical towns, temples & palaces**
Lombok and Sumbawa Though not comparable with similar places on Bali, the **Mayura Water Palace and Gardens** and **Pura Mayura** in Mataram-Cakranegara on Lombok are worthwhile and so too is the **Taman Narmada** and the **Waktu Telu Temple** and the **Sultan's Palace**, a wonderfully decrepit old wooden palace in Sumbawa Besar.
East Nusa Tenggara Sumba: this is one of the most interesting islands with well-preserved tribal villages, stunning traditional architecture, a fascinating cultural tradition largely untouched by the 20th century, megaliths, spectacular rituals, outstanding ikat woven fabrics, and miles of totally unspoilt and deserted golden sandy beaches. **Flores**: a beautiful island with many active volcanoes. There are interesting traditional cultures in the **Manggarai** district round **Ruteng**, and the **Ngada** villages near **Bajawa**. Visit **Larantuka** for its Catholic Easter festivities. **Sikka** on the south coast below Maumere, **Ngella** and the **Wolotopo** area east of Ende are all weaving centres.

Bali For the greatest concentration of things 'cultural' in Indonesia from dances to funeral ceremonies and traditional villages. **Lombok**: Traditional villages - the traditional Sasak villages of **Sade** and **Rembitan** are fairly touristy these days. **Culture**
East Nusa Tenggara Central and west Flores for its **traditional villages**; Larantuka in east Flores for its unique **Christian cultural tradition**; **whaling** in Lamalera. **Sumba** for its traditional villages (see above).

Bali The Museum **Bali** in Denpasar has one of the best – and best presented – provincial collections. **Neka Museum** in Ubud. **Subak Museum** in Tabanan, dedicated to traditional farming practices. **Museums**
East Nusa Tenggara The **Blikan Blewut** Museum outside Maumere; Kupang's good Museum of **East Nusa Tenggara**.

Bali Has an array of products including **paintings**, **jewellery**, **woodcarving**, **silver**, **musical instruments**, **batik** and **garments** often skilfully designed for Western tastes. **Shopping & handicrafts**
Lombok Crafts: the quality of many of the crafts produced is high, particularly the pottery in the villages of **Banyumulek**, **Penunjak** and **Penakak**; also look out for textiles.
East Nusa Tenggara Flores, Sumba, Timor, and the Alor and Solor archipelago, for their varied traditional textiles.

Essentials

When to go

The climate of Indonesia's eastern isles varies considerably from island to island. In general, the further east you travel the drier it becomes and the more marked and longer the dry season. Bali is a tropical island with comparatively high rainfall. The dry season here runs between May and October, and the wet season from November to April. However, rain falls throughout the year and the seasons are not nearly as marked on Bali as on the islands to the east. Travelling from Lombok, through Sumbawa, to Flores and Sumba and Timor, it quickly becomes apparent why the great Victorian naturalist Alfred Russel Wallace was so struck by the changes in vegetation and fauna he witnessed. The islands of the 'Far East' have a dry season which extends over half the year or more, from April to October. And here, unlike Bali, the dry season is truly dry. Because the vegetation is sparser, when the rains do come they can make travel tricky. But don't be put off: hotel prices are less during the wet season and it is rare for roads to be washed away.

Tours and tour operators

Local tour operators are listed in town entries & in the practical introductions to each major island or island group

Arc Journeys, small group or bespoke tours to Southeast Asia and elsewhere, arc@travelarc.com, www.travelarc.com

Asian Journeys, a range of tours by a well established company, mail@asianjourneys.com, www.asianjourneys.com

Bali Barong Tours, PO Box 7066, Northridge, CA 91327, T818-3685648, F818-3684725, www.balibarongtours.com

Dragoman, adventure and cultural tours and expeditions to Southeast Asia and beyond, wl@dragoman.co.uk, www.dragoman.co.uk

Exodus, small group walking and trekking holidays, adventure tours and more, sales@exodustravels.co.uk, www.exodus.co.uk

Explore Worldwide, small group adventure tours across the world, including Southeast Asia, www.explore.co.uk

Footprint Adventures, trekking and wildlife trips to Southeast Asia and wider, sales@footprint-adventures.co.uk, www.footprint-adventures.co.uk

Gecko, small group adventure tours to Southeast Asia, geckotravel@cs.com, www.geckotravel.co.uk

Guerba, adventure and discovery holidays, www.guerba.co.uk

Silk Steps, tailor made and group trips to several destinations in Asia, info@silksteps.co.uk. www.silksteps.co.uk

Symbiosis, small group expeditions to Southeast Asia, info@symbiosis-travel.co.uk, www.symbiosis-travel.co.uk

Teaching and Projects Abroad, offers work and experiences while you travel, info@teaching-abroad.co.uk, www.teaching-abroad.co.uk

Indonesian Tourist Promotion offices overseas

Australia *Level 10,5 Elizabeth Street, Sydney NSW 2000, Australia.*
T61-02-2333630,
F61-02-233629,3573478.
Japan *2nd Floor Sankaido Building, 1-9-13 Akasaka, Minatoku, Tokyo 10, Japan. T03-358553588, 35869736, F03-35821397.*
Asean 10, Collyer Quay, 15-07 Ocean Building, Singapore 0104.
T65-02-5342837, F65-02-5334287.
Taiwan *5th Floor, 66 Sung Chiang Road,*

Taipei, Taiwan ROC. T02-5377620, F02-5376621.
Europe *Wiessenhuttenstrasse 17, D-6000 Frankfurt/Main, Germany. T69-233677/78, F69-230840.*
United Kingdom *3-4 Hanover Street, London W1 9HH, England.*
T44-71-4930030,4930334, F44-71-4931747.
North America *3457 Wilshire Boulevard, Los Angeles, CA 90010, USA.*
T1-213-3872078, F1-213-3804876.

Essentials

The Imaginative Traveller, adventure tours to the world, including Southeast Asia, info@imaginative-traveller.com
Worldwide Adventures Abroad, adventure tours organized for/in small groups, abroad@globalnet.co.uk, www.adventures-abroad.com

Finding out more

Useful websites
More websites are
listed on page 65

http://www.tourismindonesia.com/ Homepage of Tourism Indonesia with modest amounts of information but little detail. Some odd material like tax laws and out of date cabinet line-ups. But still worth a browse.

http://www.i-2.co.id/ie40.asp Indonesia Interactive I2, the country's first information portal. Lots of information to trawl here and good links.

http://indonesia.elga.net.id/ Another very wide-ranging site with lots of background on the country, although not specifically tourist-oriented.

http://www.visit-indonesia.com The official website of the Indonesian tourism promotion board.

http://www.accessindo.com/travel/body_index.html Information on hotels, tours, guidebooks, travel forums, tips and more.

http://www.mawar.inn.bppt.go.id/ Indonesia homepage based in Jakarta but good place to start a search of Websites for Indonesia.

http://www.travelbali.com The 'official Bali website', with plenty of accommodation listed, by region, cost or activity, Bali Newsletter provides information on the latest goings on, restaurant and events listings.

http://www.bali-paradise.com To quote Jack Daniels, of Bali Discovery: "A veritable 'Funk and Wagnals' of Bali Travel run by the unsinkable Melina Caruso in Bali".

http://www.balidiscovery.com/ For anyone looking for a tour, you could start by looking at *Bali Discovery Tours*. Run by Jack Daniels, who writes a weekly Bali Update newsletter, which is distributed electronically to over 10,000 people worldwide. For the very latest happenings in Bali, subscribe to the newsletter.

http://www.bali-travelnews.com Another good source of information for Bali.

http://www.balihotels.com A good starting point if you are looking for accommodation, with around 300 hotels across the island.

Language

The national language is **Bahasa Indonesia**, which is written in Roman script (see page 426). Bali has its own language, as do many of the islands of the east. However, the effect of Indonesia's national education policy – an attempt to glue together a hugely varied population of 200 million people – has meant that there are few people under 50 who don't speak Bahasa. English is the most common foreign language, although there are Dutch speakers amongst the older generation.

Bahasa Indonesia is a relatively easy language to learn, and visitors may have a small but functional vocabulary after just a few weeks. Unlike Thai, it is not tonal and is grammatically very straightforward. However, this does not mean it is an easy language to speak well. A small number of useful words and phrases are listed in the box below. There are many cheap, pocket-sized Indonesian-English dictionaries available in Indonesia. They are fine for the odd request for a towel or a slightly cleaner room, but anyone wishing to learn more will find them disappointing. The best dictionary is John Echols and Hassan Shadily's twin volume edition but it is hardly handy in terms of size and weight and is mostly used by scholars of Indonesia. For visitors interested in studying Bahasa Indonesia in more depth, the Cornell course, though expensive, is recommended. Cassettes are available from Southeast Asia Publications Office, East Hill Plaza, Ithaca, New York 14853, USA, T 607 2553827.

Language
courses in
Indonesia

The best way to learn Indonesian is to study it intensively in Indonesia. Most courses are put on by language schools and institutes in Jakarta and Yogyakarta (the latter, Indonesia's so-styled 'cultural capital'). In Bali, courses are run by the Bali Language and Cultural Centre, Jl Tukad Pakerisan 80, Denpasar, T0361-239331.

Before you travel

Entry requirements

All visitors to Indonesia must possess passports valid for at least six months from their date of arrival in Indonesia and, in theory, they should have proof of onward travel. Many visitors find that immigration officials are happy with some indication that sufficient funds (eg TCs) are available to purchase a return flight. **Passports**

Visas are **not** required for nationals of ASEAN countries (Brunei, Laos, Malaysia, Myanmar, Philippines, Singapore, Thailand and Vietnam), Argentina, Australia, Austria, Belgium, Brazil, Canada, Chile, Denmark, Egypt, Finland, France, Germany, Greece, Iceland, Ireland, Italy, Japan, Kuwait, Liechtenstein, Luxembourg, Malta, Mexico, Morocco, the Netherlands, New Zealand, Norway, Saudi Arabia, South Korea, Spain, Sweden, Switzerland, Taiwan, Turkey, UAE, UK, USA and Venezuela. Tourists may stay for a maximum of two months (non-extendable). Entry or exit must be through one of the so-called 'Gateway' cities. These are Ambon, Bali, Balikpapan, Bandung, Batam (Riau), Biak, Jakarta, Kupang, Manado, Mataram, Medan, Padang, Pekanbaru, Pontianak and Surabaya airports; the seaports of Ambon, Batam (Riau), Belawan (Medan), Benoa (Bali), Dumai, Jakarta, Manado, Padangbai (Bali), Semarang, Surabaya and Tanjung Pinang (Riau); and the single visa-free land crossing at Entikong in Kalimantan. If entering **or leaving** the country through any other city, a visa is required. These can be obtained from any Indonesian embassy or consulate, are only valid for one month, but can be extended (apply at an immigration office). **Visas** *Note that for the places covered in this book only Denpasar airport & Benoa port on Bali, Mataram Airport on Lombok, & Kupang in Timor are 'Gateways'*

For nationals of countries other than those listed above, visas can be obtained from any Indonesian embassy or consulate (see box next page), but are valid for one month only (extension possible). Two passport photographs and a small fee are required, plus a confirmed onward flight.

Business visas People intending to work in Indonesia need to take their passport, two photos and a covering letter from their company to an Indonesian embassy or consulate. The application takes 24 hours to process, maximum stay five weeks.

Visa extension Jl Teuku Umar I, Jakarta, T349811. Note that extensions are not possible on the standard 60 day tourist pass. It is necessary to leave the country, and then re-enter. Financial penalties for over-staying are steep. If you are unavoidably delayed and unable to leave the country, immigration officers may allow a couple of days' leeway but only in exceptional circumstances.

None required unless visitors have been in a cholera, yellow fever or smallpox infected area six days prior to arrival. **Vaccinations**

Other health problems Malaria tablets and mosquito repellent are essential. **Warning**: do not go diving if you are taking Larium (Mefloquine). Some local residents swear by *Minyak Gosok Tawan* (lemon balm oil) or *Minyak Kayu Putih* (camphor oil) to keep mosquitoes at bay. Tiger Balm is also good for itchy bites. **NB** There are no strong mosquito repellents available outside Jakarta. The locally produced *Autan* is not terribly effective. An American company has designed a tailored mosquito net which covers the wearer in fine mesh and offers protection as you move around; contact *Ben's Bug Armor*, T00-1-510 540 4763. *See Health section page 52 for further information on recommended vaccinations, malaria prophylaxis & other health advice*

Essentials

 Embassies and consulates overseas

Note not all Indonesian embassies are listed below. For a full listing of embassies of the world, including Indonesia see: http://www.embassyworld.com/embassy/indonesia1.htm

Argentina, Chile, Uruguay and Paraguay, Mariskal Ramon Castila 2901, 1425 Buenos Aires, Argentina. T0054-11-8016622, 8016655, 8017142, F8024448. Tx18704 INDON AR. Cable: INDONESIA BUENOS AIRES.

Australia: Embassy, in Australia, 8 Darwin Avenue, Yarralumla, Canberra - ACT 2600. T0061-2-2508600, F2508666. Cable: PERWAKILAN.

Consulate, 236-238 Maroubra Road, Maroubra, NSW – 2035. T3449933, T297741 (Commercial Office).

Consulate, 72 Queen's Road, Melbourne VIC-3004. T5252755, F5251588, TxAA35223 KRIMEL.

Consulate, 134 Adelaide Tce, East Perth, WA-6004. T2215858, F2215688.

Consulate, 18 Harry Chan Avenue, Darwin, NT 0800. T410048, F412709. Postal Address: PO Box 1953, Darwin NT. 0801.

Austria, A-1180 Wien, Gustav, Tschermakg 5-7, AUSTRIA.

Brazil, Bolivia and Peru, Setor Embaixada Sul Avenida, Das Nacoes Yuadra, 805, Lote 20 Caixa Postal 08934, Brasilia. T055-61-2430102, 2430233, 2444904, F2431713, Tx612541 EDIB BR, 611079 EDIB BR, Cable: Indonesia Brasil.

Canada: Embassy, 287 MacLaren Street, Ottawa, Ontario, Canada K2P 0L9. T001-613-2367403, F5632858.

Consulate, Toronto 129 Jarvis Street, Toronto, Ontario, M5C 2H6, Canada. T001-416-3604020, F3604295.

Consulate, Vancouver 1455 West Georgia Street, 2nd Floor, Vancouver, B.C. V6G 2T3. T001-604-6828855, F6628396.

Representative on the ICAO Council, 1000 Sherbrooke Street West # 986, Montreal, Quebec, H3A 3G4. T001-514-2858276.

People's Republic of China, Sanlitun Diplomatic Office Building B, Beijing, 100600 China. T0086-10-5325484-9, F5325366. Telex: 221035 KBRIB CN, Cable: INDONESIA BEIJING

Finland, Kuusisaarentie 3, 00340 Helsinki, Finland. T00358-9-458 2100, F4582882. www.iit.edu/~syafsya/finland/helsinki1.html

Germany, Bernkasteler Str. 2, D-53175, Bonn. T0049-228-382990.

Japan: Embassy, Higashi Gotanda 5-2-9, Shinagawa-ku, Tokyo, Japan. T0081-3-34414201, 3441-4209. F34471697. TxINDONJ-22920. Cable: INDONESIA TOKYO

Consulate, Kato Building 3rd floor, Kyomachi 76-1, Chuo-ku, Kobe 605, Japan. T0081-78-3211656, F3920792. Tx5624166, INDKOBJ, Cable: PERWAKIN KOBE.

Consulate, Hokkaido Island 883-3 Chome 4-Jo, Miyayanomori, Chuo-ku,

What to take

Travellers usually tend to take too much. Almost everything is available in Bali – and often at a lower price than in the West. However, the islands of Nusa Tenggara are less well supplied, although most things can be obtained in the larger towns.

Suitcases are not appropriate if you are intending to travel overland by bus. A backpack, or even better a travelpack (where the straps can be zipped out of sight), is recommended. Travelpacks have the advantage of being hybrid backpacks-suitcases; they can be carried on the back for easy porterage, but they can also be taken into hotels without the owner being labelled a 'hippy'. **NB** For serious hikers, a backpack with an internal frame is still by far the best option for longer treks.

In terms of **clothing**, dress in Indonesia is relatively casual – even at formal functions. Suits are not necessary except in a few of the most expensive restaurants. However, though formal attire may be the exception, dressing tidily is the norm. Women particularly should note that in many areas of Indonesia, they should avoid offending

Essentials

Sapporo, Japan. T0081-11-2516002 (day), 6434531 (night)
Consulate, Kyushu Island Kyuden Bldg.1-82, Watanabe-Dori, Chuo-ku, Fukuoka, Japan. T0011-92-7613031.
Kenya, Utalli Hous 3rd Floor, Uhuru Highway/Loita Street, PO Box 48868, Nairobi, Kenya. T00254-2-215874/5, 215848, F340721. Tx23171 INDO KE, Cable: INDONESIA NAIROBI.
Democratic People's Republic of Korea, 5 Foreigner's Building Moon So Dong, Taedongkang, District Pyong Yang, Democratic People's Republic of Korea, PO Box 178, T00850-2-817425, Tx35030 INDON KP, Cable: INDONESIA PYONG YANG.
Laos, Route Phone Keng, Boite Postale 277, Vientiane R.D.P.L, Laos. T00856-2373.2370, Tx4333 INDVTELS, Cable: INDONESIA VIENTIANE.
Myanmar and Nepal, 100, Pyidaungsu Yeiktha Road, PO Box 1401 Yangon, Myanmar. T0095-1-81174, 81358, Tx21355 TINDON BM, Cable: PERWAKIN YANGON.
Netherlands, T. Asserlaan 8, 2517 KC The Hague. T0031-70-3108151.
New Zealand, 70 Glen Road, Kelburn, Wellington, New Zealand. T0064-4-4758697/8/9, F4759374. Tx3892 (INDON NZ).
Sri Lanka & Malvides, No. 1, Police Park Terrace-Colombo-5, Sri Lanka. T0094-1-580113, 580194, Tx21223 KBRI CE, Cable: INDONESIA COLOMBO.

Turkey, Abdullah Cevdet Sok No. 10, PK.C 42 Cankaya-06680 Ankara, Turkey. T0090-312-4382190/91/92, 4388712, F4382193. Tx067-43250 INDO TR, Cable: INDONESIA ANKARA.
United States of America: Embassy, 2020 Massachussetts Ave, N.W. Washington, DC 20036. T001-202-7755200.
Consulate, Two Illinois Center 233 North Michigan Avenue Suite 1422 Chicago, Illinois 60601, USA. T001-312-9380101, F9383148. Tx210222 INAC UR, Cable: INDONESIA CHICAGO.
Consulate, 1111 Columbus Avenue, San Francisco, CA 94133. T001-415-4749571, F4414320.
Consulate, Texas c/o Thomas E. Jamail, Jr. (Bidang Penerangan), 10900 Richmond Avenue, Houston, TX 77042. T001-713-7851691, F7809644, kjrihous@accesscomm.net
Consulate, 5 East 68th Street, New York, NY 10017. T001-212-8790600.
Consulate, Los Angeles, kjri@kjri-la.com www.kjri-la.com
Vietnam, 50 Ngo Quyen Street, Hanoi, Vietnam. T0084-4-256316, 253353, 253324, 252788, F259274. Tx411434 INDOHA VT, Cable: INDONESIA HANOI.
Zimbabwe, 3 Duthie Avenue, Belgravia, PO Box 8296 Causeway, Harare, Zimbabwe. T00263-732561/737447, F737479. Tx22451 INDONHR ZW.

Muslim sensibilities and dress 'demurely' (ie keep shoulders covered and wear below-knee skirts or trousers). This is particularly true in Sumbawa. Note that this does not generally apply in beach resorts (see also note on page 28). It is usually warm (except in highland areas), so only one thin sweater or sweatshirt is usually necessary. Cotton clothes are most appropriate: they are light, dry quickly, and are cool. A sarong is useful when bathing in public or lounging in the evening – but it is best to buy one after arrival.

There is a tendency, rather than to take inappropriate articles of clothing, to take too many of the same article. Laundry services are cheap, and the turn-around rapid. It is also worth remembering that clothes are cheap should something fall apart or get lost.

Bumbag; earplug; First Aid kit (see also 'Health' section page 52); insect repellent **Checklist** and/or electric mosquito mats, coils; international driving licence; passport (valid for at least 6 months); photocopies of essential documents; short wave radio; spare passport photographs; sun protection; sunglasses; Swiss Army knife; torch; umbrella; wet wipes; zip-lock bags.

Those intending to stay in budget accommodation might also include: Cotton sheet sleeping bag; money belt; padlock (for hotel room and pack); sarong (or buy on arrival); soap; student card; toilet paper; towel; travel wash.

For women travellers: a supply of tampons (although these are available in most towns); a wedding ring for single female travellers who might want to help ward off the attentions of amorous admirers.

Customs

Duty free allowance Two litres of alcohol, 200 cigarettes or 50 cigars or 100 grammes of tobacco along with a reasonable amount of perfume.

Currency regulations A limit of 50,000Rp can be carried in or out of the country. There are no restrictions on the import or export of foreign currency, either cash or TCs.

Prohibited items Narcotics, arms and ammunition, TV sets, radio/cassette recorders, pornographic objects or printed matter, printed matter in Chinese characters and Chinese medicines. In theory, approval should also be sought for carrying transceivers, movie film and video cassettes. Photographic equipment, computers, typewriters and tape recorders should also be declared on arrival, although for tourists this is not assiduously enforced.

Money

Currency The currency in Indonesia is the **Rupiah** (Rp). 1Rp equals 100 sen. Denominations of notes are 100Rp, 500Rp, 1,000Rp, 5,000Rp, 10,000Rp, 20,000Rp and 50,000Rp, coins are minted in 25Rp, 50Rp, 100Rp and 500Rp denominations. **NB** When taking US$ in cash, make sure that the bills are new and crisp, as banks in Indonesia can be fussy about which bills they accept (Flores and Sulawesi are particularly bad). Larger denomination US$ bills also tend to command a premium exchange rate. Note, finally, that during the recent period of extreme exchange rate volatility places outside main centres tended to give poor rates. Shop around: there can be great variations between exchange rates offered by different banks and money changers. Current rates for rupiah from the *Bank of Indonesia* are available on http://www.bü.co.id/english/headline/ex_rates.htm#TODAY; alternatively, check http://www.oanda.com/converter/classic

The Indonesian currency has been very volatile over the last two years. At one point in the recent past, the rupiah had lost 85% of its value against the US$.

In more out of the way places it is worth making sure that you have a stock of smaller notes and coins – it can be hard to break larger bills.

Credit cards Major credit cards are accepted in larger hotels, airline offices, department stores and some restaurants although this method of payment is often subject to a 3% surcharge. Visa and MasterCard are the most widely accepted. It is not so easy to use credit cards to get cash advances, although major banks in the main cities may do it – and especially in Java and Bali. Banks in larger towns and tourist centres across the archipelago have ATMs (Automatic Teller Machines) which provide credit card advances. Again, Visa and MasterCard are most widely taken and the cirrus system is also offered by many banks. If you are visiting very remote areas for a long period, it can make sense to obtain Indonesian Post Office TCs in one of the big cities. These are then easily changed into rupiahs in any post office in the country.

Banks, credit card cash withdrawals

Bank Bali	MasterCard, Cirrus
Bank Internasional Indonesia (BII)	MasterCard, Visa, Cirrus
Bank Central Asia (BCA)	MasterCard, Visa, Cirrus
Lippo Bank	MasterCard, Cirrus
BNI	MasterCard, Cirrus

For **lost credit cards** call the following toll free numbers or visit the websites:
Visa: T001-803-1-933-6294 or www.visa.com
American Express cards and TCs: T001-803-61005 or www.americanexpress.com
MasterCard: T001-803-1-887-0623 www.mastercard.com
Western Union: www.westernunion.com

Credit card fraud: we have received increasing numbers of reports of credit card fraud, particularly from Bali and usually centred on restaurants - even the best. It seems that waiters copy the cards electronically.

Travellers' cheques Travellers' cheques (TCs) can usually be changed in larger towns and tourist destinations. In smaller towns and more out of the way spots it may not be possible to change TCs. The US$ is the most readily acceptable currency, both for TCs and cash and it is best to carry US$ denominated TCs if travelling outside the major tourist centres. If staying in tourist centres TCs denominated in any major currency will do but note that rates for US$ tend to be better simply because most transactions are in US$. Occasionally money changers charge a commission – check beforehand. If changing cash, note that banks like bills in pristine condition, and a better rate is often given for larger denomination notes – eg US$50 or US$100.

American Express TCs denominated in US$ are probably the easiest to change. We have had reports that Thomas Cook Cheques are not always accepted by banks in provincial towns, especially those out of the main tourist centres. Money changers often give better rates than banks. Hotels will sometimes change TCs (usually in popular tourist destinations), but rates vary a great deal from competitive to appalling, so it is worth checking.

Banks Two of the better banks, at least for most visitors' needs, are *BNI* (Bank Negara Indonesia) and *BCA* (Bank Central Asia). *BNI* is reliable and efficient and most of their branches will change US$ TCs. They also give one of the best rates and have offices across the archipelago. *BCA* is also very efficient and they are usually likely to change TCs denominated in 'unusual' (from the Indonesian perspective) currencies. But *BCA* does not have such a wide distribution of branches. Another bank which deals with foreign currencies efficiently is *Bank Ekspor Impor*.

As an international tourist destination, it is easier to change money – either cash or TCs in all major currencies – in Bali than any other spot in Indonesia. All the tourist centres offer money changing facilities at competitive rates. Cash advances can be obtained on Visa cards from *BCA* in Denpasar. However, the airport rates are not as competitive as in-town rates. The very best rates in Indonesia are from the money changers in Kuta; the larger denomination notes get a better rate (in other words, the dollar rate for a $100 bill is significantly better than that for a $10 bill). Always check the amount you receive very, very carefully as scams are in abundance.

Cost of living Providing US$ estimates of costs of living in Indonesia has been tricky over the last few years. In 1997, US$1 would buy you 2,500Rp. By mid-1998 this had spiralled down (or up, if you were a tourist, that is) to more than 13,000Rp. The exchange rate as this book went to press was 9,343Rp to US$1 (GBP1 bought 13,266Rp). In other words, visitors to Indonesia over the last few years have found their Dollars, Francs, Pounds, Yen and Guilders have gone an awful lot further – notwithstanding some periods of rapid inflation.

Visitors staying in first class hotels and eating in hotel restaurants will probably spend 300,000Rp a day and upwards. Tourists staying in cheaper a/c accommodation, and eating in local restaurants will probably spend about 150,000Rp a day. A backpacker, staying in fan-cooled guesthouses and eating cheaply, might expect to be able to live on 30,000Rp a day. A meal in a simple warung should cost 5-10,000Rp, in a local restaurant about 10-20,000Rp, and in a swish hotel coffee shop 20,000Rp+. Of course it is best not to calculate your budget simply by multiplying the number of days you intend to stay by the figures given above. A long bus journey, a trip by air, a couple of days' diving, or the need to hire a guide on a trek, for example, would throw such careful calculations right out. Finally, a word of caution. Because of the volatility of the domestic currency, coupled with rapid inflation, prices have been highly unstable. Or rather they have escalated – at least in rupiah terms. While the bus and other prices quoted here were collected during 1999 and 2000, there is every chance that you will find that they have increased, sometimes markedly. But just remember, it is still a lot cheaper than a couple of years back!

Getting there

Air

Most people using this book will arrive at Bali's international airport, Indonesia's most important gateway after the capital, Jakarta. *Garuda*, the national flag carrier, flies between Bali and Europe, the US, other Asian cities and Australia and New Zealand, often via Jakarta. Most of the major European carriers reduced the number of flights they operated to Indonesia during the recent troubles and the downturn in tourism; these have still to return to pre-crisis levels of frequency. There are three flights a day between Singapore and Denpasar, three flights a week between Singapore and Mataram, Lombok (with Silkair, part of SIA). There are also connections between Kupang (Timor) and Darwin (Australia).

The economic crisis led to a sharp fall in the number of Indonesians travelling abroad and the political crisis and widely reported communal violence led to a sharp fall in foreign tourists entering Indonesia. As a result many carriers cut the frequency of flights to Indonesia. However on 1 January 2001 the government are planning to lift the US$105 outbound tax currently levied on Indonesian nationals and permanent residents (an effort to raise revenue during the depths of the economic crisis). As a result some commentators are forecasting a 40% rise in flights to Indonesia by Asian and European carriers as they meet the expected increase in demand.

From Australasia Direct flights to Bali from Darwin, Cairns, Brisbane, Sydney, Melbourne, Adelaide, Perth and Auckland. *Ansett Airlines* flies once a week, on Wed, between Bali and Broome, Western Australia.

From Europe At the time of writing the only direct flight from Europe to Bali is once a week with *Lauda Air*. There are easy connections from London via Vienna, and onward connections from Bali to Australia with Ansett. Garuda operates a frequent service between Jakarta and Denpasar, though there has been a reduction in this service; flights may be cancelled at short notice and most flights depart fairly full so you can no longer rely on getting a seat at the last minute. You can also fly from Europe to Singapore and change planes for an onward connection to Bali; there are flights approximately every 2 hrs between Singapore and Jakarta, and three flights a day between Singapore and Denpasar.

Direct flights to Bali from most capital cities including Hong Kong, Bangkok, Singapore, **From the**
Taipei, Seoul, Tokyo, Osaka, etc. **Far East**

There are many direct flights from Singapore, Bangkok or Kuala Lumpur; also from **From Southeast**
Manila with *Garuda* and *Philippine Airlines*. Three flights a week between Singapore **Asia**
and Mataram (with *Silkair*, part of SIA).

From Los Angeles fly direct with *Garuda*. **From the USA**

Boat

Visitors can enter Indonesia by sea through two ports on Bali - Benoa and Padangbai.
An increasing number of cruise liners stop at Bali, although there are no regular
international connections.

For those interested in booking a passage on a cargo ship travelling to Indonesia,
contact the *Strand Cruise Centre*, Charing Cross Shopping Concourse, The Strand,
London WC2N 4HZ, T020-78366363, F020-74970078. Another company booking
berths on freighters is *Wagner Frachtschiffreissen*, Stadlerstrasse 48, CH-8404
Winterthur, Switzerland, T052-2421442, F052-2421487.

Road

There are no international road crossings to the places covered in this book.

Touching down

Airport information

Denpasar's (Bali) Ngurah Rai Airport is at the south end of the island, just south of **International**
Kuta. It is one of Indonesia's 'gateway' cities, with international connections with **airports**
Australia, Hong Kong, Europe, Singapore, Japan and North America.

Lombok's Selaparang Mataram Airport lies north of Mataram and 20 mins south
of Senggigi Beach. At present the only direct **international connection** is a daily
flight to Singapore with Silk Air.

West Timor's El Tari Airport in Kupang is 14 km northeast of the town and has
international connections with Darwin, Australia.

30,000Rp on international flights. Anywhere between 5,500 and 11,000Rp on **Airport tax**
domestic flights, depending on the airport. (Airports/provincial governments are
allowed some leeway in setting their own taxes.) Domestic tax is usually included in
the cost of the ticket – and it should be indicated on the ticket.

Tourist information

The Directorate General of Tourism (head office in Jakarta) is administratively under the **Tourist offices**
Department of Tourism, Post and Telecommunications, which has offices throughout
the country. These offices are known as Kanwil Depparpostel. Each of Indonesia's
provinces also has its own tourist offices, known as Deparda or Dinas Pariwisata.

Indonesia Government Tourist Offices *Department Of Tourism*, Post And
Telecommunication, Jl Merdeka Barat No. 16-19, Jakarta 10110. T062-021-3838412,

Essentials

Touching down

Hours of business Hours of business are highly variable; there are not even standard opening hours for government offices. The listing below is a rule of thumb:
Banks: foreign banks 0800-1200 Mon-Fri and 0800-1100 Sat; local banks 0800-1300, 1330-1600 Mon-Sat. Banks in hotels may stay open longer.
Businesses: most businesses open 0800/0900-1200, 1300-1600/1700 Mon-Fri.
Government offices: 0800-1500 Mon-Thu, 0800-1130 Fri and 0800-1400 Sat.
Museums: 0830 or 0900-1400 Tue-Thu, 0900-1100 Fri, 0900-1300 Sat and 0900-1500 Sun, closed Mon.
Shops: 0900-2000 Mon-Fri, 0900-1300 Sat, sometimes on Sun. In smaller towns shops may close for a siesta between 1300 and 1700.

Official time All the islands included in this book come under Central Indonesia time, GMT+8 (which, for the record, includes South and East Kalimantan and Sulawesi as well as Bali and Nusa Tenggara).

Voltage 220 volts, 50 cycles in the big cities; 110 volts in some areas. Plugs are usually rounded and two pin; sometimes sockets are recessed. It is easy enough to find adaptors in local electrical shops. More expensive hotels often have 3-pin plugs. Power surges are not common and well protected electrical equipment such as lap-top computers can be used.

Weights and measures Metric, although local units are still in use in some areas.

3838417, Telex : INTOUR IA, F02-021-3848245. *Directorate General Of Tourism* (DGT) Jl Merdeka Barat No. 16-19, Jakarta 10110, T062-021-3838217, 3838220, Telex: INTOUR IA, Cable : INTO JAKARTA, F062-021-3867589, 3860828.

Bali *Regional Office of Tourism*, Post and Telecommunication X, ali, Komplex Niti Mandala, Jl. Raya Puputan, Renon, Denpasar 80235. T0361-225649, 233474, F0361-233475. *Provincial Tourist Service East Java*, Jl S. Parman, Niti Mandala, Denpasar 80235, T0361-222387, 226313.

West Nusa Tenggara *Regional Office of Tourism,* Post and Telecommunication XX, West Nusa Tenggara, Jl. Singosari No. 2 Mataram 83121. T(0364) 32723, 34800, F(0364) 37233. *Provincial Tourist Service West Nusa Tenggara*, Jl Langko No. 70, Ampenan 83114. T0364-21730, 21866.

East Nusa Tenggara *Regional Office of Tourism*, Post and Telecommunication XI, East Nusa Tenggara, Jl. Ir. Soekarno No. 29, Kupang 85112. T(0391) 21160, 31452, F(0391) 21160. *Provincial Tourist Service East Nusa Tenggara*, Jl Jend. Basuki Rachmat 1, Kupang 85117, T0391-21540, 21824.

Disabled travellers
As a poor country, Indonesia has almost no infrastructure to enable people with disabilities to travel easily. Pavements are frequently very high, 9 inches or so, uneven and ridden with holes and missing slabs. Buildings, including shops and museums are frequently reached via steps with no ramps for wheelchair access. Public transport is frequently cramped and overcrowded. Some of the Western-owned hotels at the top end of the market do go out of their way to provide wheelchair access and facilities for disabled visitors. For travel to this area, it would be best to contact a specialist travel agent or organization dealing with travellers with special needs. In the UK, contact *RADAR* (The Royal Association for Disability and Rehabilitation), 12 City Forum, 250 City Road, London, EC1V 8AF, T020-72503222, T020-72504119. In North America, *Society for the Advancement of Travel for the Handicapped* (SATH), Suite 610, 347 5th Avenue, New York, NY 10016, T212-4477284.

Gay & lesbian travellers
Indonesia is surprisingly tolerant of homosexuality given that it goes against the tenets of both Muslim and traditional Balinese religions. Homosexuality is not illegal; the age of consent is 16 years for men and women. Indonesian men are generally

more affectionate in public which allows foreign gay men to blend in more easily. Bali is the only island with an established gay area centred on Kuta, with certain bars, restaurants and areas which are patronized by, but not exclusive to, gay people. Few Indonesian men make a living as 'rent boys'; however, as a supposedly wealthy foreigner you will be expected to pay for meals, transport and accommodation. For more information contact: *Yayasan Yusada Bhakti*, Jl Belimbing Gang Y4, Denpasar.

Anyone in full-time education is entitled to an **International Student Identity Card** (ISIC). These are issued by student travel offices and travel agencies across the world and offer special rates on all forms of transport and other concessions and services. The ISIC head office is: *ISIC Association*, 479 Herengracht, 10-17-BS, Amsterdam, T31-204421280. **Student travellers**

Women travelling alone face greater difficulties than men or couples. Young southeast Asian women rarely travel without a partner, so it is believed to be strange for a Western woman to do so. Western women are often believed to be of easy virtue – a view perpetuated by both Hollywood and local films. To minimize the pestering that will occur, dress modestly – particularly in staunchly Muslim areas such as Sumbawa and in more out-of-the-way spots where locals may be unfamiliar with tourists. Comments, sometimes derogatory, will be made however carefully you dress and act; simply ignore them. Toiletries such as tampons are available in Indonesia's main cities but may not be in more out of the way places. **Women travellers**

A tourist visa does not give you the right to work. In a country on the brink of financial chaos, with high unemployment, job opportunities are extremely limited. Teaching English is the best option, often for room and board rather than cash. If you have a specialist skill such as being a diving instructor, you might find work in that field. **Working in the country**

Rules, customs and etiquette

As a rule, Indonesians are courteous and understanding. Visitors should be the same. As foreigners, visitors are often given the benefit of the doubt when norms are transgressed. However, it is best to have a grasp of at least the basics of accepted behaviour. In tourist areas and large cities, Westerners and their habits are better understood; but in remote areas you should be more aware of local sensibilities. There are also some areas – such as Sumbawa – that are more fervently Muslim than other parts of the country. With such a diverse array of cultures and religions, accepted conduct varies. Specific cultural notes are given in the appropriate introductory sections. Generally speaking, the more popular an area is (as a tourist destination) the more understanding local people are likely to be of tourist habits. But this is not to imply that anything goes. It is also true that familiarity can breed contempt, so even in places like Bali it is important to be sensitive to the essentials of local culture. **Conduct**

The economic and political crises in Indonesia, the Australian-led UN force in East Timor, and the sense that the West has taken advantage of a poor and ravaged country has also led to more suspicion and enmity than was hitherto the case. This is particularly true of West Timor, and of some areas of Nusa Tenggara. While the great majority of Indonesians are welcoming to foreigners it is worth remembering that the country and its people have been through a traumatic experience over the last few years.

Penalties are harsh for trafficking even modest quantities. Expect a lengthy jail term at the very least. *Prisoners Abroad* is a charity dedicated to supporting UK nationals in prisons abroad. As the charity writes: "Arrest, trial and imprisonment are devastating in a familiar environment, supported by family and friends. Abroad it is much worse." Young men and women caught with drugs may find themselves facing sentences of 10 years or more, often in appalling conditions. Volunteers can help *Prisoners Abroad*, **Drugs**

Essentials

☞ *MTV has a lot to answer for!*

Even in remote island areas the sight of an oversized satellite dish is common. Juxtaposed with thatched and corrugated rooftops, television is beamed in from around the world fuelling aspirations of 'development' and affluence. It has become the chief medium of cross-cultural communication. Indonesian middle class situation dramas are avidly watched, as are steamy French films. 'Animal Hospital' on the Australia Channel invokes bewildered amusement at the high tech medical care and silk cushion pampering of household pets.

And then there is MTV. Once the BBC World Service was the voice of the West, often a lifeline for countries where information and human rights are in small doses. Now MTV pumps out 24 hour images, largely of those perennial favourites 'sex, drugs and rock and roll'. Britney Spears in a plastic, red catsuit is, by default, the West's contemporary cross-cultural emissary. No more gunboat diplomacy and stiff upper lips; today it is pouting rock stars and cosseted pets. Reading between the lines, many Indonesians perceive the message of MTV as individual freedom –

and in the case of older Indonesians, individual freedom gone beserk. In a culture where sex is largely taboo as a topic of open discussion, semi-naked, beautiful women seem to be causing some confusion.

Lyrics are not subtitled, and the subtitles (if any!) of the MTV play list are eclipsed by the scenes of 'romantic' interplay and cavorting Toni Braxtons in underwear. So if you are a lone woman traveller experiencing lewd behaviour, and/or harassment, blame MTV! The communications era may have created a global village but some issues get lost in translation. Perceptions of Western sexuality and negative female stereotypes are perpetuated and when lone female orang putih are hassled we have, in a sense, only ourselves to blame. Messages are misconstrued in a context where there is little other societal information to provide balance. Indeed a lone white woman is often considered to be of the 'anytime, anywhere, anyhow' variety. Although this is irritating, when turning down offers of "gigi gigi" the looks of genuine surprise and disappointment at not finding a nymphomaniac on tour, is some recompense.

and similar organizations, by becoming a pen pal, donating a magazine subscription, or sending books, for example. If you or a friend find yourself in the unfortunate position of being in jail, or facing a jail term, then contact the charity at: *Prisoners Abroad*, Freepost 82, Roseberry Avenue, London EC1B 1XB, UK, T020-5616820, (if telephoning from abroad then the code is +4420). Further information on the charity and its work can also be obtained from the above address.

Calmness Like other countries of Southeast Asia, a calm attitude is highly admired, especially if things are going wrong. Keep calm and cool when bargaining, or waiting for a delayed bus or appointment.

Dress Most of the population of Indonesia are Muslim - more than 90% overall - and women should be particularly careful not to offend. Dress modestly and avoid shorts, short skirts and sleeveless dresses or shirts (except at the beach). Public nudity and topless bathing are not acceptable. While the country as a whole is predominantly Muslim (but it is not an Islamic state), the islands covered by this book are rather more mixed in terms of the religious affiliation of their populations. Lombok, Sumbawa, West Timor and Sumba are largely Muslim. Bali is Hindu and Flores is Christian.

Clothing Light clothing is suitable all the year round, except at night in the mountains. Shorts, miniskirts and singlets should be limited to beachwear only. Proper decorum should be observed when visiting places of worship; shorts are not permitted in mosques, shoulders and arms should be covered, and women must cover their heads. Formal dress for men normally consists of a batik shirt and trousers; suits are rarely worn. Local dress varies according to region but the standard (so far as there is one) is *batik* for men and *kebaya* for women.

If you are invited to somebody's home, it is customary to take a gift. This is not opened until after the visitor has left. Most small general stores have a range of pre-wrapped and boxed gifts appropriate for a variety of occasions including weddings. These are usually items of china or glasses. **Gifts**

The head is considered sacred and should never be touched (especially those of children). Handshaking is common among both men and women, but the use of the left hand to give or receive is taboo. When eating with fingers, use the right hand only. Pointing with your finger is considered impolite; use your thumb to point, beckon buses (or any person) with a flapping motion of your right hand down by your side. When sitting with others, do not cross your legs; it is considered disrespectful. In addition, do not point with your feet and keep them off tables. Shoes are often not worn in the house and should be removed on entering. **Heads, hands & feet**

Jam karet or 'rubber time' is a peculiarly Indonesian phenomenon. Patience and a cool head are very important; appointments are rarely at the time arranged. **Punctuality**

Public displays of affection between men and women are considered objectionable. However, Indonesians of the same sex tend to be more openly affectionate, holding hands for example, than in the West. **Open affection**

Indonesia has the largest Muslim population of any country in the world. **Mosques** are sacred houses of prayer; non-Muslims can enter a mosque, so long as they observe the appropriate customs: remove shoes before entering, dress appropriately (neatly and fully covered, avoiding singlets, shorts or short skirts), do not disturb the peace, and do not walk too close to or in front of somebody who is praying. During the fasting month of Ramadan, do not eat, drink or smoke in the presence of Muslims during daylight hours. **Religion**

Bali has remained a **Hindu** island (see page 236), and remnants of Hinduism are also evident in parts of central and East Java. To enter a temple or *pura* on Bali it is often necessary to wear a sash around the waist (at some temples a sarong is also required); these are available for hire at the more popular temples, or can be bought for about 1,200Rp (7,000Rp for a sarong). Modest and tidy dress is also required when visiting Hindu temples; women should not enter wearing short dresses or with bare shoulders. Do not use flash-guns during ceremonies. Menstruating women are requested not to enter temples.

Christianity is a growing religion in East Nusa Tenggara (page 321).

Although not a religion, **Pancasila** is – or was – the state ideology. However, now that Suharto has gone and the New Order has become an Old Order pancasila does not have the resonance it once did. Even so, most people were brought up believing that it was the glue holding this disparate group of peoples together (see page 410).

For a more comprehensive background to do's and don'ts in Indonesia see: Draine, Cathy and Hall, Barbara *Culture Shock! Indonesia*, (Times Books: Singapore).

Tipping is not usual in Indonesia. A 10% service charge is added to bills at more expensive hotels (in addition to tax of 11%), and in upmarket restaurants; these days an increasing number of smaller restaurants in tourist areas add a service charge. Porters expect to be tipped about 500Rp a bag. In more expensive restaurants where no service is charged, a tip of 5-10% is sometimes appropriate. Taxi drivers (in larger towns) appreciate a small tip (200-300Rp). *Parkirs* always expect payment for 'watching' your car – 500Rp. **Tipping**

Safety

Despite the recent media coverage of riots and other disturbances in Indonesia, it remains a safe country and violence against foreigners is rare (but see below for a check list of places that have seen civil disturbances in recent months). However, there have been numerous reports of an increase in thefts and robberies during the economic crisis as people struggle to survive in extremely difficult times. Inevitably, tourists – by definition, wealthy – have been targeted. Some visitors have taken to private transport (hire cars, taxis and the like) and flying to avoid overnight buses and trains, where the majority of thefts take place. Those who cannot afford the costs of private transport and air travel should take particular care on buses and trains, especially on the more popular tourist routes. 'Shuttle buses' which specialize in carrying travellers and backpackers on Bali and Lombok are usually safer than public buses when it comes to petty theft. Thefts are also common in shopping centres and other places where tourists congregate.

Theft and deception were a problem even before the economic crisis. It is advisable for travellers to carry all valuables in a moneybelt. Avoid carrying large amounts of cash; travellers' cheques can be changed in most major towns. Pickpockets frequent the public transport systems. Reports of robbery on the overnight trains through Java (if this is the way you are getting to Bali) are common. Take great care of your belongings on these longer journeys on public transport. Keep a close watch on your bags going through security checkpoints at airports; some travellers have reported that their bags were stolen before they could retrieve them after having passed through the x-ray machine. Do not leave valuables in hotel rooms; most of the more expensive hotels will have safety deposit boxes. Many guesthouses have 'open air' bathrooms, ie with only a partial roof. A favoured means of entering rooms is over the bathroom wall and through the bathroom door, therefore it is essential to lock bathroom doors in this type of accommodation. Petty theft is a growing problem in all places frequented by travellers. Hikers on Gunung Rinjani have recently been targeted by thieves; improved policing has been promised and during our most recent visit in mid-2000 the problem appeared to be under control.

Single women should take particular care – it is unusual for women to travel alone and those who do will find Indonesians concerned for their safety. There is a notion held by too many Indonesians that Western women, by definition, are loose, so pestering males may be a problem (see the box 'MTV has a lot to answer for!' on page 28). Be firm, but be polite. Older women travelling alone will not be faced with such problems and will be treated with great respect.

Beware of the confidence tricksters who are widespread in tourist areas. Sudden reports of unbeatable bargains or closing down sales are the usual ploys.

The following areas of Indonesia covered by this book saw disturbances during 1998, 1999 and 2000. Note, however, that these were localized, usually short-term, and almost never affected foreign visitors (bar journalists, that is). West Timor, especially near the border with East Timor is currently highly unstable and in early September 2000 three UN personnel were murdered. Bali also experienced some violence but it was quickly contained. In the south of Bali this was targeted primarily at the Chinese, whilst the violence in the north of the island reflected the greater volatility associated with the stronger Muslim presence in this area. Lombok was also a source of communal violence at the beginning of 2000 (see below for more details on Lombok). For latest information of conditions in Indonesia, see the British Foreign & Commonwealth Office's travel advisory website (http://www.fco.gov.uk/travel/), and/or the US State Department's equivalent site (http://travel.state.gov/travel_warnings.html). Note, however, that these tend to be written by diplomats based in capital or other major cities and they tend to be rather generic in their advice.

Lombok The riots of January 2000 saw tourists chartering helicopters out of Lombok, whilst even those Indonesians not involved with the issues at hand took up weapons in Mataram in case any marauding gangs passed by. Inevitably, the tourist industry was significantly affected by this internationally reported outbreak of violence, and during our last visit in 2000 tourist numbers were down and hotel rates highly negotiable – that is if you feel comfortable with milking this misfortune. Many local people are quite clear that agents provocateur from elsewhere in the country precipitated the violence in defence of Muslims in Maluku (the Spice Islands). If this is so then just as soon as these people leave the islands things should settle down to their formerly pretty amicable state of inter-communal affairs (and it seems, in mid-2000, that this was already the case). All locals, whether Muslim, Christian or Hindu were consciously trying to put foreigners at ease during mid-2000. All over Lombok local neighbourhood watch style groups formed to protect residents and property. HQ Praya will get your stolen goods back within the day! Hence crime decreased considerably during 2000.

Where to stay

Tourist centres usually have a good range of accommodation for all budgets. Bali, for example, has some of the finest hotels in the world – at a corresponding price – along with excellent middle and lower-range accommodation. However, visitors venturing off the beaten track may find hotels restricted to dingy 'Chinese' establishments and over-priced places catering for local businessmen and officials. The best run and most competitively priced budget accommodation is found in popular tourist spots – like Bali, along the backpackers' trail in Lombok and Flores, and at out of the way places popular with surfers such as Hu'u on Sumbawa. It is almost always worth bargaining in Chinese hotels, and in middle and upper grade establishments. This is particularly true for hotels in tourist destinations which attract a fair amount of local weekend business: the weekday room rate may be as much as 50% of the weekend rate. Cheaper places may not give discounts, although as a general rule it is worth negotiating. All hotels are required to display their room rates (for every category of room) on a *daftar harga*, or price list. This is invariably either in public view in the reception area or will be produced when you ask about room rates. Note that Indonesians prefer to be on the ground floor, so rooms on higher floors are usually cheaper.

Terminology can be confusing: a **losmen** is a lower price range hotel and, in some areas, losmen are also known as **penginapan**; a **wisma** is a guesthouse, but these can range in price from cheap to moderately expensive; finally, a **hotel** is a hotel, but can range from the cheap and squalid up to a Hilton. **NB** The government has introduced a ruling requiring all tourist accommodation to have Indonesian names rather than use Western words. Thus the *City Guesthouse* might be renamed *Wisma Kota*; the *Samudra Beach* would become the *Pantai Samudra*. It seems that this edict is not being assiduously enforced and many hotels are ignoring it – or at least adopting it in a rather half-baked way. Nonetheless, be prepared for hotel name changes and also some variation on name use.

There is a 'star' system in use in Indonesia and it can give a rough guide to the price of the establishment (although it is a rating of facilities not of quality). The '*melati*' (flower) system is for cheaper hotels; while the '*bintang*' (star) system is for higher rated, and therefore more expensive, hotels. As in most countries 5 star (luxury) is top of the range.

Essentials

👉 Hotel price guide

L over US$100. Luxury: hotels in this bracket number a handful and are to be found only in Jakarta and Bali. All facilities, combined with sumptuous rooms and excellent service.

AL US$50-100. International class: only to be found in a few cities and tourist destinations. They should provide the entire range of business services (fax, translation, seminar rooms, etc), sports facilities (gym, swimming pool, etc), Asian and Western restaurants, bars, and discotheques.

A US$25-50. First class: will usually offer good business, sports and recreational facilities, with a range of restaurants and bars.

B 75,000-150,000Rp. Tourist class: in tourist destinations, these will probably have a swimming pool and all rooms will have air-conditioning and an attached bathroom. Other services include one or more restaurants and 24-hours coffee shop/room service. Most will have televisions in the rooms.

C 50,000-75,000Rp. Economy: rooms should be air-conditioned and have attached bathrooms with hot water. A restaurant and room service will probably be available but little else.

D 30,000-50,000. Budget: rooms are unlikely to be air-conditioned although they should have an attached bathroom or mandi. Toilets may be either Western-style or of the 'squat' Asian variety, depending on whether the town is on the tourist route. Toilet paper may not be provided. Many in this price range, out of tourist areas, are 'Chinese' hotels. Bed linen and towels are usually provided, and there may be a restaurant.

E 15,000-30,000. Guesthouse: fan-cooled rooms, often with shared mandi and Asian 'squat' toilet. Toilet paper and towels are unlikely to be provided, although bed linen will be. Guesthouses on the tourist route have better facilities and are sometimes excellent sources of information, offering cheap tours and services such as bicycle and motorcycle hire. Places in this category vary a great deal, and can change very rapidly. Other travellers are the best source of up-to-the-minute reviews.

F under 15,000. Guesthouse: fan-cooled rooms, shared mandi and 'squat' toilet. Rooms can be tiny, dark and dingy, with wafer-thin walls. There are also some real bargains in this bracket. Standards change very fast and other travellers are the best source of information. Homestays are usually also in our E-F categories. The difference between a guesthouse (or losmen) and a homestay is that in the latter guests live within the family house, while in the former they sleep separately.

NB More expensive hotels often quote their room rates in US$. Depending on the exchange rate there may be a currency overlap between hotel categories L, AL and A (all quoted here in US$) and B and below (quoted in rupiah).

Accommodation
For a list of hotels on Bali & to book online, visit www.hotels.ains. net.au/bali

Hotels listed in this book are graded under eight categories, according to the *average* price of a double/twin room for one night. It should be noted that many hotels will have a range of rooms, some with air conditioning (a/c) and attached bathroom facilities, others with just a fan and shared facilities. Prices can therefore vary a great deal. The best rooms in any hotel are usually termed 'vip'. If a hotel entry lists 'some a/c', then these rooms are likely to be in the upper part of the range, perhaps even in the next category. Hotels in the middle and lower price categories often provide breakfast in the room rate. In the more out-of-the-way places or in hotels geared to Indonesians this is usually fried rice or something similar. White bread, margarine and chocolate vermicelli is also strangely popular as a breakfast pick-me-up. In the more expensive hotels, service charge (10%) and government tax (11%) are added onto the bill; they are usually excluded from the quoted room rate. More expensive hotels tend to quote their prices in US$. (This was not much of an issue when the rupiah/US$ exchange rate was stable, but in mid-1997 the rupiah weakened dramatically. While hotels that priced their rooms in rupiahs became significantly 'cheaper' for many foreign visitors, those that quoted their rates in US$ did not.) **NB** During the off-season, hotels in tourist destinations may halve their room rates, so it is always worthwhile bargaining or asking whether there is a 'special' price. Hotels which cater primarily to the tour market display high room rates as part of their agreement with the tour companies; an independent traveller walking in off the street (known as FIT in the trade – Frequent Independent Traveller) should not pay much more than half the official rate except in the high season. There is a new category of hotel in Bali called 'boutique' hotels; these are small upmarket hotels, usually with 50-100 rooms, which charge the same as the larger hotels but have fewer facilities. They claim to offer a more intimate ambience.

Self catering This is a growing option on Bali, particularly in the south between Jimbaran and Nusa Dua, and around Sanur and Seminyak. Self catering developments usually consist of either a development of bungalows in landscaped grounds or of apartments, with pool. They can be rented on a short or long term basis and some offer excellent value for money. Individual bungalows are also available to rent in areas such as Seminyak, Jimbaran, Sanur and Ubud. (See relevant sections for more information.)

For private villas for rent on Bali visit www.baliholidays.com

Peculiarities of Indonesian hotels include the tendency to build rooms without windows and, more appealingly, to design middle and lower range hotels around a courtyard.

Baths and showers are not a feature of many cheaper losmen, except on Bali. Instead a **mandi** – a water tank and ladle – is used to wash. The tub is not climbed into; water is ladled from the tub and splashed over the head. Some bathrooms will also have a shower attachment, occasionally with hot water although more often not. The traditional Asian toilet is of the squat variety. (Toilets are euphemistically called **kamar kecil** – the universal 'small room' – or **way say**, as in the initials 'WC'.) These can take some time to become accustomed to and many visitors never become entirely happy with the system, swaying precariously over the hole as their thigh muscles begin to ache. Water scooped from a mandi, or a large water jar, is used to 'flush' the bowl. In popular tourist destinations, and also in larger more cosmopolitan towns (even if they are not favoured tourist destinations), Western toilets are beginning to replace the Asian variety. On Bali very few of the cheap accommodations have squat toilets; Western toilets are the norm. They are seen, in some quarters, as a sign of progress. Toilet paper is not traditionally used; the faithful left hand and water suffice. Some travellers take their own supply of toilet paper – although be aware that not all systems can deal with toilet paper. The division between 'Western' and 'Asian' is not clear cut and it is not uncommon to find bathrooms which mix 'n' match according to whim: a hot water shower, cold water mandi and Asian loo, for example. In cheaper accommodation you are expected to bring your own towels, soap, toilet paper and the bed may consist only of a bottom sheet and pillow with no top sheet (so it is useful to bring your own if you want to keep the mosquitoes at bay).

Bathing & toilets

Camping is not common in Indonesia and even in national parks camping facilities are poor and limited. Indonesians find it strange that anyone should want to camp out when it is possible to stay in a hotel. National Parks are the only places tourists are likely to camp and facilities are basic. (You may need permission from the PHPA office which can usually be arranged on the spot.)

Camping

Essentials

Getting around

Air

Domestic airlines This is the most convenient and comfortable way to travel around Indonesia *Garuda* and *Merpati*, now sister-companies, service all the main provincial cities. *Merpati* tends to operate the short-hop services to smaller towns and cities, particularly in Eastern Indonesia.

The other main domestic airlines are *Bouraq, Mandala* and *Sempati* (see route map, page 363). Note that Sempati was declared bankrupt in 1999 but its routes are likely to be taken over by a new airline, *Indonesian Airlines* (see the next paragraph for more details). *Bouraq's* network is concentrated in Kalimantan and Eastern Indonesia (including Nusa Tenggara); *Sempati's* (or rather, its possible successor) is centred on the islands of Kalimantan, Sumatra, Java and Sulawesi; while *Mandala* has the most restricted network, serving only a handful of cities. Smallest of all are *DAS*, *SMAC* and *Deraya* which tend to service smaller towns in the Outer Islands. On some routes, *Bouraq, Mandala* and *Sempati* offer fares that are marginally cheaper than *Garuda/Merpati* but there is very little in it. There are also non-commercial air services such as the *Missionary Aviation Fellowship* (MAF) and *Associated Missions Aviation* (AMA) which offer non-scheduled flights to more out of the way spots. **NB** These are not commercial airlines and can refuse passage. See page 258 for an air route map of Nusa Tenggara.

The economic crisis threw Indonesia's airline industry into turmoil. Many routes were cut or the frequency of flights was reduced as economic hardship reduced the numbers of people flying. *Sempati*, (started up under Suharto family patronage) with massive debts that it was unable to service, was bankrupted. However a number of new airlines are on the verge of beginning (or have begun) operations as Indonesia's increasingly deregulated industry (another product of the economic crisis) enticed new investors into the fray. At the time of writing only seven of the original 13 domestic airlines start-ups which applied for licences to operate in Indonesia, are still on course, several of them with familiar names from the distant past, attempting to rise 'phoenix-like' from the ashes of their bankruptcies. During 2000 it is expected that *Mentari Airlines* will begin operations in Eastern Indonesia (Nusa Tenggara and Maluku); *Indonesian Airlines* is due to take over many of Sempati's routes (concentrated in Kalimantan, Sumatra, Java and Sulawesi), while *Pelita Airlines* which has been operating charter services for some years (it is owned by *Petamina*, the national oil company), is also due to begin commercial, scheduled operations. *Awair International* was the first of these new airlines to start up using Airbus A310 aircraft on a network that includes Denspasar, Jakarta and Surabaya. *Lion Airlines* was next, using B737-200 (the oldest 737 variant) flying between points in Sumatra and Jakarta with plans to expand regionally to Singapore and KL with a proposed fleet of 4 aircraft. Five other airlines hope to launch services this year primarily on domestic routes; these include *Bayu Indonesian Air, Rusmindo Internusa Air* and *Jataya Air*, in addition to *Indonesian Airlines* and *Pelita Air Services* mentioned above. As this should make clear, expect considerable change in Indonesia's airline industry.

Safety and maintenance Safety standards are reasonable, though Indonesian airlines do have their share of accidents. Indonesia heads the Southeast Asian region's list of poor performers by a clear margin, and Indonesia's worst performer is domestic carrier Merpati Nusantara. However, when you consider the number of flights and the conditions under which they are flown, in this the world's largest archipelago, the result is not quite as bad as it sounds. However with such a wave of start-up airlines, none with a proven safety record and many flying ancient planes, there is scope for a further deterioration in the country's air safety record.

By international standards, flights in Indonesia are cheap. It is also considerably cheaper buying tickets in Indonesia than it is purchasing them abroad. Offices in larger towns will usually accept credit card payment, although smaller branch offices in out-of-the-way places will often only take cash payment. Some airlines give student reductions; others don't. It is worth carrying an international student card (ISIC) and producing it when booking a ticket. Note that there can be difficulties booking seats on some legs (particularly in Nusa Tenggara). During holiday periods (for example the Islamic festival Lebaran when the entire nation seems to be on the move, and the traditional holiday period of August) flights are booked up some time ahead. That said, 'no shows' are many and it is always worth going to the airport even if the plane is said to be 'full'. It is essential to reconfirm tickets.

Garuda/Merpati offers a **Visit Indonesia Decade Pass**. The basic pass is for three 'stretches' (legs) and costs US$300 (plus 10% VAT). Each additional stretch costs a further US$100, up to a maximum of seven. The pass is valid for 60 days, with a minimum stay of five days, and can be used on all Garuda/Merpati routes except 'pioneer' services (perintis). These passes are obtainable by non-Indonesian citizens outside Indonesia in Japan, Hong Kong, Australia, New Zealand, Europe and US and are non-refundable. They are also available in Indonesia but whether you are purchasing in or out of the country, you must possess an incoming *Garuda International* ticket. Note that conditions on air passes periodically change and should be checked carefully before booking.

Train

There are no train services on Bali or the islands of West and East Nusa Tenggara.

Bus

Road transport in Indonesia has improved greatly in recent years, and main roads on most of the islands are generally in reasonably good condition. It should be noted that in many areas in Indonesia during the rainy season and after severe storms, even main roads may be impassable.

For details on road transport & conditions in a specific area, see the relevant regional introduction

Most Indonesians, as well as many visitors, get around by bus. Although bus travel is not always quick or comfortable, it is the cheapest (and often only) way to travel in Nusa Tenggara. Buses – and particularly non-a/c buses – are often overfilled and seats are designed for Indonesian, rather than Western bodies. A/c buses are generally less cramped. 'VIP' (pronounced as it is spelt – 'vip') buses are more comfortable still. There are also *bis pariwisata* – tourist buses – which have more space and may stop-off at *objek wisata* (tourist sights) *en route*. There is a range of bus alternatives:

bis ekonomi – speaks for itself really; the bottom rung of the bus ladder. Slow, uncomfortable, often full, but cheap. A great way to meet Indonesians and to interface with farm animals, but probably not recommended for long journeys.

bis patas – express buses, non-a/c. Marginally more comfortable than *ekonomi*, and also faster.

bis malam – (over)night buses. Usually a/c (and cold), probably the fastest buses, tend to arrive at their destinations very early in the morning.

bis pariwisata – tourist buses. More leg room, priced slightly cheaper than VIP buses but not as comfortable. Often minibuses rather than large coaches. Some stop off at tourist sights *en route*.

bis VIP – 'luxury' buses; a/c, more leg room, better service, usually driven with a little more care and attention.

The seats at the front of buses are the most comfortable, but also the most dangerous (crash-wise). In May 1993, it was reported that the police had asked bus drivers to pray

👉 *Bus prices*

	Journey time	Fare
Sumbawa		
Sumbawa Besar-Dompu		2,000Rp
Dompu-Hu'u		2,000Rp
Flores		
Bajawa-Labuanbajo	12 hours	15,000Rp
Bajawa-Ruteng	6 hours	7,500Rp
Bajawa-Ende	5 hours	7,500Rp
Lombok/Sumbawa		
Mataram-Sape	10 hours	52,000Rp (incl ferry)

NB *the prices quoted here were collected in mid-2000. But prices vary according to service (level of comfort, age, whether direct or not etc) and with the Indonesian economy in such a parlous state change more than was the case in the past.*

before setting off. Some people recommend booking two seats for comfort, although on non a/c buses it is difficult to lounge over two seats free from guilt when the vehicle is packed. Roads are often windy and rough, and buses are badly sprung (or totally un-sprung). Despite harrowingly fast speeds at times, do not expect to average much more than 40 km/hour. Overnight buses (*bis malam*) are usually faster and recommended for longer journeys. However, a/c *bis malam* can be very cold and a sarong or blanket is useful. Their other disadvantages are that the scenery passes in the darkness and they invariably arrive at anti-social, inconvenient times of day (or night). **NB** Watch out for pickpockets.

The key word when travelling by bus is: patience. On non-a/c buses be prepared for a tedious 'trawl' around town (for up to an hour) collecting passengers, until the bus is full to overflowing. Buses stop regularly for refreshments at dubious looking roadside restaurants, hawkers cram the aisle, selling hot sate, fruit, sweets, sunglasses, magazines, even pornographic playing cards. Loud music and violent videos keep the passengers either in heaven or purgatory. As most Indonesians have still to be convinced that smoking is bad for your health ("that's only true with Western cigarettes, *kreteks* [Indonesian clove cigarettes] are good for you") or that some people might find it distasteful, buses – and especially a/c buses – are also often fogged with cigarette smoke. The buses themselves are usually plastered with perplexing names such as 'No Problem – Banana on the Road', 'Sweet Memory', 'No Time for Love', 'Pash Boy's' and 'Khasoggi'. But, despite the drawbacks, buses are not only the cheapest and often the only way to get about, they are also one of the best ways to see the scenery and to meet Indonesians.

In many towns, bus companies have their offices at the bus terminal. However, this is not always true, and some long-distance buses may depart directly from a bus company's office located in another part of town to the terminal. Larger towns may also have several bus terminals, serving different points of the compass. These are often out of town, with regular bemos linking the various terminals with one another and with the town centre. In smaller towns, buses will sometimes pick up passengers from outside their losmen or hotel (although occasionally passengers may be asked for a surcharge). They may also drop passengers outside a losmen at the other end of the journey.

Tickets can be obtained from bus company offices or through travel agents; shop around for the best fare; bargaining is possible. It is sensible to book a day or so ahead for longer journeys. During Ramadan and at Lebaran all forms of public transport are packed. Estimated journey times are often wildly inaccurate. Although it is possible to book 'through' tickets, involving a change of vehicle in some town *en route* to your destination, this is not always the quickest, and almost certainly not the cheapest way to get from A to B. It can involve a long wait for a connecting bus and because the ticket ties you to one company (or its associated company) it is not possible to switch between firms. Connecting tickets, strangely, also tend to work out more expensive than buying two single tickets.

NB Bus fares vary a great deal depending on level of service (a/c, reclining seats, express etc), the size of the vehicle (coach or minibus), the number of seats, the time of departure, the age of the vehicle, and between bus companies (which is related to their reputation for safety and timeliness).

In the main tourist areas of Bali and Lombok look out for **shuttle buses**. These operate almost exclusively for the benefit of foreigners connecting the most popular destinations, with a fixed daily timetable. They may pick up and drop off passengers at their hotels, often for a small extra charge, and take a very great deal of the hassle out of ground travel, though you miss much of the local colour.

Bicycling

We have had a number of letters from people who have bicycled through various parts of Indonesia. The advice below is collated from their comments, and is meant to provide a general guideline for those intending to travel by bicycle. There may be areas, however, where the advice does not hold true. (Some of the letters we have received even disagree on some points.) Cycling round Bali is becoming increasingly popular.

Touring, hybrid or mountain bikes are fine for most roads and tracks in Indonesia – take an ordinary machine; nothing fancy.

Bike type

Readily available for most machines, and even small towns have bicycle repair shops where it is often possible to borrow larger tools such as vices. Mountain bikes have made a big impact in the country, so accessories for these are also widely available – although their quality might not be up to much. What is less common are components made of unusual materials – titanium and composites, for example. It is best to use common accessories. It may also be worthwhile forging a good relationship with a bike shop back home just in case a spare is not available – and then it can be couriered out. It is better to have a 'free' rear wheel, as opposed to a free hub and cassette, as the latter are generally not available, while free rear wheels are widely sold.

Spares

The view seems to be that it depends on the area. In Nusa Tenggara people are generally very welcoming and warm. In Bali bicyclists tend to be ignored. Officials, though, may view independent cyclists with some suspicion. Cars and buses often travel on the hard shoulder, and few expect to give way to a bicycle. Be very wary, especially on main roads. In general the principle throughout Indonesia is that the biggest vehicle has right of way, which means cyclists have to keep their wits about them and give way to just about everyone else.

Attitudes to bicyclists

The maps in this guide are not sufficiently detailed for bicycling and a good, colour map is useful in determining contours and altitude, as well as showing minor roads. Nelles produce a dedicated map of Nusa Tenggara. There are a large number of good maps of Bali, produced by Nelles, Periplus as well as many local companies.

Road conditions

Expect to pay a surcharge of about one third to a half of the cost of the ticket for buses and ferries. They are used to taking bicycles (although the more expensive a/c tour buses may prove reluctant). Most taxi drivers are not so keen on carrying bicycles – be ready to throw it in the boot and have bungee cords close at hand to secure.

Taking bikes on public transport

Essentials

☞ *Driving in Indonesia*

Renting a self-drive car in Indonesia has several advantages: it is a flexible, relatively quick, convenient and comfortable means of travel, and is a good way of experiencing the countryside and getting to out-of-the-way spots. But there are several dangers worth highlighting. As in many other Southeast Asian countries, 'might is right' – smaller vehicles give way to larger ones. A driver flashing his headlights normally means 'don't mess with me'. Although Indonesians are a very courteous people, this does not apply when in a car. Traffic does not always remain in the allotted lanes – it is best to adopt a strategy of follow-the-leader and go with the flow. Cutting in is an accepted way of changing lanes. After driving in Indonesia many people leave firmly beliving that the guiding principle adhered to by most road users is that 'Time is money and lives are cheap'.

If involved in an accident, it is best to go to the nearest police station to report the incident, rather than waiting at the scene. Signposting is generally poor, so be sure to get a good map. Often the best way to find the names of roads is to look at signs on shops, mosques, schools, hospitals, and so on. Many towns have complicated one-way systems, which take a bit of negotiating. Every town has its army of semi-official traffic wardens – often dressed in orange jumpsuits – waiting with whistle poised to usher motorists into a parking spot. All 'parkir' must be paid for. Petrol is cheap and Pertamina stations are found on all main highways.

Many international airlines take bicycles free-of-charge, provided they are not boxed. Take the peddles off and deflate the tyres. Domestic airlines sometimes charge, although there does not seem to be a hard-and-fast rule.

Equipment   **Useful** Pollution mask if travelling to large cities; basic toolkit – although there always seems to be help near at hand, and local workshops seem to be able to improvise a solution to just about any problem – including a puncture repair kit, spare tubes, spare tyre, pump; good map of the area; bungee cords; first aid kit; water filter.

Unnecessary A tent is generally not needed. Every small town will have a guesthouse of some description. Nor is it worth taking a stove, cooking utensils, sleeping bag, food. It is almost always possible to get food and a place to sleep – and cheaply, too. The equipment is simply a burden. The exceptions to this are the really back-of-beyond areas of Indonesia. A 'D' lock is not really necessary – they are hefty and a simple cable lock will suffice. Many bicyclists take their machines into their rooms at night.

Car hire

Cars can be hired for self-drive (see box next page) or with a driver, but mainly in Bali and Lombok. Chauffeur-driven vehicles are available by the hour or by the day, and cost about 15,000Rp/hour for use within a city, rather more if travelling out of town. For an out-of-town trip expect to pay about 200,000Rp (you would also be expected to buy the driver his lunch, drinks and such like.) A cheaper alternative is to simply charter a bemo for the day.

Generally, self-drive cars are only available at the more popular tourist destinations (eg Bali and Lombok) and in the bigger cities; expect to pay about US$40-50/day depending on the company, and the condition and type of vehicle. In Bali and Lombok, there are numerous small operations that offer cars and jeeps for hire and prices in Bali and Lombok are probably the lowest of all. For car rental offices, see the appropriate town entry. International groups like *Avis* and *Hertz* operate in more popular tourist destinations.

Other local transport

Becaks or bicycle rickshaws are one of the cheapest, and most important, forms of **Becaks**
short-distance transport in Indonesia. Literally hundreds of thousands of poor people
make a living driving becaks. They are a good – and sedate – way to explore the
backstreets and alleys of a city and can be chartered by the hour or for a particular
journey. Bargain hard and agree a fare before boarding.

These are small buses or adapted pick-ups which operate fixed routes. The name **Bemos**
originates from 'motorized becak' (*becak motor*). The bemo is gradually being replaced
by the larger oplet (see below). Bemos usually run fixed routes for fixed fares (it varies
between towns, but around 500Rp) but can also be chartered by the hour or day.

Trucks converted into buses with bench seats down each side. They are now only in **Bis kayu**
use on minor roads on some islands in Nusa Tenggara, such as Flores. Slow and
uncomfortable, they often ply unsealed roads.

These come in various shapes and sizes. *Dokars* are two-wheeled pony carts carrying **Horsecarts**
two to three passengers found, for example, in Padang, West Sumatra. In Lombok
dokars are known as *cidomos*, while in Bima-Raba (Sumbawa) they are proudly named
Ben Hurs. *Andongs* are larger four-wheeled horse-drawn wagons, carrying up to six
people. Horse-drawn transport is still very common in the countryside, and 'stands' of
carts can be seen arrayed at most markets.

Available at many beach resorts and increasingly in other towns. Rates per day vary **Motorbike hire**
according to size and condition of the machine, but range from 25-50,000Rp. It is
illegal to ride without a helmet, although this can just be a construction worker's hard
hat. Many machines are poorly maintained, so check brakes and lights before paying.
The pointers on driving in Indonesia in the car hire section above, and in the box, apply
equally to driving motorbikes (if not more so). The most likely place to find bikes for
hire is from guesthouses and losmen geared to foreign tourists.

These are motorcycle taxis – a form of transport which is becoming increasingly popular. **Ojeks**
Ojek riders, often wearing coloured jackets, congregate at junctions, taking passengers
pillion to their destination. Agree a price before boarding and bargain hard.

Larger versions of bemos carrying 10-12 passengers. They have a bewildering number **Oplets**
of other names and in rural areas tend to be called *Colts*. In larger cities bemos/colts
often follow fixed routes. They are sometimes colour coded, sometimes numbered,
sometimes have their destinations marked on the front – and sometimes all three. For
intra-city trips there is usually a fixed fare – it varies between towns, but around 500Rp
– although it is worth asking one of your fellow passengers what the *harga biasa*
(normal price) is, or watch what is being handed to the driver or his sidekick by fellow
passengers. In the countryside, routes can vary and so do fares; be prepared to bargain.
Oplets can also be chartered by the hour or day (bargain hard).

Taxis are metered in the major cities. Unmetered taxis can be shared for longer **Taxis**
journeys. **NB** Drivers cannot usually change large bills. All registered taxis, minibuses
and rental cars have yellow number plates; black number plates are for private
vehicles, and red are for government-owned vehicles. Pirate taxis (with black number
plates) tend to operate at airports, supermarkets and in city centres.

In some of the more popular tourist destinations, guesthouses and some tour **Bicycles**
companies hire out bicycles. These vary a great deal in quality – check the brakes

Essentials

before you set off! See above for some general pointers of bicycling in Indonesia. Expect to pay about 20,000Rp/day for a locally or Chinese-built mountain bike.

Sea

Boat The national shipping company is *PELNI*, standing for *Pelayaran Nasional Indonesia*. PELNI's fleet of ships are a critical component in Nusa Tenggara, linking the myriad islands that make up this disjointed region. The company's head office is at Jl Gajah Mada 14, Jakarta, T021-6334342, F3854130. For ticket offices, see relevant town entries. Note that many travel agents also sell *Pelni* tickets and although they levy a small surcharge may be far more convenient. Pelni operates an expanding fleet of modern passenger ships which ply fortnightly circuits throughout the archipelago (see timetables). The ships are well run and well maintained, have an excellent safety record, and are a comfortable and leisurely way to travel. Each accommodates 500-2,250 passengers in five classes, has central a/c, a bar, restaurant and cafetería. In 1999 there were 21 ships in the *Pelni* fleet with one more vessel due to join in 2000.

First Class cabins have attached bathrooms and TV sets. Classes I-IV are single sex – unless a group takes the whole cabin. Class II has 4 bunks per cabin, Class III, 6 bunks and Class IV, 8 bunks. Fares include all meals (no matter what class), and classes I-IV are cabin classes, while class V is 'deck' class (in fact, in a large a/c room where mattresses can be rented for 2,500Rp). Note that even First Class cabins are 'inside', ie they have no portholes. All classes tend to be chilly so don't get caught with nothing more than a pair of shorts and a t-shirt. It may be possible to leave bags at the ship's information desk. Booking ahead (max, seven days) is advisable

Pelni ports

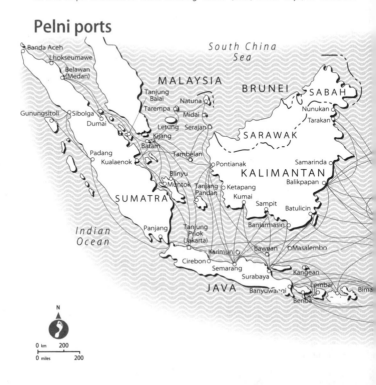

although in smaller ports of call it may only be possible to make reservations four days in advance. Get hold of an up-to-date *Pelni* timetable when you arrive. Even with this to hand, it is advisable, when planning a trip, to check in a big *Pelni* office that departure dates are the same as given on the timetable. Often the smaller agents only work on the basis of the timetable, which may not necessarily be accurate. When queueing for tickets, it is sometimes worth following the locals' example and pushing your way to the front, or at least actively defending your position in the queue; this may ensure that you actually get a berth and a mattress. Having said that, it sometimes can seem like a free-for-all once you are on board and you will need to grab the first cabin you can find.

In addition to these ships, *Pelni* also operates a so-called 'pioneer' service – *Pelayaran Perintis* – serving smaller, more out-of-the-way ports. Perintis vessels are important means of travel in Maluku for example. These ships have no cabins but take passengers 'deck' class. Like their more illustrious sister vessels, they are generally well run and safe, if not always comfortable. Finally, there are the mixed cargo boats and ships which go just about everywhere. Passage can be secured just by visiting the port and asking around. **NB** Safety equipment may not be up to standard, and level of comfort is minimal.

A new fast ferry service was inaugurated to eastern Indonesia from Benoa Harbour in Bali in mid-2000. The 70-m, 925 passenger ship *Barito*, with a top speed of 36 knots, leaves every Friday afternoon at 1800 hours on a 16 hour voyage to Bima (Sumbawa) and Kupang (Timor). Every Sunday at midday the Barito makes a 7 hour hop to the port of Surabaya in eastern Java. For more information contact **Gama Dewata Bali Tours** at T0361-263568 or T0361-232704, F0361-263569.

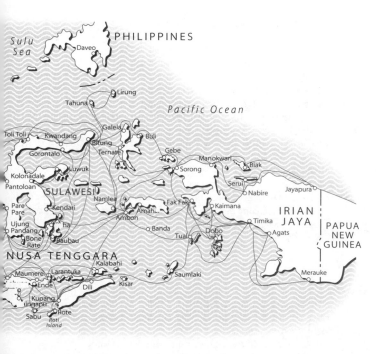

Keeping in touch

Communications

Email &
internet access

Email has caught on fast in Indonesia, and any town of any size has its cyber café. This is especially true of tourist destinations. To remain in email contact with people back home while travelling sign up for a free account with one of the email service providers such as: **Hotmail**:   http://www.hotmail.com;   **Yahoo**:   http://mail.yahoo.com;   **Rocketmail**: http://www.rocketmail.com; **NetAddress**: http://www.netaddress.usa.net

You'll be asked for a name and password. As you travel you can download your emails at any of the growing number of cyber cafés.

Postal services

The postal service is relatively reliable; though important mail should be registered. Every town and tourist centre has either a *kantor pos* (post office) or postal agent where you can buy stamps, post letters and parcels; in many cases they also provide poste restante services. For poste restante, have your letters addressed using your surname first, underlined and in capitals if possible. (Otherwise you may find your letters filed under your Christian name). Kantor pos keep official government hours : Mon-Sat 0800-1400. Postal agents open much longer hours, often until 2200 daily.

Faxes and telexes can be sent from major hotels and *Perumtel*, *Telekom* and *Wartel* offices, found in most major towns. These are often open 24 hours. Post and telex/fax offices are listed under Post & telecommunications in each town entry.

Telephone
services

Indonesia has a comprehensive telecommunications network which links the islands throughout the country and boasts its own satellite (Indosat). Every town has its communication centres (*Warpostel*) where you can make local, interlocal (between other areas within Indonesia) and international calls and faxes. Most Warpostels open early in the morning and operate until around midnight. Interlocal calls are cheaper after 2100, so centres tend to be very busy then. International calls have a cheap rate between midnight and 0800, and all Sat and Sun. Calls are expensive. There is a wide network of card phones and coin phones (taking 50Rp and 100Rp coins) throughout Jakarta and other main towns and cities in hotels, shopping centres, street corners. Telephone cards (*Kartu telepon*) are sold in Warpostel's, supermarkets and a wide range of shops. Sold according to number of units at the rate of 82.5Rp per unit, so that a 100 unit card costs 8,250Rp. Cards come in the following units: 60, 100, 140, 280, 400 and 680.

International calls can be made from card phones and from *Perumtel*, *Telekom* and *Wartel* offices which are often open 24 hours. Direct international dialling and collect calls can be made from here. **International enquiries**: 102. **Operator**: 101. **Local enquiries**: 108. **Long distance enquiries**: 106. **International country code**: 62. Local telephone codes are given in each entry under the heading 'Post and telecommunications'.

Media

Newspapers

English language newspapers are the *Indonesia Times*, *Jakarta Post* (which carries international news from Reuters reports and English football league reports) and *Indonesia Observer/Sunday Observer*. With Indonesia's halting progress towards democratization, one of the outcomes is the emergence of a much more independent and combative press. Of the international newspapers available in Indonesia, the *Asian Wall Street Journal* and the *International Herald Tribune* can be purchased in Jakarta and some other major cities and tourist destinations; so too can the Singapore *Straits Times*. Among English language magazines, the most widely available are the

Economist, Time, Newsweek and the Hong Kong-based *Far Eastern Economic Review*. The latter provides the most comprehensive regional coverage and is well-informed.

Bali The *Jakarta Post* is now published on Bali so should be available early in the day, and there is talk of also publishing a Bali supplement. The free English language *Bali News* is published once a fortnight and can be found at many hotel desks. The *Bali Echo* magazine has interesting, often well-informed articles on Indonesian and Balinese culture, history, the environment, high society, social events and a practical section; distributed free in upmarket hotels. *Bali Plus* has information on tourist sites, a calendar of festivals and cultural events, practical information and maps; distributed at the airport and upmarket hotes. The *Bali Advertiser*, aimed at the expatriate community, has a 'community events' section listing everything from local meetings of Alcoholics Anonymous and local support groups, to sports events, aerobics classes, elementary and international schools and church services, as well as a real estate section listing properties available to rent, items for sale including cars, and an employment section; distributed in supermarkets and some hotels. All these are complimentary.

Radio *Republik Indonesia* (RRI) broadcasts throughout the country. News and **Radio** commentary in English is broadcast for about an hour a day. Shortwave radios will pick up Voice of America, the BBC World Service and Australian Broadcasting. See page 68 for BBC and VoA frequencies.

Indonesia has put satellites into geostationary orbit so that television pictures can be **Television** received anywhere in the archipelago. The vast 'parabolas' outside many houses, including shacks which may not even have piped water, testifies to the power of television and the priorities of many Indonesian households. Televisi Republik Indonesia (TVRI) is the government-run channel. There are also four private stations – although these rigorously toe the government line when it comes to reporting news. Hotels also usually receive satellite TV and if they have a significant foreign clientele they may well tune into English language channels. CNN, BBC, Star, Television Australia, Malaysian, Philippine and Thai television can all be received in Indonesia.

Food and drink

Food

Although Indonesia is made up of a bewildering array of ethnic groups dispersed over 5 million sq km of land and sea, the main staple across the archipelago is rice. Today, alternatives such as corn, sweet potatoes and sago, which are grown primarily in the dry islands of the East, are regarded as 'poor man's food', and rice is the preferred staple.

Indonesians will eat **rice** – or *nasi* (milled, cooked rice) – at least three times a day. Breakfast often consists of left-over rice, stir-fried and served up as *nasi goreng*. Mid-morning snacks are often sticky rice cakes or *pisang goreng* (fried bananas). Rice is the staple for lunch, served up with two or three meat and vegetable dishes and followed by fresh fruit. The main meal is supper, which is served quite early and again consists of rice, this time accompanied by as many as five or six other dishes. *Sate/satay* (grilled skewers of meat), *soto* (a nourishing soup) or *bakmi* (noodles, a dish of Chinese origin) may be served first.

In many towns, sate, soto or bakmi vendors roam the streets with pushcarts containing charcoal braziers, ringing a bell or hitting a block (the noise will signify what he or she is selling), looking for customers in the early evenings. These carts provide the cheapest food, anything from *soto ayam* (chicken noodle soup), to *bakso*

Restaurant price guide

Expensive 50,000Rp+.
Hotel restaurants and exclusive restaurants.

Mid-range 50,000-20,000Rp.
Restaurants in tourist class hotels and more expensive local restaurants.

Cheap 20,000-10,000Rp.
Coffee shops and basic restaurants.

Very cheap under 10,000Rp.
A warung or roadside stall.

(meatballs), or noodles often of a sickly greenish hue. Somehow the pushcarts selling sweet items such as cakes or fried bananas in batter look more appealing. In Bali the pushcart vendors are often refugees from East Java, particularly those that frequent the Kuta area in the south. These pushcarts are known as **kaki lima** – literally 'five legs'. There are two schools of thought as to the origins of the term. Most people maintain that they are named after the three 'legs' of the cart plus the two of the vendor. But pedagang (vendor) kaki lima (abbreviated to PK5 in newspaper reports) also refers to hawkers who peddle their wares from stalls and from baskets hung from shoulder poles. The second interpretation of the term maintains that kaki lima in fact refers to the pavement, which formerly used to have a width of 5 ft. This is a less obvious, and rather more attractive interpretation.

Larger foodstalls where there is too much to cart around tend to set up in the same place every evening in a central position in town. These **warungs**, as they are known, may be temporary structures or more permanent buildings, with simple tables and benches. In the larger cities, there may be an area of warungs, all under one roof. Often a particular street will become known as the best place to find particular dishes like martabak (savoury meat pancakes) or gado gado (vegetable salad served with peanut sauce). Some of the tastiest and cheapest meals can be found in the small warungs popular with locals; however, portions will be small and consist mainly of rice with a few tasty vegetables, and any meat may well be tough and gristly. Rice (nasi), egg noodles (mie) and rice-flour noodles (bakmi) form the basis of the cheaper Indonesian meals such as nasi goreng (fried rice) and mie goreng (fried noodles). Good value at local restaurants is nasi campur (pronounced 'champur'), which is mixed rice served with whatever the cook has to hand: tasty vegetables, fish, meat, chicken or tempe and tahu, krupuk (deep fried rice or tapioca crackers the best of which are flavoured with prawn) and fried egg. The busier the restaurant the more variety of ingredients will be available and the better your nasi campur will be. Nasi campur can be hard to find in tourist restaurants probably because it represents 'too good' value for money. It is common to see some warungs being labelled wartegs. These are stalls selling dishes from Tegal, a town on Java's north coast – Warung Tegal = warteg. More formalized restaurants are known simply as rumah makan, literally 'eating houses', often shortened to just 'RM'. Another term for cheaper restaurants is 'Depot', which is often rather appropriate. A good place to look for cheap stall food is in and around the market or pasar (from the Arabic bazaar); night markets or pasar malam are usually better for eating than day markets.

Feast days, such as Lebaran marking the end of Ramadan, are a cause for great celebration and traditional dishes are served. Lontong or ketupat are made at this time (they are both versions of boiled rice – simmered in a small container or bag, so that as it cooks, the rice is compressed to make a solid block). This may be accompanied by sambal goreng daging (fried beef in a coconut sauce) in Java or rendang (curried beef) in Sumatra – and by people with Javanese or Sumatran roots in many other areas of the country. Nasi kuning (yellow rice) is traditionally served at a selamatan (a Javanese celebration marking a birth, the collection of the rice harvest or the completion of a new house).

Balinese cuisine and food on Bali

Visitors to Bali are more likely to encounter Indonesian, Chinese and Western cuisine than Balinese. However things are getting better. As a result of the growth in upmarket tourism to Bali more restaurants specializing in excellent Balinese cuisine are appearing, but their food does not come cheap. Ubud is undoubtedly the best place for good Balinese food at every price level.

The truly outstanding Balinese cooking is mostly served at festive occasions and religious ceremonies. The best known dish is **babi guling**, suckling pig roasted on a spit and stuffed with chilli pepper, red onion, turmeric, ginger, candlenuts, garlic, salt and pepper, all mixed with coconut oil. The skin is rubbed with turmeric to give it an attractive brown glaze. The pig is cooked on a wood fire and turned continually for about three hours. At ceremonies most of the pigs are way past the suckling stage. Another dish visitors may come across is **bebek betutu**, smoked duck cooked very slowly in an earth oven. Other dishes include: **Lawar**, a mixture of spicy, raw meat; **be tumbus**, boiled fish served in a spicy, tomato sauce; and **tum**, beef ground with spices, wrapped in a banana leaf and steamed.

Everyday Balinese home cooking consists primarily of rice with assorted spicy vegetables, fish or meat. Food is cooked in the morning, then covered and eaten cold during the day as required. Coconut is frequently used to provide some of the most delicious flavours. Most of the tourist hotels offer a Balinese feast which may or may not approximate to the real thing.

Coconuts are central to Balinese cooking. There are more than 10 varieties of coconut found on Bali. Coconut oil is used for frying; ground coconut is an essential ingredient in many sauces, marinades, ground meat, sate, vegetable dishes, and in santen which is coconut cream. The young coconut provides a sweet, refreshing drink and when fermented it becomes the alcoholic beverage tuak.

There are more than 100 types of vegetable eaten in Bali including **bayem** which is similar to spinach, **pusuh biu** the flower of the banana plant, **kekalan** tender young banana shoots, **buah pete** bean pods, **paku** edible ferns, **kacang** beans, **ubi** sweet potatoes, **bawang pere** leaks, and **bangkuwang** which is water chestnut. **Avocados** are ubiquitous and the leaves of many plants including sweet potato, acacia, papaya, peanut and mango are used in cooking. In the cooler climate of the mountainous interior, more familiar temperate vegetables such as tomatoes, cabbage, cauliflower and beans also grow in abundance.

Popular puddings include **bubur injin** (rice pudding made with black rice, coconut milk and brown palm sugar) and **pisang goreng** (fried banana in batter).

Other cuisine on Bali

Ordinary tourist fare can be disappointing. Meals tend to be rather bland and geared to perceived tourist tastes. Portions are often small, and quality is very variable; one day you might have an excellent meal but the next day the exact same item on the menu could be altogether inferior. Again the exception is Ubud, where many small restaurants serve excellent reasonably priced Indonesian, vegetarian, Asian and international food.

Vegetarians will find plenty of tasty dishes; tofu and tempe (fermented beancurd), are widely available. In the main tourist centres you are more likely to find Mexican or Italian food than Balinese cooking. Pizza is currently the 'in' food with pizza parlours springing up everywhere including in the five-star hotels.

In addition to familiar tropical fruits, strawberries are grown extensively in Bedugul and grape vines are cultivated along the north coast. Some of the best tropical fruit is grown along the northern coastal strip; this area is where the best mangoes grow. The tastiest salak are grown in the foothills of Gunung Agung near Sibetan and the season runs from December to March.

Essentials

Tempe: soybean cake

Tempe *has recently become a popular health food in the West, but its origins are Indonesian. It is believed to have originated in Java about 100 years ago, with the establishment of the soybean trade with China. In Indonesia, it is used as a meat-substitute by poorer communities, providing a cheap meal, rich in protein. During the Second World War, tempe became familiar to prisoners in Japanese prison camps. It is an easily digestible nutritious food, because it is fermented before being eaten. It contains no cholesterol or saturated fats, but does* contain the vitamin B12. It is made by injecting cooked soybean with a fungal spore. The soybean is packed in banana leaves (now, more usually, plastic bags) and left to ferment. A solid white cake is formed, looking rather like a cheese, which is then cut into slices and may be deep fried *(tempe goreng) or simmered in spicy coconut milk (pechel tempe – an East Javan speciality). Visitors to Indonesia are most likely to come across tempe in* gado-gado, *where it is served, along with a hard-boiled egg, on top of vegetables.*

In addition to rice, there are a number of other common ingredients used across the country. Coconut milk, ginger, chilli peppers and peanuts are used nationwide, while dried salted fish and soybeans are important sources of protein. In coastal areas, fish and seafood tend to be more important than meat. As Indonesia is over 80% Muslim, pork is not widely eaten, although Chinese restaurants usually serve it and in some areas, such as Bali and Christian Flores, it is much more in evidence.

Commonly found **spices** include *cabe/tabia* red chilli, *kesuna* garlic, *bawang merah* red onion, coconut, fermented fish paste, *jahe* ginger, ground peanuts, *sra* shrimp paste, *nyuh* coconut, *tingku* candlenuts, *kunyit* turmeric, *ketumbah* coriander, and *celagi* tamarind. *Basa genep* is a popular ready-mixed spice found in the shops and consisting of 30-40 different ingredients. On the table of every warung you will find the spicy, chili based sauce *sambal*, *kecap asin* which is like soy sauce and *kecap manis* which is sweet and thicker. Every family grows a few chilli plants and has its own secret recipe for *sambal*; the larger the chilli pepper the less hot it is likely to be; young chillies are green turning red as they become hotter and mature. *Pedas* means hot! It is the seeds of the chilli which are the source of the 'hot' effect; if you find your mouth is on fire eat some plain rice, cucumber or bread, this is much more effective than drinking water or beer. Squeezing lemon over a hot dish is said to make it taste milder.

Regional cuisines Although Indonesia is becoming more homogeneous as Javanese culture spreads to the Outer Islands, there are still distinctive regional cuisines. The food of **Java** itself embraces a number of regional forms, of which the most distinctive is **Sundanese**. *Lalap*, a Sundanese dish, consists of raw vegetables and is said to be the only Indonesian dish where vegetables are eaten uncooked. Characteristic ingredients of Javanese dishes are soybeans, beef, chicken and vegetables; characteristic flavours are an interplay of sweetness and spiciness. Probably the most famous regional cuisine however is **Padang** or **Minang** food, which has its origins in West Sumatra province. Padang food has 'colonized' the rest of the country and there are Padang restaurants in every town, no matter how small. Dishes tend to be hot and spicy, using quantities of chilli and turmeric, and include *rendang* (dry beef curry), *kalo ayam* (creamy chicken curry) and *dendeng balado* fried seasoned sun-dried meat with a spicy coating). In **Eastern Indonesia**, seafood and fish are important elements in the diet, and fish grilled over an open brazier (*ikan panggang* or *ikan bakar*) and served with spices and rice is a delicious, common dish. There are large numbers of Chinese people scattered across the archipelago and, like other countries of the region, **Chinese** restaurants are widespread.

Drink

Water must be boiled before it is safe to drink. If boiling it yourself be aware that some organisms (such as the one which causes amoebic dysentery) can survive up to five minutes of boiling so anything less could be dangerous. Hotels and most restaurants, as a matter of course, should boil the water they offer customers. Ask for *air minum*, literally 'drinking water', *air putih* or *air mendidih* (boiled water). You may have to try both *air putih* and *air mendidih* to get what you want; in some places if you ask for *air mendidih* you will get boiling hot water rather than the previously boiled water. On Bali *air putih* usually means cold but previously boiled water. Many restaurants provide a big jug of boiled water on each table. But in cheaper establishments it is probably best to play safe and ask for bottled water. Note that some tourist restaurants may be reluctant to provide it since it is free. (You should not be charged for *air putih* unless ice is added.)

Over the last few years '**mineral water**' – of which the most famous is *Aqua* ('aqua' has become the generic word for mineral water) – has become increasingly popular. It is now available from Aceh to Irian Jaya in all but the smallest and most remote towns. There have been some reports of empty mineral water bottles being refilled with tap water: check the seal before accepting a bottle. The cheapest place to buy bottled water is in supermarkets and Matahari Department Stores; it comes in 500 ml, 1500 ml and 6 l containers as well as giant kegs. The 6 l size is not necessarily cheaper than 4 x 1500 ml size.

Western **bottled and canned drinks** like *Sprite*, *Coca-Cola*, *7-Up* and *Fanta* are widely available in Indonesia and are comparatively cheap. Alternatively most restaurants will serve *air jeruk* – citrus **fruit juices** – with or without ice (*es*). The **milk of a fresh coconut** is a good thirst quencher and a good source of potassium and glucose. Fresh fruit juices vary greatly in quality; some are little more than water, sugar and ice. Ice in many places is fine, but in cheaper restaurants and away from tourist areas many people recommend taking drinks without ice.

Javanese, Sumatran, Sulawesi or Timorese **coffee** (*kopi*), fresh and strong, is an excellent morning pick-you-up. It is usually served sweet (*kopi manis*) and black; if you want to have it without sugar ask for it *tidak pakai gula*. The same goes for other drinks habitually served with mountains of sugar (like fruit juices). If you plan to buy coffee at the supermarket be aware that the cheaper brands are mixed with rice flour which causes an unpleasant bloating effect and is very inferior. **Milk** (*susu*) is available in tourist areas and large towns, but it may be sweetened condensed milk. **Tea** (*teh*), usually weak, is obtainable almost everywhere. Another refreshing drink is hot ginger tea.

Although Indonesia is a predominantly Muslim country, alcoholic drinks are widely available. The two most popular **beers** – light lagers – are the locally brewed *Anker* and *Bintang* brands. Locally brewed beer is good, the breweries having benefited from European collaboration in the early years. Good **wine** is much harder to come by. Two sweetish red wines are produced on Bali from locally grown grapes and are widely available on the island. Both vinyards are under British tutelage. One wine, marketed under the name 'Hatton', sells for about 80,000Rp; the other hasn't yet got a licence but is sold in beer bottles and has been described, probably rather euphemistically, as tasting 'like Bordeaux'! Imported **spirits** like whisky and gin are usually only sold in the more expensive restaurants and hotels. They are comparatively expensive – about 8-10,000Rp for a large bottle in a restaurant. There are, however, a number of local brews including *brem* (rice wine), *arak* (rice whisky) and *tuak* (palm wine).

Tipping & tax in restaurants Expect to pay a 21% tax and service charge in the more expensive restaurants, particularly in tourist areas of Bali and Lombok. Even the cheaper restaurants serving foreigners may add 10% to the bill.

Essentials

Essentials

Indonesian food glossary

Arak *A strong spirit made from distilled sugar palm or rice*
asam *tamarind; sold in a solid block, or still in the brown pod*
atpokat *avocado*
ayam *chicken*
ayam goreng *fried chicken*
babek *duck*
babi *pork*
bakar *roast*
bakmi *rice flour noodles*
bakso *meat balls*
belimbing *star fruit*
bifstik *beef steak*
Brem *sweet rice wine*
cabe *chilli*
cumi cumi *squid*
dadar *omelette/pancake*
daging *beef/meat*
durian *durian*
es *ice*
es krim *ice cream*
garam *salt*
goreng *stir fry*
gula *sugar*

gulai *curry soup*
ikan *fish*
istemiwa *'special' – nasi goreng istemiwa has a fried egg and other additions*
jeruk *generic term in Java and Bali for citrus fruit*
jeruk bali *pomelo*
jeruk manis *orange*
jeruk nipis *lime*
kacang *generic term for bean or nut*
kacang *peanut sauce*
kacang buncis *french bean*
kacang kedele *soybean*
kacang tanah *peanut*
kambing *lamb/goat*
kangkung *'greens' grown in water*
kayu manis *cinnamon*
kecap asin *salt-soy sauce*
kelengkeng *lychee*
kemiri *macadamia nut*
kenari *a shade tree which produces a nut similar to an almond*
kepiting *crab*
ketimun *cucumber*

Shopping

Indonesia offers a wealth of distinctive handicrafts and other products. Best buys include textiles (batik and ikat), silverwork, woodcarving, puppets, paintings and ceramics. Bali has the greatest choice of handicrafts; fashion and children's clothes are also good buys and several international designers have shops in the new upmarket malls. It is not necessarily the case that you will find the best buys in the area where a particular product is made; the larger cities, especially Jakarta, sell a wide range of handicrafts and antiques from across the archipelago at competitive prices.

Tips on buying Early morning sales may well be cheaper, as salespeople often believe the first sale augers well for the rest of the day. Except in the larger fixed price stores, **bargaining** (with good humour) is expected; start bargaining at 50-60% lower than the asking price. Do not expect to achieve instant results; if you walk away from the shop, you will almost certainly be followed, with a lower offer. If the salesperson agrees to your price, you should really feel obliged to purchase – it is considered very ill mannered to agree on a price and then not buy the article.

Antiques There are some good antique shops in Bali and a few other towns in Nusa Tenggara, but bargains usually need to be 'rooted out' by visiting little out-of-the-way shops. Antiques include Dutch memorabilia and Chinese ceramics (Indonesia was on the trade route between China and India), as well as various local products. **NB** There are also a huge number of fakes on the market.

Essentials

kodok *frog*	**papaya (kates)** *papaya*
kopi *coffee*	**pisang** *banana*
kopi bubuk *ground coffee (with grounds)*	**rambutan** *rambutan*
	rebus *boil*
kopi saring *filtered coffee*	**roti** *bread*
krupuk *deep-fried tapioca crackers*	**salak** *brown, pear shaped fruit, with a shiny, snake-like skin. The flesh is white, segmented and dry. Balinese salak are considered to be the sweetest*
kuah *gravy*	
kue *cake*	
kunyit *turmeric*	
lombok *chilli*	**sambal** *chilli paste*
lontong *compressed rice, usually served with sate*	**santen** *coconut milk*
	sawi *Chinese cabbage*
madu *honey*	**sayur** *vegetables*
mangga *mango*	**semangka air** *watermelon*
manggis *mangosteen*	**sereh** *lemon grass*
manis *sweet*	**serundeng** *grated coconut roasted with peanuts*
merica *black pepper*	
mie *noodles*	**sop** *soup*
nangka *jackfruit, eaten ripe as a fruit or unripe cooked as a vegetable*	**tahu** *soybean curd*
	telur *egg*
nasi *rice*	**tempe** *fermented soybean cake (see box)*
nasi putih *plain white rice*	**Tuak** *wine made from rice, sugar palm or coconut*
nenas *pineapple*	
pala *nutmeg*	**udang** *shrimp*
panggang *grill*	**udang karang** *lobster*

Batik
Centres of batik-making are focused on islands not covered by this book, especially Java. However batik is nonetheless widely available in Bali, Lombok and the other islands of Nusa Tenggara. The traditional hand-drawn batiks (**batik tulis**) are naturally more expensive than the modern printed batiks.

Clothing
Very reasonably priced Western-style clothes can be found in most of the bigger cities. Large department stores and markets are the best places to browse. Children's clothes are also very good value (although dyes may run). Bali offers the best fashion clothing. (See shopping sections in the Bali chapter for more information.)

Ikat
This dyed and woven cloth is found on the islands of Bali, Lombok and Nusa Tenggara (Sumba, Flores, Timor, and the smaller islands of the Alor and Solor archipelagos), although it is not cheap and is sometimes of rather dubious quality. For more information see page 181.

Jewellery
Gems mined in Indonesia include diamonds and black opals from Kalimantan and pearls from Maluku. Contemporary-style jewellery is made in Bali (although some is of poor quality).

Metalwork
The traditional Malay sword, the *kris* is the most popular buy. Both antique and modern examples are available.

Painting
Ubud (Bali) has, since the 1930s, been a centre for local artists and is a good place to buy tropical-style paintings (see page 234).

| **Wayang puppets** | Wayang is a Javanese and Balinese art form and puppets are most widely available on these two islands. |

Weaving Baskets of all shapes and sizes are made for practical, everyday use, out of rattan, bamboo, sisal and nipah and lontar palm. The intricate baskets of Lombok are particularly attractive.

Woodcarving This ranges from the clearly ersatz and tourist oriented (Bali), to 'primitive' pieces from some areas of Nusa Tenggara. The greatest concentration of woodcarvers work in Bali producing skilful modern designs as well as more traditional pieces.

Holidays and festivals

See below for a separate listing of Muslim holidays and festivals. **NB** these holidays are subject to change. See also page 238.

National holidays and other festivals

January **Tahun Baru,** New Year's Day (1st: public holiday). **New Year's Eve** is celebrated with street carnivals, shows, fireworks and all-night festivities. In Christian areas, festivities are more exuberant, with people visiting each other on New Year's Day and attending church services.

January/ February **Imlek,** Chinese New Year (movable, 24th-25th January 2001, 12th-14th February 2002). It is not an official holiday, but many Chinese shops and businesses close for at least two days. Within the Chinese community, younger people visit their relatives, children are given *hong bao* (lucky money), new clothes are bought and any unfinished business is cleared up before the New Year.

March/April **Wafat Isa Al-Masih,** Good Friday (movable: public holiday, 13th April 2001, 29th March 2002). **Nyepi** (movable: public holiday, 26th March 2001). **Balinese Saka New Year** (1995 = 1917). **Kartini Day** (21 Apr). A ceremony held by women to mark the birthday of Raden Ajeng Kartini, born in 1879 and proclaimed as a pioneer of women's emancipation. The festival is rather like mothers' day, in that women are supposed to be pampered by their husbands and children, although it is women's organizations like the Dharma Wanita who get most excited. Women dress in national dress.

May **Waisak Day** (movable: public holiday). Marks the birth and death of the historic Buddha; at Candi Mendut outside Yogyakarta a procession of monks carrying flowers, candles, holy fire and images of the Buddha walk to Borobudur. **Kenaikan Isa Al-Masih** or Ascension Day (movable: public holiday).

August **Independence Day** (17th: public holiday). This is the most important national holiday, celebrated with processions, dancing and other merry-making. Although it is officially on 17th, festivities continue for a whole month, towns are decorated with bunting and parades cause delays to bus travel, there seems to be no way of knowing when each town will hold its parades.

October **Hari Pancasila** (1st). This commemorates the Five Basic Principles of Pancasila (see page 410). **Armed Forces Day** (5th). The anniversary of the founding of the Indonesian Armed Forces, with military parades and demonstrations.

Christmas Day (25th: public holiday). Celebrated by Christians – the Bataks of   December
Sumatra, the Toraja and Minahasans of Sulawesi and in some of the islands of Nusa
Tenggara, and Irian Jaya.

Islamic holidays

NB Muslim festivals are lunar and move forward 10 or 11 days each year. Dates for the
year 2001 are given here and those for 2002 noted at the end of this section. A website
providing details of public holidays and religious festivals in Indonesia (and
elsewhere) is: http://www.holidayfestival.com

Idhul Adha (movable, 6th: public holiday) celebrated by Muslims to mark the 10th day   March
of Zulhijgah, the 12th month of the Islamic calendar when pilgrims celebrate their
return from the Haj to Mecca. In the morning, prayers are offered and later, families
hold 'open house'. This is the 'festival of the sacrifice' and is the time when burial graves
are cleaned, and an animal (a cow or goat) is sacrificed by those who can afford it to be
distributed to the poor. This commemorates the willingness of Abraham to sacrifice
his son. Indonesian men who have made the pilgrimage to Mecca (the Haj) wear a
white skull-hat. The Haj is one of the five keystones of Islam.

Muharram (movable, 26th: public holiday), Muslim New Year. Marks the first day of the   March
Muslim calendar, and celebrating the Prophet Muhammad's journey from Mecca to
Medina on the lunar equivalent of AD 16 July 622. Religious discussions and lectures
commemorate the day.

Garebeg Maulad (or Maulud Nabi Muhammed, birthday of the Prophet Mohammad)   June
(movable, 4th: public holiday,) to commemorate Prophet Muhammad's birthday in AD
571. Processions and Koran recitals in most big towns. Celebrations begin a week before
the actual day and last a month, with *selamatans* in homes, mosques and schools.

Al Miraj (or Isra Miraj Nabi Muhammed) (movable, 15th). The ascension of the Prophet   October
Mohammad when he is led through the seven heavens by the archangel. He speaks
with God and returns to earth the same night, with instructions which include the five
daily prayers.

Awal Ramadan (movable, 17th-18th) the first day of Ramadan, a month of fasting for   November
all Muslims. During this month Muslims abstain from all food and drink (as well as
smoking) from sunrise to sundown – if they are very strict, Muslims do not even
swallow their own saliva during daylight hours. It is strictly adhered to in more
conservative areas like Aceh and West Sumatra, and many restaurants remain closed
during daylight hours – making life rather tiresome for non-Muslims. Every evening
for 30 days before breaking of fast, stalls are set up which sell traditional Malay cakes
and delicacies. The only people exempt from fasting are the elderly, those who are
travelling, and women who are pregnant or are menstruating.

Idul Fitri (Aidil Fitri) or **Lebaran** (movable, 16th-17th: public holiday) is a two day   December
celebration which marks the end of the Muslim fasting month of Ramadan and is a period
of prayer and celebration. In order for Hari Raya to be declared, the new moon of Syawal
has to be sighted; if it is not, fasting continues for another day. It is the most important time
of the year for Muslim families to get together; Indonesians living in towns and cities return
home to their village, where it is 'open house' for relatives and friends, and special delicacies
are served. Mass prayers are held in mosques and squares. This is not a good time to travel.
Trains, planes and buses are booked up weeks in advance and hotels are also often full.

Essentials

Islamic festivals Idul Fitri, 6th December; Idhul Adha, 23rd February; Muharram, 15th March; Garebeg
for 2002 Maulad, 25th May; Al Miraj, 5th October; Awal Ramadan, 6th November.

Health

The traveller to Indonesia is inevitably exposed to health risks not encountered in
North America, Western Europe or Australasia. All of the countries have a tropical
climate; nevertheless the acquisition of true tropical disease by the visitor is probably
conditioned as much by the rural nature and standard of hygiene of the countries
concerned than by the climate. There is an obvious difference in health risks between
the business traveller who tends to stay in international class hotels in large cities and
the backpacker trekking through rural areas. There are no hard and fast rules to follow;
you will often have to make your own judgements on the healthiness or otherwise of
your surroundings.

Medical care Medical care is very variable; medical culture is quite different from the other
neighbouring countries, although there are some good hospitals in Jakarta and other
main cities. The likelihood of finding a doctor who speaks English and a good standard
of care diminishes very rapidly as you move away from the big cities. In the rural areas
there are systems and traditions of medicine wholly different from the Western model
and you may be confronted with less orthodox forms of treatment such as herbal
medicine and acupuncture. At least you can be sure that local practitioners have a lot
of experience with the particular diseases of their region. If you are in a city it may be
worthwhile calling on your embassy to provide a list of recommended doctors.

Medicines If you are a long way away from medical help, a certain amount of self-administered
medication may be necessary and you will find many of the drugs available have
familiar names. However, always check the date stamping (sell-by date) and buy from
reputable pharmacists because the shelf life of some items, especially vaccines and
antibiotics, is markedly reduced in hot conditions. Unfortunately, many locally produced
drugs are not subjected to quality control procedures and so can be unreliable. There
have, in addition, been cases of substitution of inert materials for active drugs. With the
following precautions and advice you should keep as healthy as usual. Make local
enquiries about health risks if you are apprehensive and take the general advice of
European, Australian or North American families who have lived or are living in the area.

Before travelling

Take out medical insurance. You should also have a dental check-up, obtain a spare
glasses prescription and, if you suffer from a long-standing condition, such as diabetes,
high blood pressure, heart/lung disease or a nervous disorder, arrange for a check-up
with your doctor who can at the same time provide you with a letter explaining details
of your medical disorder. Check the current practice for malaria prophylaxis
(prevention) for the countries you intend to visit.

Vaccination & Smallpox vaccination is no longer required. Neither is cholera vaccination, despite the
immunization fact that the disease occurs – but not at present in epidemic form – in some of these
countries. Yellow fever vaccination is not required either, although you may be asked
for a certificate if you have been in a country affected by yellow fever immediately
before travelling to Indonesia. The following vaccinations are recommended:

Typhoid (monovalent) One dose followed by a booster 1 month later. Immunity
from this course lasts 2-3 years. An oral preparation is also available.

A miracle of nature: the devil's powder

Quinine has saved more lives than any other medicine used for the treatment of infectious diseases. It comes from the bark of the Cinchona tree, native to Peru, where the Indians used the ground bark to treat fever. In 1632 an Augustinian monk living in Peru wrote describing how effective this treatment was in curing fever. Word spread, and by 1640 Jesuits' or Peruvian bark as it was then called, had reached Europe where malaria was widespread.

At that time many Protestants said they would rather die than take the Jesuits cure. Cromwell called it the "devil's powder" and though dying of malaria refused to use it. Without the bark of the Cinchona tree and its alkaloids, European colonial expansion in Southeast Asia would not have been possible. Indeed the 'Chemical News' of 1867 states that without quinine many countries would have been uninhabitable to Europeans, the Panama Canal would not have been built, and the outcome of the American War of Independence may have been influenced by Washington's purchase of the drug to supply his troops.

By the early 19th century the bark was becoming increasingly scarce and expensive such was the demand for the miracle drug. The Peruvian authorities were naturally anxious to maintain their monopoly on the Cinchona tree. However, in 1836, under the auspices of the Director of Kew Gardens in London, two Britons, a

naturalist and a clerk with the East India Company, set off on a perilous journey into the high Andes intent on procuring Cinchona seeds and saplings. Their mission was a success and plantations were established in India. In 1820 the pure chemical derivative, quinine, was isolated from the bark; this made dosing easier - 0.5 gm of pure quinine rather than 30 gm of bark - and prevented charlatans from selling the adulterated bark.

At this time another Englishman, Charles Ledger, whilst travelling in the Andes in search of alpaca wool discovered that a particular species of the tree, Cinchona Ledgeriana, had the highest levels of quinine in its bark. Having failed in his attempt to interest British botanists in his find he sold the seeds of Ledgeriana to the Dutch who set up plantations in Java and soon held the monopoly in production of quinine. As production increased the price dropped from US$100 per kilo in 1880 to US$7 per kilo in 1893. Synthetic anti-malarial drugs were developed following the Japanese invasion of Java during the Second World War.

The Cinchona plantations in the East are still a major source of quinine. The trees are harvested after eight to 12 years and stripped of their bark; about 5,000 tons of bark are processed each year. The Cinchona belongs to the same family, Rubiacea, as coffee and gardenia.

Poliomyelitis This is a live vaccine generally given orally but a full course consists of three doses with a booster in tropical regions every 3-5 years.

Tetanus One dose should be given, with a booster at 6 weeks and another at 6 months. 10 yearly boosters thereafter are recommended.

Meningitis and Japanese B encephalitis (JVE) There is an extremely small risk of these rather serious diseases; both are seasonal and vary according to region. Meningitis can occur in epidemic form; JVE is a viral disease transmitted from pigs to man by mosquitoes. For details of the vaccinations, consult a travel clinic.

Infectious hepatitis (jaundice) This is common throughout Indonesia and, more widely, in Southeast Asia. It seems to be frequently caught by travellers. The main symptoms are stomach pains, lack of appetite, nausea, lassitude and yellowness of the eyes and skin. Medically speaking there are two types: the less serious but more common is hepatitis A for which the best protection is careful preparation of food, the avoidance of contaminated drinking water and scrupulous attention to toilet hygiene. Human normal immunoglobulin (gammaglobulin) confers considerable protection against the disease and is particularly useful in epidemics. It should be obtained from a reputable source and is certainly recommended for travellers who intend to travel and live rough. The injection should be given as close as possible to your departure and as the dose depends on the likely time you are to spend in potentially infected areas, the manufacturers' instructions should be followed. A vaccination against hepatitis A has recently become generally available and is safe and effective. Three shots are given over 6 months and confer excellent protection against the disease for up to 10 years. Eventually this vaccine is likely to supersede the use of gammaglobulin.

The other, more serious, version is hepatitis B which is acquired as a sexually transmitted disease, from a blood transfusion or an injection with an unclean needle, or possibly by insect bites. The symptoms are the same as hepatitis A but the incubation period is much longer.

You may have had jaundice before or you may have had hepatitis of either type before without becoming jaundiced, in which case it is possible that you could be immune to either hepatitis A or B (or C or a number of other letters). This immunity can be tested for before you travel. If you are not immune to hepatitis B already, a vaccine is available (three shots over 6 months) and if you are not immune to hepatitis A already, then you should consider having gammaglobulin or a vaccination.

Children should, in addition to the above, be properly protected against **diphtheria**, **whooping cough, mumps** and **measles**. Teenage girls, if they have not had the disease, should be given a **rubella** (German measles) vaccination. Consult your doctor for advice on **BCG** inoculation against tuberculosis: the disease is still common in the region.

On the road

Aids Aids is increasingly prevalent in Indonesia and in many of the other countries of Southeast Asia. Thus, it is not wholly confined to the well known high risk sections of the population ie homosexual men, intravenous drug users, prostitutes and the children of infected mothers. Heterosexual transmission is probably now the dominant mode of infection and so the main risk to travellers is from casual sex. The same precautions should be taken as when encountering any sexually transmitted disease. In some Southeast Asian countries, Thailand is an example, almost the entire population of female prostitutes is HIV positive and in other parts intravenous drug abuse is common. Indonesia, although it does not seem to have so serious an AIDS problem on its hand as Thailand and places like Cambodia and Myanmar, does have the potential for considerable growth in HIV infections rates. The AIDS virus (HIV) can be passed via unsterile needles which have been previously used to inject an HIV positive patient, but the risk of this is very small indeed. It would, however, be sensible to check that needles have been properly sterilized or disposable needles used. The chance of picking up hepatitis B in this way is much more of a danger. Be wary of carrying disposable needles. Customs officials may find them suspicious. The risk of receiving a blood transfusion with blood infected with the HIV virus is greater than from dirty needles because of the amount of fluid exchanged. Supplies of blood for transfusion are supposed to be screened for HIV in all reputable hospitals so the risk should be small. Catching the virus which causes AIDS does not necessarily produce an illness in itself; the only way to be sure if you feel you have been put at risk is to have a blood test for HIV antibodies on your return to a place where there are reliable laboratory facilities. However, the test does not become positive for many weeks.

Malaria is prevalent in Indonesia. Malaria remains a serious disease and you are **Malaria** advised to protect yourself against mosquito bites as above and to take prophylactic (preventative) drugs. Start taking the tablets a week before exposure and continue to take them 4 weeks after leaving the malarial zone. Remember to give the drugs to babies and children, pregnant women also. The *Medical Advisory Services for Travellers Abroad* (MASTA) advises against taking anti-malarial drugs if you are visiting only Bali; the risk of adverse side-effects is greater than the danger of catching the disease. If you are visiting any of the other islands of Nusa Tenggara you should definitely take prophylactic medication.

The subject of malaria prevention is becoming more complex as the malaria parasite becomes immune to some of the older drugs. In particular, there has been an increase in the proportion of cases of falciparum malaria which are resistant to the normally used drugs. It would not be an exaggeration to say that we are near to the situation where some cases of malaria will be untreatable with presently available drugs.

Before you travel you must check with a reputable agency the likelihood and type of malaria in the countries which you intend to visit. Take their advice on prophylaxis but be prepared to receive conflicting advice. Because of the rapidly changing situation in the Southeast Asian region, the names and dosage of the drugs have not been included. But Chloroquine and Proguanil may still be recommended for the areas where malaria is still fully sensitive. At least one informed source considers Indonesia to fall in this category; ie you should be adequately protected by taking Chloroquine and Proguanil. Doxycycline, Metloquine and Quinghaosu are presently being used in resistant areas. Halofantrine Quinine and tetracycline drugs remain the mainstays of treatment. The mainstay of malaria prevention is to avoid being bitten! Cover yourself with an insect repellent, particularly during the hours between dusk and dawn; those containing DET are most effective (see below). Citronella, an essential oil, used in a base of moisturizer, or in candles, is highly effective as a deterrent to mosquitoes. Also B12 tablets (found in high concentrations in beer and garlic) may help to prevent bites, although this has not been clinically proven. The bonus with this approach is that there are no long or short term side effects.

It is still possible to catch malaria even when taking prophylactic drugs, although this is unlikely. If you do develop symptoms (high fever, shivering, severe headache, and sometimes diarrhoea) seek medical advice immediately. The risk of the disease is obviously greater the further you move from the cities into rural areas, with primitive facilities and standing water.

Full acclimatization to tropical temperatures takes about 2 weeks and during this **Heat & cold** period it is normal to feel relatively apathetic, especially if the humidity is high. Drink plenty of water (up to 15 litres a day are required when working physically hard in the tropics). Use salt on your food and avoid extreme exertion. Tepid showers are more cooling than hot or cold ones. Large hats do not cool you down but do prevent sunburn. Remember that, especially in highland areas, there can be a large and sudden drop in temperature between sun and shade and between night and day so dress accordingly. Loose-fitting cotton clothes are best for hot weather. Warm jackets and woollens are often necessary after dark at high altitude.

These can be a great nuisance. Some, of course, are carriers of serious diseases such as **Insects** malaria, dengue fever or filariasis and various worm infections. The best way of keeping mosquitoes away at night is to sleep off the ground with a mosquito net and to burn mosquito coils containing Pyrethrum. Aerosol sprays or a 'flit gun' may be effective as are insecticidal tablets which are heated on a mat which is plugged into the wall socket (if taking your own, check the voltage of the area you are visiting so that you can take an appliance that will work; similarly, check that your electrical adaptor is suitable for the repellent plug; note that they are widely available in the region).

You can, in addition, use personal insect repellent of which the best contain a high concentration of diethyltoluamide (DEET). Liquid is best for arms and face (take care around eyes and make sure you do not dissolve the plastic of your spectacles). Aerosol spray on clothes and ankles deter mites and ticks. Liquid DET suspended in water can be used to impregnate cotton clothes and mosquito nets. The latter are now available in wide mesh form which are lighter to carry and less claustrophobic to sleep under.

If you are bitten, itching may be relieved by cool baths and antihistamine tablets (take care with alcohol or when driving), corticosteroid creams (great care – never use if any hint of septic poisoning) or by judicious scratching. Calamine lotion and cream have limited effectiveness and antihistamine creams have a tendency to cause skin allergies and are therefore not generally recommended. Bites which become infected (a common problem in the tropics) should be treated with a local antiseptic or antibiotic cream such as Cetrimide, as should infected scratches. Skin infestations with body lice, crabs and scabies are unfortunately easy to pick up. Use gamma benzene hexachloride for lice and benzyl benzoate for scabies. Crotamiton cream alleviates itching and also kills a number of skin parasites. Malathion lotion is good for lice but avoid the highly toxic full strength Malathion which is used as an agricultural insecticide.

Intestinal upsets

Practically nobody escapes intestinal infections, so be prepared for them. Most of the time they are due to the insanitary preparation of food. Do not eat uncooked fish, vegetables or meat (especially pork), fruit without the skin (always peel fruit yourself), or food that is exposed to flies (particularly salads). Tap water may be unsafe, especially in the monsoon seasons and the same goes for stream water or well water. Filtered or bottled water is usually available and safe but you cannot always rely on it. If your hotel has a central hot water supply, this is safe to drink after cooling. Ice should be made from boiled water but rarely is, so stand your glass on the ice cubes instead of putting them in the drink. Dirty water should first be strained through a filter bag (available from camping shops) and then boiled or treated. Bringing the water to a rolling boil at sea level is sufficient. In the highlands, you have to boil the water a bit longer to ensure that all the microbes are killed (because water boils at a lower temperature at altitude). Various sterilizing methods can be used and there are proprietary preparations containing chlorine or iodine compounds. Pasteurized or heat-treated milk is now fairly widely available as is ice cream and yoghurt produced by the same methods. Unpasteurized milk products, including cheese, are sources of tuberculosis, brucellosis, listeria and food poisoning germs. You can render fresh milk safe by heating it to 62°C for 30 minutes followed by rapid cooling or by boiling. Matured or processed cheeses are safer than fresh varieties.

Fish and shellfish are popular foods throughout Indonesia but can be the source of health problems. Shellfish which are eaten raw will transmit food poisoning or hepatitis if they have been living in contaminated water. Certain fish accumulate toxins in their bodies at certain times of the year, which give rise to illness when they are eaten. The phenomenon known as 'red tide' can also affect fish and shellfish which eat large quantities of tiny sea creatures and thereby become poisonous. The only way to guard against this is to keep as well informed as possible about fish and shellfish quality in the area you are visiting. Most countries impose a ban on fishing in periods when red tide is prevalent, although this is often flouted.

Diarrhoea

Diarrhoea is usually the result of food poisoning, but can occasionally result from contaminated water. There are various causes – viruses, bacteria, protozoa (like amoeba), salmonella and cholera organisms. It may take one of several forms coming on suddenly or rather slowly. It may be accompanied by vomiting or severe abdominal pain, and the passage of blood or mucus (when it is called dysen tery).

All kinds of diarrhoea, whether or not accompanied by vomiting, respond favourably to the replacement of water and salts taken as frequent small sips of some kind of rehydration solution. There are proprietary preparations consisting of sachets of oral rehydration electrolyte powder which are dissolved in water, or make up your own by adding half a teaspoonful of salt (3.5 grams) and 4 tablespoons of sugar (40 grams) to a litre of boiled water. If it is possible to time the onset of diarrhoea to the minute, then it is probably viral or bacterial and/or the onset of dysentery. The treatment in addition to rehydration is Ciprofloxacin (500 mg every 12 hours). The drug is now widely available as are various similar ones. Ciprofloxacin can be taken as a one-off dose or more commonly as a course of 3, 5 or 7 days. It is an antibiotic, so it is important to complete the course.

If the diarrhoea has come on slowly or intermittently, then it is more likely to be protozoal, ie caused by amoeba or giardia, and antibiotics will have no effect. These cases are best treated by a doctor as should any diarrhoea continuing for more than 3 days. If there are severe stomach cramps, the following drugs may help: Loperamide (Imodium, Arret) and Diphenoxylate with Atropine (Lomotil). The drug usually used for giardia or amoeba is Metronidazole (Flagyl) or Tinidazole (Fasigyu).

The linchpins of treatment for diarrhoea are rest, fluid and salt replacement, antibiotics such as Ciprofloxacin for the bacterial types, and special diagnostic tests and medical treatment for amoeba and giardia infections. Salmonella infections and cholera can be devastating diseases and it would be wise to get to a hospital as soon as possible if these were suspected. Fasting, peculiar diets and the consumption of large quantities of yoghurt have not been found useful in calming travellers' diarrhoea or in rehabilitating inflamed bowels. Oral rehydration has, especially in children, been a lifesaving technique and as there is some evidence that alcohol and milk might prolong diarrhoea they should probably be avoided during, and immediately after, an attack. There are ways of preventing travellers' diarrhoea for short periods of time when visiting these countries by taking antibiotics but these are ineffective against viruses and, to some extent, against protozoa. This technique should not be used other than in exceptional circumstances. Some preventatives such as Enterovioform can have serious side effects if taken for long periods.

Sunburn & heat stroke The burning power of the tropical sun is phenomenal, especially in highland areas. Always wear a wide-brimmed hat, and use some form of sun cream or lotion on untanned skin. Normal temperate zone suntan lotions (protection factors up to 7) are not much good. You need to use the types designed specifically for the tropics or for mountaineers or skiers, with a protection factor between 7 and 15 or higher. Glare from the sun can cause conjunctivitis so wear sunglasses, particularly on beaches.

There are several varieties of heat stroke. The most common cause is severe dehydration. Avoid this by drinking lots of non-alcoholic fluid, and adding salt to your food. Heatstroke results when the body's cooling system breaks down. Symptoms include a very high body temperature, flushed red skin, an erratic pulse, reduced perspiration; this is a serious condition that in extreme cases can result in death. Immediate treatment is to lower the patient's body temperature to 102° F by wrapping in towels or sheets soaked in cold water, with use of a fan if available, or having a tepid bath; hospital treatment may be needed. Spending too long, unprotected, under the hot sun can also result in heatstroke.

Snake & other bites & stings If you are unlucky enough to be bitten by a venomous snake, spider, scorpion, centipede or sea creature, try (within limits) to catch or kill the animal for identification. Reactions to be expected are shock, swelling, pain and bruising around the bite, soreness of the regional lymph glands, nausea, vomiting and fever. If in addition any of the following symptoms should follow closely, get the victim to a doctor without delay: numbness, tingling of the face, muscular spasms, convulsions, shortness of breath or haemorrhage. Commercial snake-bite or scorpion-sting kits may be available but these are only useful against the specific type of snake or scorpion for which they are designed. The serum has to be given intravenously so is not much good unless you have had some practice in making injections into veins. If the bite is on a limb, immobilize it and apply a tight

Essentials

bandage between the bite and the body, releasing it for 90 seconds every 15 minutes. Reassurance of the victim is very important because death from snake bite is very rare. Do not slash the bite area and try to suck out the poison because this sort of heroism does more harm than good. Hospitals usually hold stocks of snake-bite serum. The best precaution is to not walk in long grass with bare feet, sandals or in shorts.

When swimming in an area where there are poisonous fish such as stone or scorpion fish (also called by a variety of local names) or sea urchins on rocky coasts, tread carefully or wear plimsolls/trainers. The sting of such fish is intensely painful. This can be relieved by immersing the injured part of the body in water as hot as you can bear for as long as it remains painful. This is not always very practical and you must take care not to scald yourself, but it does work. Avoid spiders and scorpions by keeping your bed away from the wall, look under lavatory seats and inside your shoes in the morning. In the rare event of being bitten, consult a doctor.

Rabies Remember that rabies is endemic in many Southeast Asian countries. At the time of writing there was an outbreak of rabies on Flores, with several deaths from the disease. Rabies vaccine is in short supply on the island; if you are planning to visit Flores check that your inoculation is up to date. A full immunization course takes a month to complete. One obvious piece of advice is to avoid all animals that are behaving strangely. If you are bitten by a domestic or wild animal, do not leave things to chance. Scrub the wound with soap and water and/or disinfectant, try to have the animal captured (within limits) or at least determine its ownership where possible, and seek medical assistance at once. The course of treatment depends on whether you have already been satisfactorily vaccinated against rabies. If you have (and this is worthwhile if you are spending lengths of time in developing countries) then some further doses of vaccine are all that is required. Human diploid cell vaccine is the best, but expensive: other, older kinds of vaccine such as that derived from duck embryos may be the only types available. These are effective, much cheaper and interchangeable generally with the human derived types. If not already vaccinated then anti-rabies serum (immunoglobulin) may be required in addition. It is wise to finish the course of treatment whether the animal survives or not.

Dengue fever Dengue Fever is a viral disease transmitted by mosquito and causes severe headaches and body pains; there are four types of the disease. It has reached almost epidemic proportions in some Southeast Asian countries. In Indonesia there have been major outbreaks during the rainy season in Java, Kalimantan and Sumatra. The mosquito that transmits Dengue Fever bites during daytime and occurs in urban tropical areas. It is important to use repellent and avoid likely exposure during the first hours of sunrise and prior to sunset when most mosquitoes feed. People with any influenza type symptoms should seek treatment immediately. Following an incubation period of 7-10 days symptoms of fever, malaise, aches and pains and occasional rashes may occur. Severity of disease is greatest in children under 15 years. Adults who have had dengue fever once before are at greater risk from exposure to a different strain of the disease which can cause complicated types of dengue known as haemorrhagic fevers. There is no treatment, you must just avoid mosquito bites.

Other common problems **Intestinal worms** are common and the more serious ones, such as hook worm can be contracted by walking barefoot on infested earth or beaches.

Influenza and respiratory diseases are common, perhaps made worse by polluted cities and rapid temperature and climatic changes – accentuated by air-conditioning.

Prickly heat is a very common itchy rash, best avoided by frequent washing and by wearing loose clothing. It can be helped by the use of talcum powder, allowing the skin to dry thoroughly after washing.

Athlete's foot and other fungal infections are best treated by sunshine and a proprietary preparation such as Tolnaftate. Cuts, bites and grazes: even the most minor scratches can easily become infected and be difficult to heal in a tropical climate. Coral cuts are particularly susceptible to infection. All cuts should be thoroughly cleansed as soon as possible with soap and water or a hydrogen peroxide solution, and treated with an antiseptic solution; betadine is widely available. An antibiotic cream should also be considered. If the wound becomes red, swollen or begins to throb a three-day course of antibiotic pills should be considered sooner rather than later. Superficial cuts are best left uncovered. It may be best to avoid swimming in pools and the sea.

When you return home

On returning home, remember to take anti-malarial tablets for 4 weeks. If you have had attacks of diarrhoea, it is worth having a stool specimen tested in case you have picked up amoebic dysentery. If you have been living rough, a blood test may also be worthwhile to detect worms and other parasites.

You may find the following items useful to take with you from home: suntan cream, **Basic supplies** insect repellent, flea powder, mosquito net, coils or tablets, tampons, condoms, contraceptives, water sterilizing tablets, anti-malaria tablets, anti-infective ointment, dusting powder for feet, travel sickness pills, antiacid tablets, anti-diarrhoea tablets, sachets of rehydration salts, a first aid kit and disposable needles (also see page 54).

Further information

Information regarding country-by-country malaria risk can be obtained from the World Health Organization (WHO) or in Britain from the Ross Institute, London School of Hygiene and Tropical Medicine, Keppel Street, London WC1E 7HT which also publishes a highly recommended book: *The Preservation of Personal Health in Warm Climates*. The Centres for Disease Control (CDC) in Atlanta, Georgia, USA will provide equivalent information, T404 639 3311. The organization MASTA (Medical Advisory Service for Travellers Abroad) based at the London School of Hygiene and Tropical Medicine (T020-76314408) will provide up-to-date country-by-country information on health risks. Further information on medical problems overseas can be obtained from *Travellers Health, how to stay healthy abroad*, edited by Richard Dawood (Oxford University Press, 1992). This is highly recommended, especially to the intrepid traveller. A more general publication, with hints on health and much more besides, is John Hatt's new edition of *The Tropical Traveller* (Penguin, 1993).

Health websites *MASTA*, http://www.masta.org/home.html (UK). Provides up-to-date country-by-country information on health risks. If you want more information on malaria try the *Malaria Foundation International* website http://www.malaria.org This site is a mine of information on every aspect of malaria. Two other tropical health oriented sites are www.uclh.org/htd, the site for the *Hospital for Tropical Diseases in London*, and www.tropicalscreening.com. The *CDC* (see above) also have a useful website at http://www.cdc.gov/cdc.html The *British FCO* (Foreign and Commonwealth Office) have a travellers advice site at http://www.fco.gov.uk which also includes some health related information, as does www.nhsdirect.nhs.uk. For a website with a child health focus check out www.medicineplanet.com *E-med*, T020-73502079, www.e-med.co.uk, is a new company that can provide medical advice to travellers whilst they are abroad. Having subscribed, send them an email to doctor@e-med.co.uk, describe your symptoms and you will receive advice from a GP within 2 hours.

Essentials

Further reading

Magazines

Asiaweek (weekly). A lightweight *Far Eastern Economic Review*; rather like a regional *Time* magazine in style.

The Far Eastern Economic Review (weekly). Authoritative Hong Kong-based regional magazine; their correspondents based in each country provide knowledgeable, in-depth analysis particularly on economics and politics.

Books on Southeast Asia

Clad, James *Behind the Myth: Business, Money and Power in Southeast Asia*, (1989, Unwin Hyman: London). Clad, formerly a journalist with the *Far Eastern Economic Review*, distilled his experiences in this book; as it turned out, rather disappointingly – it is a hotch-potch of journalistic snippets.

Conrad, Joseph *Lord Jim*, (1900, Penguin: London). The tale of Jim, who abandons his ship and seeks refuge from his guilt in Malaya, earning the sobriquet Lord.

Conrad, Joseph *Victory: An Island Tale*, (1915, Penguin: London). Arguably Conrad's finest novel, based in the Malay Archipelago.

Conrad, Joseph *The Rescue*, (1920, Penguin: London). Set in the Malay Archipelago in the 1860s; the hero, Captain Lingard, is forced to choose between his Southeast Asian friend and his countrymen.

Dingwall, Alastair *Traveller's Literary Companion to South-east Asia*, (1994, In Print: Brighton). Experts on Southeast Asian language and literature select extracts from novels and other books by Western and regional writers. The extracts are annoyingly brief, but it gives a good overview of what is available.

King, Ben F and Dickinson, EC *A Field Guide to the Birds of South-East Asia*, (1975, Collins: London). Best regional guide to the birds of the region.

Reid, Anthony *Southeast Asia in the Age of Commerce 1450-1680*, (1988, Yale University Press: New Haven). Perhaps the best history of everyday life in Southeast Asia, looking at such themes as physical well-being, material culture and social organization.

Reid, Anthony *Southeast Asia in the Age of Commerce 1450-1680: Expansion and Crisis*, (1993, Yale University Press: New Haven). Volume 2 in this excellent history of the region.

Books on Indonesia

The books listed here are not necessarily focused on Bali and the islands of Nusa Tenggara. They are included because they provide an insight into different aspects of Indonesian life.

Western novels & biography Conrad, Joseph: Perhaps the finest novelist of the Malay archipelago, books include *Lord Jim* and *Victory*, both widely available in paperback editions from most bookshops.

Couperus, Louis *The Hidden Force*, (1994, Quartet Books: London). A translation of this Dutch novel originally written in 1900, Couperus was a dandy, who liked to shock. His book deals with the culture clash of locals and colonials and the underlying corruption and decadence of the colonial way of life. All a little dated now but caused a stir at the time of writing.

Koch, CJ *The Year of Living Dangerously*, (1978). Average novel transformed into a well-received film; romance based in Java during the 1965 attempted coup.

Van der Post, Laurens *The Seed and the Sower*, (1963, Penguin: London). The semi-autobiographical account of Laurens van der Post's internment in a Japanese prisoner of war camp outside Bandung. Was made into a film starring David Bowie: *Merry Christmas Mr Lawrence*.

Van der Post, Laurens *The Night of the New Moon*, (1970, Penguin: London). Like his better-known *The Seed and the Sower*, this is based on his internment in a Japanese prisoner of war camp; it is rather more introspective and philosophical, though.

Lubis, Mochtar *Twilight in Djakarta*, (1957). One of the finest works of modern **Indonesian** Indonesian fiction; tells of the poverty and destitution in 1950s Jakarta; journalist Lubis **literature** was imprisoned for his writings. **available in**

Lubis, Mochtar *A Road with No End*, (1968, Hutchinson). Originally published in **English** Indonesia in 1952, and regarded as one of the classics of Indonesian literature, it draws heavily on French existentialist philosophy. The novel tells the story of Isa, a teacher in Java, and the turmoil of the early years of independence.

Lubis, Mochtar *Tiger!*, (1991, Select Books: Singapore). A novel based in Sumatra first published in Indonesia in 1975.

Toer, Pramoedya Ananta *This Earth of Mankind*, (1979, Penguin: Ringwood, Australia). Along with the other three books in this series – *Child of all Nations*, *Footsteps*, and *Glass House* – this represents some of the finest of modern Indonesian writing. It tells the story of the writer Minke caught between the Dutch and modernity, and his own people and tradition. Toer was imprisoned on Buru Island between 1965-79 and his books remain banned in Indonesia.

Barley, Nigel *Not a Hazardous Sport*, (1988, Penguin: London). A humorous and **Travel** entertaining book in which anthropologist Barley heads off to Toraja and convinces a team of builders to travel to London to construct a traditional house for the Museum of Mankind.

Bickmore, Albert S *Travels in the East Indian archipelago*, (1869, OUP: Singapore). Published at the same time as Wallace's much more famous tome, this is not nearly as important a text but, written by an American, it does provide a very different gloss. Republished in 1991 by OUP, Singapore.

Bird, Isabella *The Golden Chersonese*, (1883 and reprinted 1983, Murray, reprinted by Century Paperback: London). The account of a late 19th century female visitor to the region who shows her gumption facing everything from natives to crocs.

Lewis, Norman *An Empire of the East*, (1994, Jonathan Cape: London). Norman Lewis' latest travel book in which he explores three politically sensitive areas: East Timor, Irian Jaya and Aceh, North Sumatra. Given the regions to which he selected to travel, beneath the languid surface it is, inevitably, a highly critical book; well written and seemingly innocently provocative.

Mjoberg, Eric *Forest Life and Adventures in the Malay Archipelago*, (OUP: Singapore).

Naipaul, VS *Among the believers* (1981). A rather self-indulgent account of Naipaul's visit to Indonesia.

Wallace, Alfred Russel *The Malay Archipelago* (1869). See the comments under Natural history, below.

Wilcox, Harry *Six Moons over Sulawesi*, (1989, OUP: Singapore). First published in 1949 as *White Stranger: Six Months in Celebes*, it recounts the six months' sojourn of Harry Wilcox in Toraja, who went to there to recover from the horrors of the war.

Chapman, F Spencer: *The Jungle is Neutral*. An account of a British guerrilla force **History** fighting the Japanese in Borneo – not as enthralling as Tom Harrisson's book, but still worth reading.

Harrisson, Tom *World Within*, (1959, Hutchinson: London). During World War Two, explorer, naturalist and ethnologist Tom Harrisson was parachuted into Borneo to help organize Dayak resistance against the occupying Japanese forces. This is his extraordinary account.

Essentials

Loeb, Edwin M *Sumatra: its History and People*, (1972 – first published 1935, OUP: Kuala Lumpur). Despite being over 50 years old this book is still worthwhile reading, and the best of its type.

Milton, Giles (1999) *Nathaniel's nutmeg*, London: Hodder & Stoughton. A fascinating account of the world of exploration opening up in the 17th century, and the history of the European search for spices culminating in the exchange of the tiny island of Run by the British for present day Manhattan held by the Dutch. Despite perilous journeys, fortunes were made at a time when ten pounds of nutmeg cost less than an English penny to buy, but could be sold for more than £2.10s in London. Highly readable and well-researched, full of extraordinary anecdotes, this book gives an enthralling evocation of the life of a sailor and adventurer in these times.

Raffles, Thomas *The History of Java*, (1817, OUP: Singapore). The first history of Java, fascinating for Raffles' observations, sections have still yet to be bettered; available as a reprint, but large, cumbersome and expensive.

Ricklefs, MC *A History of Modern Indonesia, c1300 to the Present*, (1981, Macmillan: London). Dense but informative, and probably the best modern history of Indonesia. A new edition has recently been published.

Van der Post, Laurens *The Admiral's Baby*, (1997, London: John Murray). Sir Laurens van der Post's last book – the story of the role that the British played in Indonesia in the immediate aftermath of World War Two and in which he played a central role. Much of the book concentrates on the attempts to restrain Indonesians from militancy in their desire to secure independence, while emphasizing to the Dutch that the past can not be recreated.

Natural history Cranbrook, Earl of *Riches of the Wild: Land Mammals of South-East Asia*, (1987, OUP).

Flannery, Tim *Throwim Way Leg, adventures in the jungles of New Guinea*, (1998, London: Weidenfeld & Nicholson). Vivid and memorable account of the author's adventures as a field biologist in the jungles and mountains of New Guinea, one of the earth's last frontiers. Here he chronicles his hilarious and sometimes dangerous encounters as he searches for new species of wildlife and discovers animals previously known only as ice-age fossils. Throwim Way Leg is New Guinea pidgin meaning 'to go on a journey', and describes the thrusting first step of what may become a very long trek.

Holmes, Derek and Nash, Stephen *The Birds of Java and Bali*, (1989, OUP: Singapore). Manageable, lightweight book with good colour illustrations.

Wallace, Alfred Russel *The Malay Archipelago: the Land of the Orang-utan and the Bird of Paradise; a Narrative of Travel with Studies of Man and Nature* (1869). A classic of Victorian travel writing by one of the finest naturalists of the period. Wallace travelled through all of island Southeast Asia over a period of eight years. The original is now re-printed.

Whitten, Tony and Whitten, Jane *Wild Indonesia*, (1992, New Holland: London). Illustrated large format coffee-table book but with good text written by specialists on Indonesia's natural history. Provides background to the country's major national parks and characteristic species and forest formations. Wonderfully illustrated.

The *Ecology of Indonesia* (listed below) series has expanded so that it now consists of seven volumes amounting to a total of around 6,000 pages. Heavy stuff and expensive (at around £50 each), but definitive.

Whitten, Anthony and Whitten, Jane (edits.) *Indonesian Heritage: Wildlife* and *Indonesian Heritage: Plants*, (1996, Singapore: Editions Didier Millet). Two volumes in the encyclopedia of Indonesian heritage series. Large format, full of colour illustrations and specially commissioned artwork, written in an accessible style by experts in the field.

Whitten, Anthony *et al. The Ecology of Java and Bali* (1997). Nearly 1,000 pages of information.

Monk, Kathryn A. *et al. The Ecology of Nusa Tenggara and Maluku* (1997). Almost 1,000 pages long.

Tomascik, Tomas and Mah, Anmarie Janice (1997) *The Ecology of the Indonesian seas*. Two volumes.

Barnes, RH *Sea Hunters of Indonesia: Fishers and Weavers of Lamalera*, (1996, Oxford: Clarendon Press). Oxford anthropologist Bob Barnes has been working among the people of Lamalera for many years and this is the culmination of his studies. In many ways it is an old fashioned work in terms of approach: a meticulous documentation of the lives and livelihoods of these people of East Nusa Tenggara. Extensive information on whaling.

Budiardjo, Carmel *Surviving Indonesia's Gulags*, (1996, London: Cassell). The author of this book is a Jewish Londoner who married an Indonesian, moved to Jakarta and worked as a civil servant and university lecturer during Sukarno's presidency. She was imprisoned in 1967 and the book recounts her horrific time in gaol. She now lives in London again and continues to campaign enthusiastically for human rights in Indonesia despite her age of over 70. She was awarded the Right Livelihood Award – a sort of alternative Nobel Peace Prize – in December 1995.

Belo, Jane (edit) *Traditional Balinese Culture*, (1970, Columbia University Press: New York). Collection of academic papers mostly focusing upon dance, music and drama.

Covarrubias, Miguel *Island of Bali*, (1937, Cassell: London), (reprinted 1987, OUP: Singapore). The original, full treatment of Bali's culture; despite being over 50 years old it is still an excellent background to the island and is highly entertaining.

Geertz, Clifford *Agricultural Involution: the Process of Ecological Change in Indonesia*, (1963, University of California Press: Berkeley). Classic book by perhaps the foremost anthropologist of Indonesia; looks at rice and shifting cultivation and conditions in 19th and 20th century Java; some of his views have been vigorously attacked in recent years. Hard to get hold of.

Lansing, J Stephen *Priests and Programmers: Technologies of Power in the Engineered Landscape of Bali*, (1991, Princeton University Press: Princeton). An anthropological account of Bali's irrigation system; interesting for rice fans.

Rigg, Jonathan (edit.) *Indonesian heritage: The Human Environment*, (1996, Singapore: Editions Didier Millet). A volume in the encyclopedia of Indonesian heritage series. Large format, full of colour illustrations and specially commissioned artwork, written in an accessible style by experts in the field.

Schwarz, Adam *A Nation in Waiting: Indonesia in the 1990s*, (1994, Boulder: Westview Press). An excellent, readable and well informed account of Indonesia's contemporary economy and politics. Adam Schwarz was the *Far Eastern Economic Review's* correspondent in Jakarta.

Stuart Fox, David *Once a century: Pura Besakih and the Eka Dasa Rudra Festival*, (1982, Penerbit Citra Indonesia: Jakarta).

Vatikiotis, Michael *Indonesian Politics under Suharto*, (1993, London: Routledge). When this book was written Vatikiotis was Jakarta bureau chief of the *Far Eastern Economic Review* and the book demonstrates an intimate knowledge of Indonesian politics and politicians. It is said he had to move posts because he simply became too close to influential Indonesians.

Waterson, Roxana *The Living House: An Anthropology of Architecture in South-East Asia*, (1990, Singapore: OUP). Although this is an academic anthropological work it is written in a style and presented in a format that makes it comparatively accessible. The colour and black and white illustrations combine with an excellent text to make it an invaluable companion (although it is rather heavy) for anyone interested in traditional houses.

Geography, anthropology, politics & development

Essentials

Arts   Djelantik, AAM *Balinese Paintings*, (1990, OUP: Singapore). Concise history of Balinese painting also covering the major contemporary schools of art.

Eiseman, Fred and Eiseman, Margaret *Woodcarvings of Bali*, (1988, Periplus: Berkeley).

Eiseman, Fred *Bali: Sekala and Niskala*. Volume 1 *Essays on Religion, Ritual and Art*, and volume 2 *Essays on Society, Tradition and Craft*, (1989 and 1990, Periplus: Berkeley). Considered by many to be the most informative books on the Balinese way of life. Sekala is what you see: a colourful world of ceremony, ritual, dance and drama. Niskala is what you don't see: the all pervading forces of the occult; gods, demons, magic – which are every bit as real to the Balinese. Highly recommended.

Jessup, Helen I *Court Arts of Indonesia*, (1990, Asia Society Galleries: New York). Lavishly illustrated book produced for the Festival of Indonesia exhibition; good background on the pieces displayed.

Saunders, Kim Jane *Contemporary tie and dye textiles of Indonesia*, (1997, Kuala Lumpur: Oxford University Press).

Warming, Wanda and Gaworski, Michael (1981) The world of Indonesian textiles, Serindia Publications: London. Summarizes all the processes of production and provides an outline of the major regional styles; illustrated.

Encyclopedias   An illustrated 15 volume encyclopedia of Indonesia is being published by Editions Didier Millet in Singapore. The large format books, covering history, natural history, economy, society and ritual, languages and literature, and art and architecture will run to over 1 million words with 8,500 images including maps, photographs and specially produced artwork.

Other books   Draine, Cathie and Hall, Barbara *Culture Shock! Indonesia*, (1986, Times Books: Singapore). A good summary of do's and don't's with some useful cultural background.

Horridge, Adrian *Sailing craft of Indonesia*, (1986, OUP: Singapore). Illustrated with concise, useful text.

Magazines   *Far Eastern Economic Review*, perhaps the most authoritative weekly magazine to the Southeast Asian region; they have correspondents based in Jakarta.

Inside Indonesia, published quarterly by the Indonesia Resources and Information Programme (IRIP) in Australia. Generally outspoken and radical (ie anti-government) in tone; excellent for background information on issues usually not covered in the press. For information on subscribing write to Inside Indonesia, PO Box 190, Northcote 3070, Australia.

Films   *Merry Christmas Mr Lawrence*. A film starring David Bowie based on Laurens van der Post's novel *The Seed and the Sower*, a semi-autobiographical account of his internment in a Japanese prisoner of war camp outside Bandung.

The Year of Living Dangerously. Well received film based on the romantic novel by CJ Koch based in Java during the 1965 attempted coup.

Maps   Nelles: publish a good series of maps of the major islands and island groups including Bali and Nusa Tenggara.

Periplus Travel Maps: recent series of maps to the major islands including some to individual provinces – such as Bali. Good on tourist site information and often with good insert city maps.

Travel Treasure Maps, Knaus Publications: arty map series concentrating on the major tourist destinations – including Bali.

Country maps *Nelles Indonesia* (1:4,000,000); *Nelles Java and Bali* (1:650,000); *Nelles Java and Nusa Tenggara* (1:1,500,000); *Nelles Bali. Gescenter International Indonesia Malaysia* (1:2,000,000); *Periplus Bali; Periplus Lombok*.

Other maps *Tactical Pilotage Charts* (TPC, US Airforce) (1:500,000); *Operational Navigational Charts* (ONC, US Airforce) (1:500,000). Both of these are particularly good at showing relief features (useful for planning treks); less good on roads, towns and facilities.

Locally available maps Maps are best purchased in Bali although you may be lucky to pick them up in other towns. Often the quality of information is poor.

Map shops In London, the best selection is available from *Stanfords*, 12-14 Long Acre, London WC2E 9LP, T020-78361321; also recommended is *McCarta*, 15 Highbury Place, London N15 1QP, T020-73541616.

Essentials

The internet

www.city.net/regions/asia
Pointer to information on Asian countries.
http://www.pata.org/
The Pacific Asia Travel Association, better known simply as PATA, with a useful news section arranged by country, links to airlines and cruise lines, and some information on educational, environmental and other initiatives.
http://webhead.com/asergio/asiaregion.html
Travel information on the Asian region.
http://www.yahoo.com/Regional Countries/[name of country]
Insert name of country to access practical information including material from other travel guides.
http://www.city.net/regions/asia/
Links to numerous country sites in Asia, including maps and some travel information, such as a traveller's health advisory.

General tourism-related websites

http://www.lib.utexas.edu/Libs/PLC/Map_collection/asia/htm
Up-to-date maps of Asia showing relief, political boundaries and major towns.
http://www.nationalgeographic.com/resources/ngo/maps/atlas/asia/asia.html
National Geographic's cartographic division, which takes maps from their current Atlas of the world.
http://www.expediamaps.com/
US biased but still pretty comprehensive. Key in a town and wait for it to magically appear.

Maps

www.rainorshine.com/
A simple but effective weather site with five-day forecasts for 800 cities worldwide.

Weather

http://travel.state.gov/travel_warnings.html
The US State Department's continually updated travel advisories on its Travel Warnings & Consular Information Sheets page.
http://www.fco.gov.uk/travel/
The UK Foreign and Commonwealth Office's travel warning section.

Travel advisories

http://www.cdc.gov/travel/index.htm
Managed by the Center for Disease Control and Prevention (CDC) in Atlanta, this is one of the best health sites, providing detailed and authoritative information including special sections on such diseases, ailments and concerns as malaria, dengue fever, HIV/AIDS, rabies and Japanese encephalitis.
www.singapore.com/pata
Pacific Asia Travel Association – lots of information on travel in the Pacific Asian region including stats, markets, products etc.

Travel & health

http://www.tripprep.com/index.html
Shoreland's Travel Health Online provides health advice by country.

Hotel Sites www.branch.com:80/silkroute/
Information on hotels, travel, news and business in Asia.

Cyber Cafés www.netcafeguide.com/
Around 2000 cybercafes in 113 countries are listed here and it also provides discussion
forums for travellers and a language section.

Newspapers, http://www.isop.ucla.edu/eas/web/radio-tv/htm
news & the For information on Asian radio and television broadcasts access. Includes free
media downloadable software.
http://www.inesmedia.com
Site with links to 150-odd on-line newspapers in Asia and the Middle East.

Currencies http://www.oanda.com/converter/classic
Select your two currencies by clicking on a list, and wham - the exchange rate is provided.

Business- www.none.coolware.com/infoasia/
related websites Run by Infoasia which is a commercial firm that helps US and European firms get into Asia.

General sites http://pears.lib.ohio-state.edu/asianstudies/asian studies.html
Huge range of links with information on topics from sports and travel to economics
and engineering.
http://www.nbr.org
Centre for papers on Asia covering strategic, economic and political issues.
www.agora.stm.it/politic
List of sites with a political focus; searchable by country; links with political parties,
governments etc.
http://libweb.library.wisc.edu/guides/SEAsia/library.htm
'Gateway to Southeast Asia' from University of Wisconsin, numerous links.
http://www.pactoc.net.au/index/resindex.htm
Covers all Pacific, but good links into Southeast Asian material; emphasis on academic
issues rather than travel.
www.pactoc.net.au/index/resindex.htm
Pacific talk homepage with lots of topics and links.
www.aseansec.org
Homepage of the Asean secretariat with material on regional economies, meetings
and so on.
libweb.library.wise.edu/guides/SEAsia/library.htm
The 'Gateway to Southeast Asia', lots of links.

History & http://www.asiasociety.org
culture Homepage of the Asia Society with papers, reports and speeches as well as nearly
1,000 links to what they consider to be the best educational, political and cultural sites
on the Web.

Environment http://nautilus.org
Homepage of the Nautilus Institute which focuses on issues connected with the
environment and sustainability in the Asia-Pacific region.
www.volcanoes.usgs.gov
General site on volcanoes with lots of background information.

www.visit-indonesia.com
The official website of the Indonesian tourism promotion board.

www.accessindo.com/travel/body_index.html
Information on hotels, tours, guidebooks, travel forums, tips and more.

www.travelmole.com
A useful site for general travel information; also provide a free electronic newsletter. Good links.

www.mawar.inn.bppt.go.id/
Indonesia homepage based in Jakarta but good place to start a search of websites for Indonesia.

www.umanitoba.ca/indonesian/homepage.html
Another homepage with good links to other servers and broad range of information.

www.ndio.co.id
Indonesia's National Development Information Office; good for stats and other ephemera.

www.iias.leidenuniv.nl
This site links with the International Institute of Asian Studies in the Netherlands; material tends to be more academic and research associated.

www.halcyon.com/FWDP/help.html
Site of the Centre for World Indigenous Studies; focus tends to be rather America-centric, but still a good place to start for those interested in Fourth World (tribal) issues.

www.ics.bc.ca/ica/membert.html
Site of the Indonesia-Canada Alliance NGO Partnerships; focus is on indigenous peoples in Indonesia and Canada.

www.pip.dknet.dk/~pip1917/publicat.html
Site of the International Work Group for Indigenous Affairs (IWGIA); good links with related sites and good source of articles.

www.dra.nl/~broeke/
Dutch website on India and Indonesia. Good links to other Indonesian sites and also on Indonesians in Holland.

www.pactok.net/docs/inside/index.htm
The home page of Australian-based campaigning magazine *Inside Indonesia* including some articles and index.

www.nla.gov.au/1/asian/indo/
Indonesia home page of the National Library of Australia – excellent.

www.indopubs.com/archives
An alternative news service for Indonesia reporting all those things you won't read about in the *Jakarta Post*.

www.iit.edu/~syafsya
An Indonesian super-site with excellent links to Indonesian language newspapers.

www.travelbali.com
The 'official Bali website', with plenty of accommodation listed, by region, cost or activity, Bali Newsletter provides information on the latest goings on, restaurant and events listings.

www.bali-paradise.com
To quote Jack Daniels, of Bali Discovery: "A veritable 'Funk and Wagnals' of Bali Travel run by the unsinkable Melina Caruso in Bali.

www.balidiscovery.com/
For anyone looking for a tour, you could start by looking at Bali Discovery Tours. Run by Jack Daniels, who writes a weekly Bali Update newsletter, which is distributed electronically to over 10,000 people worldwide. For the very latest happenings in Bali, subscribe to the newsletter.

Indonesia
websites

Essentials

www.bali-travelnews.com
Another good source of information for Bali.
www.balihotels.com
A good starting point if you are looking for accommodation, with around 300 hotels across the island.

Short wave radio (KHz)

British Broadcasting Corporation (BBC, London) *Southeast Asian service* 3915, 6195, 9570, 9740, 11750, 11955, 15360; *Singapore service* 88.9MHz; *East Asian service* 5995, 6195, 7180, 9740, 11715, 11750, 11945, 11955, 15140, 15280, 15360, 17830, 21715.
Voice of America (VoA, Washington) *Southeast Asian service* 1143, 1575, 7120, 9760, 9770, 15185, 15425; *Indonesian service* 6110, 11760, 15425.
Radio Beijing *Southeast Asian service (English)* 11600, 11660.
Radio Japan (Tokyo) *Southeast Asian service (English)* 11815, 17810, 21610.

Bali

3

Bali

72	Denpasar		**189**	North from Denpasar to Lake Bratan
78	**South Bali**		**195**	**North Coast, Buleleng Regency**
109	Nusa Penida and Nusa Lembongan		**198**	Singaraja
113	The Bukit Peninsula and Nusa Dua		**201**	West of Singaraja
128	**North and east from Denpasar**		**217**	**The West**
130	Ubud		**224**	**Background**
147	North of Ubud		**224**	History
149	Gianyar to Mount Batur via Bangli		**228**	Land and environment
158	Pura Besakih and Mount Agung		**231**	Art and architecture
161	East Bali and Regency of Kerangasem		**235**	Culture
			249	Modern Bali

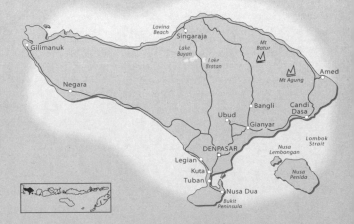

Bali is the original magical Isle. From the earliest years after its bloody incorporation within the expanding territories of the Dutch East Indies in the early 20th century, Westerners have been entranced by the heady combination of a fabulous landscape and a mesmerizing culture. Streams cascade down impossibly green mountainsides from sacred crater lakes, while dance dramas are performed to please the Gods. Artists and the artistically-inclined settled, worked and died amidst the rice fields and temples, reluctant to leave their Garden of Eden.

The advent of cheap air travel has brought increasing numbers of visitors interested more in the attractions of the beach than of the temple and theatre. Today hundreds of thousands of people visit Bali, many scarcely aware of the world beyond the sun lounger and the cocktail shaker. But while Bali may have changed – and the notion that Bali is on the verge of being 'ruined' is a constant motif in writings about the island from the 1930s – the singular magic of the place has not been erased.

Denpasar

Phone code: 0361
Colour map 1, grid B2

Once the royal capital of the princely kingdom of Badung, there is little evidence now of Denpasar's past. Situated in the south of the island, about 5 km from the coast, Bali's capital has grown in the past 10 to 15 years from a sleepy village to a bustling city. Today, the town has a population of over 450,000 and is Bali's main trade and transport hub, with its central business area centred around Jalan Gajah Mada. Puputan Square pays homage to the tragic end of the Rajah and his court in 1906; it is named after the 'battle to the death' – or puputan – against a force of Dutch soldiers on the morning of the 20 September (see page 226).

Ins and outs

Getting there Ngurah Rai airport is several kilometres south of Denpasar, beyond Kuta. There are good links from here with other destinations in Indonesia, and there are some international flights too (see the Essentials section of this book). The Ubung bus terminal is 4 km or so north of the town centre. Buses leave here for major destinations in Java, including Jakarta, Yogyakarta and Surabaya. There are also buses eastwards to Mataram, on Lombok.

Getting around As Bali's capital, Denpasar is well connected with the rest of the island. No fewer than 5 terminals provide bemo services to various parts of the island and minibuses run between the different terminals. Metered taxis are also abundant in Denpasar. There are two **tourist offices**: *Denpasar Tourist Office*, on Jl Surapati 7, T223602 (open 0700-1400 Mon-Thu and Sat, 0700-1100 Fri) provides a free map, calendar of events and Bali brochure; and *Bali Government Tourism Office*, on Jl S Parman, T222387.

Bali, distances between cities (km)

	Amlapura	Bangli	Besakih	Candi Dasa	Denpasar	Gianyar	Gilimanuk	Karangasem	Klungkung	Kuta Beach	Lake Batur	Legian	Lovina Beach	Ngurah Rai Airport	Nusa Dua	Singaraja	Tanah Lot
Bangli	26																
Besakih	41	20															
Candi Dasa	13	52	50														
Denpasar	85	47	70	72													
Gianyar	54	16	39	41	31												
Gilimanuk	219	181	201	206	134	165											
Karangasem	-	41	38	13	85	54	219										
Klungkung	38	26	23	27	47	16	181	38									
Kuta Beach	95	57	80	82	10	41	144	95	57								
Lake Batur	50	20	38	71	67	40	135	50	46	77							
Legian	97	59	82	84	12	43	146	97	59	2	79						
Lovina Beach	97	86	106	139	89	102	79	97	112	99	66	101					
Ngurah Rai Airport	98	60	83	85	13	44	147	98	60	3	80	5	102				
Nusa Dua	109	71	94	96	24	55	158	109	71	14	91	16	113	11			
Singaraja	97	79	97	110	78	99	90	97	105	88	59	90	11	91	110		
Tanah Lot	118	80	103	105	33	64	124	118	80	43	100	45	89	46	57	78	
Ubud	67	29	52	54	23	13	157	67	29	33	40	35	106	36	47	95	56

Bali highlights

Temples *The most important and impressively situated temple is* **Besakih** *on Mount Agung (page 158).* **Uluwatu** *is perched on a cliff-top on the Bukit Peninsula (page 121), while the coastal temple* **Tanah Lot** *(page 189) is the most photographed sight on Bali. Other notable temples include* **Taman Ayun** *at Mengwi (page 190) and* **Kehen** *at Bangli (page 152).*

Other historical sights *Within easy reach of Ubud are* **Goa Gajah** *or Elephant Cave (page 131), the ancient stone carvings at* **Yeh Pulu** *(page 132), the mysterious monumental burial chambers of* **Mount Kawi** *(page 147) and the holy springs at* **Tirta Empul** *(page 149). The royal bathing pools of* **Tirtagangga** *are in the east (page 178). The* **Museum Bali** *in Denpasar (page 73) has a good collection of ethnographic and archaeological exhibits.*

Beaches *The main beach resort areas are* **Kuta** *(page 79),* **Sanur** *(page 97) and* **Nusa Dua** *(see page 123);* **Candi Dasa** *(page 169) and* **Lovina Beach** *(page 201) are smaller and less developed.*

Shopping *Bali is a shopper's paradise; fashions in* **Kuta** *(page 83), craft villages north of* **Sanur** *(page 128), paintings and crafts in and around* **Ubud** *(page 130).*

Natural sights *Among the most notable, is the extraordinary volcanic landscape of* **Mount Batur** *(page 155); the upland, almost alpine, area centred on* **Lake Bratan** *(page 191); the terraced rice fields of the south and east and the countryside around* **Ubud** *(page 130); and the* **Bali Barat National Park** *(page 218).*

Sports *Surfing (see page 15), white water rafting (page 135), snorkelling, golf (pages 127 and 194) and diving (page 14) are the most notable.*

Culture & performance *Balinese dancing around Ubud (page 143), and the* **Bali Aga village** *of Tenganan (page 170).*

Sights

Denpasar is not a particularly attractive town and does not have much in the way of 'sights'. The major tourist attraction is easily found, in the centre of town and is a focus for local hawkers. The Museum Bali was established in 1931 and is situated on the east side of Puputan Square. The entrance is on Jalan Mayor Wismu. The museum, built in 1910, mirrors the architecture of Balinese temples and palaces and is contained within a series of attractive courtyards with well-kept gardens. The impressive collection of prehistoric artefacts, sculpture, masks, textiles, weaponry and contemporary arts and crafts was assembled with the help of Walter Spies, the German artist who made Bali his home. The artefacts on display are apparently only a small proportion of the museum's collection. Labelling could be better and there is no guide to the museum to help the inquisitive visitor. Nevertheless, it gives an impression of the breadth of the island's culture. ■ *T222680. 0800-1700 Tue-Thu, Sat and Sun, 0800-1530 Fri, closed Mon. Adult 500Rp, children 200Rp.*

Museum Bali

Next door to the museum is the new **Pura Jaganatha**, a temple dedicated to the Supreme God *Sang Hyang Widi Wasa*. The statue of a turtle and two nagas signify the foundation of the world. The complex is dominated by the *Padma Sana* or lotus throne, upon which the gods sit. The central courtyard is surrounded by a moat filled with water-lilies and the most enormous carp.

Pura Masopahit From an archaeological perspective, Pura Masopahit is the most important temple in Denpasar. The main gateway to the pura faces the main street, but the entrance is down a side road off the west end of Jalan Tabanan. The temple is one of the oldest in Bali, probably dating from the introduction of Javanese civilization from Majapahit in the 15th century, after which it is named. It was badly damaged during the 1917 earthquake, but has since been partly restored. Note the fine, reconstructed, split gate with its massive figures of a giant and a garuda.

Taman Werdi Budaya Art Centre The Taman Werdi Budaya Art Centre on Jalan Nusa Indah was established in 1973 to promote Balinese visual and performing arts. It contains an open-air auditorium, along with three art galleries. Arts and crafts are also sold here. Activity peaks during the annual Bali Festival of Art held from mid-June for a month. ■ *0800-1700 Tue-Sun, closed on Mon. 250Rp.*

Essentials

Sleeping

Until 1950s, Denpasar was the place where most tourists stayed; today it is largely frequented by domestic tourists – foreign visitors either head for the beaches or inland to Ubud. Nonetheless, there is an adequate range of accommodation

A *Natour's Bali*, Jl Veteran 3, T225681, F235347. 75 rooms, a/c, restaurant, pool, central location, built in the 1930s, it was the first hotel on Bali, rather frayed now but it does retain some charm. **B-C** *Chandra Garden*, Jl Diponegoro 114, T226425. 38 rooms, some a/c, popular with Indonesians, price includes breakfast. **B-C** *Pemecutan Palace*, Jl Thamrin 2, T223491. Some a/c, a reconstruction of a palace which was destroyed here by the Dutch in 1906, rooms are shabby. **C-D** *Pura Alit*, Jl Sutomo 26, T428831, F288766. Some a/c. **D** *Adi Yasa*, Jl Nakula 23, T222679. This place seems to have gone downhill. Recent visitors have reported that the rooms are dirty. Price includes breakfast. **D** *Dewi*, Jl Diponegoro 112, T226720. **D-E** *Dharmawisata*, Jl Imam Bonjol 89, T222186. Pool, clean rooms with own mandi.

Eating **Cheap** *Hong Kong*, Jl Gajah Mada 89, a/c, a tour group stop, wide selection of Chinese dishes, empty fish tanks, some international dishes. *Atom Baru*, Jl Gajah Mada 106-108, Chinese, popular with the locals. *Kakman*, Jl Teuku Umar (half way to Kuta), excellent Indonesian.

Nusa Indah *Warung Wardani* for cheap, genuine Balinese food. Recommended. Several *warungs* are to be found within the Kumbasari market.

Entertainment **Cinemas** *Wisata Complex*, Jl Thamrin 69, T423023.

Dance *SMKI* (untill recently called *KOKAR*), based in Batubulan, is a conservatory of dance. Students perform many different styles of traditional dance, accompanied by a gamelan orchestra. The *Werdi Budaya Art Centre* gives Kecak dance performances every day from 1830-1930.

Indonesian Language Courses *IALF, The Indonesian Australian Foundation*, JL Kapten Agung 17, T221782. Runs regular language courses in Denpasar, Sanur. Ubud and Legian.

Festivals **Mid-June to mid-July** The *Werdi Budaya Art Centre* presents an **Annual Arts Festival**, with demonstrations of local music, dance and performance. Hotels or the tourist office will supply a calendar of events.

Shopping **Department stores** *Duta Plaza*, Jl Dewi Sartika, *Tiara Dewata* and *Matahari* both have a good range of goods, including reasonably priced children's clothes, English language books and some handicrafts. The former also has a public swimming pool.

Handicrafts The *Sanggraha Kriya Asta*, T222942, 7 km east of the centre of town, is a government handicrafts shop, selling batik, jewellery, paintings and woodcarvings. The prices are set and quality is controlled. They will organize free transport to the shop from your hotel if telephoned. There are also a number of handicraft shops on Jl Thamrin, and on the 3rd floor of the Kumbasari Market (see 'Markets', below).

Markets The biggest market in town (and the biggest on Bali) is the **Kumbasari Market**, off Jl Dr Wahidin, on the banks of the Badung River. It is a great place to browse, with a range of goods including textiles and handicrafts.

Textiles A large selection of textiles is to be found in the shops along Jl Sulawesi.

Bali

Denpasar

To Tanah Lot, Bedugul, Singaraja & Ubung

Wangaya Hospital

Jl A Yani

Jl Kartini

Jl Setiabudi

Jl Nangka

Jl Suli 8

Jl Pattimura

Stadium

Garuda & Merpati Offices

Jl Supratman

To Gianyar

Jl Kedondong

Jl Kamboja

Jl Kapungdung

Jl Melati

Jl Nusa Indah

Jl Sutomo

Jl Dr Wahidin

Jl Kartini

Sports Centre

Jl Gadung

10

Jl Palawa

Jl Durian

Jl Merapi

Jl G Merapi

Jl Thamrin

Gajah Mada

Jl Veteran

St Joseph's

Night Market

Werdi Budaya Art Centre

Kumbasari Market

Batara Guru Statue

Jl Surapati

Bouraq Airlines

Jl Hasanuddin

Puputan Square

Jaganatha

Museum Bali

Jl Hayam Wuruk

Jl G Batu Karu

Indonesian Australian Language Foundation

Jl MJ Sutoyo

Jl Gn Kidul

Chandra Garden

Tiara Dewata Shopping Complex

Jl Letda Kajeng

Jl Diponegoro

River Badung

Jl Imam Bonjol

Jl Nusakambangan

Night Market

Jl Dr Monginsidi

Jl Dr Sudirman

To Kuta

Jl Yos Sudarso

Jl Hajar Dewantara

Matahari Dept Store

Jl D Sartika

Jl Teuku Umar

Paket Pos

University Udayana

Jl Panjaitan

Immigration Office

Jl Diponegoro

Sanglah Public Hospital

Jl Raya Puputan

Jl Dr Kusuma Atmaja

To Airport & Kuta

Night Market

To Sanur

Jl Buton

Jl Waturenggong

To Benoa

N

0 metres 300
0 yards 300

■ Sleeping	8 Suli Inn	🚌 Transport
1 Adi Yasa	9 Viking	1 Gunung Agung Terminal
2 Dirgapura	10 Wisma Taruna	2 Kereneng Terminal
3 Djaja		3 Suci Terminal (Bemos)
4 Natour's Bali	● Eating	4 Tegal Bemo Station
5 Oka	1 Atom Baru	5 Bemo Terminal
6 Pemecutan Palace	2 Hong Kong	
7 Rai	3 Prambanan Fried Chicken	

Tour operators *Arha Bali Rafting*, Jl Muding Indah 11/4 Kerobakan, T427446, F427339, rafting on Klungkung River US$65-75, price including pick-up from your hotel and lunch. *Ayung River Rafting*, Jl Diponegoro 150B 29, T238759, F224236, rafting on Ayung River, US$63, including hotel pick-up and meal, also mountain cycling and trekking available. *Grand Komodo Tours & Travel*, PO Box 3477, T287166, F287165, tours to Komodo and Lombok, from US$390 for 3 days to US$730 for 8 days, including full board but not air fares. *Bali Vacanza*, Jl Laksamana VI/1.4, T261576, F231652, 1 or 2 day trips to Yogyakarta and Lombok. *Waka Experience*, Jl Imam Bonjol No 335 X, T0361-723629, 723659, F722077. Members of the Cousteau Society. They organize *Wakalouka* luxury cruises on a catamaran to their upmarket resort on the island of Lombongan, taking 9 hrs (leaves Benoa harbour at 0900 for the 2 hr journey) which includes 5 hrs at their luxury reef club with swimming pool, watersports and games room; also included is a village tour, and the price of US$86 (children half price) includes transfers, gourmet Indonesian meal with wine and beer, sunset cocktails and all soft drinks. Also *Wakalouka Land Cruises* into the interior by Land Rover, taking in remote rice paddy, ancient quarries and hot springs, and a rustic restaurant in the heart of the rainforest where food is cooked over traditional mud ovens and served on immaculate starched tablecloths, with Italian designer cutlery, US$83 per person covers the day-long trip and includes all the food and drink you want, including refreshments from the capacious hampers carried on top of the Land Rover. Recommended. *Bali Safari Rafting*, Jl Hayam Wuruk 88a, T221315, F232268, organizes rafting on Telaga Waja River, US$65 including transfers, buffet lunch, refreshments, insurance.

Transport

As Denpasar is the transport hub of the island, it is easy to get to most of the main towns, beaches & sights from here

Local Bemo: a few of the original, rickety and under-powered 3-wheeler bemos still travel between the main bemo terminals (1000Rp), criss-crossing town, although much more common these days are Japanese built mini buses. It is also possible to charter these bemos for trips around town. From the terminals – of which there are several – bemos travel to all of Bali's main towns: the Ubung terminal, north of town on Jl Cokroaminoto, for trips to **West Bali**, **North Bali** and **Java**; Tegal, west of town, near the intersection of Jl Imam Bonjol and Jl G Wilis, for journeys to **South Bali**; Suci, near the intersection of Jl Diponegoro and Jl Hasanuddin, for **Benoa Port**; Kereneng, at the east edge of town off Jl Kamboja (Jl Hayam Wuruk) for destinations around town and for **Sanur**; while Batubulan, east of town just before the village of Batubulan on the road to Gianyar, for buses running east and to central Bali (see page 35 for more details). **Dokar**: pony-drawn carriages, now on the verge of extinction and/or asphyxiation. **Ojek**: motorcycle taxis, and the fastest way around town; ojek riders can be identified by their red jackets (1,000Rp minimum). **Taxi**: there are numerous un-metered cars that can be chartered by the hour or day, or which can be hired for specific journeys. Bargain hard. There are also some metered taxis. *Praja Bali Taxi*, pale blue taxis all operate with meters and make no extra charge for call-out service, T701111.

Air See page 34 for details.

Road Bemo: these provide transportation from Denpasar's 5 terminals to most places on the island (see page 39 and above). Mini buses run between the various terminals (1000Rp). **Bus**: connections with **Java** from the Ubung terminal, just north of Denpasar on Jl Cokroaminoto. Express and night bus offices are concentrated near the intersection of Jl Diponegoro and Jl Hasanuddin, for example, *Chandra Ticketing*, Jl Diponegoro 114, T226425. Journey time and departure times for night and express buses are as follows: **Jakarta** 30 hrs (0630-0700), **Surabaya** 11 hrs (0700 and 1700-2000), **Malang** 10 hrs (1800-1930), **Yogyakarta/Solo** 16 hrs (1500-1600), **Semarang** 15 hrs (1600), **Bandung** 25 hrs (0700), **Bogor** 24 hrs (0700), **Blitar** 15 hrs (1900).

Airline offices *Bouraq*, Jl Sudirman 19A, T223564. *Garuda*, Jl Melati 61, T222788. *Mandala*, Jl
Diponegoro 98 (Kerta Wijaya Plaza), T222751, F231659. *Merpati*, Jl Melati 57, T235358. *UTA*, Jl
Bypass Ngurah Rai, T289225. **Banks** *Bank Bumi Daya*, Jl Veteran 2. *Bank Dagang Negara*, Jl
Gajah Mada 2. *Bank Negara Indonesia*, Jl Gajah Mada 20. *Diners Club*, Jl Veteran 5, Denpasar,
T227138. **Visa & Mastercharge:** *Bank Duta*, Jl Hayam Wuruk 165, Denpasar, T226578.
Communications Post office: Jl Raya Puputan, Renon. Open 0800-1400 Mon-Thu, 0800-1200
Fri, 0800-1300 Sat. *Poste Restante* available here. *Paket Pos* (packing service & parcel post): Jl
Diponegoro 146. **Communications centre:** Jl Teuku Umar 6. **Embassies &
consulates** Australia, Jl Mohammad Yamin 51, T235093. **France**, Jl Rayan Sesetan 46, T233555.
Germany, Jl Pantai Karang 17, T288535, F288826. **Japan**, Jl Pemuda, Renon, T227628. **Norway**, Jl
Jayagiri VII/10, T234834. **Medical services** Emergency dental clinic: Jl Pattimura 19, T222445.
Hospitals: *Sanglah Public Hospital*, Jl Kesehatan Selatan 1, T227911. *Wangaya Hospital*, Jl
Kartini, T222141. 24 hr on-call doctor and ambulance, Jl Cokroaminoto 28, T426393. This is the
main hospital with the best emergency service. Some staff speak English. Bali's only
decompression chamber for divers is located here. Bear in mind that medical facilities are not up
to western standards. For any serious medical problem Singapore is the best place to go.
Optician: *International Optical*, Jl Gajah Mada 133, T226294. Pharmacy: *Apotik Kimia Farma*, Jl
Diponegoro 123, T227812. **Places of worship** Catholic: *Church of St Joseph* on Jl Kepundung
(1730, Sat, 0830, 1730, Sun). Evangelical Church : Jl Melati. Protestant Church: Jl Surapati. **Useful
addresses** Emergencies: 24-hr helpline, T228996. **Immigration office**: Jl Panjaitan, off Jl
Puputan Raya, T227828. **Police**: HQ, Jl Supratman, T110.

Bali

South Bali

Most visitors to Bali stay in one of the resorts at the south end of the island. Most famous is **Kuta**, *the original backpackers' haven, together with its north extension,* **Legian**, *both of these are fairly noisy, crowded, downmarket resorts. Much nicer is* **Seminyak** *further north, which is still relatively rural. To the south of Kuta is a newly developed zone of hotels and restaurants named* **Tuban**. *Further south still is* **Jimbaran**, *a large village, as yet unspoilt, with one of Bali's top resorts nearby –* The Four Seasons, *which overlooks Jimbaran Bay – and its new international neighbour, the* Bali Inter-Continental. *Sanur is on Bali's east coast and offers largely middle range accommodation, though some newer budget places to stay have recently opened.* **Serangan**, *or Turtle Island is a short distance offshore. Rather further off the east coast, in the Lombok Strait, are the two islands of* **Nusa Penida**, *with limited and very basic accommodation, and* **Nusa Lembongan**, *with a growing number of upmarket hotels; both are also accessible on a day trip.*

South Bali

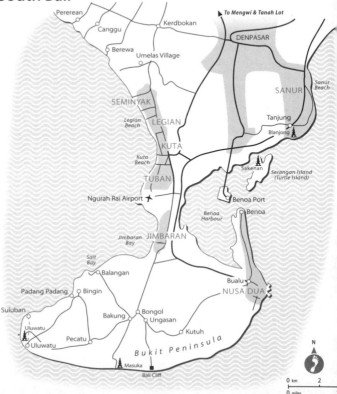

Kuta

Kuta was the main port and arrival point for foreigners visiting south Bali for over 100 years from early in the 18th century until first Benoa, and then the airport at Denpasar usurped its role. The town prospered as a hub of the slave trade in the 1830s, attracting an international cross section of undesirables. Its current role as a tourist centre can be traced back to the arrival of hippies and surfers in the 1960s, when it was a popular staging post on the overland route from Europe to Australia.

Phone code: 0361
Colour map 1, grid B2

The first pub was opened in Kuta in 1930 by an American, Ketut Tantri; in the same decade another American couple opened the first hotel on the beach. Nonetheless, the author and Bali-phile Miguel Covarrubias wrote in 1937 that Kuta and Sanur were "small settlements of fishermen who brave the malarial coasts". It was not until the 1960s that large numbers of Western travellers 'discovered' Kuta. Since then, it has grown into a highly developed beach resort with a mind-boggling array of hotels, restaurants and shops. While Sanur is no longer a backpackers' haven, there are still many cheap losmen in Kuta as well as a growing number of middle to high range accommodation.

Bali

Getting around Traffic in Kuta frequently comes to a standstill, despite the one-way system. The main drag, containing most of Kuta's shops, is Jl Legian, which runs north-south (traffic travels one way south). Jl Pantai meets Jl Legian at the notorious 'Bemo Corner' and is the main east-west road to the south end of the beach (with traffic going one way west). The beach road is northbound only. There is a Government **Tourist Information Office**, on Jl Bakungsari, T756176, open daily 0800-1300, 1500-1800.

The town Many people dislike Kuta. Crowded beyond belief, with an infrastructure at breaking point, as space runs out accommodation owners have taken to building multi-storey concrete blocks of rooms to let, often in what were once pretty Balinese gardens. In the rainy season the drainage system is hopelessly inadequate and some areas of Kuta become flooded and virtually impassable for several days at a time.

With the downturn in the economy petty theft is becoming more of a problem. Locals accuse 'refugees' from eastern Java of being behind this increase in crime. Look out for groups of young children, both boys and girls, particularly in front of the *Hard Rock Hotel*, who will swarm over you, often waving an old newspaper or beaded jewellery to distract your attention while rifling through your pockets or money belt. If your hotel has a safe, it is worth leaving your money belt there – prominently displayed money belts, not surprisingly, seem to act as a magnet for thieves.

The beach Kuta Beach is a fine beach; a broad expanse of golden sand where local officials have taken fairly unsuccessful steps to limit the persistence of hawkers. It is because of its accessibility that it is popular with surfers, although better waves can be found elsewhere. It is an excellent spot for beginners and recreational surfers. Boards can be hired on the beach and there are usually locals who will offer their insider's knowledge of surf conditions. Strong and irregular currents can make swimming a little hazardous – look out for the warning notices and coloured flags which indicate which areas are safe for swimming on any particular day; the currents change from day to day. The sand is white to the south, but grey further north. The hordes of hawkers can be very aggressive, selling trinkets and offering hair-plaiting, manicure and massage services. The beach faces west, so is popular at sunset. There are allegations that levels of contamination in the sea at Kuta are above internationally accepted safety levels, though many people are happy to swim in the sea with no apparent ill effects. Several groups are trying to encourage local action to combat the problem including the Wisnu Foundation (see section 'Green Bali'), and several of the large hotels including *The Hard Rock* are actively involved in various schemes that include educating the local population by targeting schools.

Sleeping
It is advisable to book accommodation during the peak periods of Jul/Aug & at Christmas & New Year, as hotels are often full. There are countless places to stay in Kuta

Taxi drivers are often reluctant to drive down Poppies Gangs I and II. Except when the area is flooded during the rainy season, Poppies Gang 11 is perfectly driveable so it is worth trying to find a driver who will drop you by your chosen accommodation.

AL *Hard Rock Hotel*, Jl Pantai, Kuta, T761869, F761868, rock@ hardrockbeachclub.com The first ever *Hard Rock Hotel* opened in May 1998, and is *the* place to stay in Kuta. Aimed at families and rock fans alike, it attracts people of all ages and nationalities. 418 rooms and suites situated around tropical gardens with sea or garden views. All rooms with a/c, fridge, safe, ceiling mounted TV, CD/cassette player, IDD, tea/coffee-making facilities, internet access (Nintendo games can be hired). Vast free-form swimming pool, the largest on Bali, centred around a sand island with its own beach area, water slides and underwater music. Semi-professional recording studio where you can record your own CD with backing group and professional sound recordist. Million dollar audio-visual system in lobby featuring nightly live entertainment. In-house radio station (soon to be broadcast throughout Bali), karaoke rooms, rock information centre, internet centre, 7 restaurants and bars, all

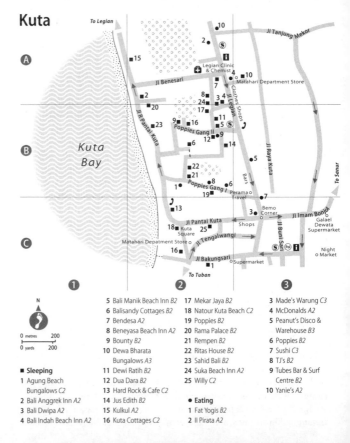

Kuta

To Legian

Kuta Bay

To Sanur

To Tuban

N
0 metres 200
0 yards 200

■ **Sleeping**
1 Agung Beach Bungalows *C2*
2 Bali Anggrek Inn *A2*
3 Bali Dwipa *A2*
4 Bali Indah Beach Inn *A2*
5 Bali Manik Beach Inn *B2*
6 Balisandy Cottages *B2*
7 Bendesa *A2*
8 Beneyasa Beach Inn *A2*
9 Bounty *B2*
10 Dewa Bharata Bungalows *A3*
11 Dewi Ratih *B2*
12 Dua Dara *B2*
13 Hard Rock & Cafe *C2*
14 Jus Edith *B2*
15 Kulkul *A2*
16 Kuta Cottages *C2*
17 Mekar Jaya *B2*
18 Natour Kuta Beach *C2*
19 Poppies *B2*
20 Rama Palace *B2*
21 Rempen *B2*
22 Ritas House *B2*
23 Sahid Bali *B2*
24 Suka Beach Inn *A2*
25 Willy *C2*

● **Eating**
1 Fat Yogis *B2*
2 Il Pirata *A2*
3 Made's Warung *C3*
4 McDonalds *A2*
5 Peanut's Disco & Warehouse *B3*
6 Poppies *B2*
7 Sushi *C3*
8 TJ's *B2*
9 Tubes Bar & Surf Centre *B2*
10 Yanie's *A2*

reasonably priced, serving excellent Indonesian, Mediterranean, Asian, American and Japanese, food, including a New York-style deli, and a sushi bar. Great sunset views over the sea from the 2nd and 3rd floors. Health club (free to guests) and spa with state of the art gym equipment. Children's club with full day's programme of activities, and crèche. Recommended.

A *Bali Anggrek Inn*, Jl Pantai, PO Box 435, T751265, F751766. A/c, restaurant, large pool, facing the beach, average rooms. **A** *Indah*, Poppies Gang II, T753327, F752787. Pool, central location for shopping, price including breakfast. **A** *Kulkul*, Jl Pantai, PO Box 97, T752520, F752519. A/c, restaurant, pool, on the beach road, well designed hotel with attractive rooms. Recommended. **A** *Poppies I*, Poppies Gang I, PO Box 378, T751059, F752364. A/c, pool, lovely garden, well-run hotel with cottage accommodation, very popular. **A** *Rama Palace*, Jl Pantai, PO Box 293, T752063, F753078. On the beach road, a/c, restaurant, pool, standard accommodation. **A** *Sahid Bali*, Jl Pantai, PO Box 1102, T753855, F752019. A/c, restaurant, pool, large hotel on the beachfront. **A** *Sol Inn*, 118 Jl Legian, T752167, F754372. New 1st-class hotel built in the centre of Kuta, 124 rooms, a/c, mini-bar, satellite TV, in-house movie, balcony, en suite bathroom, pool, Japanese restaurant, Indonesian restaurant, pub, 2 bars, simple but attractive pastel décor. **A-B** *Mutiara*, Poppies Gang I, T752091. Some a/c, attractive pool, nice garden, clean rooms.

B *Agung Cottages*, Jl Raya Legian, T751147. Some a/c, restaurant, good pool. Recommended. **B** *Aneka Beach*, Jl Pantai, T752067, F752892. A/c, pool, on the beach road, 3-storey hotel plus some thatched bungalows, attractive grounds. **B** *Bakungsari*, Jl Bakungsari, PO Box 1044, T755396, F752704. A/c, pool, built around a central swimming pool, clean rooms. **B** *Bali Bungalows*, PO Box 371, T755285, F751899. A/c, pool, near *Rama Palace* on the beach road, nice grounds. **B** *Bruna Beach*, PO Box 116, T751565, F753201. A/c, on beachfront road, average rooms, price including breakfast. **B** *Five One Cottages*, behind Poppies Gang I, a/c, small pool, hot water. **B** *Flora Beach*, Jl Bakungsari 13A, PO Box 1040, T751870, F751034. A/c, pool, new hotel with attractive pool and clean, well-designed rooms, one of the better of the mid-range hotels. Recommended. **B** *Kuta Cottages*, Jl Bakungsari, PO Box 300, T751101. Pool, small hotel. **B** *Melasti*, Jl Kartika Plaza, PO Box 295, T751335, F751563. A/c, pool, on the beach, may be rather overpriced and living on its reputation, south end of Kuta. **B** *Satriya*, Poppies Gang II, T752741. Pool, hot water, clean rooms, price including breakfast. Recommended. **B** *Willy*, Jl Tengalwangi 18, T751281, F752641. Small, attractive pool, central location in Kuta, attractive rooms, built around a garden. Recommended. **B-C** *Agung Beach Bungalows*, Jl Bakungsari, T751263. Some a/c, pool, good location south of Jl Pantai. **B-C** *Dewa Bharata Bungalows*, Jl Legian, T/F751764. Clean rooms with a/c or fan, private bathroom all with hot water, shower and Western toilet, attractive gardens with good sized swimming pool, price includes meagre breakfast, not as well run as it used to be but still worth considering if you want a decent sized pool. *Dewa Bharata Bungalows* in Candi Dasa owned by same people. **C** *Jesen's Inn III*, Jl Bakungsari 19, T751561. Off the main road in a large palm-filled courtyard, rooms in the new wing are best. **B-C** *Dewi Ratih*, Poppies Gang II, T751694. Some a/c, small pool, hot water, price includes breakfast.

C *Barong Cottages*, Jl Legian, T751488, F751804. A/c, pool, 3-storey accommodation, nice garden, price including breakfast. **C** *Sorga Cottages*, off Poppies Gang II, some a/c, good pool, price including breakfast. **C-D** *Dharma Yudha*, Jl Bakungsari, T751685. Some a/c, friendly, but rooms are rather dark. **C-D** *Lasi Erawati*, Poppies Gang I, T751665. Fan, clean, nice garden. Recommended. **C-E** *Rita's House*, Poppies Gang I, T751760, F236021. 12 reasonably priced rooms with fan or a/c and private mandi with Western toilet, set around small garden, clean and relaxing.

D *Bali Manik Beach Inn*, Poppies Gang II, T752740. Own bathroom, clean, with a verandah in front of each room, price includes breakfast. Good value. **D** *Balisandy Cottages*, Poppies Gang II, T753344. 2-storey bungalows with private mandi, Western toilet, fan, set in spacious coconut grove away from the noise of Kuta, attractive décor, very clean and quiet. Good value and recommended. **D** *Bamboo Inn*, Gang Kresek 1, Jl Bakungsari, T751935. Friendly, clean, but not very close to the beach, price including breakfast. **D** *Kuta Suci*, just off Poppies Gang II, T752617. Small but clean rooms. **D** *Masa Inn*, Poppies Gang I, T752606. Fan, clean (motorbike hire). **D** *Rempen*, T753150. Just off Poppies Gang 1. Perfectly adequate, fairly basic rooms in 3-storey block. Price includes simple breakfast. **D** *Sareg*, Jl Pantai Kuta, basic, Western toilets, clean. Recommended. **D-E** *Bendesa*, T751358. North of Poppies Gang II just off Jl Legian. Set in large gardens, 35 rooms; the new rooms are bright and clean, older rooms are very basic and not particularly good value. All with private bathroom, Western toilet, shower. Price includes breakfast and tea all day. **D-E** *Dua Dara*, Jl Legian, Poppies Gang II, T754031. Well run, spotlessly clean simple rooms with fan, private bathrooms with shower and Western toilet, attractive small garden with family temple, price includes breakfast, safety deposit boxes available. Recommended.

E *Bali Dwipa I*, T751446/752247. Just north of Poppies Gang II, one of the nicer budget places in the area. 48 rooms in a 3-storey block with small garden and attractive atrium. Rooms are simple but clean with private bathrooms, shower and Western toilets. Special longstay rates available, price including breakfast, friendly atmosphere and staff. Recommended. **E** *Bali Indah Beach Inn*, T752509. Just north of Poppies Gang II, basic but clean rooms, private bathrooms with shower and Western toilet (some without toilet seat), very friendly management, price including breakfast. **E** *Beneyasa Beach Inn*, just north of Poppies Gang II. T754180. 50 rooms set round gardens which sometimes flood in the wet season providing nice breeding grounds for mosquitoes! Rooms are simple but clean with private bathroom, Western toilet and shower. **E** *Jus Edith*, off Poppies Gang II to the south, basic but cheap and very popular. **E** *Komala Indah I*, opposite Poppies Cottages, Poppies Gang I, rooms with own bathroom. **E** *Mekar Jaya*, north of Poppies Gang II, Basic but clean, rooms could do with redecoration. Private bathroom, shower, Western toilet (most without seats). **E** *Pension Arka Nini*, Jl Buni Sari 7. Very comfortable beds, toilet and mandi in room, price including good breakfast, friendly management, clean and quiet rooms, despite central location. **E** *Suka Beach Inn*, Just north of Poppies Gang II, T752793. One of the nicest of the budget places in this area. 54 rooms, some new, set around pretty gardens. Rooms are clean with private bathroom, shower and Western toilet. Very friendly management. Price includes breakfast. Motor bikes for hire. Popular. Recommended.

Eating

Most of the restaurants in Kuta offer a range of food, including Indonesian & international, so we have not split restaurants by cuisine categories

Mid-range *Bebek Mas*, street-front of *Melasti Beach Bungalows*, Jl Kartika Plaza, T752750. Owned by Dutch chef Wim Hilgers. Seafood salad, crab and grapefruit salad, fettucini senora bianca, all recommended. Excellent Bebek Betutu (Balinese duck). Pasta night on Mon, Schnitzel night on Wed, Rifsttafel on Thu, Indonesian buffet on Sun. No a/c and the mosquitoes are bad. *Edelweiss*, on Jl By-Pass between Kuta and Nusa Dua. Run by Otto King, previously chef at *Nusa Dua Beach Hotel*. Austrian and international dishes, good steaks. *Hard Rock Hotel*, Jl Pantai. 7 restaurants and bars (see hotel entry), prices to suit every budget. *Hard Rock Café*, Jl Pantai, on 2 floors facing the sea. Serves American food, live bands each night.

Cheap *Aromas of Bali*, Jl Legian. Vegetarian food in a garden setting. *Indah Sari*, Jl Legian, near Bemo Corner. Indonesian grilled seafood. *Poppies*, Poppies Gang I. Attractive garden, good food (mostly international). Popular and recommended. *SC*, Jl Legian. Seafood, Chinese. *Sushi Restaurant*, Jl Legian, just up from Bemo Corner. Good, reasonably priced Japanese food. *TJ's*, Poppies Gang I. Good Mexican food and excellent margaritas. *Un's*, Poppies Gang I. Indonesian, travellers' food, seafood, both only average quality.

Very cheap *Bobbies*, towards Legian, to left of Jl Legian. Excellent value food, particularly the pizzas, and good breakfasts. Recommended. *Crown*, T754719. The fish on the menu here has been recommended. *Golden Palace International*, Poppies Gang II. Good lasagnes, opposite here is a small, popular and very cheap restaurant, with pizza, fried rice etc and cheap beer. *Made's Warung*, Jl Pantai. The oldest eating establishment on Kuta, serving Asian and travellers' food and still very popular. Recommended. *Murni's Warung*, Poppies II, halfway down Poppies II opposite *Kori Restaurant*. Incredibly cheap and tasty nasi campur, also fruit juices and coffee. This is where the locals eat. *Tree House*, Poppies Gang I. Travellers' food. *Yunna*, Poppies Gang II. Travellers' food, popular. *Burger King*, Jl Legian. *Il Pirata*, Jl Legian. 24-hr pizzeria. *Locanda Fat Yogi*, Poppies Gang I. Bakery and Italian restaurant with good pizzas. Recommended. *Mini's*, Jl Legian. Popular Chinese restaurant, with good seafood.

Club Bruna, Jl Pantai (beach road, see 'Discos'). *Bali Rock*, Jl Melasti. *Lips Bar*, Jl Legian Raya – country and western music. *Sari Club*, Jl Legian. *The Bounty*, Jl Legian, popular Australian drinking-hole, with jugs of Margueritas and videos, happy hours 1800-1900, 2200-2300. Every Tues and Sat a pub crawl leaves *Peanuts*, on Jl Legian at 1830. Arrives at *Casablancas* (Jl Buni Sari – just south of Bemo Corner) at about 2200, where there is often live music. *Hard Rock Café*, Jl Pantai, expensive drinks, live (good) bands, big crowds, music starts about 2300 and goes on until 0200. *Tubes Bar*, a surfers hangout and excellent source of surfing information.

Bars
Kuta probably has the 'best' nightlife on Bali. Most of the bars are on Jl Legian

Balinese performing arts Kecak, legong, Ramayana dance and Balinese music; performances take place at many of the major hotels.

Entertainment

Discos *Peanut's*, Jl Legian (4,000Rp entry fee). *Warehouse* (next door to *Peanuts*), free entry. *Bruna Reggae Pub*, Jl Pantai, live local music starts at 2330 (8,000Rp entry fee). *Spotlights* and *Cheater's*, both on Jl Legian. Open-air discos at *Gado-Gado* (closed Mon and Thu) and *Double Six* (open Mon, Thu and Sat), both north of Legian, off Jl Dhyanapura and Jl Legian Cottage. Both these two are open from 2400-0400 (10,000Rp entry fee).

Best buys Kuta is undoubtedly the best place on Bali to shop for clothing; the quality is reasonable (sometimes good), and designs are close to the latest Western fashions, with a strong Australian bias for bright colours and bold designs. There is a good range of children's clothes shops. Silver jewellery is also a good buy (although some of it is of rather inferior quality). In addition, Kuta has a vast selection of 'tourist' trinkets and curios: leather goods, woodcarvings, mobiles, batik. Quality is poor-to-average. The boys hawking watches at an asking price of up to 200,000Rp, buy them in Surabaya for 15,000Rp a kilo! Almost all the hawkers and stall holders are from Java. They are unskilled workers who live in cardboard boxes and often bring their troubles with them, which has led to a rise in petty crime, and has sorely tried the fabled tolerance of the Balinese. The new Kuta Square shopping centre has a variety of designer boutiques and a large *Matahari* department store (the cheapest place to stock up on food, drinking water and fruit).

Shopping

Children's clothes shops *Hop on Pop*, Jl Pantai 45. *Kuta Kidz*, Bemo Corner; *Outrageous*, Jl Legian Kaja 460.

Jewellery Several shops on Jl Legian and Jl Pantai. *Shiraz Silver*, on Jl Bunisari, has some attractive silver jewellery.

Bali

Leather Leather goods are generally poor quality but cheap and attractive – if you are buying a bag, check the handles are strong. *A-Sodig*, 3 Kuta Theatre St, sells made-to-measure leather jackets and trousers, and has good value boots and shoes.

Men's clothes Shirts at *Aladdin's Cave*, Jl Legian and in several shops around Bemo Corner.

Swimwear & sportswear Jl Pantai, and from the surfing shops on Jl Legian and Jl Bakungsari.

T-shirts A multitude of shops along Jl Legian; good designs from *Tony's* on Jl Bakungsari.

Women's clothes shops Mostly along Jl Legian and Jl Pantai. Lots of lycra, available from *Coconut Tree*, Jl Legian. Outrageous sequined garments from *Dallas*, Jl Legian 496. Batik jump-suits and jackets from *Aladdin's Cave*, Jl Legian; *Bali Design*, good quality cotton fashions.

Sports **Bungy Jumping** *Bali Bungy Co*, Jl Pura Puseh, Legian Kelod, T752658, open daily 0800-midnight, the first bungy jumping company in Bali – the unsightly 45 m metal tower from which jumps are made is clearly seen from quite a long way away, free pick-up service is offered.

Diving *Aquamarine Diving*, Jl Raya Seminyak 56, Kuta, T730107, F735368, 81-23944162 '(mobile), www.aquamarinediving.com This company is owned and run by an Englishwoman, Annabel Thomas, a PADI instructor. It offers a personal service, uses Balinese divemasters who speak English (and Japanese) and has well-maintained equipment. PADI courses up to divemaster can be provided in English, German, Spanish, French and Japanese.

Massage Numerous masseurs – with little professional training – roam the beach; more skilled masseurs can be found at hotels or specialist clinics around Kuta.

Surfing Kuta is famous for its surfing, although the cognoscenti would now rather go elsewhere (see page 15). Surfboards are available for rent on the beach. Surf equipment is available from *The Surf Shop*, Jl Legian. *Amphibia Surf Shop*, Jl Legian; and *Ulu's Shop*, Jl Bakungsari. They will all provide information on currents, tides and latest surfing reports.

Swimming Small pool and spa in historic building, centre of Kuta, opposite the Art Market, adult 3,000Rp, child 1,500Rp, towels and lockers for hire. Waterbom Park in Tuban is nearby (see Tuban entry).

Bali Adventure Tours, Jl Tunjung Mekar, T751292, F754334. An organized company **Tour operators**
owned by long term Australian resident (the owner of *Yanies Restaurant* in Legian),
they can help you with rafting or kayaking trips, mountain biking or trekking,
US$40-56, including pick-up from hotel, lunch and insurance. *Gloria Tours &*
Travel Services, Jl Raya Kerobokan 2, T730272, F730273, Bali sight-seeing tours, island
tours, car rental. *Lila Tours Ltd*, Natour Kuta Beach Hotel, Jl Pantai Kuta 1, T761827,
F761826, lilatur@indosat.net.id Locally owned and run tour company. *Perama*, Jl
Legian 16, T751551, *Perama* organize shuttle buses all over the island and are one of
the cheapest companies. Ask for a Member's Card and you will receive 10% discount
on all journeys. Alternatively keep your used Perama ticket and show it when buying
your next ticket for a 10% discount.

Local Bemos: run from Bemo Corner up Jl Pantai to Legian (1,000Rp); and from just **Transport**
east of Bemo Corner, to Denpasar's Tegal terminal. Note that these days many bemo *11 km from Denpasar,*
drivers are reluctant to pick up Westerners except for a highly inflated fare. Bemos for *4 km from the airport*
charter also hang around Bemo Corner. **Bicycle hire**: 10,000Rp per day. **Car hire**:
arrange through hotels, or one of the rental agencies in town, approximately
80,000Rp per day; there are also private cars (with drivers) that can be chartered by
the hour or day, or for specific journeys. Bargain hard, expect to pay about 60,000Rp
per day. Drivers can be found around Bemo Corner. **Motorbike hire**: arranged
through travel agents, hotels or from operations on the street, from 20,000Rp per day.

Road Bemo: to Tegal terminal in **Denpasar** and from there, change to other terminals for next destination. **Shuttle bus**: to most tourist destinations on the island; shop
around for best price. **Taxi**: 15,000Rp to the airport.

Airline offices *Garuda*, Natour Kuta Beach Hotel, Jl Pantai, T751179. Mon-Fri 8am-5pm, Sat and **Directory**
Sun 9am-1pm. **Banks** Plenty of money changers on Jl Legian and its side streets. Very few, if any
are licensed, and most are masters of sleight of hand and deception: BE WARNED! You should take
a calculator with you and count the money you receive very, very carefully. *Matahari* has a foreign
exchange booth on the ground floor with reasonable rates. Also a handful of banks. Branches of
Lippo Bank and *Danamon* in *Galael Plaza* (on road into Kuta from Denpasar). **Communications**
Postal agent: Jl Legian; *poste restante* service. **Post Office**: Jl Raya Kuta, south of Jl Bakungsari.
Telecommunications centre: Jl Legian, near Poppies Gang II. **Embassies &**
consulates **Netherlands**, Jl Imam Bonjol 599, T751094, F752777. **Medical services** Clinic:
Legian Clinic, Gang Benasari (off Jl Legian before Jl Melasti), T758503. Helpful staff who speak
good English. The doctors do not charge but any treatment starts at 75,000Rp plus the cost of
medicines. Jl Raya Kuta 100, T753268, 24 hrs on call. *American CDC*, T(Atlanta)404-639-3311, web
site: http://www.cdc.gov/cdc.html **Places of worship** Protestant service: 1000 Sun, Gang
Menuh, Jl Legian.

Legian

It is hard to say where Kuta ends and Legian begins, as the main shopping *Phone code: 0361*
street, Jl Legian dominates both places. However, Legian is more than just a
name and it does have its own identity, though it is becoming more and more
like Kuta. Like Kuta, Legian is a shopping haven, but the shops are slightly
more upmarket, there are fewer drinking holes and more arts and crafts shops,
as opposed to clothing. North of Legian you reach Seminyak which starts at Jl
Double Six; the beach here is much less crowded, wide and sandy with a few
mostly mid- to upmarket hotels dotted along it, the most prestigious of which
is the *Oberoi*. Jalan Pura Bagus Tarunais also known as Rum Jungle Road. Jalan
Dhyana Pura is also known as Jalan Abimanyu.

Legian & Seminyak

To Denpasar, Balisani Suites & Batubelig Beach Bungalo

To Bali Intan Village

To Puri Ratih

Petitenget Temple

JI Kayu Aya

24 Hour Clinic

JI Lasmana

JI R Krobokan

JI Seminyak

SEMINYAK

JI Sarinande

JI Dhyana Pura (JI Abimanyu)

Alas Arum Supermarket

Santo Mikael

Bintang Supermarket

Bungee Jumping

JI Double Six

Taxi Stand

JI Nakula

Legian Beach

LEGIAN

JI Pura Bagus Taruna

Swiss Consulate

JI Legian

Logi Supermarket

JI Padma Utara

JI Padma

JI Melasti

To Kuta & Airport

N

0 metres 300
0 yards 300

■ **Sleeping**
1 Adika Sari Bungalows D2
2 Ananda Bungalow B1
3 Bali Agung Village C1
4 Bali Holiday Resort C1
5 Bali Intan E2
6 Bali Legian Resort C2
7 Bali Mandira E2
8 Bali Oberoi B1
9 Bali Padma E2
10 Bali Reski Asih B1
11 Balisani & Sinar Indah D2
12 Bunga Seminyak C1
13 Century Saphir Bali C2
14 Dewi Tirta C2
15 Dhyana Pura C1
16 Garden View D2
17 Imperial C1
18 Jayakarta D2
19 Kesuma Sari, Sarinande Beach Inn & Vila Kresna C1
20 Laut Biru D2
21 Legian B1
22 Legian Beach D3
23 Legian Village E2
24 Mesari Beach Inn & Horse Riding Stables C2
25 Ned's Hideaway C2
26 Oka D2
27 Orchid Garden D2
28 Pandawa Bungalows C2
29 Pondok Sarah & Dynasty Bungalow C2
30 Peter's Place B1
31 Puri Cendana C1
32 Puri Hijau Lestari D2
33 Puri Mangga D2
34 Puri Naga D2
35 Raja Gardens C2
36 Ramah Village C2
37 Resor Seminyak B1
38 Sari Uma Cottages C1
39 Suri Wathi E2
40 Taman Ayu A1
41 Three Brothers D3
42 Vila Rumah Manis C3
43 Villa Lalu C3
44 Villa Lumbung A2

● **Eating**
1 Benny's Café D3
2 BL Café C2
3 Do Drop Inn D3
4 Goa 2000 C3
5 Kin Khao C2
6 La Lucciola B1
7 Raja Laut C2
8 Ryoshi Legian C2
9 Warisan A2

AL *Bali Padma Hotel*, Jl Padma 1, T752111, F752140, padma@
denspasar.wasantara.net.id On Legian beach, this large hotel has 400 rooms and cottages set in lush tropical gardens beside the sea. Usual facilities of a hotel in this class including pool, tennis courts and spa. **AL-A** *Legian Beach Hotel*, Jl Melasti, T751711. Large hotel popular with tour groups and families. **AL-A** *Hotel Puri Raja*, Jl Padma Utara, T754828, 755902, F754202. This has a good location beside the sea. 72 rooms with a/c, HW, fridge, TV, telephone. 2 large pools, gardens leading down to beach. 24-hr restaurant and room service. Good value with off-season discount.

A *Bali Mandira*, Jl Padma, T751381, F752377. A/c, restaurant, large pool, close to sea, free airport pick-up. Recommended. **A** *Jayakarta Hotel formerly Kuta Palace*, Jl Pura Bagus Teruna, PO Box 244, T751433, F752074. A/c, 5 restaurants, 2 pools, tennis, fitness centre, all facilities, facing the beach, large hotel with 2-storey blocks of accommodation and some family bungalows. A bustling tour group hotel. **A** *Legian Garden Cottages*, Jl Legian Cottage, T751876. A/c, pool, quiet except when the *Double Six Disco* is operating. **A** *Puri Tantra Beach Bungalows*, Jl Padma Utara 50 X, T/F753195. 6 attractive Balinese style bungalows with large bedroom/living room, storage room, kitchen (fridge but no cooker), HW and ceiling fan, verandah. Pretty tropical gardens, with Hindu temple in the grounds (you might be lucky and witness a traditional ceremony here), lead down to the beach. No pool. Safety deposit box and library. One of the most peaceful places to stay in Legian. Very helpful owner. Long stay discount available. Recommended. **A** *Rama Garden Cottages*, Jl Padma, T751971, F755909. 30 a/c rooms, artistic Balinese décor, mini-bar, private terrace, pool, restaurant. **A-B** *Adika Sari Bungalows*, Jl Padma Utara, north of Jl Padma, T751413, F755898. 23 clean, new rooms with a/c, HW. Set in cramped gardens with pool, 5 mins' walk from beach. Rates negotiable off season. **A-B** *Puri Hijau Lestari*, (formerly *Evergreen Puri*), access via beach road south of Jl Double Six, T730386. Looking rather neglected, 22 rooms with a/c or fan, cold water only. Garden but no pool. Its main attraction is that it is right on the beach. **A-B** *Puri Mangga Bungalows*, Jl Legian Cottages/Arjuna 23, T730447, F730307 (Att Indigo). 6 rather gloomy bungalows with kitchen, living room, HW, fan, etc. Long term rates available, short term rates are overpriced. Around 10-15 mins' walk to beach. **A-B** *Sinar Indah Beach Cottages*, Jl Padma Utara, T755905, 756008. 20 rooms plus 6, 2-storey bungalows (US$320 monthly. Kitchen, living room, private small garden). Attractive, new and very clean, fan, HW, garden, 3 mins' walk from beach. Use of *Hotel Balisani* swimming pool for 5,000Rp. Good value, price includes breakfast and tax. **A-B** *Sing Ken Ken*, Jl Double Six, T730980, F780535. A short walk from the beach. Cramped grounds with average rooms. HW, a/c. Low season discount.

B *Garden View*, Jl Padma, T751559, F753265. A/c, pool, quiet location, a walk to the beach. **B** *Laut Biru*, access via beach road S of Jl Double Six, T730289, F730590. 24 bungalows with kitchen, living room, 1 and 2 bedrooms, etc. Price reflects the lack of luxury. Garden, beside sea, friendly staff. **B** *Legian Village*, Jl Padma, T751182. Some a/c, pool, popular. **B** *Orchid Garden Cottage*, Jl Pura Bagus Taruna 525, PO Box 379, T751802. Small hotel, attractive gardens, clean. **B-C** *RJ's*, Jl Rum Jungle, T751922. Pool, good value, good food. **B-C** *Three Brothers*, quiet hotel with cottages in a traditional Balinese garden courtyard, attractive and better value than its equivalent in Kuta.

C *Lumbung Sari*, Jl Three Brothers, T752009. Rather squashed in between other developments, cottage with kitchen (**D**) no fan. **C-D** *Suri Wathi*, 12 Jl Menuh, T753162. Good value, simple rooms. Fairly quiet with nice pool.

D *Legian Beach Bungalow*, Jl Padma, T751087. Good discount for longer stay. **D** *Oka*, Jl Padma, T751085. Small, clean, but hemmed in by other buildings. **D** *Puri Damai Cottage I*,

Jl Padma, T751965. Popular. **D** *Sari Yasa Beach Inn I*, Jl Rum Jungle, T752836. Basic but OK rooms.

E *Sri Beach Inn*, with bathroom, quiet.

Eating *Benny's*, Jl Pura Bagus Taruna, great range of coffee. *Do Drop Inn*, Jl Legian, steak-house, bar and restaurant. *Koko's Warung*, Jl Pura Bagus Taruna, Indian food. **Mid-range** *Poco Loco*, Jl Padma Utara, in the quieter northern end of Legian, popular, terraced Mexican restaurant, open evenings only. *Ryoshi Legian*, Jl Melasti, T761852. Popular Japanese restaurant serving a varied selection of favourites: Sushi, sashimi, noodles, tempura, yakitori, teriyaki, donburi and bento. Open 1100 to midnight.

Bars *Bali@CyberCafé and restaurant*, Jl Pura Bagus, Taruna, T361761326, hchua@ idola.net.id, http://www.singnet.com.sg/~hchua/café.htm The first internet café on Bali, with 3 networked PCs, scanner, laser printer, colour printer etc. Also serves cheap food. An off-shoot of the Singapore café. *Do Drop Inn*, Jl Legian.

Shopping **Handicrafts** 'Antiques' and Indonesian fabrics at the north end of Jl Legian.

Swimwear and sportswear Several good shops on Jl Legian and side streets.

Tour operators *Perama*, Jl Padma, for travel agent services. *Bali Jaran Jaran Kensana*, *Logi Gardens Hotel*, T975298, organize pony trekking around Tabanan, daily rate per person US$55, including hotel pick-up, tuition, buffet lunch, insurance.

Directory **Banks** Branch of *Lippo* bank and plenty of money changers along Jl Legian. **Embassies & consulates** Switzerland, c/o *Swiss Restaurant*, Jl Pura Bagus Taruna, T751735.

Tuban

Phone code: 0361
Colour map 1, grid B2
Although quieter and more up-market than Kuta, Tuban is still fairly built up. Lying just north of the airport and south of Kuta, the town is spread along busy Jl Kartika Plaza and one of its main attractions is the convenience of its close proximity to the airport. At the lower end of the market, Tuban represents poor value compared to the Kuta/Legian area. There are a string of up-market hotels overlooking the bay beside a reasonable sandy beach, which cater mainly to tour groups. Tucked down side streets away from the beach are some budget places to stay which would be convenient if you arrive late at night or have an early airport departure. There is limited access to the beach down a few public paths between the big hotels; the most useful path is on the extreme left just inside the entrance to the *Bali Dynasty Hotel*. Due to the stiff competition in Tuban, it is worth enquiring about promotion rates. Buffet theme nights are also worth finding out about; they are often good value and may include entertainment. The large hotels have pools, sports and recreation facilities. and most also have organized cultural activities, kiddie clubs and lobbies with live Gamelan music.

As mentioned elsewhere, many unskilled migrant labourers have descended on Bali hoping to take advantage of its relative prosperity. Some set up as hawkers and stall holders in Tuban. However, for once Balinese tolerance was stretched to the limit, and in April 1999 a group of local Balinese decided to take action. Dressed in traditional Balinese costume, a large group forcibly ejected the migrants and destroyed their stalls. The local government has now promised to look into the situation and there is talk of setting aside an open space specifically for these stall holders.

AL *Bali Dynasty Resort*, Jl Kartika Plaza, PO Box 2047, T752403, F752402. 225 rooms, a 4-star hotel under *Shangri-La* management, set in luscious gardens, a short walk from white, sandy beach, all rooms with a/c, satellite TV, tea and coffee-making facilities, mini-bar, robes and slippers, other facilities include free-form pool with kiddies section, poolside bar and restaurant, Chinese restaurant, tennis, indoor games room, beauty salon, boutique and disco/karaoke, promotion rates sometimes available, good value food, ideal for families. **AL** *Holiday Inn Bali Hai*, Jl Wana Segara 33, T753035, F754548. 195 rooms, complimentary airport transfer, built in 1992 in style of traditional Balinese architecture, decorated with beautiful carvings and antiques from the owner's private collection, spacious rooms with a/c, fridge, tea and coffee-making facilities, balcony, some non-smoking rooms and disabled facilities, pleasant shady pool with swim-up bar, kiddy pool, tennis, fitness centre, watersports facilities, theme buffets every night (free for under 6s), Ratna Satay terrace has a bar and specializes in satay, live Balinese music plays for sunset. **AL** *Ramada Bintang Bali*, Jl Kartika Plaza, T753292, F753288. 400 rooms, 5-star facilities, attractive lobby overlooking exotic gardens, non-smoking rooms on 3rd floor only, disabled facilities, beauty salon, fitness centre, boutiques, private beach with lifeguard/security officer, pool is complete with a thundering cascade, a hot whirlpool and cold dip, also kids pool and swim-up

Sleeping

All rooms with private bathroom & Western toilet unless otherwise stated

Bali

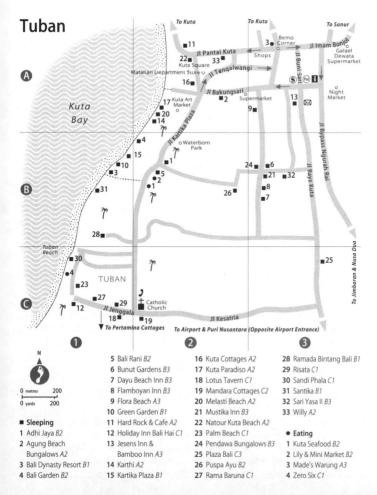

Tuban

Sleeping
1 Adhi Jaya *B2*
2 Agung Beach Bungalows *A2*
3 Bali Dynasty Resort *B1*
4 Bali Garden *B2*
5 Bali Rani *B2*
6 Bunut Gardens *B3*
7 Dayu Beach Inn *B3*
8 Flamboyan Inn *B3*
9 Flora Beach *A3*
10 Green Garden *B1*
11 Hard Rock & Cafe *A2*
12 Holiday Inn Bali Hai *C1*
13 Jesens Inn & Bamboo Inn *A3*
14 Karthi *A2*
15 Kartika Plaza *B1*
16 Kuta Cottages *A2*
17 Kuta Paradiso *A2*
18 Lotus Tavern *C1*
19 Mandara Cottages *C2*
20 Melasti Beach *A2*
21 Mustika Inn *B3*
22 Natour Kuta Beach *A2*
23 Palm Beach *C1*
24 Pendawa Bungalows *B3*
25 Plaza Bali *C3*
26 Puspa Ayu *B2*
27 Rama Baruna *C1*
28 Ramada Bintang Bali *B1*
29 Risata *C1*
30 Sandi Phala *C1*
31 Santika *B1*
32 Sari Yasa II *B3*
33 Willy *A2*

Eating
1 Kuta Seafood *B2*
2 Lily & Mini Market *B2*
3 Made's Warung *A3*
4 Zero Six *C1*

bar, 5 restaurants including *Coconut Wharf* (recommended for Italian food), tennis, children's playground, all rooms a/c, mini-bar, satellite TV, in-house movie, balcony. **AL** *Santika Beach*, Jl Kartika Plaza, T751267, F751260, santika@ denpasar.wasantara.net.id A/c, restaurants, 2 pools, tennis, rather featureless but pleasant enough. **AL-A** *Risata Bali Resor*, Jl Jenggala, T753340, F753354. Bustling with tour groups despite being less attractive and less good value than some other nearby hotels. 146 rooms with the usual facilities: a/c, HW, IDD, TV, fridge, tropical gardens, pool, restaurant etc. Balinese stage for weekly cultural programme. Not beside the sea, 5 mins' walk to beach.

A *Bali Garden*, Jl Kartika Plaza, PO Box 1101, T752725, F753851. A/c, restaurant, pool, extensive facilities. **A** *Bali Rani*, Jl Kartika Plaza, PO Box 1034, T751369, F752673. One of the latest additions to the Tuban area, 104 rooms, each with a/c, satellite TV, in-house movie, mini-bar, balcony, facilities include free-form pool and children's pool, Chinese restaurant, French bakery, pub. **A** *Dayu Beach Inn*, off Jl Kartika Plaza, T752263. 19 clean rooms with a/c or fan, HW, small pool, bar. **A** *Green Garden*, Jl Kartika Plaza 9, T754570. 25 comfortable, tiled rooms with wood furniture, a/c, fridge, TV, balcony overlooking small pool with waterfall, good Chinese seafood restaurant. **A** *Kartika Plaza*, Jl Kartika Plaza, PO Box 3084, T751067, F752475. A/c, 5 restaurants, large pool, part of the *Aerowisata* chain, facilities include squash courts, tennis, fitness centre, huge reception, some cottage-style accommodation. **A** *Kuta Paradiso Hotel*, formerly *Sol Paradiso* (no longer part of Sol Group), T761414, F756944, kutapar@denpasar.wasantara.net.id Primarily for tour groups. Usual facilities, pool, a/c, restaurant. **A** *Palm Beach Resor*, Jl Pantai Banjar Segara 1, T751661/2/752431, F752432. 99 bright rooms with pretty views and the usual facilities: a/c, HW, TV, fridge, etc. Set in peaceful gardens with pool, 5 mins' walk from beach. Rate includes breakfast. **A** *Pendawa Bungalows*, off Jl Kartika Plaza, T752387, T/F757777. Down a lane leading away from the beach, just south of the Kartika Plaza, 38 clean rooms, the cheapest of which are a bit grim, all with private bathroom and Western toilet. A/c or fan, some cold water only. Set in pretty gardens with very small pool. Tax and breakfast extra. A bit overpriced these days. **A** *Putra Jasa*, Jl Kuta Beach, PO Box 3121, T751161. Formerly *Pertamina Cottages*, 5-star hotel, a/c, satellite TV, mini-bar, restaurants including the *Borsalino* for Italian food and *Yashi*, a Japanese restaurant, pool, children's pool, good sports facilities, rooms arranged in rather dated villas (4 rooms/villa), suites available. **A** *Hotel Rama Baruna*, Jl Jenggala (formerly Jl Wana Segara), T751557, F751768. One of the better hotels catering to the tour group market. Usual facilities: HW, a/c, tropical gardens, pool, restaurant etc. Open air Balinese theatre for weekly cultural programme. Not beside the sea, 4 mins walk to beach. Reasonable value. **A-B** *Puspa Ayu*, off Jl Kartika Plaza, T756721. 15 rooms with a/c or fan, HW. Fan rooms a bit gloomy. Overpriced.

B *Karthi Inn*, Jl Kartika Plaza, T754810, F751708. Dated but comfortable, a/c, TV, pool with sunken bar, open-air Chinese restaurant. **B** *Sandi Phala*, off Jl Jenggala, T753708/9, F754889. The best value hotel with a beachside location, though rooms are rather plain and could do with redecoration, a/c, HW. Peaceful location, pool set in grassy gardens. Restaurant overlooking sea.

C *Alit's Kuta Bungalows*, Jl Puri Gerenceng, Tuban, T751968, F288766. 35 rooms. Convenient for airport. **C** *Bunut Gardens*, off Jl Kartika Plaza, T752971, 974732. 8 average rooms in quiet location; fan, HW, nice views from upstairs room. Also 4 rooms with shared mandi. **C** *Flamboyan Inn*, off Jl Kartika Plaza, T/F752610. 15 clean and attractive rooms with a/c and HW set in pleasant gardens with very small pool. 15 mins' walk to beach across busy main road. Overpriced on the rack rate but price is negotiable. **C** *Mandara Cottages* , Jl Kartika Plaza, T751775. Small pool, open-air bathrooms.

Recommended. **C** *Mustika Inn*, off Jl Kartika Plaza. T753298. The nicest of the budget places. 4 clean new rooms with pleasant views from upstairs rooms. No garden. Price includes continental breakfast, 10% tax extra. **C** *Puri Nusantara Cottages*, Jl Raya Tuban 56, T752996. Right by the airport, so very convenient. 35 spotless rooms, with fan and cold water only, set in large well-tended gardens. Left luggage facility. Prompt pick-up service to and from the airport, usually only up until about 2200 (depending on when the driver goes home). Price includes morning coffee. **C** *Sari Yasa Beach Inn II* (though some way from the beach!), off Jl Kartika Plaza, T752825. Basic, not very attractive rooms with private bathroom. 15 mins' walk to beach.

Mid-range *Kaisar*, Jl Kartika Plaza, Balinese and Indonesian dishes. *Coconut Wharf,* **Eating** *Bintang Bali*, Jl Kartika Plaza, poolside Italian restaurant, good pasta dishes, pizza and cocktails. Recommended. *Kuta Sea Food*, Jl Kartika Plaza, opposite *Bintang Bali*, theatre and restaurant, dancing performances (2200-2100) while you dine – mostly Chinese food, steamboat and seafood basket are popular, children's menu available, a definite tourist spot and a little grubby with it. *Bali Sea Food*, Jl Kartika Plaza, next door to *Kuta Sea Food*, similar in concept, but a bit cleaner, interesting menu features snapper with Thai sauce, Bali fish with Sumatra dressing, free pick-up from hotel offered. *Lotus Tavern*, Jl Wana Segera, open-air restaurant under alang-alang roof, candle-lit after dark, good salads, homemade pasta, wood-oven pizza, friendly atmosphere, pick-up from hotel offered. Recommended. *Metro Club*, Jl Kartika Plaza, more of a nightclub than restaurant with happy hour from 1600 to 1900, wide range of dishes from Mexican tacos to Indonesian satay. 50,000-8000 *Zero Six* T753196. Good location on beach in quiet area. Italian, Indonesian, Chinese and Western food, including pizza, fish and New Zealand steak.

Cheap *Croissants de France*, Jl Kartika Plaza, French bakery serves breakfast and snacks 0700-1100.

O'Brien's Fun Pub, Holiday Inn Bali Hai, a 'sporty' pub, open 1700-0100, happy hour **Bars** 1800-1900.

Disco *BB Discotheque*, *Bintang Bali Hotel*, 1900-0200, fashion shows every Tue and **Entertainment** Fri; *Waves Discotheque*, *Bali Dynasty Hotel*.

Kuta Square Relatively new shopping precinct on the boundary with Kuta, with a **Shopping** range of Western designer boutiques, internet cafés, restaurants and a large Matahari department store and supermarket (this is the best place to get fresh fruit, no bargaining and prices are better than the market).

Plaza Bali, department store, duty-free shop (selection of perfumes and cosmetics, clothing and pricy liquor), restaurant, venue for Balinese dancing.

Diving *Bali Dolphin Divers*, *Bali Garden Hotel*, Jl Kartika Plaza, T752725. They also **Sports** provide fishing, parasailing, jetskiing and waterskiing facilities. *OMI Dives*, Kompleks *All the big hotels along* Ruko, Indah Permai Blok C5, Jl By Pass Ngurah Rai, T757484, F772982. Diving tours *Jl Kartika Plaza have* locally and on islands, US$65-95 for the day including two tanks, lunch box, instruc- *watersports facilities,* tion and insurance. *pools & tennis courts*

Swimming *Waterbom Park*, Jl Kartika Plaza, T755676, F753517, waterbom@ denpasar.wasantara.net.id Within walking distance of Tuban hotels, open daily 0900-1800, over 600 m of water slides, water volleyball, spa offering traditional massage etc., gardens, restaurant, lockers and towels for hire (children under 12 must be accompanied by an adult).

Tour operators *Surya Candra*, Jl Wana Segara 25x, T754557, sightseeing around Bali, car rental.

Transport **Air** Airline reservations: *Garuda* at *Natour Hotel* on boundary with Kuta (see Kuta section).

Directory **Banks** Bank opposite the *Bintang Bali*, money changers along Jl Kartika Plaza and Jl Wana Segara, most hotels change money too but rates are not so good. **Places of worship** Sunday school for children every Sun 1100, *Kuta Retreat House*, Tuban. **Useful addresses Immigration**: south of town on the road to the airport, Jl Ngurah Rai, Tuban, T751038. **Police station**: Jl By-Pass, Tuban, T751598.

Seminyak

Phone code: 0361

This area to the north of Legian begins at Jl Double Six and runs northwards into unspoilt ricefields. Seminyak offers a glimpse of how beautiful Kuta must have been before mindless development destroyed it. With a fabulous coast-line, spectacular sunsets and views of the mountains of North Bali on a clear day, it is still relatively quiet and unspoilt. However, month by month more development appears and in time it will become, one fears, just like Kuta and Legian. Many new houses are being built as second homes for residents of Jakarta, mainland China and Westerners from Europe, Australia and the US. Westerners prefer traditional, thatched roof homes whereas Asians like mod-ern, more solid, construction methods!

There is good surfing but be warned: the sea here can be lethal. There are strong undercurrents and riptides – and no lifeguards.

Travelling north from Seminyak you pass through **Petitenget** with its large temple made of white coral (covered in moss so not looking white at all). Fur-ther north still the village of **Batubelig** is in an undeveloped area, with a luxury hotel and a small guesthouse; again this is a surfing rather than swimming beach. Unless you are a keen walker you will probably need to hire a car if stay-ing in this area.

Sleeping
■ *Legian map, page 86*
Accommodation in Seminyak often includes a kitchen & long-stay rates are frequently available

Long a favoured haunt of ex-pats, particularly those involved in the export of furniture, crafts and garments, some of the accommodation in Seminyak is in bungalows and houses available to rent monthly or long term. Look for signs along the streets, notices in the *Wartel* on Jl Dhyanapura or the small number of real estate agents. For shorter stays there are only a handful of budget accommodation options, with most properties in the mid to upper range. There are several real estate agencies that provide longstay and holiday rentals. *Intouch*, Jl Raya Seminyak 22, T731047/8, F730683, intouch@denpasar.wasantara.net.id They handle holiday rentals, sales and leasing. Also check out Rudy's Wartel in Jl Dhyanapura which has a useful travellers' information board including accommodation, particularly long-stay bungalows in Seminyak area.

L *Puri Ratih*, Jl Puri Ratih, PO Box 1114, T751546, F751549, Seminyak. A/c, restaurant, pool, all suites, with own kitchen, living-room and garden, excellent facilities, owned by RCI, the timeshare group. **L** *The Legian*, Jl Lasmana, Seminyak, T730622, F730623, legian@gmhhotels.com Tall (far too tall), ugly building, a real blot on the coastal landscape of Seminyak. Built in 1997. Expensive, 70 large suites with well equipped kitchenette, elegant but rather dark and austere, all facing the sea. Pool, restaurant, bar, spa. Part of the Chedi group of hotels. **L-AL** *Bali Imperial*, Jl Dhyanapura, T754545, F751545. A/c, restaurant, pools, tennis, Japanese-owned hotel on a beach-front plot, opened 1992 with 121 luxurious rooms and one of the most inviting swim-ming pools in South Bali. **L-AL** *Bali Oberoi*, Jl Kayu Aya, PO Box 3351, T730361, F730791. North end of Legian on a peaceful stretch of sandy beach, surrounded by 5 ha of formal gardens, built in 1972, the Oberoi was one of Bali's first luxury class hotels, and has attracted a prestigious clientele over the years, including David Bowie, John Denver, Art Garfunkel, Mick Jagger, Roman Polanski and Gianni Versace – to name but a few, many of the newer hotels in its category have borrowed features of the Oberoi, particularly the stone-walling, thatched alang-alang roofs and the arrangement of accommodation in private villas. The Luxury Lanai rooms are 4 independent rooms under one roof, with the expected facilities including satellite TV, video, stereo, mini-bar, a/c and a luxurious marble finished bathroom, complete with sunken bath, that opens onto a small, walled garden. Luxury villas are also available, twice the size and twice the price, some with private pools, resort facilities including pool (no paddling pool), health club, beauty salon, boutique, 500 m of private beach, tennis, small amphitheatre for regular Balinese performances, 2 restaurants. Recommended.

AL *Vila Rumah Manis*, Jl Nakula 18, Seminyak, T730606, F730505. It's hard to know why anyone would stay in this cramped, overpriced hotel. Perhaps the appeal is having your own private villa with minute private garden and plunge pool. Even the communal swimming pool is small and noisy. A/c, HW, IDD, fridge etc. Restaurant and bar. Popular with Australian tour groups. 25 mins' walk to beach via a dangerously busy side street off Jl Legian. **AL** *Villa Lumbung Hotel*, Jl Raya Petitenget 1000X, Petitenget, Batubelig, T730204, F731106. In a very peaceful location just north of Seminyak. 18 rooms in 2 storey *lumbung* style bungalows with thatched roofs, and 2 villas (with 3 bedrooms, living room and kitchen in private garden), scattered around pretty tropical gardens, built in 1997. Attractive décor; downstairs rooms have open-air bathrooms. A/c, HW, restaurant, bar, free-form swimming pool. 15 mins' walk to beach. **AL-A** *Ananda Bungalows*, Jl Kayu Aya, Basangkasa, north of Seminyak, T730526, F731563, aps@indo.net.id Newly built in Balinese village style, in peaceful setting on the northern edge of Seminyak. 1 and 2-storey bungalows with living room, kitchen, verandah and small private garden, a/c in bedroom only. Rooms are darkish, and rather plain. Pretty gardens, smallish free-form pool. Nice views over ricefields from upstairs rooms which are brighter. 10 mins' walk to beach. Price negotiable, includes breakfast. **AL-A** *Bali Agung Village*, Jl Dhyanapura, T730367, F730469. 32 attractively decorated bungalows in beautiful tropical gardens with small pool. A/c, HW, fridge, IDD, restaurant, bar, cultural performances. Peaceful location on northern edge of Seminyak, 15 mins' walk to beach. Popular with specialist tour companies therefore often full. **AL-A** *Ramah Village*, Gang Keraton, off Jl. Raya Legian, Seminyak, T/F731071/730793 (in Hamburg, Germany: T+49-40-221048, F221725), Balirama@jad.telkom.net.id In a quiet location beside a single remaining ricefield, down a small lane off Jl Legian. Opened in 1992 and beginning to show its age. 16 bungalows, some with 2 bedrooms, set in verdant gardens. Fan only, HW, kitchen, large verandah, fairly clean. Plunge pool. Long-stay rates available. 20 mins' walk to beach. Owned by German photographer. Tax and breakfast extra. **AL-A** *Resor Seminyak*, formerly *Pesona Bali*, Jl Lasmana, Seminyak, T730814, F730815, pesonahti@indosat.net.id Built in 1988, peaceful location beside sea. Two storey building set in extensive gardens, only the deluxe rooms have sea view. A/c, pool, 24 hr restaurant. Strong currents make swimming dangerous directly in front of the hotel. **AL-A** *Villa Kresna*, Jl Sarinade 19, off Jl Dhyanapura, T730317, F732847. Newly built. 2 rooms, 5 suites and 2 villas in a small, slightly cramped compound with small pool. A/c or fan, most with HW, unusual but pleasant hand painted pastel décor. German owner, coffee shop serving German and international food. 3 mins' walk to beach. A little overpriced. **AL-A** *Villa Lalu*, off Jl Legian (opposite Alus Alum Supermarket), Seminyak, T731051, F731052, vilalalu@dps.mega.net.id 7 studios (5 without kitchens), very tastefully furnished, single-storey villas in very peaceful location, set around open gardens and good-sized pool. Large, bright rooms, well-equipped kitchen a/c and fan, HW, IDD, TV, verandah. 24-hr childcare service. 20 mins' walk to beach. Recommended.

A *Century Saphir Bali Hotel*, Jl Abimanyu (also known as Jl Dhyanapura), Seminyak, T730573, F730518, saphir@dps.mega.net.id Clean, mid-range, typical tour group hotel, 127 rooms, 2 restaurants, pool, 24 hr room service, spa, tennis court. 10 mins' walk to beach. **A** *Dhyana Pura Hotel*, Jl Dhyanapura, T730442, F730463, dhyana-p@indosat.net.id 125 rooms, older rooms are a bit drab, a/c, HW, fridge, IDD. Pool, large gardens. Free airport transfers and shuttle to Kuta. Restaurant, bar, 24 hr room service. Conference facilities for up to 300 people. 10 mins' walk to beach. Nothing special. **A** *Peter's Place* (as yet unnamed though may be called *Puri Manis*), next to *Oberoi Hotel*, T733255. 3 bungalows set in gardens with swimming pool, 3 mins' walk to beach. Fantastic value but usually full with long-stay guests who pay up to 5 million rupiah a month, or 1-1.5 million rupiah a week (Peter doesn't take advance bookings). **A** *Raja Gardens*, Jl Camplung Tanduk off Jl Dhyanapura, T730494, F732805. 6 attractive, Balinese style rooms set in lovely gardens with good-sized pool. Fan and cold water only. Not directly on beach, 3 mins' walk down path. Price does not include tax or breakfast. A bit overpriced. **A** *Sarinade Beach Inn*, Jl Sarinade 15, off Jl Dhyanapura, T730383/733604, F733605. 14 rather plain rooms, a/c or fan, HW, TV, minibar. Central, rather cramped courtyard, with pool but no garden. Restaurant, free airport transfers and shuttle to Kuta. 3 mins to beach. Price includes tax and breakfast. Overpriced, but may be negotiable down to Rp140,000 for a double. **A-B** *Bunga Seminyak Cottages*, Jl Camplung Tanduk off Jl Dhyanapura, T730239, F730905. 7 rooms and suites in good beachside location, set in pretty gardens with smallish pool. Rooms vary enormously, the suites are large and attractively decorated with marble bathrooms, whereas the rooms are rather small and drab. Cold water only, a/c. Price negotiable. Good value for the best rooms, price includes continental breakfast and tax. **A-B** *Hotel Puri Cendana*, Jl Dhyanapura, T730869, F730868. 6 cottages consisting of 24 rooms, 12 of which are two-storey with living room downstairs and bedroom upstairs, all with a/c, mosquito net, HW. Set in tropical gardens with pool (only open between 1100-1900), restaurant. 4 mins' walk to beach. Breakfast and tax extra. **A-B** *Taman Ayu Cottage*, Jl Pantai Petitenget, Kerobokan, T730111/2, F730113. In quiet village location N of Seminyak, surrounded by ricefields (at the moment but no doubt earmarked for future development). 41 rooms, clean but in need of some redecoration, a/c, HW, TV, balcony or verandah. Upstairs rooms have good views. Pool, restaurant, bar. 15 mins' walk to beach. Price negotiable.

B-C *Bali Reski Asih*, Jl Sari Dewi, T731045/6, F730342, 483359. In quiet location, 400 m from tarmac road down rough track. 16 rooms with fan, some with HW or kitchens. Pretty gardens, pool. Price includes tax but not breakfast.

C *Kesuma Sari*, Jl Sarinade off Jl Dhyanapura, T233601, 730575. 6 rooms, not particularly attractive, in cramped grounds; rooms are clean and bright but in need of redecoration. 5 mins' walk to beach. **C** *Pandawa Bungalows*, Jl Raya Seminyak 36 B, T730359. 5 well-maintained, 2-storey bungalows set in pretty gardens just off the main road. Upstairs bedroom, downstairs living room, bathroom, cold water only, fan. Good value, often full. **C-D** *Mesari Beach Inn*, Jl Camplung Tanduk off Jl Dhyanapura, T/F730401. This must be the best value in Seminyak. 10 rooms and bungalows right on the beach, set in large, well-tended gardens. No pool. Fairly basic but a great location.

D *Ned's Hideaway*, Gang Bima 3 (off Jl Legian), T/F731270. Down a quiet lane off the main Legian/Seminyak road. Excellent value traveller's budget accommodation, described, predictably, by David the Aussie host as "an Aussie type of motel, guest house and bar". 14 clean, simple rooms with HW, fan, bathroom in a 2-storey block. Set in pretty garden with restaurant and bar. 20 mins' walk to beach. Price includes tax and breakfast.

Long stay (monthly rates only) *Sari Uma Cottages*, Jl Sarinade 3, Seminyak, T/F730916, 730496, Cell0811392808. 5 bungalows with 2 bedrooms, fully equipped kitchen, living room. 12 mins' walk to beach. Price includes gardener and maid service. Coffee shop on the premises. 5 million Rp per month. **A** (per night) *Pondok Sarah* (sign just north of Jl Double Six), T732142, F732143. 14 very attractive, newly built bungalows with 1, 2 or 3 bedrooms, kitchen, living room, fan, hot water, and small plunge pool. Peaceful location in north Legian. Italian owned. *Dynasty Bungalow*, north of Jl Double Six, T754074. House to rent long term with private garden in peaceful location. *Rudy's Wartel* on Jl Dhyanapura has a useful travellers' information board with information on accommodation including long-stay bungalows.

AL *Balisani Suites*, Jl Batubelig, Kerobokan, T730550, F730141, balisani@ dps.mega.net.id Owned by time share company RCI but open to all. 126 rooms and suites in peaceful seaside location. Built in Balinese village style, attractively decorated with antique-style furnishings, though bedrooms are darkish. A/c, TV, minibar, IDD and terrace/balcony. Swimming pool, 4 restaurants and bars, 24-hr room service. Free shuttle to Kuta and airport transfers. **A** *Intan Bali Village*, PO Box 1089, Batubelig Beach, T752191, F752475. A/c, several restaurants, 2 pools, extensive sports facilities, large central block with some bungalow accommodation. Caters almost exclusively to tour groups with little to attract the independent traveller. **B** *Batubelig Beach Bungalows*, Jl Batubelig 228, Kerobokan, T30078. 3 well-built and attractively furnished thatched roof bungalows with kitchen, large bedroom and bathroom, HW, a/c set in garden. Peaceful location 3 mins' walk to beach. Dutch owner with Javanese wife. Ferri the manager, from Flores, speaks good English and is very helpful. Breakfast not included in rates. Longstay rates available. *Sastika Restaurant* on premisese, very cheap and good value.

Sleeping in Batubelig

Mid-range *Kafe Warisan*, Jl Raya Kerobokan (the continuation of Jl Legian north of Seminyak), T731175. Expensive restaurant set in an area of diminishing paddy fields, serving excellent French and Mediterranean food. Open for lunch, but more romantic for candlelit dinners. Art gallery on the premises and bar. Very popular with the local ex-pat crowd. *Cin Cin*, Jl Dhyana Pura, friendly open-air restaurant on roadside, good salads, emphasis on German dishes, pool for use of clients. *La Lucciola*, Jl Kayu Aya, most people go here for the fantastic setting especially the sunset views. Spacious open-air building with a vast alang-alang roof, set on a quiet stretch of beach at the northern end of Seminyak, food varies in quality but can be very good, primarily Italian food. Popular with ex-pats and wealthy Balinese, this is the trendy place to be seen in these days. Open until 2300. *Poco Loco*, Jl Padma Utara, terraced Mexican restaurant. *Ryoshi Seminyak*, Jl Raya Seminyak (the northern continuation of Jl Legian), T731152. Popular Japanese restaurant serving a varied selection of favourites: sushi, sashimi, noodles, tempura, yakitori, teriyaki, donburi and bento. Open 1100-midnight.

Eating

Cheap *Kin Khao Thai*, Jl Seminyak 37, authentic Thai food (with Thai chef), reasonably priced, modest portions. *Raja Laut*, Jl Dhyanapura. Good, primarily seafood restaurant, also serving Indonesian and Western dishes at reasonable prices. *Café BL*, Jl Dhyanapura. T732169, 732917. Good, reasonably priced food, artistically presented. Fish, Indonesian, European.

Communications Several *Wartel* in the area, one of the best is *Rudy's* on Jl Dhyanapura.

Directory

Canggu

This area of coastline, only 20 minutes north of Legian is slowly being developed and (at the moment) offers peace and rural tranquillity, traditional villages untouched by tourism, and frequent ceremonies and festivals at one of its many temples or on the beach. The area features in historical and mythical tales concerning the third king of Bali in the 14th and 15th centuries and his beautiful 'Bangawan Canggu Keris' with magical powers. Particularly important and colourful ceremonies are held at Batu Bulong Temple on the beach of the same name in early July and at the end of August (you will also see spectacular sunsets from here). This temple, with its sacred spring 'Tirta Empul' features in the Lontar chronicles in the Temple of Batur near Kintanami.

At the moment accommodation consists of three overpriced resort hotels (prices negotiable except during high season) catering to package tourists and one losmen. However, more hotels are nearing completion and more losmen will appear. Some of Denpasar's 'wealthy' have chosen to live in this area and have built large, stylish homes.

Canggu district offers unspoilt, grey sand beaches, with the possibility of excellent surfing (easy 1 to 2 m-high waves off left and right-hand reef breaks), as well as swimming. The following beaches are all part of Canggu: Pererean, Banjartengah, Canggu, Tegal Gundul, Padang Linjong, Batu Bulong and Berewa. The villages from which the beaches draw their names are inland and most offer simple homestays, just ask around, local people are very friendly and helpful.

The drive to Canggu is very beautiful as you pass endless lush green paddy fields, coconut and banana palms, cows grazing and only the occasional picturesque, small village full of temples and shrines. It is still very much a rural area, and very peaceful with the sound of the running water from the paddy fields blending with the sound of the waves on the deserted beaches (of course if you stay in a resort hotel with air-conditioning you may miss some of this!).

Sleeping **Pererean Beach** A completely undeveloped stretch of beach with only **D** *Sunset Club Losmen*, 4 new, simple rooms with large, attached bathroom with Western toilet (one of the bathrooms has 2 papaya trees growing in it!), breakfast and tax not included, upstairs restaurant (very cheap) with good views of coast, very peaceful and unspoilt. **Canggu Beach** A hotel will be open by the time this guide is published.

Transport To reach Canggu you will need your own transport. Follow the main road north from Legian until you pick up signs for Canggu. The beach signposted 'Canggu Beach' is in fact Pererean Beach. To reach 'Canggu Beach' itself turn left at the T-junction in Canggu village and keep going to the beach. If in doubt ask for directions.

Berewa Beach

Swimming in the sea here can be dangerous A very peaceful location (the drive from Kuta takes about 30-45 minutes; as yet there is no coast road) with an unspoilt beach backing onto ricefields, friendly local people and few tourists. There are a few Christian families in the villages in this area. These Christians were poor people persuaded to join the faith in the hopes of material benefits, their Christianity being but a thin veneer since they lead lives indistinguishable from other Balinese, although you may notice Christian crosses and motifs woven from palm leaves at the entrance to their properties. There are a few unpretentious restaurants hoping to attract tourists from the local hotels; except during high season these are usually only open for dinner. There are also a few small shops near the hotels, and more shops serving the local community in the small village of **Tegalgundul**, 20 minutes walk away, these close in the afternoon and open again towards dusk. Watch out for the dogs. No nightlife. The main temple here is 'Pura Dang Khayangan', there has been a temple here since the 16th century.

There are 3 hotels here which cater primarily for tour groups. With attractive and very peaceful locations beside the sea, they all offer the usual facilities: private bathrooms, a/c, TV, poolside bars, etc. Prices should be negotiable off season. Breakfast and tax extra. **AL** *Villa Ani Ani*, T/F65-755-2588, F755-3315, evilldes@singnet.com.sg 4 secluded villas in a private compound with swimming pool and open-air eating pavilion. Set in tropical gardens, each villa is well decorated in traditional Balinese style. 3 bedrooms, kitchen, bathroom a/c. Fully staffed including resident chef. **A-AL** *Dewata Beach Hotel*, Banjar Berewa, Desa Canggu 80361, PO Box 3271, Denpasar 80032, T0361-730263, F0361-730290, dewatabh@indo.net.id The best of the hotels at this beach, 168 rooms and suites, in the main building and in 2-storey cottages. Facilities include swimming pool, seasports, beach volleyball, tennis courts and children's playground, massage, reasonably priced restaurants, bars, including karaoke, theatre for Balinese dances. Free shuttle bus to Kuta. Honeymoon packages. **A** *Bolare Beach Bungalows*, PO Box 3256 80, 032 Denpasar, T/F0361-730258. Probably the best value, rather ornate rooms with a/c, bathroom etc, could do with a little maintenance, facilities include restaurant, travel agency, car hire, swimming pool etc. **A** *Legong Keraton Beach Cottages*, PO Box 617, Kuta, T0361-730280, F730285. Very ornate rooms, not to everyone's taste, restaurant, swimming pool, free airport transfer.

Sleeping

Horse riding at Umelas Village Horse riding is available at Umelas Stable north of Seminyak in a rural area beside the sea. Jl Lestari No 9x, Br Umalas, Kerobokan, T0361-731402, F731403. Lessons for all abilities from beginners to advanced including dressage. 1-3 hr treks through the ricefields or along the beach at sunset. Tours include hotel pick-up and US$25,000 insurance. Prices from US$25 for an hour's group trek to US$70 for a 3-hr individual trek. Dressage/beginners lesson: US$25/30 for group/individual.

Sport

Sanur

The first of Bali's international resorts, Sanur falls midway between the elegant, upmarket Nusa Dua and the frenetic, youthful Kuta. Attracting a more sedate, middle-aged clientele, many on package tours, Sanur's attractions are its white sand beach, restaurants and shopping. This is also a centre for watersports with surfing, snorkelling by Serangan Island, and diving. Noticeably more expensive than Kuta, hotels tend to be mid-range to upmarket though there are some pretty, more reasonably priced small guesthouses and an increasing number of cheaper homestays. Nightlife here does not compare to that of Kuta, although there are outstanding restaurants and several discos. The road parallel to the beach is lined with money changers, tourist shops (selling clothing and jewellery), tour companies, car rental outlets and shipping agents.

Phone code: 0361
Colour map 1, grid B2

Like Kuta, Sanur was once a malaria-infested swamp which local people, bar a few intrepid fishermen, tended to avoid. In the past, the villages around Sanur had a reputation for producing some of the best dancers and story-tellers. The area has long been associated with powerful black magic, with shamans and *leyak* (evil spirit/witch) who are feared throughout Bali; a Balinese from elsewhere on the island will seek the protection of a guardian spirit before visiting Sanur. Sanur is also home to the most highly respected *balian* (healers) and priests; a large number of Brahmin families live here.

History In May 1904 the Chinese steamer *Sri Koemala* was wrecked off Sanur and looted by the local Balinese. The Dutch used the failure (and subsequent outright refusal) of the King of Badung to offer compensation for this 'outrage' as justification for blockading the principality. On the 15 September 1906, there followed an armed invasion by the Dutch on the beaches of Sanur, which was unopposed by the peaceful local Brahmanas (the priestly caste). However, an army arrived from Denpasar to confront the Dutch the following morning. Fighting lasted for much of the day, resulting in the death of a handful of Dutchmen and hundreds of Balinese. After the skirmish, the Dutch remained at Sanur for a few days – apparently giving concerts for the local inhabitants – before setting out for Denpasar and the King of Badung's palace. The rest, as they say, is history (see page 226).

Barely two decades after the Dutch military invasion of Sanur, the beginning of another invasion took root: tourism. Intrepid travellers from the West began to arrive, enticed by tales of a tropical paradise. Early residents included the anthropologist Margaret Mead, the writers Jane Belo and Vicki Baum, and the artists Walter Spies and Theo Meier. Many foreigners built homes in the area and to this day Sanur attracts many long term expatriates who live in exclusive private estates primarily in the Batu Jimbar area, as well as foreign consulates and diplomats. Bali's first, and perhaps ugliest, international hotel was built here (the *Bali Beach*) in 1966 financed by Japanese war reparation funds. The tower, nine storeys tall, was built as a monument to President Sukarno's progressive Indonesia. It ultimately served a more useful purpose when the local Banjar decided that its height offended the gods and a law was brought in stipulating that no building on the island could be higher than a coconut palm (about four-storeys), though judging by some recent developments it would appear that palm trees are now growing taller by the year. Before long, hotels sprang up along the beachfront and the era of mass tourism was underway.

The local Banjur is still strong and influential. A village co-operative was established to ensure some of Sanur's profits benefited the local community. Income is derived from a tax on all building projects, an art market, community owned land and other ventures.

Sights The **Le Mayeur Museum** is just to the north of the *Bali Beach Hotel* and is named after the famous Belgian artist Adrien Yean Le Mayeur, who arrived in Bali in 1932. He was immediately captivated by the culture and beauty of the island, made Sanur his home and married a local beauty, Ni Polok, in 1935. He died in 1958. The museum contains his collection of local artefacts and some of Le Mayeur's work. The interior is dark and rather dilapidated, making the pieces difficult to view – a great shame because Le Mayeur's impressionistic works are full of tropical sunlight and colour. Le Mayeur's paintings were a great influence on a number of Balinese artists, including the highly regarded I Gusti Nyoman Nodya. ■ *Small admission charge. 0800-1400 Tue-Thu and Sun, 0800-1100 Fri, 0800-1200 Sat.*

Kite flying is a popular activity, especially in Aug, when strong trade winds are blowing & competitions take place. Teams gather with huge kites that require the united effort of several men to launch

To the south of Sanur, on the route to the main road, is the **Pura Blanjong** (on the left-hand side of the road). It houses the **Blanjong Inscription**, an inscribed cylindrical stone pillar, discovered in 1932 and believed to date from 914. The inscription is written in two languages, Sanskrit and Old Balinese, and was carved during the reign of King Kesari, a Buddhist King of the Sailendra Dynasty (who may also have founded the Besakih temple). It supports the view that there was an Indianized principality on Bali at a very early date. The inscription itself, though difficult to decipher, refers to a military expedition.

The Green Turtle

The Green turtle (Chelonia mydas) is the only species of five turtle found in Indonesia which is not protected by law. Indeed Indonesia is the only country where the green turtle does not enjoy protection. The reason is that the population of this species is regarded as sufficiently large in Indonesia to ensure its survival.

While turtle eggs are regarded as a delicacy throughout Indonesia, turtle meat is not eaten by most Indonesians as it is regarded as haram – 'unclean' under Islamic dietary laws. However turtle meat is highly popular in Bali where it is often consumed during religious ceremonies. It is thought that by the 1950s green turtles were already scarce in the waters around Bali due to over-hunting and demand for the animals meant that they were being harvested as far away as Maluku and the far islands of East Nusa Tenggara. During the 1970s it is thought that 20,000 turtles were being imported into Bali each year, with some 30,000 in 1978 alone. The provincial government, under pressure from environmental groups, tried to reduce the number to 5,000 and to limit the outlets where turtle meat is sold. However, these efforts have been comparatively desultory and in 1993 18,000 turtles were imported.

Temples made of coral are dotted along Sanur beach. The presence of primitive, pyramid shaped structures at many of these temples suggests their origin dates back to prehistoric times. At the southern, south-facing end of Sanur beach is the **Pura Mertasari**, a small temple under a canopy of trees which is considered to harbour exceptionally powerful forces of black magic. The *odalan* festival of this temple falls at the most favoured time in the Balinese calender, two weeks after the Spring equinox. An unusual ritual trance dance, the *baris cina* (Chinese dance), is performed on the night of the festival. The dancers wear old Dutch army helmets and bayonets and the evening can end with a dramatically violent dance movement. A nearby village, **Singhi**, is home to the Black Barong, the most powerful Barong in Bali, made from the black feathers of a sacred, rare bird.

On a clear day there are fantastic views of several mountain ranges to the north, including Mount Agung and Mount Batur, especially beautiful at sunset and sunrise. There is a path running along the beach for the entire length of Sanur though in places it is beginning to collapse. The beach varies in width along its length and disappears completely in some places; it is at its best in front of the *Grand Bali Beach Hotel*, *The Hyatt*, an area that includes the *Tanjung Sari* and adjacent hotels, and at the southern end. At Batu Jimbar, where the ex-pat crowd have built their beautiful seaside villas, the beach disappears completely. There are several roads and tracks leading down to the beach from Jl Danau Tamblingan along its length, including Jl Pantai Karang where the German consul is situated, and Jl Segara Ayu.

Serangan Island or Turtle Island is, as the name suggests, famous for its turtles which are caught in the surrounding sea, raised in pens, and then slaughtered for their meat – which explains why they are becoming rarer by the year. The formerly common green turtle is now said to be virtually extinct in the area. The beaches on the east coast of the island are best, with offshore coral providing good snorkelling. One of Bali's most important coastal temples is the **Pura Sakenan** in Sakenan village, at the north end of the island. The temple was founded at the end of the 15th century and contains a rare prasada (*prasat*) or stepped stone tower. Stylistically, this is a combination of the Javanese candi and pre-Hindu megalithic stone altar. Like Uluwatu on the Bukit

Excursions

Peninsula, it is constructed of hard coral. Pura Sakenan's *odalan* or anniversary festival, held at Kuningan (the 210th day of the Balinese calendar) is thought by many to be one of the best on Bali. ■ *Getting there: boats can be chartered from Sanur or from Nusa Dua and Benoa. Usually visitors leave from a jetty just south of Kampung Mesigit and 2 km southwest of Sanur. From here there are regular public boats to Serangan Island (600Rp); the problem is that tourists are often forced to charter a boat for far more; share if possible and bargain furiously. It is easier, and often just as cheap, to go on a tour. It is also possible to wade out to the island at low tide.*

Nusa Lembongan (see page 109) lies just off the coast. ■ *Boats leave every morning for the island from close to the Bali Beach Hotel, 1 hr (17,000Rp). Perama now run a boat service to the island departing twice a day in high season at 10.30 and 16.30, in low season usually only the morning departure. The 27 km crossing takes about 40 mins. Departures from Nusa Lembongan are at 09.00 and 15.00 in high season. Perama office in Sanur is at Pino Restaurant, T287594.*

Tours The major hotels on the beach all have tour companies which organize the usual range of tours: for example to **Lake Bratan** (where waterskiing can be arranged); to **Karangasem** and **Tenganan**, to visit a traditional Aga village; to **Ubud**; white-water rafting on the **Agung River**; to the temples of **Tanah Lot** and **Mengwi**; to the **Bali Barat National Park**; to **Besakih Temple**; the *Golden Hawk* tall ship runs day trips to **Lembongan Island** (see page 109), as do *Island Explorer Cruises*, Ena Dive Center, Jl Tirta Ening 1, T287945, F287945, who also organize dolphin tours off Nusa Dua and provide watersports equipment, including PADI diving. *Sobek*, the 'adventure' tour company are based in Sanur at Jl Tirta Ening 9, T287059. They can arrange bird watching and sporting activities (see 'Sports', page 107).

Sleeping Accommodation on Sanur is largely mid to high-range, though recently a number of
See map page 102 new and attractive budget guest houses have opened along Jl Danau Tamblingan which offer excellent value for money. Much of the guest house accommodation is overpriced and disappointing, particularly compared to other parts of Indonesia, but also to Bali. Fan rooms are hard to come by as most places have installed a/c in order to charge much higher prices. Prices are frequently geared to European tour groups who form the largest group of visitors; except during high season you should never have to pay more than 50% of the listed price, and even then many places still seem overpriced. Unless otherwise stated, all accommodation includes private bathroom and Western toilet.

L-AL *Tanjung Sari*, Jl Danau Tamblingan, PO Box 3025, Denpasar, T288441, F287930. A/c, restaurant, small pool, opened in 1967, 29 bungalows with own sitting-room and outside pavilion, some tastefully decorated others hideous. Very much in need of renovation, very overpriced, disappointing and living off its reputation now that the original owner has died and his son is in charge. Gardens lead down to reasonable beach. **AL** *Bali Beach*, PO Box 275, Denpasar, T288511, F287917, J 320107. North end of the beach, 523 rooms, a/c, restaurant, 3 large pools, 9-hole golf course, 10-pin bowling, tennis, the original international hotel in Bali, built in the 1960s as a showpiece, with the backing of President Sukarno, a high-rise block completely out-of-place but thanks to it a law was introduced banning any building taller than a (giant!) coconut palm. Rooms in the high-rise block are a bit scruffy, though they have lovely sea views. The more recently built bungalows, to the south, are more attractive though hot water is alleged to be a problem sometimes. Good facilities and fronting an excellent section of beach. Internet access in lobby (expensive). **AL** *Bali Hyatt*, Jl Danau Tamblingan , PO Box 392, T281234, F287693. A/c. This hotel has the best location in

Sanur, peaceful, beside an excellent beach and surrounded by 36 acres of exquisite tropical gardens created by renowned landscape designer Made Wijaya (an Englishman who has lived in Bali for many years and taken a Balinese name). Two lovely pools, with grottoes, traditional Balinese stone carvings and an open air, heated jacuzzi. Imposing, Wantilan style reception hall, library, 5 restaurants serving Asian and Western specialities. Many of the staff, who include a priest and a noted local artist, have been with the hotel since it was built almost 26 years ago and they have a friendly dignity which adds to the hotel's attraction. The hotel is decorated with many pieces of fine Balinese antique furniture and paintings. The Spa, designed as a Balinese village surrounded by gardens, has recently been voted one of the world's top five spas by *Cosmopolitan* magazine. It offers a full range of Western and traditional treatments lasting from 2-5 hrs. A wide range of sports activities including tennis, badminton and watersports including windsurfing, scuba diving, water-skiing, snorkelling and deep-sea fishing are also available. A daily programme of cultural activities including a temple visit and garden tour; the plants and trees have name plaques so you can identify the tropical plants. *Camp Sanur* provides a full day of activities for children including sports, arts and crafts, Balinese music and dance lessons. Recommended. **AL** *Natour Sindhu Beach*, Jl Pantai Sindhu 14, PO Box 181, T288351, F289268, n.sindhu@denpasar.wasantara.net.id 60 darkish, bungalow-style rooms with verandah, large rather plain gardens leading down to beach. Pool, restaurant, a/c, minibar, telephone. **AL** *Puri Santrian and Griya Santrian*, Jl Danau Tamblingan 47 & 63, T288181, F288185, santrian@denpasar.wasantara.net.id 190 (60 newly built rooms) a/c, fridge, IDD phone, 2 pools, several restaurants, watersports, central 3-storey block and some bungalows set in gardens, standard (cheapest) rooms dark and disappointing. Right on a good stretch of beach. **AL** *Raddin Hotel*, Jl Mertasari, T288833, F287303, 287772, radsanur@indosat.net.id Situated at the southern end of Sanur on a good white sand beach. 195 attractive rooms in 3-storey lumbung style bungalows (a separate room on each floor) with the usual facilities. 2 pools, tennis court, watersports. 3 reasonably priced restaurants and a bar. **AL** *Radisson Suites*, Jl Bypass Ngurah Rai 83, Sanur, T281481, F281482. 84, 1, 2 and 3 bedroom, fully furnished apartments in a secure resort setting, ideal for families and self-catering. Set around attractive landscaped gardens and pool. Restaurant, poolside BBQ, fitness centre, laundry and self-service launderette, minimart, underground car park. Room service and grocery delivery. A/c, modern kitchen, satellite TV, IDD tel. Kids Club. Guests have full privileges at the *Radisson Hotel*. Free shuttle bus linking hotel, suites and beach. **AL** *Sanur Beach*, Jl Danau Tamblingan, PO Box 3276, T288011, F287566, sanurbch@indosat.net.id South end of beach, a/c, several restaurants (fish restaurant recommended), 2 lovely pools, sports facilities include fitness centre, 524 rooms, cheaper rooms small and functional with small balcony, deluxe rooms more attractive, all rooms are in a 3-storey block. Primarily for tour groups. Part of the Aerowisata chain of rather over-large hotels. OK but not intimate. *Garuda* office is now located here. **AL-A** *Laghawa Villas*, See Laghawa Beach Inn, below, JL Danak, Tamblingan, T288494, F289353. 3 villas with kitchen, living room, etc. Long-stay rates available. **AL-A** *Radisson Bali Indonesia*, Jl Hang Tuah 46, PO Box 3807, T281781, F281782, radbali@indosat.net.id This popular, luxury new hotel offers excellent value for money. 329 nicely decorated rooms, a/c, fridge, tea and coffee making facilities. Landscaped pool area. Shuttle bus to Radisson managed beach which has showers and refreshments. Excellent programme of cultural activities including complimentary tours to local sights. Sports including tennis and free introductory scuba diving lesson; the hotel is adjacent to a 9-hole golf course. Very helpful and friendly hotel staff. 5 restaurants and cafés including the Sanur Harum with tasty, very reasonably priced Chinese food; excellent buffet breakfast. Spa offering a full range of Western and traditional Balinese treatments. Fitness centre managed by internationally acclaimed Weider, using advanced scientific equipment and operated to the highest standards.

Sanur

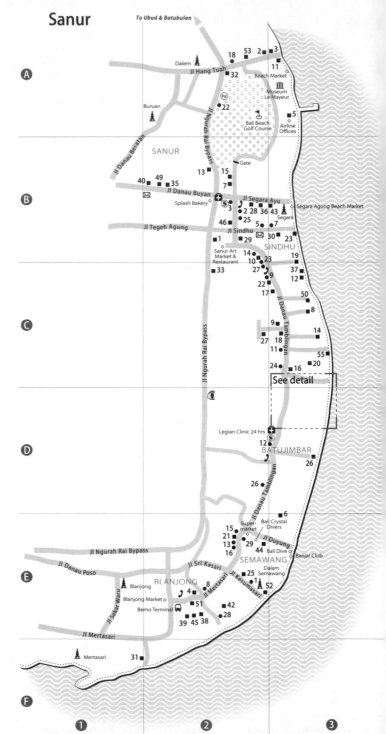

To Ubud & Batubulan

Dalem

Jl Hang Tuah

Buruan

SANUR

Jl Danau Beratan

Jl Danau Buyan

Splash Bakery

Jl Tegeh Agung

Jl Ngurah Rai Bypass II

Pol

Beach Market

Museum Le Mayeur

Bali Beach Golf Course

Airline Offices

Gate

Jl Segara Ayu

Segara

Segara Agung Beach Market

Jl Sindhu

SINDHU

Sanur Art Market & Restaurant

Jl Danau Tamblingan

Jl Ngurah Rai Bypass

See detail

Legian Clinic 24 hrs

BATUJIMBAR

Jl Danau Tamblingan

Bali Crystal Divers

Super-market

Jl Duyung

Bali Dive

Banjar Club

SEMAWANG

Jl Ngurah Rai Bypass

Jl Sri Kesari

Dalam Semawang

Jl Danau Poso

Jl Sekar Waru

Blanjong

BLANJONG

Blanjong Market

Bemo Terminal

Jl Mertasari

Jl Kesumasari

Jl Mertasari

Mertasari

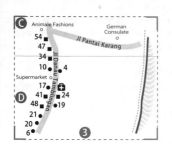

N

Not to scale

■ **Sleeping**
1 Abian Srama *B2*
2 Alit's Beach
  Bungalows *A2*
3 Ananda *A3*
4 Ari Putri *E2*
5 Bali Beach *A3*
6 Bali Hyatt *E3*
7 Bali Warma *B2*
8 Besakih Bungalows *C3*
9 Bumas *C3*
10 Coco, Luisa & Yulia
   Homestays *B2*
11 Diwangkara *A3*
12 Gazebo *C3*
13 Griya Ayu Inn *B2*
14 Griya Santrian Beach *C3*
15 House for rent *B2*
16 Julia Homestay *C3*
17 Kalpathara *C3*
18 Keke Homestay *C3*
19 La Taverna *B3*
20 Laghawa Beach Inn *C3*
21 Lestari Homestay *E2*
22 Made's Pub
   & Homestay *C3*
23 Natour Sindhu Beach *B3*
24 Orchid Villa *D3*
25 Palm Garden *E2*
26 Paneeda View *D3*
27 Pondok Wisata Prima *C2*
28 Puri Kelapa *B2*
29 Puri Mango
   Guesthouse *B2*
30 Queen Bali *B3*
31 Raddin *F1*
32 Radisson Bali Indonesia
   A2
33 Radisson Suites *C2*
34 Ramayana *D3*
35 Rani *B2*
36 Ratna *B2*
37 Respati Bali *C3*
38 Santrian *E2*

39 Sanur Beach *E2*
40 Sanur Indah *B2*
41 Sapanami Homestay *D3*
42 Sativa Sanur Cottages
   E2
43 Segara Village *B3*
44 Segara Agung *E2*
45 Semawang Beach *E2*
46 Sumi's Bungalows *B2*
47 Swastika *C3*
48 Taman Agung *D3*
49 Taman Sari *B2*
50 Tanjung Sari *C3*
51 Trophy Ayu & Pub *E2*
52 Villa Kesumasari *E2*
53 Watering Hole
   Guesthouse &
   Restaurant *A2*
54 Wirasana *C3*
55 Wisma Werdhapura *C3*

● **Eating**
1 Abian Boga *E2*
2 Bacu Warung *B2*
3 Bahagia's *B2*
4 Bali Indah *D3*
5 Borneo *B2*
6 Café Batu Jimbar *D3*
7 Carlo *B3*
8 Donald's Café *E2*
9 Jak's Kafe *C2*
10 Kaka Tua Warung *D3*
11 Kita *C3*
12 Kul Kul *D3*
13 Legong & Bar *E2*
14 Lotus Pond *B2*
15 Nelayan *E2*
16 Oka's *E2*
17 Penjor *D3*
18 Pino & Perama Bus *A2*
19 Rest & Eat *D3*
20 Ryoshi Sanu *D3*
21 Santai Internet *D3*
22 Several Warung *A2*
23 Swastika *B2*
24 Swastika Garden *C3*
25 Taman Istana *B2*
26 Telaga Naga *D2*
27 The Village *C2*
28 Trattoria da Marco *E2*
29 Warung Agung *E2*

Kids club with a range of specially designed activities to keep children occupied throughout the day. Special Guest Information service providing a wealth of information about Bali, invidually tailored to suit every interest. Convention centre with 9 conference rooms and capacity for up to 1500 delegates. Throughout the year there are special offers which represent outstanding value, check their website at www.radisson.com

A *Ari Putri Hotel*, Sanur Beach Street, Banjar Semawang, T289188, F289190. 41 rooms with a/c, HW, minibar, balcony. Restaurant, bar, smallish pool. Popular with tour groups. **A** *Bali Sanur Bungalows*, Jl Danau Tamblingan 45, PO Box 3306, T288423, F288426, besakih@indosat.net.id (mark for the attention of Bali Sanur Bungs). A/c, 79 standard bungalow rooms are poorly lit and slightly claustrophobic, with verandahs surrounded by luxuriant vegetation providing plenty of shade. Well-kept, pretty mature gardens which run down to beach, restaurant, 2 smallish pools. Primarily for tour groups. **A** *Bumi Ayu*, Jl Bumi Ayu, PO Box 3511, T289101, F287517. Restaurant (excellent service), nice pool, attractive mature gardens with plenty of shade. 58 bungalows with Balinese style décor, slightly claustrophobic, poorly lit rooms, a/c, verandah. Recommended. Well run, but too far from the beach, 15 mins' walk. Primarily tour groups. **A** *Bumas Hotel*, Jl Bumi Ayu 4, T286306/7, F288341. 74 large clean but darkish rooms with a/c, HW, verandah. Pretty gardens with 2 good pools. Primarily a tour group hotel. A bit overpriced, price includes tax and breakfast. **A** *Diwangkara*, Jl Hangtuah, T288577, F288894. 40 Balinese style rooms beside the sea, not much beach. Rooms are large and clean, but darkish with verandah, gardens and pool. A/C HW. Lovely views from seaside restaurant. **A** *Hotel Bali Warma*, Jl Wira HBB 2, T285618, 285619, 285623, F285154. 20 rooms, bright new and clean. A/c, HW, fridge, small garden with pool. Quiet location, 12 mins' walk to beach. Price

Bali

includes breakfast and tax and may be negotiable. **A** *Hotel Kesumasari*, Jl Danau Tamblingan 22. Attractive rooms with a/c or fan, HW, some with fridge, verandah/balcony, nice views from upstairs rooms. Restaurant, pool, pretty gardens. Better value than many in Sanur, and more spacious. Rate includes continental breakfast only. **A** *Hotel Taman Agung Beach Inn*, Jl Danau Tamblingan 146, T288549, T/F289161. 27 fairly pleasant, clean rooms, 23 with a/c, 4 with fan, most with HW. Newer rooms have no verandah/balcony and no view. Attractive gardens, pool, 5 mins' walk to beach. Price includes continental breakfast. **A** *La Taverna*, Jl Danau Tamblingan 29, PO Box 3040, T288497, F287126. Discounts available, restaurant (recommended), pool, 34 rooms are well decorated with traditional furnishings and character, attractive gardens leading down to sea and a not particularly good beach, friendly and obliging staff. More attractive than most Sanur hotels of this type. Popular with tour groups. **A** *Palm Garden* (*Taman Palem* in Indonesian), Jl Kesuma Sari 3, Semawang, T287041, F289571, plmgrd@indosat.net.id Towards southern end of Sanur. 19 pleasant rooms, fan or a/c, fridge, restaurant, small pool. Cramped grounds. Price includes breakfast and tax but overpriced. **A** *Paneeda View Beach Hotel*, Jl Danau Tamblingan 89, T288425/289045, F286224/288300. Excellent location by sea, 44 pleasant cottages, a/c, HW, large pretty gardens running down to meagre beach. Lovely views from reasonably priced seaside restaurant. Good value for Sanur. **A** *Puri Kelapa Garden Cottages*, Jl Segara Ayu 1, T286135, F287417. 47 rooms, a/c, HW, fridge. Upstairs rooms are bright with views over garden but downstairs rooms are darkish. Smallish pool. Overpriced. **A** *Queen Bali Hotel*, Jl Sindhu, T288054. An unprepossessing property, rooms are tatty and very dark. A/c, HW. **A** *Ratna Beach Hotel*, Jl Segara Ayu 10, T289109, F288413. 34 rather basic rooms. Cramped grounds, small pool, overpriced. **A** *Sativa Sanur Cottages*, Jl D Tamblingan 45, PO Box 3163, T/F287881. 50 rooms a/c, crammed around smallish pool, attractive, thatched reception hall, accommodation is in fairly attractive, thatched cottages. No direct access to beach (15 mins' walk). Overpriced. **A** *Segara Desa* (*Segara Village*) Jl Segara Ayu, T288407. 2 mins' walk to sea. Clean attractive rooms, fridge, A/c, HW. Pleasant gardens, smallish pool, 2 restaurants, tennis court. **A** *Surya Beach*, Jl Mertasari, T288833, F287303, T021-5706421. South end of beach, a/c, restaurant, pool, sports facilities, large hotel with 2-storey cottage-style accommodation.

A-B *Laghawa Beach Inn*, Jl Danau Tamblingan, Sanur, T288494, F289353, laghawa@indo.net.id 30 very clean rooms with fan or a/c, HW, set in pretty large gardens leading down to the beach. Pool, restaurant, bar. **A-B** *Gazebo Cottages*, Jl Danau Tamblingan 35, T288212, F288300. 76 pleasant rooms in a range of styles with some older rather attractive unusual rooms, some 2-storey; a/c, fridge, restaurant (unimpressive) but with good views, 3 smallish pools, large, attractive Balinese-style gardens leading to beach. Peaceful, better value than many in Sanur. **A-B** *Hotel Segara Agung*, Jl Duyung 43, Semawang, T288446, 286804, F286113. 12 new, clean and attractive rooms in bungalows with a/c or fan, some with cold water only. Set in pretty gardens with smallish pool, restaurant and bar. 3 mins' walk to beach. Friendly staff. Rate includes continental breakfast only. Good value. Recommended. **A-B** *Orchid Villa*, Jl Danau Tamblingan, T289162. 3, 2-storey villas, one a/c and 2 with fan. Attractively decorated with views from upstairs balcony, however, lounge and upstairs bedrooms are open air on one side (this might create security and mosquito problems). No direct access to beach. Long-stay rates available. **A-B** *Pondok Wisata Prima* (*Prima Cottages*), Jl Bumi Ayu 15, T286369, F289153. 14 rooms, a/c or fan, HW. Rooms are clean and simple, darkish downstairs, nice views from upstairs balconies. Quiet location, small pool in pretty gardens. 20 mins' walk to beach. Price includes tax only. **A-B** *Respati Bali*, Jl Danau Tamblingan 33, T288427, F288046. A/c and fan rooms. 24 rooms, simply decorated, darkish. Rooms near the street are close to a busy restaurant and tend to be noisy. Small pool, pretty gardens running down to narrow beach. Overpriced. **A-B** *Swastika Bungalows*, Jl Danau Tamblingan 128, T288693, F287526. 81 attractive Balinese-style rooms, clean, open air bathrooms, a/c or fan, 2 pools, quiet location set back from road, 15 mins' walk from the beach, pleasant gardens, popular, central for shops and restaurants. **A-B** *Trophy Ayu Bungalows*, T285010, 286230, F287663. At the southern end of Sanur in a cramped noisy location. 12 rooms, 3 apartments and 3 bungalows with a/c and HW. Small pool, restaurant and bar. Price includes breakfast but not tax. Long-stay rates available, no direct beach access. **A-B** *Villa Kesumasari*, Jl Kesumasari 6, T287824, F288876. Small clean rooms with either a/c plus HW, TV and fridge; fan plus HW; or fan and cold water. Set around concrete courtyard, 1 min's walk from beach. Price includes breakfast and tax, but seems overpriced for the more expensive rooms. **A-C** *Made's Homestay and Pub*, Jl Danau Tamblingan 74, T/F288152. 15 pleasant rooms which would benefit from redecoration, 6 with a/c, 9 with fan, all with HW. Set in garden with small pool. Breakfast and tax extra.

B *Alit's Beach Bungalows*, Jl Hang Tuah 41, T288560, F288766. North end of Sanur. 85 rather drab, but clean bungalows, some 2-storey, with verandahs or balconies, a/c, HW, some with fridge. Smallish pool, large complex of traditional Balinese design, large Balinese-style gardens run down to sea, no beach. Restaurant, bar with pool table. Price includes tax and breakfast. **B** *Ananda Hotel*, Jl Hang Tuah 43, T288327. 20 rooms with fan or a/c. At the northern end of Sanur beside a busy path, adjacent to an unattractive stretch of sea with no beach. Could be noisy. Restaurant and bar. **B** *Hotel Wirasana*, Jl Danau Tamblingan 138, T288632, F288561, wirasana@ indosat.net.id 18 spotless rooms with a/c or fan, HW. Set in large gardens. Guests can access the internet, and have use of the Hotel Swastika pool next door. 15 mins' walk to beach. Good value. **B** *Kalpatharu*, Jl D Tamblingan 80, T/F288457. Some a/c, cold water only, restaurant, small hotel, rooms are rather hemmed-in, lacking character. **B** *Puri Mango Guest House*, Jl Danau Toba 15, Sindhu Sanur, T288411, 281293, F288598. 20 new, spotless rooms with a/c or fan, most with HW. Upstairs rooms have bright open outlook. Small pool, 5 mins' walk to sea. Price includes breakfast which can be taken at the owner's restaurant 5 mins' walk away beside the sea. **B** *Ramayana*, Jl Danau Tamblingan 130, PO Box 3066, T288429. Same ownership as *Swastika*. 20 small rooms, very clean with verandahs, a/c, nice garden. Small, family-run hotel, away from the beach (15 mins' walk) but you have use of the pools at *Swastika*, can be noisy. Rate includes breakfast but tax is extra. **B** *Santai*, Jl Danau Tamblingan 148, T287314. Some a/c, restaurant, pool, away from beach but better value in this price range, central location. **B** *Sumi's Bungalows*, Jl Danau Tamblingan 14A. T285012. 5 bungalows and 8 small, but new and spotless rooms with fan and mosquito net. Set back from the road in small garden with pool. An attractive place and excellent value. Long-stay rates available. Recommended. **B** *Watering Hole*, Jl Hangtuah 37, T288289. 24 large, newly renovated rooms. Fan or a/c, fridge, balcony/verandah. Small garden. Front rooms could be noisy. Price includes tax but not breakfast. Good value for Sanur. 3 mins' walk to sea. Good restaurant. **B** *Werdhapura Wisma*, behind Laghawa Beach Inn, Jl Danau Tamblingan, T288171, 286711. Fantastic value if you don't mind the lack of a pool. 60 attractive, clean rooms with a/c, HW, set in lovely large gardens beside the sea, with sea views from some of the verandahs. Very friendly staff. Restaurant with sea views. Very peaceful location. Government owned so it occasionally fills up with government employees. Price includes breakfast and tax. Recommended.

B-C *Abian Srama*, Jl Bypass, T288415, F288673. Some a/c, small pool, bad location, away from the beach, but well-run. **B-C** *Griya Ayu Inn*, Jl Danau Buyan IV, no 24, T288313, F288654. Quiet place at the back of the *Kentucky Fried Chicken*, more upmarket rooms have a/c, cheaper bungalow-style rooms with garden, very clean, no

Bali

hot water, friendly people. **B-C** *Penginapan Lestari Homestay*, Jl Danau Tamblingan 188, T288867. 10 clean but basic rooms, 3 a/c, 7 with fan, set in attractive gardens, 10 mins' walk to beach. Friendly staff, long-stay rates available. Good value.

C *Yulia 2 Homestay*, Jl Danau Tamblingan 57, T287495. 6 clean rooms with fan. Price includes breakfast and tax. Excellent value. Recommended.

The following three budget places are in descending order of price and attractiveness, but all offer excellent value for money: **C** *Yulia 1 Homestay*, Jl Danau Tamblingan 38, T288089. 12 simple but clean rooms set in small, pretty gardens with family temple. Price includes tax and breakfast. **D** *Coco Homestay*, Jl Danau Tamblingan 42, T287391. 8 simple but attractive and spotless rooms set around small courtyard garden. Long-stay rates available. Price includes breakfast and tax. Recommended. **D** *Luisa Homestay*, Jl Danau Tamblingan 40. T289673. 11 new rooms, basic but clean. No garden. Friendly owner. About the cheapest place in Sanur. Price includes breakfast and tax.

D-E *Hotel Taman Sari*, Jl Danau Buyan, some a/c, good rooms for the price of the cheaper end of what is available here, rate includes breakfast. **D-E** *Sapanami Homestay*, Gang Taman Agung 4, off Jl Danau Tamblingan. Possibly the cheapest place in Sanur. Very friendly Dutch owner often in residence. 8 rooms, 4 with own bathroom and shower, cold water only, fan, cheapest rooms have squat toilets. Use of kitchen. Off street parking. Price includes tax.

Eating Many of the best restaurants in Sanur are concentrated at the south end of the beach, on Jl Danau Tamblingan. The 4 big hotels, namely the *Hyatt*, the *Radisson*, the *Bali Beach* and the *Sanur Beach* all have several good restaurants and many of the smaller hotels have good restaurants too with competitive prices. One reader has suggested that the turnover in all the restaurants on Jl Danau Tamblingan is low and therefore, the food is not always fresh.

Expensive *Kita*, Jl Danau Tamblingan 104, average Japanese food.

Mid-range *Bali Moon*, Jl Danau Tamblingan 19. Italian, attractive setting in an open-air pavilion, good food. *Café Batu Jimbar*, Jl Danau Tamblingan 152, T287374, opposite Batu Jimbar estate. Pleasant open-air restaurant with a good choice of healthy dishes. The vegetables are grown in their own vegetable garden at Bedugul. Popular with local ex-pats. *Made's Bar and restaurant*, Jl Danau Tamblingan 51, seafood, Italian, Indonesian, generous portions, good food and atmosphere. Recommended. *Paon*, Jl Danau Tamblingan (not far from *Bali Hyatt*), seafood and steaks. *Tanjung Sari Hotel*, Jl Danau Tamblingan, excellent Indonesian and International food (French cook) served in elegant, peaceful surroundings, drinks at candlelit tables on the beach provide a romantic atmosphere. *Telaga Naga*, part of the *Hyatt Hotel* across the road, serves excellent, reasonably priced Chinese and Szechuan food in a romantic setting surrounded by lotus ponds, pavilions and gardens. Open evenings only 1830-2300. *Ryoshi Sanur*, Jl Danau Tamblingan 150, T288473. Popular Japanese restaurant serving a varied selection of favourites: sushi, sashimi, noodles, tempura, yakitori, teriyaki, donburi and bento. Open 1100-midnight. *The Village Kampung*, Jl Danau Tamblingan 66. T/F285025. New, popular restaurant opened by Austrian chef. Western food, daily and weekly specials including a business lunch of 2 courses for 35,000Rp; also occasional special 4 course dinners with live music. Open 0900-midnight. Recommended.

Cheap *Kalimantan*, Jl Pantai Sindhu 11, T289291, good atmosphere, good food (especially good breakfasts), good service and thousands of books waiting to be

Bali

borrowed. Owned by an American, Bob Kendall. *Mina Garden*, Jl Danau Tamblingan. Balinese, Indonesian, Italian and international, Balinese dance. Recommended. *Sanur Harum Chinese Restaurant at Radisson Bali Indonesia*, Jl Hang Tuah 46, very reasonably priced.

Very cheap *Jawa Barat*, south end of Jl Danau Tamblingan, Indonesian. *Mira*, opposite *Hotel Ramayana*, cheap and good value. *Terrazza Martini*, on the beach at the south end, small restaurant serving good Italian food. *Trattoria Da Marco*, on the beach at the south end, Italian. Recommended. *Watering Hole*, Jl Hangtuah 37, good Indonesian and Western food.

Dance The *Sanur Beach Hotel* offers a buffet dinner with Legong (Mon), Ramayana Ballet (Wed), Genggong/frog dance (Sun) all at 1930. The *Tanjung Sari Hotel* has legong dance and gamelan performances on Sat nights. The *Penjor* restaurant (near the *Bali Hyatt Hotel*) stages legong dance performances on Tue, Thu and Sun 1930-2100, frog dance every Mon 2015, joged dance every Wed 2015 and janger dance every Fri 2015.

Entertainment

Disco *Rumours*, Jl Sindhu, 2200-0400 (happy hours 2200-0100).

Jazz *Gratan Bar*, Bali Hyatt Hotel, live music nightly, 2100-0100; *Olgas Lounge*, *Surya Beach Hotel*, 2000-1200.

Massage On the beach, or at *Sehatku*, Jl D Tamblingan 23, T287880, 10,000Rp for a traditional massage.

Sauna/spa *Sehatku*, Jl D Tamblingan 23, T287880, 40,000Rp.

Meditation The *Bali Usada Meditation Center* in Sanur offers courses in meditation including courses specifically aimed at controlling the impact of negative memories and emotions, and dealing with addictions. Contact the *Bali Usada Meditation Center*, By Pass Ngurah Rai 23, Sanur, T0361 289209, F287726, usada@balimeditation.com, http://www.balimeditation.com

Diving *Bali Marine Sports*, Jl Raja Bypass, Blanjong, T287872, F287872; *Baruna Watersports* at the *Bali Beach Hotel*, T288511, *Sanur Beach*, T288011 and *Bali Hyatt*, T288271, they are expensive but very professional, with well maintained equipment and very safe procedures; *Oceana Dive Centre*, Jl Bypass 78, T288652, F288652.

Sports

Golf 9-hole course at the *Bali Beach Hotel*, green fee US$50 (50% discount for *Bali Beach Hotel* guests), one price for 9 holes, 18 holes or all day. Club hire: half set US$15.50, full set US$22.50, golf shoes US$4.50, caddy US$2.50.

Jungle skirmish (aka Paintball) *Bali Splat Mas*, T289073, 2 approximate 5-hr sessions a day, US$45 per session.

Mountain biking *Sobek*, organize various trips around the interior, T287059.

Sea kayaking *Sobek*, T287059.

Surfing The reef here has one of the world's best right-hand breaks but it is only on for about 28 days a year. Surfing in Sanur is best in the wet season Oct-Apr, and is possible with any tide depending on the size and direction of the swell. Beware of strong currents and riptides in high winds. To the north of Sanur the right-hand break in front of the Grand Bali Beach Hotel is a fast 4 to 5 m with some good barrels but is best on a mid or high tide and needs a large swell. Opposite the *Tanjung Sari Hotel* at high tide there is the possibility of a long, fast wall. For the biggest waves hire a jukung to take you out to the channel opposite the *Bali Hyatt*, very good right handers on an incoming tide.

Ten-Pin Bowling   At the *Bali Beach Hotel*, 3,500Rp per person per game.

Watersports   Equipment available from the bigger hotels or on the beach. Typical prices per person: jet ski US$15 per 15 mins; parasailing US$10 per round; glass bottom boat US$15 (min 2); windsurfing US$8 per hr; water skiing US$15 per 15 mins; deep sea fishing US$240 included (maximum 6 people for full day).

Whitewater rafting   *Sobek*, T287059.

Shopping   **Batik**   *Popiler*, in Tohpati, 5 km north of Sanur beach, on the road to Batubulan. Recommended.

Clothing   *Animale* on Jl Danau Tamblingan (see map) has the best selection of reasonably priced, good quality fashions. *Pisces*, Jl Sanur Beach (near the *Bali Hyatt*) has good designs.

Ikat   *Gego*, Jl Danau Toba 6, ikat and handwoven fabrics; *Nogo*, Jl Tamblingan 98, high quality ikat made in Gianyar and sold for 14,000Rp per metre for plain colours and 16,000Rp per metre for designs, plus ready-made clothing. They also sell batik.

Jewellery   *Bali Sun Sri*, Jl Bypass Ngurah Rai (out of town) has a wide selection of silver jewellery and good designs; *Pisces*, Jl Sanur Beach (near *Bali Hyatt*) sells a limited range of contemporary silver jewellery.

Leather and rattan bags   *The Hanging Tree*, Jl Tamblingan.

Supermarkets   *Galael Dewata* on the By-Pass road, has closed down. The best supermarket these days is *Alas Arum* on Jl Danau Tamblingan at the northern end of Batu Jimbar near Swastika Bungalows. This is a fairly large supermarket with a good selection of imported food, and is also the best place to buy fruit; prices are much better than the market where tourists are unlikely to get a bargain.

Tourist trinkets   T-shirts, bags, batik, at the north end of Jl Tanjung Sari.

Tour operators   *Perama*, Warung Pino, T287594. Shuttle bus service all over the island.

Transport   **Local Bemo**: short hops within Sanur limits cost 1000Rp. **Bicycle hire**: the *Bali Hyatt*
6 km from Denpasar   *Hotel* has mountain bikes for hire. **Car hire**: larger national and international firms tend to be based at the bigger hotels; there are also many smaller outfits along the main road. Big companies charge about, $45 per day, smaller ones about 80,000Rp per day. Note that cars cannot be taken off the island. *Avis*, *Bali Hyatt Hotel*, T288271 ext 85023; *Bali Car Rental*, Jl Ngurah Rai 17, T288550; *National*, *Bali Beach Hotel*, T288511 ext 1304.

Road Bemo: regular connections on green bemos with **Denpasar's** Kreneng terminal and on blue bemos with Tegal terminal (both 2000Rp); also regular connections with the Batubulan terminal, north of Sanur (2000Rp). To airport, 25,000Rp. **Taxi**: most hotels will arrange airport transfer/pickup and will charge the same as, or often more than taxis for the service (25,000Rp).

Airline offices All of the following have offices in the Bali Beach Hotel. *Ansett Australia*,
T289636/7; *Cathay Pacific*, T286001; *Japan Airlines*, T287576; *KLM*, T287577; *MAS*, T288511;
Qantas, T751471; *Northwest Airlines*; *Lufthansa* open Mon-Fri 0900-1700 (closed for lunch
1200-1300), Sat 0900-1130; *Continental Micronesia*; *Qantas* Tel Toll Free 001 803 61 786;
Air France T287734 Open Mon-Fri 0900-1700 (closed for lunch 1230-1330), Sat 0900-1230.
British Airways (which no longer flies to Indonesia) are part of the Oneworld Alliance represented
by Qantas on Bali, or can be contacted in Jakarta Tel 021 521 1500. *Garuda* have moved their office
to the *Sanur Beach Hotel* at the southern end of Sanur, T288011. Opening hours are Mon-Fri
0800-1700, Sat 0800-1200. **Banks** There are several along the main street.
Communications Perumtel telephone service: on the corner of Jl Tanjung Sari and Jl Sindu.
Post Office: Jl Danau Buyan. **Postal agent**: Jl Tamblingan 66 (opposite *Taverna Bali Hotel*);
including poste restante. **Wartel telephone service**: corner of Tanjung and Segara Ayu.
Approximate rate to USA and Europe 5,000Rp per min. **Embassies & consulates** *Australia*, Jl
Prof M Yamin 4, Renon (near Sanur), T235092,F231990; *France*, Jl Bypass Ngurah Rai 35X, Sanur
T285485; *Germany*, Jl Pantai Karang 17, T288535, F234834 (0800-1200 Mon-Fri); *Norway* and
Denmark, Jl Jaya Giri VIII/10, Renon (near Sanur), T235098; *Japan*, Jl Raya Puputan, Renon (near
Sanur), T227628 F231308; *Sweden & Finland*, *Segara* Village Hotel, Jl Segara Ayu. T288407/8,
288021. **Medical facilities** Dentist: Dr Alfiana Akinah, Jl Sri Kesari 17. Doctor: *Bali Beach Hotel*
from 0800-1200 daily. Or ask at any major hotel such as *The Hyatt*, *Radisson* etc. Bali's first
international standard hospital is planned to open in April 2000 in the Sanur area. Charges will
range from 50,000Rp up to 400,000Rp per night for a VIP room. **Places of worship** Catholic:
church service at *Bali Beach Hotel*, 1800 Sat and *Bali Hyatt Hotel* 1900 Sat (times may vary).
Protestant: Bali Beach, 1800 Sun. **Useful addresses** Police: Jl By-Pass, T288597.

Nusa Penida and Nusa Lembongan

These two islands off Bali's southeast coast in the Lombok Strait are relatively *Phone code: 0361*
isolated from the 'mainland' and have not experienced the same degree of *Colour map 1, grid B2*
tourist development.

Nusa Lembongan the smaller of the two is encircled by beautiful white sand **Nusa**
beaches with stunning views of Mount Agung on Bali, especially at sunset. A **Lembongan**

Nusa Lembongan

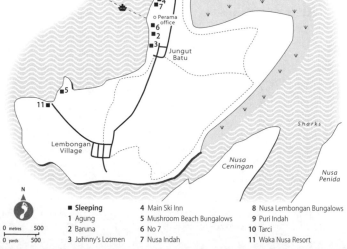

To Sanur

o Perama office

Jungut Batu

Sharks

Lembongan Village

Nusa Ceningan

Nusa Penida

N

| 0 metres | 500 |
| 0 yards | 500 |

■ **Sleeping**
1 Agung
2 Baruna
3 Johnny's Losmen

4 Main Ski Inn
5 Mushroom Beach Bungalows
6 No 7
7 Nusa Indah

8 Nusa Lembongan Bungalows
9 Puri Indah
10 Tarci
11 Waka Nusa Resort

favourite haunt of backpackers for years Nusa Lembongan has now been discovered by mainstream tourism and new upmarket places to stay are proliferating, along with a growing number of sporting and entertainment options. There is good surfing along the north shore, and the surrounding reefs with their clear waters and good visibility offer some of the best snorkelling and diving within easy reach of Bali. You may choose to arrange dives with an operator on Bali, although there is now a PADI dive operation based on the island, see below. Tourism will in time impact on the rural tranquillity of this island but for the time being it seems that the harvesting of seaweed for export – primarily to Hong Kong for the cosmetics industry – will remain the island's main source of income. An arid, scrubby island which supports few crops, mainly tobacco, peanuts, beans and corn; most of Nusa Lembongan's food has to be brought over from Bali, 12 km distant and many of the island's 3,000 inhabitants work on mainland Bali.

Measuring only 4 km by 2 km the island is easily explored on foot. It is a pleasant place to stay for a few days and there are no cars just motorbikes. The main village is **Desa Lembongan** but most people stay in accommodation along the beach north of **Jungut Batu**. A tarmac road runs between the two villages, a distance of about 3 km. At low tide the seaweed beds are worth a visit. There is a track running right round the island which makes for a pleasant walk. For a cool, damp interlude you can explore the underground house on the edge of Lembongan village, a network of caves, rooms and passages. Bring your own torch; the local kids will offer to act as guides. Boats for rent 5,000Rp per hour, 150,000Rp per day, motorbikes 12,000Rp per day.

The small island of **Nusa Ceningan** can be easily reached from Nusa Lembongan by hiring a boat. There is just one small village, no accommodation, but there are beaches with good surfing, snorkelling and diving; there are sharks in the waters here but they rarely attack.

Nusa Penida The far larger sister island of Nusa Penida is rugged and barren, with steep cliffs along its south shore and sandy beaches to the north. It has a reputation among the Balinese as a cursed place and criminals and outcasts used to be sent here to live out their days. Perhaps because of its reputation, Nusa Penida has not yet been caught up in the tourist mêlée and there is only basic losmen accommodation available in the main town **Sampalan**, and the village of

Nusa Penida

Toyapakeh where boats from Bali arrive although it might also be possible to persuade a local to take you in at other villages. Ask the *kepala desa* (headman). Most visitors come for the day only and visit the white sand beaches of the north coast. Very few make it to the sheer limestone cliffs of the south coast. The bat filled cave at Karengsari may be a place of interest for some.

Bali Hai Cruises, Benoa Harbour, T720331, F720334, balihai@indosat.net.id, **Tours** www.bali-paradise.com/balihai Bali Hai operate professionally run cruises from Benoa Harbour to Lembongan. Under Australian management, the one hour crossing is made in a high-tech, fully a/c catamaran – you barely notice you are in a boat. There are three cruise options: A (US$80) sails to a pontoon off Lembongan from where you can snorkel, banana-boat ride, view the reef through a semi-submersible boat and snorkel (extra charge), before buffet lunch served on catamaran deck; B (US$68) sails to beach club on Lembongan, buffet barbecue, relax around pool, snorkel from beach; C (US$38) sunset cruise, buffet and disco/karaoke. Cruise B has the added attraction of being able to visit the island, taking in seaweed farms, Lembongan village and an underground house that was built by a local priest. Cruise A is strictly for those in search of watersports and action. Recommended. *Bali Hai* have recently introduced daily ocean rafting cruises operated from a 12.6 m 'RIB' (Rigid Inflatable Boat) carrying up to 28 passengers and capable of speeds up to 70 km per hour. An early morning Dolphin or a full day tour to the islands of Nusa Lembongan, Nusa Ceningan and Nusa Penida.

Wakalouka Cruises, Benoa Harbour, T0361-723629, 723659, F722077. Two hour crossing from Benoa Harbour in luxury sailing catamaran to the *Wakanusa Resort* on Lembongan. The trip costs US$86 (children half price) and includes tour of Lembongan village, snorkelling, buffet lunch, glass bottom boat to view coral reef, morning and afternoon refreshments, hotel transfers. Recommended.

Sea Rover, Jalan Segara Werdi 6, Harbour Beno is one of the numerous small companies operating day trips to Lembongan in simple motorboats, the tours cost under US$40, but the experience is downmarket.

The *Golden Hawk*, a tall ship over 100 years old sails from Benoa Harbour to Lembongan for day trips, US$88 for all inclusive trip – pick up from hotel, lunch, snorkel gear, glass bottom boat etc (scuba diving equipment and lessons can be arranged). *Golden Hawk Cruises* operate from Jalan Danau Poso 20A, Sanur, T/F28658.

Island Explorer Cruises, Jalan Sekar Waru 8, Sanur, T289856, F289837, organize day trips and an overnight package on sailing yacht and motorboats. Fishing, snorkelling, barbecue lunch provided (US$59-69).

Essentials

A *Coconuts Beach Resort*, newly opened with upmarket rustic bungalows and breathtaking sea views. **A** *Hai Tide Huts* run by Bali Hai Cruises, T720331, F720334, www.bali-paradise.com/balihai, balihai@indosat.net.id 6 large thatched roofed, 2-storey lumbung style rooms, with a/c. All overlooking the beach with panoramic ocean views with Mount Agung in the background. Watersports, free-form swimming pool, bar and restaurant. **A** *Nusa Lembongan Resort*, T413375, F413376, sales@nusa-lembongan.com, www.nusa-lembongan.com Opened in mid-1999, boutique hotel set in gardens overlooking Sanghiang Bay. 12 villas, 7 ocean view and 5 garden view, with a/c and the usual upmarket facilities, built in the traditional manner using natural materials. Included in the design is a wooden deck perched above the ocean, used for fishing, sunbathing and for a romantically sited restaurant and

Sleeping: Nusa Lembongan

All the accommodation is beside the sea, with fabulous sunset views over Bali & Mt Agung

bar. **A** *Waka Nusa Resort*, booking office Benoa Harbour, T723629/723659, F722077. Gated compound on the southwest coast of the island. 10 luxury bungalows contained in tiny private garden, simple but artistic décor, alang-alang roofs, polished woods, natural fabrics, pool, restaurant. Recommended. **B** *Pondok Baruna*, Jungutbatu, F288500. Recently renovated, 8 rooms with Western bathrooms, beachfront restaurant. **C-D** *Nusa Lembongan Bungalows* (booking office on Kuta at Jl Pantai Legian, T53071), price including breakfast, attractive, clean and spacious rooms. **C-E** *Agung*, good restaurant, clean, thatched-roof bungalows, some with private mandi. **C-E** *Main Ski Inn*, 2-storey bungalows set in garden, upstairs rooms have balconies with sea views, can be noisy due to the restaurant serving good, cheap food overlooking the sea. **C-E** *Tarci*, 2-storey bungalows, some with private mandi, restaurant which also serves good and cheap food, beside the beach. **E** *Johnny's Losmen*, basic accommodation near the village.

Eating   Most places to stay have their own restaurant, *Tarci* has a good reputation or try the fish at the *Main Ski Inn*.

Shopping   **Textiles**   Distinctive weft ikat cotton cloth is produced on Nusa Penida; usually in the form of a red *kamben*.

Sports   **Scuba Diving** *World Diving Lembongan*, Pondok Baruna, Jungutbatu, F288500 (correspondence to Mark Micklefield, Jl Danau Maninjau, Gang 111 no 7, Sanur). New dive operation on Nusa Lembongan though the company has been in operation for many years based in Sanur. Full range of PADI approved courses, English Divemaster. The islands of Nusa Lembongan and Nusa Penida offer a range of diving conditions and regular sightings of sharks, turtles and large rays.

Transport   **Local Bemos**: run fairly regularly between Toyapakeh and Sampalan, with a more limited service to Suana and Klumpu. To really see the island you will need a motorbike.

Sea Boat: regular connections to Nusa Penida from either Padangbai or Kesamba, docking near Sampalan at (respectively) Buyuk or Toyapakeh (the boats from Kesamba are small junks), 1 hr. Locals pay 4,000Rp but the boatmen demand 15,000Rp from foreigners. For Nusa Lembongan they leave every morning from near the *Bali Beach Hotel* (Sanur Beach) and dock at Jungut Batu. The public boats leave very early from 0500 depending on the tide. It is a 10 min walk from the accommodation north of Jungut Batu to the spot on the beach where the boats come in; no jetty, you wade over to the boat. There are also early morning boats between Nusa Penida and Nusa Lembongan. The best way to get to Nusa Lembongan is with *Perama* who have two boats a day from Sanur. Schedules change so check for up-to-date times. Currently boats leave Sanur at 1030 and 1615, and leave Nusa Lembongan at 0900 and 1500. In the low season there may only be one boat a day, in the morning. The 27 km crossing takes about 40 mins, 17,500Rp. Departures from Sanur are 1030 and 1630 in high season. Perama office in Sanur is at Warung Pino, T287594 – *Perama's* shuttle bus service from the popular tourist destinations on Bali, links up with the boats – pick up a copy of their timetable for full details. A faster way to reach the island is by catamaran which takes about 30 mins. There are also a growing number of cruise options from mainland Bali costing between US$50-100, see page 40.

The Bukit Peninsula and Nusa Dua

The Bukit Peninsula starts 4 km south of Kuta, with just a narrow isthmus connecting it to the mainland, and extends over an area roughly 10 km from north to south and 18 km east to west. It is known locally as The Bukit or Bukit Badung. The area is of little use agriculturally and naturally, has been earmarked for tourist development. The latest area to be developed is on the south coast east of Uluwatu at Pecatu where the new Pecatu Indah Resort is being built. The Bukit landscape is dotted with several failed ventures: the concrete carcasses of luxury resorts that lie abandoned and falling into disrepair, some never completed.

Phone code: 0361
Colour map 1, grid B2

Ins and outs

Public transport only goes to the main population areas of Jimbaran, Nusa Dua and Benoa. Myriad tour companies offer trips to Uluwatu, but otherwise you will need your own transport to explore this area, much of which can more easily be reached by motorbike than car.

Getting around

The area

Most of the bukit (meaning hill in Indonesian) is dry rocky terrain with scrubby vegetation and little surface water. Popular with surfers since the early 1970s, it boasts some of the best surfing in Southeast Asia, and ranks in the top 10 of world surfing destinations. These days, thanks to the drilling of bore holes and a water treatment plant, the east coast has been developed into a verdant luxury resort fronted by clean sandy beaches. The peninsula is also the location of one of Bali's finest temples, **Uluwatu**, spectacularly located on a west-facing clifftop, especially enchanting at sunset. Good roads lead to Nusa Dua and Uluwatu, while rough roads and tracks lead to idyllic, isolated beaches, limestone caves and dramatic cliffs rising up to 100 m straight out of the sea. The remains of ancient temples can still be seen in remote coastal spots in the west and south.

On the west side of the isthmus is **Jimbaran Beach**, and on the east side, **Benoa**. The purpose-built luxury resort area of **Nusa Dua**, also lies on the east side, to the south of Benoa. The Bukit Peninsula is a barren, arid, limestone tableland – the Dutch called it Tafelhoek – which once lay under the sea but now rises to 200 m. Geologically, this barren landscape has more in common with Nusa Penida and provides a tremendous contrast with the lushness of the rest of south Bali. The soils are sandy and infertile, rainfall is less abundant and highly seasonal allowing crops of cassava and sorghum which are made into flour, and peanuts, rice, beans, corn, bananas, coconuts, and oranges to grow in the wet season only. Some cattle are also raised here.

It was considered such an unpleasant place to live that criminals were once banished to the Bukit Peninsula. At one time herds of buffalo and wild banteng foraged here, as well as deer, pheasant and wild boar, and the area served as a hunting ground for local rulers.

In 1969 the Indonesian government commissioned a French consultancy firm to draw up a report on the future development of Bali. The resulting report became the master plan for the island's tourist industry. The plan envisaged that tourist development would be confined to designated resort areas, thus preventing tourists from intruding too much on daily life. Central to this strategy was the creation of Nusa Dua: an extraordinary area of large four and five star hotels and immaculately kept gardens on the east coast of the Bukit Peninsula. Deep bore holes were sunk to provide ample supplies of fresh water, the area was landscaped and replanted, and a highway was built from the airport – the most expensive road ever to have been built on Bali. Although there can be little doubt that the development has isolated the tourists from the locals – a good thing some might maintain – it has also meant that only larger hotels and businesses have benefited from the tourist dollars. The only way that a Balinese businessman of limited means can set-up in the 'amenity core' of Nusa Dua is by hiring a stall from the Tourist Authority. Even the bulk of the food is imported.

The only 'sight' on the Bukit Peninsula is the **Uluwatu Temple** (see page 121), magnificently positioned on a clifftop overlooking the sea at the southwest extremity of the peninsula. Much of the west coast has remained relatively undeveloped because of the steep cliffs. But the excellent surf for which this area is renowned draws large numbers of surfers to the west coast. At the neck of the peninsula is the sandy Jimbaran Bay, which is set to become the next target for tourist development.

Jimbaran

About 15 minutes' drive south of Kuta, this is perhaps the nicest of the upmarket resorts in south Bali. The location is superb: a grand sweeping bay, a fine white sand beach (one of the best beaches on Bali), and spectacular sunsets. On a clear day you can see the hills of Tabanan in the distance.

Jimbaran Bay is a spiritual place of deep religious significance to local Balinese. For this reason, although it is sandwiched between the airport and Nusa Dua, the bay was passed by until recently and represented a small enclave of peace surrounded by activity. But over the last few years developers have moved in, despite local protestations, and it is possible that eventually it could be transformed into another bustling resort. Six hotels and a time-share property have already been built and more are planned.

Jimbaran is a large, relatively prosperous, tidy village with a population of 3,500. Few foreigners venture into the village and the people seem rather more polite than in other tourist areas. This village is also renowned for the Barong dance, **Barong Ket**, staged by its residents, many of whom go into a trance during the performance. The dance season lasts for about six months of the year during which time performances are held approximately every 15 days. Sekan Barong is the name given to the group of people, numbering about 100, who are responsible for all aspects of the barong, including the masks and costumes, and who meet monthly to discuss details of the performance, finances and so on. It is people from this group who habitually go into trance and are called *babuten*. Asked how they feel about going into trance most people say they find it very tiring, do not enjoy the experience and would like to stop; afterwards they are embarrassed at having made a public spectacle of themselves and for having lost control. The feeling is that they have been taken over by a negative force which they could not prevent. The spectators' view is that the *babuten* is possessed by a malevolent spirit who dictates their actions, and that you should be careful of these people while they are in trance. Fred Eiseman, author of many books on Balinese culture including the notable *Bali Sekala & Niskala* lives just outside the town at 8a Jl Bukit Permai and sells his books from his home.

In the middle of the village, set in its own large grounds, is the impressive **Ulun Siwi Temple**, dating from the 17th century. It was built by Cokorda Mungga, a Mengwi raja at a time when this area was part of Mengwi regency. The 11-tiered meru indicates the temple's importance and the strength of religious feeling at the time it was built. During the rainy season the pavements on the outskirts of town can be very slippery.

This is very much an upmarket resort with good luxury accommodation but very little for the budget traveller; the few cheap places seem overpriced for what they offer. There are also a few villas available to rent both long and short term (see map for location of Villa Batu and Bukit Permai Villa Rini).

Sleeping

L *Four Seasons Resort*, T701010, F701020. Built in 1992 to a design incorporating the best of Balinese pavilion design, voted as one of 'the 10 Healthiest Hotels in the World' by *Tatler Travel Guide* (UK 1996) and 'No 1 Resort in the World' by Condé Nast *Traveler* (USA 1996), this is a resort that is hard to beat – the only problem is summoning the

Jimbaran Bay

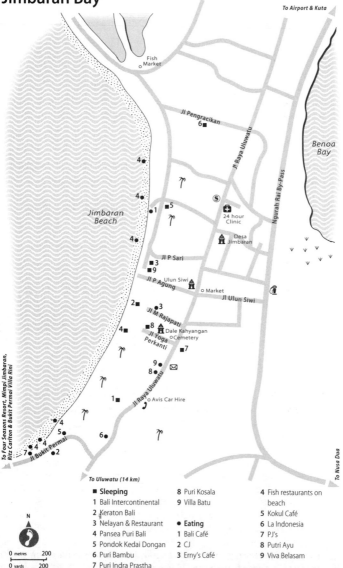

Bali

■ **Sleeping**
1 Bali Intercontinental
2 Keraton Bali
3 Nelayan & Restaurant
4 Pansea Puri Bali
5 Pondok Kedai Dongan
6 Puri Bambu
7 Puri Indra Prastha
8 Puri Kosala
9 Villa Batu

● **Eating**
1 Bali Café
2 CJ
3 Erny's Café
4 Fish restaurants on beach
5 Kokul Café
6 La Indonesia
7 PJ's
8 Putri Ayu
9 Viva Belasam

0 metres 200
0 yards 200

will to leave it and see the rest of the island. About 150 beautiful villas, each sur-rounded by a stone wall, are set on the slope above Jimbaran bay, entered by a tradi-tional courtyard gate, the walled enclosure contains 3 pavilions: 1 free-standing pavilion – an open-air living/dining area, and 2 joined pavilions which contain the sleeping area and a luxurious bathroom with an outdoor shower area and an over-sized Victorian bath tub which stands on a solid marble plinth, the sleeping area has a/c and fan, satellite TV and in-house movies, VCR and CD sound system, each villa also has its own plunge-pool and sun-deck, the resort facilities feature beautifully landscaped gardens, 2 pools, outdoor jacuzzi, supergrass tennis courts, spa with sauna, library/lounge, and 2 first-class restaurants including *PJ's* – a beachside place serving Mediterranean food, specializing in exotic pizza cooked in wood-burning oven. **L** *The Ritz-Carlton Hotel*, Jl Bukit Permai. T702222, F701555. Luxury hotel with the usual facilities but suffers from its rather poor location.

L-AL *Bali Inter Continental Resort*, Jl Uluwatu 45, T701888, F701777, bali@ interconti.com, www.interconti.com/bali   Set right on the bay with a long stretch of beach frontage with 500 m of spectacular sea views, this hotel has the best location in Jimbaran. A rather grand hotel designed in the style of an ancient Javanese water pal-ace, with a vast and impressive entrance lobby. Attractively furnished rooms with verandahs, set in extensive 35-ha landscaped gardens, 3 pools, the largest of which is vast and close to the beach, 3 outdoor jacuzzis, sports centre, spa, 5 restaurants including a first-class Japanese teppanyaki bar. Conference facilities. Daily programme of cultural and sporting events, including a horticultural tour of the gar-dens. One of the most environmentally conscious hotels with its own sophisticated water treatment plant and the only hotel on Bali with tap water you can drink. **L-A** *Mimpi Jimbaran*, T701070, F701074. A small, exclusive development of 14 studios, 4 apartments and 3 villas designed and managed to very high standards, the apart-ments and villas have kitchens, on a hillside overlooking Jimbaran Bay, with beautiful gardens, restaurant and poolside bar, the villas have their own private pools, monthly rates available, tennis, conference facilities, 15 mins from airport. Recommended.

AL *Keraton Bali*, Jl M. Rajapati, T701961, F701991, german@ denpasar.wasantara.net.id 99 cottages in typical Balinese style, rooms are only aver-age, with a/c, fridge, IDD etc. Set in gardens leading down to the sea, 3 restaurants and bars, pool, sports facilities including sailing and fishing. Popular with tour groups. **AL** *Pansea Jimbaran*, T701605, F701320, panseabl@indosat.net.id 41 fairly attractive cottages with fan and a/c, minibar, safe etc. 2 restaurants, pool, superb location over-looking Jimbaran bay. **AL-A** *Puri Kosala*, Jl Yoga Perkanti 2, T701673/702575, F702576. 6 beautifully furnished bungalows with marble floors, a/c and fan, HW, fridge etc. Set in very pretty gardens with large pool, in a very peaceful location 3 mins' walk from the beach. Well managed with friendly staff. Price includes breakfast, tax extra. **A** *Nelayan Jimbaran Bungalows and Homestay*, Jl Pantai Jimbaran 3, T/F702253. 10 rooms consisting of 6 bungalows and 4 homestay. Rooms are large, but fairly dark with a/c but cold water only, homestay rooms are more basic and smaller but brighter, all are set at the back of the restaurant and can be noisy. Tiny garden. Two mins from beach. About the closest Jimbaran gets to budget accommodation but overpriced compared to other parts of Bali. **A** *Puri Bambu*, Jl Pengeracikan, Kedonganan, T701377, 701468/9, F701440. Down a side road, 6 mins' walk to the beach, this is one of the cheaper hotels in Jimbaran. 38 rooms, clean, fairly new and plain, with a/c, HW, minibar, TV, bal-cony/verandah, etc. Pool in central courtyard, restaurant, bar, free shuttle bus to airport and Kuta. Price includes breakfast, 50% discount off season.

B *Pondok Kedai Dongan*, Jl Pantai Kedonganan 118X, T/F752667. Brand new in 1999, just across the road from the beach. 9 rooms with a/c and HW. Great views from upstairs restaurant. **B** *Puri Indra Prastha*, Jl Uluwatu 28A, T701552, 701544. One of the cheapest places to stay in Jimbaran, on the main road in town, 5 mins' walk to the beach. 11 rooms, clean but dark and fairly basic, with a/c or fan, and verandah, set around central courtyard overlooking pool. Restaurant, reasonable sized pool, price includes breakfast, 10% tax extra.

Eating

Fish warungs right on the beach have sprung up in the last few years starting with just 9 in 1996. Now they cover increasingly large areas of beach in 2 separate places: adjacent to the town and further south between the *The Four Seasons Resort* and *Intercontinental Hotel*. Open for lunch and dinner, but particularly popular in the evening when bus loads of locals and tourists arrive. Diners choose their freshly caught fish, which is priced per kilo, and sit at tables outside on the beach or in tents while the fish is cooked, then served with salad, sauces and rice followed by fruit salad for an inclusive price. Of these *Bali Café* in the first area is one of the better warungs and operates to high standard of cleanliness. At the southern end, just over the bridge, *Bagus Café* is popular with expats.

Mid-range *PJ's* (see *Four Seasons Resort* above) great views over Jimbaran bay.

Cheap *Nelayan Restaurant*, Jl Pantai Jimbaran 3. Good sea views from this upstairs restaurant which serves fish, Western and Indonesian food. *Pondok Kedai Dongan*, Jl Pantai Kedonganan 118X, T/F752667. Good views from upstairs restaurant.

Transport

Road Bemo: connections with **Denpasar's** Tegal terminal. **Car hire**: several of the larger car hire companies are in Jimbaran on the Jl By Pass Nusa Dua. *Golden Bird Bali*, Jl Raya By Pass Nusa Dua 4, T701111, F701628, offers a range of transport services from car rental (Suzuki jeep, Toyota Kijang) to chauffeur driven cars (Volvo). They are one of the largest car rental companies on the island so they offer good break-down service, insurance etc. *Golden Bird* also manage the blue taxis on the island – amongst the few taxis you will find with meters. Recommended. *Toyota Rent a Car*, Jl By Pass Nusa Dua, T701747, F701741, specialize in Toyota vehicles, namely Kijang, Starlet and Corollas.

Benoa

Benoa consists of a small fishing village called Tanjung Benoa, at the tip of a finger of land extending north from Nusa Dua; and is not to be confused with utilitarian Benoa port across the water. To travel between Tanjung Benoa and Benoa Port by land would take about an hour, though there are occasional boats which make the crossing in about 20 minutes.

Phone code: 0361
Colour map 1, grid B2

The area between Tanjung Benoa and Nusa Dua, is becoming increasingly popular and in recent years many new places to stay have opened at all price levels including several well-known international hotel chains (some hotels here claim to be in Nusa Dua for added cachet). Benoa has a good reputation for the quality of its watersports, including diving; and this is its principle attraction as the area is rather flat and uninteresting, and on the wrong side of the island for sunsets. However, as yet unspoilt by tourism, the village of Tanjung Benoa is worth a visit and many of the villagers earn their living as fishermen.

Sights

There is an interesting Chinese temple which you can visit if you are suitably dressed, as well as a mosque, a Hindu temple, and a market. The tourist area of Tanjung Benoa covers four different banjars which provide excellent gamelan orchestras for the cultural activities that take place regularly at the big hotels here. You might catch them rehearsing in the evenings. The residents of each banjar speak with a slightly different accent and are thus readily distinguishable to the local people.

Benoa

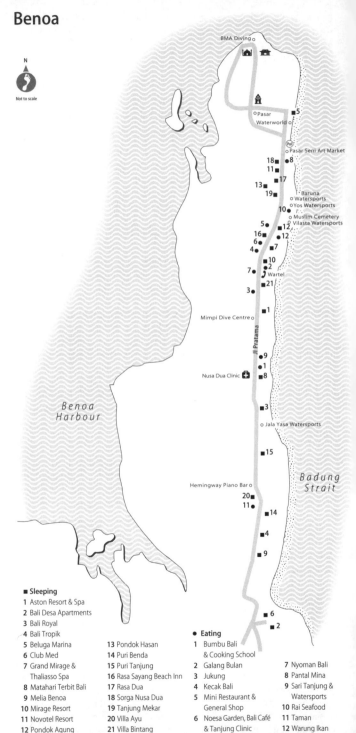

N
Not to scale

BMA Diving

■ 5

Pasar
Waterworld

Pasar Seni Art Market

18 ■   ● 8
11 ■
          17 ■
13 ■
19 ■   Baruna
                Watersports
                Yos Watersports
          10 ● Muslim Cemetery
                Vilasta Watersports
5 ●   ● 12
16 ●   ● 12
6 ●   ● 7
4 ■
          ■ 10
7 ●   ■ 2
          ♪ Wartel
          ■ 21
3 ●
          ■ 1

Mimpi Dive Centre

Jl Pratama

                ● 9
                ● 1
Nusa Dua Clinic   ■ 8

          ■ 3

          Jala Yasa Watersports

          ■ 15

Hemingway Piano Bar

20 ■
11 ●   ■ 14

          ■ 4

          ■ 9

Benoa
Harbour

Badung
Strait

Bali

          ■ 6

          ■ 2

■ Sleeping

1 Aston Resort & Spa
2 Bali Desa Apartments
3 Bali Royal
4 Bali Tropik
5 Beluga Marina
6 Club Med
7 Grand Mirage &
  Thaliasso Spa
8 Matahari Terbit Bali
9 Melia Benoa
10 Mirage Resort
11 Novotel Resort
12 Pondok Agung
13 Pondok Hasan
14 Puri Benda
15 Puri Tanjung
16 Rasa Sayang Beach Inn
17 Rasa Dua
18 Sorga Nusa Dua
19 Tanjung Mekar
20 Villa Ayu
21 Villa Bintang

● Eating

1 Bumbu Bali
  & Cooking School
2 Galang Bulan
3 Jukung
4 Kecak Bali
5 Mini Restaurant &
  General Shop
6 Noesa Garden, Bali Café
  & Tanjung Clinic
7 Nyoman Bali
8 Pantal Mina
9 Sari Tanjung &
  Watersports
10 Rai Seafood
11 Taman
12 Warung Ikan

All rooms with private bathroom and Western toilet unless otherwise stated. Jl **Sleeping**
Pratama is a busy road, without pavements, and at its narrower sections walking
along it is not for the faint hearted. Watersports are available at all the **A** and **B** category accommodations.

AL *Aston Bali Resort*, Jl Pratama 68X, T773577, F774954. New international hotel. 187
rooms, beside sea with pool, restaurant, bar and watersports. **AL** *Bali Tropik*, PO Box
41, T772130, F772131, btropik@indosat.net.id Located at the southern end of the
Benoa peninsula. 103 attractive rooms in Balinese style with good views from upstairs
balconies. All with verandah/balcony, a/c, IDD, TV. 3 restaurants and bars, medium
sized pool set in large gardens adjacent to an eroded area of beach. Daily programme
of free events, free non-motorized watersports. Staff are very friendly and efficient.
Catering mainly to tour groups; price includes all meals and tax. **AL** *Grand Mirage*,
T772147, F772148. A/c, restaurant, pools, new, big and brash. **AL** *Melia Benoa*, Jl
Pratama, T771714, F771713, meliabenoa@denpasar.wasantara.net.id Typical international hotel catering to tour groups, opened in 1997. 128 rooms, restaurant, bar,
pool, watersports, beside sea. Free shuttle to Kuta. Low season discount.
AL *Novotel Benoa Bali* (*Coralia Resort*), Jl Pratama, T772239, F772237. Beautifully
designed hotel with excellent resort facilities, one of the most attractive resort hotels
in Bali. This is a notable example of the new Asian architecture evoking tradition in its
use of natural materials, coconut wood, thatch and soft adobe patinas, and with
abundant evidence of skilled craftsmanship in its method of construction. Great
attention has been paid to design detail and creating a mood-enhancing environment, including the use of creative lighting and state of the art air conditioning. Set in
landscaped tropical gardens which lead down to the beach. 180 extremely attractive
rooms, with a/c, minibar, tea/coffee making facilities, unlimited free drinking water,
private garden or balcony. 12 luxurious beach cabanas beside the sea with private
garden and entertainment system. 3 imaginative swimming pools including large
jacuzzi pool, fitness centre with sauna and massage, floodlit tennis court, games
room, library, art gallery, tour desk, meeting rooms and an excellent programme of
watersports. Outdoor theatre for cultural performances of traditional dance and
music, which take place each evening, and are lit in the traditional manner by a coconut oil lamp which creates a wonderfully evocative setting; these performances are
free to all hotel guests with no obligation to dine (unlike many resort hotels). Free
daily programme of events. Excellent children's club providing a full day's activities,
and separate kids' pool. 3 restaurants and bars. The hotel is actively sponsoring local
environmental programmes and traditional theatre and music groups. Recommended. **AL** *Suites Hotel Bali Royal Resort* (formerly *Bali Royal*), Jl Pratama. T771039,
F771885. (In Vienna, Austria, T0043-1-9145851, F9113770). Built in 1991. 13 Balinese
style rooms with open plan bathroom, a/c, HW, minibar, TV, telephone, safety deposit
boxes. Small pool in gardens leading down to beach. Restaurant serving Indonesian,
international and Austrian cuisine, room service. Austrian owner in residence. Very
peaceful but overpriced.

A *Hotel Puri Tanjung*, Jl Pratama 62, T772121, F772424. 64 clean, simple rooms with
a/c, HW, TV, telephone, verandah/balcony. Large gardens leading down to beach,
pool area in need of some refurbishment. Restaurant. Rate includes breakfast and tax.
Low season discount. **A** *Hotel Villa Bintang*, Jl Pratama, T772010, F772009,
vl_bintang@denpasar.wasantara.net.id 54 large rooms including 2 villas, a/c, HW,
TV, fridge, balcony, IDD. 3 restaurants serving Indonesian, Japanese and Continental
cuisine. 24-hr coffee shop and room service, bar. Catering primarily to tour groups;
attractive gardens beside sea with large pool. Watersports. Rates negotiable.
A *Matahari Terbit Bali*, Jl Pratama, T771019, F772027, nyomanbali@
denpasar.wasantara.net.id 20 new attractively furnished bungalows, a/c, HW, fridge,

TV. Also family villa (US$225 per night) with 3 bedrooms and open air living room. Lovely gardens with small pool beside beach; marine sports. Beach front café, *Bumbu Bali Restaurant* (see below). In the grounds are a kulkul tower, traditional farming implements and a relocated rice barn. Free airport transfer. Recommended. **A** *Puri Benoa* (formerly **Puri Joma Bungalows**), Jl Pratama 15B, T771634, F771635, pbenoa@denpasar.wasantara.net.id 10 new, completely refurbished bungalows decorated in Balinese style with large rooms, open air bathroom; a/c, HW, TV, verandah. Restaurant beside sea. Smallish pool, set in pretty tropical gardens leading down to beach. Good value. **A** *Taman Damai*, T772514, F773589. Or Contact *Bali Air Marine Sport* near the village. Located 200 m down track off main road. 5 bungalows for rent, 1 bedroom (without kitchen) and 2 bedrooms (with kitchen), large bathroom, fan, mosquito nets, HW. Bungalows are new, clean and simply furnished. Pretty gardens, small pool, parking. Free airport pick-up for stays of one week or more. Friendly caretaker speaks English. Good value.

A-B *Sorga Nusa Dua*, Jl Pratama (northern end of Benoa peninsula), T771604/772413, F77139. Under new management and undergoing complete renovation. 54 attractive, large, very clean rooms, a/c, HW, TV, fridge, telephone, large verandah/balcony. Good sized pool set in pretty gardens, tennis courts. Restaurant serving Japanese, Indonesian and European food. Price includes tax and breakfast, negotiable off season. Friendly owners. **B** *Bali Resort Palace*, Jl Pratama, T772026, F772237. A/c, restaurant, pool. **B** *Villa Ayu*, Jl Pratama 61D, T772828/773703, F771242. 4 new, clean rooms, plus 2 family rooms with kitchen. All with a/c, HW. Small pool in small gardens. Price includes tax and breakfast.

B-C *Pondok Agung Homestay*, Jl Pratama 99, T/F771143. 7 clean newish rooms with a/c or fan, HW, use of kitchen, satellite TV. 2 upstairs verandahs overlooking pretty garden. Tax included, breakfast extra. **B-D** *Rasa Sayang*, Jl Pratama 88X, T771643. 11 rooms with a/c, 8 with fan, verandah, safety deposit box. Attractive entrance, small gardens. Rates include breakfast and tax. 10 mins' walk to beach. Good value.

C *Tanjung Mekar Homestay*, Jl Pratama, T772063. 4 new, spotless rooms, with spring beds, fan, cold water only, balcony. Friendly owner. Price includes breakfast, 10% tax extra. 10 mins' walk to beach. Good value.

D *Pondok Hasam*, T772456. Perfectly adequate clean rooms. **D** *Rasa Dua*, Jl Pratama, T771571. Basic place, rooms with fan, private bathroom. Price includes tax only.

Eating **Mid-range** *Bumbu Bali*, excellent Balinese food. The owner, Heinz Von Holzen, owns 2 other good restaurants in Tanjung Benoa, the **Kecak** (cheap) and *The Nyoman* (very cheap), Jl Pratama, T772704. Open 0900-2400, Indonesian, Chinese and European food and seafood, free transport in Nusa Dua area (recommended); and a cooking school. For information about these: hvhfood@indosat.net.id

Cheap *Galang Bulan Bar and Restaurant*, Jl Pratama 70, T773708. Indonesian, Chinese, Japanese, European and seafood, free transport in Nusa Dua area. *Warung Ikan* (fish market restaurant) open 0600-2300. *Kecak*, see above. **Very cheap** *The Nyoman*, see above. *Taman Sari Restaurant*, Thai, Indonesian and European food. *Hemingway Piano Bar*, open 2000 onwards. There are a growing number of cafés and restaurants on the beachfront and along Jl Pratama opposite the hotels.

Entertainment **Discos** *Cool Bar*, *Grand Mirage Hotel*, open 2100-2400.

Cooking Ex-pat Heinz Von Holzen has established an excellent cooking school at his *Bumbu Bali* restaurant. For more information contact hvh@indosat.net.id

A growing number of car hire outlets and shops selling tourist accessories and groceries are opening along Jl Pratama. **Shopping**

Marine activities and watersports The catamaran Quicksilver operates regular **Sports** tours to Nusa Penida leaving from the harbour at Tanjung Benoa. When choosing a dive centre it would be best to choose one with a PADI Certification. The following all have outlets in Benoa: *Baruna* T753820, F753809; *Yos Diving* T773774; *Vilasta* T775122 ext 62; *Beluga Marine*; *Jala Yasa*.

Tours: *Tour Devco* T231592 organize trips on a tall ship to Nusa Lembongan; price **Tour operators** includes lunch and watersports equipment. *The Bali International Yacht Club*, T288391, also organizes yacht and fishing trips to the islands. *Bali Hai Cruises* and *Wakalouka Cruises* specialize in trips to Lembongan Island from Benoa Port (see page 111).

Road Bemo: connections with **Denpasar's** Suci terminal. **Sea Boat**: Benoa Port **Transport** was built by the Dutch in 1906 and is the main port of call for cruise ships and yachts as well as the place to come for anyone hoping to sign on as crew. A new fast ferry service was inaugurated to eastern Indonesia from Benoa Harbour in Bali in mid-2000. The 70-m, 925 passenger ship *Barito*, with a top speed of 36 knots, leaves every Fri afternoon at 1800 hours on a 16 hour voyage to **Bima** (Sumbawa) and **Kupang** (Timor). Every Sun at midday the *Barito* makes a 7 hour hop to the port of **Surabaya** in eastern Java. For more information contact *Gama Dewata Bali Tours* at T0361-263568 or T0361-232704, F0361-263569. The *Pelni* Line ships which visit Bali dock here on their circuits around the Indonesian Archipelago and it is also the jumping off point for hydrofoils to Lombok. The *Mabua Express* leaves Benoa twice a day for **Lembar** (Lombok). Travelling time is 2½ hrs and costs US$25 and 30 depending on class (children 2-12 years half price), T721212, F732615 (on Lombok T0370-81195, F81124) for details. Current departure timetable: leaves Benoa 0800, leaves Lembar 1730. A/c, aircraft type seats. The *Pelni* ships *Tatamailau*, *Awu*, *Dobonsolo* and *Tilongkabila* dock here. For Pelni information, T721377.

Clinic: Tanjung Clinic, T773843, open 24 hrs; see map. Nusa Dua Clinic, 24 hrs, see map. **Directory**

Uluwatu Temple

Pura Uluwatu, also known as Pura Ulu Atu, is considered – despite its small size – one of Bali's *sadkahyangan* – the six most important temples on the island. Its full name, *Pura Luhur Uluwatu* literally means 'high headland', an apt name as the temple is spectacularly situated on the south tip of the Bukit Peninsula, perched on a cliff 70 m above the sea. The area used to be closed to visitors, and was jealously guarded by The Prince of Badung. The pura's inhospitable location also kept the curious away. Today it is easily accessible but can be very crowded and you may have to contend with an army of hawkers and unpleasant, but sacred, monkeys.

Pura Uluwatu may have been constructed during the 11th century, although it **History** was substantially rebuilt in the 16th century – and as a result is rather difficult to date. The temple was owned by the Prince of Badung (today's Denpasar) and he alone was allowed to visit it. Once a year the Prince travelled to Uluwatu to make his offerings, a journey that he made until his death at the hands of the Dutch in 1906 (see page 226). It is said that part of the temple fell into the sea 18 months before the massacre at Denpasar – an event which was therefore prophesied.

The site Uluwatu has several unusual features; it is built of hard grey coral, which means that the temple's decoration has survived the centuries of weathering remarkably well. Secondly, the *candi bentar* or split gate is shaped in the form of a stylized *garuda* (mythical bird) rather than with smooth sides, as is usual. Also unusually, two statues of Ganesh flank the inner gateway. It was at Uluwatu that the famous Hindu saint, Danghyang Nirartha, is reputed to have achieved *moksa*, or oneness with the godhead. ■ *Entry by donation. Keep clear of the monkeys on the steps up to the entrance.*

Beaches There are several good surfing beaches near Uluwatu, including **Bingin**, **Nyang Nyang** (on the south coast) and **Padang Padang** (just south of Jimbaran Bay) (see page 114). Most involve a walk of up to 2 km down stony tracks.

Sleeping The popular surfing spots have warungs nearby, often at the cliff top from where steep steps lead down to a narrow beach and the surf. These offer standard Indonesian and Western food, and surfers often sleep in the very basic accommodation available at the warung or on the floor if nothing better is available.

L-AL *Bali Cliff Resort*, Jl Pura Batu Pageh, Ungasan, T771992, F771993, info@balicliff.com or bcr@indosat.net.id Stunning location perched on the edge of a cliff overlooking the Indian Ocean at the southern tip of Bali, a very romantic setting. Set in pretty gardens with ponds, walkways and an outdoor theatre for the occasional cultural performance. Accommodation is either in the main hotel or in private villas with pools. A travelator carries guests the 250 ft down to sea level and a small white sand beach which disappears at high tide. Canadian and Japanese chefs provide excellent and reasonably priced food in 5 restaurants which offer fish, international, Indonesian, Italian and Japanese food and a pizzeria. One of the restaurants is situated at the bottom of the cliff in an ancient cave; here you can enjoy a buffet dinner and kecak dance every Sat night. 2 of the best pools in Bali; one superbly located at the cliff edge whose waters merge into the blue of the distant horizon, the other a full Olympic size swimming pool which is never crowded. Fitness centre, children's playground, games room. Art market set in a replica of a traditional Balinese village where you can watch

Uluwatu

Adapted from Kempers, AJB,
Monumental Bali, Periplus, Singapore (199...

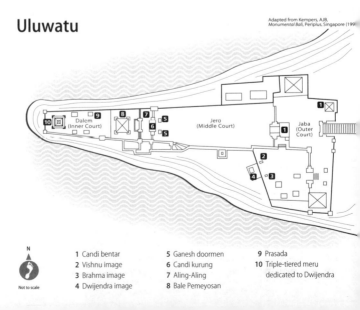

N

Not to scale

1 Candi bentar	5 Ganesh doormen
2 Vishnu image	6 Candi kurung
3 Brahma image	7 Aling-Aling
4 Dwijendra image	8 Bale Pemeyosan

9 Prasada
10 Triple-tiered meru
dedicated to Dwijendra

artists and craftsmen at work. Free shuttle bus to airport, Kuta and Nusa Dua. Convention facilities for up to 600 people. Good surfing here. Recommended. **D** *Gobleg Inn*, off the track to the beach.

There are several places to stay inland near **Bongol**, on the road leading to the *Bali Cliff Resort* and Uluwatu Temple, 20 mins' drive from the airport:

A *Bukit Inn Villa Koyo*, T702927. Small, modern hotel with a/c. **A** *Jimbaran Resort Hills*. Modern hotel with Western facilities. **C** *Ugly Boys*, 3 kms north of Ungasan. The cheapest accommodation in the area, popular with surfers, bar and café.

Bali Cliff Resort, Sunday brunch which includes the use of the resort's spectacular cliffside pool. See hotel entry for more information about the hotel's excellent restaurants.

Eating

Road Minibus: minibuses (C1) leave from **Kuta** for Uluwatu; connections with Denpasar's Tegal terminal.

Transport
20 km from Kuta

Nusa Dua

Nusa Dua is a 'planned resort', developed with assistance from the World Bank and funds from private developers. Building started in 1973 and the first hotels opened here in 1983. The barren landscape of the Bukit Peninsula has been transformed into a tropical haven: 5-star hotels, beautiful gardens, tennis courts, horse riding and a golf course. The intention was to build a resort which would be isolated from the 'real' Bali and, in so doing, protect the locals from the excesses of international tourism. To make way for the resort, the few farmers who scratched a living from the reluctant soil were unceremoniously turfed out and an enclave created.

Phone code: 0361
Colour map 1, grid B2

The entrance to the resort area is through huge split gates. There are no ugly high-rise blocks here, and none of the dirt and poverty associated with a Third World country. Overall the effect may seem rather sterile and some visitors will find the ambience rather boring. Being on the east side of the island you also miss out on the dramatic sunsets that are such a feature of many other resorts on Bali. Within the resort precinct, reached by roads running through the manicured lawns of the development, is the Galleria complex with travel agencies, airline offices, banks, a post office, restaurants, art shops, a supermarket, performing arts shows – in short, everything that a Western tourist could want. Or at least that is what the consultants thought. What Nusa Dua does not provide is any insight, indeed any sense, of what life in Bali is like. Tourists are sheltered and pampered, but if you wish for more, it is necessary to venture beyond the Bukit Peninsula to Bali proper or at the very least to **Buala** village just outside the entrance to Nusa Dua, a brief seven minutes' walk. It is a clean village with a range of small shops, the inevitable stalls selling tourist goods, banks, a *Wartel*, restaurants and a Tragia supermarket that is better value than the one in the Galleria complex in Nusa Dua. You might even encounter a temple festival taking place in the village.

On the beach, the surf is gentle along the northern part of the shore, but the waves become bigger to the south. Both areas are popular with surfers. If you are not staying at one of the hotels, the beach is easily accessed east of the Galleria complex or further south at the end of the strip of luxury hotels, with parking lots at both places. That said, if you are not a surfer, there is nothing especially attractive about this beach, except for its cleanliness and the relative absence of hawkers.

Sleeping

The hotels below provide a wide variety of sports facilities – waterskiing, windsurfing, scuba diving, fishing, parasailing, horse riding & tennis

L *Amanusa*, PO Box 33, T772333, F772335. Latest in the luxurious Aman group, set high above the Badung Straits, away from the concrete of Nusa Dua, with sea views only marred by the towers of the *Hilton*, 'epic' architecture, cathedral-like lobby perfumed by giant vases of tuber rose, accommodation in 35 Balinese style bungalows, 2 dozen roses to welcome guests, a/c, 4-poster bed, CD, satellite TV, mini-bar, sofa set into bay window, spacious dressing room, marble bathroom with sunken bath overlooking lotus pond, outdoor shower, sun-patio with canopied day bed, some suites with private pools, resort facilities including the largest swimming pool on Bali, state-of-the-art Italian restaurant, local cuisine at terrace restaurant, complimentary afternoon tea served in terrace bar, library, tennis, mountain bikes, buggy service to beach or golf course. Recommended.

L-AL *Nusa Dua Beach*, PO Box 1028, T771210, F771229. A/c, 4 restaurants, pool, now owned by the Sultan of Brunei, it recently underwent a US$20 mn plus refurbishment, the lavish entrance is through split gates into an echoing lobby with fountains, lush gardens and painstakingly recreated traditional Balinese buildings, good sports facilities, including a new spa centre, the new 'palace' extension is for the truly well-heeled.

L-AL *Sheraton Laguna*, PO Box 2044, T771327, F771326. Part of the Sheraton 'Luxury Collection'. One of the more luxurious hotels in Bali, voted in the 'Top 5 best resorts in Asia' by Conde Nast Traveller Magazine. The emphasis is on providing an intimate and relaxed atmosphere in surroundings of elegance and luxury, with personal service

Nusa Dua

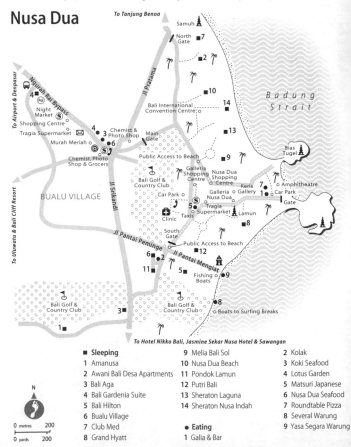

■ **Sleeping**
1 Amanusa
2 Awani Bali Desa Apartments
3 Bali Aga
4 Bali Gardenia Suite
5 Bali Hilton
6 Bualu Village
7 Club Med
8 Grand Hyatt
9 Melia Bali Sol
10 Nusa Dua Beach
11 Pondok Lamun
12 Putri Bali
13 Sheraton Laguna
14 Sheraton Nusa Indah

● **Eating**
1 Galia & Bar
2 Kolak
3 Koki Seafood
4 Lotus Garden
5 Matsuri Japanese
6 Nusa Dua Seafood
7 Roundtable Pizza
8 Several Warung
9 Yasa Segara Warung

N

0 metres 200
0 yards 200

including 24 hr butler service. 269 fine rooms and 18 sumptuous suites. The hotel has been totally refurbished with an outstanding spa and health club. Another feature is the 5 ha of swimmable freshwater lagoon with specially created beach, to which some of the rooms have their own private access; this is one of the largest pools in Bali. 3 bars and restaurants including 'fine dining' at the Mayang Sari which features Balinese and International dishes, and is surrounded by lagoons and waterfalls. Wheelchair access. Recommended.

AL *Awani Bali Desa Apartments*, on the northern edge of Nusa Dua at the boundary with Tanjung Benoa. T772688, F772678, awaniss@indosat.net.id 28 very attractively decorated 2 and 3 bedroom villas with living room, marble floored dining room, well equipped kitchen, 2 bathrooms, hall, a/c, satellite TV, IDD, verandah, maid room, daily maid service. Some 2-storey villas with upstairs sea views. Pool, tennis court, garage, no direct beach access but use of *Club Med* beach, 3 mins' walk. Free airport transfers. Rates negotiable, long-stay rates available, good value for this area. **AL** *Bali Hilton International*, T771102, F771616, information@balihilton.com or blihil@indosat.net.id 538 rooms some with great sea views. Designed to resemble a Balinese water palace with an imposing entrance and the grandest lobby in Bali, built in the Wantilan style. Set in 30 acres, the grounds feature lagoons, fountains, stone statues and carved reliefs relating to the Hindu epics. Each evening there is a cultural performance in the Balinese theatre with excellent buffet dinner. Live gamelan orchestra in the lobby. Special children's facilities including club and playground. Weider fitness centre with latest equipment and cardiovascular monitor, spa, and sauna. Daily programme of activities, sports tuition, covered tennis courts, squash, pool, full range of watersports, adjacent to 18 hole golf course. 6 restaurants and bars including Japanese, and pub with live music and dancing. Conference facilities for 700+600 people with full technical support, and business centre. 24 hr health clinic. Ayodya club offers 75 rooms and suites with upgraded facilities and private pool. Special rooms for disabled visitors. **AL** *Grand Hyatt*, PO Box 53, T771188, F771084. A/c, restaurant, 5 pools, opened April 1991, large and very plush, with extensive and elaborate grounds. **AL** *Hotel Nikko Royal Bali*, Jl Raya Nusa Dua Seletan, Nusa Dua Selatan, T773377, F773388, sales@nikkobali.com Dramatic location at the edge of a 40 ft cliff. 395 well designed rooms and suites although the public areas of this Japanese owned hotel have rather clinical décor. All rooms with balcony, a/c, mini bar, tea/coffee making facilities, safe deposit box, IDD etc. 4 restaurants and 4 bars, health club, 4 inter-connected pools with 30 m water slide, tennis, watersports, camel riding (contact Tel ext 210). 1 hr camel rides through tropical bushland and along the beach (adults US$33, children [12 and under] US$17), activities for children. **AL** *Jasmine Sekar Nusa Resort*, Jl Raya Nusa Dua Selatan. T773333, F775765, Jasmine@indosat.net.id One of the new boutique hotels, currently 53 bungalows with plans to expand to 161. Built in Balinese Kampung style, each attractively decorated room is situated in a very small, enclosed courtyard with seating, pond and fountain, but absolutely no views and rather claustrophobic. Rooms have a/c, HW, tea making facilities, minibar. Reasonably priced spa. The best feature of the hotel is its hilltop pool (one of 2 pools) and restaurant (mid-range), both with far-reaching views. 20 mins' walk to beach. Aimed at the tour group market, prices are very high for independent travellers. **AL** *Melia Bali Sol*, PO Box 1048, T771510, F771360. A/c, several restaurants (recommended), large and attractive pool, beautiful gardens, owned by a Spanish chain of hotels, a fact reflected in the design which is rather Mediterranean, good sports facilities. **AL** *Putri Bali*, PO Box 1, T771020, F771139. A/c, restaurant, pool, set in attractive landscaped grounds, all facilities, and some cottage-style accommodation. **AL** *Sheraton Nusa Indah*, PO Box 36, T771906, F771908. Excellent, recently refurbished family resort. A/c, set in 25 acres of tropical gardens beside the sea with lagoons, a small aviary, iguana park and mini zoo. 369 very attractively decorated rooms each with separate seating area and balcony, tea/coffee making facilities, modern a/c, etc, many rooms face the ocean. There are 12 family suites with adjoining rooms, 2 bathrooms, nanny's bed, fluffy toys and Nintendo games system. An additional 23 suites have separate eating and pantry facilities. The 4 restaurants serve excellent, reasonably priced food, and include a Japanese and a fish restaurant. 3 beach pavilions beside the sea for lazing or for a private sunset dinner. Large pool with hidden cove and waterfall; fitness centre with cardiovascular equipment, sauna and massage; a full range of watersports. The hotel provides an outstanding programme of activities for children, the best of any hotel on the island; called the 'Little Stars Club' it includes a computer lab, 15 play stations, a/c 'class rooms' for lessons in Balinese music, dance and art, a sleeping area, a supervised baby-sitting area for toddlers, swimming pool, playground and a mini-zoo. The aviary which is supervised by a vet, offers sanctuary to rescued birds. Wheelchair access. The largest conference centre on Bali, with capacity for 2500 in the main hall, plus an additional 8 halls, with state of the art equipment, multilingual business centre, banqueting facilities, and theme parties. Guests can use the facilities of the *Sheraton Laguna* next door. A security guard here, Ms Ni Made Wahyuni, is an international gold medallist in the martial art of Pencak Silat. This Indonesian form of self-defence is based on the movements of the tiger and the monkey and is studied by a growing group of devotees around the world. **AL** *Bali Aga*, 8 Jl Nusa Dua Selatan. T776688, F773636, baliaga@indo.net.id Another new boutique hotel with no outstanding features. Situated in a 3-storey block, 15 mins' walk from the beach. 62 rooms with a/c, safe, TV, IDD, tea making facilities, minibar. Two pools, spa, 2 restaurants, 24 hr coffee shop and room service. Only interested in the tour group market.

A *Club Med*, PO Box 7, T771246, F771831. A/c, on the boundary with Benoa. 2 restaurants, 3 pools, excellent sports facilities and cultural activities, and caters well for children. **A** *Hotel Bualu Village*, PO Box 6, T771310, F771313, htlbuala@indosat.net.id One of the cheaper hotels in Nusa Dua, smaller and more personal but not nearly as luxurious; neither is it on the beach (10 mins' walk or use the hotel shuttle bus which runs every 15-30 mins). A 2-storey building with 48 rooms, each with verandah or balcony, a/c, IDD, TV, minibar. Set in gardens, with 2 restaurants, bar, 2 pools, tennis, children's play area.

B *Lamun Guesthouse*, T771983, F771985. 24 fairly basic rooms in need of refurbishment, with a/c but only cold water. 12 mins' walk to beach. Restaurant and bar. Used as a training centre by the Hotel and Tourism Training Institute. Very friendly staff. Easily the cheapest place in Nusa Dua but you are not getting much for your money.

Eating All the hotels have a range of restaurants serving Indonesian, Balinese, other Asian cuisines and international food. The *Amanusa* has a first class Italian restaurant as well as local cuisine served in their terrace restaurant. Quality is generally good but prices are far higher than anywhere else in Bali – presumably because the management feel they have a captive clientele. *Galleria Nusa Dua Shopping Complex* houses some restaurants at varying prices.

Mid-range *Matsuri Japanese Restaurant*, Galleria Nusa Dua Shopping Complex, T772267. Serves fairly expensive but often disappointing Japanese food. Open 1130-2300. *Sheraton Nusa Indah* has an elegant and very reasonably priced restaurant, *The Capsicum Café*, which serves excellent meals. In Buala village there is a growing number of restaurants that cater for clientele from the *Nusa Dua* hotels which are more reasonably priced, and there are cheap but clean local eateries near the Tragia supermarket. On the public beach south of the hotels there are several cheaper warung selling fish dishes and the usual tourist fare (nasi goreng, sandwiches etc). Originally catering to Western surfers these have become increasingly popular with hotel guests. **Cheap** *Prahu Yasa Segala Warung*, at the end of Jl Pantai Mengiat (between the Putri Bali Hotel and the Hilton).

Bars *Players Bar*, *Nusa Dua Beach Hotel*, happy hours 1900-2100, games room; *Lila Cita*, Grand Hyatt, open 1800-0200, happy hours 1800-2000, good cocktails.

All the hotels have an outdoor theatre where nightly cultural performances take place, often in conjunction with dinner and for diners only. Some of the restaurants in the *Galleria Nusa Dua Shopping Complex* put on shows of Balinese dancing in the evening. A Barong procession wends its way through the shopping complex in the late afternoon during high season. **Entertainment**

Nusa Dua Annual Festival for one week spanning the end of Aug/beginning Sep. All events are free and open to hotel guests in the Nusa Dua area. The programme of mainly traditional Balinese cultural events includes a religious procession, demonstrations showing the preparations for traditional ceremonies and Balinese food, and exhibitions of art and handicrafts. Each evening performances of both traditional and modern Balinese dances and gamelan music take place at sunset in the Amphitheatre. Special children's progamme of events. **Festivals**

Clothes The *Galleria Nusa Dua Shopping Complex* is the largest shopping complex on Bali and has smart clothing boutiques, jewellers, a duty-free store and supermarket. Several international designers have shops in the complex including: Dolce and Gabana, Armani, Versace, and Benetton. One of the best clothes shops is *Animale*, a current favourite with Westerners, and its prices are very reasonable. There is a large **Batik Keris** department store which sells clothes and handicrafts. As can be expected, prices are higher than elsewhere on the island, but the quality is good. The complex also boasts the best sports and golf shop in Bali – golf sets available for rent (US$20). There is a free shuttle bus running between the major hotels and the shopping complex on a fixed schedule. There is also a bus that runs every 40 mins and costs 2,000Rp per person. **Shopping**

Diving *Bali Marine Sports*, Club Bualu, T771310; *Barrakuda Bali Dive*, *Bali Tropik Palace Hotel*, T772130, F772131; *Baruna Watersports* at the *Melia Bali Sol*, T771350, and Nusa Dua Beach, T771210. *Waterworld* at *Sheraton*, T777281, 774971, or visit their counter on the beach in front of the hotel. Prices are typically: US$298-375 for a PADI open water course, US$75 for an introductory dive at Nusa Dua, for certified divers US$65 at Nusa Dua Reef, US$125 for 2 dives at Nusa Penida, US$100 at Padangbai, Tulamben or Amed, US$125 at Menjangan Island. **Sports**

Watersports Most of the leading watersports companies are represented in Nusa Dua at the luxury hotels. Typical rates and sports on offer are: Jet ski US$20-35 for 15 mins, price depends on how powerful the machine is; snorkelling US$25 per hr (minimum 2 people); yacht cruises US$1,000-1,800 for 3-6 hrs; fishing US$80 for 4 hrs; windsurfing US$15-25 per hr for hire of board, instruction available from US$60 for 3 hrs; sailing US$20 per hr; banana boat/parasailing US$15 a ride; glass bottom boat US$20 a ride; waterski US$25 for 15 mins. You can get cheaper rates if you approach the company directly rather than go through your hotel.

Golf 18-hole *Bali Golf and Country Club* (opened 1991, designed by Nelson and Wright), T771791, F771797 for details. Tee-times from 0630-1600. Green fees, which include mandatory golf cart, US$142 for 18 holes, US$85 for 9 holes. Beautiful sea-side setting. Attractive clubhouse and pool.

Local Car hire: *Avis*, *Nusa Dua Beach Hotel*, T771220 ext 739, and *Club Med*, T771521. **Taxi**: taxis and hotel cars will take guests into Kuta and elsewhere; prices are high. **Transport** *27 km from Denpasar, 9 km from airport*

Road Bemo: from Jl Pantai in **Kuta** to Nusa Dua; and regular connections from **Denpasar's** Tegal terminal.

Places of worship Interdenominational church service at the *Nusa Dua Beach Hotel*, Sun 1730. Catholic Mass: Bali Sol, Sun 1800. **Directory**

Bali

North and east from Denpasar

Bali

Craft villages on the road from Denpasar to Ubud

After 22 km climbing steadily through picturesque paddy fields & past steep-sided ravines, the road arrives at the hill resort & artists' colony of Ubud

A number of craft villages, each specializing in a different craft, from production of wood and stone carvings to gold and silver jewellery, line the busy main road north from Denpasar to Ubud. The concentration of workshops here is extraordinary – much of the products are exported around the world. Most have been centres of production for many years – Miguel Covarrubias in his book *Island of Bali* notes that they had a reputation for the quality of their work in the 1930s. Since then the demands of the tourist industry have caused the mass production of second-rate pieces to become common. Nonetheless there are still some fine works to be found.

Batubulan
Phone code: 0361

This ribbon-like village, stretched out for about 2 km along the road is 8 km from Denpasar. It is renowned for its stone carving, although the production of carved wooden Balinese screens and doors is very much in evidence. In addition, there is a sizeable pottery industry here. **Barong**, **kecak** (fire dance) and **kris dances** are performed every day at the north end of the village. ■ *Times vary, 0900-1030, 1800-1930*. One of Bali's principal performing arts academies – *KOKAR/SMKI* – is based in Batubulan. Just outside Batubulan is the **Taman Burung Bali Bird Park**. ■ *T299352. 0900-1800*.

Celuk & Batuan
Phone code: 0361

Celuk, 4 km on from Batubulan and 12 km from Denpasar, supports large numbers of gold and silversmiths who sell their jewellery from countless shops and showrooms along the road. Much of the work is inferior, although there are some shops selling slightly better quality jewellery; for example, *Runa*, *Dede's*, Jl Grianyar 18 and *Banjar Telabah*. It is worth bargaining in these shops. Another 4 km north from Celuk is another woodcarving village, Batuan. A range of products are on sale although the artists have a particular reputation for the quality of their carved wood panels.

Mas
Phone code: 0361

Finally, Mas, 20 km from Denpasar and 2 km south of Ubud, is a woodcarving village. In the mid-1980s this was the centre of woodcarving in Bali; now the industry is far more dispersed. Nevertheless, some of the finest (unpainted) works are still produced here and it is possible to watch the artists at work. Although there are numerous wood carvers based here, the workshop of *Ida Bagus Tilem* – the *Tilem Gallery*, T975099, is recommended. His pieces are expensive, but Tilem's father was an accomplished artist, and his son's work is also highly regarded. The workshop of *Ketut Puja*, T975096, has also been recommended.

Kemenuh
Phone code: 0361

Kemenuh village, about 9 km southeast of Ubud, is another important wood carving centre offering a range of pieces including huge mythical beasts, fine art and the usual Balinese objects at more competitive prices than Mas.

Sleeping B *Sua Bali Lodge*, Kemenuh village (Sua Bali is signposted from the Gianyar road, 7 km east of Ubud), T/F32141. 6 cottages in large grounds with private facilities, run by Ida Ayu Agung Mas, who has studied in Germany and now teaches at Udayana University, Bali. Her aim is to create the natural atmosphere of Bali in her lodge. The lodge offers language tuition in both Balinese and Indonesian and is a unique opportunity to learn about the customs and culture of Bali. The founder set up the lodge with the aim of preserving the local environment and culture. To this end 70% of supplies come from the local village and funds have been given to the village for development and social projects. The lodge recently won first prize in a competition organized by the German Government to reward tourist enterprises worldwide that were socially and environmentally responsible.

Around Ubud

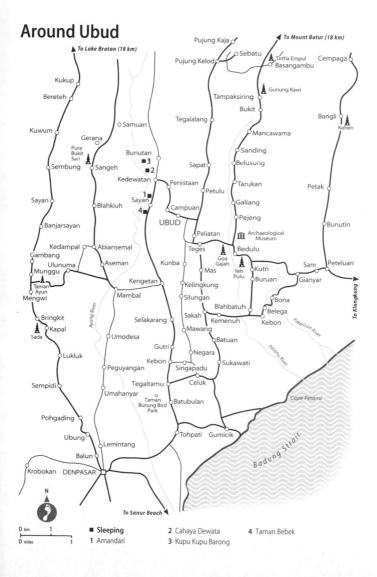

■ **Sleeping**
1 Amandari
2 Cahaya Dewata
3 Kupu Kupu Barong
4 Taman Bebek

Ubud

Phone code: 0361
Colour map 1, grid B2

During the rainy season Ubud gets much more rain than the coastal resorts & can be very wet & much cooler

Ubud is a rather dispersed community, spread over hills and valleys with deep forested ravines and terraced ricefields. A spring near Ubud is the source of AQUA, the most popular of Indonesia's bottled waters. For many tourists, Ubud has become the cultural heart of Bali, with its numerous artist's studios and galleries as well as a plentiful supply of shops selling clothes, jewellery and woodcarving. Unfortunately the town has succumbed to tourism in the last few years with a considerable amount of development, often of surprising ugliness, including a few concrete monstrosities, glitzy bars and restaurants draped in neon. Traffic congestion has also become a major problem. Increasing numbers of hotels, restaurants and shops are destroying the rural character of this once beautiful area as 'Ubud' spreads further and further into the surrounding countryside.

Ins and outs

Getting there Public bemos stop at the central market at the point where Jalan Wanasa Wana (Monkey Forest Road) meets Jl Raya, in the centre of Ubud. Peraman, T96316, which runs shuttle buses to the main tourist destinations, has a depot 15 mins walk away from the centre of town on Jl Handman. They are increasingly reluctant to pick up or drop off at travellers' accomodations. *Nomad* also runs shuttle buses from their office adjacent to *Nomad restaurant* to the main tourist destinations, T975520. Their service is not as comprehensive as *Perama's* but they tend to be cheaper. Public bemos run from Ubud to Batubalan for connections south to Kuta, Sanur etc; Gianyur for connections east to Padangbai and Candi Dasa and north to Singaraga and Louina and Kintaman. *Perama* and *Nomad* run regular shuttle buses to the airport. There is often a surcharge for departures before 0900.

Bina Wisata **tourist office** is on Jl Raya Ubud (opposite the Puri Saren), open 1000-2000. Good for information on daily performances and walks in the Ubud area but otherwise not very helpful.

History

Ubud was one of the more powerful of the principalities that controlled Bali before the Dutch extended their control over the whole island at the beginning of this century. Though primarily an upland rice-growing area it also gained an early reputation for the skill of its artists, particularly for the intricacy of their work. Perhaps it was the latent artistic temperament of the people of Ubud, coupled no doubt with the beauty of the place, that caused many of the entranced Western artists to base themselves here. The painter Walter Spies was invited to Bali by the Prince of Ubud, Raka Sukawati, and was so entranced with the place that he settled here – becoming the first of a series of bohemian Westerners to make Ubud their home (see page 233). These residents, in turn, attracted such luminaries as Charlie Chaplin, Noel Coward, the Woolworth heiress Barbara Hutton, and the American anthropologist Margaret Mead. In 1936, Spies, Bonnet (another artist) and the Prince established *Pita Maha*, the first artists' co-operative on the island. Since then Ubud has remained a centre of the arts in Bali, particularly painting, and many of the finest Balinese artists are based here or in the surrounding villages. Because of the influence of Spies, Bonnet and the artists' co-operative, there is a distinct style to much of the work. Paintings tend to be colourful and finely worked depictions of the natural world.

Sights

Much of the charm and beauty of Ubud lies in the natural landscape. There are few official 'sights' in the town itself – in contrast to the surrounding area (see 'Excursions' below). The **Museum Puri Lukisan** is in the centre of Ubud and has been recently renovated. Two of the buildings here contain examples of 20th century Balinese painting and carving (and that of Europeans who have lived here). The third building, to the back of the compound, has a changing exhibition, organized by an artists' co-operative. Fifty artists exhibit one or two pieces each; it is a showcase for their work. All work is for sale, but visitors are advised just to look at work here and then to visit the artist's studio, where they will be offered a wider range of work, at discounted prices. ■ *500Rp. 0800-1600. See entertainment below for more information.*

Antonio Blanco, a Western artist who settled in Ubud has turned his home into a gallery. The house is in a stunning position, perched on the side of a hill, but the collection is disappointing and includes an array of his 'erotic art', where the frames are more interesting than the actual pictures. Blanco – unlike Spies and Bonnet – has had no influence on the style of local artists. Most people visit his house to meet the man, rather than to see his work. He is an eccentric character who is interesting to talk to about Balinese life. He may try to interest you in his recently published autobiography. ■ *500Rp. To get there, walk west on the main road and over a ravine past Murnis Warung – the house is immediately on the left-hand side of the road at the end of the old suspension bridge.*

The **Museum Neka**, 1½ km from town, up the hill past Blanco's house, six Balinese-style buildings contain a good collection of traditional and contemporary Balinese and Javanese painting as well as work by foreign artists who have lived in or visited Bali. There is a good art bookshop here and a good restaurant with views over the ravine. ■ *1,000Rp. 0900-1700, Mon-Sun.*

At the south end of Jl Monkey Forest is the forest itself, which is overrun with monkeys. An attractive walk through the forest leads to the **Pura Dalem Agung Padangtegal**, a Temple of the Dead. ■ *Admission to forest 1,000Rp.* Back in town on Jalan Raya Ubud, opposite Jalan Monkey Forest, is the **Puri Saren**, with richly carved gateways and courtyards. West of here behind the Lotus Café is the **Pura Saraswati**, with a pretty rectangular pond in front of it.

Do NOT enter the forest with food – these monkeys have been known to bite. You will only have 48 hrs to get to Jakarta for a rabies injection

Excursions

There are villages beyond Ubud which remain unspoilt and it is worth exploring the surrounding countryside, either on foot or by bicycle. Around Ubud, particularly to the north in the vicinity of Tampaksiring, and to the east near Pejeng and Gianyar, is perhaps the greatest concentration of temples in Bali. The most detailed and accurate guide to these pura is AJ Bernet Kempers's *Monumental Bali* (Periplus: Berkeley and Singapore, 1991). **Sangeh** and the **Pura Bukit Sari** are two temples about 25 km west of Ubud, but easier to reach via Mengwi (see page 190).

Craft villages line the route to Batubulan & Denpasar (see page 128)

Goa Gajah or 'Elephant Cave', lies about 4 km east of Ubud, via Peliatan, on the right-hand side of the road and just before Bedulu. The caves are hard to miss as there is a large car park, with an imposing line of stallholders catering for the numerous coach trips. The complex is on the side of a hill overlooking the Petanu River, down a flight of steps.

Hewn out of the rock, the entrance to the cave has been carved to resemble the mouth of a demon and is surrounded by additional carvings of animals,

Goa Gajah
See plan next page

plants, rocks and monsters. The name of the complex is thought to have been given by the first visitors who mistakenly thought that the demon was an elephant. The small, dimly lit, 'T'-shaped cave is man-made. It is reached by a narrow passage whose entrance is the demon's mouth. It contains 15 niches carved out of the rock. Those on the main passageway are long enough to lead archaeologists to speculate that they were sleeping chambers. At the end of one of the arms of the 'T' is a 4-armed statue of Ganesh, and at the end of the other, a collection of lingams.

The **bathing pools** next to the caves are more interesting. These were only discovered in the mid-1950s by the Dutch archaeologist JC Krijgsman, who excavated the area in front of the cave on information provided by local people. He discovered stone steps and eventually uncovered two bathing pools (probably one for men and the other for women). Stone carvings of the legs of three figures were uncovered in each of the two pools. These seemed to have been cut from the rock at the same time that the pools were dug. It was realized that the heads and torsos of three buxom nymphs which had been placed in front of the cave entrance belonged with the legs, and the two halves were happily re-united. Water spouts from the urns held by the nymphs, into the two pools.

Stairs lead down from the cave and pool area to some meditation niches, with two small statues of the Buddha in an attitude of meditation. The remains of an enormous relief were also found in 1931 (by Conrad Spies, the painter and Walter Spies' cousin), depicting several stupas. To get there, walk down from the cave and bathing pools, through fields, and over a bridge. The complex is thought to date from the 11th century. ■ *1,050Rp (500Rp extra for camera), children 300Rp. Dress – sarong. Getting there: a short ride by bemo from Ubud or from the Batubulan terminal outside Denpasar; alternatively, join a tour.*

Yeh Pulu Yeh Pulu is 2 km east of Goa Gajah, beautifully set amongst terraced rice fields, and a short walk along a paved path from the end of the road. This is a peaceful place, free from crowds and hawkers. It also happens to be the location of the local bath house and launderette, which has resulted in a profusion of plastic 'Rinso' bags littering the stream. Yeh Pulu is one of the oldest holy places in Bali, dating from the 14th or 15th century. Cut into the rock are 20 m of vigorous carvings depicting village life intermingled with Hindu and Balinese gods: figures carrying poles, men on horseback, Krishna saluting, wild animals and vegetation. Originally these would have been plastered over – and perhaps painted – although almost all of the plaster has since weathered away. A small cell cut into the rock at the south end of the reliefs is thought to have been the abode of a hermit – who probably helped to

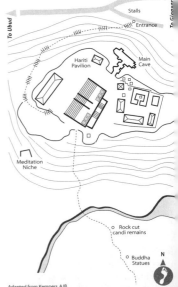

Goa Gajah

Stalls

To Ubud

To Gianyar

Entrance

Hariti Pavilion

Main Cave

Meditation Niche

Rock cut candi remains

Buddha Statues

N

Not to scale

Adapted from Kempers, AJB, *Monumental Bali*, Periplus, Singapore (1991)

maintain the carvings. The site was 'discovered' by the artist Nieuwenkamp in 1925 when he was sketching nearby. Until 1937 when the site was renovated, water from the overhanging paddy fields washed over the carvings causing significant erosion. There is also a small bathing pool here. An old lady looks after the small shrine to Ganesh and ensures a donation is placed there.

Bernet Kempers, in his book *Monumental Bali*, interprets the sequence of carvings as follows, beginning at the top. There is an opening piece, followed by five 'scenes':

Opening: a standing man with his arm raised opens the yarn. This is probably Krishna, who as a young shepherd protected his friends from an irate Indra by using Mount Govardhana as an umbrella.

Scene I: a man carries two vessels (probably of palm wine) on a pole over his shoulders and is led by a woman of high status towards a hut where an old woman waits at a pair of double doors.

Scene II: here, an old woman rests in a cave while a man, to her left, approaches with a hoe over his shoulder. Behind him sits an ascetic dwarf with a turban. On the far right is a demon with fangs and a large sacrificial ladle.

Scene III: surrounded by trees, a man on a horse gallops towards two figures, with weapons raised, who are attacking a bear (?) while a fourth man advances from behind. In the lower right corner a frog with a sword fights for his life against a large snake.

Scene IV: two men, their hunting trip completed and successful, carry a pair of dead bears on a pole.

Scene V: a woman holds a horse's tail while two monkeys play on her back. She is either trying to restrain the horse and rider, or they are helping to pull her up a hill.

■ *550Rp. Dress – sarong and sash (for hire at site). It is probably possible to visit this site at any time, as there are no 'entrance gates'. Getting there: Yeh Pulu is 350 m off the main Ubud-Gianyar road just south of the Tampaksiring turning, and is signposted to Bendung Bedaulu. Bemos from Ubud will drop passengers at the turning; it is an easy walk from there to the site.*

Sleeping and eating At the beginning of the path there is a restaurant, and close by is the **E** *Lantur Homestay*.

Gianyar Regency contains a number of important archaeological sites, the majority located near **Pejeng**, 4 km east of Ubud. This sacred area, inhabited since the Bronze age, contains over 40 temples as well as massive stone statues, carvings, sarcophagi, Buddhist sanctuaries, bathing sites and bronze artefacts. A number of artefacts have been removed to museums as far afield as Amsterdam, but many have remained *in situ*, beside rivers, in paddy fields or in nearby temples. Pejeng was once the centre of a great kingdom which flourished between the 9th and 14th centuries before falling to the Majapahit. These days it is home to many Brahmin families.

The road north from Bedulu

An important archaeological discovery was made in early 1999. A sarcophagus, estimated to be 2,000 years old dating from the megalithic period, was found buried in a garden. Measuring 130x102 cms with highly sophisticated mask carvings on its cover, the sarcophagus contained another egg-shaped coffin measuring 94x64 cms. This is the first double sarcophagus ever discovered in Indonesia. Inside the second coffin were the remains of an adult in the foetal position wearing items of jewellery suggesting an individual of some social standing in the community. The quality of carving of the images on the cover of the sarcophagus suggests a high level of artistic development on the island 2,000 years ago. This is perhaps a partial explanation for the high concentration of artisans still to be found in the Gianyar area.

The small, poorly labelled, **Purbakala Archaeological Museum**, consisting largely of a collection of sarcophagi, neolithic tools and Hindu relics, is 400 m north of Bedulu. About 200 m further north still is the **Pura Kebo Edan** or 'Mad Bull Temple', a rather ramshackle and ill-kept temple. Among the monumental weathered stone figures in the courtyard is a statue of Bima dancing on a corpse, its eyes open, protected under a wooden pavilion. The figure – sometimes known as the 'Pejeng Giant' – is renowned for its 'miraculous' penis, pierced with a peg or pin (used to stimulate women during intercourse, a feature of sexual relations across the region). Snakes curl around the figure's wrists and ankles, and his face is covered by a mask, attached with ribbons around the back of the head. Although the figure was thought to be an image of Bima – and it is in all likelihood demonic – it is probably more accurately interpreted as an incarnation of Siva. ■ *Admission by donation. Dress: sarong.*

Pura Pusering Jagat (the 'Navel of the World' Temple), is 50 m off the main road, a short distance north from Kebo Edan. **Pura Panataran Sasih** lies another 250 m north in Pejeng and is thought to date from the 9th or 10th century. This temple was the original navel pura of the old Pejeng Kingdom. The entrance is flanked by a pair of fine stone elephants. Walk through impressive split gates to see the '**Moon of Pejeng**' (*sasih* means 'moon'). It is housed in a raised pavilion towards the back of the compound and is supposedly the largest bronze kettle-drum in the world (see box page 144). In Balinese folklore, the drum is supposed to have been one of the wheels of the chariot that carries the moon across the night sky. The wheel fell to earth and was kept (still glowing with an inner fire) in the temple. It is said that one night a man climbed into the tower and urinated on the drum, extinguishing its inner fire, and paid for the desecration with his life. Visitors should on no account try to climb the tower for a better look at the drum. The drum is believed to date from the 3rd century BC, although no-one is absolutely sure – certainly, it has been housed here for centuries. It may be a Dongson drum from Vietnam or it may be a later example produced elsewhere. The fine decoration on this incomparable piece of bronze work was first recorded – in a series of brilliantly accurate drawings – by the artist WOJ Nieuwenkamp in 1906 (although it was mentioned in a book by the blind chronicler GE Rumphius published in 1705). A collection of 11th century stone carvings are also to be found here. ■ *Admission by donation. Dress – sarong. Getting there: by bemo from Ubud or from the Batubulan terminal outside Denpasar.*

Tours **Bird watching** walks around Ubud with *Bali Bird Walks* (possible sightings include Java Kingfisher, Bar-winged Prinia, Black-winged Starling, Java Sparrow, Scarlet-headed Flowerpecker), T975009, based at the Beggar's Bush pub, Tjampuhan, Ubud, US$30, including lunch and shared use of binoculars. Tours on Tuesday, Friday, Saturday and Sunday 0900.

Day tours around the island can be booked from Jl Raya Ubud. Good choice of tours including temples, sunsets and volcano. From 30,000Rp to 45,000Rp full day. Beware of bus drivers taking you to a pre-arranged place for lunch where the prices are high and the alternatives nil.

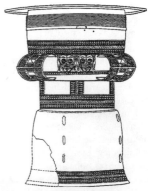

The Moon of Pejeng

Mountain biking downhill all the way back from Mount Batur (90,000Rp) and Jungle Mountain trekking (85,000Rp) both with *Sobek Expeditions* (see below). Some places down Jl Monkey Forest do tandems. Expect to pay between 5-10,000Rp per day.

Whitewater rafting down the Ayung River with *Sobek Expeditions*, T287059, F289448, for a 2 hour trip with time to swim in the pools under the waterfalls while the raft waits, buffet lunch included; this is a well-organized, professionally run outfit, US$70 per person. Also *Bali Adventure Tours*, T751292, see page 85. *Bali Widya*, T976309 full day with meals, insurance and showers US$65 and well recommended for a full day's entertainment. They also claim to go 'that bit further' than their competitors!

Essentials

Ubud has a wide choice of good value, clean and generally high quality accommodation in often romantic and well-designed bungalows. Except in the more expensive hotels, breakfast is included in the rates. Remember to book ahead in peak seasons.

Sleeping
See maps pages 129, 136 & 138

L *Amandari*, Kedewatan, 2 km northwest of town, T975333, F975335, amandari@ indosat.net.id Restaurant, pool, magnificently positioned, set alone above the Aynug River among paddyfields, excellent service (personal staff for each of the 29 bungalows), beautiful rooms with private garden each protected by high walls. The ultimate hotel if money is no object – one honeymooner called it 'heaven on earth'. Recommended. **L** *Kupu Kupu Barong*, Kedewatan, T975478, F975079. Northwest of town, restaurant, pool, lovely position overlooking the Agung River, superb service and rooms, no children under 12 years. **L-AL** *Pita Maha*, Jl Sanggingan, Campuhan, T974330, F974329, pitamaha@dps.mega.net.id The sophisticated sister of the *Hotel Tjampuhan* has 24 self-contained, traditional bales (villas), the architect is a member of the Ubud royal family and the quality of workmanship meets regal standards especially in stone masonry and woodcarving. Stunning views over the Oos River valley and to Mount Agung. All villas are the ultimate in luxury, very spacious with king-size beds, a/c, fan, minibar, satellite TV, CD, bathroom adjoining exotic garden, indoor and outdoor living areas, some rooms with private pools. Spectacular spring-water pool lapping over the edge of the ravine, open-air pavilion restaurant with ravine views, complimentary sarong and 'brem barong' drink – come here to be pampered. Recommended. **L-AL** *The Chedi Ubud*, Desa Melinggih Kelod, Payangan, Gianyar, T975963, F975968. A/c, restaurant, pool, health spa, library, new hotel with 65 rooms, quietly sophisticated, exquisite views, private garden and walkways, located north of Ubud village. **AL** *Kamandalu*, Jl Tegallalang, Banjar Nagi, 2 km from Ubud centre (complimentary shuttle service), T975825, F975851, kamandal@indo.net.id, www.kamandalu.com 58 luxurious, self-contained villas, built in traditional Balinese style, surrounded by ricefields overlooking the Petanu River valley, villas are complete with a/c, fan, fridge, satellite TV/in-house movies, CD player, 4-poster bed, deluxe bathroom with open-air Bale Benjong shower, top of the range villas have private pools and jacuzzi, the large main pool is free-form with a swim-up bar and paddling pool attached, herbal spa is one of the new additions to the hotel – couples can go together for Indonesian/new age massage, good new restaurant, *Petulu*, with top chef specializing in spicy Asian food as well as high class international cuisine. Recommended. **AL** *Waka di Ume*, Jl Sueta, Desa Sambahan, T96178, F96179. A few kilometres above Ubud set amongst rice paddies, recently completed, it is as its brochure says "a very different resort" designer primitive style – natural fabrics, copper, slate, bamboo 'alang-alang', bleached wood, and antiques artistically mixed with primitive farming tools. Spacious rooms, white muslin draped 4-poster, fan only, white bath robes, bamboo slippers, luxurious marble bathroom. Roof top restaurant serves genuine Balinese food, cascading swimming pool set amongst palms, stone statues and tropical flowers, overlooking the rural valley, meditation chapel with music/TV/library, sauna, steam baths, traditional massage, an oasis of tranquillity. Recommended.

A *Cahaya Dewata*, Kedewatan, in between the Amandari and Kupu Kupu Barong (out of town), T/F975495. Excellent restaurant, pool. Recommended. **A** *Champlung Sari*, Jl Monkey Forest 58. Smart hotel with 58 very comfortable rooms with TV, fridge and stone bathrooms. Despite its size service remains personal and friendly. Recommended. **A** *Dewi Sri*, Jl Hanoman, Padangtegal (near the intersection with Jl Monkey Forest), T975300, F975005. Pool, 2-storeyed thatched bungalows amid the ricefields, well-run. Recommended. **A** *Merpati Inn*, Jl Andong, T973083, F975862. This hotel is a little out of town. Very bright and clean, with a large pool, pricey. **A** *Padma Indah Cottages*, Campuan, T975719, F975091. A/c, restaurant, pool, cottages could sleep 4, attractive cottages but badly managed. **A** *Prada Guest House*,

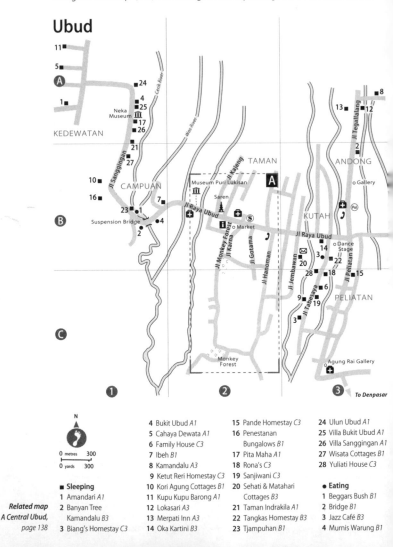

Ubud

Sleeping
1 Amandari *A1*
2 Banyan Tree Kamandalu *B3*
3 Biang's Homestay *C3*
4 Bukit Ubud *A1*
5 Cahaya Dewata *A1*
6 Family House *C3*
7 Ibeh *B1*
8 Kamandalu *A3*
9 Ketut Reri Homestay *C3*
10 Kori Agung Cottages *B1*
11 Kupu Kupu Barong *A1*
12 Lokasari *A3*
13 Merpati Inn *A3*
14 Oka Kartini *B3*
15 Pande Homestay *C3*
16 Penestanan Bungalows *B1*
17 Pita Maha *A1*
18 Rona's *C3*
19 Sanjiwani *C3*
20 Sehati & Matahari Cottages *B3*
21 Taman Indrakila *A1*
22 Tangkas Homestay *B3*
23 Tjampuhan *B1*
24 Ulun Ubud *A1*
25 Villa Bukit Ubud *A1*
26 Villa Sanggingan *A1*
27 Wisata Cottages *B1*
28 Yuliati House *C3*

Eating
1 Beggars Bush *B1*
2 Bridge *B1*
3 Jazz Café *B3*
4 Murnis Warung *B1*

Related map
A Central Ubud,
page 138

Jl Kajeng 1, T/F975122, pradaku@indola.net.id, www.angelfire.com/co/pradha/ Newly created guesthouse in traditional Balinese décor with Western influences, relaxed environment. Thoughtful touches add to the charm of the rooms, excellent service, well-priced. Highly recommended. **A** *Pringga Juwita*, off Jl Jawa Ubud, T/F975734. Small but secluded pool, fan, well designed bungalows set amongst flowing water gardens, rooms comfortable with obvious care taken, stone baths, breakfast extra. Recommended. **A** *Siti Bungalows*, Jl Kajeng 3, T975699, F975643. 8 sizeable rooms, with 4-poster beds, set around small lake, give this hotel a peaceful atmosphere, telephone, small pool. **A** *Taman Bebek Villas*, 2 km south of Amandari Hotel on Sayan-Ubud Rd, T/F975385. 8, 1- or 2-bedroomed bungalows, with sitting areas and kitchenettes, a family-style homestay set in a beautiful garden above the Ayung River. Recommended. **A** *Tjampuhan*, Jl Raya Campuhan, PO Box 198, Gianyar, T975368, F975137. At west end of Jl Raya Ubud, over the river and up the hill, this hotel was originally the artist Walter Spies' home, restaurant, small spring-fed pool, stunning setting on the side of a ravine, watery gardens (complete with frogs), bungalows built in layers up the ravine, romantic rooms with old wooden beds and pleasant sitting areas, plans afoot to revitalize its faded elegance, in the meantime the 'Raja' rooms are the best. **A** *Ubud Village Hotel*, Jl Monkey Forest, T975571, F975069. Lovely rooms set among beautiful gardens, large pool (open to non-residents), good restaurant. **A** *Ulun Ubud*, Sanggingan, T975762, F975524. Simple restaurant, pool, traditional Balinese style, attractive position on steep hillside facing the Campuan River, people work at the bottom of the gorge chipping out stones for carving, women carry the rocks on their heads up to the road. **A** *Villa Bukit Ubud*, by Neka Museum, Sanggingan, T975371, F975787. Restaurant with good views and good value food, good pool, pleasant a/c bungalows on edge of ravine, Balinese thatch roofs and surprising suburban comfort inside, a/c, hot water, good for families. Recommended. **A** *Villa Sanggingan*, just south of Neka Museum, Sanggingan, T974274, F974275. Lovely pool and breakfast room, good views, rooms away from the road are quieter.

A-B *Oka Kartini*, Jl Raya Ubud, T975193, F975759. Pool, small hotel with friendly staff, rooms are a little over-elaborate but thoughtfully designed, rooms with a/c in **A** price range, pleasant bar with marble tables and art gallery next door. Recommended.

B *Agung Cottages*, Jl Gautama 18, T975414. Separate bungalows set amidst beautiful gardens. Large rooms with front terraces. Recommended. **B** *Cendana Cottages*, Jl Monkey Forest, T973243. Large rooms overlook ricefields and give a feeling of space and tranquillity, open bathrooms with hot water, restaurant. **B** *Fibra Inn*, Jl Monkey Forest, T975451, F975125. Pool, good rooms and open-air bathrooms, hot water. Recommended. **B** *Grand Ubud Hotel*, Jl Monkey Forest, T974053, F975437. Lovely large rooms with good service, the pool is small. **B** *Gusti's Garden Bungalows*, Jl Monkey Forest, T973311. Good sized rooms with excellent views over fields and forest, hot water; pool in peaceful setting. **B** *Lokasari Guesthouse*, Jl Raya Andong, T/F975476. Slightly out of town on main road, good 2-storey family apartments with kitchen area and alfresco bathroom. Art gallery and café. **B** *Mumbul Inn*, T975995, F976478. Lovely views overlooking river. Peaceful and tastefully decorated rooms, with marble floors and baths, well priced. **B** *Nick's Pension*, off Jl Monkey Forest, this was once the popular place to stay in Ubud but has now gone to seed. Still in a fantastic position, hidden within the jungle, therefore peaceful and secluded. Overpriced and the rooms could do with redecoration. **B** *Pertiwi Bungalows*, Jl Monkey Forest, T975236, F975559. Restaurant, pool, lovely rooms, open-air bathroom. Recommended. **B** *Pringga Juwita Inn*, off Jl Raya Ubud and next to *Pringga Juwita Water Garden Cottages*, T/F975734. Bungalows in pleasant garden on edge of rice fields. **B** *Sehati*, Jl Jembawan 7, T975460. Lovely cool rooms overlooking a leafy ravine, bathrooms with hot water and Western toilet. Recommended. **B** *Sri Bungalows*, Jl Monkey Forest,

Central Ubud

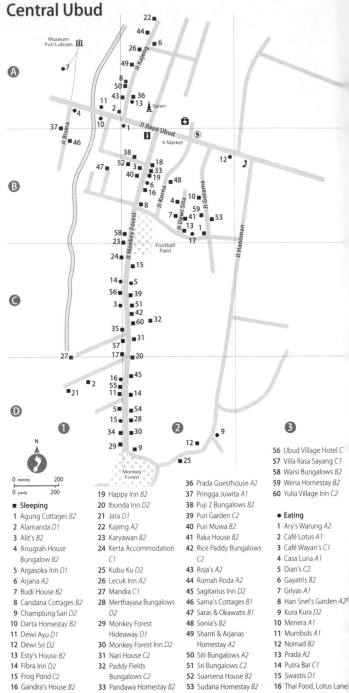

■ **Sleeping**

1 Agung Cottages *B2*
2 Alamanda *D1*
3 Alit's *B2*
4 Anugrah House Bungalow *B2*
5 Argasoka Inn *D1*
6 Arjana *A2*
7 Budi House *B2*
8 Candana Cottages *B2*
9 Champlung Sari *D2*
10 Darta Homestay *B2*
11 Dewi Ayu *D1*
12 Dewi Sri *D2*
13 Esty's House *B2*
14 Fibra Inn *D2*
15 Frog Pond *C2*
16 Gandra's House *B2*
17 Grand Ubud *C1*
18 Gusti's Garden Bungalows *B2*

19 Happy Inn *B2*
20 Ibunda Inn *D2*
21 Jata *D1*
22 Kajeng *A2*
23 Karyawan *B2*
24 Kerta Accommodation *C1*
25 Kubu Ku *D2*
26 Lecuk Inn *A2*
27 Mandia *C1*
28 Merthayasa Bungalows *D2*
29 Monkey Forest Hideaway *D1*
30 Monkey Forest Inn *D2*
31 Nari House *C2*
32 Paddy Fields Bungalows *C2*
33 Pandawa Homestay *B2*
34 Pande Permai Bungalows *D1*
35 Pertiwi Bungalows *C1*

36 Prada Guesthouse *A2*
37 Pringga Juwita *A1*
38 Puji 2 Bungalows *B2*
39 Puri Garden *C2*
40 Puri Muwa *B2*
41 Raka House *B2*
42 Rice Paddy Bungalows *C2*
43 Roja's *A2*
44 Rumah Roda *A2*
45 Sagitarius Inn *D2*
46 Sama's Cottages *B1*
47 Saras & Okawatis *B1*
48 Sonia's *B2*
49 Shanti & Arjanas Homestay *A2*
50 Siti Bungalows *A2*
51 Sri Bungalows *C2*
52 Suarsena House *B2*
53 Sudana Homestay *B2*
54 Ubud Inn Cottages *D2*
55 Ubud Terrace Bungalow *D1*

56 Ubud Village Hotel *C*
57 Villa Rasa Sayang *C1*
58 Warsi Bungalows *B2*
59 Wena Homestay *B2*
60 Yulia Village Inn *C2*

● **Eating**

1 Ary's Warung *A2*
2 Café Lotus *A1*
3 Café Wayan's *C1*
4 Casa Luna *A1*
5 Dian's *C2*
6 Gayatris *B2*
7 Griyas *A1*
8 Han Snel's Garden *A2*
9 Kura Kura *D2*
10 Menera *A1*
11 Mumbuls *A1*
12 Nomad *B2*
13 Prada *A2*
14 Putra Bar *C1*
15 Swastis *D1*
16 Thai Food, Lotus Lane & Mendras Café *D1*
17 Tutmak *B2*

T975394. Moderate sized rooms with hot water and pool, room walls a little grubby but overall a decent place to stay. **B** *Taman Indrakila* (was *Wisata Cottages*), Sanggigan, T/F975017, tikila@bali-paradise.com, www.bali-paradise.com/tamanindrakila Only 15 rooms in this idyllic 'hotel on the hill' with lovely views and an 'away from it all' setting. Well decorated rooms have their own balcony, some overlooking Mount Agung. Large sitting area around pool. Recommended. **B** *Ubud Inn Cottages*, Jl Monkey Forest, T975071, ubud_inn@indosat.net.id Well established cottages dotted around the large pool, variously priced rooms, simply furnished with low bamboo beds, some a/c; large family rooms with space to breathe. **B** *Villa Rasa Sayang*, Jl Monkey Forest, T975491. Large rooms overlooking pool (open to non-residents), peaceful atmosphere despite its central position. **B** *Yulia Village Inn*, Jl Monkey Forest, clean and well presented rooms, check for special prices, a little overpriced otherwise.

B *Villa Kerti Yasa*, Nyuh Kuning Village, T974377, F974377, reservations@villakertiyasa.com. Only 5 years old – small, friendly hotel in craft village of Nyuh kuning, around 5 min walk from the Monkey Forest and 10 min from Ubud itself. **B-C** *Artini*, hidden cottage, new, attractive rooms set amongst rice paddies off Jl Hanoman, same ownership as *Artini I* and *II*, bathrooms with hot water and Western toilet. **B-C** *Homestay Indraprastha*, 40 Jl Hanoman, T975549. Well-run minor homestay with clean rooms in beautiful, quiet garden bordering ricefields. Good service. Excellent breakfast included. Airport pick-up service available. **B-C** *Ibunda Inn*, Jl Monkey Forest, T97352. A travellers' Mecca. Basic clean rooms, good pool, popular with younger residents. **B-E** *Matahari Cottages*, Jl Jembawan, T975459. More expensive rooms are well-designed and secluded, some hot water. Recommended.

VILLA KERTI YASA

Nyuh Kuning Village
UBUD BALI

Hotel
Restaurant
Swimming Pool
& Spa

Balinese style in a traditional artisans' village – 5 minutes from the Monkey Forest Sanctuary

Tel/Fax: **(62-361) 974 377**

Email:
reservations@villakertiyasa.com
www.villakertiyasa.com

C *Argaosoka Inn*, Jl Monkey Forest, T973221. Large rooms overlooking the forest, each with ceiling fan and mosquito net. Outdoor breakfast room with fantastic views, laundry service, friendly management. **C** *Bali Breeze*, Jl Hanoman. Accommodation is in thatched cottages ('pondok'), the larger can sleep 6, with balcony and patio. Lovely garden and views over paddy fields. Attached cold water shower, free tea and coffee, room rate includes breakfast. Recommended. **C** *Bali Ubud Cottages*, T975058, F286971. This place comes recommended by recent guests. **C** *Gria Jungutan*, Jl Monkey Forest, T975752. Very peaceful setting overlooking the forest, hot water, laundry service. **C** *Kori Agung*, Penestanan-Campuan, T975166. A little out of town, off the main road, but lovely rooms with verandah, cold water showers only. Recommended. **C** *Kubu Ku*, Jl Monkey Forest, at the end of the road, set in the middle of paddy fields with lovely rooms. **C** *Lecuk Inn*, Jl Kajeng 15, T/F973445. Moderate rooms with balconies overlooking the river, outside bathrooms means showering with the mosquitoes and geckos. **C** *Mandia*, 30 m off Jl Monkey Forest, T870571. Lovely garden atmosphere. Recommended. **C** *Monkey Forest Hideaway I & II*, Jl Monkey Forest. All rooms overlook the forest and rice terraces; some rooms in Monkey Forest Hideaway II with views overlooking Mount Agung. Breakfast balcony provides a focus and feeding point for the forest monkeys in the early morning. Travel centre, car hire. Recommended. **C** *Nari House*, Jl Monkey Forest, T975070. Small, personal hostel offering clean attractive rooms, all with hot water and an excellent breakfast. **C** *Nuriani Guesthouse*, just off Jl Hanoman, T975346. 12 clean, attractive rooms, small garden, bathrooms with hot water and Western toilet, upstairs rooms have views of rice paddies. **C** *Nusa Indah*, well built bungalows. **C** *Penestanan Bungalows*, Campuan, T975604, F975603. Small pool, a little out of town, set scenically on a hill overlooking paddy fields, good rooms, hot water. **C** *Puri Garden*, Jl Monkey Forest, T975395. Lovely water garden, good rooms, fan. Recommended. **C** *Puri Indah*, attractive accommodation, one of the better places. **C** *Puri Muwa*, Jl Monkey Forest, T975046. Well-decorated rooms in this pleasant, family run hostel, price includes breakfast. **C** *Pondok Impian*, Jl Hanoman, comes recommended by several visitors, the wok has an excellent reputation. **C** *Rumah Roda*, Jl Kajeng 24, T975487. Clean rooms with hot water and friendly management. Excellent breakfasts. **C** *Shanti Homestay*, Jl Kajeng 5. Spacious but basic rooms, friendly management who are keen to relay information about the surrounding area. **C** *Siddhartha's Shelter*, Penestanan Kaja (Campuan), T975748. West of town, set among paddy fields. **C** *Sonia's House*, Jl Karna 7, T975535. Variously priced bungalows, each with private balcony or sitting area, giving the place an individual feel, watch out for some stinking mattresses but overall a good place to stay. Pool, some a/c. **C** *Warsi Bungalows*, Jl Monkey Forest, T/F975311. Located opposite playing field, small hostel with hot water, fan and a recommended breakfast. **C** *Wisata Cottages*, Campuan, near Neka Museum, T/F950177. Pool, lovely position with views over paddy fields.

C-D *Family House*, Banjar Tebesaya 39, T974054. Expanding homestay with new rooms, each with elegant 4-poster beds, breakfast included, hot water, a cut above the rest for the price. **C-D** *Ketut Reri Homestay*, Jl Tebasaya, T975591, small and friendly hostel with clean rooms, hot water, and tea and coffee all day. **C-D** *Rona's*, Jl Tebasaya 23, T973229. Short distance from town, poular, friendly family environment with lots of children around. Many guests there on long-stay basis – excellent rates negotiable, kitchen available, good grounds, restaurant and beauty parlour where you can have a petal bath and a massage. Recommended. **C-D** *Sama's Cottages*, Jl Birma, T973481. Clean comfortable rooms in a relaxed setting overlooking the rice fields, good value. **C-D** *Sanjiwari*, Jl Tebesaya 41, T/F973205, nithi@denpasar.wasantara.net.id Large, clean balcony rooms with cold water only, good views, kitchen available. **C-D** *Ubud Terrace Bungalows*, Jl Monkey Forest, T975690. Situated in a quiet grove, friendly management, attractive décor, private bathrooms with hot water and Western toilet, upstairs rooms have good sunset views.

D *Adinda Bungalows*, Jl Hanoman 64 (just off Hanoman in an alleyway). Attractive outlook over the ricefields to Mai bar, good beds, clean showers, balconies, tea all day long, giant breakfasts, bikes for rent, ticketing for bus journeys and shows arranged. Recommended. **D** *Agungs*, off Jl Raya Ubud (by *Nomad's restaurant*), friendly owner, but rooms are a little overpriced. **D** *Alamanda*, 50 m off Jl Monkey Forest, T980571. Peaceful setting with exceptionally helpful staff, there seem to be more helpers than residents. Rooms are spacious and cool, bathrooms very clean, use of kitchen and fridge, hot water. Recommended. **D** *Arganas*, Jl Kajeng. 8 rooms with alfresco mandi, clean but simple comfort, run by a friendly family, well priced. **D** *Baruna*, simple rooms, one of the cheaper places. **D** *Biang's Homestay*, Jl Tebsaya, T973207. 5 basic but cheap and clean rooms, small bathrooms, friendly staff that are keen to practise their English. Café specializing in vegetarian food. **D** *Darta Homestay*, Jl Godtama, T980571. 4 basic rooms that are nothing to write home about, but are cheap and functional, fan, price includes breakfast. **D** *Dewangga*, off Jl Monkey Forest (by the football field). Attractive setting, nice garden, good rooms, open-air bathroom, friendly staff, breakfast included. Recommended. **D** *Dewi Ayu*, Jl Monkey Forest, T976119. Large airy rooms set within a colourful, well kept garden, fan, hot water, cheap and efficient laundry service. **D** *Frog Pond*, Jl Monkey Forest, next to playing field. Basic but clean rooms with outside mandi, relaxed atmosphere makes this a good place to spend time in. **D** *Gandra's House*, Jl Monkey Forest, T976529. Set off road so quiet, decent colourful rooms with fan, some bathrooms with bath, breakfast (with brown bread), good value. **D** *Jata 3*, 25 m from Alamanda, T973249. Small but quiet rooms with mosquito nets, rural setting down a side road, hot water, breakfast. **D** *Kajeng*, Jl Kajeng 29, T975018. Rooms with verandahs overlooking a ravine and duck pond, clean with attractive open-air mandis. **D** *Karyawan*, Jl Monkey Forest. Lovely gardens, clean. Recommended. **D** *Lecuk Inn*, Jl Kajeng 15. Open-air mandi, including breakfast, friendly people, big rooms with a terrace, attractive setting by river and lovely gardens. **D** *Merthayasa Bungalows*, Jl Monkey Forest (bottom of), standard rooms with hot water provide a comfortable stay, 2 large family rooms good for groups on a budget. **D** *Monkey Forest Inn*, Jl Monkey Forest, good value clean rooms with fan, HW and breakfast, laundry. Recommended for travellers passing through. **D** *Mushroom Beach*, simple accommodation in excellent location. **D** *No 7*, attractive room, pretty garden. **D** *Paddy Fields*, off Jl Monkey Forest (opposite *Café Wayan*). Attractive position overlooking rice paddy, good breakfast, friendly owners. Recommended. **D** *Pramesti Cottages*, Jl Monkey Forest. 3 attractive 1- or 2-room cottages set in garden with pond, each room with balcony and small terrace, set back from the street in a rural setting – you hear the frogs at night – hot water and breakfast included. Recommended. **D** *Puri-Pusaka*, opposite Central Market, T975132. Good rooms with ensuite bathroom and Western toilets, price negotiable and it includes breakfast in the restaurant next door. **D** *Rice Paddy Bungalows*, convenient central location in Jl Monkey Forest, modern rooms, clean, upstairs rooms have views over rice paddies. **D** *Sagitarius Inn*, Jl Monkey Forest. Set back from the road so very peaceful yet still central, rooms are newly painted, large and good value. **D** *Sama's*, off Jl Raya Ubud (by *Miro's restaurant*), wonderful position among paddy fields, 3 rooms, clean, charming owner. Recommended. **D** *Shanti Homestay*, Jl Kajeng 5, new homestay, friendly. **D** *Sri*, Jl Monkey Forest, T975394. Very clean. Recommended. **D** *Wena Homestay*, Jl Godtama, T975416. Four good, homely rooms decorated with colourful local artwork and bathrooms lined with multi-coloured tiles. This hostel is a cut above the rest, breakfast included. Recommended.

D-E *Ibu Arsa*, Peliatan (east of town), older rooms are rather dark, the newer rooms are characterful with attractive open bathrooms, friendly. Recommended. **D-E** *Nyoman Astana's Bungalows*, Peliatan (next to *Siti Hotel*), attractive cosy rooms (the newer ones are more expensive) with attached bathrooms and hot water, beautiful quiet garden, price including a generous breakfast, excellent value for money. Recommended. **D-E** *Suarsena House*, Jl Arjuna, clean and central, more expensive rooms with large bathrooms.

E *Alit's*, Jl Monkey Forest, nice garden, clean rooms, friendly. **E** *Anom*, Jl Arjuna, central, only 3 rooms, but good. **E** *Anugrah House*, Jl Dewi Sita. Good, clean budget accommodation. Price includes breakfast. **E** *Arjana*, Jl Kajeng 6, T978233. Quiet, clean rooms, good bathrooms. Recommended. **E** *Budi*, Jl Dewi Sita, off Jl Monkey Forest, T973307. 4 rooms set above the road, therefore quiet with a feeling of isolation and space. Rooms are clean and large, recommended for the price. **E** *Esty's House*, Jl Dewi

Sita, T980571. 6 excellent rooms with fan in quiet area, bathrooms large and clean, breakfast included. Recommended. **E** *Kubu Roda*, off Jl Raya Ubud (by *Miro's restaurant*), 3 rooms, fan, friendly owners. **E** *Pandawa Homestay*, Jl Monkey Forest, good value, big rooms. **E** *Pande Homestay*, Peliatan (east of town), friendly, clean. **E** *Puji 2*, Gunung Arjuna (off Jl Monkey Forest), private bathroom – shower and Western toilet, mosquito nets, large breakfast included, comfortable and the cheapest around. **E** *Puri Muwa*, Jl Monkey Forest, T975046. Well-decorated rooms. **E** *Raka House* (off Jl Meluti – near the football field), 3 or 4 rooms. Recommended. **E** *Roja's*, Jl Kajeng 1, attractive bungalows, well kept garden. Recommended. **E** *Sara's*, off Jl Monkey Forest (next to *Okawati's restaurant*), mandi, verandah and large breakfast, good value. Recommended. **E** *Sudana Homestay*, Jl Gotama, T976435. 3 light, pleasant rooms with fan, family run and welcoming environment, good budget accommodation. **E** *Sukerti*, Jl Bima, Banjar Kalah (near intersection with Jl Raya Ubud), clean and very friendly. **E** *Wayan Family Homestay*, Jl Hanoman, only 5 rooms with en suite bathroom and hot shower and Western toilet, very clean, set in a pretty garden. Price includes breakfast, very friendly owners. Recommended. **E** *Yuliati House*, Jl Tebsaya, T974044. Well-presented, clean budget rooms. Hostel lays on Balinese dancing in the evening which is a good way to meet other travellers. Recommended.

Eating

Food in Ubud is good, particularly international food. Most restaurants serve a mixture of Balinese, Indonesian & international dishes

Expensive *Saffron*, *Banyan Tree*, Kamandalu, good quality spicy Asian food, interesting menu. Recommended. *Café Lotus*, Jl Raya Ubud, overlooks Puri Saraswati Palace, international (particularly Italian), pleasant situation and good atmosphere but somewhat tarnished by the draining of the famous lotus ponds (closed Mon). *Café Wayan*, Jl Monkey Forest, international, some seafood, very popular, delicious desserts (if you can fit them in), Balinese buffet on Sun evenings, particularly recommended are the traditional Balinese ceremonial dishes for two to share (order 24 hrs in advance), tables arranged in a series of outdoor kiosks.

Mid-range *Han Snel's Garden Restaurant*, Jl Kajeng, north of Jl Raya Ubud, very attractive setting and charming owners, generous, though pricey, servings (closed Sun). Recommended. *Thai restaurant*, Jl Monkey Forest, T977484. Recently opened, good food and ambience. Young Indonesian owner, Thai food cooked by a Thai chef. Excellent service and presentation. *Tjampuhan Hotel restaurant*, west end of Jl Raya Ubud, Indonesian and international, pleasant ravine-side setting. *Bridge Café*, near Antonio Blanco's House, positioned under suspension bridge offering good views, buffet at lunchtimes, large portions and excellent service. *Ryoshi Ubud*, Jl Raya Ubud, T976362. Popular Japanese restaurant serving a varied selection of favourites: sushi, sashimi, noodles, tempura, yakitori, teriyaki, donburi and bento. Open 1100-2400.

Cheap *Ary's Warung*, Jl Raya Ubud (opposite the temple complex), international and Indonesian food served in relaxed, occasionally bohemian atmosphere, with musical accompaniment, frequented by the Ubud cognoscenti, recommended for food but rather close to the main street. *Pradha Restaurant*, Jl Kajeng 1. Stylish Balinese décor in this small, intimate restaurant with good food and service. Off the main tourist route. *Bumbu*, Suweta No 1, pleasant terrace off the main drag, good value food, excellent presentation, friendly service. Recommended. *Café Bali*, Jl Monkey Forest (bottom end of football field), international, attractive setting Recommended. *Café Rona*, 23 Tebasaya, good tomato soup! *Casa Luna*, Jl Raya Ubud, opposite Museum Puri Lukisan, good range of International dishes, recommended (but small portions). *Dian's*, Jl Monkey Forest, well-cooked range of dishes, pleasant place for a drink. *Gayatri's*, Jl Monkey Forest, inexpensive and good for children. Recommended. *Ibu Rai*, Jl Monkey Forest (next to the football field), Balinese and international. Recommended. *Jaya Restaurant*, Jl Monkey Forest, good reasonably priced Indonesian and Western food. *Monkey Café*, Jl Monkey Forest, T96246. Small 2-storey café looking out onto paddy fields. Vegetarian menu with Indonesian and Western dishes, including Balinese Nasi Campur and Rijstaffel (excellent value). Simple, clean, cheap, carefully prepared food. Highly recommended. *Mumbul's Garden Terrace*, Jl Raya Ubud (close to the *Puri Lukisan Art Museum*), T975364. For excellent salads, international and Balinese food, timing for serving dishes erratic. Recommended. *Nomad*, Jl Raya Ubud, T975131. International and Balinese including Balinese duck and suckling pig, good guacamole. *Nuriani Restaurant*, Jl Hanoman, T975558. Excellent reasonably priced Indonesian and Western food with pretty views over the paddy fields especially at sunset. Recommended. *Pondok Tjampuhan*, next to *Blanco's House*, pizza, Indonesian, Chinese, good position overlooking ravine. *Ubud Raya*, Jl Raya Ubud (east end), Javanese, Japanese and international. Recommended. *Bagus Café*, Jl Raya Ubud, Peliatan (southeast of the centre), Balinese specialities. *Griya's*, Jl Raya Ubud, barbecued chicken is recommended, but poor service. *Kura Kura*, Jl Monkey Forest (at the end, near Jl Padangtegal), Mexican. *Lilies*, Jl Monkey Forest. Recommended. *Miro's*, in garden set above Jl Raya Ubud, generous helpings and beautiful presentation, good food at very reasonable price, candle-lit at night, very atmospheric. Recommended. *Murni's Warung*, overlooking ravine at west end of Jl Raya Ubud, at the Ubud end of the old suspension bridge, Indonesian and international (mostly American), an old-time favourite, good service, mixed reports some people think this is the best place to eat in Ubud, others find their food is nothing special (closed Wed). *Travellers' Café*, 16 Jl Hanoman, T977165. More than just another restaurant; a place where you can leave your pack whilst finding accommodation. Good 'travellers' book for latest tips from other travellers. International newspapers available. The manager, Mr Nyoman Wardana is a good source of in-depth information about Balinese culture and current events. *Yudit Restaurant and Bakery*, Jl Monkey Forest, pizzas and good bread. Recommended. *Jazz Café*, Jl Sukma 2 Tebesaya. T976594. Good live music Tue and Fri. Good food and coffee. Run by Nina from England. Recommended.

Very cheap *Mai Bar*, Jl Hanoman 60, big restaurant with a beautiful garden near the paddy fields, artwork on the walls, decorative ceramics to eat off, music and fashion-shows, even the waitresses are decorative, rice dishes, soups and coffee. Recommended. *Metri's*, Jl Hanoman, excellent bakery with brown bread and cakes and good food, very friendly owner. Recommended. *Tutmak Restaurant*, Jl Dewi Sita, small, friendly and inexpensive with good service and excellent food, large portions guaranteed, popular with travellers.

Bars

Putra Bar, Jl Monkey Forest, well priced food (cheap to mid-range) and drink. Attracts travellers, great for evening entertainment such as live Reggae music or films on wide screen. *Jazz Café*, Jl Tebesaya, atmospheric surroundings make this a relaxed place for a drink or meal (cheap), with enticing menu and children's menu. Live music.

Beggar's Bush, near *Hotel Tjampuhan*, west of town on Jl Raya Ubud, English pub (some food). *Salzbar*, Jl Monkey Forest, live music on Tue and Thu. *Nomad*, Jl Raya Ubud, open late.

Entertainment

Artists' colonies Ubud has perhaps the greatest concentration of artists in Indonesia, exceeding even Yogya. Many will allow visitors to watch them at work in the hope that they will then buy their work. The *Pengosekan Community of Artists* is on Jl Bima.

Dance There are numerous performances every day of the week; most begin at between 1900 and 2000 and cost 5,000Rp. A board at the *Bina Wisata Tourist Centre*, Jl Raya Ubud (opposite the palace), lists the various dances, with time (most performances start at 1930 or 2000), location and cost (almost entirely 7,000Rp). There are

Bronze kettledrums of Vietnam

One of the most remarkable and intriguing of metal objects found in Southeast Asia is the bronze kettledrum. These were first produced in Northern Vietnam and Southern China in the 4th century BC and were associated with the Dongson culture. However, they have also been discovered widely distributed across island Southeast Asia – as far east as the island of Alor in Nusa Tenggara and Irian Jaya. In total, around 30 kettledrums have been found in Indonesia. Some of the examples were probably traded from Vietnam; others may have been made in situ. Whatever the case, they are skilfully produced using the lost wax process, wonderfully decorated, and were clearly objects of considerable value and prestige.

Strictly speaking they are not drums at all but percussion instruments, as they have no membrane. In Indonesia they are known as nekara. They consist of a hollow body, open at the bottom, and covered at the top with a metal tympan. In size, they range from 0.4-1.3 m in diameter, and 0.4-1.0 m in height. The top is often highly decorated with birds, houses, canoes carrying the dead to the afterlife, dancers and drummers. A question which has never been satisfactorily answered is what they were used for. The fact that they are often surmounted by three-dimensional figures of frogs has led some authorities to postulate that they were used to summon rain. Hence their other name: rain drums. Helmet Loofs-Wissowa believes that they were royal regalia – used by chiefs as an indicator of rank and status. Recently a drum was unearthed in East Java with the crouched skeleton of a child inside leading some to suggest that this was a royal burial and the drum was included as an indicator of rank. There is a fine collection of drums in the National Museum, Jakarta.

almost nightly performances at the *Puri Saren* at the junction of Jl Raya Ubud and Jl Monkey Forest. Performances including legong, Mahabharata, barong, kecak, Ramayana ballet and wayang kulit (7,000Rp). At the Museum Puri Lukisan, there is a children-oriented troupe who perform gamelan and barong dances every Sun at 1030. Admission: 2,000Rp for museum entrance plus a donation.

Massage *Mentari Massage Service Centre*, No 1 Anoman St, T97400. Professional massage, not a 'beach-rub', very popular, book in advance. *The Bodywork Centre*, Jl Hanoman 25, Padangtegal. T975720. This place offers everything from massage and milk bath to hair cuts and pedicures.

Videos There is a very popular *Video Bar* on the far side of the football field on Jl Monkey Forest. Two shows a night of Western films. Laser disc videos at *Menara Restaurant*, Jl Raya Ubud. Laser disc at *Putra Bar*, Jl Monkey Forest.

Shopping
Ubud offers a good range of crafts for sale

Batik & ikat *Ibu Rai* travel agent near Lilies restaurant on Jl Monkey Forest. *Kunang Kunang*, Jl Raya Ubud. *Lotus Studio*, Jl Raya Ubud. *Binal Art Studio*, Jl Tebesaya 48, lovely batiks made on site and to order.

Books *Ubud Bookshop*, Jl Raya Ubud (next to *Ary's Warung*) for a good range of English language books on the region; *Ubud Music*, Jl Raya Ubud, selection of English language books and local music; *Ganesha Bookshop*, Jl Raya Ubud, near Post Office. Owned and operated by a well-known writer/actor/musician, Ketut Yuliarsa and his wife, Anita, the Ganesha Bookshop houses a vast collection of second-hand books including some antiquarian editions on Bali and Indonesia, in addition to its extensive collection of new books on Indonesian topics. Also CDs and tapes of Indonesian ethnic music and a collection of local instruments including gongs, cymbals, flutes and gamelan which sometimes gives rise to a spontaneous Balinese 'jam' session. T976339,

ganesha@bali-paradise.com, www.bali-paradise.com/ganesha *Book Exchange*, 3
Jl Monkey Forest, 1 on Jl Gotama.

Clothing *Bali Rosa*, on Jl Raya Ubud, towards Campuan, for accessories (bags, belts,
beaded pumps). Recommended. *Balika*, Jl Monkey Forest for fashion clothing.
Hare Om, Jl Monkey Forest for well-designed but expensive hand-painted silk scarves
and shirts. *Lotus Studio* for unusual designs and great hats; the market on the corner
of Jl Raya Ubud and Jl Monkey Forest offers a range of 'travellers' clothes – t-shirts,
batik etc. *Mutiara Art Company*, Jl Raya Ubud, good value batik shirts, mostly rayon
but some cotton too, interesting designs. Recommended.

Jewellery There are a number of shops along Jl Raya Ubud. Good designs but the
quality is not always very high – it looks better than it feels.

Dongson drum

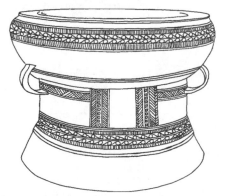

Dongson drum & mantle, bronze (79cm in width, 63cm high).
Unearthed, Northern Vietnam 1893-94.

Paintings Ubud painters have a distinctive style, using bright colours and the depiction of natural and village scenes (see page 234). There is a large selection of paintings to be found in the town and galleries are concentrated along the east section of Jl Raya Ubud. It is possible to visit the artists in their homes; enquire at the galleries.

Pottery Near the post office, just off Jl Raya Ubud.

Shoes *Bali Rosa*, Jl Raya Ubud, for 'pumps'. *Hare Om* for a range of individually designed suede shoes. For hand-made shoes, there is a place on Jl Mejuti, down the hill on the left. They also repair shoes here.

Wind chimes Shop specializing in wind chimes at the end of Jl Monkey Forest in the paddy fields – worth a visit.

Woodcarving Concentrated on the Peliatan road out of town. The so-called 'duck man' of Ubud (Ngurah Umum) is to be found on the road to Goa Gajah, with a selection of wooden fruits and birds. Recommended shop near the *Bamboo restaurant*, off Jl Monkey Forest, facing the football field.

Sports **Mountain biking** See 'Tours', page 135.

Swimming Some hotel pools are open to non-residents, prices for a full day range between 5,000-20,000Rp. *Ubud Village*, Jl Monkey Forest, 20,000Rp (for the day; you can come and go as you like), *Gusti Garden* 10,000Rp; *Pande Permai* 10,000Rp; *Ubud Terrace Bungalows*, large pool, 5,000Rp; *Visa Rasa Sayong* 5,000Rp; *Puri Saraswati Bungalows* 10,000Rp. Also try the *Andong Inn*, Jl Andong 26A; *Champlong Sari Hotel*, and *Okawatis Restaurant*, Jl Monkey Forest.

Whitewater rafting See 'Tours', page 135.

Tour operators Double check airline tickets bought here; there have been complaints that despite assurances that flights are confirmed, on reaching the airport, visitors have found they are not. *Cahaya Sakti Utama*, Jl Raya Ubud, T975131, F975115; *Ibu Rai*, Jl Monkey Forest 72, T975066, recommended; *Kurnia*, Jl Raya Ubud, T975020 for buses to Lombok and around Bali, tours and car rental; *Nominasi*, Jl Monkey Forest 67-71, T975065.

Bird watching US$30 including lunch. Tours on Tue, Fri, Sat and Sun 0900. Day tours around the island: book from Jl Raya Ubud, good choice of tours including temples, sunsets, volcano. From 30,000Rp to 45,000Rp full day. Beware of drivers taking you to a pre-arranged place for lunch where prices are high and the alternative nil.

Transport **Local Bicycle hire**: bicycles are the best way to get about (apart from walking); there are several hire places on Jl Monkey Forest, 3,000Rp per day. **Car hire**: hire shops on Jl Monkey Forest, 80,000Rp per day plus insurance for Suzuki 'jeep'; 100,000Rp per day for larger Toyota Kijang. **Motorbike hire**: several outfits on Jl Monkey Forest, from 30,000Rp per day.

Road Bemos: leave from the Pasar Ubud in the centre of town, at the junction of Jl Monkey Forest and Jl Raya Ubud; regular connections with **Denpasar's** Batubulan terminal (1,000Rp), airport (4,000Rp). **Bus**: there are 'shuttle' (in fact not as regular as the name implies) buses to **Kuta**, the **Ngurah Rai Airport** (10,000Rp), **Candi Dasa**, **Padangbai**, **Sanur**, **Denpasar**. Details are available at the travel or tour agents. Perama cut back their bus service in the wake of the economic crisis and currently run 11 buses a day to the airport, Kuta and Sanur; 7 buses a day to Ubud, 3 buses a day to

Lovina; 3 buses a day to Padangbai, Candi Dasa, 1 a day to **Tirtagangga**, **Tulamben** and **Yeh Sanih** and 2 buses a day to **Mataram** and **Senggigi**. Fares are 7,500Rp to the airport, 20,000Rp to Lovina, 15,000Rp to Padangbai and Candi Dasa, 35,000Rp to Mataram and Senggigi. Perama operates to the main tourist destinations on Bali and Lombok. They have an office on Jl Hanoman, T973316. **Taxi**: taxis congregate at the Pasar Ubud in the centre of town.

Perama has an office near the boat landing.

Banks Numerous money changers will change cash and TCs and offer rates similar to banks. **Directory**
Communications Perumtel (for fax, telex and international telephone): Jl Andong (close to intersection with Jl Raya Ubud) and Jl Raya Ubud (near *Nomad Bar and restaurant*), or on the road to Petulu, at the east end of Jl Raya Ubud. **Postal agents**: *Nominasi*, Jl Monkey Forest 67 and Jl Raya Ubud. **NB** they sometimes charge very high 'service charges'. **Post Office**: Jl Jembawan 1 (road running south off Jl Raya Ubud, opposite Neka Gallery); poste restante. **Useful addresses** Medical: Ubud Clinic, Jl Raya Campuhan (near Beggar's Bush), T974911, F975298, ubudclinic@usa.net.id, 24 hr medical service and dentist. **Police**: on the road to Petulu, east end of Jl Raya Ubud.

North of Ubud

Four kilometres east of Ubud is the small town of Bedulu, close to which are the sights of Goa Gajah and Yeh Pulu (see page 131). Ten kilometres north of Bedulu, on the road to Lake Batur, shortly after the village of Tampaksiring off the main road on the right hand side, are two popular tourist destinations: the temples of Mount Kawi and Tirta Empul. By continuing north from here, the road runs up a steep-sided valley to Mount Batur and the town of Penelokan.

Gunung Kawi

Gunung Kawi, literally the 'Mountain of the Poets', is one of the most impressive, and unusual, temples in Bali. A steep rock stairway, with high sides leads down to the bottom of a humid, tree-filled, ravine. At the bottom lies the temple. The whole complex was literally hewn out of the rock during the 11th century, when it was thought to have been created as the burial temple for King Anak Wungsu and his wives, who probably threw themselves on his funeral pyre.

The site You descend 315 steps to a massive rock archway, and from there to the nine tombs which face each other on either side of the Pakerisan River. These two rows of candis, four on the south side and five on the north, were cut out of the rock. It is believed that the five on the north bank of the river were for the King and his four wives, whilst the four on the south bank may have been for four concubines. They resemble temples and are the earliest

Gunung Kawi

Queen's Tombs

Entrance

Royal Tombs

Pura

Main Cloister

Pakerisan River

Second Cloister

Tenth Cloister

Third Cloister

Not to scale

Adapted from Kempers, AJB, *Monumental Bali*, Periplus, Singapore (1991)

Bali

traces of a style of architecture which became popular in Java in the following centuries. As such they may represent the precursor to the Balinese *meru* (see page 191). Balinese mythology maintains that Empu Kuturan, a royal prince, carved these shrines with his fingernails. Over the years there has been disagreement over the function of the candis. The art historian C Lekkerkerker in 1920 postulated that the corpses were left in the cells to be eaten by wild animals, picked-over by birds, and to putrefy and degenerate. Rather later, Bernet Kempers argued that they were not tombs at all, but merely symbols of death.

East of the five candis on the far side of the river is a cloister of various courtyards and rooms, also carved out of the rock. They were created for the Buddhist priests who lived here (perhaps reflecting its Buddhist origins, visitors are asked to remove their shoes before entering). Still farther away, on the other side of the river, is the so-called 'tenth tomb'. The local people call this tomb 'the priest's house' and it was not discovered by Western archaeology until 1949 when Krijgsman revealed the site. The tenth tomb is, in all likelihood, a monastery and consists of a courtyard encircled by niches. To get to the tenth tomb take the path across the paddy fields that runs from the rock-hewn gateway that leads down into the gorge; it is about a 1 km walk. ■ *1,000Rp. Dress – sash or sarong required.*

Sleeping There is accommodation close by in Tampaksiring eg *Gusti Homestay*. Tampaksiring also has a number of good jewellery workshops.

Transport **Road Bemo**: connections with **Denpasar's** Batubulan terminal or from Ubud to Tampaksiring. It is about a 3 km walk from here, passing Tirta Empul (see below), although bemos also make the journey to the temple site.

North & east Bali

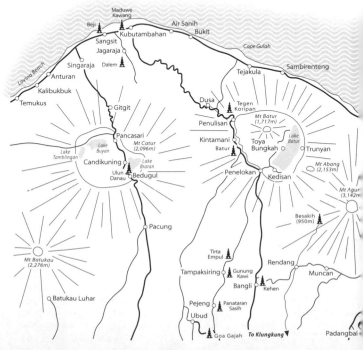

Tirta Empul

Tirta Empul is 2 km north of Tampaksiring, 1 km on from Mount Kawi. The temple is one of the holiest sights on Bali and is a popular pilgrimage stop, evident by the maze of trinket stalls that has to be negotiated on the way out of the complex.

Tirta Empul is built on the site of a holy spring which is said to have magical healing powers. In the past, barong masks were bathed here to infuse them with supernatural powers during the dance. Originally constructed in 960, during the reign of Raja Candra Bayasingha, the temple is divided into three courtyards, and has been extensively restored with little of the original structure remaining – bar a few stone fragments. The outer courtyard contains two long pools fed by 30 or more water spouts, each of which has a particular function – for example, there is one for spiritual purification. The holy springs bubble up in the inner courtyard. During the *Galungan Festival*, sacred *barong* dance masks are brought here to be bathed in holy water. ■ *1,050Rp (500Rp extra for a camera).*

Road Bemo: take a bemo from **Denpasar's** Batubulan terminal or Ubud towards **Transport** Tampaksiring. The temple is 2 km north of the town centre; either walk or catch a bemo. From here it is a 1 km walk to Mount Kawi (see above).

Gianyar to Mount Batur via Bangli

East of Ubud is the royal town of Gianyar, which has little of interest to attract the tourist. Fifteen kilometres north of Gianyar, at the foot of Mount Batur, is another former royal capital, Bangli, with its impressive Kehen Temple. A further 20 km leads up the slopes of Mount Batur to the crater's edge – one of the most popular excursions in Bali. Along the rim of the caldera are the mountain towns of Penelokan and Kintamani, and the important temples of Batur and Tegen Koripan. From Penelokan, a road winds down into the caldera and along the west edge of Lake Batur. It is possible to trek from here up the active cone of Mount Batur (1,710 m), which thrusts up through a barren landscape of lava flows. North from Penulisan, the road twists and turns for 36 km down the north slopes of the volcano, reaching the narrow coastal strip at the town of Kubutambahan.

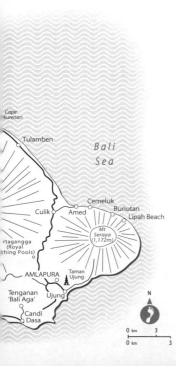

Gianyar

Gianyar is the former capital of the kingdom of Gianyar. During the conquest of Bali, this principality sided with the Dutch and so escaped the massacres that accompanied the defeat of Denpasar, Klungkung and

Phone code: 0361
Colour map 1, grid B2

Pemetjutan. In the centre of Gianyar, on Jl Ngurah Rai, is the **Agung Gianyar Palace**, surrounded by attractive red brick walls. This is the best example of a traditional Balinese Puri to be found on Bali and continues to be used by the royal family in much the same way as it always has been. Features include courtyards and pavilions with Dutch, Indian and Portuguese influences. The building of palaces on Bali reflected the esteem in which the royal families of Bali were held by the Hindu population of the island. The building of grand palaces was at its zenith between the 16th-19th centuries but ended with the arrival of the Dutch. At the turn of the century, the Regency of Gianyar formed an alliance with the Dutch in order to protect itself from its warring neighbours. As a result, the royal palace was spared the ravages and destruction, culminating in *puputan*, that befell other royal palaces in South Bali during the Dutch invasion. The rulers of Gianyar were allowed a far greater degree of autonomy than other rajas; this allowed them to consolidate their wealth and importance resulting in the regency's current prosperity and the preservation of the royal palace. It is not normally open to the public, but the owner, Ide Anak Agung Gede Agung, a former politician and the rajah of Gianyar, does let visitors look around his house if you ask him. The bemo station is 5 mins' walk to the west of the palace, also on Jl Ngurah Rai. Traditionally regarded as Bali's weaving centre, there is only a limited amount of cloth on sale these days. Gianyar's other claim to fame is that it is said to have the best *babi guling* (roast suckling pig) on the island. Gianyar **tourist office** (*Dinas Pariwisata*), is on Jl Ngurah Rai 21, T93401. The office provides visitors with pamphlets on sights in the regency.

Sleeping **B** *Agung Gianyar Palace Guesthouse*, within the Palace walls.

Entertainment **Dance** At 1900, every Mon and Thu, a cultural show including dinner is staged at the *Agung Gianyar Palace*, T93943/51654.

Sports **Mountain biking** Down into the volcano on the 'Batur Trail', organized by *Sobek Expeditions*, T287059 (US$45 including lunch), pickup from all the resorts.

Transport Twenty-seven kilometres from Denpasar. **Road Bemo**: regular connections with **Denpasar's** Batubulan terminal.

Bangli

Phone code: 0366
Colour map 1, grid B2

Bangli, the former capital of a mountain principality, is a peaceful, rather beautiful town, well maintained and spread out. Set in a rich farming area in the hills, there is much to enjoy about the surrounding scenery, especially the captivating views of the volcanic area to the north including Mount Agung and Mount Batur. Both the town itself and the countryside around afford many opportunities for pleasant walks. The area claims to have the best climate on Bali and the air is cooler than on the coast. Despite these attractions Bangli is not on the main tourist routes and all the more charming for that. There is a tourist offce, however, *Bangli Government Tourism Office*, on Jl Brigjen Ngurah Rai 24, T91537. Open 0700-1400 Mon-Sat. Very friendly and helpful, but little English is spoken and they are not really geared up for foreigners. Free booklet and map.

History The name Bangli derives from '*bang giri*' meaning red forest or mountain, and like so much else on Bali, derives from local folklore. With a history dating back to at least the 13th century, Bangli regency was founded by the Gelgel-based, Majapahit dynasty and despite never being the strongest of Balinese kingdoms, over time it gained its independence. During the 19th century Bangli was frequently at war with neighbouring kingdoms as each sought to increase its power and extend its influences. During this time Bangli lost control of the mountainous area around Mount Batur to the powerful ruler of Buleleng. In the early 1840s many of Bali's rulers signed co-operation agreements with the Dutch. However, it became clear that the Dutch had no intention of honouring the spirit of these agreements and would use ruthless force to extend their authority on the island, particularly in Buleleng to the north. This provided an opportunity for the ruler of Bangli to gain revenge for the annexation of his lands, and by siding with the Dutch he was able to regain Batur. At the same time he annexed the regencies of Mengwi and Gianyar. For much of the second half of the 19th century the regencies of Gianyar and Bangli were at war. However, in the face of the common threat posed by the Dutch, who were intent on extending their control to the south of the island, these two regencies agreed to resolve their differences. Following the capitulation of the regencies of Badung and Tabanan to the Dutch, Bangli and also Klungkung, became Dutch protectorates; the ruler of Bangli was allowed to remain as titular head. By 1909 all of Bali was under Dutch control.

Balinese believe that Bangli is the haunt of *leyaks*, witches who practise black magic. In Bali, misfortune or illness, is frequently attributed to leyaks, who often

Bangli

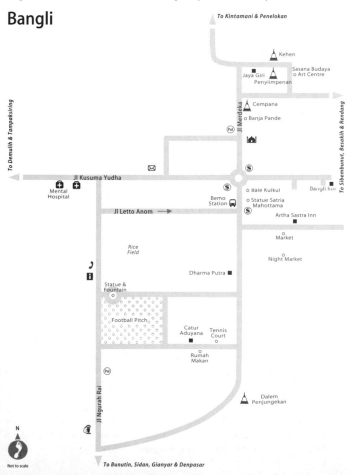

intervene on behalf of an enemy. In order to overcome this the Balinese visit a *balian*, a shaman or healer, who often has knowledge of the occult. As a result of the presence of leyak in the area, Bangli has a reputation for the quality of its *balian* with supplicants arriving from all over the island, dressed in their ceremonial dress and bearing elaborate offerings. The people of Bangli are the butt of jokes throughout Bali as Bangli is the site of the island's only mental hospital, built by the Dutch.

Sights   There is a **market** every three days in the centre of town. Locally grown crops include cloves, coffee, tobacco, vanilla, citrus fruit, rice, cabbages, corn and sweet potatoes; some of which are exported. Bangli lies close to the dividing line between wet-rice and dry-rice cultivation.

Most people come to Bangli to visit the **Pura Kehen**, one of Bali's more impressive temples and one of the most beautiful, set on a wooded hillside about 2 km to the north of the town centre. The Pura was probably founded in the 13th century. There is some dispute over the true origin of the temple because inscriptions within the compound have been dated to the 9th century. It is the second largest on Bali and the state temple of Bangli regency. Elephants flank the imposing entrance, leading up to three terraced courtyards, through finely carved and ornamented gateways decorated with myriad demons. The lower courtyard is dominated by a wonderful 400-year-old *waringin* tree (*Ficus benjamina*) with a monk's cell built high up in the branches. It is here that performances are held to honour the gods. The middle courtyard houses the offertory shrines, while the top-most courtyard contains an 11-tiered *meru* with a carved wood and stone base. The elaborate woodwork here is being beautifully restored and repainted by craftsmen. In the wall below, guides will point out the old Chinese plates cemented into it. Curiously, some of these depict rural England, with a watermill and mail coach drawn by four horses. Every three years in November (Rabu Kliwon Shinta in the Balinese calendar) at the time of the full moon (purnama) a major ceremony, Ngusabha, is held at the temple. ■ *1,000Rp per person plus 1,000Rp for a car. The temple is on the back road to Besakih and Penelokan. Outside there are stalls selling snacks and sarongs.*

The **Sasana Budaya Arts Centre** stages performances of traditional and modern drama, music and dance, as well as art and cultural exhibitions. It is one of the largest cultural centres on Bali, located about 100 m from the Pura Kehen. Ask at the tourist office for information on performances. Bangli is particularly noted for its dance performances. These include Barong Ngunying, performed at important temple ceremonies, such as Galungan, which tells of the fight between the illustrious King Udayana, who ruled Bali in the 11th century, and his wife Queen Guna Pria Dharma Patni. The king is represented by Barong as the good spirit, while the queen is represented by Rangda as the force for evil! However, the reason the queen turns into a wicked witch is because her husband of many years falls in love with, and marries, another woman and she is angry and seeks revenge. After a violent battle the king succeeds in driving his wife away, Barong vanquishes Rangda, good triumphs over evil. The rulers are represented by chickens (symbolizing dynamism), stupidity is represented by the consumption of arak, and goodness by Tirta (holy water). Various forms of *Baris*, a ritual war dance where the all-male performers imitate the actions of soldiers in battle, often wearing a characteristic peaked helmet, are also performed. The Baris dances performed in Bangli developed in the more remote, highland areas and include *baris dapdap* where the men perform in pairs holding shields made of dapdap wood shaped like the large, curling wings of a bat (the wood of the dapdap tree symbolizes strength and everlasting life). Bangli also has one of the largest gamelan orchestras on Bali, captured from the ruler of Klungkung by the Dutch who gave it to Bangli.

In the centre of town is the **royal palace** which houses eight branches of the former royal family. Built about 150 years ago and largely restored by the present descendants, the most important section is the Puri Denpasar where the last ruler of Bangli lived until his death almost 40 years ago. The temple of the royal ancestors is situated on the northwest side diagonally opposite the *Artha Sastra Inn*; important ceremonies are still held here.

There is an impressive **Bale Kulkul** in the centre of town, three storeys high and supported on columns made of coconut palm wood; it is about 100 years old. There are in fact two kulkuls, *kulkul lanang* which is male, and *kulkul wadon* which is female. In times past the kulkul was sounded to summon the people, or act as an alarm warning of impending danger. The people of Bangli consider these kulkul to be sacred, and they are used during important temple festivals.

At the other end of town the **Pura Dalem Penjungekan**, temple of the dead, is also worth a visit. The stone reliefs vividly depict the fate of sinners as they suffer in hell; hanging suspended with flames licking at their feet, being castrated, at the mercy of knife wielding demons, being impaled or having their heads split open. The carvings are based on the story of Bima on his journey to rescue the souls of his parents from hell. The destructive 'Rangda' features extensively. In the centre there is a new shrine depicting tales of Siwa, Durga, and Ganesh. The temple is in a parkland setting with possibilities for walks.

Bukit Demulih at an altitude of about 300 m, and the village of Demulih, lie to the south of the Tampaksiring road 3 km west of town (about 1 hour's walk). The small, pretty village has some well-carved temples, and a kulkul tower by the bale banjar. From here the villagers will show you the track up the hill at the top of which is a small temple; en route you pass a sacred waterfall. If you walk along the ridge you will come to other temples and fine views over the whole of south Bali. ■ *Getting there: walk or take a bemo bound for Tampaksiring, get off after about 3 km, take the narrow, paved road south for 1 km to Demulih village.* **Excursions**

A pleasant walk east of Bangli leads to **Sibembunut**. This road continues towards Rendang through sculpted wet-rice terraces and deep gorges; just to the north, rice is grown using dry-rice cultivation techniques.

There is a **bamboo forest** 3 km north of Bangli near Kubu village, with different varieties of bamboo. The local people believe the area is suffused with magic because of the eerie sound the wind makes when it blows through the bamboo, and the strange, green tinge of the light.

The **Pura Penataran Agung** at Bunutin just off the main road about 6 km south of Bangli could be of interest. It has a pleasant lakeside setting and an unusual shrine with four doors, one facing in each direction of the four winds. This Muslim connection traces back in local folklore to a sickly Hindu prince who was advised by a balian, a traditional healer, that in order to recover his health he should build a shrine at the village of Bunutin to honour a Muslim ancestor of his who was said to have lived there. The prince recovered and to this day his family eschew eating pork.

Bukit Jati, near Guliang about 2 km south of Bunutin, is another hill to climb for splendid views and scenic walks.

Sidan, just north of the main Gianyar to Klungkung road, 10 km south of Bangli, is notable for its **Pura Dalem** which has some of the most vivid, spine-chilling depictions of the torture and punishment that awaits wrong-doers in hell. The carvings show people having their heads squashed, boiled or merely chopped off, and the wicked and evil widow Rangda dismembering and squashing babies. ■ *1,100Rp. There is a car park opposite the temple, and a stage where dance performances sometimes take place.*

Sleeping **C** *Bangli Inn*, Jl Rambutan No 1, Bangli 80661. T/F91419. New hotel, 9 rooms which are clean and simple, with private bathroom, Western toilet. Friendly staff, but limited English. Price includes breakfast. **D-E** *Artha Sastra Inn*, Jl Merdeka 5, T91179. 14 rooms. Located in the inner court of the royal palace with plenty of atmosphere, although don't expect anything as grand as a European palace, Balinese palaces are not that grand. This is the place to stay in Bangli. The more expensive rooms are very clean, simple, with private bathroom and Western toilet; cheaper rooms have shared mandis with squat toilets. Rooms have beautiful carved wooden doors painted in red and gold, and are set around a central courtyard virtually unchanged from its days as a palace. There are walls and arches of carved stone, a 'customary room' which is open to the central courtyard, much old carved wood, and some interesting old photos of the Bangli royal family. Restaurant (cheap). Run by the grandson of the last raja who is a doctor, you are more likely to meet the manager who speaks good English. Price includes breakfast. Recommended. **E** *Catur Aduyana Homestay*, Jl Lettu Lila 2, T91244. 7 rooms. Clean and pleasant homestay located 1 km to the south of the town centre. 3 rooms with private mandi, squat toilet, 4 rooms with shared mandi, squat toilet. Breakfast of tea/coffee and bread included. Friendly owner speaks no English. **E** *Losmen Dharma Putra*. Room rate including breakfast, a good, friendly, family-run losmen. **E-F** *Jaya Giri Homestay*, Jl Sri Wijaya 6, T92255. Pleasant, quiet location by the Pura Kehen, above Bangli town. Entrance is past the pay point for entry to the temple; just tell them you are going to the homestay and they will let you through for free. 6 rooms, though 4 were unavailable when we visited. Rooms are very dark and basic, 2 with private mandi, all squat toilet. Price includes breakfast.

Eating There are warungs beside the bemo station in the centre of town, and a good night market opposite the *Artha Sastra Inn* with the usual staple Indonesian/Balinese stall food including noodles, rice, nasi campur, satay, etc. Near the *Catur Aduyana homestay* opposite *'Yunika'* is a clean Rumah Makan. Foodstalls near the Pura Kehan sell simple snacks.

Transport **Road Bemo**: many, but not all, bemos are 'colour coded'. These days there are a plentiful supply of bemos running throughout the day and most places are accessible by bemo if you are prepared to wait and do some walking. There are regular services between: **Denpasar's** Batubulan terminal, many connect through to **Singaraja**; the market in **Gianyar** (these bemos are usually blue); and **Klungkung**. Blue bemos wait at the Bangli intersection on the main road between Gianyar and Klungkung at Peteluan; so it's easy to change bemos here. The road climbs steadily up to Bangli with good views to the south. Generally, orange bemos run between Bangli and **Kintamani**; between Bangli and **Rendang** bemos are generally black or brown and white; bemos also run between Bangli, **Besakih** and **Amlapura**, all fairly regularly from 0600 to 1700; fewer in the afternoon. The road from Bangli to Rendang is good but winding, with little traffic; it is also very pretty with deep ravines, streams and overhead viaducts made of bamboo and concrete.

Directory **Banks** Several banks including *Bank Rakyat Indonesia*, Jl Kusuma Yudha, T91019, in the centre of town by the Bale Kulkul will change cash and TCs, open 0700-1600 Mon-Fri and 1000-1400 on Sat. **Communications** Post office: Jl Kusuma Yudha 18, T91195. *Wartel*: just north of the tourist office, T91303 and on Jl Merdeka T91001, open 24 hrs. **Medical services** *General Hospital*, Jl Kusuma Yudha 27, T91020. Chemists: *Apotik Kurnia Farma*, Jl Kusuma Yudha, and in Toko Obat Rhizoma, Jl Bridjen Ngurah Rai. **Useful services** Petrol Station: at the start of town on Jl Brigjen Ngurah Rai.

Mount Batur

The spectacular landscape of Mount Batur is one of the most visited inland areas on Bali. Despite the hawkers, bustle and general commercialization, it still makes a worthwhile trip. The huge crater – 20 km in diameter – contains within it Lake Batur and the active Mount Batur (1,710 m), with buckled lava flows on its slopes. The view at dawn from the summit is stunning with both Mount Agung (3,142 m) and Mount Abang (at 2,153 m the highest point on the caldera rim surrounding Mount Batur) in almost perfect alignment, and further east Mount Rinjani on Lombok. The original Mount Batur, which first erupted thousands of centuries ago, must have been immense. The initial explosion was followed several thousand years later by a second resulting in a double caldera, still visible in places. Mount Batur, as seen today, is the result of successive eruptions starting 10,000 years ago. It stands 700 m above the caldera floor in the middle of the vast valley left by the original eruption; only 200 m on average above the level of the surrounding caldera rim. Although these days Mount Batur is less destructive than Mount Agung, it is the most active volcano on Bali having erupted 20 times during the past 200 years.

See map, page 148
Colour map 1, grid B2

In 1917, an eruption killed over 1,000 people and destroyed 65,000 homes and more than 2,000 temples. The lava flow stopped at the foot of the village of Batur's temple, which the local people took as a good omen and continued to live there. In 1926, the village of Batur, and its temple, were completely destroyed by another eruption. This time the village moved to a safer site. In August 1994 Mount Batur erupted again, after 18 years of dormancy. The eruption was not a major event; it lasted for a period of five days and ash was deposited on the village of Kintamani about 6 km away. The volcano's shape tells a geological tale of great violence though – making more recent eruptions minor by comparison, notwithstanding the lives lost. The double caldera, with one caldera lying within the second, "is the product of two cataclysmic eruptions each of which would certainly have destroyed large parts of Bali", as Graeme Wheller, a geologist, says in an article in *Inside Indonesia*. The older explosion occurred between 40,000 and 100,000 years ago; the more recent, some 23,500 years ago. Perhaps it is this constant battle with combative nature which has made the inhabitants of the area less welcoming, and more surly, than those of other parts of the island. It is dangerous to generalize, but many visitors leave the slopes of Mount Batur with a sense of relief.

Lake Batur in the centre of the caldera is considered sacred, as it is thought to be the fountainhead of the water that flows into Bali's ricefields. A local legend recounts that the Goddess of the Crater Lake, Dewi Danu and her male counterpart, the God of Mount Agung, rose from the depths of the lake and extended their power over the lands and waters of Bali. Dewi Danu and the God of Mount Agung are complementary; female and male, and occupy the two highest peaks on the island, Agung and Batur.

A steep road winds down the crater side and then through the lava boulders and along the west shore of Lake Batur. There are hot springs here and paths up the sides of Mount Batur, through the area's extraordinary landscape. Treks begin either from **Purajati** or **Toya Bungkah** (there are 4, 5 or 6 hour treks,), or around the lake (guides are available from the *Lake View Cottages* in Toya Bungkah). Aim to leave Toya Bungkah at about 0330. After reaching the summit it is possible to hike westwards along the caldera rim, though this hike is not for the faint-hearted as the ridge is extremely narrow in places with steep drops on both sides. The cinder track passes several of the currently most active craters, lava flows and fumaroles. In the north and east of the caldera the

Trekking

Bali

landscape is quite different. The rich volcanic soil, undisturbed by recent lava flows, supports productive agriculture. The vulcanology institute on the rim of the caldera monitors daily seismic activity.

Trunyan

Numerous visitors have written to us saying how unfriendly the villages of this area are. They report a distinct lack of hospitality, an oppressive & unpleasant air – even palpable hostility

Boats can be hired from the village of **Kedisan** on the south shore of Lake Batur – be prepared for the unpleasant, hard-line sales people here – or from Toya Bungkah, to visit the traditional Bali Aga village (see page 178) of Trunyan and its cemetery close by at Kuban, on the east side of the lake.

The Bali Aga are the original inhabitants of Bali pre-dating the arrival of the Majapahit; records show that the area has been inhabited since at least the 8th century. Legend recounts that the village was founded at the place where an ancient banyan tree grew, its fragrant smell reminiscent of incense having attracted the goddess of the lake, Dewi Danau. The name may come from *taru menyan* meaning wood and perfume. Trunyan's customs are different from Tenganan (see page 170) – but these differences can only be noted during festival time, which tend to be rather closed affairs. Despite its beautiful setting beside Lake Batur with Mount Abang rising dramatically in the background, a visit can be disappointing. Most people come to visit the cemetery to view the traditional way of disposing of corpses. Like the Parsees of India, the corpses are left out to rot and be eaten by birds rather than being buried or cremated. It is claimed that the smell of rotting corpses is dissipated by the fragrance of the sacred banyan tree. The idea behind this custom is that the souls of the dead are carried up towards heaven by the birds; this flight to heaven propitiates the gods and results in improved prospects for the souls in their reincarnation in the next life. The corpses are laid out on enclosed bamboo rafts, but very likely all you will see is bones and skulls. The cemetery is only accessible by boat; make sure you pay at the end of your journey otherwise the boatman may demand extra money for the return journey. The villagers are unfriendly and among the most aggressive on Bali; with a long tradition of begging for rice from other parts of the island as they were unable to grow their own, they now beg or demand money from tourists.

Penelokan & Kintamani

On the west rim of the crater are two villages, Kintamani and Penelokan. Large-scale restaurants here cater for the tour group hordes. The area is also overrun with hawkers selling batik and woodcarvings – some so vociferously as to scare the most hardened visitor. Penelokan is perched on the edge of the crater and its name means 'place to look'. About 5 km north of here, following the crater rim, is the rather drab town of Kintamani, which is a centre of orange and passionfruit cultivation. The town's superb position overlooking the crater makes up for its drabness. Ged's trekking is based here; they can advise on the best walks in the area and provide a guide for the more dangerous routes up to the crater rim.

Pura Batur

Just south of Kintamani is Pura Batur, spectacularly positioned on the side of the crater. This is the new temple built as a replacement for the original Pura Batur which was engulfed by lava in 1926. Although the temple is new and therefore not of great historical significance, it is in fact the second most important temple in Bali after Pura Besakih. As Stephen Lansing explains in his book *Priests and Programmers* (1991), the Goddess of the Crater Lake is honoured here and symbolically the temple controls water for all the island's irrigation systems (see page 229). Ultimately therefore, it controls the livelihoods of the majority of the population. A nine-tiered meru honours the goddess and unlike other temples it is open 24 hours a day. A virgin priestess still selects 24 boys as priests who remain tied as servants of the temple for the rest of their lives. The most senior is regarded as the earthly representative of the goddess, with whom he is magically linked.

Pura Tegeh Koripan is the last place on the crater rim, on the main road 200 m **Pura Tegeh**
north of Penulisan. Steep stairs (333 in all) lead up to the temple which stands **Koripan**
at a height of over 1,700 m above sea level next to a broadcasting mast. The
temple was first visited by a European at a relatively early date – a scientist, Dr J
Jacobs, climbed up to the temple in 1885. However, after that first visit, the
local population forcibly kept foreigners away from the temple and it was only
in 1918 that the archaeologist Nieuwenkamp managed to gain admission and
become its second Western visitor. The temple contains a number of highly
weathered statues, thought to be portraits of royalty. They are dated between
1011 and 1335. Artistically they are surprising because they seem to anticipate
later Majapahit works. The whole place is rather run down at the moment,
though there are some signs that repairs are being attempted. ■ *1,000Rp.*
Mon-Sun. Getting there: catch a bemo running north and get off at Penulisan.

Toya Bungkah **C** *Lake View*, Gunawan. **C-D** *Under the Volcano*, good restaurant, **Sleeping**
clean rooms, friendly management. **D** *The Art Centre* (or *Balai Seni*), Toya Bungkah,
quite old but still a good place to stay. **F** *Nyoman Pangus Homestay*, the accommodation here is fine, but the food is poor value, with small portions, and the people
rather unfriendly – like the village. **Penelokan** **B-D** *Lake View Homestay*, basic but
good views over the lake. **C-D** *Gunawan Losmen*, clean, private bathroom, fantastic
position. **Kintamani** **B** *Surya Homestay*, great position, new, more comfortable
rooms now available. **D** *Segara Bungalow*. **C** *Puri Astina*, large clean rooms.
Losmen Sasaka, stunning views over the crater and lake.

Segara, in Kedisan, across road from boat jetty, clean, serves excellent lake fish, **Eating**
friendly staff.

Road **Bemo**: from **Denpasar's** Batubulan terminal to **Bangli** and then another to **Transport**
Penelokan. Some bemos drive down into the crater to Kedisan and Toya Bungkah.
Bus: regular coach services from **Denpasar** (2-3 hrs).

Alternative routes from Ubud to Mount Batur

If you have your own transport and are starting from Ubud, you can turn left at
the end of Ubud's main street and take the back road heading north. This leads
through an almost continuous ribbon of craft villages, mainly specializing in
woodcarving, with pieces ranging in size from chains of monkeys to full size
doors and 2 m high *Garudas*. There are good bargains to be found in this area
off the main tourist track. Follow the road through Petulu, Sapat and
Tegalalong and continue northwards.

The road, its surface not too good in places, climbs steadily through rice
paddies and then more open countryside where cows and goats graze, before
eventually arriving at the crater rim – 500 m west of Penelokan.

The area around Mount Batur is considered very sacred and comprises
numerous temples, small pretty villages and countryside consisting of rice fields
littered with volcanic debris. There are several rugged backroutes from Ubud
through this region. One of the most interesting villages is **Sebatu** northeast of
Ubud near Pura Mount Kawi, reached via a small road leading east from the
northern end of **Pujung Kelod**. This village has a number of temples and is
renowned for the refined quality of its dance troupe, its gamelan orchestra and
for its wood carving. The dance troupe has revived several unusual traditional
dances including the telek dance and makes regular appearances overseas. **Pura
Gunung Kawi** is a water temple with well maintained shrines and pavilions, a
pool fed by an underground spring and open air public bathing.

From Mount Batur to the north coast

See map, page 148 From Penulisan the main road runs down to the north coast which it joins at Kubutambahan. It is a long descent as the road twists down the steep hillsides and there are many hairpin bends.

If exploring the northeast coast, a very pleasant alternative is to take the minor road which turns directly north just short of a small village called Dusa. The turning is not well signed – ask to make sure you are on the right road.

This is a steep descent but the road is well made and quiet. The road follows ridges down from the crater of Mount Batur, with steep drops into ravines on either side. The route passes through clove plantations and small friendly villages with stupendous views to the north over the sea. Behind, the tree-covered slopes lead back up to the crater.

The road eventually joins the coast road near Tegakula. Turn left, northwest, for Singaraja and Lovina, and right, southeast, for the road to Amlapura (see page 176).

Pura Besakih and Mount Agung

The holiest and most important temple on Bali is Pura Besakih, situated on the slopes of Bali's sacred Mount Agung. Twinned with Mount Batur to the northwest, Agung is the highest mountain on the island, rising to 3,140 m. It is easiest to approach Besakih by taking the road north from Klungkung, a distance of 22 km. However, there are also two east-west roads, linking the Klungkung route to Besakih with Bangli in the west and Amlapura in the east. Although little public transport uses these routes, they are among the most beautiful drives in Bali, through verdant terraced rice paddys.

Besakih

See also map, page 148 Pura Besakih is not one temple, but a complex of 22 puras that lie scattered over the south slopes of Mount Agung at an altitude of about 950 m. Of these, the central, largest and most important is the Pura Penataran Agung, the Mother Temple of all Bali. It is here that every Balinese, whatever his or her clan or class, can come to worship – although in the past it was reserved for the royal families of Klungkung, Karangkasem and Bangli. The other 21 temples that sprawl across the slopes of Mount Agung surrounding the Mother Temple are linked to particular clans. **Mount Agung** is an active volcano, and last erupted in 1963 killing 2,000 people. Graeme Wheller, in an article in *Inside Indonesia* published at the end of 1994, claims that "Gunung Agung is a disaster waiting to happen – again". The 1963 explosion, in his view, is set to repeat itself with even greater human repercussions. The population is now considerably denser and the scale of investment much greater. He claims that not only would thousands be at risk but the tourist industry would be devastated for months afterwards. There are three observatory stations that monitor the state of the mountain, but these are very poorly equipped and under-funded. When – it is not considered to be a question of 'if' – the mountain does erupt, it could be with very little warning. The traditional *lontar* manuscripts (see page 200) sometimes name the mountain *To Langkir* meaning Uppermost Man, or 'The Abode of the Gods' and the area has been a sacred spot for several centuries.

The **Pura Penataran Agung**, which most visitors refer to as Pura Besakih, is dedicated to Siva and was probably a pre-Indic terraced sanctuary. An indication that the pura is of great antiquity and pre-dates the arrival of Hinduism in Bali is the use of Old Indonesian and Old Balinese to name some of the gods that are worshipped here. Since then, it has seen many changes. It seems that the temple was enlarged during the reign of King Dharmavangsa (1022-1026). But the most significant changes occurred after 1343 when Gajah Mada of the Majapahit Kingdom of Java, sent a force to subdue the 'infamous and odious' ruler of Bali. With the victory of the Majapahit army, viceroys were sent from Java to rule the island. A descendant of one of these men established himself as the Prince of Gelgel, and this royal family became closely associated with Besakih, making it their ancestral *pura*. The *merus* were probably added at this time.

From the entrance gate, it is a 10 minute walk up to the temple, past a long row of souvenir stalls. Although it is possible to walk up and around the sides of the temple, the courtyards themselves are only open to worshippers. It is the spectacular position of this *pura*, rather than the quality of its workmanship, which makes it special: there are views over fields to the waters of the Lombok Strait.

Temple layout

Pura Besakih consists of three distinct sections (for general background to Balinese temple layout see page 231). The entrance to the forecourt is through a *candi bentar* or split gate, immediately in front of which – unusually for Bali – is a *bale pegat*, which symbolizes the cutting of the material from the heavenly worlds. Also here is the *bale kulkul*, a pavilion for the wooden split gongs. At the far end of this first courtyard are two *bale mundar-mandir* or *bale ongkara*, their roofs supported by single pillars.

Pura Besakih

Entering the central courtyard, almost directly in front of the gateway, is the *bale pewerdayan*. This is the spot where the priests recite the sacred texts. On the left-hand wall is the *pegongan*, a pavilion where a gamelan orchestra plays during ceremonies. Along the opposite (right-hand) side of the courtyard is the large *bale agung*, where meetings of the Besakih village are held. The small *panggungan* or altar in front and at the near end of the bale agung is used to present offerings to the gods. The similar *bale pepelik* at the far end is the altar used to present offerings to the Hindu trinity – Vishnu, Brahma and Siva. These gods descend and assemble in the larger *sanggar agung* which lies in front of the bale pepelik.

From the central courtyard, a steep stone stairway leads to the upper section, which is arranged into four terraces. The first of these terraces in the inner courtyard, is split into an east (right) and west (left) half. To the right are two large *merus*; the meru with the seven-tiered roof is dedicated to the locally venerated god Ratu Geng, while the 11-tiered meru is dedicated to Ratu Mas. The 3-tiered *kehen* meru

Bali

The 1979 festival of Eka Dasa Rudra at Pura Besakih

The once-a-century Eka Dasa Rudra is the most important Hindu festival in Indonesia. It is held when, according to the Hindu saka calendar (see page 239), the year ends in two zeros. However, it can also be held when natural, political or economic calamity or disturbance is such that one needs to be called. Such was the case in 1963 (saka 1884), when it was deemed necessary to hold the festival following the events of the Indonesian revolution (1945-1949). An Eka Dasa Rudra had not been held for several centuries, and it was widely felt that one was due. Indeed, so many years had elapsed that the Balinese had forgotten, in large part, how to hold the festival and had to re-invent the celebration. However, shortly before the great sacrifice, scheduled for 8 March, Mount Agung began to erupt, leading to extensive death and destruction. Perhaps it was fortunate that saka 1900 (AD 1979) was to fall only 16 years later, allowing the Balinese to atone for any wrongs that might have been committed.

Eka Dasa Rudra is not just one festival, but a series of many. The most important is the purification sacrifice, or Taur Eka Dasa Rudra, which occurs on the last day of a saka century – saka 1900 fell, for

example, on 28 March 1979. The magnificence of the Eka Dasa Rudra can be imagined by magnifying immeasurably the colourful every day festivals held in Bali's smaller temples; offerings on a massive scale, flowers in great piles, and janurs and colourful banners fluttering from the temple's shrines. During the course of the festival large numbers of animals were brought up to Besakih for sacrifice – about 60 species in all. It was not a reassuring sight for conservationists, as among the creatures were tiger cubs and rare eagles. President Suharto made an appearance at the ceremony and, unlike 1963, it ended with no incident or eruption. DS Fox writes at the back of his book about the festival Once a century: Pura Besakih and the Eka Dasa Rudra Festival (1982):

"It is impossible to imagine the Balinese world in another 100 years able to support an Eka Dasa Rudra as extravagant as the 1980 [sic] festival: Will there still be baby tigers and eagles for the animal sacrifices? Will the Balinese still be willing to spend millions of man-hours weaving a spectacle of such scale? Will the tenacity of Balinese culture survive the severe pressures of 21st century life?"

is used to store the temple treasures. On the left-hand side is a row of four merus and two stone altars. The tallest meru, with seven tiers, is dedicated to Ida Batara Tulus Sadewa. Up some steps, on the second terrace is another 11-tiered *meru*, this one dedicated to Ratu Sunar ing Jagat or Lord Light of the World. There are also a number of bale here; the bale in a separate enclosure to the left is dedicated to Sira Empu, the patron god of blacksmiths. Up some more stairs, to the third terrace is yet a further 11-tiered meru, dedicated in this instance to Batara Wiscsa. On the final terrace are two *gedongs* – covered buildings enclosed on all four sides – both dedicated to the god of Mount Agung.

At the back of the complex there is a path leading to three other major puras: **Gelap** (200 m), **Pengubengan** (2.5 km) and **Tirta** (2 km). There are over 20 temples on these terraced slopes, dedicated to every Hindu god in the pantheon. ■ *0800, Mon-Sun. 3,000Rp for which you get a fistful of different tickets – an entry ticket, a camera ticket, a compulsory insurance ticket ... then, thinking it is safe to go back into the water...another ticket office on the climb up the hill where you have to sign in and are invited to make a further donation (ignore the vast sums that are claimed to have been donated). As the temple is an ill-kept shambles one assumes that someone is creaming off a fair proportion. Guides available (about 2,000Rp). Best time to visit: early morning, before the tour groups.*

Climbing Mount Agung trips can be organized by the *Lake View Cottages* in Toya **Tours**
Bungkah, the price (100,000Rp up to US$25 or more) includes a guide, pick-up, trans-
port to base camp, but no food.

There are a total of 70 festivals held in and around Pura Besakih each year, with every **Festivals**
shrine having its own festival. The two most important festivals are occasional ceremonies: The **Panca Wali Krama** is held every 10 years, while the **Eka Dasa Rudra** is
held only once every 100 years and lasts for 2 months. In fact, two Eka Dasa Rudra festivals have been held this century (see box above for explanation).
January New moon of 7th lunar month.
March/April Nyepi (movable, full moon of 10th lunar month), the Balinese Saka
new year, a month-long festival, which is attended by thousands of people from all
over Bali, centering on the triple lotus throne.

Road Bemo/minibus: regular minibuses from **Klungkung**; from **Denpasar** catch a **Transport**
bemo from the Batubulan terminal to Klungkung and then get a connection on to *22 km from Klungkung,*
Besakih (via **Rendang**). But bemos are irregular for this final leg of the journey and it *60 km from Denpasar*
makes more sense to charter a bemo for the entire trip or rent a car or motorbike
(chartering a bemo makes good sense in a group).

East Bali and Regency of Karangasem

*The greatest of the former principalities of Bali is Klungkung and its capital still
has a number of sights which hint at its former glory. But it is worth driving east of
here into the Regency of Karangasem: to the ancient Bali Aga village of
Tenganan, 3 km outside Candi Dasa, then inland and northeast to Amlapura
(Karangkasem), with its royal palace (40 km from Klungkung), then 7 km north
to the royal bathing pools of Tirtagangga. From here the road continues north following the coast all the way to Singaraja (almost 100 km from Amlapura). Few
tourists make the drive, which is peaceful and very beautiful, passing black sand
beaches and coconut groves, see page214.*

*An area of great beauty dominated by Mount Agung (3,140 m), Bali's highest
and most sacred volcano, Karangasem is one of the most traditional parts of Bali
and one of the most rewarding areas to explore. During the 17th and 18th centuries Karangasem was the most powerful kingdom on Bali. Its sphere of influence
extended to western Lombok, and the cross cultural exchanges which resulted
endure to this day. During the 19th century, the regency co-operated with the
Dutch thus ensuring its continued prosperity.*

*The massive eruption of Mount Agung in 1963 devastated much of the regency
and traces of the lava flows can still be seen along the northeast coast, particularly
north of Tulamben.*

Ins and outs

Bear in mind that all times are necessarily approximate and can vary enormously **Getting there**
depending on traffic conditions from Denpasar, particularly on the main road from **& away**
Klungkung to Denpasar. **Buses** run most frequently in the morning starting early
(from 0500 or 0600), and continue until about 1700 or later; on major routes. The frequency of buses is improving all the time.
From Denpasar (Batubulan terminal) to: Gianyar 1 hr; Klungkung 1 hr 25 mins;
Padangbai 1 hr 50 mins; Candi Dasa 2 hrs 10 mins; Amlapura 2½ hrs; Bangli 1 hr 20
mins; Singaraja (Sangket terminal) 4 hrs.

From Gianyar to: Klungkung 25 mins; Padangbai 50 mins; Candi Dasa 1 hr 10 mins; Amlapura 1½ hrs; Ubud 25 mins; Bangli 20 mins; Singaraja (Sangket terminal) 3 hrs.
From Amlapura to: Candi Dasa 20 mins; Tirtagangga 10 mins; Amed 30 mins; Tulemban 40 mins; Rendang 1 hr 20 mins; Besakih 1 hr 35 mins; Sideman 1 hr 15 mins; Singaraja (Penarukan terminal) 2 hrs 20 mins.
From Candi Dasa to: Denpasar (Batubulan terminal) 2 hrs 10 mins; Padangbai 20 mins; Amlapura 20 mins; Tirtagangga 30 mins; Ubud 1 hr 35 mins; Besakih 2 hrs.

Several companies run tourist shuttle buses linking Padangbai, Candi Dasa, Tirtagangga and Tulemben with Ubud, Kuta, Sanur (and Nusa Lembongan by boat), Kintamani, Lovina, Bedugul and Air Sanih; Mataram, Bangsal, the Gili Islands, Kuta Lombok and Tetebatu on Lombok. One of the best is *Perama* with offices in all the above places; allow 3 hrs to get to Denpasar airport from Candi Dasa.

By boat: from Padangbai: there is a round-the-clock (leaving every 2 hrs) ferry service to Lembar port on Lombok taking 4-5 hrs. Small boats make the crossing to Nusa

Karangasem

*Related map
Amed & Tulamben
area, page 183*

Traditional villages and festivals of Karangasem

Karangasem has several traditional villages rarely visited by tourists where unique and ancient forms of dance and music are still a part of village life. Any of the following villages are worth exploring, especially at festival time: **Bugbug**, **Perasi**, **Jasi**, **Ngis**, **Timbrah**, **Bungaya**, **Bebandem** and **Asak**. The main festivals are held at the time of the full moon, the appearance of penjors lining the roads is an indication of a forthcoming celebration; ask around for details. One important festival is **Usuba Sumbu**, an agricultural ceremony held in some of the above villages between the months of May and August. Another important festival takes place in June/July at these villages to pay tribute to the village ancestors; other festivals take place in January/February and March/April. These festivals often last for several days and are accompanied by sacred dances and traditional music with the performers dressed in exquisite ritual dress.

The heirarchy and ritual life of some of these villages dates back to the days of the Bali Aga, the original people of Bali. While perhaps not quite as fascinating as the village of Tenganan, these villages have retained an authenticity which Tenganan has lost due to the impact of tourism. Perasi is a pretty village with lots of flowers, flame trees and jacaranda, and a good beach called Bias Putih (which means white sand).

Bali

Penida very early every morning taking about 1 hr 20 mins. From Kusumba: small boats leave early every morning for Nusa Penida and Nusa Lembongan, 1 hr 15 mins.

While you can reach most of these villages by public bemo it is better to hire a car. There are many scenic backroads which climb up into the hills offering spectacular views when the weather is fine; be warned that some of these minor roads are in dreadful condition with numerous, huge potholes. The road leading up from Perasi through Timbrah and Bungaya to Bebandem is especially scenic and potholed. A much better road with outstanding views leads west from Amlapura to Rendang; *en route* you pass through an area famed for its salak fruit and in the vicinity of Muncan you will find beautiful rice terraces. From Rendang you can continue on up to Pura Besakih.

Getting around

Klungkung

Klungkung was the centre of another of the numerous principalities that made up Bali before the Dutch conquest of the island. It was also the oldest and most powerful, and the last to fall to the Dutch, which happened in 1908 when the Dewa Agung of Klungkung had a force sent against him – in this case, under the pretext that he had been 'insolent'. Like the kings of Denpasar and Pemetjutan, the Dewa Agung opted to fight and die rather than surrender. Another *puputan* or 'fight to the death' took place (see page 226) in the main street in Klungkung, and the King and his entire family were killed by the Dutch forces. On the side of the road approaching from Ubud are a series of tunnels, bored by the Japanese occupying army in the Second World War.

Phone code: 0366
Colour map 1, grid B2

The **Puri Semarapura** was once the symbolic heart of the kingdom of Klungkung. All that remains of this palace on Jalan Untung Surapati are the gardens and two buildings; the rest was destroyed in 1908 by the Dutch during their advance on the capital and the ensuing *puputan*. The **Kherta Ghosa** or Hall of Justice, built in the 18th century by Ida Dewa Agung Jambe, was formerly the supreme court of the kingdom of Klungkung. It is famous for its ceiling murals painted in traditional, wayang style, with vivid illustrations of

Sights
Klungkung is also known by its former name Semarapura (particularly as the destination on buses)

Bali

heaven (towards the top) and hell (on the lower panels). As a court, the paintings represent the punishment that awaits a criminal in the afterlife. The murals have been repainted several times this century. Miguel Covarrubias describes the nature of traditional justice in Bali in the following terms:

"A trial must be conducted with the greatest dignity and restraint. There are rules for the language employed, the behaviour of the participants, and the payment of trial expenses. It is interesting that the court procedure resembles that of cockfights in its rules and terminology. On the appointed day the plaintiff and the defendant must appear properly dressed, with their witnesses and their cases and declarations carefully written down. ... When the case has been thoroughly stated, the witnesses have testified and the evidence has been produced, the judges study the statements and go into deliberation among themselves until they reach a decision. Besides the witnesses and the material evidence, special attention is paid to the physical reaction of the participants during the trial, such as nervousness, change of colour in the face, or hard breathing."

The Kherta Ghosa was transformed into a Western court by the Dutch in 1908, when they added the carved seats, as they found sitting on mats too uncomfortable. It is said – although the story sounds rather dubious – that one of the Rajahs of Klungkung used the Kherta Ghosa as a watch tower. He would look over the town and when his eyes alighted on a particularly attractive woman going to the temple to make offerings, he would order his guards to fetch her and add the unsuspecting maid to his collection of wives.

Adjoining the Kherta Ghosa is the **Bale Kambangg** (or Floating Pavilion), originally built in the 18th century, but extensively restored since then. Like the Kherta Ghosa, the ceiling is painted with murals; these date from 1942.

Further along the same road, just past a school, is the attractive **Taman Gili** also built in the 18th century. This consists of a series of open courtyards with finely carved stonework, in the centre of which is a floating pavilion surrounded by a lotus-filled moat. ■ *1,000Rp.*

To the east of the main crossroads in the centre of town – behind the shopfronts – is a bustling **market**, held here every three days and considered by many to be the best market on Bali, and also a large monument commemorating the *puputan* (see page 226).

Excursions **Kamasan village**, 4 km southeast of Klungkung, is an important arts centre where artists still practise the classical Wayang style of painting. Most of the artist families live in the banjar Sangging area of town. Artists from this village painted the original ceiling in the Kerta Gosa in Klungkung in the 18th century as well as the recent restoration, using the muted natural colours (reds, blacks, blues, greens and ochres) typical of this school.

Goa Lawah or 'bat cave', is one of the state temples of Klungkung. There are tunnels here which are reputed to lead as far as Pura Besakih. As the name suggests, the temple is overrun by bats and corresponding smells. *Getting there*: take a bemo heading for Padangbai or Candi Dasa.

Boats leave for **Nusa Penida** and **Nusa Lembongan** from the fishing village of Kusamba, 8 km southeast from Klungkung. On the beach are huts and shallow troughs used in salt production. The fishing fleet consists of hundreds of brightly painted outrigger craft with triangular sails, which operate in the Lombok Strait (similar to the *lis-alis* of Madura). They are fast and manoeuvrable, and can make way in even the lightest breezes. Boats leave Padangbai for Nusa Penida only.

Sleeping **E** *Ramayana Palace*, Jl Diponegoro (east edge of the town on road to Candi Dasa), T21044. Restaurant.

Textiles Although good examples are not easy to find, Klungkung is the centre of the production of royal *songket* cloth, traditionally made with silk but today more often from synthetics. The cloth is worn for ceremonial occasions and characteristically features abstracted floral designs, geometric patterns, wayang figures and animals. It takes 2 months to weave a good piece.

Road Bemo: regular connections with **Denpasar's** Batubulan terminal and points east – **Besakih, Amlapura, Candi Dasa**.

Boat **Kusamba**, from where there are boats to **Nusa Penida**.

Communications Post Office: to the west of the Kherta Ghosa.

Padangbai

Padangbai has a beautiful setting overlooking a crescent-shaped bay with *Phone code: 0363* golden sand beach, colourful *jukung* (fishing boats) and surrounded by verdant hills. This is the port for ferries to Lombok and boats to Nusa Penida (see page 109) and is a hive of excitement when ferries arrive and depart. When there are no ships calling, the town is quiet and relaxed. It is one of the best deep-water harbours in Bali, and many tankers ride at anchor in the approaches. There are beaches on either side of the town. Walking south from the pier and bus station follow the road until you come to a tatty sign on the left indicating the rough, steep path that leads up and over the hill to **Pantai Cecil**, (400 m approximately, 15 minutes' walk). This is a beautiful, undeveloped white sand beach surrounded by grassy hills, the perfect setting for a quiet swim or evening stroll. There are two beachside warungs.

Padangbai

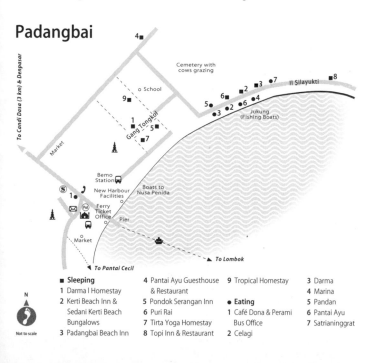

■ **Sleeping**
1 Darma I Homestay
2 Kerti Beach Inn &
   Sedani Kerti Beach
   Bungalows
3 Padangbai Beach Inn

4 Pantai Ayu Guesthouse
   & Restaurant
5 Pondok Serangan
6 Puri Rai
7 Tirta Yoga Homestay
8 Topi Inn & Restaurant

9 Tropical Homestay

● **Eating**
1 Café Dona & Perami
   Bus Office
2 Celagi

3 Darma
4 Marina
5 Pandan
6 Pantai Ayu
7 Satrianinggrat

N

Not to scale

Sleeping   The most attractive rooms are in town. However, the best location is to the north along the bay where rooms and bungalows are surrounded by gardens and coconut groves and are quieter; they are in need of refurbishment, though, and are overpriced for what they offer.

B-D *Puri Rai* (formerly *Rai Beach Inn*), 7 Jl Silayukti, T41385/6/7, F41386. Has attempted to go upmarket but rooms are very overpriced, rather spartan and unattractive, rooms and 2-storey bungalows (these have drab, plywood floors and easy access for mosquitoes), with fan or a/c, private mandi with Western toilets but not always toilet seats, restaurant (cheap). **D** *Pondok Serangan Inn*, Jl Segara, T41425. Clean, modern, 1st floor rooms with fan, private mandi, Western toilet, attractive, 1st floor balcony seating area with views of town and sea, pot plants and family shrine. Recommended. **D** *Topi*, east side of bay, restaurant, isolated position, clean and comfortable basic rooms but creaky floors and thin walls makes for little privacy. **D-E** *Darma I Homestay*, Jl Silayukti Gang Tongkol No 6, T41394. In town, well run, very clean, modern rooms with private mandi and Western toilet, fan and mosquito nets, 1st floor balcony seating area with lovely sea views, good value. Recommended. **D-E** *Jati Wangi Inn*, Melanting 5 (owner at I Wayan Wista near market), clean, cool, friendly. **D-E** *Kerti Beach Inn*, Jl Silayukti, T41391. Outside town with garden, rooms are basic and need redecorating, private mandi with Western toilets, fan. **D-E** *Padangbai Beach Inn*, Jl Silayukti, one of the best locations, outside town, set in large grounds, but rooms are fairly basic, the more expensive rooms with private mandi and Western toilet are OK, but the cheaper rooms are pretty grim with private squat toilet and shared shower. **D-E** *Pantai Ayu Guesthouse*, Jl Silayukti, T41396. Set on a hill overlooking Padangbai and the sea with fabulous views and flower filled garden, well run, clean but rooms are a little older than some, private bathrooms, Western toilets, 3rd floor restaurant (cheap). Recommended. **D-E** *Satrianinggrat*, Jl Silayukti No 11, T41517. Outside town, in quiet garden location with pleasant view of coconut grove, behind restaurant, 4 new rooms with private mandi (no wash basin), Western toilet, fan, not particularly well built, somewhat overpriced. **D-E** *Sedani Kerti Beach Bungalows*, cottages and plain rooms on the beach front. **E** *Tirta Yoga Homestay* (opposite *Darma I Homestay*), Jl Silayukti Gang Tongkol, T41415. Set in pretty, small garden with shrine, clean rooms with fan, private mandi, Western toilet, new rooms are good value, older rooms smelt damp. **E** *Tropical Homestay*, Jl Silayukti 1A, T41398. Good (new) rooms, attractive courtyard, friendly staff, choice of breakfast, quite noisy, rooms with fan, private mandi, Western toilet.

Eating   **Mid-range** *Pandan*, not by sea but set in pretty gardens backing onto coconut
All offer Indonesian   grove. *Pantai Ayu*, Jl Silayukti, on the beach, also 3rd floor restaurant in guest house
& Western food   with fabulous views over Padangbai and sea, see accommodation, great seafood, money changer. *Topi Inn*, upstairs, with views. *Marina Restaurant* has lovely sea views, several small warungs along sea front.

Transport   **Road Bemo**: Padangbai is 2½ km off the main coastal road; connections with Denpasar's Batubulan terminal, Candi Dasa and Amlapura. **Bus**: from the bus station you can catch long distance buses west to Java and east to Sumbawa and Lombok.

Sea Boat: ferries for Lembar on Lombok leave daily, every 2 hrs and takes 4-5 hrs , 4,800Rp, 9,300Rp in 1st class (children half price). The busiest departure is 0800 which is not a problem if one of the 2 large ultra-modern ferries is doing that sailing; otherwise try to get on as early as possible to secure a decent seat. Boats also depart for Nusa Penida (tourists pay 15,000Rp).

Padangbai to Candi Dasa

For many people Bali is at its best and most rewarding away from the tourist centres. Along the road leading from Padangbai to Candi Dasa there are several hotels and bungalow-style accommodation which offer peace and quiet in secluded settings with beautiful sea views. (The rice paddies in these parts sprout an interesting selection of scarecrows in different styles!) Breakfast is included in the price except at the luxury hotels.

Balina Beach lies midway between Padangbai and Candi Dasa (approximately 4 km from the latter) adjacent to the village of Buitan, which runs this tourist development as a co-operative for the benefit of the villagers. It is a slightly scruffy black sand beach with a definite tourist feel to it. Sengkidu village and beach 2 km further east have more charm. Sometimes there are strong currents.

Manggis & Balina Beach
Phone code: 0363

Bali

The village of **Buitan** has a public telephone and several small warung/restaurants and shops; the road to the beach and the accommodation is signposted. Perhaps the highlight of this village is the large advertisement promoting the advantages of artificial insemination in pig breeding. The village of **Manggis**, inland and to the west of Buitan, is known locally for its associations with black magic; it is said to be the haunt of *leyaks*, witches with supernatural powers. There is a road from here leading up to **Putung**, 6 km away, with spectacular views over the Lombok Strait.

At present there are two upmarket accommodations; the simpler, cheaper places seem to have disappeared.

L *Amankila* (outside Candi Dasa near the village of Manggis) T41333, F41555 (reservations through *Amanusa* at Nusa Dua T0361-771267, F771266). Opened mid-1992, one of the renowned Aman group of hotels, in an outstanding location spread out over the hillside with stunning sea views. Designed with simple elegance to create a

Sleeping

Manggis, Balina Beach & Sengkidu

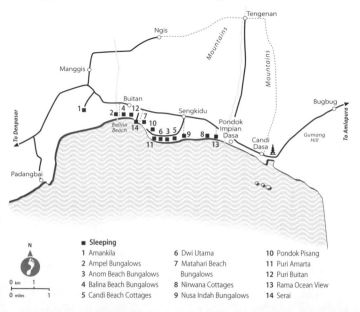

■ Sleeping		
1 Amankila	6 Dwi Utama	10 Pondok Pisang
2 Ampel Bungalows	7 Matahari Beach	11 Puri Amarta
3 Anom Beach Bungalows	Bungalows	12 Puri Buitan
4 Balina Beach Bungalows	8 Nirwana Cottages	13 Rama Ocean View
5 Candi Beach Cottages	9 Nusa Indah Bungalows	14 Serai

calming and peaceful milieu, and with only 35 guest pavilions and 3 vast swimming pools on different levels of the hill, it is easy to imagine you are the only guest in residence. The guest pavilions are set amongst coconut and frangipani trees, separated by marble walkways, and each has a view over the Lombok Strait. The cove at the bottom of the hill is only accessible from the hotel, providing one of the few private beaches on Bali. The library includes a good range of books on Bali and Indonesia. 2 restaurants (expensive to mid-range), the main restaurant has views and good reasonably priced food; the food at the beach club is disappointing. Many cultural activities, watersports, tours etc, impeccable service. Voted hotel of the year by *Tatler* magazine and possibly the most remarkable of the Aman hotels on Bali – but prices to match. **AL** *Serai*, Buitan, Manggis, Karangasem 80871, T41011, F41015. A luxury class hotel set in a coconut grove beside the sea in total seclusion, 58 rooms (superior, deluxe and suites), a good location but the décor is rather functional, large swimming pool, restaurant, boutique, satellite TV, airport transfer. **A-B** *Balina Beach Bungalows (Pondok Pantai Balina)*, Balina Beach, Manggis, Postal reservations: *PT, Griyawisata Hotel Management*, Wijaya Grand Centre Blok G No 20-21, Jl Darmawangsa Raya, Jakarta 12160, T021-41002/3/4/5, F41001. 42 Balinese style bungalows set in large, tropical gardens with beautiful sea views, each bungalow has a private, Western style bathroom with hot water and fan or a/c, and a verandah, the bungalows are set in the grounds away from the sea, restaurant (cheap), bar and café overlooking the sea, small swimming pool, sea sports, snorkelling, scuba diving, fishing and sailing can be arranged, tours, car/motorbike hire, currency exchange, the most attractive of the 2 places to stay at Balina Beach, but other places offer better value. **A-B** *Puri Buitan*, Balina Beach, Manggis, Postal reservations: PO Box 3444, Denpasar 80034, T/F0361-223718, (at hotel) T41021. 34 rooms in a featureless modern hotel, rooms are functional, lacking in character, but clean, with fan or a/c, private Western style bathrooms, deluxe rooms have a sea view, restaurant (cheap) overlooking the smallish pool, access to pebbly beach, not particularly attractive, or good value. **C-D** *Matahari Beach Bungalows* (formerly *Sunrise Beach Bungalows*), Buitan, Manggis, Postal address: PO Box 287, Denpasar 80001, T41008/41009. Signposted from the main road, follow a steep path down the hill for about 50 m, beautiful setting in a large coconut grove beside the sea, with a beach suitable for swimming though occasionally there is a current, and offering complete seclusion, 11 fairly attractive bungalows and rooms with private bathroom, Western toilet, fan, very clean, some large family rooms with 3 beds, several of the cheapest rooms have a shared ceiling so your neighbours will probably hear your every movement, breakfast included, meals available if required, Ketut, the owner, speaks good English and is very helpful, he used to be in the tourist industry so is knowledgeable about Bali. **D-E** *Ampel Bungalows*, Manggis Beach, 6 km from Candi Dasa, just off the main road, T41209. A peaceful, rural setting overlooking rice paddies and the sea, 4 simple, very clean bungalows, with private mandi, Western toilet and verandah with seating, the black sand beach is 5 mins' walk as is Balina Beach with a selection of restaurants, price including breakfast, very friendly owners, signposted from the main road shortly after the *Amankila Hotel*.

Sengkidu Village

Phone code: 0366 Two kilometres west of Candi Dasa, is an authentic Balinese village as yet unravaged by tourism. The pretty backstreets lead down to the sea and beach along which a hotel and five bungalow accommodations have so far been built. If arriving by bemo, ask the driver to let you off in the centre of the village by the temple and sign for *Candi Beach Cottage*. Follow the signpost to the right of the temple; the track leads to the beach and accommodation, 400 m. Surrounded by coconut groves and tropical trees, Sengkidu offers an attractive alternative to Candi Dasa and is more pleasant and more interesting than Balina Beach.

The village itself has a number of shops, fruit stalls and a temple where festivals are celebrated; foreigners are welcome to participate if they observe temple etiquette and wear the appropriate dress, otherwise they can watch.

A *Candi Beach Cottage*, reservations: PO Box 3308, Denpasar 80033, T41234, F41111. **Sleeping** Luxury hotel set in large, scenic tropical gardens, in a quiet location beside sea with access to beach, offering everything you would expect from a hotel in this class, popular with tour groups, elegant rooms with a/c, minibar, satellite TV, IDD telephone, private bathrooms, private terrace or balcony, seaside restaurant (**3-2**), bar, large swimming pool, children's pool, tennis courts, fitness centre, games room, etc, scuba diving, snorkelling, tours, money exchange, car rental, medical clinic. **A-B** *Anom Beach Bungalows*, T/F0361-233998. 18 bungalows and rooms, attractively decorated, with fan or a/c, some with mini-bar, private bathroom with hot water, small pool, seaside restaurant (cheap), access to beach, airport transfer available, watersports, tours, car hire, very overpriced, the grounds are not particularly attractive, the rooms do not face the sea. **C-D** *Pondok Bananas (Pisang)*, T41065. Family-run, set in a large coconut grove beside the sea with access to beach, very peaceful and secluded, 400 m beyond the other accommodations, might suit an artist or writer looking for long term accommodation, 4 spotless rooms/bungalows built to a high standard in Balinese style, with private modern bathrooms with hot water, including a 2-storey bungalow with downstairs living area and upstairs bedroom. **D** *Puri Amarta* (*Amarta Beach Bungalows*), T41230. 10 bungalows set in large, attractive gardens beside the sea and beach, well-run and very popular, liable to be full even off-season with many guests returning year after year, bungalows face the sea and are very clean with private bathroom, Western toilet, good breakfast included in price, restaurant (cheap) beside sea. **D-E** *Dwi Utama*, T41053. 6 very clean rooms, not facing sea, with fan, private bathroom, shower and Western toilet, beachside restaurant (cheap), access to good, small beach, well-tended, small garden, peaceful, good value. **D-E** *Nusa Indah Bungalows*, Sengkidu, signposted and reached via a separate track to the left of the temple, set in a peaceful location beside the sea, amidst coconut groves and rice paddies, 7 clean, simple bungalows facing the coconut grove with private mandi, Western toilet, fan, verandahs with seating, access to small, rocky beach, beachside restaurant (cheap).

Cheap *Dwi Utama* (in addition to its beachside restaurant) and shop which also acts **Eating** as a Post Office. *Baliarsa Restaurant*. See also under accommodation.

Candi Dasa

Candi Dasa is smaller, more intimate and offers better value for money than *Phone code: 0363* the main seaside resorts of Bali. It also provides an excellent base from which to explore the sights of East Bali.

The gold and black sand beach has been badly eroded, washed away by the sea due to the destruction of the reef for building materials, despite the unsightly concrete groynes and piers, which were constructed to prevent this happening. However, the lack of beach has saved Candi Dasa from over development. Even so, it is at its best off season. There is no surf, so swimming is safe. **Candi Dasa temple** is on the opposite side of the road from the lagoon. There are good walks in the area, either round the headland east to a deserted black-sand beach, only possible at low tide, or up over the hills to Tenganan. You can also climb Gumang Hill, by following the main road out of town to the east, for spectacular views of the surrounding countryside and across the strait to Lombok. The small temple at the top of the hill is the site of a major festival every two years at the time of the full moon in October (see below).

The village Candi Dasa gets its name from the temple on the hill overlooking the main road and the fresh water lagoon; the ancient relics in this temple indicate that there has been a village on this site since the 11th century. The word 'dasa' means 10 and refers to the 10 holy teachings of the Buddhist 'Tripitaka'. There are in reality two temples, one dedicated to Siva and the other to Hariti, giving rise to an unusual situation whereby one site serves both Hindus and Buddhists. Childless couples come here to pray to Hariti for children.

Traditionally fishermen in these parts have gone out fishing each day from 0400 until 0800, and again in the afternoon from about 1430 until 1800. Although most people on Bali fear the sea as a place of evil spirits and a potential source of disaster, those who live near the sea and earn their living from it consider it a holy place and worship such sea gods as *Baruna*. The boats they use, *jukung*, are made from locally grown wood and bamboo which is cut according to traditional ritual practice. The day chosen for cutting down the tree must be deemed favourable by the gods to whom prayers and offerings are then made, and a sapling is planted to replace it. Carved from a single tree trunk without using nails and with bamboo outriders to give it stability, the finished boat will be gaily coloured with the characteristic large eyes that enable it to see where the fish lurk. The design has not changed for thousands of years; it is very stable due to the low centre of gravity created by the way the sail is fastened. These days there are fewer fish to catch and many fishermen augment their living by taking tourists out snorkelling on the reef. *Jukung* cost about 850,000Rp.

In the rice field by the road to Tenganan are two ingenious **bird-scaring devices** operated by a man sitting in a thatched hut. One is a metre-long bamboo pole with plastic bags and strips of bamboo; when the man pulls on the attached rope, the pole swings round causing the bamboo strips to make a clacking noise and the plastic bags to flutter. The other consists of two 4-m-long bamboo poles which are hinged at one end, with flags and plastic bags attached; when the attached rope is pulled, the two poles swing round with flags and plastic bags waving.

Excursions The village of **Tenganan**, 3 km north of Candi Dasa, is reputed to be the oldest on Bali – and is a village of the Bali Aga, the island's original inhabitants before the Hindu invasion almost 1,000 years ago (see box page 178). The walled community consists of a number of longhouses, rice barns, shrines, pavilions and a large village meeting hall, all arranged in accordance with traditional beliefs. Membership of the village is exclusive and until recently visitors were actively discouraged. The inhabitants have to have been born here and then to marry within the village; anyone who violates the rules is banished to a neighbouring community. Despite the studied maintenance of a traditional way of life, the inhabitants of Tenganan have taken the decision to embrace the tourist industry. It is in fact a very wealthy village, deriving income not only from tourism but also from a large area of communally owned and worked rice paddys and dryland fields.

Tenganan is one of the last villages to produce the unusual **double ikat** or *geringsing*, where both the warp and the weft are tie-dyed and great skill is needed to align and then weave the two into the desired pattern (see box page 181). The cloth is woven on body-tension (back-strap) looms with a continuous warp; colours used are dark rust, brown and purple, although newer pieces suffer from fading due to the use of inferior dyes. Motifs are floral and geometric, and designs are constrained to about 20 traditional forms. It is said that one piece of cloth takes about five years to complete and only six families still understand the process. Note that much of the cloth for sale in the village does not originate *from Tenganan. ■ Admission to village: by donation, vehicles prohibited. Getting there: it is possible to walk the 3 km to Tenganan; take the road heading north, 1 km to the west of Candi Dasa – it ends at the village. Alternatively, walk or catch a bemo heading west towards Klungkung, get off at the turning 1 km west of Candi Dasa and catch an ojek up to the village. Tours to Tenganan are also arranged by the bigger hotels and the tour agents on the main road. Bemos run past the turn-off for the village from Denpasar's Batubulan terminal.*

About 13 km southwest of Candi Dasa is the temple and cave of **Goa Lawah** (see page 164). ■ *Getting there: regular bemos run along the coast.*

Boats leave for **Nusa Penida** from Padangbai (see page 165).

The royal bathing pools of **Tirtagangga** (see page 178) and the town and palace of **Amlapura** (see page 176) are both within easy reach of Candi Dasa.

Three small islands with coral reefs are to be found: 30 minutes by boat from Candi Dasa. They make a good day trip for snorkelling or diving. Samuh village co-operative keeps goats on the largest of these islands, called **Nusa Kambing (goat island)**. Every six months the goats are transported back to the mainland by boat. Quite a sight if you are lucky enough to witness it. ■ *Getting there: most hotels and losmen will arrange a boat for the day.*

There are many very reasonably priced places to stay available. Most accommodation is sited adjacent to the beach on the seaward side of the main road. At the eastern end of Candi Dasa, where the main road bends to the left, a small road (Jl Banjar Samuh, there is no name sign but there are many signs indicating accommodations including *Puri Bagus* and *Genggong*) leads off on the right lined with accommodation on the seaward side. Known as Samuh village, this slightly rural area is perhaps the most attractive place to stay. Expect power cuts if you visit during the rainy season unless yours is one of the many places which have their own generators. Most include breakfast in their rates. Most hotels with swimming pools allow non-residents to use their pools for a charge of 6,000Rp per person.

Sleeping

Candi Dasa West

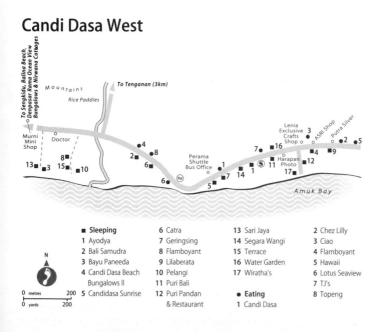

■ **Sleeping**		
1 Ayodya	6 Catra	13 Sari Jaya	2 Chez Lilly
2 Bali Samudra	7 Geringsing	14 Segara Wangi	3 Ciao
3 Bayu Paneeda	8 Flamboyant	15 Terrace	4 Flamboyant
4 Candi Dasa Beach	9 Lilaberata	16 Water Garden	5 Hawaii
Bungalows II	10 Pelangi	17 Wiratha's	6 Lotus Seaview
5 Candidasa Sunrise	11 Puri Bali		7 TJ's
	12 Puri Pandan	● **Eating**	8 Topeng
	& Restaurant	1 Candi Dasa	

0 metres 200
0 yards 200

Bali

Bali

AL *Puri Bagus* (east of lagoon), T51223, F52779. A/c, restaurant, pool, good rooms and attractive open-air bathrooms, but overpriced, shadeless pool area. **A** *Rama Ocean View*, T51864, F51866. A/c, restaurant, pool, on the road into Candi Dasa about 1 km from the town 'centre', tennis and fitness centre, good pool, overpriced catering mainly to tour groups, restaurant (mid-range). **A-B** *Ida Beach Village*, Jl Banjar Samuh, postal address: PO Box 3270, Denpasar, T41118/9, F41041. Designed as a Balinese village, each bungalow is built in traditional style and set in its own small, private courtyard, very attractive rooms with a/c, hot water, telephone and Western-style bathroom, some 2-storey bungalows with downstairs living room, swimming pool and access to beach, beachside restaurant (cheap). Recommended. **A-B** *Kubu Bali Bungalows*, T41532, 41256, F41531. These bungalows have a breathtaking location extending up the hill behind the *Kubu Bali* restaurant with spectacular seaviews, each attractively furnished bungalow has a Western bathroom with hot water, a/c, refrigerator, telephone and ceiling fan, and a verandah with seating, set in extensive, beautiful, tropical water gardens with live gamelan music playing all day, there is a coffee shop and swimming pool set high on the hill with the same inspiring views, you will need to be fairly fit to reach the topmost suites, 4-star restaurant located on the high street, with the *Baliku Restaurant* beside the sea just across the main street, airport transfer available, highly recommended. **A-B** *Nirwana Cottages*, Candi Dasa Beach, Sengkidu, Amlapura 80871, T41136, 41903 F41543, nirwanacot@ denpasar.wasantara.net.id Situated outside Candi Dasa on the south side, 300 m from the main road down a dirt track, 12 spotless bungalows built in the traditional Balinese style offering peace and tranquillity, set in a coconut grove beside a quiet beach with beautiful sea views. A/c, HW, house phone, complimentary tea/coffee/drinking water in each room, deluxe rooms with refrigerator, large pool with sunken bar, transport to/from airport available on request, seasports and tours

Candi Dasa East

	6 Dutha Cottages	17 Puri Pepaya	2 Astawa
7 Gandhi Ashram	18 Puri Pudak Bungalows	3 Gloria
8 Gengong Cottage	19 Puri Oka	4 Kubu Bali
9 Ida Beach Village	20 Rama Ocean View	5 Legend Rock Café
0 metres 100	10 Ida's	21 Ramayana	6 Lila Arnawa Theatre
0 yards 100	11 Kelapa Mas &	22 Satria	& Restaurant
	Restaurant	23 Sekar Orchid	7 Raja's
■ **Sleeping**	12 Nani Beach Inn	Bungalows	8 Warung Nyoman
1 Agung Bungalows	13 Natia	24 Sindhu Brata	9 Rasmini Warung
2 Barong	14 Pandawa	25 Srikandi	10 Srijati
3 Candi Dasa Park	15 Pondok Bamboo		
Resort	& Restaurant	● **Eating**	
4 Dewa Bharata	16 Puri Bagus	1 Asoka	
5 Dewi			

available by arrangement, car hire, *Seaside Restaurant* (cheap), no music in order to pre-serve the peaceful atmosphere here. Owned by Mrs Widagdo Fleming, who is married to a German. This place is run to the highest standards at very reasonable prices. Highly recommended. **A-B** *Resor Prima Candidasa*, Jl Banjar Samuh, PO Box 01, Manggis 80871, T/F204440. A rather unattractive hotel catering mainly to tour groups, the 28 rather dark rooms face each other away from the sea, a/c, HW, fridge, TV, pool, beach access. **A-B** *Water Garden*, PO Box 39, T35540. Restaurant, pool, individual cottages, set on the hillside in lovely gardens, each cottage has its own verandah overlooking a pri-vate lily pond, simple rooms with HW, very attractively laid out. Recommended.

B *Candi Dasa Beach Bungalows II*, Jl Raya Candi Dasa, T35536, F35537. A/c, 2 restau-rants, pool, 2-storey blocks, set in beautiful garden, views from rooms vary, beach here is only so-so, food recommended. **B** *Samudra Indah*, T35542, F35542. A/c, pool, on the south edge of town, nice pool, comfortable but featureless rooms with hot water. **B-C** *Dewa Bharata Bungalows* (also has branch in Kuta, see Kuta section), T41090, 41091, F41091. Popular, located in the centre of town beside the sea, 24 attractive bungalows in well-tended tropical gardens, rooms with a/c or fan, HW, pri-vate bathrooms with Western toilets, swimming pool beside the sea, open air, rea-sonably priced, beachside restaurant (cheap) with beautiful sea views offering Western, Indonesian and Chinese food. **B-C** *Puri Oka*, T41092, F41093. Small pool, simple but attractive rooms, with attached bathrooms and hot water, very pleasant restaurant overlooking the sea, the tiny beach here evaporates at high tide and there is no swimming – although outrigger trips can be arranged to the islands off-shore for snorkelling, very overpriced. **B-D** *Puri Pudak* (east of lagoon), T41978. Well-designed, clean bungalows, with fan, private bathrooms, some with HW, attractive garden, beside sea but with no direct access which is a major drawback, a little overpriced. **B-D** *Sindhu Brata* (beside lagoon), T41825. Some a/c and hot water, clean with pri-vate bathroom, set in large attractive garden beside the sea with beach, restaurant (cheap) with sea views.

C *Pondok Bamboo*, T41534, F41818. In centre of town beside the sea, average rooms all with private bathroom, Western toilet, some with HW, new swimming pool and seaside restaurant with grand sea views should be finished late 1996. **C** *Pondok Impian Dasa*, opposite the turning to Tenganan, T41897, F0361-96335. New accommodations in bungalows and lumbungs (2-storey Balinese style build-ings) set in rather plain gardens, with small sea frontage (no real beach) at the point where a slightly dirty village stream flows into the sea. Rooms are not particularly attractive, bathrooms have hot water and Western toilets. Swimming pool. Seaside restaurant (cheap). **C-D** *Bayu Paneeda Beach Inn*, T41104. Peaceful location to west of town beside the sea with fabulous sea views, bungalows with private bathrooms (Western toilet) and fan, deluxe rooms with a/c and baths with hot water, restaurant (cheap) with good sea views. **C-D** *Genggong Cottage*, Jl Banjar Samuh, T41105. 12 rooms set in large gardens with beach, rooms are clean but simple with fan, private mandi, Western toilet and shower, 2 rooms have hot water, rooms are overpriced but you are paying for the beach, a rare asset in Candi Dasa. **C-D** *Ida's*, T41096. This place consists of just 5 bungalows set in a large coconut grove beside the sea with access to its own small beach (due to the contours of the land and the direction of the sea cur-rent, less of the sandy beach was lost at Ida's following the destruction of the coral reef). Ida's was the second homestay to open in Candi Dasa in 1975, 2 large 2-storey bungalows and 3 smaller single storey bungalows beautifully built in the traditional Balinese style with rattan floors, bamboo walls and screens, mosquito nets and pri-vate bathrooms. An underground stream in the garden supplies fresh water. In the gardens are 2 old rice barns brought here from a nearby village and rebuilt to provide a traditional style rest area for guests. The 50 coconut palms produce 600 coconuts in

Bali

2 months; (there is a local saying 'Coconuts have eyes' meaning that a falling coconut will not hit you!), manager/owner is Ida Ayu Srihati and her German husband both of whom have lived in the USA for many years, and are an excellent source of local knowledge; Ida herself is related to the Klungkung royal family. Highly recommended, reservations advisable. **C-D** *Kelapa Mas*, PO Box 103, Amlapura 80801, T41047. Located on the eastern edge of town in a beautiful, large, traditional Balinese garden with a shrine, beside the sea with its own small area of beach, spotless bungalows, some overlooking the sea, with private bathrooms, Western toilets, deluxe rooms with a/c, bathtubs, hot water, library and secondhand book shop, (cheap) restaurant offering excellent food including seafood, Balinese specialities and performances of the Legong Dance on certain evenings, English language Indonesian newspapers can be read in the lobby. Excellent value. Recommended. **C-D** *Sekar Orchid Beach Bungalows*, Jl Banjar Samuh, PO Box 113, Candi Dasa, Bali 80851, T41086. 8 attractive rooms with private bathroom, Western toilet, some with hot water and bathtub, fan, set in large, pretty gardens beside the sea with a beach except at high tide, very well run and spotlessly clean, safety deposit box, Wendy the Javanese owner has lived in England and Germany and speaks both languages, a very secure accommodation which is an important consideration given the growing number of thefts from tourist bungalows in Candi Dasa. Recommended. **C-E** *Barong*, Jl Banjar Samuh, T41127. Set in attractive gardens beside the sea, simple rooms with large comfortable bamboo beds, fan and in the cheaper rooms minimal furniture and weatherbeaten, 'no maintenance' private bathrooms open to the skies with Western toilets, you can listen to the waves crashing at night or hear the magical frog chorus at the start of the rainy season, you might even find a frog in your bathroom!, the more expensive rooms face the sea and have enclosed bathrooms, be mindful of security as there have been thefts, good breakfast.

D *Agung Bungalows*, T235535. Good value for location in centre of town, situated beside the sea with access to beach, basic bungalows with private bathroom (Western toilet), set in large gardens with coconut palms. **D** *Bunga Putri* (east of lagoon), at the north end of the bay, past the fishing boats, restaurant, peaceful undeveloped setting, good rooms. Recommended. **D** *Puri Pandan*, PO Box 126, Amlapura 80801, T41541. Rooms average, bathrooms better than average with hot water. **D** *Srikandi* (east of lagoon), T53125. Clean rooms but rather close together, popular, new restaurant (cheap) beside sea serving Indonesian and Western food. **D-E** *Dutha Cottages*, Jl Banjar Samuh, T41143/5. 10 rooms beside the sea but with no direct access, fairly basic but clean, with private mandi, Western toilet, shower, set in coconut grove with pretty gardens. **D-E** *Nani Beach Inn*, Jl Banjar Samuh, simple rooms with private mandi, Western toilet, shower, set in coconut grove. **D-E** *Pandawa Homestay* (just east of lagoon), T41929. Closely spaced bungalows with fan and private bathroom, some with hot water, access to sea via tiny beach. **D-E** *Pepaya Bungalows*, Jl Banjar Samuh, T41567. Clean, simple rooms with fan and attractive private bathroom, Western toilet, set in large gardens but not beside the sea, attached to the *Asoka Restaurant*. **D-E** *Ramayana*, Jl Banjar Samuh, T/F41778. 3 simple but attractive bungalows with private mandi, Western toilets, shower, verandahs with outside seating and hammocks. Beside the sea with access to small beach where the local fishermen land their catch and keep their boats. Under new management so standards may have slipped. **D-E** *Satria* (east of lagoon), attractive rooms, nice bathrooms, good value, but not on the beachside, popular with local Balinese men.

Gandhi Ashram, overlooking the lagoon at eastern end of town, this ashram is run according to Gandhian principles and guests follow strict codes of behaviour, by invitation to those who are genuinely interested in Gandhi's teachings, there are bungalows and more basic rooms, this was the first homestay to open in Candi Dasa, run by Ibu Gedong Oka.

Out of town D-E The following are all situated outside of town to the west in a peaceful setting with access to the sea, well-sited for visits to Tenganan. Inland there are beautiful views of rice terraces and mountains, with possibilities for walks. These rice paddies are communal land owned by Tenganan village; you can watch the villagers rhythmically working the fields as if living in a different age, adjacent to but oblivious of the tourist world across the road. They all offer similar accommodation consisting of basic bungalows with private bathrooms and Western toilets, fan, at similar prices, and in descending order of preference: *Terrace Beach Bungalows*, nice setting beside beach; *Taruna Homestay*, rooms could do with redecoration, good sea views, tea and coffee available all day; *Flamboyant Bungalows*, beside sea, rooms could do with redecoration, tea available all day; *Sari Jaya Sea Side Cottage*, T41149. Average rooms in attractive gardens beside the sea; *Pelangi Homestay*, T41270. Bungalows set in attractive gardens, not beside the sea but with easy access via adjacent accommodation.

There are a variety of well-priced restaurants dotted along the main road with similar menus; seafood is the best bet. Most restaurants cater to perceived European tastes which can be disappointing for anyone who likes Indonesian food. Many of the above accommodations have restaurants, often with sea views. The following are also recommended though quality and ingredients can vary enormously from day to day; you might have a delicious meal one day, order the exact same dish the next day and be very disappointed.

Eating
Several restaurants including Kelapa Mas, Bali Tropical & Astawa offer dance performances & gamelan recitals in the evenings

Mid-range *Kubu Bali*, good seafood and Chinese and Indonesian specialities.

Cheap *Astawa*, popular though you are paying for the décor. *Kelapa Mas*, good value and sometimes excellent food. *Legend Rock Café*, Western and Indonesian. *Pandan*, on the beach, daily Balinese buffet, reasonably priced international food. Recommended. *Raja's Restaurant and Cocktail Bar*. *TJ's Café*, Mexican, good food, friendly. Recommended.

Very cheap *Rasmini Warung*, a genuine warung serving simple Indonesian food and the best Nasi Campur in town though quality varies from day to day, excellent value.

Dance Balinese dance performances staged nightly at 2100 at the *Pandan Harum* near the centre of town. Many restaurants offer performances of Balinese dance and gamelan music in the evenings, see under 'Eating'. The best performances are at the newly opened *Lila Arnaud* which has been designed as a theatre with a proper stage, prices include dinner. Several places have nightly shows of Western films on video; best of these is *Raja's* whose Australian owner imports the latest films.

Entertainment

Crafts *Geringsing*, on the main road, sells double ikat cloth from Tenganan and other Balinese arts and crafts. *Lenia*, T41174, a good place to see *ata* baskets, these baskets are made from a locally grown vine which is much more durable than rattan, water resistant, it is claimed these baskets can last for up to 100 years, *Lenia* also has a small selection of Sumba blankets and other quality crafts.

Shopping

Books The best place for books is the *Candidasa Bookstore* which has a reasonable selection of books on Bali and Indonesia as well as secondhand books, magazines and newspapers. This is one of the few places where books on Indonesia are for sale at reasonable prices. Daily papers arrive in the afternoon and are cheaper here as well. The lady who runs it speaks excellent English and is very friendly and helpful. *Kelapa Mas* has a good selection of secondhand books.

Fruit A growing number of shops are realizing that travellers like to buy fresh tropical fruit. There is also a small stall opposite the lagoon which sells reasonable quality produce though they are reluctant to bargain. If you wonder why the papayas often taste disappointing it is because they are picked whilst still unripe and then stored in ashes to soften them.

Groceries *Asri*, fixed price store for film, food and medicine.

Tailor The Chinese lady who runs the Candi Dasa bookstore is also a tailor. She speaks excellent English and is very helpful.

Sports **Diving** *Stingray Dive Centre*, *Puri Bali Homestay*. *Baruna Watersports*, *Puri Bagus Hotel*, T0361-753820/751223, F753809/ 752779, prices start from US$40 for 1 dive PADI course (4 days), US$300. Also available fishing and watersports. **Snorkelling** Rent snorkels from hotels and charter a boat to go out to a reef.

Tour operators Several travel agents book tours, reconfirm tickets and sell bus tickets to major destinations in Java.

Transport **Local** Bicycle, motorbike and car hire from hotels, losmen and from shops along the main road.

Road Bemo: regular connections with **Denpasar's** Batubulan terminal, **Amlapura** and **Klungkung**. **Shuttle bus**: more expensive, but quicker, shuttle buses link Candi Dasa with **Denpasar**, **Ubud**, **Kuta**, **Lovina**, **Kintamani**, **Padangbai**, **Tirtagangga**, **Tulamben** and **Lombok** (7,500-20,000Rp). *Perama* is one of the best with an office in Candi Dasa. T41114/5.

Directory **Banks** There are several money changers offering reasonable rates. **Communications** Postal agent: opposite the *Candi Dasa Beach Bungalows*.

Amlapura (Karangasem)

Phone code: 0363
Colour map 1, grid B2

At one time Amlapura, capital of the Regency of Karangasem, was the seat of one of the most powerful states in Bali. Today, this may be hard to believe – it is a quiet and attractive town, with wonderful views of Mount Agung from its clean landscaped streets. Little happens here. Earthquakes which accompanied the massive eruption of Mount Agung in 1963 caused much damage and in order to protect the town from future devastation the name of the capital was changed from Karangasem to Amlapura to confuse the evil spirits who had wreaked this havoc. Several palaces are to be found in Karangasem, the most accessible being the **Puri Agung**, or Puri Kanginan, to the east of the main north-south road, Jalan Gajah Mada. The last king of Karangasem was born at the Puri Agung. Entrance to the palace is through tall gateways. To the south are a cluster of buildings, which would have been offices and artist's workshops. Another gateway takes the visitor out of this first compound and a door to the south leads into the major part of the palace. A pillared building faces south onto a *bale Kembang* or floating pavilion. The buildings are all rather run-down, and are rather architecturally eclectic, with European, Balinese and Chinese elements and motifs. There are interesting photographs from the early part of this century and some rather tatty furniture. ■ *Small admission charge. 0800-1700 Mon-Sun.* There is a **market** to the south of the palace; the stallholders seem strangely reluctant to bargain.

The ruined water palace of **Ujung** is very beautiful in its romantic decrepitude. **Excursions** It lies 8 km south of town towards the coast and was built by the last King of Karangasem. The hills of Lombok can be seen from the site which is in a beautiful position at the edge of the sea with the huge volcanic cone of Mount Agung inland. Most of the buildings were destroyed during an earthquake in 1963. The palace must have been splendid in its time. Now, you can wander among the large lotus ponds, still part full, and explore the ruined pavilions. The bridges leading over the water to the old temple have all collapsed, and columns lean at crazy angles. Parts of the balustrades, their intricate carvings still intact, litter the ground. Although the rice terraces and steps up to the central pavilion above the ponds are intact, the palace has the air of an ancient lost city. No crowds or hawkers – eminently suitable for those with fertile imaginations. There are plans to have the palace restored. On the nearby beach, the colourful fishing boats are very picturesque, with children frolicking here every evening. ■ *Getting there: bemos leave from the station near the market (south of the palace).*

Tirtagangga royal bathing pools are 7 km north of town (see next page).

Bebandem is the scene of an important cattle market held every three days, as is usual with Balinese markets. On market day stalls are set up selling everything from medicines to sarongs. Ironsmiths take up their positions along the main road producing cockfighting spurs, keris knives, farm tools etc. The animals start their journey to the village at dawn, often on foot, and the activity is over by 0900. ■ *Getting there: by bemo from Amlapura.*

Abian Soan is a small peaceful village 4 km west of Amlapura with accommodation. **E** *Homestay Lila*, is a genuine family homestay in a rural setting beside the main Amlapura to Bebandem road. The garden is full of fruit trees and wandering chickens, geese and pigs. The five bungalows are characterful but a little primitive, with private mandis and squat toilets except for one seatless Western toilet. The garden extends down to a river with a small waterfall.

There are walks through the ricefields and a hill, **Bukit Kusambi**, a few kilometres away with views of Mount Agung, Mount Seraya and Mount Rinjani in the distance, climb it at dawn to watch a spectacular sunrise. Surprisingly, the family speak very limited English. ■ *Getting there: take a bemo from the turn-off outside Amlapura bound for Rendang and get off after 3½ km. By car follow the road west to Rendang for 3.2 km, Homestay Lila is signposted on the main road. There is car parking in a neighbour's drive, though the gate is frequently shut.*

E *Homestay Sidha Karya*, Jl Hasannudin. **E** *Lahar Mas Inn*, Jl Gatot Subroto 1. Small, **Sleeping** friendly people. **E** *Losman Kembang Remaja*, 200 m along the road to Bebandem

Bemo stops for onward connections from Amlapura

Bali

The Bali Aga: the original Balinese

In pre-history, Bali was populated by animists whose descendants today are represented by the Bali Aga, literally 'Original Balinese'. The Aga are now restricted to a few relic communities in North and East Bali, particularly in the regency of Karangkasem. Most have been extensively assimilated into the Hindu-Balinese mainstream. Miguel Covarrubias visited the Aga village of Tenganan in the 1930s, a village which even then was extraordinary in the extent to which it was resisting the pressures of change. He wrote:

"The people of Tenganan are tall, slender and aristocratic in a rather ghostly, decadent way, with light skins and refined manners. ... They are proud and look down even on the Hindu-Balinese nobility, who respect them and leave them alone. They live in a strange communistic... system in which individual ownership of property is not recognized and in which even the plans and measurements of the houses are set and alike for everybody".

Even today, a distinction is still made between the Bali Aga and the Wong Majapahit. The latter arrived from Java following the fall of the Majapahit Kingdom at the end of the 15th century.

In former years, the Aga were probably cannibalistic. It has been said that Aga corpses used to be washed with water which was allowed to drip onto a bundle of unhusked rice. This was then dried and threshed, cooked, moulded into the shape of a human being, and served to the relatives of the deceased. The eating of the rice figure is said to symbolize the ritual eating of the corpse, so imbibing its powers.

outside of town, T21565. Fairly basic rooms with private mandi, squat toilet, few Westerners stay here.

Eating **Cheap** *RM Surabaya*, adjacent to the market, good Chinese and Indonesian dishes, popular with local expats, good value. *Pasar Malam*, near the main market serves good local food. Restaurants close early at about 2100.

Transport **Road Bemo/minibus**: the bemo terminal is on Jl Kesatrian. Regular connections with **Denpasar's** Batubulan terminal and to **Manggis, Culik, Padangbai, Klungkung, Tirtagangga** and **Singaraja**. See map for bemo stops outside the main town for onward connections.

Directory **Banks** *Bank Rakyat Indonesia*, Jl Gajah Mada. **Communications** Post Office: Jl Gatot Subroto 25.

Tirtagangga

Phone code. 0363
Colour map 1, grid B2

Northwest of Amlapura by 7 km is the site of the royal bathing pools of Tirtagangga. Built in 1947 by the last king of Amlapura, they were badly damaged by the earthquake of 1963 but have since been restored. The pools occupy a stunning position on the side of a hill, overlooking terraced ricefields. At harvest times the fields are full of people gathering the golden rice, and carrying it on poles back to the villages to dry. The complex consists of various pools (2 of which visitors can swim in), fed by clear mountain streams with water spouting from fountains and stone animals. It is popular with local people as well as visitors and is a peaceful place to retreat to except at weekends and holidays when young Balinese arrive en masse on their motorbikes. ■ *500Rp, plus 2,000Rp to swim in the upper pool, 1,000Rp in the lower pool, children half price. Mon-Sun.*

There are many walks in the hills around Tirtagangga; the scenery is superb **Excursions** and there are several traditional villages worth visiting: **Abadi**; **Tanah Lingis** with its interesting music group which sings in rhythms imitative of a gamelan orchestra, this musical form originated in Lombok and on Bali is found only in Karangasem; **Budakling** with a Buddhist tradition that pre-dates the arrival of Hinduism on Bali, this village also produces good quality gold and silver pieces. There are spectacular walks up **Mount Agung** one of which starts from the village of **Tanaharon**.

About 8 km northeast of Tirtagangga is temple **Pura Lempuyang** situated at an altitude of 1,060 m, one of the more important temples on Bali. It is a steep climb, so make an early start to avoid the heat and enjoy the views before the clouds roll in. All these villages have traditional festivals during the year. Your accommodation can help you plan walks.

As you follow the main road out of town up the hill towards Amed and Tulemben you **Sleeping** come first to *Puri Sawah Bungalows and Restaurant*. Further up the hill is *Kusumajaya Inn* and finally *Prima Bamboos Homestay*; of these 2 places *Prima* offers better, cleaner, newer, more attractive rooms, with slightly better views, at lower prices than *Kusumajaya*. Continue on this road for 1½ km from Tirtagangga then take the first left to reach two simple places to stay; *Geria Semalung* and *Pondok Batur Indah* have idyllic locations with stunning views over Tirtagangga to the coast. A short 10 min walk across the paddy fields from the centre of Tirtagangga in the direction of the coast will bring you to Cabe Bali (reached by car/bemo on the main Amlapura to Tirtagangga road, both routes are signposted). The other places to stay are in Tirtagangga. All include breakfast in their price.

B *Cabe Bali*, Temege, Tirtagangga, T/F22045, http://members.aol.com/cabebali Immaculate property run by a very friendly lady from Munich, Barbara Soetarto, this is one of the nicest places to stay in Karangasem. Set in glorious gardens with sea views, refreshing breezes, fruit trees and swimming pool. 3 beautifully decorated bungalows, with Slumberland beds, luxury bathrooms. Every room has views of both Mount Agung, and the coast with Nusa Penida in the distance. The café/restaurant (mid-range to cheap) is set in an open air pavilion surrounded by ponds. Barbara will take interested guests around the gardens explaining the names, and herbal uses where applicable, of the plants. *Getting there by car/bemo*: coming from Amlapura, 5 km from town turn left at the sign where the road bends sharply right, in Temege village, on the main road to Tirtagangga; follow a very rough track for 1 km. Airport pickup available, free if you stay a week. Highly recommended. 12 min walk from the centre of Titagangga along a narrow path beside the dykes. **B-C** *Puri Sawah* (formerly *Rice Terrace*), PO Box 110, Amlapura 80811, T21847, F21939. Run by Liz from Guernsey and her Balinese husband Made, the 2-storey bungalow was built to a very high standard to accommodate friends and family visiting from the UK. The upstairs bungalow is decorated very tastefully in Balinese style with a balcony offering glorious views over the rice paddies, private bathroom with squat toilet. The attractive downstairs bungalow has private bathroom with hot water, bath and Western toilet. 4 additional rooms have been built in two 2-storey bungalows with private bathrooms with cold water and Western toilets, the restaurant (mid-range to cheap) offers excellent Indonesian and Western food and is well known for its filled baguettes, and you can even get baked beans on toast! The owners have land near Amed which they are planning to develop. Highly recommended.

C-D *Geria Gemalung*, Desa Ababi, Abang, Karangasem. No telephone, F21044. Situated just outside Tirtagangga: follow the main road heading north towards Amed for 1.4 km, turn left and follow this road for about 600 m turn left at the sign and follow the mud track for about 200 m to this family owned accommodation. A very peaceful, verdant setting on the edge of a ravine overlooking Tirtagangga with dramatic views to the coast. 6 clean, simple rooms with private bathrooms and verandahs overlooking pretty gardens surrounded by woodland; 4 are new with Western toilets, 2 older rooms with squat toilet. Very friendly owners, speak English. Restaurant (cheap) serving Balinese vegetarian food. Price includes breakfast. A little overpriced. **C-D** *Kusumajaya Inn*, T21250. Rooms in need of refurbishment (ants are a problem), no fans, all rooms with private bathroom and Western toilet, one with hot water, set in pretty gardens with grand views over the rice paddies to the distant sea, this view is shared by the functionally decorated, but cheap restaurant, trekking available, there are 99 rather gruelling steps up to the Inn from the road. **D** *Prima Bamboo Homestay and Restaurant*, T21316, F21044. 7 rooms, well run, clean, set in immaculate gardens with bamboo windchimes, terrific views of rice paddies and the coast, all rooms with fan, private mandi with Western toilet, outside verandahs to enjoy the view, very peaceful, restaurant (cheap), climbs of Mount Agung and other treks can be arranged, owner is a keen chess player. Recommended. **D** *Tirta Ayu Homestay*, within the water garden itself, rather overpriced for 6 unexciting rooms, though the most expensive room is attractive with a large bathroom, a great position. Rooms are clean with private bathrooms, Western toilet, set around lovely, very peaceful gardens, 2-3 times a month there is a Holy Water Ceremony in the grounds of the water gardens in the afternoon, ask owner for information, price includes access to the water gardens and swimming pools, restaurant (mid-range) overlooking water gardens with cool breezes (see below).

D-E *Dhangin Tamin Inn*, PO Box 132, Amlapura 80811, T22059. Rooms are attractive, very clean but rather dark, set around a pretty courtyard, all with private mandi and Western toilet, fan, safety deposit box available, restaurant (very cheap). **D-E** *Pondok Batur Indah*, Tanah Langis. 1 km past Geria Semalung, follow the rough mud track for about 300 m, in same ownership as *Rijasa*, 500 m from town centre by foot following a path through paddy fields (ask for directions at *Rijasa*), 1½ km by road, 4 basic rooms with private mandi, views. **D-E** *Pondok Wisata Dau*, T21292. Reached across paddy fields just above the water palace in a peaceful setting, modern house with 3 clean, new but featureless rooms, only 1 with private mandi, squat toilets, if there is no one at home ask at *Rama Tirtagangga Restaurant* in town near the entrance to the water palace. **D-E** *Rijasa Homestay and Restaurant*, T21873. Clean but drab and basic rooms with private mandi (Western toilet), set round simple gardens, owner can provide a map and information about local walks, restaurant (very cheap) the *Nasi Campur* has been recommended, off season prices negotiable.

Eating **Cheap** *Good Karma*, same ownership as *Good Karma Bungalows* at Amed, just outside the pools, friendly people, food recommended. *Tirta Ayu Restaurant*, T21697. An open-air restaurant within the water garden, with a fabulous position overlooking the pools and the terraced paddy fields beyond.

Very cheap *Kusumajaya Inn and Prima*, on the hill with great views over the whole panorama down to the sea, good spot for lunch. *Nasi Campur* (see *Rijasa Homestay* above) has also been recommended.

Transport **Road Minibus/bemo**: connections with **Amlapura**, **Culik**, **Kubu**, **Singaraja**. From **Denpasar's** Batubulan terminal catch a bemo to Amlapura and get off at the intersection just before Amlapura to catch a connection up the hill to Tirtagangga. Tirtagangga is easily reached by public bemo as a day trip from **Candi Dasa** (where there is a much better choice of budget price accommodation), 30 mins door to door. Perama now operates to Tirtagangga with connections to its route network on Bali

Cloth as art: Ikat in Southeast Asia

Ikat is a technique of patterning cloth characteristic of Southeast Asia and is produced from the hills of Burma to the islands of Eastern Indonesia. The word comes from the Malay word mengikat which means to bind or tie. Very simply, either the warp or the weft, and in one case both, are tied with material or fibre so that they resist the action of the dye. Hence the technique's name – resist dyeing. By dyeing, retying and dyeing again through a number of cycles it is possible to build up complex patterns. Ikat is distinguishable by the bleeding of the dye which inevitably occurs no matter how carefully the threads are tied; this gives the finished cloth a blurred finish. The earliest ikats so far found date from the 14th-15th centuries.

To prepare the cloth for dyeing, the warp or weft is strung taut on a frame. Individual threads, or groups of threads are then tied tight with fibre and leaves. In some areas wax is then smeared on top to help in the resist process. The main colour is usually dyed first, secondary colours later. With complex patterns (which are done from memory, plans are only required for new designs) and using natural dyes, it may take up to 6 months to produce a piece of cloth. Prices are correspondingly high – in Eastern Indonesia for example, top grade cloths can easily exceed 1,000,000Rp (US$500), and ritual cloths considerably more. Today, the

pressures of the market place mean that it is more likely that cloth is produced using chemical dyes (which need only one short soaking, not multiple long ones as with some natural dyes), and design motifs have generally become larger and less complex. Traditionally, warp ikat used cotton (rarely silk) and weft ikat, silk. Silk in many areas has given way to cotton, and cotton sometimes to synthetic yarns. Double ikat, where incredibly both the warp and the weft are tie-dyed, is produced in only one spot in Southeast Asia: the village of Tenganan in Eastern Bali.

Warp ikat

Sumatra (Bataks)
Kalimantan (Dayaks)
Sulawesi (Toraja)
East Nusa Tenggara (Savu, Flores, Sumba, Roti)

Weft ikat

Sulawesi (Bugis)
Northeast Java
East Sumatra
Bali
Burma (Shans)
Thailand
Laos
Cambodia

Double ikat

East Bali

and Lombok including Candi Dasa and Lovina. Perama stops in the central parking area. From Candi Dasa catch a bemo to Amlapura and ask to be let off at the turning for Tirtagangga (see map). There are many bemos here, you won't have to wait long for a connection to Tirtagangga.

Amed

For peace and quiet, this area on the east coast, north of Tirtagangga has much to offer. The drive from Culik via Amed to Lipah Beach is quite spectacular especially on the return journey with Mount Agung forming a magnificent backdrop to the coastal scenery. Numerous coves and headlands, with colourful fishing boats complete the vista and offer endless possibilities for walks and picnics. The area became popular because of the good snorkelling and diving available here, the reef is just 10 m from the beach with some good coral and a variety of fish. Amed is developing slowly with new guest houses, hotels, restaurants and dive centres opening every year, some with spectacular hillside

Phone code: 0363
Colour map 1, grid B3

Bali

Mount Agung

Mount Agung is Bali's tallest and most sacred mountain, home of the Hindu gods and dwelling place of the ancestral spirits, it dominates the spiritual and physical life of the island. It is awe-inspiring with its magnificent summit dominating the landscape over much of Bali. All directions on Bali are given in relation to this much revered mountain. Toward the mountain is called 'kaja', away from the mountain is 'kelod'. In a country where direction is of immense significance, this is the site of the most important of the nine directional temples (see page 231). Water from its sacred springs is the holiest and most sought after for temple rites. According to local legend, the god Pasupati created the mountain by dividing Mount Mahmeru, centre of the Hindu universe, in two making Mount Agung and Mount Batur.

Standing 3,014 m high, at its summit is a crater about 500 m in width. In 1969, after lying dormant for more than 600 years, the volcano erupted causing massive destruction; over 1,600 people died in the eruption, a further 500 in the aftermath and 9,000 were made homeless. For a week the mountain spewed ash covering much of the island, and casting a cloud over East Java. Even today the scars left by the destruction are visible in the shape of lava flows and deep ravines. Much was read into the fact that the eruption took place at the time of Bali's greatest religious festival, Eka Dasa Rudra; this is a very superstitious community. One theory is that the mountain erupted because the priests were pressured into holding the ceremony before due time, to coincide with an important tourism convention that was taking place on Bali.

Climbing Mount Agung Since this is a sacred mountain, access to Mount Agung is restricted during religious ceremonies, particularly in March and April. In any case the arduous climb should only be attempted during the dry season, May to October; even then conditions on the summit can be quite different from the coast. There are several routes up Mount Agung but the two most popular depart from Besakih and Selat. The latter is shorter but you will not be able to reach the very highest point on the mountain, and views of part of the island are hidden behind the summit. You should be well prepared, the mountain is cold at night and you will need warm clothes, water, some food, a good torch and decent footwear. You will also need a guide, and should aim to reach the summit before 0700 to witness the spectacular sunrise; after 0800 the clouds may begin to build up, obscuring views.

From Besakih: this route takes you to the summit providing the best views in all directions. The longer of the two ascents, this climb takes about 6 hours, with another 4-5 hours for the demanding descent. You start out in forest but once you reach the open mountain it becomes extremely steep. Guides can be hired at Besakih through the tourist office who can also arrange nearby accommodation. Expect to pay about US$40 per person, this includes offerings at temples along the route.

From Selat: by following this route you reach a point about 100 m below the summit, which obscures all-round views. However, the climb only takes 3 to 4 hours; aim to start your climb by 0300 or 0400. From Selat, take the road to Pura Pasar Agung then climb through forest before reaching the bare mountain. Guides can be arranged both in Muncan and Tirtagangga, as well as Selat. One recommended guide is I Ketut Uriada, a teacher who lives in Muncan; he can be contacted at his shop in that village. Costs start at about 40,000Rp, which includes temple contributions and registering with the local police. In Selat ask the local police about guides, they should be able to advise. In Tirtagangga ask at your accommodation; rates here tend to be higher, US$35 per person which should include transport. There is good accommodation in Selat (see accommodation, page 188) or your guide may arrange cheaper accommodation at his home.

locations and stunning views of Mount Agung. At present much of the accommodation lies beyond Amed at Lipah Beach, reached along a dreadful, potholed road, part of which has been washed away. There is much talk of laying a new road in the near future!

Lipah Beach itself is an extremely average grey sand public beach with some litter. Own transport is recommended. There are restrictions to prevent property from being built within 100 m of the beach in order to preserve the beauty of the area, but already these are being flouted.

The area called Amed is in fact a 15 km stretch from Culik to Selang village, encompassing the villages of Amed, Cemeluk (also spelt Jemeluk), Bunutan and Selang. At present the first accommodation you come to is 5.7 km from Culik. If you go during the dry season you can watch the local men making salt; they also work year round as fishermen setting off at 0500 and returning about 1000, and then going out again at 1500. It is possible to go out with them. As there is no irrigation system, farming is mainly done in the wet season when the men raise crops of peanuts, corn, pumpkin and beans, on the steeply sloping hillside inland from the road, to sell in the market at Amlapura. In dry spells, all the water needed for the crops is carried by the women up the steep slope, three times a day; a back-breaking chore. Most of the land is communally owned by the local Banjar.

AL-A *Hotel Indra Udhyana*, Bunutan, T0361-241107, F234903. Brand new luxury **Sleeping** hotel, built in Balinese style, perched on the rock face right beside the sea. Set in landscaped gardens with views of Mount Agung with Mount Rinjani on Lombok in the distance. 35 bungalows each with a view and a private garden. Restaurant (mid-range) on 3 levels. Small conference hall. Medium sized swimming pool with

Amed & Tulamben area

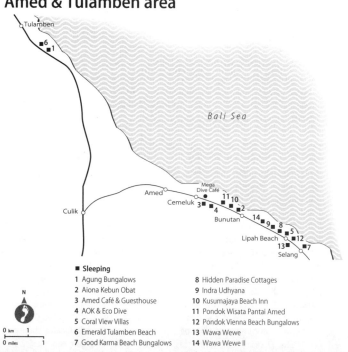

■ Sleeping
1 Agung Bungalows
2 Aiona Kebun Obat
3 Amed Café & Guesthouse
4 AOK & Eco Dive
5 Coral View Villas
6 Emerald Tulamben Beach
7 Good Karma Beach Bungalows

8 Hidden Paradise Cottages
9 Indra Udhyana
10 Kusumajaya Beach Inn
11 Pondok Wisata Pantai Amed
12 Pondok Vienna Beach Bungalows
13 Wawa Wewe
14 Wawa Wewe II

sunken bar. The beach moves completely over the course of a year, appearing beside the hotel in Jul and Aug, then moving to the east about 100 yds away. **A-B** *Coral View Villas* (in same ownership as *Hidden Paradise Cottages* next door, below, same address and T/F), 19 bungalows in attractive garden beside sea, new with attractive décor, private open-air bathrooms, hot and cold water, fan or a/c, seaside bar and restaurant (mid-range to cheap), swimming pool, children's play area. Friendly staff, excellent food. **A-B** *Hidden Paradise Cottages*, Lipah Beach, PO Box 121, Amlapura, Bali, T0361-431273, F0361-423820 and 0363-21044. 16 bungalows in attractive gardens beside public beach, with private bathrooms (Western toilets), with fan or a/c, hot water, swimming pool, restaurant (mid-range to cheap), diving and snorkelling, transport available. **B-C** *Wawa-Wewe II*, PO Box 124 Karangasem, 7 new attractive villas beside sea, fan, cold water only, mosquito nets, restaurant price includes excellent breakfast, good value. Recommended. **C** *Kusumajaya Beach Inn*, Amed Jemeluk (also spelt Cemeluk) (same ownership as *Kusumajaya* at Tirtagangga), near Amed in unspoilt rural setting beside sea, more attractive location than Lipah Beach, new Balinese-style bungalows in large, slightly unkempt gardens, with private bathrooms, shower, Western toilet, fan, restaurant (cheap) overlooking the sea with beautiful views. Recommended, although staff can be less than helpful. **C-D** *Amed Beach Cottage*, (Pantai Amed) Cemeluk. T/F0361-288192. Good location in large gardens running down to the sea. 4 large, simple, new rooms (with more due) with private bathroom, Western toilet, verandah overlooking garden with sea views. Rooms are rather dark. Owned by the *Mega Dive Centre*. Restaurant (mid-range to cheap) beside beach. Price includes breakfast and tax. **C-D** *Good Karma Beach Bungalows*, Lipah Beach, owner is planning to change name to *Pala Karma Beach Bungalows*, set in rather scrubby garden beside public beach, more expensive bungalows have attractive new décor, private bathrooms with shower and Western toilets, cold water, fan; cheaper bungalows are very close together and have squat toilets, restaurant (cheap) overlooking sea. **C-D** *Pondok Vienna Beach Bungalows*, Lipah Beach, 1 Wayan Utama, PO Box 112, Bali, bungalows in beachside garden setting with fan, private bathrooms (Western toilet) and cold water, restaurant (cheap), watersports available. **D** *Aiona Kebun Obat (Health Garden)*, Bunutan. Pos Keliling, Desa Bunutan, 80852 Abang. T0361-974865. 2 basic, bamboo bungalows with private mandi, squat toilet, in large overgrown gardens beside the sea. No electricity. Swiss owned. Offers traditional Balinese healing, massage, meditation and sells locally made health products. Vegetarian restaurant (mid-range to cheap). When we visited the owner was in Europe and the place looked rather neglected and overpriced. **D** *Amed Café Hostel (Pondok Kebun Wayan)*, 5-7 km from Culik, Amed. Perched on the hillside overlooking the sea, this accommodation offers good value for money. 11 simple, attractively furnished rooms with fan, mosquito net, most (9) with private bathrooms, Western toilet. Restaurant (cheap), excellent food, try the curry cooked by Wayan, the manager's wife. Live gamelan music is sometimes played, otherwise they have an interesting collection of taped gamelan music. In high season they also have performances of local dances. Swimming from the beach just across the road, good snorkelling, and diving 15 m from the shore. Ketut the manager is a former school teacher (of Indonesian), speaks excellent English (also a little German and Japanese) and is a mine of information. In high season (Jul and Aug) aim to arrive by 1100. Highly recommended. **D** *Wawa-Wewe*, Lipah. F22074, rodanet@denpasar.wasantara.net.id 4 very attractive bungalows with private bathroom, Western toilet. Set in pretty gardens with good snorkelling and swimming from the beach across the road. The owners, Deborah from England and her husband Made are very friendly and knowledgeable about the local area and Balinese customs. (They also have a house available to rent nearby.) Small shop selling sarongs, jelly shoes (to protect your feet when you go swimming) and woodcarvings. Deborah is knowledgeable about Balinese crafts. Occasional performances of local dances and gamelan music. Book exchange. Restaurant (mid-range to cheap) serving excellent local and Western cuisine, with play area for children. The name *Wawa-Wewe* is a local Balinese saying which roughly translates as *comme ci comme ca*. Price includes breakfast and tax. Highly recommended. **F** *AOK and Eco Dive*, Cemeluk. Run by 'mad' Mike from England. Crash pads, basic, very cheap with shared facilities.

Eating Several new restaurants are opening to cater to the increased number of visitors. One of the best is *Wawa-Wewe* (see accommodation entry). The restaurant at *Amed Café* also serves delicious food (see under accommodation).

Sports **Diving** *Mega Dive Center*, Cemeluk. T/F0361-288192. PADI courses, diving trips to all the main diving areas around Bali. US$30 for one dive. There is a Second World War shipwreck lying about 20 m off-shore in shallow water, accessible to both divers and snorkellers.

Transport **Car** 45 mins to Amed from Candi Dasa. **Bemo** From **Amlapura** catch a bemo heading north to Culik and Singaraja. Change bemos at Culik; until noon there are a limited number of bright red bemos running along the coast east to Amed and Lipah, after 1200 you can catch an ojek or try and hitch a lift, otherwise it is a long walk. Perama stops at Culik. From here you can catch a bemo to Amed. There is a regular bemo service up to midday but in the afternoon you may have to rely on ojek , motorcycle taxis.

Culik to Tulamben Returning to the main road at Culik, the drive north following the coast road affords stunning views of Mount Agung (you can easily understand why the mountain is worshipped by the Balinese) and enchanting seascapes. This eastern coast of Bali is drier than other parts of the island, the lush jungle vegetation giving way to scrub and open vistas. You can still see remnants of the lava flows from the eruption of Mount Agung in 1963 that caused widespread devastation in the regency of Karangasem.

Tulamben

Tulamben, an established dive centre, attracts divers because of the wreck of the American Liberty ship which sank just 40 m from the shore; lying in shallow waters it offers good snorkelling as well. The location is very scenic with Mount Agung towering to the west of the deep blue sea, though the beach consists of grey/black pebbles with some litter. Tulamben lies about 9 km north of Amed. Like Amed, Tulamben is attracting a sprinkling of new hotels, guesthouses and dive centres each year.

Phone code: 0361
Colour map 1, grid B2

Sleeping **AL-B** *Mimpi Resort Tulamben* (reservations: Kawasan Bukit Permai, Jimbaran, Denpasar 80361, T701070, F701074). Sister resort to *Mimpi Jimbaran*, new, beautifully designed complex of cottages with private courtyards and cheaper rooms set in glorious, landscaped gardens with fabulous views of Mount Agung which provides a spectacular backdrop especially at sunset. Well-equipped diving facilities offering PADI courses, the wreck of the American Liberty ship lies just 400 m along the beach from the hotel (40 m out from the shore). Snorkelling in front of the hotel. Climbs of Mount Agung can be arranged. Large freshwater swimming pool fed by underground spring, this is also used to teach novice divers, restaurant (mid-range) with sea views, the beach itself is pebbles. Recommended. **A** *Emerald Tulamben Beach Hotel*, T462673, F462407, tohpati@idola.net.id Spectacularly located, new, hotel; Japanese owned. Attractive rooms, some with sea views, with usual upmarket facilities including mini bar, kettle, safe. The large, tropical gardens have a magnificent setting with the sea on one side and Mount Agung rising majestically on the other. You can hear both the sound of the waves and a waterfall built in the grounds. There is a 9-hole golf course and swimming pool with sunken bar. Restaurant (expensive to mid-range) with seaviews, international, Indonesian, Chinese and Japanese food, coffee shop, pizza hut. Activities include: scuba diving, snorkelling, fishing, sailing, aroma massage, horseback riding (the two horses roam the gardens) and off road motor bike. Helicopter pad. Recommended.

B-C *Bali Sorga Bungalows*, formerly Paradise Palm Beach Bungalows, (reservations: *Friendship Shop*, Candi Dasa, T0363-41052). Good setting beside sea (pebble beach) with attractive gardens, but rather overpriced reflecting its location as a Mecca for divers, 20 rooms, 4 with a/c and hot water, all rooms with private bathroom (Western toilet and shower) and fans, diving arranged at sites off East and North Bali, prices from US$45 for one dive at Tulamben up to US$100 at Nusa Penida and Menjangan Island. **C** *Puri Aries*, across the road from the beach, one of the newer guest houses here. **C** *Puri Madha*, close to the wreck of the Liberty ship, clean, functional rooms. **D** *Agung Cottages*, c/o of *Agung Cottages* at Candi Dasa, same ownership 0363-41535. From the south this is the first accommodation you come to before you reach Tulamben (see map). The only budget accommodation in the area. 6 brand new, simple bungalows with bright, clean rooms, all with private bathroom, Western toilet. The gardens stretch down to the sea and a shingle beach. Very peaceful with outstanding views of Mount Agung. Breakfast and tax included in price. **D** *Ganda Mayu Bungalows and Restaurant*, 8 bungalows ranging from rather basic to attractive depending on price, all with private bathroom (Western toilets) and fan, situated beside the sea with beachside restaurant, diving can be arranged, one of the cheapest places to stay at Tulamben. **D** *Pondok Matahari*, rooms are a little basic.

West of Amlapura

See map, page 148 The road running west from Amlapura up into the foothills of Mount Agung is one of the most scenic on Bali with stunning views of the sacred mountain, the coast to the south and spectacular terraced ricefields especially near **Muncan**. The road deteriorates between Putung and Muncan, with a multitude of potholes, but is perfectly passable. Ten kilometres west of Amlapura is Bebandem (see page 177). Turn right shortly after leaving Bebandem to reach the village of **Jungutan**; nearby is the **Tirta Telaga Tista**, one of three water palaces built by the rulers of Karangasem. Not exactly a palace, more a man-made lake fed by an underground spring, in a pretty and peaceful rural setting. Continuing along the main road you get to **Sibetan**, famed for the quality of its salak fruit. Salak can be identified by their brown skin which has the appearance of snakeskin, and is in season from December to March; inside, the fruit is crisp with a slightly medicinal flavour. The road here is lined with salak palms, growing about 3½ m high with sharp prickles; further up the mountain slopes there are teak and clove plantations.

Transport Public bemos run regularly between Singaraja and Amlapura and Klungkung and Denpasar passing through Tulamben, Perama stop in Tulamben en route between Padangbai, Candi Dassa, Air Sanin and Lovina.

Shortly after leaving Sibetan is **Putung** and a turning on the left for the *Pondok Bukit Putung*, perched on the edge of a cliff with magnificent views to the coast. In the evening the Burung Merpati bird makes a quite magical song by inflating its neck. There is now a road running from the village down to Manggis on the coast, a distance of about 8 km. Back on the main road you pass through the village of **Duda**, which holds an important ceremony at the time of the full moon in October.

Not long after leaving Duda is the turning for Iseh and Sideman on the left. This road travels south down hill through glorious scenery with views to the coast, eventually reaching Klungkung. **Iseh** is home to some unique rituals. At the time of the harvest full moon, in the Pura Dalem, trance dances take place in which the dancers represent animals such as puppies, snakes and pigs, and even kitchen utensils such as pots and potlids, as well as evil spirits. After passing through Iseh you come to **Sideman**, 29 km from Amlapura, where there are now several places to stay (see 'Sleeping' below) and a good quality weaving factory, the *Pelangi Workshop*, where you can watch the process and buy *endek* from the weavers. Other workshops produce the expensive 'kain songket' using silk interwoven with gold and silver thread. (It has been alleged by a leading German magazine that dye from the weaving factories is poisoning the underground water supply which affects places as far away as Kuta.) Traditional varieties of rice are still grown here. There are endless possibilities for walks in an area where you feel you have stepped back 100 years in time; the local people seem gentle and very friendly as they go about their lives in a manner unchanged since their forebears, gathering firewood and farming in the time honoured way.

Sideman & Iseh have some of the best views in Bali

Situated in the hills 12 km north of Klungkung, this is one of the most beautiful areas of Bali. Not only are the ricefields some of the most breathtaking on the island but Mount Agung rises in awesome majesty dominating the landscape in an almost mystical way; while to the south there are views to the coast and the sea in the distance. The area was favoured by the artists Walter Spies and Theo Meyer who lived here in the 1930s, and the dramatic views from this area inspired some of his most outstanding Balinese landscapes. The house they lived in is available for longterm rentals; enquire at *Patal Homestay* (see 'Sleeping', page 188). The writer Anna Mathews also stayed here for a year at the time of the 1963 eruption of Mount Agung. Her book '*Night of Purnama*' is an evocative account of life in the village prior to the eruption and the experience of living through that dramatic period.

Back on the main road you pass through **Selat**, 11 km from Rengdang and 21 km from Amlapura, a village that was badly destroyed by the 1963 eruption. This is the point of departure for the shorter of the two climbing routes up Mount Agung (see page 182), and there is good, reasonably priced accommodation here (see 'Sleeping', Putang). **Pura Pasar Agung**, one of Bali's nine directional temples, is located nearby, signposted from the main road. The road up to the temple climbs steeply past countryside scoured by lava flows. There is a car park just below the steps leading up to the temple, which has been completely rebuilt since its destruction in 1963.

The nearby village of **Padangaji** has a 'Gambuh' school; *gambuh* is a classical dance/drama with music that is slow and courtly. The road continues to **Muncan** passing through some of the most breathtaking *sawah* landscapes on Bali, at their best just before the planting of the young rice seedlings when the fields are flooded. This is a peaceful area with ravines, streams and the sounds of running water and birdsong. Just before Muncan you'll notice a sign: 'Antiques made to order'(!) and 5 km further on you reach Rendang and the road up to Besakih. From here you can cut across to Bangli or turn south to Klungkung; a steady stream of bemos connect Rendang with these two towns and with Amlapura.

C-D *Pondok Bukit Putung*, Duda, Selat, Karangasem, T/F23039, reservations: *Balina Beach*, Manggis, Karangasem, T0363-41002-5, F41001; or direct as above. Perched on the edge of a cliff with spectacular panoramic views of the ricefields below and the east coast of Bali. 5 rather basic bungalows with private bathroom, Western toilet

Sleeping at Putung
Phone code: 0366

Bali

(some without seats). Some rooms are dark, the whole complex is a bit rundown and badly in need of redecoration. Restaurant (cheap) with lovely views. Good walks in the cooler mountain air, 750 m above sea level.

Transport 22 km by road west of Amlapura, 10 km west of Bebandem. The village can be reached via bemo from **Amlapura** to **Bebandem** (500Rp) change to a bemo heading for **Selat**, ask to be dropped at the turn off for Putung 1 km before **Duda** village, from here it is 1½ km to the bungalows and restaurant. Much easier by car.

Sleeping at Sideman
Phone code: 0366

All the properties in this area are owned by the local ruler, of the Satria caste, or his relatives. **A** *Patal Homestay*, 6 km from the main Amlapura-Rendang road, 1 km before Sideman village, T2001/23005, F23007. The outstanding place to stay in this area. Stunning views of Mount Agung to the north; to the south are panoramic views over the countryside to the coast. 2 huge, bright, older rooms with private bathrooms, Western toilet, cold water only. Newly built family suite with 3 rooms, 2 en suite bathrooms with hot water, large covered verandah. Beautiful, luxuriant gardens with many fruit trees and a family temple. Price includes full board. The family were friends of Walter Spies and Theo Meyer, who stayed at their house in Iseh in the 1930s. This house is available to rent but usually taken on a long let. The owner Ida Ayu Mas Andayani speaks excellent English. Very popular, many guests book in advance a month at a time. For Jul/Aug you need to book by January. Highly recommended. **A** *Sideman Homestay*, T23009, F23015. On right at the start of the village coming from the north, just before *Pelangi Weaving*; superb views to south coast. Rooms however are in need of renovation, very dark, private bathrooms with Western toilets. Supremely overpriced. **A-B** *Subak Tabola Inn*, PO box 119, Klungkung, Bali 80701. T/F23015. Signposted from the main road 1½ km before the centre of Sideman, coming from the north. Follow a dreadful, rutted track for 1½ km, ignore the distances on their optimistic signs. Stunning location with views of both Mount Agung and the distant sea. 11 bungalows in what might be described as simple luxury. The Swiss joint-owners have aimed to create an upmarket establishment offering peace and seclusion. The large rooms are simply, but attractively, decorated with mosquito nets, private bathrooms, Western toilet, cold water only, despite the cool evenings at this altitude. Exceptionally peaceful setting; listen to the frog chorus at night, the sound of the cowbells and bamboo bird scarers by day. The pool is filled with water from the village spring and guests complain about the lack of any filtration or purification. Students at the 'Gambuh' school in nearby Padangaji provide performances and gamelan recitals. Restaurant (expensive to mid-range). Excellent Indonesian and international food, beautifully situated with views and cool breezes. Reservations essential in Jul/Aug. On Wed a tour group usually visits so it may be full. Choice of B&B, half or full board. Recommended.

Sleeping at Selat
Phone code: 0366

C-D *Pondok Wisata Puri Agung*, T23037 or c/o Jl Gili Biaha 3, Denpasar, T0361-223663. On the main road through the village. Situated in the foothills of Mount Agung with fabulous views of the mountain, next to ricefields. 9 newly built rooms, attractively furnished, with private bathrooms, western toilet. A good place to stay if you are planning to climb the mountain. Manageress lives behind the property and may take time to rouse.

Transport Bemos: regular bemos, usually green, run from **Amlapura** via **Bebandem** and Selat to **Rendang**, and from **Klungkung** (also called by its old name Semarapura). From Rendang connections to **Bangli** (black or brown and white bemos usually) and on to **Gianyar** (blue bemos) and **Denpasar**. Klungkung to Bebandem green bemos run regularly throughout the day.

North from Denpasar to Lake Bratan

Fifteen kilometres northwest of Denpasar is the town of Kapal. Shortly after
Kapal, in the village of Bringkit, the road branches; west for Tanah Lot and
Gilimanuk, and north for Lake Bratan, Singaraja and Lovina Beach. The
coastal temple of Tanah Lot is 10 km off the main road and is a popular tourist
attraction. The other arm of the fork runs north for 2 km to Mengwi (with its
impressive temple complex). Continuing north, the road climbs through
breathtaking terraced paddy fields to Lake Bratan, one of three crater lakes that
fill part of a massive caldera. Mount Catur lies to the north of the lake and is the
highest peak in the area at 2,096 m.

*See maps pages
129 & 148*

Bali

The meru and pottery-making town of Kapal is best-known for its red-brick
Pura Sada which lies just south of the main road, past the bend near the market place (it is signposted). The pura is an important shrine of the former
dynasty of the kingdom of Mengwi. Inside the enclosure is an unusual
10-m-high *prasada* or *prasat* (possibly explaining its name 'Pura Sada'), similar in style to Javanese candis, and dedicated to the king's ancestors. An earthquake in 1917 all but destroyed the prasada and the *candi bentar* or split gate.
In 1949, it was carefully restored by local craftsmen. The sculptures that decorate the prasada were all carved after 1950.

Kapal

Transport 15 km from Denpasar. **Bemo**: regular bemos from the Ubung terminal,
just northwest of **Denpasar**.

Tanah Lot

The coastal temple of Tanah Lot, perched on a rock at the edge of the
shore-line and 30 km northwest of Denpasar, is probably the most photographed sight in Bali. The temple is one of the *sadkahyangan* – the six holiest
shrines – and is said to have been built after the Hindu saint Danghyang
Nirartha spent a night here and subsequently suggested that a temple be constructed on the spot.

*Phone code: 0361
There are good
coastline walks south
from Tanah Lot*

   The temple itself is small, and hardly remarkable artistically, with
two-tiered merus and several other pavilions. What makes it special, and so
popular, is its incomparable position. Built on a rock outcrop just off the coast,
it can only be reached at low tide. The surrounding rocks are said to be inhabited by sea-snakes but this does nothing to deter the hordes of visitors who
clamber over the rocks and stroll along the beach. The profusion of trinket
stalls, warungs and hawkers can be overpowering and detracts from the overall
ambience of the location, but it is still well worth the visit, particularly in the
late afternoon, when the sun sets behind the temple (and photographers
line-up to catch the moment). ■ *1,500Rp. Facilities here include a money
changer, restaurant and post office.*

A *Mutiara Tanah Lot Hotel and Restaurant*, T812939, F812935. Some a/c, bungalows
are arranged out the back in a garden. They have attached bathrooms with hot water
and the room rate includes breakfast. **A-B** *Dewi Sinta*, T812933, F813956. Some a/c,
large restaurant with some villas out the back. The villas, with hot water, have an
attractive position overlooking ricefields, close to the walkway to Tanah Lot and a
pitching wedge from the new golf course. The hotel also has a small pool – which is
open to non-residents – and a mini-library. There is a US$10 surcharge during the
peak months from 22 Dec-8 Jan. **B** *Bali Wisata Bungalows*, Yeh Gangga Beach,

Sleeping

T261354. A/c, restaurant, saltwater pool, a dozen small bungalows close to rice paddies, the beach on one side and a pura on the other, 1 hr walk from Tanah Lot along the beach; to the cognoscenti: Bali as it used to be – quiet, relaxed, peaceful, only drawback is that the currents here are too strong for swimming in the sea. Recommended. **D** *Losmen Puri Lukisan Tanah Lot*, (close to the public parking areas and tucked behind a painting gallery). Handful of rooms and the cheapest place to stay here.

Shopping The village of **Kediri** holds a big animal market at the Pasar Hewan with cattle, goats, pot-bellied pigs, ducks and unhappy looking chickens bound together in bunches by their ankles; all in all probably not a place for animal lovers.

Transport **Road Bemo**: connections with **Denpasar's** Ubung terminal, north of town to **Kediri**
30 km Denpasar and then another from Kediri to Tanah Lot be sure to leave Tanah Lot by 1400 in order
See section 'The West' to catch a connecting bemo from Kediri back to town. The turning for the temple is
for the route up 20 km northwest of Denpasar on the road to Negara and Gilimanuk. From here it is a
the west coast from 10 km drive down a lovely road through paddy fields to the sea.
here, page 217

Mengwi

Phone code: 0361 Mengwi, on the road north from Kapal towards Lake Bratan and Singaraja, is a
Colour map 1, grid B2 market town which hosts an important cattle market every Wednesday and
Sunday. Otherwise it is unremarkable, save for the **Pura Taman Ayun**. This
impressive temple, with its classic design, lawns and ponds is free from crowds
and hawkers (especially before 1000), making it worth the visit. It was built for
the founder of the Mengwi Kingdom in 1634. Surrounded by a moat, it consists, characteristically, of a series of three courtyards. The tallest gate leads
into the back courtyard, where there are two rows of *palinggih-palinggih* or
shrines for visiting deities on the north and east sides, each with ornate pillars
and beautifully carved doors. On the west side are a number of *bales* or pavilions. The courtyard also contains a stone altar (*paibon*) with reasonable relief
carvings. To the left of the main entrance there is a poor 'Museum of Complete
Cremation' (admission by donation). There are two restaurants nearby, the
Bali Green Restaurant and the Sari Royal Garden. ■ *Take the turning to the
right opposite the colt station to get there.*

Excursions **Sangeh** nutmeg forest is 15 km north of Mengwi (it is also known as 'monkey
forest' because of the many monkeys found here) and is the sight of the **Pura
Bukit Sari**. The temple was built at the beginning of the 17th century by the son
of the King of Mengwi as a meditation temple. Today it is a *subak* (or irrigation)
temple. ■ *Getting there: although the forest and temple are closest to Mengwi it is
difficult to get there on public transport except by returning to Denpasar's Ubung
terminal and taking another bemo north – which means a total journey of nearly
40 km. With private transport, it is easy to take the road east towards Kedampat.*
  Pura Luhur is an isolated mountain temple situated on the slopes of Mount
Batukau (or 'shell' mountain), amidst tropical forest. ■ *Getting there: it is not
easy to reach by public transport – it is best to charter a bemo from Denpasar or
Mengwi, turning north at Tabanan. The final climb is steep.* On the way, visit the
hot springs at **Penatahan**, **AL** *Yeh Panes*, Jl Batukaru, Desa Penatahan,
T262356. These natural hot springs are part of a spa resort, with simple chalets,
wooden floors and balconies, standing on a hillside overlooking swimming pool
and spa area. The spa comprises a series of nine enclosed hot-spring rock pools
with jacuzzi jets. Massage available. Towels and lockers for hire. Open air restaurant overlooking river. Tennis courts. Lunch and use of spa is US$48 per person.
If you stay at the resort, use of the spa and breakfast is included in the room rate.

The Balinese pagoda: the meru

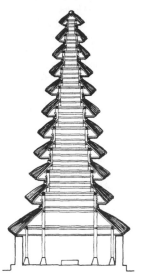

Perhaps the most characteristic feature of Balinese architecture is the meru. These are multi-tiered (but always odd in number) pagoda-like towers made of wood and coir thatch. As the name suggests, they symbolize the cosmic Hindu-Buddhist mountain, Mount Meru (as do candis and prasada/prasats). The underworld is represented by the lower section, the world of men by the middle section, and the heavens by the towering, tapering roofs. There are clear stylistic links between merus and the brick candis of Java, as well as with similar buildings in Nepal. Whether the idea of making the upper portions from perishable materials was introduced from Java is not clear. Certainly, there are structures today in Java which consist only of a base, indicating that there may have been an upper portion of wood or thatch.

After a drawing by PAJ Moojen, 1926

Pura Yeh Gangga is an attractive temple 15 km from Mengwi off the road north to Lake Bratan. Unusually, the base of the merus are constructed of stone, rather than wood, with porcelain set into the walls. A stone inscription discovered within the compound can be dated to 1334. ■ *Getting there: take a bemo running north towards Lake Bratan from Mengwi or Denpasar's Ubung terminal and ask to be let off just after the village of Bereteh (and before Kukup). Take the turning to the left and walk through the village of Paang to Perean, where the pura can be found (a walk of about 1½ km).*

Road Bus: connections with **Denpasar's** Ubung terminal; buses turn off the main road to Gilimanuk at Bringkit, and fork north. Alternatively, big buses travel the main road from Denpasar to Gilimanuk from Denpasar's Ubung terminal; ask to be let off at the turning to Mengwi and Bedugul (in the village of Bringkit); bemos wait at this junction and run north.

Transport
18 km from Denpasar

Lake Bratan and Lake Buyan

The beautiful, almost alpine, Lake Bratan is surrounded by the crater walls of the now extinct volcano, Mount Catur. This is a peaceful spot to visit, with cool evenings and away from the hassle of the beach resorts. Because of the altitude, it is much cooler here than at the coast. There are attractive walks around the lake and boats can be hired. On its west shore is the stunningly positioned and mystical, **Pura Ulun Danau Bratan**, which seems to almost float on the water (indeed, in the 1970s it was at risk of sinking beneath the rising waters of the lake). The temple, set in well kept gardens, was built in 1633 by the King of Mengwi to honour the Goddess of the Lake who provides water for irrigation. Along with the temple at Lake Batur (see page 155), the Pura Ulun Danau Bratan, is the most important of the various irrigation temples on Bali.

Lake Bratan
Phone code: 0368

Restaurant within the temple gardens for lunch and snacks. ■ *Admission charge and parking fee. 0800-1900 Mon-Sun. Toilets: 200Rp.* Outside the walls of this Hindu temple is a stupa with seated Buddha images in its niches, revealing Bali's Buddhist roots.

Bedugul South of Candikuning, on the south lip of the crater is the small town of **Bedugul**. There is a good permanent fruit, vegetable, flower and spice market here every day. There are many lovely walks in the hills round here. The wet season lasts longer than on the coast and this area can be very wet indeed; best months are May-October with daytime temperatures averaging 20°C, night time 16-18°C, maximum temperature is rarely above 24°C. The coldest, wettest month is January when temperatures average 16°C.

Near Bedugul, at an altitude of 1,240 m, the road passes the **Bali Botanical Gardens**, Kebun Raya Eka Karya Bali. Opened in 1959 as a branch of the National Botanical Gardens in Bogor, the gardens cover nearly 130 ha on the slopes of Mount Pohon (*pohon* means tree in Indonesian). Over 650 species of tree and 450 varieties of orchid, some rare, grow here, though unfortunately few are labelled. It is a beautiful and very peaceful area especially on weekdays, and is also a good place for birdwatching. There are some temples in the grounds (see the map at the entrance), the most interesting of which is Pura Teratai Bang; the sulphur in the earth here is believed to be beneficial for skin ailments which attracts some to the gardens. ■ *1000Rp plus 3,000Rp for cars. Weekdays 0700-1630, weekends 0800-1630. Getting there: 1½ hrs' drive from Lovina; a narrow road leads west from the corn-on-the-cob sculpture just on the outskirts of Bedugul to the gardens.*

Lake Buyan North from Lake Bratan, the road crosses the floor of the crater and as the road climbs up over its north walls, **Lake Buyan** comes into sight. This is another lake of great natural beauty and is the proposed site of a national park. Curious platforms about 50 m from the shore are used by the locals for fishing. To get to the lake, stop the bemo by the entrance to *Lake Buyan Cottages* (there is a barrier on the left hand side, travelling north), just before the road starts to climb out of the crater. There is a small surfaced road, passing a dilapidated temple on the right, to a car park where drinks are sold and fishing-rods are for hire. From here, it is possible to walk around the lake, if the water level is not too high. There are no watersports, so it is very peaceful. Coffee is grown on the hillsides around the lake.

Just 2 km north of Lake Bratan is the site of the **Handara Kosaido Country Club** and golf course, voted one of the world's 50 most beautiful courses (see below for details).

Air Terjun Gitgit Air Terjun Gitgit lies about 15 km north of Lake Bratan, near the village of Gitgit. Well signposted from the main road, with a car park and rest area, a path leads the 500 m to this waterfall, sometimes described as the most dramatic waterfall on Bali. Although not much more than 40 m in height it is quite impressive, especially in the wet season, as it falls dramatically into a pool where the locals swim. According to local folklore if you visit the falls with your boy/girl friend the relationship will not endure. ■ *Admission on main road 500Rp, 15 mins walk to the falls. Getting there: take a bemo heading for Singaraja; coming from Singaraja take a bemo from the southern bus terminal, Sangket.*

Bedugul Tropical mountain climate with a temperature range from 18-24° C. Rainy season Nov-Apr. Accommodation here is often disappointing and somewhat overpriced. **A-AL** *Pacung Mountain Resort*, Jl Raya Pacung, Baturiti T21038/9, 0361-262461/2, F21043, Pacungmr@Denpasar.Wasantara.net.id 9 km south of Bedugul (60 mins' drive from Singaraja, 2 hrs from airport) on the main road with view over steep valley and terraced ricefields, beneath the peaks of Batukaru and Pohen mountains. 50 bungalows and small but comfortable rooms arranged on steep valley side, linked by walkways and steps, a/c, satellite TV, mini bar, IDD, en suite bathroom, resort facilities including heated pool (a consideration at this altitude), jogging track, health club, gift shop, 24-hr coffee shop, restaurant very popular with passing coach tours, good value buffet lunch, rather quiet in the evening, banking and postal service, jungle treks. Recommended. **B** *Bedugul*, T0361-226593; 21197, F21198. Bland resort hotel beside lake, plain, rather drab rooms in need of renovation, clean bathrooms with Western toilets, most have view across the lake, noisy during the day, also some cottages, one of which has a 3-way view, watersports and curio shops. Canteen-like restaurant popular with tour groups. **B** *Bukit Permai*, T23663. On left of road at lip of crater before road descends into Bedugul, cottage-type accommodation, some rooms have fireplaces, but they smoke badly, compelling occupants to open windows and lose any benefit of the warmth, well-kept garden, excellent views towards Denpasar – awkward for lake visits without own transport. **D** *Hotel Bukit Stroberi*, T0361-21442/21265. On main road by turn-off for *Bedugul Hotel*, 10 very basic, small rooms, with grim Western toilets, noisy during the day, excellent view towards Denpasar but not close to the lake. Price includes tax and breakfast.

Close to Bedugul market there are 3 cheaper places to stay, all within 10 mins' walk of lake, but no view of lake. **D** *Ibu Hadi*, T23497. Restaurant, new building, clean rooms, very steep staircase. Recommended. **D** *Mawar Indah*, T21190. Small, simple rooms, scrub garden (both the above are down the road with the Botanical Garden gateway). **D-E** *Sari Artha Inn*, T21011, just after market on left, noisy, but convenient location for transport and lake, no lake view. Best rooms are on the hill away from the main road, clean with private mandi. Rooms by the road may be noisy. Reasonably priced.

Candikuning On reaching the lakeshore for the first time, there are 2 similar places to stay. Stop the bemo/bus here. **B-D** *Ashram Guesthouse*, T22439, F21101. Some a/c, restaurant (cheap and not recommended). A lovely lakeside setting with views of the lake temple from some verandahs, this is the best place to stay for views of lake. Rooms are spread out up the hill which was an old paddy terrace (over 100 steps to rooms at top), and are a little drab and soulless; the most expensive rooms have hot water with bath and Western toilet, cheapest rooms have shared mandi and squat toilet, most rooms have cold water only making them a bit pricey considering that temperatures are coolish here in the mountains. Price depends on the views. Well kept gardens with tennis court, friendly staff, very relaxing. High season Jun/Aug and Dec/Jan, reservation necessary 1 month in advance, price includes breakfast and tax. Recommended. **C-D** *Lila Graha*, restaurant, cottage type rooms, shady gardens, overlooks lake, above road.

Pancasari Bemo station here, approximately 2 km beyond temple. **L-AL** *Bali Danau Buyan* (formerly *Lake Buyan Cottages*), Jl Raya Bedugul, T0362-21351/23739, F21388. 5 km north of Lake Bratan, 2 km from Handara Country Club. 9 luxurious individual cottages, each with 2 bedrooms, living room with fireplace, dining room with kitchen area and terrace, furnished to a high standard. 1 cottage with Japanese style rooms. Beautiful setting in immaculate gardens with views across Lake Buyan; tennis courts and putting greens. **A** *Handara Country Club*,

Sleeping
Near Lake Bratan
Phone code: 0368

It is important to be dropped off at your hotel, otherwise you may have quite a walk. Hotels listed are divided into 4 sections, with southernmost places listed first

Bali

entrance on right just before village, T28866/88944. Some bungalows, tennis, fitness centre, golf course, beautiful location, but rather overpriced. **A** *Pancasari Inn*, T53142. Just north of *Handara Country Club* on left hand side, tennis, no lake views, last place to stay before road climbs out of the crater. **B** *Bukit Mungsu Indah* (before Bedugul, at Baturiti), price includes breakfast.

Air Terjun Gitgit   C-D *Gitgit Hotel*. Fairly new and clean, situated amidst lush vegetation, rooms are fairly plain. All have private bathrooms with Western toilet, some with hot water. Restaurant (cheap).

Eating   **In Bedugul close to market**   *Ananda, Bogasari* and warungs.

Closer to the lake   *Ashram Guesthouse, Lila Graha* or *Taliwang Bersaudara* (simple Lombok restaurant), good value, views across lake; *Perama Ulundanu*, in temple complex, lunch only, although they might be persuaded to open for dinner.

Sports   **Golf**   *Handara Country Club*, 18 holes, designed by the Australian golfer Peter Thomson; green fees 90,000Rp, clubs for hire, T28866. One of the 50 best golf courses in the world.

Watersports There are 3 locations to hire boats: **1)** temple complex (pedalo) 7,500Rp per 30 mins, circuit of lake in motorboat (15 mins) 4 people 14,000Rp, 5 people 17,500Rp; **2)** layby next to *Ashram Guesthouse*, rowboat 7,500Rp per 30 mins; **3)** *Bedugul Hotel* offers jetskiing (US$10 per 15 mins), waterskiing (US$10), parasailing (US$10), and motorboats (US$15 per 30 mins).

Transport   **Road**   **Bemo**: to Singaraja from **Pancasari** – it should be possible to flag down passing bemo rather than wait for them to fill up. Regular 'express' bemos leave from **Denpasar's** Ubung terminal for Singaraja (see below), passing through **Bedugul** and **Lake Bratan** *en route*, (1½ hrs). Perama stops here. The office is at the Sari Artha Inn, T21011 on the left just past the market heading north.

53 km from Denpasar, 35 km from Mengwi

Lake Tamblingan & Munduk   To the west of Lake Buyan lies Lake Tamblingan and a little further west still is the village of Munduk. This beautiful area lies 500 m-1,500 m above sea level and is part of a new scheme where visitors can stay in simple bungalows and can learn the ways of the Balinese people.

Sleeping   *Puri Lumbung* (a *lumbung* is a Balinese rice barn and the houses have been built in a similar way). Visitors can learn anything from carving a wooden door frame to cooking a Balinese meal. Weaving, music playing (and the making of the instruments), learning about traditional medicines or repairing a fishing net are all part of the 'cultural experience'. For more information write to *Puri Lumbung*, Balai Pendidikan dan Latihan Pariwisata Bali (BPLP), Kotak Pos 2, Nusa Dua, Bali 80363.

North Coast, Buleleng Regency

The north coast is a different world from the rest of Bali. Fewer rivers water this side of the island and there is less rainfall; as a result, the lushness of the south is replaced by savanna forest. The mountains to the south create a dramatic backdrop to the coastal scenery, providing an escape from the heat and opportunities for walks and drives while enjoying stunning views. Lying in the rain shadow of these mountains, the north is drier and less humid. Its primary attractions include its beaches, long stretches of black sand with safe swimming and some of the island's best snorkelling and diving, particularly off Pulau Menjangan. The sunsets can be spectacular, with Java's highest volcano, Mount Semeru, illuminated in the iridescent afterglow of the setting sun. Culturally the north should not be underestimated either.

Ins and outs

Getting there & around

From the south by car Coming from the south over the mountains, the road from Lake Bratan is a long and twisting descent through clove and coffee groves. Singaraja, being the former Dutch capital of Bali and Nusa Tenggara, remains an important local town but has only a few attractions to entice the visitor. Ten kilometres west from here is the resort of Lovina Beach. The road continues west following the north coast all the way to Gilimanuk (and the ferry for Java). The road east from Singaraja passes a number of important temples built in distinctive North Balinese style (see section 'East of Singaraja'). The drive along the north coast eastwards and then south, passing by Tulemben and Amed, to Amlapura is very beautiful and peaceful, passing black sand beaches and coconut groves. The distance from Singaraja to Amlapura is almost 100 km. Beautiful walks can be taken in the hills behind Singaraja with views over the coast to the sea.

Bus Bear in mind that all times are necessarily approximate and can vary enormously depending on traffic conditions. Buses run most frequently in the morning starting early (from 0500 or 0600), and continue until about 1700, continuing later on major routes. The frequency of buses is improving all the time.

    From Singaraja South: (Sangket bus station) to **Denpasar** (Ubung Terminal) 3 hrs, **Bedugul** 1½ hrs, **Gitgit** 25 mins, **Ubud** 3 hrs. **West**: Banyuasri bus station, to **Gilimanuk** 2 hrs, to **Lovina** 20 mins, to **Pemuteran** 1½ hrs, to **Surabaya** 9 hrs. **East**: (Penarukan bus station) to **Denpasar** (Batubulan terminal) 3 hrs 30 mins, **Amlapura** 2 hrs 15 mins, **Kintamani** 1 hr 40 mins, **Penelokan** 2 hrs, **Sangsit** 15 mins, **Air Sanih** 25 mins, **Sawan** 35 mins.

Shuttle bus *Perama* currently offers the best service. They have two offices in Lovina, in Kalibukbuk and Anturan, T41161/41104. From **Lovina** and **Air Sanih** there are connections with **Kuta**, **Sanur** (with a boat connection to Nusa Lembongan), Ubud, **Kintamani**, **Bedugul**, **Tulamben**, **Tirtagangga**, **Candi Dasa**, **Padangbai**, the **airport** and **Lombok**. They can also arrange tickets for Surabaya, Malang, Yogyakarta and Jakarta on Java, and Bima/Sape on Sumbawa.

History

Up until this century it was the north of Bali which had the greatest contact with the outside world. Prior to the building of Denpasar airport, Singaraja was the principal port and main entry point to the island. Lying on the main trading routes from Java eastwards, the area served as an entrepôt for Bugis, Arab and Chinese traders who brought not only their products but also their religion and culture; many settled here, making the north coast their home. European influence also reached the north earlier than other parts of Bali and to this day parts of the north have a colonial feel, particularly Singaraja.

For most of its history the north has been geographically isolated from the south by the chain of volcanic mountains that run from east to west across the northern part of Bali. It was only as recently as the early part of the 20th century that roads were built through the mountains, which has allowed the region to develop a somewhat distinct culture.

Although there have been scattered settlements on the north coast from earlier times, the earliest written reference dates from the 10th century. During the 17th century, the region rose to prominence when Ki Gusti Ngurah Panji Sakti founded the Buleleng regency, centering his kingdom at the palace he built in Singaraja. He set about extending his sovereignty to include Jembrana, much of Karangasem and parts of east Java. In the early 18th century the marriage of his daughter to the ruler of Mengwi further extended the dynastic power and for most of the century the joint regency of Buleleng and Mengwi prospered. However, rivalry amongst the princely successors allowed the ruler of Karangasem to usurp control in the early 19th century. The Dutch arrived in 1814 anxious to secure Bali in the face of an increasing British presence in the region. Following two unsuccessful campaigns in 1846 and 1848 they established control after a bloody battle at Jagaraga in which the brave Balinese, armed only with kris' and spears, were unable to withstand the military superiority of the invaders; thousands of Balinese died as against about 30 Dutch soldiers. Notwithstanding their defeat the Balinese continued to retaliate against Dutch rule over the next few decades.

North Bali (Buleleng Regency)

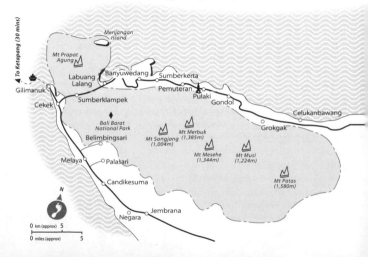

In order to secure their authority and ensure the profitability of Bali the Dutch set about improving the infrastructure. Roads were built, irrigation improved and cash crops such as coffee and spices were introduced. A member of the Buleleng royal family was appointed regent but under the authority of the Dutch. Under the Dutch, Buleleng once again became powerful. Singaraja became the seat of colonial administration with jurisdiction ultimately over the whole of Bali and Lombok. The area thus came under Western influence more than half a century earlier than the south; it took the best part of 60 years before the south was subjugated, in 1909. Increasingly, European writers, traders and scholars began to visit and some settled. During the Second World War the Japanese also made Singaraja their headquarters when they invaded the island. However, with the building of an airport near Denpasar the Dutch moved their administrative capital to the more populous south. Benoa and Padangbai have now taken over as the main ports.

Village life in the north is not as rigidly defined; the family, rather than the banjar, is the focus of an individual's life to a greater extent than further south. This is partly because, with little wet rice cultivation, there is not the same need for mutual help and interdependence amongst the predominantly farming community. The class system is not as strong, either, partly as a result of the many outside social and religious influences the north has experienced, including the longer period of Dutch occupation. The Dutch in particular set out to control Balinese society, making changes where it suited them, often in total disregard of the class system; for example in schools a high caste boy might be made to sit next to a lower caste girl, something that would never happen in traditional Balinese society. Women in Buleleng were the first on the island to cover their breasts as the Dutch were concerned about the effect of bare breasts on their soldiers. But not all aspects of Dutch rule were bad. Buleleng's villagers were the first to be vaccinated against smallpox, and slavery was abolished here earlier than in other parts of the island. The slave trade had been Bali's economic mainstay throughout the 17th and 18th centuries.

The cosmopolitan nature of Buleleng's society, isolated from the south by the mountainous terrain, has also had an impact on culture and the arts, creating styles which are unique and distinctive. Many new forms of **dance**,

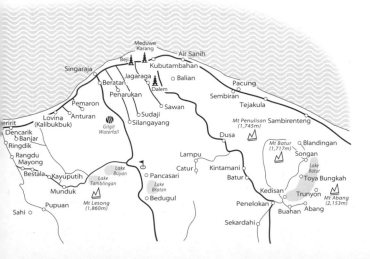

music and **art** originated here. The frenzied gamalan style *gong kebyar*, now the predominant form on the island, originated in the north in 1915, influenced by Western musical forms including jazz. *Kebyar* replaced the slow, gentle, stately *gong gede* and today there are only a handful of *gong gede* orchestras left on the island. Buleleng's dance troupes are held in high esteem and several new dance styles originated here including a highly suggestive *Joged*. This erotic dance is even alleged to have ruined marriages at the height of its popularity, in the 1960s and 1970s, such was the erotic intensity of the movements performed by the young girl dancers. These days the dance is performed by a single dancer wearing a headdress made of gilded leather and decorated with flowers. She dances erotically for a time, then with the fan she is holding, she taps one of the male members of the audience as an invitation for him to join her, and she presents him with a sash which must be tied around his waist. *Janger*, another dance, is performed by two rows of boys and girls facing each other and is very popular with Balinese youth; each sings in turn, usually about love, with much joking and use of slang. Crafts such as weaving, metalwork and pottery also show distinct regional variations; as do the flamboyant temple carvings.

There is less **rice** cultivation in the drier north where the rich volcanic soils support crops of soybeans, peanuts, maize and tobacco as well as fruit. Some of the island's best grapes, mangoes and durian are grown here. Cattle are also a significant export. In season the growers sell mangoes from big baskets by the roadside; though if you are thinking of buying be aware that if the fruit is too hard and unripe it will never become sweet.

Singaraja

Phone code: 0362
Colour map 1, grid B2

Singaraja is the second largest city in Bali with a population in excess of 100,000 and the capital of the regency of Buleleng. It was the original Dutch capital of Bali and the other islands of Nusa Tenggara, and remained the administrative centre of this region until 1953. During this period it was a relatively important harbour and trading post, but has since declined in significance. The main ports for Bali are now Benoa and Padangbai and a new harbour has been built further along the north coast to the west at Celukanbawang. Since colonial times Singaraja has been an important educational and cultural centre, and with two universities in the town there is a sizeable student population. The name Singaraja means lion king, and the lion, symbol of bravery, courage and determination, is the emblem of Buleleng.

Ins and outs

Getting there As Bali's second city, Singaraja is well connected to other destinations on the island with buses leaving from 3 terminals serving different areas. The only out-of-island services are to Surabaya, on Java. Night buses leave from the Banyuasri terminal.

Getting around Bemos link Singaraja's 3 bus terminals There are also horse-drawn dokars and ojeks providing trips around town. The **tourist office** is on Jl Veteran 23, T61141. The staff are very helpful and speak good English (ask for Nyoman Swela or Putu Tasraujiya). Maps of Buleleng, Lovina and Singaraja, as well as brochures detailing places of interest. Open 0800-1600 Mon-Thu and Sat, 0800-1100 on Fri, and 0800-1400 on Sun.

Sights

Singaraja is for the most part an attractive town with a lingering colonial feel, some well-preserved colonial architecture, and tiny winding backstreets in the southern part of town which make for pleasant wandering. In addition to its Dutch heritage there are remnants of Chinese and Muslim influence particularly in the area behind the now decaying harbour where you can still see the old Chinese-style roofs behind the modern shopfronts. By the waterfront there is a **Chinese temple** (called *klenteng*), one of the few on Bali, with a Hindu temple nearby, and to the south a mosque. The descendants of Chinese, Arab and Bugis settlers still live in this area along streets nicknamed Kampong Arab and Kampong Bugis. On the western side of town there is an old **Chinese cemetery** beside the sea near Pantai Lingga at Bukit Suci, which means hallowed hill. In 1995 Singaraja won a nationwide award for the cleanest and best maintained town in Indonesia. People here are extremely friendly and helpful.

The centre of town lies at the intersection of Jl Gajah Made and Jl Jen A Yani; here you will find banks, post office, telephones, accommodation, restaurants and the **market** which turns into a night market full of foodstalls in the evenings.

Bali

Singaraja

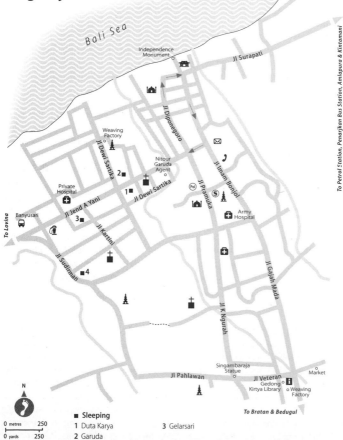

■ Sleeping
1 Duta Karya   3 Gelarsari
2 Garuda

On Jl Veteran, next door to the tourist office, is the **Gedong Kirtya**, a manuscript library founded by the Dutch in 1928 when it was named the Kirtya Liefrinck van der Tuuk. It contains Bali's best collection of palm leaf illustrated books or *lontars* which record local myths, magic formulas, literature and dances. Many were taken from the palace in Lombok during the Dutch campaign at the beginning of this century. Some of the Lombok manuscripts originated in Java, from where they were rescued during the disintegration of the Majapahit Empire. The palm leaves are cut into lengths of about 50 cm and then incised with a sharp blade and the incisions filled with a mixture of soot and oil to accentuate the marks. They are then bound together using lengths of cord and protected between two wooden boards.

Excursions Singaraja could be used as a base for visiting the sights of the north coast to the east and west of town, however accommodation is limited and most visitors prefer to base themselves in either Lovina Beach 10 km to the west of town, or Air Sanih 17 km to the east, both of which offer a greater choice of accommodation, restaurants and activities and also provide a pleasant seaside location.

The temples of the north are interesting for their distinct north style of architecture; in general they are artistically 'busier', exhibiting much more elaborate and dense carving. For details on excursions, see pages 201, 212 and 212 (headings for west, south and east of Singaraja).

Essentials

Sleeping Accommodation in Singaraja largely caters for Indonesian businessmen and tends to be in the centre of town; the main street running east-west, Jl Jend Yani, in particular has a number of these 'business' hotels. *Tresna homestay*, which used to be popular with travellers, has closed.

B-D *Wijaya*, Jl Sudirman, T21915. A/c, range of good accommodation. **D-E** *Duta Karya*, Jl Jend A Yani, T21467. Some a/c, adequate. **E** *Garuda*, Jl Jend A Yani 76, T41191. Price includes breakfast. **E** *Gelarsari*, Jl Jend A Yani, T21495. **E** *Sakabindu*, Jl Jend A Yani, T21791.

Shopping **Textiles** Singaraja is known for its finely detailed ikats, both cotton and silk weft ikat; there are 2 weaving factories which are worth a visit to view the cloth they produce. At 42 Jl Dewi Sartika the ***Berdikari weaving factory*** (open 0800 to 1800 daily) produces exquisite reproductions of traditional Buleleng cloths, some made of silk. If you go in the morning you can see the process whereby the thread is spun and then woven into cloth. You can buy here as well; the high prices reflect the quality of the work. Towards the south of town just off Jl Veteran 22, behind the Gedong Kertya, is the ***Puri Sidar Nadi Putra weaving factory*** situated in the former royal palace, Puri Kawan (open 0800 to 1600), which produces high quality pieces of ikat from silk and cotton, with a shop attached.

Tour operators *Nitour*, Jl Jend A Yani, T22691.

Transport
78 km from Denpasar, 11 km from Lovina Beach

Road Bus: Singaraja has 3 bus stations, Penarukan on the east edge of town on Jl Surapati for destinations to the east. (**Amlapura** mostly yellow buses, **Kubu** and **Kintamani**), Banyuasri on the west edge at the intersection of Jl Jend Sudirman and Jl Jend A Yani for destinations west of the town (**Lovina** and **Gilimanuk**) and Sangket (officially called Sukasada) on the south edge of town on Jl Mayor Metra for destinations south (**Denpasar** and **Bedugul**). **Night buses** (bis malam) leave from the Banyuasri terminal at approximately 1800 for Surabaya, arriving in **Surabaya** about 0400 (bus companies have their offices at *Taman Lila*, Jl Jend A Yani 2). **Bemos**: link the 3 terminals, fares within town are 400Rp. There are also some horse drawn dokar.

getaway tonight on

www.exodus.co.uk

The Different Holiday

2

1

exodus
9 Weir Road
LONDON
SW12 0BR

BUSINESS REPLY SERVICE
Licence No SW4909

Directory

Airline offices *Nitour*, Jl Jend A Yani 59, T22691 is the *Garuda* agent in Singaraja. **Banks** Several banks along Jl Ngurah Rai and Jl Jend A Yani, including *Bank Rakyat Indonesia*. **Communications** **General Post Office:** Jl Gajah Mada 158, Singaraja 81113; poste restante service. The **Telephone Office:** next to the post office, reasonable rates, overseas rates are displayed, and helpful staff. Open 24 hrs. **Medical services** **Chemists:** there are several chemists along Jl Ngurah Rai at nos 23, 27 and 28, also Singaraja Farma on Jl Jend A Yani. **Hospitals:** There are several hospitals in Singaraja. *General Hospital (Rumah Sakit Umum)*, Jl Ngurah Rai, T22046/22573. *Rumah Sakit Umum Angkatan Darat (RSAD)*, a military hospital which also treats members of the public, also on Jl Ngurah Rai, T22543. *Rumah Sakit Kerta Usada*, a private hospital with a dental section, Jl Jend A Yani 108, T22396.

West of Singaraja

Bali

Lovina

Lovina, an 8 km stretch of grey sand, is the name given to an area that begins 7 km west of Singaraja and includes six villages and their associated beaches: from east to west they are Pemaron, Tukad Mungga, Anturan, Kalibukbuk, Kaliasem and Temukus, all of which merge into one another. Lovina is one of the larger beach resorts on Bali and caters to all ages and price groups from backpackers and a few remnant hippies to an increasingly upmarket and package tour oriented clientele. Kalibukbuk is the heart of Lovina, the busiest, most developed part, with the greatest number of tourist facilities and nightlife. If you are looking for somewhere more peaceful try the area to the east which is currently less developed, more rural and peaceful.

Phone code: 0362

The **tourist office** is next door to the police station. Open daily 0800-2000. They are very helpful, speak good English, supply maps, booklets and during high season can help you to find accommodation. Also offer tours and car hire at competitive prices, eg a full day tour, 0900-1800, for two people, taking in the area around Lovina and up into the hills around Bedugul, costs 60,000Rp.

The beach

The beach itself is quite narrow in places and the grey/black sand is not the prettiest, but the waters are calm, so swimming is very safe and there is reasonable snorkelling on the reef just off-shore. The beach is interspersed with streams running into the sea where some villagers wash in the evening. Several areas are the preserve of the local fishermen whose dogs can be menacing if you are out for a walk, particularly in the evening. You can usually scare them off by bending down to pick up a few stones, only the most persistent wait for you to actually throw the stone at them. Hawkers are not as bad as they used to be but can still be a nuisance.

There are plans to build a by-pass to take the heavy traffic that currently passes right through the centre of Lovina; it is not certain when, or if, this will happen. Equally uncertain are the plans to build an airport to handle light aircraft to the west near Pemuteran.

The most popular outing is an early morning boat trip to see the **dolphins** cavorting off the coast; there are two schools of dolphin which regularly swim off the coast. In the Kalibukbuk area the fishermen run a co-operative which fixes the number of people in each boat and the price, currently 10,000Rp; snorkelling is not included in the price. If you book through your hotel you will pay more for the convenience but the price may include refreshments and the opportunity to go snorkelling afterwards. Boats set off at about 0600 and the tour usually lasts 90 minutes. You'll be travelling in the fishermens' boats (many earn more from tourism than fishing these days), made from a single, hollowed out tree-trunk with bamboo outriders on each side to act as stabilizers; bear in mind that there is no shade on the boats. People have mixed reactions to the experience. If yours is the first boat to reach the dolphin area then you may be rewarded with 12 dolphins leaping and playing, but as other boats arrive the dolphins may be chased away.

Bull races Bull races, *sapi gerumbungan* take place on Independence Day, 17 August and on some other national holidays such as Singaraja Day 31 March, check exact dates at the tourist office. The Balinese name for the races is derived from the huge wooden bells *gerumbungan* which the bulls (*sapi* in Indonesian) wear around their necks during the races. These bull races are unique to Buleleng and originated as a religious ceremony to propitiate the gods before planting the new rice crop. The specially trained bulls, decorated with colourful ornaments and silk banners, and with equally well dressed drivers, were originally raced over a flooded ricefield, usefully ploughing the field as they competed. Recently the event has been held on playing fields in the village of Kaliasem to the west of Kalibukbuk, primarily as a tourist attraction. However, in 1995 to commemorate the 50th anniversary of Indonesian Independence, the regional government decided to hold the event in its original form on a flooded ricefield in the village of Banjar, and they plan to make this an annual event. The winner is not necessarily the fastest; the appearance of the bull and driver are an important consideration when the judge decides the overall winner.

Excursions About 5 km to the west there are waterfalls at the village of **Labuhan Haji**, and a Buddhist monastery near the village of **Banjar Tegeha** with hot springs nearby. To the south there are cool highland areas with **lakes** and **botanical gardens** in the area surrounding Bedugul and Mount Batur; it can be very wet here except at the height of the dry season. To the east is **Singaraja**, the capital of the district, and beyond Singaraja, there are interesting temples and other cultural sites, and the gamelan village of **Sawan**. (More information in the relevant sections.)

Sleeping
■ *on maps pages 203 & 205*

The central area of Kalibukbuk has the greatest concentration of accommodation, the widest choice of restaurants and nightlife, and most of the tourist facilities; however, it is becoming increasingly busy and built up. Some of the side roads to the east in the Anturan area offer more attractive and peaceful surroundings. To the west of Kalibukbuk towards Temukus the road runs close to the beach, so accommodation here can be noisy; there are some new, attractive places here with beachfront locations, though prices seem a bit high.

Lovina started as primarily a backpackers' resort with the result that many of the older hotels with the best, beachfront sites have rooms which do not always justify the price. The resort is now going upmarket with a growing number of new star-rated hotels taking the place of some of the older, basic losmen. Several hotels cater largely for the package tour market; these tend to be rather featureless and uninspiring offering poor value for money. Surprisingly, it is not only luxury hotels that charge for breakfast in Lovina, even at budget level you may have to pay. Some of the hotel swimming pools are tiny, little more than plunge pools. Premium prices charged for a beachside location though it is not the prettiest beach and hawkers and fishermen may hassle; the sunsets can be memorable though. Accommodation along the main road on the side away from the beach is cheapest. Mosquitoes can be a problem, not all bungalows provide nets. During high season, Jul, Aug and the Christmas/New Year period, accommodation tends to be full with some people without reserved rooms being forced to spend their first night sleeping on the beaches.

AL *Hotel Damai*, new hotel in the hills overlooking Lovina. To reach it turn south in Kalibukbuk by the *Khi Khi* restaurant at the sign for Kayuputih (see map), continue along a fairly narrow road climbing into the hills for about 10 mins until you see the hotel on your right. Stunning location with spectacular views to the coast; the setting is rural and very peaceful, with landscaped tropical gardens and temperatures a little cooler than sea level, even at high noon there is a refreshing breeze. The 8 bungalows have been built to the highest standards with 4-poster beds, sunken lounge, luxury bathroom, a/c, mini bar. Small pool with adjacent bar, restaurant (expensive) providing gourmet food (at gourmet prices) with an extensive wine cellar; the chef trained with Paul Bocuse.

Lovina Beach

■ **Sleeping**
1 Aditya Beach Bungalows
2 Agus
3 Aldian Palace
4 Aneka Lovina
5 Bali Lovina Beach Cottages
6 Bali Taman Beach
7 Banyualit Beach
8 Baruna Beach Cottages
9 Celuk Agung
10 Krisna
11 Lila Cita
12 Mandiri Homestay
13 Mas Lovina Beach
14 Padma
15 Pantai Bahagia
16 Perama
17 Permai Beach Cottages
18 Pringa
19 Puri Bagus
20 Puri Bedahulu
21 Ray Beach Inn 2
22 Samudra
23 Sol Lovina
24 Suci Jati
25 Suna
26 Toto
27 Yudha

Related map
A Kalibukbuk,
page 205

= = = = = Private access to hotel

Bali

Pemaron (approximately 2 km west of Singaraja) **AL** *Puri Bagus Lovina*, PO Box 225, T21430, F22627. Sister hotel to the *Puri Bagus Candi Dasa*, and of equally high quality, newly opened and the best of the upmarket hotels in Lovina. Beautiful location beside sea, set in peaceful, secluded tropical gardens with fountains, gamelan music and large pool, thatched Balinese style bungalows provide attractive, bright rooms with outdoor as well as indoor bathrooms in case guests wish to shower under the stars, verandah, satellite TV, mini bar, a/c. 2 suites with private pool, kitchen and dining room; facilities are as expected in a hotel of this class and include 24-hr room service, library, boutiques, meeting room, restaurants and bar, sports facilities include sailing, scuba diving/diving school, fishing, windsurfing, cycling, trekking etc. 4 white ducks, the hotel's mascots, wander the grounds and guests are welcome to any eggs they find, tax and breakfast extra. **A-C** *Baruna Beach Cottages*, T41745, F41252. Beside the sea with good sea views, though the public beach is none too peaceful, smallish pool, rooms are over-priced and some would benefit from redecoration, cheapest rooms are dark and pokey, all with private bathroom, Western toilet, some a/c and hot water, tax and breakfast extra. **B-D** *Aldian Palace Hotel*, T25519. Very average hotel, not a good location, beside the road with no access to beach and no pool, 34 rooms with private bathroom and Western toilet, some with a/c, hot water and TV, restaurant and bar.

Tukad Mungga (approximately 7 km from Singaraja) **A-C** *Bali Taman Beach*, PO Box 149, T41126, F41840. A rather average upmarket hotel, disappointing for the price, beside the sea with smallish pool, tennis courts, 28 rooms, all with private bathrooms, Western toilets, some a/c, hot water, rooms near road could be noisy, rates include tax and continental breakfast. **B-D** *Puri Bedahulu*, T41731/23861. 11 rooms, set in tropical gardens beside the beach which can be noisy, rooms with private bathroom, Western toilet, fan, 2 with a/c and hot water, some rooms are small and rather dark, price includes breakfast, 10% tax extra. **C-E** *Yudha* (formerly *Simon Seaside Cottages*) PO Box 151, T41183, F411160. 20 rooms set in gardens beside sea, rooms have been attractively redecorated and include a new wing, all rooms have fans, private bathrooms with West-ern toilet, upstairs rooms have balconies with beautiful sea views, tax is included but breakfast is extra, owner speaks excellent English and is knowledgeable and helpful. **D** *Pantai Bahagia* (formerly *Happy Beach Inn*), no phone, beside sea, basic rooms with private bathroom and Western toilet. **D-E** *Permai Beach Cottages*, T41471, F41224. 17 rooms set in gardens in a quiet location down a side road leading to the beach, a swim-ming pool is due to be built. Simple, clean rooms with private bathroom, Western toilet, fan, some with a/c, hot water and spring mattresses, good value and the cheapest a/c in Lovina, dive centre on premises. **E** *Suci Jati* (formerly *Jati Reef Bungalows*), same owner-ship as *Hotel Yudha*, PO Box 151, T41052, F41160. 16 rooms, set in large gardens next to beach, owner plans to renovate, in the meantime this offers basic but reasonably priced accommodation, all with private mandi and Western toilet, breakfast extra.

Anturan (8½ km west of Singaraja) **A-B** *Hotel Celuk Agung*, PO Box 191, T41079, F41379. 28 rooms set in immaculate, large gardens in very peaceful location surrounded by rice paddies (crickets and frog chorus at night), several mins' walk from the beach, clean and well-maintained, rooms with verandah/balcony, private bathrooms, Western toilet, bath, hot water, some with Balinese style décor, a/c, satellite TV and fridge, restaurant (mid-range to cheap), large swimming pool, floodlit at night, tennis courts, staff are very helpful and friendly and will occasionally put on an impromptu gamelan concert, price includes tax and continental breakfast. Recommended. **D-E** *Lila Cita*, superb location beside sea but rooms are badly in need of renovation though they are clean. Private mandis, most with Western toilets, fan, upstairs rooms with balconies and fine sea views, price includes breakfast and tax. **D-E** *Perama Hotel*, T41161/41104. Small, basic rooms set around small Balinese style garden beside road, can be noisy as this is the location of the *Perama* shuttle bus operation, restaurant (cheap).

Banyualit (9 km west of Singaraja) **AL** *Hotel Mas Lovina Beach* (formerly *Las Brisas*, sister hotel *Bali Danau Buyan* near Bedugul), Jl Raya, F41236. Set in immaculate, completely secluded, tropical gardens with beautiful sea views, 10 spotless bungalows with full self-catering facilities, living room, dining room, fully equipped kitchenette, bathroom with hot water, a/c, satellite TV, large beachside pool and restaurant. **A** *Hotel Aneka Lovina*, Jl Raya Seririt, T41121/2, F41827. Catering largely for tour groups, set in lovely tropical gardens beside the sea, rooms face each other with a small verandah and are attractively furnished with satellite TV and mini bar, facilities include restaurant, karaoke bar and small pool. **A** *Sol Lovina* (formerly *Palma Beach Inn*), T41775, F41659. Part of the Sol Group offering typical package tour accommodation, rooms face each other and facilities include fridge, TV, telephone, beachside location with large pool, tennis courts, meeting room, restaurant, coffee shop, bar, 24-hr room service, breakfast and tax extra. **B-C** *Banyualit Beach Inn*, PO Box 116, T41789, F41563. 20 rooms, seaside location with attractive pool, rooms are a bit overpriced, but clean, cheaper rooms are in semi-detached bungalows so you might hear your neighbours, all with private bathroom, Western toilet, fan or a/c, some with hot water, satellite TV and fridge, rates include continental breakfast and tax. **C-D** *Hotel Kalibukbuk*, T41701. Reasonably priced beside the sea though rooms are nothing special, cheaper rooms face away from the sea, the more expensive, upstairs rooms have pleasant sea views, all with private bathrooms, Western toilet, fan or a/c, price includes tax and breakfast. **D** *Ray Beach Inn 2*, T41088. Same ownership as *Ray Beach Inn 1* in Kalibukbuk, set in small garden several mins' walk from beach, simple, clean, accommodation in new 2-storey building with shared terrace/balcony and 1 detached bungalow, all with private bathrooms, Western toilet, fan or a/c, restaurant (mid-range to cheap).

Kalibukbuk (10 km west of Singaraja) **A-B** *Bali Lovina Beach Cottages*, T22385/23478, F23478. 34 overpriced rooms adjacent to a good beach with pool, 6 bungalows have sea views, a/c, hot water, fridge and TV, the remaining a/c rooms

Bali

Kalibukbuk, Lovina Beach

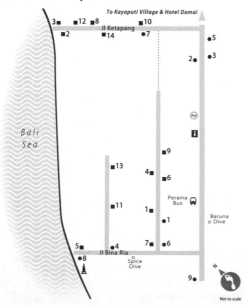

■ Sleeping
1 Angsoka
2 Astina
3 Bayu Kartika Beach Bungalows
4 Harris Homestay
5 Nirwana
6 Padang
7 Pulestis Beach
8 Puri Bali Bungalows
9 Puri Manik Sari
10 Rambutan Beach Cottages
11 Ray Beach Inn I
12 Rini
13 Susila Beach Inn
14 Taman Lily

● Eating
1 Bali Apik
2 Chonos
3 Ciri Warung
4 Kakatua
5 Khi Khi
6 Nick's Warung
7 Sanary
8 Sea Breeze
9 Wina

face each other and are clean but dark, 4 fan rooms are small and basic, tax and breakfast extra, restaurant (mid-range to cheap). **B-C** *Bayu Kartika Beach Bungalow*, T41055, F41219. Superb beachside location, one of the few new places beside the sea in this price range. 20 simple rooms with verandahs, private bathrooms, Western toilet, mosquito nets. A/c rooms have open-air bathrooms, hot water and good sea views, fan rooms have cold water only and face sideways, overlooking the area the fishermen moor their boats, so may well be noisy early morning. Large gardens with plans to build a pool. Restaurant with sea views. Price includes tax and continental breakfast. Very friendly staff, manager plays gamelan. Long stay discount available. Recommended. **B-D** *Nirwana*, clean but no mosquito protection, nice rooms overlooking a garden, rather overpriced. **B-D** *Puri-Bali Bungalows*, T41485. 20 bungalows in garden setting with small pool, rooms are dark and simple, with private bathroom, Western toilet, some with a/c, hot water. **B-D** *Rambutan Beach Cottages*, PO Box 195, T41388, F41057. Set in large, pretty gardens with small plunge pool, 18 simple but clean rooms with verandah, private bathroom, Western toilet, cold water in all but the most expensive rooms, fan, cheaper rooms face the car park, overpriced, restaurant (mid-range to cheap). **B-D** *Rini Hotel*, T41386. Set in tropical gardens, 20 spotlessly clean rooms, cheaper rooms are dark and basic, some with squat toilets, more expensive rooms are attractive but not particularly good value, one enormous room with large peaceful verandah, all rooms have private bathrooms, fan, some hot water, Swiss owner, restaurant (mid-range to cheap). **B-E** *Angsoka Hotel*, T41841, F41023, angsoka@singaraja, wasantara.net.id 38 rooms, a popular place set in pretty tropical gardens with a small pool, there is a large range of rooms and prices, all with verandah, private bathroom, cheapest rooms have squat toilets, the most expensive rooms have baths, hot water and a/c, have a look at several rooms as price is not necessarily an indication of how attractive the room will be: the newer rooms are much nicer and much better value, look out for the two *Pisang Seribu* banana trees which produce a thousand tiny bananas which take 3 months to ripen, one is growing just past the pool, the other by the restaurant, price includes breakfast and tax. Recommended. **C-E** *Puri Manik Sari*, T41089. Bright, new, clean accommodation set in immaculate garden, 8 simple, reasonably priced rooms with private bathrooms, Western toilet, fan, cheaper rooms near road may be noisy, price includes breakfast and tax. Recommended. **D** *Pulestis Beach Hotel*, T41035. 14 rooms, set in gardens, rooms are rather dark and drab but reasonably priced, all with private bathrooms, Western toilets. **D-E** *Astina*, very clean but no mosquito protection, some private mandis, dark rooms, but good value and run by friendly people. **D-E** *Harris Homestay*, T41152. A genuine homestay run by Betty from Germany who is very helpful and friendly, 5 attractively decorated, spotlessly clean rooms with private mandi, shower, squat toilet, mosquito nets, fan, good mattresses, price includes breakfast and tax. Recommended. **D-E** *Ray Beach Inn 1*, T41087 (same ownership as *Ray Beach Inn 2* in Banyualit). Basic accommodation in 2-storey block with shared verandahs/balconies; upstairs balconies have pleasant views and rooms are small but brighter and less claustrophobic than some of the cheaper places in this area, all rooms with private bathroom, Western toilet, shower, fan or a/c, price includes tax and breakfast. **D-E** *Susila Beach Inn*, T61565. Price includes breakfast, friendly people but basic accommodation.

Temukus (11-13 km west of Singaraja) **A-C** *Aditya Beach Bungalows*, PO Box 134, T41059, F41342. 75 rooms, a large hotel set in attractive gardens beside the sea, the most expensive bungalows have good sea views from their verandahs, garden view rooms are a bit dark, cheaper rooms suffer from road noise and need renovation, all rooms have hot water, a/c or fan, attractive raised pool with sea views, restaurant (mid-range to cheap), breakfast and tax extra. **B-C** *Padma Hotel*, T/F41140, padma@ singaraja.wasantra. net.id 17 rooms, this new, clean hotel suffers from road noise and is overpriced, rooms are featureless with drab furnishings and tiny verandahs, a/c or fan, hot water, beside the sea with small pool, restaurant (mid-range to cheap), price includes continental breakfast, tax extra. **C-D** *Agus*, T41202. 11 rooms, attractive beachside location but suffers from road noise, rooms are clean and bright with private bathrooms, Western toilet a/c or fan, restaurant (mid-range to cheap). **C-D** *Puri Tasik Madu*, towards Temukus, T21585. Restaurant, dark but characterful with 4-poster beds but nasty furniture, friendly owners. **D** *Villa Delima*, Villa Delima, Jl Seririt, T41141, delima@lovina.com Refurbished in 1999, 8 en-suite rooms, big, clean, good value, restaurant open until late. **D** *Samudra*, PO Box 15, some a/c, hot water. **E** *Toto*, 4 or 5 rooms, noisy bungalows near the road, better ones on the beach, good value.

Mid-range to cheap *Nick's Warung*, good fish. *Sea Breeze (Laut Angin)*, good Indonesian and European food but pricier than some places, English owner. *Bali Pub*, good fresh fish. Recommended. *Bali Apik*, specializes in pizzas and breakfasts as well as Indonesian and Chinese food. *Ciri Warung*, next to *Khi Khi Restaurant*, on non-beach side of the road, good Balinese food but meat can be tough (*nasi campur*). *Wina Restaurant*, excellent Chinese and Indonesian food. Recommended. *Puri Jaman Lorina*, excellent food, good value. *Sanary*, good Chinese food. *Susila*, fresh seafood (snapper, crab, squid) and Indian. Specialities including various thalis, lassi and chapaties.

Eating
Many of the restaurants at Lovina serve good, & reasonably priced, seafood

Bali

Villa Delima is a pretty hotel serving the budget traveller and is located just outside the hustle and bustle of Central Lovina on Bali's north coast. The hotel boasts good-sized, comfortable rooms, a pleasant bar-restaurant and is ideally situated for touring the peaceful northern part of Bali.

• *8 spacious double/twin rooms with en-suite facilities and fans*
• *patio or balconies for all rooms* • *shady courtyard with sun traps*
• *spacious car/coach park*

Jalan Seririt, Temukus, Lovina Beach, Bali, Indonesia.
www.lovina.com/delima/ Tel:+62 (0)362 41141 E-mail: delima@lovina.com

Bali

Entertainment	**Live music** At *Wina's* and *Malibu*.

Videos Evening showings at *Malibu* and *Wina's*, both popular.

Sports **Boat tours** Organized by the *Bali Lovina Beach Cottages*; other larger hotels and tour and dive companies.

Diving Trips to **Menjangan Island** are easily organized from here (see page 212). *Spice Dive*, Kaliasem, US$45-60 for 2 dives all including; introductory training and 1 dive US$45; 5 day certification course US$230. *Spice Dive* also arrange offshore snorkelling trips (25,000Rp). Seems the best company on Lovina, with well maintained equipment and helpful, friendly staff, owner's wife is English. *Baruna*, Jl Seririt, Kalibukbuk, T41084, PADI Dive Centre Introductory (US$80) and 4-day open water certificate course US$300, 2 dives US$50, also offers fishing and watersports. *Lovina Marine Resort* and *Bali Lovina Beach Cottages* organize diving expeditions.

Fishing Most hotels and losmen offer fishing trips (10,000Rp).

Golf The only golf course in the north at present is the *Bali Handara Koseido Country Club*, at Pancasari near Bedugul. Approximately US$75 for a round of golf.

Sailing Boats available for hire.

Snorkelling Average snorkelling just off the beach. Snorkel hire 5,000Rps for 2 hrs; better marine life at Menjangan Island (25,000Rp for a day trip with *Spice Dive*). Equipment available from the *Bali Lovina Beach Cottages*, boat owners and dive shops, not all of equal quality.

Swimming At the *Bali Lovina Beach Cottages*, 5,000Rp to non-residents. Most big hotels will let non-residents use the pool for between 5-10,000Rp if you look presentable.

Transport
11 km from Singaraja

Local Car/motorbike/bicycle hire from several of the hotels; eg *Rambutan* have motorbikes for hire. *Perama* have reasonably priced car hire with insurance included. The tourist office also offers car hire. Be prepared for some hard bargaining; most hire companies quote in dollars. A 5/6 seat minibus with English speaking guide costs about US$20 a day (0830-2100), US$10 for half a day.

Road Bus: from **Denpasar's** Ubung terminal catch an express bus to Singaraja, 1½-2 hrs. The bus stops at **Singaraja's** Banyuasri terminal, from where there are regular buses to Lovina. There are also regular buses and minibuses from **Gilimanuk**, taking the north coast route, 1½ hrs (buses from Java will drop passengers off at Gilimanuk to catch a connection to Lovina – sometimes including in the cost of the ferry and bus ticket). **Shuttle bus**: 12,500Rp to Kuta, 7,500Rp to Ubud, 5,000Rp to Air Sanih, 20,000Rp to **Candi Dasa**, with *Perama*. *Perama* will pick you up from your hotel, but at Lovina they will only drop you off at one of their 2 offices in the Lovina area, or along the main road in between these.

Directory **Banks** On the main road. **Communications** Postal agent on main road.

West of Lovina

The road follows the flat, narrow coastal strip all the way to Gilimanuk passing between the mountains and the sea. As you approach Pemuteran the scenery becomes more impressive with the mountains rising dramatically just to the south of the road while the sea is close by to the north. After Banyuwedang the road passes through parts of the **West Bali National Park** (no charge for road vehicles entering this portion of the park).

The village of **Labuhan Haji** is 5 km from the centre of Lovina; from here you will see signs for the **Singsing Air Terjun** (waterfall) a further 1 km away. Consisting of two falls with attendant pools where you can swim, Singsing is not as spectacular as some of the other waterfalls on Bali and is probably only worth visiting during the wet season. There is a car park with a warung nearby. The area provides pleasant walks along paths which pass other small waterfalls.

About 10 km to the west of Kalibukbuk is the turning for the villages of **Dencarik** and **Banjar**, and a sign indicating the route to Bali's only Buddhist monastery, Brahma Vihara Asrama which lies up a steep road just past the village of Banjar Tegeha. A Buddhist monastery was established here in the 1950s but the present building dates back to 1971 and was built with financial help from both the Indonesian and Thai governments; the huge temple bell was donated by Thailand. The building was damaged in an earthquake in 1976 but has been completely repaired. Architecturally it combines traditional Buddhist elements, including stone reliefs showing scenes from Buddha's life, a stupa and a statue of Buddha decorated in gold leaf, with an overall Balinese feel. Naga guard the entrance, and there is a kulkul tower; overall the temple is very colourful with bright orange roof tiles. Set in the hills with fine views to the sea, the monastery and grounds provide a peaceful and cool interlude from the heat and bustle below. Visitors are welcome but they should be appropriately dressed and act with decorum. The monastery serves as a focus for Buddhist life on the island; Bali's Chinese community make frequent visits and the Dalai Lama visited in 1982. Education is an important aspect of monastery life; various courses, including meditation, are offered (check in advance when instruction in English is available). It is possible to stay overnight but contact the monastery in advance of intended stay. A short walk west along a track from the monastery leads to Banjar Hot Springs.

These sacred hot springs are set in beautifully landscaped gardens and consist of three pools; eight naga spew the hot, sulphurous water from an underground spring into the first of the pools, from here the water overflows through the mouths of five more naga into a second pool. There are changing rooms, rather cramped and smelly, and a restaurant (cheap) which offers good food. The car park is about 400 m from the holy springs. Very popular with the local population; if possible avoid Sundays and Tuesdays when groups come. ■ *Adult 1,000Rp, child 500Rp. Getting there: both the Banjar hot springs and the monastery, which are about 1 km apart, are easily reached from Lovina; take a bemo west to Dencarik from where you can catch an ojek or make the steep climb on foot. From the village of Banjar it is a 1 km walk uphill; follow the signpost shortly after the village market.* There is also a track which connects the monastery and springs making a pleasant walk.

Sleeping **B** *Pondok Wisata Grya Sari*, Air Panas Banjar, 200 m from the hot springs, signposted from the main road, 3 km. T92303, F92966. Recently opened and set amidst lush vegetation in a peaceful location overlooking a ravine, with the sound of birdsong and running water from a nearby stream. There are lovely gardens and a refreshing breeze. Fourteen bungalows with attractive décor, spring mattresses, TV, fan, clean bathrooms with western toilet, large verandahs. Live gamelan music. Guests are entitled to free entry to the Banjar hot springs. There are plans to build a pool using water from a hot spring. Restaurant.

Seririt   Seririt is 2 km further on. Turning south, the road starts climbing into the central mountains through spectacular terraces of rice paddies. There are many picturesque villages on this quiet road, and magnificent views. If you take the right fork at Pupuan, 25 km to the south, the road contours along the narrow mountain ridges and eventually descends through villages and clove plantations to reach the main road along the south coast at Pekutatan, not far from the surfing beach at Medewi, on the main coast road from the south to Gilimanuk. The drive takes about two hours.

The area stretching from Seririt west to Pulaki is one of the island's prime grape growing regions; the best grapes are exported to Japan; some are also dried for export. Conditions are good for grape growing as the heat is mitigated by cool sea breezes, and the resultant black grapes are sweet and juicy. Two sweetish red wines are now being produced, both under British tutelage, which are widely available on the island. One marketed under the name 'Hatton' sells for about 80,000Rp; the other hasn't yet got a licence but is sold in beer bottles and has been described as tasting 'like Bordeaux'!

Pulaki   At Pulaki, approximately 55 km west of Singaraja, there is a temple perched on a cliff with fine views out to sea. The temple itself is rather drab, a modern concrete construction. It is inhabited by bag-snatching grey macaques, considered 'holy' by the Balinese, which have a special penchant for raiding motorcycles. The site has an historical connection with the 16th century Javanese priest Nirartha. Legend recounts that a town of some 8000 inhabitants lived on the site at the time of Nirartha's arrival. Their leader asked Nirartha that they be given supernatural powers which would allow them to become invisible. This was granted, and these invisible *gamang*, as they are called, exist to this day living close by in Pura Melanting. Local Balinese keenly feel the presence of the 'gamang' and make offerings to appease them.

Pemuteran   This small fishing village, 1 km west of Pulaki, lies on a sweeping bay with a
Phone code: 0362   backdrop of brooding, dormant volcanoes. These act as a rainbreak so the area receives slightly less rain, a consideration if you are travelling during the wet season. The sunsets can be fantastic with views over Java and its stunning volcanic craters including Mount Semeru. The beach is public, with fishermen going about their business and mooring their boats, though the areas in front of hotels are kept clean and are relatively peaceful.

Offshore there are reefs to swim to (five minutes by boat) which provide good snorkelling and diving; visibility is good (10-15 m) with a slight current, there is a good variety of coral, reef fish, even the occasional 'manta', and impressive drop-offs. The area is beginning to see some development with several upmarket hotels having appeared in the last two years. Reports suggest that wealthy property dealers from Java, including President Suharto's daughter, have bought up prime beachfront sites, and there are even rumours that a small airfield will be built at some time in the future to allow light aircraft to land. However, major development is probably a good way off, and at present the three hour drive from Denpasar acts as a deterrent.

Sleeping **L** *Puri Ganesha Villas*, Pemuteran, T93433, sales office T0361-261610/ 246712, F261611, www.puriganeshabali.com 4 very luxurious villas each with its own private pool and dining pavilion. Owned by an English lady, cookery classes a feature. **L-AL** *Matahari Beach Resort*, PO Box 194, T92312, F92313. The most luxurious hotel in the area, set in glorious tropical gardens beside the sea. The 32 bungalows are beautifully decorated in Balinese style using wood and thatch. The superb, marble bathrooms feature a small outdoor garden which can be floodlit at night, and include both indoor and outdoor showers for those who want to wash under the stars. Facilities include a magnificent pool, Padi diving courses (Open Water Course lasting 3-4 days 850,000Rp), dives at all the main sites around Bali (prices start at 80,000Rp for 1 dive; this is the only hotel on Bali with the right to provide direct access to Menjangan Island, Bali's best dive site), watersports, tennis, tours, massage, library. The hotel also offers classes in Balinese dance, stonecarving and drawing. Restaurant (expensive) with resident European cook and in-house bakery, outdoor raised performance area. Conference facilities for 80 people. **A-B** *Taman Sari Bali*, T92623/ T0361-288096 (travel agent), F0361-286297. 23 bungalows most attractively furnished in rustic style, set in spacious gardens beside the sea with private bathrooms, Western toilets, fan or a/c, some rooms with hot water. A very peaceful setting though rooms are a bit pricey. Restaurant (mid-range) beside the sea, portions tend to be small. Offers meditation and yoga as well as scuba diving (with Reef Seen Aquatics), sailing, hiking and tours. Popular with specialist US tour groups. Tax and breakfast extra. **A** *Taman Sari 2*, new development next door to *Taman Sari Bali* with just five bungalows. Reservations c/o *Taman Sari Bali*. **B-C** *Pondok Sari Beach Bungalows* and *Yos Dive Centre*, T/F92337. 20 modern, attractively decorated bungalows, fan or a/c, private bathrooms with Western toilet, cold water. The more expensive bungalows face the sea. Set in large pretty gardens, running down to the beach with good swimming and fabulous sunsets. Not as well managed as in the past. Restaurant (mid-range to cheap): the day we ate there the food was awful and the staff were disenchanted with their low salaries; the German owner spends most of the year in Germany with the result that standards here have slipped. The manager can organize hiking trips to **Taman Nasional Bali Barat**. Price includes tax but not breakfast.

Diving Just to the east of *Pondok Sari Beach Bungalows* is *Reef Seen Aquatics Dive Centre*, T/F92339. Manager Chris Brown is Australian and a PADI instructor. This was the first dive centre to open in this area, and offers a variety of newly discovered sites with dives to suit every level of experience; photographers are also catered for. There are safe dives off the beach as well as further afield, and he operates to high standards; not always the case in the Bali/Lombok area. Chris is very conservation minded and has launched the 'Turtle Project' to save the endangered local species. Prices range from US$30 for a single dive to US$70 for 2 people diving off Menjangan Island. The centre is easily reached by public bus from Singaraja (1½-2½ hrs, 60 km, 2,000Rp) and Gilimanuk/Cekik (1 hr, 30 km, 1,500Rp), buses run from 0500-1700.

Transport Take a bus from **Denpasar's** Ubung terminal to **Gilimanuk** (these are usually green) and then catch a connection on. From **Singaraja**, take a bemo from the Banyuasri terminal, running west towards Gilimanuk. Some buses also connect with **Amlapura** and **Klungkung**.

Labuan Lalang

About 15 km from Gilimanuk, Labuan Lalang is the most convenient base for visits to Menjangan Island (see 'Excursions' below). It will cost 2,000Rp to park your car (even if you just want to stroll down to the beach). There is a simple warung and a few basic losmen.

Excursions   **Pulau Menjangan** (Deer Island) lies just off Bali's north coast and is part of the Bali Barat National Park (see also page 218). The island is uninhabited, fringed with mangroves, very beautiful and home to the rare Java deer and Bali white mynah. There are no losmen on the island and camping is not permitted. The island is surrounded by spectacular coral reefs and offers the best diving around Bali, with excellent visibility (25-50 m) and a slight current. In addition to the good variety of coral there is also the wreck of a ship the 'Anker' and beyond 60 m you might find the rare 'Genicanthus Bellus'. The snorkelling is excellent as well. Expect to pay close to 100,000Rp for 4 hours on the island; this includes 60,000Rp for the hire of the boat, and 15,000Rp for a guide. The guides will try to rent out snorkelling equipment. The nearest dive centres are at Pemuteran about 15 km, 15 minutes' drive away; both 'Reef Seen Aquatics' (70,000Rp for a two-dive package with two people) and the *Matahari Beach Resort* (100,000Rp for two people) offer diving trips to Menjangan. All the dive centres on Bali offer trips to Menjangan but it makes a long day if you are coming from the south or east of Bali. The trip by boat from Labuan Lalang takes 30 minutes.

Pura Jayaprana, just west of Labuan Lalang is a temple built to commemorate the 17th century folk hero, Jayaprana, whose beautiful wife, Layonsari, was coveted by his stepfather, the Raja of Kalianget. The raja had Jayaprana murdered; however, Layonsari acted nobly, and spurning the advances of the king, she chose suicide rather than betray her dead husband. The temple, perched on the hillside, is primarily of interest for the superb views it affords across the sea to Pulau Menjangan.

South of Singaraja

Beratan village just south of Singaraja is the northern centre for silverware. Silversmiths make religious and household articles such as vases, large plates and jewellery. It is possible to watch them at work and buy direct from them. The choice is not great.

Air Terjun Gitgit is a waterfall 11 km south of Singaraja, worth visiting in the wet season (see page 192). *Getting there*: catch a bemo to Singaraja and then one heading towards Lake Bratan.

East from Singaraja

Sangsit &   **Pura Beji** is situated just north of the main coastal road 8 km east of Singaraja
around   and nearly 20 km from Lovina Beach, near the village of **Sangsit**. The temple is
Phone code: 0362   dedicated to the rice goddess Dewi Sri and belongs to the local *subak* or irrigation society which is served with the task of managing and allocating water resources among its members (see page 229). The association of rice, water and religion reflects the dependence of rice cultivation upon an adequate and constant supply of water, and of people upon rice for their survival. This is a fine example of North Bali's exuberant style of temple architecture. The soft pink sandstone 'candi bentar' (split gate often found at the entrance) is a flamboyant mass of fanciful carvings of plants, animals, demons and nagas, certain to keep evil spirits at bay, while the walls of the temple itself are equally alive

with carvings. Frangipani trees lend shade to the inner courtyard. Visitors are likely to be mobbed by the local children. The **Pura Dalem**, 500 m northeast, is also worth a visit. The carved reliefs show scenes from the Mahabharatha depicting Bima's journey to heaven and hell in search of his mother. On this journey he witnesses the rewards in heaven for those who have led a good life, and learns of the punishments in hell for those who have sinned. This story is one of the most popular subjects in wayang kulit. The carvings are both humorous and erotic; the erotica, enlarged genitalia, representations of coitus etc, are believed to frighten away evil spirits. ■ *Getting there: take a bemo to Singaraja and then another from Singaraja's Penarukan terminal.*

Sleeping A-D *Berdikara Cottages*, T25195. Some rooms with a/c and hot water, private bathroom with Western toilets, attractive gardens with fruit trees, with open air theatre for dance performances, price includes breakfast, bar restaurant, long stay guests are offered lessons in Balinese dancing and hand weaving; they may also eat the fruit growing in the garden.

Half a kilometre past Sangsit, 18 km from Lovina, is the turning for the villages **Jagaraga &** of Jagaraga and Sawan. The first village, Jagaraga, 4 km inland from the main **Sawan** road, is famous for two reasons. In 1849 the Dutch wiped out virtually the entire settlement in what has come to be known as the Puputan Jagaraga. This was the third attempt by the Dutch to gain control of Buleleng, as a prelude to colonizing the whole of Bali, having failed in 1846 and 1848. They arrived with troops numbering some 7000 men, and with their superior military technology defeated the brave and determined Balinese force who were armed only with kris' and lances, killing thousands while losing only about 30 Dutch soldiers. The **Pura Dalem** – a Temple of the Dead – dedicated to Siwa the destroyer, is famous for its humorous depictions in stone relief of the Dutch invaders. Scenes show them arriving in boats which are attacked by sea monsters, in aircraft involved in aerial dogfights falling from the skies, being eaten by crocodiles and drinking beer. The most famous is the depiction of two rotund Dutchmen in a Model-T Ford being held up by armed bandits. Other reliefs show scenes from village life. Many of the images relate to the evil witch Rangda, related to Siwa's wife Durga, and a central character in the Barong dance. There is also a statue of *Men Brayut* buried under a mound of offspring. Admission – suggested donation comparatively overpriced at 1,000Rp.

Sawan village, a further 4 km up the road, is the home of a well-known gamelan maker. Most days you can watch the gongs being cast and the frames and stands being intricately carved. Gamelan for sale here. ■ *Getting there: if travelling independently, turn right off the main coast road ½ km beyond Sangsit, and then travel south for 4 km to the village of Jagaraga. To get there by public transport take a bemo from Singaraja's Penarukan terminal bound for Sawan. Alternatively, take a bemo going east and get off ½ km past Sangsit at the turning for Jagaraga and Sawan; from there it is an 8 km walk uphill to Sawan (4 km to Jagaraga) or get a lift on an ojek.*

'The Temple of the Owner of the Land', is situated in the village of **Pura Maduwe** Kubutambahan, 12 km east of Singaraja, 23 km from Lovina Beach and on the **Karang** main coast road near the turning to Kintamani. Like Pura Beji, the temple of Maduwe Karang is dedicated to ensuring a bountiful harvest, though not of irrigated rice, but of dry land crops. Many consider this to be the finest of North Bali's temples; though the carvings are not quite as exuberant as the Pura Beji, there is a certain realism and humanity to these whimsical creations which set them apart from those in North Bali's other temples. Outside the

☞ Brayut family planning

A well-known Balinese folk story tells of Pan and Men Brayut, the father and mother of 18 disruptive children. The family are very poor and to make ends meet, Men weaves in addition to bringing up her huge family, whilst poor old Pan helps out round the house, doing most of the household chores. The reasons given as to why Pan and Men end up with so many children are that on the one hand, they are constantly arguing, and after each fight they make up in the 'traditional way' thus adding to the family with each conflict; additionally, Pan is unable to control his desire for Men no matter how inappropriate the time or place. Although essentially a story rooted in Hindu mythology, there is also a Buddhist connection. In this latter version of the tale, Men was originally the evil Hariti whose favourite pastime was to devour children; however, she became a Buddhist, changed her ways, and became a saviour of children and goddess of fertility. As Hariti she is associated with several temples where childless couples go to pray for children, including the Candi Dasa temple (see page 169). The Brayut family also feature extensively in traditional paintings including those of the artists of the Ubud School (I Gusti Nyoman Lempad in particular), showing scenes of everyday life in Bali, and on the walls of the Bale Kambang in Klungkung. The surname 'Brayat' may be old Javanese meaning 'burdened with too many children.' These days she is widely used by family planning campaigners as a symbol to illustrate why "having so many children is not always suitable."

temple are 34 stone figures representing characters from the Ramayana, while inside floral themes and renditions of daily life abound, including a woman taking a bath, and another making love. An interesting relief, found on the base of the inner temple wall, is the famous panel showing a Dutchman riding a bicycle with wheels made of flowers. Some people maintain that the cyclist is the artist WOJ Nieuwenkamp (1874-1950) who came to Bali in 1904 and decided to explore the island by bicycle; this was probably the first bicycle ever seen on Bali. Nieuwenkamp played an important role recording Bali's artistic heritage. The temple is laid out on a grand scale; the grounds are well-tended with an abundance of fragrant Frangipani trees. Entrance by donation. *Getting there*: by bemo to Singaraja and then another from Singaraja's Penarukan Terminal on the eastern edge of town.

Air Sanih
Phone code: 0362

Air Sanih lies 17 km east of Singaraja, on the coast. It has become quite a popular tourist spot because of its spring-fed pool. However it has retained its local village atmosphere and is, as yet, unspoilt by mass tourism; the glistening black-sand beaches remain almost empty. The main season for visitors here seems to be July and August.

Sleeping **A** *Ciliks Beach Garden*, Air Sanih, Singaraja 81172, T/F26561. Two very large, very beautiful, luxury bungalows with marble floors, very tastefully decorated, mosquito nets, attractive bathrooms with hot water and squat toilets, beside the sea with verandah and garden, and separate pavilions for relaxing, offering complete privacy. Tasty Balinese cooking, and a traditional fishing boat available for hire. **A-E** *Puri Sanih Bungalows*, some a/c, restaurant, pool. The most expensive modern bungalows are right on the beach and have their own bathrooms, the cheapest atmospheric but decrepit (rooms on the 2nd floor have lovely views of the sea), immaculate gardens, tour groups catered for, largest place to stay on Air Sanih. **C** *Graha Ayu*, 2 bungalows, new and attractive with fan, private bathroom with shower and Western toilet, price includes breakfast, unfortunately on the wrong side of the road from the beach and with no immediate access to beach once you cross the road. **D** *Sunset Graha Beach*, on a hill above Air Sanih. The restaurant has a good view of the sea, but the bungalows are set behind, facing a rather neglected garden. Large, rather kitsch rooms, with grandiose bathrooms, reasonably priced. **D** *Tara Beach Inn*. 4 bungalows with shower and Western toilet, 2 older thatched bungalows with squat toilet, all basic but with nice location beside sea, owners' dogs and children can be noisy, pub and restaurant, Australian co-owner sometimes lives in the treehouse in the garden. **D-E** *Puri Purtiwi*, on the main road 1 km east of Air Sanih; no telephone. Good beachside location; 5 rooms (plus 4 in the process of being built) set in large, grassy slightly unkempt gardens beside the sea. At the time of viewing the steps leading down to beach level, were broken leaving a 3 m drop. Rooms are clean but a little dark, with private bathroom, Western toilet. Restaurant (cheap).

Eating Mid-range: *Archipelago Restaurant*, on hill overlooking Air Sanih is more upmarket. **Warungs**: there are several warungs opposite the *Puri Sanih Bungalows*, offering reasonably priced local and Western food, good cheap nasi campur and mie goreng at first small restaurant, in shop, as you enter Air Sanih from the west, on right side of road.

Transport Buses: pass through Air Sanih en route to **Gilimanuk** in the west and **Amlapura**, **Klungkung** and **Denpasar** in the east and south, starting from early morning about 0600 until 1700, or sometimes later these days. *Perama* now operates a shuttle bus to/from Air Sanih to all its destinations; eg 5,000Rp to **Lovina**, 10,000Rp to **Candi Dasa**, 20,000Rp to **Kuta**, 15,000Rp to **Ubud**. Perama buses run between Lovina and Padangbai stopping in Air Sanih.

Cultural centres *Osho Abheeshu Meditation & Creative Centre*, F21108. Daily meditation programme creativity course US$25 for 1 day. **Directory**

Continuing east from Air Sanih, the road follows the coast, rounding Cape **East of Air Sanih** Sanih, with good views out to sea. After 7 km the road climbs to the site of **Pura Pondok Batu**, another splendidly situated temple associated with the eminent 16th century priest Nirartha. Across the road is a small shrine where Nirartha is alleged to have sat writing poetry inspired by the sea view. On one occasion he noticed that a ship had capsized; on the shore lay the bodies of the dead crew members. With his legendary ability to perform miracles he brought them back to life and as a testament to their gratitude a temple was built on this site. There is said to be a fresh water spring bubbling out of the sand, visible on the beach at low tide; people from neighbouring villages come here to get fresh water and bring their animals to drink.

At the village of **Pacung**, 6 km beyong Pura Pondok Batu, there is a signposted **Semniran** turning to the 'Bali Aga' village of Sembiran, 3 km from the main road along a narrow road. Unlike **Tenganan** and Trunyan, two other villages associated with the original 'Bali Aga' inhabitants of the island, Sembiran has few reminders of its past other than the layout of the village which differs from traditional 'Hindu' villages. It is, however, believed to be the site of the oldest megalithic settlement on Bali and is known for its sacred *Baris* dance. The village of **Julah**, 1 km to the east, also dates back to ancient times and has the oldest temple in North Bali.

Three kilometres further along the main road brings the village of Tejakula **Tejakula** famous for its elaborate though decaying horse baths. These days horses are not washed here, though the public baths are still in use. The village also has a 'Banjar Pande' where silversmiths can be seen at work.

Eleven kilometres from Air Sanih, a minor road turns inland, climbing the steep ridges to Mount Batur's crater rim at Penulisan (see page 157 for this route).

There are not so many set piece sights along this coast; the beauty lies in the natural scenery. The road passes through small rural villages, the land is much drier here and there are none of the rice terraces, so prevalent elsewhere.

Sambirenteng & further south Sambirenteng is a village on the coast, with some accommodation. The **Les waterfall** is about 6 km from here and is worth a visit. **Sleeping B** *Alamanda*, bookable through a German travel agent – *Pike Travel*, Uwi Siegfriedsen, Ostersielzung 8, 25480, Friedrichstadt, T494881-930633, F494881-930699. Booking recommended. Prices are non-negotiable and the bill is payable in US$ only, restaurant, right on the edge of the sea, 12 back-to-nature bungalows on stilts, set amongst coconut palms. Lovely, clean rooms with Western bathrooms and friendly service. German owned, and also a dive centre, equipped with full sub-aqua gear. Snorkelling on the reef just off the beach. Diving offered at Tulamben, Ulami, Amed, Menjangan and Nusa Penida as well as at Alamanda. Includes night dives, introductory dives available for 125,000Rp. Prices for two dives at each site, 95,000Rp-135,000Rp depending on site.

A 4 hour hike from the main road up to **Trunyon** is signposted 1 km north of Tianyar; Tianyar is about 15 km southeast along the main road from Sambirenteng.

Further east, the land becomes more arid and the road skirts the lower slopes of Mount Batur and the ever imposing Mount Agung, punctuated by 20-30 m wide dry water courses which have cut channels into the barren volcanic rock. Continuing southwards down the east coast you eventually come to **Tulamben**, a beachside village which has long been a Mecca for divers but which is now being developed for a broader market; several new hotels have been built in the last year (see page 185).

Bali

The West

The west of Bali, encompassing the regencies of Jembrana, Tabanan and Badung, is the least visited part of the island; most visitors merely pass through en route from the east of Bali to Java. In a number of respects the west is atypical: the area to the north is less rich agriculturally, it remains the least populated part of the island, there are no historic sights to match those of the east, and there is a strong Muslim representation with settlers from Madura, Java and Sulawesi. At the west tip and 134 km from Denpasar is Gilimanuk, the ferry port for Java. Completely encompassing the port and much of the west is the Bali Barat National Park.

   The west has some of Bali's most spectacular scenery. This is a largely rural area where most of the island's rice is grown, and there are spellbinding vistas of jade green rice terraces with misty mountains in the background. The coast has long stretches of superb, deserted beach strafed by rolling waves, good for surfing but swimming is dangerous due to strong currents and undertows. Some of Bali's prettiest and most traditional villages are also found here. With few visitors and with a paucity of accommodation the area has preserved its Balinese feel and is one of the most rewarding to visit.

Ins and outs

Getting there & around

Bear in mind that all times are necessarily approximate and can vary enormously. Coming from Denpasar times will depend on traffic jams and the number of slow-moving, heavy lorries impeding progress. **Buses** run most frequently in the morning starting early (from 0500 or 0600), and continue until about 1800; on major routes buses usually continue later than this and those connecting via Gilimanuk through to Java run virtually 24 hrs. The frequency of buses is improving all the time.

   From Denpasar Buses run from the Ubung terminal: **Mengwi** 25 mins; **Tanah Lot** (via Kediri) 45 mins, **Tabanan** 30 mins; **Lalang Linggah** (for Balian Beach) 1 hr; **Medewi Beach** 90 mins; **Negara** 2 hrs; **Cekik** (entrance to Bali Barat National Park) 2 hrs 35 mins; **Gilimanuk** 2 hrs 45 mins; **Surabaya** on Java 11 hrs; **Yogyakarta/Solo** 16 hrs; **Jakarta** 30 hrs.

   From Gilimanuk **Cekik** (for Bali Barat National Park) 12 mins; **Negara** 45 mins; **Medewi Beach** 1 hr 15 mins; **Labuan Linggah** (for Balian Beach) 1 hr 45 mins; **Tabanan** 2 hrs 15 mins; **Tanah Lot** (via Kediri) 2 hrs 20 mins; **Denpasar** 2 hrs 45 mins; **Labuan Lalang** (for Pulau Menjangan) 20 mins; **Pemuteran** 30 mins; **Lovina** 1 hr 30 mins; **Singaraja** (Banyuasri Terminal) 2 hrs.

Gilimanuk and Cekik

Phone code: 0365
Colour map 1, grid B1

Gilimanuk is the departure and arrival point for the ferry that runs between Bali and Java. There is no reason to stay here unless forced to; it is only a transit point. For archaeologists, however, Gilimanuk is important as the site of a bronze/iron age burial ground excavated in the 1960s and 1970s, thus providing evidence of prehistoric settlement on Bali. Cekik, the headquarters of the Bali Barat National Park, is 3 km south of Gilimanuk.

Excursions The **Bali Barat** (or West Bali) **National Park** was established as recently as 1984, and covers over 75,000 ha straddling both the dry north coast and the forested, tropical south. The Bali white mynah or *jalak putih Bali* (*Leucopsar rothschildi*), better known by English speakers as the Bali starling, one of the rarest birds in the world, is found here, mostly confined to Menjangan Island. It is a small white bird, with black tips to its wings and tail, and a streak of blue around its eye (easily confused with the black-winged starling, which has wholly black wings and tail). In 1990 a survey revealed that there were only 15 birds left in the wild, and many zoologists thought the population too small to recover. However, 1991 and 1992 saw a marked increase in numbers and it was thought that there were probably 40-50 in the park in the mid-1990s though by 1999 the number was down to only 31. There are also thousands in captivity. A programme to re-introduce captive birds back into the wild has begun, and a British breeder, Nick Wileman, recently successfully bred 20 Bali starlings in the UK and reintroduced four of these birds to Bali. Trapping is still a problem – with prices on the black market approaching US$1,000 or more, their capture is a considerable temptation (it is illegal but fines are rarely enforced). A visit to the bird market in Jl Veteren in Denpasar gives an indication of the high prices paid. One captive bird recently released promptly reappeared for sale at the Jakarta bird market. The wild Javan buffalo (*Bos javanicus*) is also present in small numbers. Other less rare animals include monkeys, leopard, civets and the rusa, barking and mouse deers.

West Coast

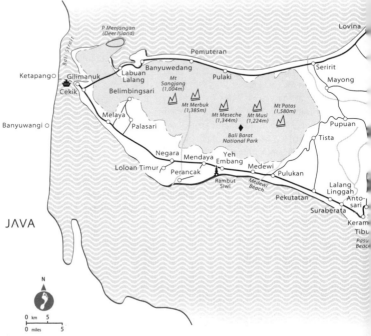

■ *The PHPA office for the Bali Barat National Park is in Cekik; there is also an office at Labuan Lalang, the jumping off point for boats to Pulau Menjangan (see page 212). Treks can be arranged from both offices, preferably a day in advance. The offices are open 0700-1600, most staff speak reasonable English and are helpful and friendly. Permits, costing 2,000Rp for one day, and information on trails can be obtained from the offices (permits are also available from the Forestry Department, Jl Suwung, Denpasar, and from Labuan Lalang). There is also a scale model of the park. NB Guides, costing from 20,000Rp depending on the length of the trek, are obligatory. Bring your own supplies when trekking as there no shops or warung at the park HQ.*

Gilimanuk There are several losmen along the main road through town to the ferry port, offering fairly basic accommodation. All in the **E** price range: *Nirwana, Nusantara 1 & 2* (the latter is off the main road about 5 mins' walk along a side road going east of the ferry terminal and is therefore a bit quieter), *Kartika Candra*. Restaurant food is pretty average as well.

Cekik Camping is forbidden within the park but there is simple accommodation at the **D-F** *National Park Guest House*, beside the PHPA Office at Cekik, T40060 for reservations. You may also be able to **camp** in the grounds of the park HQ. For more luxurious accommodation **Pemuteran** is the closest option, see page 211.

Sleeping

Bali

Road Bus: regular connections with **Denpasar's** Ubung terminal. Connections with **Singaraja** via **Lovina Beach. Sea Ferry**: to **Ketapang** on Java: there is a brand new terminal. Fares are 1,000Rp for pedestrians and 11,000Rp for vehicles. Running 24 hrs a day, ferries leave every 20-30 mins during the day, less regularly at night. The 3 km crossing takes 30 mins. **NB** During Indonesian holidays and at weekends there may be a long wait for a boat.

Transport
134 km from Denpasar, 88 km from Singaraja. 30 mins, driving time to Negara

Belimbingsari and Palasari

These two Christian villages are well worth a visit. Easily reached from the main Gilimanuk to Negara road, there are several signposted turnings, including a turn to the left 17 km from Gilimanuk at signpost, or just past Melaya village. The drive climbs through picturesque scenery along quiet roads, with possibilities for rewarding walks, passing paddy fields and buffaloes with misty mountains in the background. You may pass Christan style *penjors*, smaller and less elaborate than their Hindu counterparts, with crosses as decoration. The air is a little cooler here. Villagers are friendly and will help with directions.

Phone code: 0365

Belimbingsari, with a population of 700 Christians, is 6 km from the turn-off along a good road. The village is spotless and flower filled, and despite the Christian influence is very much culturally Balinese; the aim of these Christian communities has been to attain a religious rather than a cultural conversion. In both villages Balinese music and dance are taught but using scenes and characters from the Bible rather than the great Hindu epics, the Ramayana and Mahabarata.

Each village boasts an attractive church: of the two, the Protestant church at Belimbingsari is perhaps the more interesting and attractive. Consecrated in 1981 and costing 100 million Rp to build, its appearance is Balinese although it was designed by an Australian architect. Entry is through a Balinese split gate decorated with Christian motifs, ascending a flight of steps with statues of guardian angels, through another Balinese style gate into a beautiful tropical garden with a moat and ponds full of waterlilies. The church is circular, wooden and open to the air on all sides. The 30 m high ceiling is divided into three 'levels' representing man's progress from earth to heaven. Many symbolic elements have been incorporated representing Biblical stories and aspects of Jerusalem.

On special religious occasions, for example Easter, Pentecost, Christmas etc, full gamelan and Angklung orchestras complete with drums augment the organ. Services are at 0900 and sometimes 1900, T82252 or 42192 for information. The priest speaks English and is very informative but is frequently out visiting parishioners. In his absence you may be met by the church guardian who has limited English but is very helpful and will willingly show you round (small donation in the box).

To reach **Palasari**, the name translates as 'garden of nutmeg trees', turn right out of Belimbingsari. After 2 km turn right again, 1 km later turn left, and after 800 m turn right. Shortly after, you will catch sight of the imposing Catholic church, the largest in East Indonesia, on your left, with a picturesque backdrop of mountains.

In appearance it looks like a conventional European church with glass windows and wooden pews, despite the Balinese split entrance gate to keep out evil spirits, and the three thatched spires like *merus*. Made of pink sandstone and surrounded by immaculate gardens, it was completed in 1994. During church services or organ practice, music rings out through the village. From here it is 6.5 km back to the main road.

This area is also home to many transmigrants who moved here from heavily populated areas of south and east Bali at the end of the 1940s. The government hoped to increase agricultural output by making available to these newcomers a forested wilderness for them to cultivate. Unlike many of the transmigration projects this one was a great success.

Negara

Phone code: 0365
Colour map 1, grid B1

Negara is the capital of the regency of Jembrana and quite a large town. It is clean and attractive, with wide, flower-filled avenues and some elegant horse-drawn carriages. The town is best known for the *mekepung* or **bullock races** which are held here between July and October. The sport was introduced by migrants from the island of Madura where the *kerapan sapi* (bull races) are the main form of entertainment. Information on Negara's bull races can be obtained from the Bali Tourist Office on Jl S Parman in Denpasar. Races normally take place after the rice harvest. Few travellers base themselves in Negara; most choose one of the beachside resorts along the coast southeast of the town. There is now a dual carriageway which bypasses the town.

Loloan Timur, on the southern outskirts of Negara, is a Bugis community where a few traditional Bugis-style stilted houses still remain, particularly in Loloan Barat (west). (The house raised on stilts was designed to protect the occupants from exceptionally high tides.) Most settlers arrived from south Sulawesi, following the fall of Makassar in 1656 to the Dutch. Over the centuries they prospered as traders and pirates; Loloan became the main transit port for goods coming to Bali from Java. Up until 30 years ago the Bugis prahus were able to sail up the Ijo Gading River to drop anchor in Loloan, 4 km inland. Following the construction of the harbour at Gilimanuk, trade declined and these days unemployment is a problem with most men earning a living as 'poor' fishermen. Many women still wear the traditional Bugis veil and the men wear the *peci* hat (a sign that they are followers of Islam); they speak a Malay dialect rather than Balinese. Nearby at Pengambengan there is a small 'crocodile garden'.

Jembrana, home of the amazing Gamelan *Jegog*, is a further 3 km east of Negara.

Following the main road running along the coast southeast of Negara the first place of interest is Rambut Siwi Temple, about 8 km west of Medewi, 16 km east of Negara, off the main coast road, at the top of a cliff overlooking a black sand beach, with the surf crashing below. This is another spectacularly located temple associated with the 16th century Hindu priest Danghyang Nirartha. Nirartha came to Bali in 1546 from his home on Java with the aim of strengthening Balinese Hinduism so that it could withstand the onslaught of Islam. Leaving Java at a time when the rule of the Hindu Majapahit Kingdom was on the wane, ousted by the forces of Islam, he travelled throughout Bali teaching, building shrines and temples and gaining a reputation for his spiritual and supernatural powers. He is credited with being the founder of the most important branch of Balinese *pedandas* (high priests). Other temples associated with him include Tanah Lot and Uluwatu. **Rambut Siwi Temple**

According to legend he stopped to pray at a temple near to the site of the present day Pura Rambut Siwi soon after reaching Bali, having landed near Negara. Much taken with the beauty of this spot and its inspiring views of Southeast Java with its sacred volcanoes, he left a lock of his hair as a gift to the village. This inspired the villagers to build a temple calling it Pura Rambut Siwi, 'worship of the hair' temple. The piece of hair is now kept in the central 'meru' in the inner courtyard. The belief that hair possesses supernatural powers comes from Siwaism, one of the oldest religious sects in India and a component of Hinduism. In Indian Hinduism the two most important sects are those who worship either Siwa or Wisnu as their principal deity; in Balinese Hinduism the cult of Siwa is paramount.

This is the most important temple in Jembrana and large scale celebrations take place every full moon. It is also a wonderful place to watch the sun blazing down across the Bali Strait over Java.

Negara E *Ana*, Jl Ngurah Rai 75, T65. E *Indraloka*, Jl Nakula 13. **Sleeping**

Gamelan Jegog is a giant bamboo orchestra. These huge gamelan of 10 perform *Jegog Mebarung*, where several orchestras compete against each other in a frenzy of energy and sound; it is also a visually impressive event. Ask around for the time of a performance – there are no regular scheduled performances. **Entertainment**

100 km from Denpasar, 34 km from Gilimanuk. **Road Bus**: regular connections with Gilimanuk and Denpasar's Ubung terminal. **Transport**

Bali

Medewi Beach

Phone code: 0365 Medewi Beach is situated 22 km east of Negara, 70 km (90 mins by car) west of Denpasar and about 4 km from the village of Pulukan. Medewi is a black sand beach and is good for surfing. The surrounding area has some fine scenery; the main road running southeast follows a beautiful rocky coastline, and metre after mile of empty beach with pounding surf, and the occasional coconut plantation. There is a choice of accommodation here and three restaurants, no other facilities. *Getting there*: take a bus running east towards Denpasar and ask to be let off at *Pantai Medewi*. If driving, there is a 24-hr petrol station 3 km southeast of Medewi.

Sleeping **A-C** *Medewi Beach Cottages*, Pantai Medewi, PO Box 126, T40029/40030, F41555/40034. Set in pleasant gardens beside the beach, with a nice pool (open to non-residents 5,000Rp), rooms are spotless but rather soulless. The more expensive rooms have a/c and hot water, refrigerator, cheaper rooms are dark and overlook the road, with fan; all have Western toilets. Price does not include breakfast. The best place to stay though rather overpriced. Restaurant (mid-range). **D-E** *Tin Jaya Bungalows*, Medewi Beach. 14 rooms, set in pretty gardens leading down to the sea. Rooms are on the whole disappointing, some are dark; there is a 2-storey *lumbung* (rice barn) style building with nice views, and some new, but tiny rooms with fan. All with private mandi, some Western toilets (not always with toilet seats). Restaurant (mid-range).

Balian Beach

Phone code: 0361 Continuing down the main coast road you reach Balian Beach, about 25 km southeast of Medewi Beach (50 km west of Denpasar, 30 km west of Tabanan, 50 km from Negara) near the village of Lalang Linggah (10 km west of Antosari, 20 km east of Pulukan). This is one of the best surfing beaches on the west coast but swimming is dangerous; this is the Indian Ocean and there are rip-tides and undertows. There are many pleasant walks in the area through ricefields and plantations of cloves, vanilla, coffee, coconut and cocoa, or following the river inland. To the east past a fishing village is a large tunnel running through the cliff-face and many caves and coves.

Sleeping **A** *Sacred River Retreat*, near the village of Suraberata, Tabanan. Postal Address: No 1 Gang Keraton, Jl Raya Seminyak, T732165, F730904; Australia T02-9999-3643. A pricey New Age Resort, Australian-owned, in a peaceful location overlooking a ravine, just to the west of *Balian Beach Bungalows*. 15 attractively decorated, thatched bungalows encroached on by tropical vegetation, with mosquito nets, private bathrooms, hot water, Western toilets. Personal growth seminars, meditation, yoga, massage, art and craft classes, creativity workshops, spiritual weddings and lunar celebrations and rituals. Performances of traditional Balinese theatre, dance, music. Tours to sacred sites, mystic healers, temples etc. Horse riding, jungle walks, snorkelling. Outside seminars welcome. Tree house, waterfall, small pool. Vegetarian restaurant (mid-range). Very friendly staff. Free airport pick-up. **B-E** *Balian Beach Bungalows*, Lalang Linggah Village, T/F813017. Set in a 6 acre coconut plantation overlooking the Balian River, within 300 m of the beach. Rooms are slowly being given much needed renovation. Some rooms have lovely views, most with private mandi, mosquito nets and squat or Western toilet. Also some cheaper dorm rooms with shared bathroom. Restaurant (mid-range to cheap) and bar. Information sheet with lots of useful local information, walking maps, and travel details. Once the renovations are finished this should be a very attractive and peaceful place. Owners will send/receive faxes for guests, and arrange tours. Price includes tax, breakfast extra.

From **Denpasar** (Ubung bus station) catch a bus bound for Negara or Gilimanuk and ask **Transport**
the driver to stop at **Lalang Linggah**. Coming from the northwest (**Java**, **Gilimanuk**,
Medewi) get off the bus just after the bridge over the Balian River; all Java-Denpasar buses
pass the entrance. From **Lovina** catch a bus west to **Seririt**, change to a bus going south
through the mountains via **Pupuan**, and on to **Antosari** east of Lalang Linggah or
Pulukan to the west; change again for a bus to Lalang Linggah. 90 mins from Legian by car.

Continuing southeast towards Tabanan, capital of the Tabanan Regency, you **Kerambitan**
come to the turning for Kerambitan where you have the opportunity to stay at one *Phone code: 0361*
of the larger royal palaces. This village is notable for a tradition of wayang-style
painting, and unique music and dance forms. These include *tektekan*, a procession of men loudly playing wooden drums and cow bells, traditionally intended to
frighten away evil spirits at times of drought or epidemic. Nearby are the temples
Tanah Lot (see page 189) and **Pura Taman Ayun** at Mengwi (see page 190).

Sleeping A *Puri Anyar*, Kerambitan 82161, Tabanan, T237458/422298/812668,
F263597. The palace spreads over 2 ha with numerous garden courtyards, family temples,
bales, and some ornately carved wooden doors and archways. It was built in 1667, renovated in 1935 and part of it opened as a hotel in 1987. These days 5 branches of the royal
family related to the Tabanan royal family live here. One area has been set aside to provide
seven rooms with attached small garden and bathroom with Western toilet and hot
water. Rooms vary greatly with one rather grand formal bridal chamber, with carved Balinese style wooden bed; some, however, are small and dark and disappointing at the price.
Cultural events, music, dance and theatre are sometimes staged in a raised performance
area; these include *tektekan* (see above) and a trance drama *calonarang*. There is a small
restaurant (no menu) and dinners can be arranged. Guests can also witness village life:
making offerings, rice harvesting, games, dances etc. There is a beautiful carved wooden
carraige in the entrance courtyard. Across the road you can see the royal collection of
musical instruments which are played at special ceremonies. *Getting there*: from the main
road 3 km northwest of Tabanan turn south following signs for Kerambitan; about 6 km.

The small village of Tibubiyu, 10.4 km from main Tabanan road, about 1 km **Tibubiyu**
inland from the beach and 4 km south of Kerambitan, is a million miles away
from tourist Bali. This village has only just made it to the 20th century; the rural
community go about their daily lives and take part in the many religious ceremonies in a manner little changed from their forebears. The nearby, black sand
beach, **Pasut beach**, is renowned for its therapeutic qualities. Swimming is
probably inadvisable as there are strong offshore currents.

Yeh Gangga (Water of the Ganges), is another fine, black sand beach with
strong currents and strange offshore rock formations. *Getting there*: turn
southwest at the sign just over 1 km west of Tabanan, and follow a dreadful,
potholed road for about 10 km.

Sleeping C *BeeBees*, c/o Dewa Ayu Putu Barbara, Tibubiyu, Kerambitan 82161,
Tabanan. Fax c/o Dr Dewa Made Suamba Negara F0361-236021. 5 very simple,
2-storey thatched bungalows overlooking the ricefields, each with 'garden' bathrooms, Western toilet. Situated just outside the village in a very peaceful setting, 10
mins' walk from the sea. Many lovely walks in the area. An opportunity to live
amongst traditional rural Balinese and witness their way of life. Off-season bargaining
possible. Restaurant (mid-range). Price includes breakfast and tax. *Getting there*: from
Kerambitan: turn left at the end of the main street, then right at the Banyan tree. Soon
you will reach Tibubiyu, *BeeBees* is signed. **B-C** *Bali Wisata Bungalows*, Yeh Gangga,
T261354. In peaceful location beside the sea. 6 large bungalows, some with cooking
facilities, private bathroom with Western toilet. Small pool. Restaurant (mid-range).

Bali

Background

As far back as the 1930s, insightful commentators were predicting what lay in store for Bali. Miguel Covarrubias, for one, in his seminal book, *Island of Bali* (1937) wrote:

"Undoubtedly Bali will soon enough be 'spoiled' for those fastidious travellers who abhor all that which they bring with them. No longer will the curious Balinese of the remote mountain villages, still unaccustomed to the sight of whites, crowd around their cars to stare silently at the 'exotic' long-nosed, yellow-haired foreigners in their midst. But even when all the Balinese will have learned to wear shirts, to beg, lie, steal, and prostitute themselves to satisfy new needs, the tourists will continue to come to Bali to see the sights, snapping pictures frantically, dashing from temple to temple, back to hotel for meals, and on to watch rites and dances staged for them."

Certainly in recent years Bali has suffered from the curse of being too popular, yet somehow the island has retained its beauty, if not always its charm, and the Balinese have traditionally believed that their island belongs to the gods and they are merely custodians entrusted to ensure its well-being.

History

Balinese recorded history begins in the 10th century with the marriage of King Udayana and the East Javanese princess Mahendradatta. In 991 their union resulted in the birth of a son, named Airlangga. He was sent to Java to rule the principality of his father-in-law King Dharmawangsa of Sanjaya. When Dharmawangsa was murdered, Airlangga assumed the throne and for the next 30 years ruled his empire with great skill. As a Balinese prince he forged strong

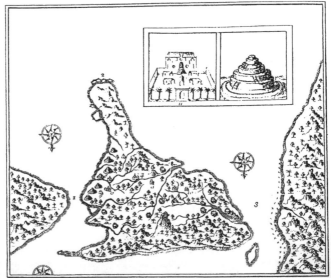

One of the first maps of Bali, Tardieu, c1760

links between his island of origin and Java, and in so doing began the pattern of Javanese cultural influence over Bali.

After 1049 when, on Airlangga's death, the kingdom of Sanjaya (or Mataram) was divided, Bali became independent once more. It remained self-governing for the next 235 years until King Kertanagara of the East Javanese dynasty of Singasari invaded in 1284. Kertanagara's domination over Bali was to last only eight years, when it was invaded by the stronger Majapahit Kingdom of Central Java. Relieved of their Singasari overlords, the Balinese were left to themselves for another 50 years. In 1343, General Gajah Mada, under the flag of Majapahit, conquered Bali, making the island a Javanese colony. Though the various Balinese principalities revolted time and again against Majapahit overlordship, they were neither individually strong enough nor sufficiently united to resist the weight of Javanese power. Even today most of Bali's nobility trace their families back to the founding fathers of Majapahit.

During the 15th century, as Islam filtered into Java, Majapahit began to decline in influence. The last Hindu prince of Majapahit crossed the Bali Strait in 1478, escaping from the Muslim onslaught to the Hindu haven of Bali. He was accompanied by priests, artists and other courtesans – as well as by large numbers of ordinary East Javanese. The prince declared himself King of Bali (his descendants are the rajas of Klungkung) and promptly divided the island up between his various supporters. These later Javanese immigrants are still referred to as *Wong Majapahit* and a shrine for *Batara Majapahit*, or the teachers of Majapahit, can be found in nearly every temple. Some commentators argue that it was because of this wholesale migration of the cream of Javanese artists and craftsmen, that Balinese art today is so strong and prolific. It was on Bali that Java's pre-Islamic artistic accomplishments were preserved.

One of Bali's most famous kings was Baturenggong who came to the throne in the middle of the 16th century and today enjoys almost mythical status. According to local chronicles, during his reign Bali was a haven of peace and prosperity and a centre for the arts. The influence of the kingdom extended west to include much of east Java and east to encompass Lombok and Sumbawa.

The Dutch arrival

The Dutch first made contact with Bali in 1597, when a fleet led by Cornelius Houtman landed on the island. His men enjoyed a long sojourn, falling in love with the people and the place. When the expedition returned to Holland, such was the wonder at the stories that the sailors told that another fleet was dispatched, in 1601, with gifts for the hospitable king. The king received these gifts with dignity, and in return presented the captain with a beautiful Balinese girl.

But this initial friendly encounter was not to be the pattern of future contacts. In 1815 Tambora Volcano erupted on Sumbawa (see page 312), and more than 10,000 people on Bali perished in the subsequent famine and plague. This was seen by the Balinese as a taste of things to come. In 1817 a Dutch ship arrived laden with goods to be traded, and in 1826, a trade agreement was signed and the first permanent Dutch representative settled in Kuta. But by then, relations between the Balinese, and what they perceived to be the arrogant, crude and ill-behaved Dutch, were already strained. In 1841, a Dutch ship ran aground and the King of Bali accepted it as a gift. This was the excuse the Dutch needed for intervention.

Five years later, the Dutch sent a large, punitive expeditionary force to conquer North Bali. The attempt failed, but the Dutch, persistent as ever, followed it with another in 1848, and yet a third in 1849. Jagaraga, the capital of the North Balinese Kingdom of Buleleng, was eventually vanquished, but not without considerable losses on both sides. The fact that Bali was divided into various different competing principalities made the Dutch campaign all the easier. Even so, an attack on South Bali at the same time led to the death of the Dutch general, and the Europeans were forced to accept a treaty which left South Bali under Balinese control. This was not the initial intention, and for the next 40 years the Dutch searched for a means of extending their influence from North Bali over the rest of the island.

To do this, the Dutch attacked Lombok in 1894, which was under the control of the East Balinese Kingdom of Karangkasem (see page 238). When Lombok fell, so too did Karangkasem, and then Bangli and Gianyar also accepted Dutch rule. But it was not until the first decade of the 20th century that the final three stubborn, recalcitrant kingdoms of Badung, Tabanan and Klungkung fell to the might of the Dutch.

This last campaign was associated with the arrival in 1904 of a new governor-general, JB van Heutz. He was determined to complete the campaign for Bali, the new Resident of Bali and Lombok recalling that when he first met van Heutz, the governor-general had run "his hand across the principalities of South Bali [saying] no more than 'this all has to be changed'". An expeditionary force sailed from Surabaya in 1906 and, anchoring off the coast of South Bali, began to shell Denpasar's royal palace. The kings remained defiant and the Dutch force had to land in order to subdue the Balinese.

The Balinese king of Denpasar quickly realized that his cause was lost. He announced that anyone who wished could accompany him in a *puputan*, or 'fight to the end'. Most men, and many women as well, heeded their King's call. They dressed in their best clothes (the women wearing men's clothes) and wore their finest gold krisses. The following extract is from Miguel Covarrubias' 1937 book *Island of Bali*:

"At nine in the morning the fantastic procession left the palace, with the Radja at the head, carried on the shoulders of his men, protected by his gold umbrellas of state, staring intently at the road in front of him, and clutching in his right hand his kris of gold and diamonds. He was followed by silent men and entranced women, and even boys joined the procession, armed with spears and krisses. They marched on through what is today the main avenue of Denpasar towards Kesiman, and when they turned the corner, the Dutch regiment was only 300 yds away. The commander, astonished at the sight of the strange procession, gave orders to halt; Balinese interpreters from Buleleng spoke to the Radja and his followers, begging them anxiously to stop, but they only walked faster. They came within 100 ft, then 70 ft, then made a mad rush

The eight regencies of Bali

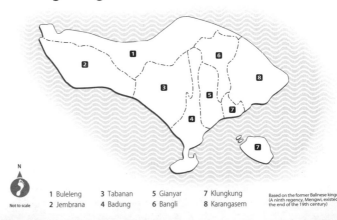

N

Not to scale

| 1 Buleleng | 3 Tabanan | 5 Gianyar | 7 Klungkung |
| 2 Jembrana | 4 Badung | 6 Bangli | 8 Karangasem |

Based on the former Balinese kingdom (A ninth regency, Mengwi, existed until the end of the 19th century)

at the soldiers, waving their krisses and spears. The soldiers fired the first volley and a few fell, the Radja among them. Frenzied men and women continued to attack, and the soldiers, to avoid being killed, were obliged to fire continually. Someone went among the fallen people with a kris killing the wounded. He was shot

The sign of the swastika

Visitors to Bali will notice swastikas intricately carved in stone patterns. This perplexes many people, but it is a sign of Balinese unity, not indicative of supporters of Germany's Third Reich.

down, but immediately another man took his place; he was shot, but an old woman took the kris and continued the bloody task. The wives of the Radja stabbed themselves over his body, which lay buried under the corpses of the princes and princesses who had dragged them over to die upon the body of their king. When the horrified soldiers stopped firing, the women threw handfuls of gold coins, yelling that it was payment for killing them.

In the battle, the entire court of the King of Denpasar – bar a few wounded women – died. The king himself is said to have adopted the position of *semadi* meditation before falling under a hail of bullets. Following this battle, the same sequence of events was to be repeated at other palaces across Bali. For many Dutch soldiers, what was an overwhelming military victory had the sour taste of moral defeat. After the second *puputan* in Badung in which the co-ruler, Gusti Gede Ngurah, died HM van Weede, who witnessed the massacre wrote, heart-wrenchingly, that he found "the prince buried under the bodies of his faithful followers, as if to show that they wanted to protect him to the death, and the most beautiful young women we had seen in Bali lay lifeless next to their children."

The King of Tabanan to the west, rather than sacrificing his army, came to negotiate with the Dutch. As a symbol of his intentions, he was shielded by a green umbrella rather than the usual gold one. When they took him prisoner, the king cut his own throat with a blunt *sirih* (betel) knife, and the crown prince took an overdose of opium. The last palace to fall was that of Klungkung on 28 April 1908. Again the king chose to die rather than surrender, together with his wives and many members of the court, he was killed in yet another *puputan*. Bali was finally subdued; although the Dutch army remained on the island until 1914. One reason the Balinese were so ready to commit mass suicide rather than surrender to the enemy was their belief that the spirit of a person who died in war would achieve Nirvana.

The problem for the Dutch was how to make the island profitable. One solution was to import and sell opium to the Balinese, particularly the royal families, at great profit to the Dutch. The use of opium was actively promoted and did even more damage to Bali's population than the preceding wars. Van Kol argued strenuously for the ending of the monopoly, writing: "The loss of opium monies will be recompensated by the increasing prosperity of the population whose productive force will no longer be paralysed, and the enormous amounts presently spent on this juice will be used for the purchase of necessities which will increase tax income. Moreover, this will be income to which no tears are attached".

After the Dutch had gained full control of Bali, they set about reorganizing the island so that they could administer it efficiently, with the minimum of fuss. They sent those few members of Bali's royal houses who had survived the various *puputan* into exile and moulded the younger princes into their colonially designated roles. Perhaps even more significantly in the longer term, the Dutch asked the senior priests to simplify the caste system. This was then frozen, removing the flexibility and mobility inherent in the original system.

The years of Dutch rule were not happy ones for many Balinese. There was a devastating earthquake in 1917, followed by a plague which decimated the island's rice crop, then an influenza epidemic, and finally the population had to contend with the economic effects of the Depression. As Adrian Vickers says in his book *Bali: a paradise created* "Bali from 1908 to 1942 ... was an island of social tensions and conflicts for the Balinese".

The Japanese occupation of the Second World War did not provide a respite from oppression. Although initially welcomed as liberators, this quickly changed as the Japanese began to target Bali's élite – who were identified with the Dutch – with considerable brutality. The end of the War shifted the conflict to one between the Dutch and their supporters, and the republicans among the island's population. But these periods of confrontation were comparatively mild when compared with the murderous months from October 1965 to February 1966.

The Communist puputan
'Puputan' means 'conclusion', or 'bringing to an end' in Balinese

During the course of the late 1950s and early 1960s, Bali became one of the strongholds of the Indonesian Communist Party – the PKI. With the failure of the attempted coup in Jakarta at the end of September 1965, a wave of violence erupted across the country (see page 409). Nowhere was it more devastating than on Bali. Adrian Vickers in his book *Bali: a paradise created* describes the progress of the massacre:

"They began in the north and west, where the Left was strongest, but by the end of this period the whole of Bali was a landscape of blackened areas where entire villages had been burnt to the ground, and the graveyards could not cope with the numbers of corpses. The military distanced themselves from the killings. They simply went into each village and produced a list of Communists to be killed, which was given to the head of the village to organize. ... After the initial struggle the killing took on a dispassionate tone. Those identified as PKI dressed in white and were led to graveyards to be executed *puputan*-style."

The numbers killed in this orgy of violence will never be known. One estimate puts the figure at an astonishing 100,000. Rivers were reported to be choked with bodies and the graveyards overflowing with corpses. Today, few on the island will talk about this dark episode, and none with relish.

Land and environment

Geography

Bali is the westernmost island of the chain that makes up the Lesser Sundas, and is one of Indonesia's smallest provinces. It covers 5,561 sq km and has a population of three million. Like the other islands of the Lesser Sundas, it rises from the deep sea as a series of spectacular volcanic peaks, the highest of which – Mount Agung – exceeds 3,000 m.

Separating Bali from Java is the narrow Bali Strait. It is 40-50 m deep, and during the last Ice Age when sea-levels were considerably lower than today, Bali would have been connected to the mainland by a land bridge, allowing animals to move freely between the two. To the east, Bali is separated from the next of the Lesser Sunda Islands, Lombok, by the far deeper Lombok Strait. At its deepest, the water depth exceeds 1,300 m – and even during the Pleistocene Ice Age the strait would have remained submerged. Wallace's Line, the division between the Asian and Australasian faunal realms, first identified by the great Victorian naturalist Alfred Russel Wallace, passes between the two islands (see page 302). Because of the depth of the water here, the strait is an important passage for nuclear submarines making the trip between the Indian and Pacific oceans.

The gift of water: rice and water in Bali

Among anthropologists, agronomists and geographers, Bali is famous for its system of irrigation. It is a three-fold fascination, bringing together impressive feats of engineering, elaborate social structures, and the guiding hand of religion.

Most of the 162 large streams and rivers which flow from Bali's mountainous interior have cut deep channels into the soft volcanic rock. This has made it impossible for farmers to dam and channel water for irrigation in the usual way. Instead, they have taken to cutting tunnels through the rock, and constructing elaborate aqueducts and bamboo piping systems to carry the water to the top of a series of terraced ricefields. From here it can flow, with gravity, from paddy field (or sawah) to paddy field.

The Balinese have been digging irrigation tunnels in this way for over a thousand years. One tunnel has an inscription recording that it was cut in AD 944. They are dug by professional tunnellers whose main difficulty is not cutting through the soft volcanic rock, but making sure they emerge in the correct place – some are over a kilometre long.

But, these feats of engineering are only half the story. The water then needs to be managed, and the tunnels, weirs and aqueducts, maintained. As American anthropologist Stephen Lansing writes in his book Priests and Programmers, "Virtually every farmer depends on an irrigation system that originates several kilometres upstream and flows in fragile channels through the lands of many

neighbours...."He notes that even a brief interruption of flow will destroy a farmer's crop. To prevent this, every rice farmer is a member of a subak or irrigation society. The subak brings together all the farmers who receive water from a common source, and this may include farmers from more than one village. The subak is designed to ensure the equitable distribution of water. Each subak is headed by a kliang subak or penyarikan subak who can call on his members to police canals, mend dykes and wiers, and generally maintain the system.

Nor does the story of rice and water end with the subak. The subaks, in turn, look to the regional water temple or pura, and the head of the pura sets the schedule of planting and harvesting. Subaks are not self-reliant; water control among the farmers of one subak is usually dependent upon those of another. The head of Pura Er Jeruk explained the system to Stephen Lansing in these terms:

"There are fourteen... subaks all of which meet together as one here. They meet at the Temple Er Jeruk. Every decision, every rule concerning planting seasons and so forth, is always discussed here. Then after the meeting here, decisions are carried down to each subak. The subaks each call all their members together: 'In accord with the meeting we held at the Temple Er Jeruk, we must fix our planting dates, beginning on day one through day ten'. For example, first subak Sango plants, then subak Somi, beginning from day ten through day twenty. Thus it is arranged in accordance with water and Pandewasan....".

Bali

One feature of life on an island that lies over the spot where two tectonic plates overlap, is great geological instability. One of the most serious earthquakes this century occurred in 1917. During January and February of that year, a series of tremors hit the east and south regions of the island, followed by the eruption of Mount Batur. When this activity came to an end on 20 February, a total of 2,431 temples had been badly damaged – including Pura Besakih on Mount Agung – 64,000 homes had been wrecked, and 1,500 people had died. The inference was clear to every Balinese: the gods were angry. It is partly for this reason that the Balinese have felt it necessary to build temples in great numbers to appease the spirits and therefore help prevent natural catastrophe. In the case of Mount Batur's 1917 eruption, though the lava engulfed the village of Batur, it stopped at the gates to the temple. The villagers took this as a good omen and refused to move, rebuilding their village at the same site. Nine years later, the volcano erupted again, this time swamping the temple and leading to one death, an old woman, who died of fright. Nonetheless, the villagers still rebuilt their village on the rim of the volcano – albeit in a safer location – courting possible future disaster.

Despite the devastating effects of periodic earthquakes and volcanic eruptions, Bali has also been blessed by nature in its rich and fertile soils and abundant rainfall. Farmers have exploited this natural wealth by creating terraces on the hillsides, cutting tunnels through the rock to carry irrigation water, and cultivating rice throughout the year (see box).

At the core of the island is a central mountain range consisting of six peaks all exceeding 2,000 m. These trap rain clouds and ensure that perennial rivers water the lower slopes. The main expanse of lowland lies to the south of this mountainous interior, and most of the rivers flow south. It is here, on the south slopes and plain, that Bali's famous terraced ricefields are concentrated. Most of the villages or *banjars* are perched on the edge of ridges, surrounded by ricefields. To the north, the lowland fringe is much narrower and the absence of rivers makes the land much drier and more suited to dry land agriculture than intensive wet rice cultivation. The west peninsula, with its poor soils, is yet more arid still.

Despite Bali's unquestioned natural fecundity, the island has begun to feel the effects of over-population. In the 1950s, about 3,000 people were leaving Bali each year to take up places on transmigration settlements in the Outer Islands; by the 1960s this had risen to 5,000. It has only been the boom in tourism since the 1970s that has prevented this stream becoming a flood, as tourism has offered young Balinese alternative opportunities outside agriculture.

Climate

Bali is hot and humid, but this is alleviated by ocean breezes and altitude. Annual rainfall averages 2,150 mm, the driest months being August and September and the wettest, December and January. Temperatures at sea-level average 26°C (average max 32°C in March, average min 29°C in July) and vary only marginally through the year; in highland areas it is considerably cooler, about 20°C. In the wet season the humidity can be oppressive.

There are two seasons: the dry season from May-October; and the wet season from November to April. But this should not deter visitors. Rain tends to fall throughout the year, but it usually comes in short, sharp showers during the afternoon and early evening. If you do get caught in a period of low pressure, the sheer volume of rain can be very limiting and it may be worth considering a move to one of the (usually) drier islands to the east. (See page 16 for best time to visit.)

Art and architecture

The American anthropologist Margaret Mead, like many other observers of Balinese life, wrote that "everyone in Bali is an artist". This extends from painting and carving, through to the dramatic arts, and into ceremony and ritual. Sometimes the sheer density of artistic endeavour can seem overwhelming. As Noel Coward wrote to Charlie Chaplin in a poem:

> As I said this morning to Charlie
> There is far too much music in Bali,
> And although as a place it's entrancing,
> There is also a thought too much dancing.
> It appears that each Balinese native,
> From the womb to the tomb is creative,
> And although the results are quite clever,
> There is too much artistic endeavour.

Most of Bali's art and architecture is linked to the 'Javanization' of the island that began in the 10th century with a marriage between two royal houses of Java and Bali. However, it was the fall of the Majapahit Empire in the 15th century and the escape of the remnants of the Majapahit court, together with many skilled artisans, that led to the greatest infusion of East Javanese art and architecture. While Java was undergoing a process of Islamization, Bali effectively preserved the Indo-Javanese cultural traditions, though adapting them to accord with existing Balinese traditions.

The Balinese pura

In Bali there are over 20,000 temples – or *pura* – and most villages should have at least three. The *pura puseh*, literally 'navel temple', is the village-origin temple where the village ancestors are worshipped. The *pura dalem* – or 'temple of the dead' – is usually found near the cremation ground. The *pura bale agung* is the temple of the great assembly hall and is used for meetings of the village. There are also irrigation temples, temples at particular geographical sites, and the six great temples or *sadkahyangan*.

As befits a country where direction is of immense significance (see box, page 237), there are **nine directional temples**, *kayangan jagat*, found at notable geographical sites around the island, particularly high up on mountains, on imposing outcrops overlooking the sea and beside lakes. These are amongst the most sacred temples on Bali and their strategic locations have been chosen to ensure that they safeguard the entire island and its people. Besakih, high on the slopes of Bali's most sacred and highest mountain, Mount Agung, is the pre-eminent of these directional temples and corresponds to the ninth directional point, ie the centre. The others, of equal importance, guard the other eight directions. Starting from the southwest they are: Pura Luhur Uluwatu, Pura Luhur Batukau on Mount Batukau, Pura Ulun Danu Batur high on edge of the crater of Mount Batur (this temple used to be beside the lake but eruptions in 1917 and 1926 caused so much destruction that it was moved to its present position with help from the Dutch colonial government), Pura Ulun Danu Bratan beside Lake Bratan, Pura Pasar Agung near Selat on the slopes of Mount Agung, Pura Lempuyang on Mount Lempuyang near Tirtagangga, Pura Goa Lawah near Padangbai, Pura Masceti near Lebih. Balinese visit the 'kayangan jagat' nearest their home village at the time of its odalan, anniversary festival, to seek protection and make offerings to the spirits. Finally, there is the mother temple, Pura Besakih.

Balinese pura are places where the gods rule supreme, and evil spirits are rendered harmless. But the gods must be appeased and courted if they are to protect people, so offerings are brought to the site. The buildings that constitute a temple are not as important as the ground, which is consecrated.

The temple complex consists of three courts (two in North Bali), each separated by walls; the front court, or *jaba*, the central court, or *jaba tengah*, and the inner court, or *jeroan*. The innermost court is the most sacred and is thought to represent heaven; the outermost, the underworld; and the central court, an intermediate place. The generalized description of the pura given below accords most closely with newer temples. Old temples, and particularly those on the north coast, tend to show differences in their configuration. **NB** Colonies of longtail macaques inhabit some temple sites; they should not be teased or fed, and certainly not purchased – as has been occurring. Macaques are social animals that suffer if removed from their family group.

Bali Pura

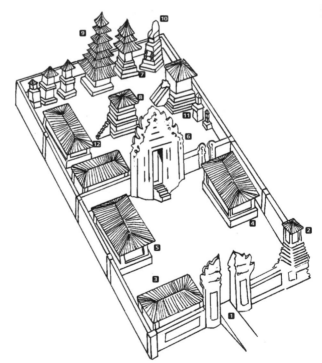

1 Candi Bentar (spilt gate)
2 Kulkul (drum tower)
3 Paon (kitchen)
4 Bale Gong
   (shed for gamelan orchestra)
5 Bale (resthouse for pilgrims)
6 Paduraksa
7 Jeroan (inner court)
8 Parungan or Pepelik
9 Meru (shrines of the gods)
10 Padmasana (stone throne for sun god Surya)
11 Sanggahs
   (secretaries of the gods)
12 Bale Piasan (sheds for offerings)

The entrance to the jaba is usually through a candi bentar, literally 'split temple' gate. The visual symbolism is clear – if the two halves of the gate are pushed together, closing the entranceway, they would form the shape of a complete candi. The split gates may represent the symbolic splitting of the material world, so that the physical body can enter the realm of the spirits. Other art historians maintain that the gates represent duality: male to the right, female to the left.

The outer court or jaba

Within the jaba are a number of structures. In one corner is the *bale kulkul* (*bale* = pavilion, *kulkul* = wooden gong), a pavilion in which hangs a large hollow, wooden, gong or drum. The kulkul is beaten during temple ceremonies and also in times of emergency or disaster – during an earthquake for example. The bale and the kulkul are often decorated. Also within the jaba, it is not uncommon to find a *jineng* – a small barn used to store rice produced from the temple's own fields (*laba pura*).

The entrance leading to the central court is through the *candi kurung*. Like the split gate, and as the name implies, this is also in the form of a candi, but in this case a wooden doorway allows visitors to pass through. In a village pura, the centre of the jaba tengah will be dominated by an open pavilion with a roof of grass or reed. This is the *bale agung* or village conference hall. There is also often a *bale* for pilgrims who wish to stay overnight in the temple.

The central court or jaba tengah

The entrance to the inner court is through a second, larger, candi kurung called the *paduraksa*. The entrance way is usually guarded by a demon's head and rises up in the form of a pyramid. In larger temples, there may be three gateways, the central one of which is only opened during ceremonies. Along the back wall of the jeroan are the most sacred of the shrines. These may have multiple roofs – as many as 11. The greater the number of roofs, the more important the god. Also on the back wall, there is a stone pillar or *tugu*. It is at the tugu that offerings are left for the *taksu*, the god who's job it is to protect the temple and through whom the wishes of the gods are transmitted to the dancer during a trance dance. In the centre of the jeroan is the *parungan* or *pepelik* – the seat of all the gods, where they assemble during temple ceremonies. Finally, along the right-hand wall of the inner courtyard, are two *sanggahs* – Ngurah Gde and Ngurah Alit. These are the 'secretaries' of the gods; they ensure that temple offerings are properly prepared. (Condensed from: East Utrecht and B Hering (1986) *The temples of Bali.*)

The inner court or jeroan

Bali's artistic renaissance

During the early decades of the 20th century, Bali became famous as the haunt of a small community of Western artists. They 'discovered' Balinese art and laid the foundations for a significant artistic flowering. Up until that point, art had been produced for the pleasure of the gods and, in some cases, for aristocratic families. Among these early Western artists, the most famous were Walter Spies, the son of a German diplomat, and the Dutchman Rudolf Bonnet. Spies, who had first worked for the Sultan of Yogya, arrived in Bali on a short visit and was so taken with the island that he decided to stay. He was also a homosexual, and there seems little doubt that he found Bali less suffocating than Europe. Homosexual activity was accepted as a pursuit among unmarried young men, and the great anthropologist Margaret Mead defended him in these terms when he was tried for homosexuality in 1939. Over the years, Spies recorded Balinese music, collected its art, contributed to academic journals, and established the Bali Museum. He also painted a handful of rich paintings, recording in minute detail Bali's natural and cultural wealth. However, Spies was not keen to teach the Balinese.

In contrast, Rudolf Bonnet was more than happy to train and advise Balinese artists in Western techniques and to transmit the European aesthetic. In 1936, Bonnet and Spies established the first artists' co-operative – the *Pita Maha* (meaning Great or Noble Aspiration) at Ubud. Balinese artists would bring works to the co-operative and Bonnet and Spies would select those they felt were good enough for sale and exhibition. This naturally led to a trend towards Western tastes and Bonnet, particularly, would offer advice to artists as to why their work had been rejected. As the art historian Djelantik writes, in "those years when the prestige of the white man was at its height, Bonnet's word was law and readily accepted". Both Spies and Bonnet remained on Bali until the Japanese occupation from 1941-45. Spies was killed when the ship carrying him to Ceylon was sunk by a Japanese bomb; Bonnet was interned by the Japanese in Sulawesi.

Spies, Bonnet and other Western artists visiting Bali viewed the Balinese as innately talented and creative, but failed fully to appreciate – or at least to take note of – the traditional strictures under which most art was produced. Balinese craftsmen worked to strict formulas and there was little room for individual invention. Production was geared to copying existing works, not to creating new ones. As court art was in decline, Spies and Bonnet encouraged Bali's artists to produce for the emerging tourist market. This allowed the Balinese greater artistic freedom, and also led to a change in subject matter; from carving gods and mythical figures, they began to produce carvings and paintings of the natural world and everyday life. At the same time, there was a shift from realism to greater abstraction and expressionism, while the gaudy colours of traditional art were replaced with softer, more natural hues. The birth of Balinese modernism can be directly linked to the influence of this small group of Western artists.

Today, art in Bali is predominantly driven by the tourist market. That which sells to foreigners determines production: output is standardized, pieces are small and easily portable, designs are selected which sell well...in short, art is now an industry in Bali.

Balinese painting

Most of the paintings produced by artists in Ubud, Batuan and Penestanan are not 'traditional'. The artists use Western materials and methods, and work to an adapted Western aesthetic. Yet, Balinese works do have a quality which sets them apart and thus makes them distinctive.

In the past, Balinese painters worked in what has become known as the *wayang* style. Adapted from the wayang kulit or shadow play, figures were painted in profile or three-quarters view, with a strict use of colour. This style of painting was used for Balinese calendars, scrolls for temples and *langse*, and large rectangular works for palaces. Today, most of the few artists still working in the wayang style live near the southeast village of Kamasan.

In *Balinese Paintings*, the art historian AAM Djelantik divides Balinese painters into seven groups:

The **Traditionalists of Kamasan** mentioned above who continue to paint in the wayang style.

The **Traditional experimentalists of Kerambitan** (20 km southwest of Tabanan) who produce wayang-style paintings but use additional colours (like blue and green) and a bolder, stronger style.

The **Pita Maha painters of Ubud** concentrate on realistically reproducing the natural world – fish, birds, frogs, tropical flora – in fresh and vibrant colours.

The **Pita Maha painters of Batuan** produce eclectic paintings; detailed scenes from Buddhist mythology, lively and innovative wayang-style images, and naive-style works – almost caricatures – that depict modern life with humour.

The **Young artists of Penestanan** make-up a group initially inspired by the Dutch painter Arie Smit who arrived in Bali in 1956; he took farm boys, and trained them, but also allowed their innate talent to emerge. The resulting works are bold and bright, naive in form, and depict everyday scenes.

The **Academicians** are artists who have received training at Western-style art schools in Java. Although the works sometimes employ Balinese or Javanese motifs and even techniques (for example, painting on batik), they are Western in inspiration and sometimes abstract.

The **Adventurers** are untrained Balinese artists who have broken away from Balinese tradition, experimenting with new styles and techniques. Their work is diverse and cannot be simply characterized.

In 1993 a new NGO, *Yayasan Mitra Bali* was established to support the small-scale handicraft producer in Bali from initial production through to the final marketing of the object. It has been estimated that there are 90,000 handicraft producers of the island, and *Yayasan Mitra Bali* is trying to promote an ideal of development which favours balanced social change and eschews the notion that development equals money. The NGO assists producers in selling their work through such international organizations as UK-based *Oxfam*, *Shared-Earth* and *Self-Help Crafts Canada*. Most craft producers who sell through shops and other outlets on Bali have to accept a 50-60% commission (this, it should be added, is roughly the same rate of commission that artists in the West have to accept); *Yayasan Mitra Bali* at the moment takes just 10%, although this is likely to rise soon. One of the NGO's workers, Agung Alit, explained in *Inside Indonesia* the objectives of his organization: "...more than ideology, more than just words, we offer producers a realistic plan for material and social progress which is not based on exploitation or ecological degradation". The offices of *Yayasan Mitra Bali* are at Jalan Sulatri 2, Denpasar, T224397.

(margin note) Supporting the Balinese handicraft industry

(margin tab) Bali

Culture

People

The original inhabitants of Bali are the Bali Aga, who still live in a handful of communities in the east of the island (see page 178). Since the intrusion of Javanese Hindu-Buddhist people and culture from the 10th century, the Bali Aga have been gradually relegated to a subordinate position. For most visitors today, the culture of Bali means that of the dominant Hindu population.

Despite population growth and considerable modernization, most Balinese still live in villages or *banjar* ranging in size from 200 to several thousand inhabitants. Family compounds or *kuren* are enclosed by high walls and are clustered around a central village courtyard. A kuren will support several families, all eating food from the same kitchen and worshipping at the same family altar. The family gods are paternal ancestors, and descent is patrilineal. The central courtyard is the place where villagers congregate for group activities; for wayang performances, village meetings, and periodic markets. In the past, each village would have been headed by a hereditary prince.

Balinese social structure is stratified in two ways. First, every individual belongs to a ranked descent group or *wangsa* ('peoples'). This system of ordering people is akin to the Indian caste system and was adopted after Javanese rule was established on the island. The nobility are divided into three castes – the *brahmanas* or priests, *satriyas* or ruling nobles, and *wesyas* or warriors.

Members of these three castes are said to be the descendants of aristocrats from the Majapahit Kingdom who settled here towards the end of the 15th century. But 90% of the population belong to the *sudras* or *jaba*; literally, the outsiders of the court. In addition to belonging to a caste, a Balinese will also belong to a far more egalitarian class structure based upon where a person lives. The *banjar* system of associations is the epitome of this (see page 238).

As dictated by Balinese tradition, a child is not placed on the floor until the 105th day of its life; he or she will be carried until able to stand and walk – never being allowed to crawl, as the Balinese believe this is animalistic. At 210 days (one Balinese year) the child is given its name. A ceremony occurs to celebrate puberty; first menstruation is followed by a tooth-filing ceremony (often occurring at the same time as the marriage ceremony). From the time of the tooth-filing ceremony, daughters are no longer the father's responsibility. Sons have their marriages financed for them by their fathers. Marriages are still sometimes pre-arranged among aristocratic families, although increasingly men want to choose their spouses (and vice versa) and mixed-caste relation-ships are occurring.

Language The Balinese language uses three different forms to indicate the caste, sta-tus or social relationship that exists between the speaker and the person being spoken to. High Balinese is used when speaking to superiors who will reply using low Balinese. Low Balinese is also used between friends and equals. Middle Balinese is a form of polite speech used to address strangers and superiors.

Balinese names Many Balinese names relate to the order of birth. For ordinary (Sudra) people Wayan is usually the firstborn, Made the second, Nyoman the third and Ketut fourth. For higher caste people, the firstborn is often called Raka, Putu or Kompiang, the secondborn Raj, the thirdborn Oka, and the fourthborn Alit. Names can also be indicative of caste; amongst Brahmans you find Ida Bagus for males and Ida Ayu for the females. Amongst the warrior caste, the Satria, Dewa and Anak Agung are common.

Religion

Except for small numbers of people in East Java, the Balinese are the only Indo-nesians who still embrace Hinduism – or at least a variant form of the Indian religion. While across Java and Sumatra, Islam replaced Hinduism, on Bali it managed to persist. Today, 95% of Balinese are still Hindu.

Known as *Hindu Dharma* or *Agama Hindu*, the Balinese religion is an unique blend of Buddhism, Hinduism and pre-Hindu animist beliefs. So, along with the worship of the Hindu trinity of Vishnu, Brahma and Siva, the Balinese also worship deified ancestors or *leluhur*, as well as deities of fertility, of the elements and of the natural world. The whole is suffused with a belief in a transcendental spiritual unity known as *Sang Hyang Widi*.

Reflecting the diverse roots of Balinese Hinduism, there is a corresponding variety of priests and other religious practitioners. There are high-ranking Brahmana priests of both Sivaite and Buddhist persuasions (Buddha is regarded as Siva's younger brother), lower order village priests or *jero mangku*, exorcists, herbal healers, and puppet masters or *dalang*.

The aim of Balinese Hinduism is to reach 'peace of spirit and harmony in the material life' by achieving a balance between philosophy, morals and ritual.

Orientation and directions

All directions on Bali are given in relation to Mount Agung, the highest and most sacred mountain on Bali, dwelling place of the Balinese gods. This is the spiritual and physical centre of the Balinese Universe. Kaja means towards the mountain, kelod means away from it. Kaja and kelod also have other directional and opposite meanings; kaja means up, kelod means down; kelod also means less sacred than kaja, and even impure. Thus kaja has a sense of everything sacred, kelod all that is profane. Kelod also means towards the sea which to the Balinese can be a dangerous and frightening place; however, directions are relative rather than absolute and while the sea is kelod in relation to Mount Agung, it is not in any way considered impure. Kangin meaning east is the second most sacred direction identified, as it is, with the sun, another manifestation of God. The opposite of kangin is kauh, towards the west. Balinese give each other directions

using these terms. Altogether there are nine directional points including centre, hence the importance of the nine directional temples (see page 231).

In keeping with the importance attached to direction on Bali, villages and temples are set out in a kaja/kelod alignment. In the village the pura puseh, *the village-origin temple where the ancestors are worshipped is at the kaja end, whereas the cemetery and* pura dalem, *temple of the dead, are kelod. In the temple, the most sacred inner part, jeroan, is kaja and also situated higher than the secular outer courtyards. Every family compound is also laid out in similar manner, the family temple being in the most hallowed location, with the head of the family living in a more kaja position than the lesser family members. The most kelod position is reserved for the animals and the rubbish. Balinese sleep with their heads pointing kaja or kangin.*

The principles of their philosophy or *tattwa* are belief in:
the existence of one God;
the soul and the spirit;
reincarnation;
the law of reciprocal actions;
the possibility of unity with the divine.

The three moral rules – or *susila* – of the religion are reasonable enough:
think good thoughts;
talk honestly;
do good deeds.

Their ritual – or *upacara* – is divided into five areas of sacrifice; ritual for the gods, the higher spirits, the Hindu prophets, for and on behalf of humans, and sacrifices for neutralizing the negative influences of the natural and supernatural worlds. Praying is also important, for which the devotee requires flowers, incense and *tirta* or holy water. Men sit on the floor with their legs crossed and their hands held together, either at the level of their foreheads (if they are praying to the Supreme God), or at the level of their lips (when praying to Sang Hyang Kala) or resting on their chests (if praying to a dead family member). In Balinese, praying is referred to as *muspa* or *mbakti*. The former means to show respect with flowers, the latter means to worship by means of devotion.

☞ *The banjar*

Every Balinese male is a member of a banjar, the basic unit of organization and local government. After marriage, a man is invited to join the banjar. This invitation is in reality a compulsion; if after the third summons, the man has not joined, he is declared 'dead' and loses most of his village rights – even the right to be cremated on the village cremation ground. The members of the banjar democratically elect one of their group to act as head (klian banjar). He enjoys the status and prestige of being head, and some other minor advantages such as additional rice during group festivities, but no cash payment for his work.

Members of the banjar are bound to assist one another in a variety of tasks. It is, in effect, a co-operative society. In any village there are likely to be a number of banjars, each drawing its members from a geographical neighbourhood. They sometimes own ricefields communally, the production going towards group festivities. Today, money owned through tourist activities – such as staging dances – also goes to the banjar, the society then redistributing it among its members. As Miguel Covarrubias wrote in 1937 (while ignoring the position of women): "Everyone enjoys absolute equality and all are compelled to help one another with labour and materials, often assisting a member to build his house, to prepare his son's wedding, or to cremate a relative".

Festivals and ceremonies

The full moon occurs approximately every 29½ days. The Denpasar Municipality Tourist Office (Dinas Pariwisata Kotamadya Denpasar), Jalan Surapati 7, publishes an annual calendar of events listing, day by day, Bali's many festivals & their location

There can be few places of comparable size that have more ceremonies and festivals than Bali. The most common are temple anniversary celebrations, odalan. Every temple on the island holds an *odalan* usually once every 210 days, one complete cycle according to the Balinese *wuku*, also known as the *Pawukon* calendar; however, some temples schedule their odalans according to the lunar calendar, the Saka, with years consisting of 354-356 days. With more than 20,000 temples, every day is a festival day, somewhere.

The major ceremonies are those of marriage and cremation, both of which are traditionally costly affairs. Also important is tooth-filing. Along with these ceremonies associated with a person's progression through his or her life-cycle, are a vast range of other rites, festivals and ceremonies.

Sesajen This is not a ceremony, so much as a ritual, but it is so commonplace that it is in some respects the most important religious activity on the island. Three times a day before meals, small woven coconut trays filled with glutinous rice, flowers and salt are sprinkled with holy water and are offered to the gods. They can be seen placed outside the front door of every house.

Eka Dasa Rudra This is the most important of Bali's festivals and is held, in theory, only once every 100 years at the 'Mother Temple' – Besakih – on Mount Agung. In 1963, the volcano erupted during the festival, killing 2,000 people. As a result, another had to be organized. It took place in 1979 and this time no catastrophe occurred (see page 158 for more details).

Panca Walikrama This festival is meant to take place once a decade at Besakih temple. However, in practice this has not happened, with only four festivals taking place this century, the last one in 1989.

Odalan The *odalan* festival celebrates the anniversary of a temple's consecration and is held over about 3 days, usually every 210 days according to the wuku, or

The Balinese calendars: saka and wuku

The Balinese use two traditional calendars in addition to the Gregorian calendar, a relatively recent addition. The Hindu saka calendar, which originated with the founding of the Saka Dynasty in South India, is based on the solar year and lasts between 354 and 356 days, divided into 12 lunar months. It is 80 years behind the Christian year, so that AD 1998 is saka 1918. Each lunar month ends with the new moon, tilem. The Balinese New Year, Nyepi, based on the saka calendar is a very important religious day, and commences on the first day of the tenth month, usually in Gregorian March.

The Balinese also use the Hindu-Javanese wuku calendar, also called pawukon or uku, based on a 210-day lunar cycle, which operates in parallel with the saka year but the years are unnumbered. This calendar is used to determine many religious festivals, market days, an individual's anniversaries and auspicious or inauspicious days for doing or avoiding certain activities. It is of immense complexity, being divided into ten separate but concurrent weeks, with from 1 day, 2 days, 3 days etc, on up to 10 days in each week. Each week has a name, of Sanskrit origin, depending on the number of days in that week; of these the 3,5 and 7-day weeks are of most significance, respectively called triwara, pancawara and saptawar. Additionally each of the 30 7-day weeks in the wuku cycle has its own individual name. Each day of each of the 10 different week systems also has a name, thus any given day may have 10 different names, with a total of 55 different day names. Every day has associated with it a deity, and both good and bad forces which are used to determine the appropriate day for carrying out any activity.

The most important days in the Balinese year, when most festivals take place, occur at the conjunction of special days in each of the two calendars, and when special days in one week-system of the wuku calendar are in conjunction with special days in another week-system. Of the latter, 6 of these conjunction days are of special importance, particularly kajeng keliwon which occurs every 15 days and is the date when many temple ceremonies and odalan occur (kajeng is the final day of the 3-day week and keliwon the final day of the 5-day week).

Some of these conjunction days have their own special names and of these Tumpek is noteworthy. It occurs six times a year in the wuku cycle. The first Tumpek honours weapons of war, especially the sacred kris, but these days cars, trucks and motorbikes (definitely all lethal weapons on Bali!) are included; even computers and faxes get a blessing. On this day, prayers are said, a priest may be called in to offer blessings; vehicles are decorated, one might almost say dressed, with ceremonial cloths, batik and brocades, and traditional bamboo baskets with religious offerings of rice etc are placed inside. On another tumpek day trees, most especially the coconut palm, are venerated and sometimes dressed in traditional Balinese clothes. On another of the 6 tumpek days domestic animals are worshipped; cows and pigs in particular are washed, decorated, given special meals, prayed over and sprinkled with holy water and rice. Even scholars have their day of veneration.

Balinese calendars, called tika, contain details of the most important days and weeks. They are read vertically starting in the top left hand corner and going down each column from left to right. Tika can be quite beautiful, especially the cloth ones with illustrations of the auspicious and malevolent forces associated with each day.

(Anyone interested in pursuing this topic should read "Bali Sekala & Niskala", volume 1, by Fred B Eiseman, Jr, which has an entire 20-page chapter as a mere introduction to the subject!)

Bali

Penjor and janur

Visitors to Bali cannot fail to notice the tall, elegant bamboo poles called penjor which bend over the roads, signifying some celebration or festival. Hanging from the slender poles are decorations made out of the yellow leaf of the coconut, known as janur. Their design varies enormously, according to the festival and to the place where they are made. So many festivals take place on Bali that there are always penjor to be seen in varying states of decay. Travelling around Bali, visitors may notice arches of palms over the gateway to a house, with janur and banana leaves on either side; this usually signifies a wedding ceremony. Fruit and flowers are placed on (or within) the janur, as offerings to the gods. Any of the following may be seen dangling from the penjor: bananas, pineapples, plastic bags filled with pink liquid, coconuts, carrots, ears of corn and janur; all symbols of fertility. These penjor take about two hours to make and look very beautiful and delicate when first erected; their beauty fades a little as they dry out and turn brown after about two days. Janurs are not unique to Bali, and can also be found in parts of Java and North Sulawesi. Reliefs depicting janur on the ninth century Hindu temple of Prambanan, in Central Java, indicate that they have been made for many centuries.

pawukon calendar, but some temples follow the saka calendar with 354-356 days. Of the 66 main temple ceremonies 40 are based on the wuku calendar and 26 on the saka. Wuku ceremonies occur at the time of the new moon, *tilem*, while saka ceremonies are usually held at the time of the full moon, *purnama*. The odalan at the nine directional temples are the grandest. This is the festival that visitors to Bali are most likely to see and it includes a great feast to which all the villagers are invited. The villagers prepare for odalan for many days beforehand by cleaning the temple, building altars and awnings, erecting flag poles, and preparing offerings. On the first day of the celebration, the ceremony starts with ritual cockfighting: the blood is a necessary offering to the gods as is the sacrifice of the most powerful fighting cock (see box, page 252). Women dress in their finest clothes – sarongs, sashes and head-dresses – and walk in procession to the temple. On their heads they carry their colourful offerings of fruit and rice cakes, arranged in beautiful and carefully balanced pyramids. The offerings remain at the temple for three days during which time they are sprinkled daily with holy water. At the end of this period, the food is taken home again and eaten.

During odalan, the men sit around the compound proudly wearing their krisses tucked into their sarongs. Over the 3 days the temple buzzes with activity; around the entrance locals set up stalls selling food and trinkets, medicine men market cure-alls, cockfights are staged, a gamelan orchestra plays, and in the evenings dance and wayang kulit performances take place. The inner courtyards are reserved for the sacred offerings and here the *pemangku* – or officiating priest – prays in front of the altars.

Kidnapping (from a Balinese painting)
Source: Covarrubias, Miguel

Caru

Caru is a blood sacrifice or purification ceremony with offerings specifically for the evil spirits. Balance is an intrinsic part of the Hindu religion, and in keeping with this, the evil forces have to be appeased just as much as the forces for good. Many of these offerings are foul smelling and in a state of decay. The undesirable parts of sacrificial animals are also included; before any animal is sacrificed a ritual takes place in which the animal is asked to forgive the slayer, and is guaranteed a better life in its next reincarnation.

Marriage

In contrast with Western marriages, the traditional Balinese marriage is preceded by the honeymoon – or *ngrorod*. The prospective couple secretly prepare for their honeymoon and, on the day they select, arrange for the abduction of the bride with the complicity of a few close friends. The girl is expected to put up a good fight, but the event is staged. When the parents discover that their daughter has been kidnapped, they send a search party to look for her; again this is for show. During their time in hiding, the couple are expected to consummate their marriage before it happens – an event which is witnessed by the gods. The marriage itself is supposed to occur within 42 days of the abduction, but not before a substantial bride-price has been paid to the parents of the girl. From this point on, the girl becomes part of her future husband's family and relinquishes her own family affiliations. She adopts the groom's ancestral gods to symbolize this. Among aristocratic families marriages were usually pre-arranged (*mapadik*).

The marriage, or *masakapan*, is held on an auspicious day selected by the priest. Invitations are sent out asking guests to bring certain types and amounts of food. The bride and groom used to have their teeth filed during the ceremony if this had not already been done (see below). While the bride is being prepared for the marriage rite, men – arranged according to status – sit, eat and chew betel nut while being entertained by professional story tellers. The rite varies from area to area, but usually the bride and groom offer food and drink to one another, and then eat together in public; an important symbolic act because in the past only married men and women were allowed to be seen eating food together. In the afternoon, the priest performs a ritual purification and blesses the couple.

Cremation

Cremation is the most important ceremony in the Balinese life-cycle. It is a time for celebration, not sorrow, and is wonderfully colourful. It is also an extremely costly affair, and people will begin to save for their cremation from middle age. Even the poorest family will need to spend about 1 million rupiah, whilst wealthy families have been known to lavish hundreds of millions of rupiah. If there is not enough money saved, families may have to wait years – sometimes more than a decade – before they can hold the cremation of a loved one, thus releasing his or her soul. To avoid the wait, poorer people may be helped out by other members of the village, or they may share in a big ceremony when a number of bodies are cremated together. Another option is to be cremated with an aristocrat who needs a retinue to accompany him to the next life. Towards the end of 1992, the Rajah of Gianyar, 71-year-old Ide Anak Agung Gede Agung, staged an elaborate cremation for his former wife, two stepmothers and two of his late father's concubines: rumour had it that the total cost to the royal house – the richest on Bali – was as much as US$1 million.

Rich people may be cremated soon after they have died, in which case the corpse simply lies in state in the family compound. If there is going to be a

● ●

Bali

Self-immolation and human sacrifice in a Dutch account of 1633

In 1633 a Dutch expedition visited Gelgel on Bali, and its members witnessed two cremations, one of a queen and another of two princes. In both cases, a number of female slaves and other courtiers also died. The English historian John Crawfurd, quoted the account of the visit and spectacle at some length in his book The Malay Archipelago *(1820). In the case of the female slaves, each was poignarded:*

"Some of the most courageous demanded the poignard themselves, which they received with their right hand, passing it to the left, after respectfully kissing the weapon. They wounded their right arms, sucked the blood which flowed from the wound, and stained their lips with it, making a bloody mark on the forehead with the point of the finger. Then returning the dagger to their executioners, they received a first stab between the false ribs, and a second under the shoulder blade, the weapon being thrust up to the hilt towards the heart. As soon as the horrors of death were visible in the countenance, without a complaint escaping them, they were permitted to fall to the ground...".

In the case of the courtiers and princesses who were cremated with the bodies of the princes, they would not allow anyone of lower status to touch them, and so had to kill themselves:

"For this purpose, a kind of bridge is erected over a burning pile, which they mount, holding a paper close to their foreheads, and having their robe tucked under their arm. As soon as they feel the heat, they precipitate themselves into the burning pile... In case firmness should abandon them... a brother, or another near relative, is at hand to push them in,

● ●

considerable time period before cremation, then the body is either buried or mummified first. When enough money has been accumulated, an auspicious day is chosen by a priest for the cremation. The body is disinterred (if buried), the bones collected up, arranged in human form, and draped with a new white cloth. The corpse is carried back to the family compound and placed in a bamboo and paper tower, richly painted and decorated. Here it is adorned with jewellery and cloths decorated with magic symbols. Various rites are performed before the ceremony to awaken and satisfy the soul. An *adegan*, a dual effigy, is carved in palmleaf and sandalwood. On the day before the cremation the effigy is taken in a grand procession to a high priest, accompanied by the dead person's relatives dressed in their finest clothes.

For the cremation itself, a large bamboo tower is built; its size and shape is dictated by the caste of the dead person. A wooden life-size bull (for men) or cow (for women) is sometimes carved. On the morning of the cremation, friends and relatives are entertained by the family of the deceased and then the body is placed inside the bamboo tower. The village *kulkul* – or gong – is struck, and the construction is carried in a noisy procession (designed to confuse the soul of the departed so that it cannot return to the family home) to the cremation ground by other members of the dead person's *banjar* or village association. The body is roughly handled as it is placed in the tower. At the cremation site, the wooden bull or cow and the corpse are set alight. After the incineration, the ashes are carried off in another raucous procession, to the nearest water, where they are thrown into the wind. The cremation is the most impressive of the Balinese ceremonies, but it is not one where any respect is shown for the corpse. The body is treated like an unclean container; it is the soul that is paramount. To illustrate the point, bodies are poked with sticks to help them burn, and are shown none of the respect evident in the funeral ceremonies of other religions.

Christianity on Bali

Within this century the impact of Christianity on Bali has been limited because in 1908 the Dutch imposed a ban on missionary activity as part of their plan to preserve traditional culture – so long as this did not interfere with the more important priority of profitable colonial enterprise. This desire to preserve Balinese culture was in part an effort to curry favour back in Holland following criticism of the violent and bloodthirsty manner in which they went about subduing Balinese resistance to their rule, and partly a realization even at this early time, that there was tremendous tourist potential for the island. To be fair there were those amongst the colonialists who genuinely appreciated this unique culture.

The history of missionary activity on Bali starts as early as 1636 when two Jesuit priests arrived on the island at the invitation of the ruler of Klungkung. However, their stay was brief largely due to the strength of Bali's native religious beliefs. Further sporadic attempts to gain a foothold on the island during the 19th century were also unsuccessful for the same reason.

In 1850, under Article 177 of the Dutch Colonial Code, all missionary activity was banned throughout Indonesia in order not to prejudice VOC (Dutch East India Company) trade. For this reason the Dutch Reformed Church agreed not to proselytize on Java. However, since the Catholic church was also actively trying to gain a foothold in the East Indies, the Dutch Protestant missionaries did not want to lose out. Therefore a decision was taken in 1854 to divide up present day Nusa Tenggara into spheres of religious influence. The Catholics were given Flores and part of Timor, and the Protestants gained access to most of the remainder including Bali.

Following the outright ban of missionary activity on Bali in 1908, Dutch attitudes softened. In 1929 Tsang To Han, a Chinese preacher from Hong Kong was allowed to minister to the religious needs of two recently arrived Chinese Christians. By 1933 Tsang had converted 300 Balinese upsetting many powerful Balinese Hindus in the process who had him expelled.

In 1935 the Dutch authorities again relented and allowed one Protestant and one Catholic priest into Bali on condition that they only ministered to their existing small flock and did not seek further converts. In order to limit their influence these religious communities were banished to a remote and uninhabited area of West Bali, the site of the present day villages of Protestant Belimbingsari and Catholic Palasari.

Today there are some 56 protestant churches of the Gereja Kristen Protestan di Bali (GKPB), the name given to the Balinese offshoot of the Dutch Reform Church, with over 6,000 members. All present day pastors are Balinese and services are held in Bahasa Indonesia and Balinese. Other Christian churches on Bali include 70 Catholic churches, a Reformed church where services are given in Batak, one for the Chinese Christian community, and evangelical and fundamentalist offshoots. The Republic of Indonesia has a Department of Religious Affairs and officially recognizes five religions: Islam, Buddhism, Hinduism, Catholicism and Protestantism.

Tooth-filing

The practice of tooth-filing was once common across island Southeast Asia. Savages, wild animals and demons have long, white teeth, so filing them down at puberty was necessary to ensure that at death a person would not be mistaken for a wild creature. In some areas of Sumatra this is taken to extremes and every tooth is filed flat; in Bali it is only the front teeth that are filed, although the rationale is the same.

In the past, not only were the front teeth filed, but they were also blackened. In theory, tooth-filing should occur at puberty, but because of the cost of staging the ceremony, it is often delayed until later in life. It is said that filing is necessary to control the six evil characteristics of the human condition, known as *sad ripu* – passion, greed, anger, confusion, jealousy and earthly intoxication. If someone dies without having had their teeth filed, the priest will often file the teeth of the corpse before cremation. Miguel Covarrubias describes a tooth-filing ceremony he witnessed in the 1930s:

"The operation is performed by a specialist, generally a Brahmana, who knows formulas by which his tools – files and whetstones – are blessed 'to take the poison out of them', to make the operation painless. The patient is laid on a *bale* among offerings, the head resting on a pillow which is covered with a protective scarf, *gringsing wayang wangsul*, one of the magic cloths woven in Tenganan, the warp of which is left uncut. The body is wrapped in a new white cloth and assistants hold down the victim by the hands and feet. The tooth-filer stands at the head of the *bale* and inscribes magic syllables (*aksara*) on the teeth about to be filed with a ruby set in a gold ring. The filing then proceeds, taking from 15 minutes to 30 minutes, endured stoically with clenched hands and goose-flesh but without even a noise from the patient."

Dance, drama and music

Dance Balinese dances, as with their music and theatre, were sacred, created as offerings to and enjoyment for the gods. It is only in recent times that troupes of 'professional' dancers performing for money have been formed. The Balinese are consummate dancers. Everyone dances, and dancing forms an essential element of private and public life accompanying, as Beryl de Zoete and Walter Spies wrote in 1938, "every stage of a man's life from infancy to the grave". Of the various dances, those most often staged for tourists are the masked dance or *topeng*, the monkey dance or *kecak*, and the dance between the witch Rangda and the mythical lion, known as the *barong*. A brief description of the various dances is given below; tourists are normally provided with a printed sheet with information on the dance(s) when they attend a performance.

Kecak – or monkey dance, is in fact a relatively recent creation invented by the German artist Walter Spies in the 1930's for a film. It was inspired by the chorus found in the sacred trance dance (or *sanghyang*), and the sound of the chattering crowd of men crouched watching a cockfight. A central person in a state of trance communicates with a god or ancestor. while the surrounding chorus of men rhythmically chant *kecak kecak kecak*, which encourages the state of trance and gives the dance its name. The dance itself is based on an episode from the Ramayana, and tells the story of when Sita is abducted by Ravana and subsequently rescued by an army of monkeys.

Barong or kris dance – is also a trance dance and while often described as the epitome of the battle between good and evil, its real purpose is to maintain harmony by balancing the forces of good and evil. Good, in the shape of the mythical *Barong*, a sacred animal, fights the evil witch *Rangda*. These dances, with their fantastic costumes, are among the most sacred and important of the Balinese dances. The Barong is the

Legong costume
Source: Cavarrubias, Miguel (1937)

Bali

guardian of the village and the purpose of the dance is to exorcise the village of evil spirits at temple festivals and when disease or disaster strike. The origin of the Barong is unknown. Almost every village has a Barong which manifests itself in different forms, of which the *Barong ket* is the most common and sacred, looking somewhat like a Chinese lion with a magnificent bulgy eyed mask and a long shaggy coat. Other manifestations include a tiger *Barong Macan*, an elephant *Barong Gajah*, a wild boar *Barong Bangkal*, a pig *Barong Celeng*, a cow *Barong Limbu*, a lion *Barong Singha* and in human form in the *Barong Lundung* where it appears as an enormous doll. At the climax of the dance Barong confronts Rangda, and Barong's followers attack her with their kris. The witch's spell turns the kris of the Barong's accomplices against themselves. However, in their trance state they are protected by the powerful magic of the Barong, and the kris can do no harm. Inside the barong costume are two men who co-ordinate their movements with great agility and often humour, much like a Chinese lion dance; indeed, it is thought that some aspects of the barong dance may be derived from the Chinese New Year lion dance. The masks themselves are believed to be infused with magic power, and are wrapped in sacred cloths and kept in the village temple. There is a special day to bless and celebrate the Barong when the streets of Bali are filled with processions of these colourful, mythological creatures. Rangda, the personification of evil, has bulging eyes and tusks and is linked to the Indian goddess Durga. She is also a source of great supernatural power and speaks in Kawi, the ancient Javanese tongue, using a whiney, sinister sounding voice. Like the barong (the word refers to both the dance and the mask), the mask of Rangda is also revered. The outcome of their confrontation is always a draw, a balance between good and evil, neither side wins and the battle goes on for ever.

Sanghyang dedari – the Dance of the Holy Angels – is the best known, and possibly the most beautiful of a type of trance dance known as *Sang* [Lord] *Hyong* [God]. Young girls perform this religious dance of exorcism, designed to rid a community of evil spirits, while a chorus of men and women provide accompaniment. The dancers are often relatives of temple servants and usually have no professional training. They are believed to be possessed by celestial nymphs, and at the end of the performance – traditionally – would walk on hot coals before being brought back to consciousness.

Legong – a Balinese dance for girls from eight to early teens (although today many tourist dances employ adult performers) which was created at the beginning of the 18th century. This is not a trance dance, but rigorous physical training is needed to perform the movements. Three dancers perform the most popular version, the *legong kraton*, a story taken from the East Javanese classic tale of Prince Panji. In this story, a bird warns the king of the futility of war, which he ignores, and is killed in battle. The dance is regarded as the finest, and most feminine, of Balinese dances and the girls dress in fine silks and wear elaborate headdresses decorated with frangipani and other flowers. The dancers do not speak or sing – the lines of the story are recounted by singers accompanied by a gamelan orchestra. Because of the demands of the dance,

The evil witch Rangda, enemy of the mythical lion Barong in the Barong dance from Balinese manuscript. Reproduced in Miguel Covvarrubia's Island of Bali (1937)

🖐 *Dance performances on Bali*

NB *This timetable is subject to change; check beforehand.*

Barong or Kris Dance

Batubulan Village, every day from 0930.
Puri Saren, Ubud, every Friday from 1830.
Catur Eka Budi, Jalan Waribang, Kesiman, every day from 0930.
Sari Wisata Budaya, Jalan By Pass Ngurah Rai, every day from 0930.
Suwung, every day, 0930-1030.
Br Abasan, Singapadu, every day, 0930-1030.

Kecak Dance

Werdi Budaya, Jalan Nusa Indah, every day from 1830.
Catur Eka Budi, Jalan Waribang, Kesiman, every day from 1830.
Padang Tegal, Ubud, every Sunday from 1800.
Puri Agung, Peliatan, every Thursday from 1930.
Ayodya Pura Stage, Tanjung Bungkak, Denpasar, every day from 1800.
Art Centre, Abian Kapas, Denpasar, every day from 1800.
Pasar Senggol, Grand Hyatt, Nusa Dua, every Tuesday from 1900.
Pelangi Stage, Nusa Dua Beach Hotel, every Sunday from 1800.
Grand Hyatt Bali, every Tuesday from 1900.
Br Buni, Kuta, every Sunday from 2000.

Kecak and Fire Dance

Bona Village, every Sunday, Monday, Wednesday and Friday from 1830.
Batubulan Village, every day from 1830.

Legong Dance

Puri Saren, Ubud, every Monday and Saturday from 1930.
Peliatan Village, Ubud, every Friday from 1930.
Pura Dalem Puri, Ubud, every Saturday from 1930.
Pasar Senggol, Grand Hyatt Nusa Dua, every Thursday from 1900.
Hongkong Restaurant, every night from 2000.
Budaya Stage, Nusa Dua Beach Hotel, every Friday from 2045.
Grand Hyatt Bali, every Saturday from 1900.
Banjar Tengah Peliatan, Ubud, every Wednesday from 1930.
Br Tegal, Kuta, every Tuesday and Saturday from 2000.

Shadow Puppet Show

Oka Kartini's, Ubud, every Saturday from 2000.

Tek-tekan Dance

Puri Anyar, Kerambitan, on request.
Puri Puri Agung Wisata, Kerambitan, on request.
Pasar Senggol, Grand Hyatt Nusa Dua, every Monday from 1900.
Grand Hyatt Bali, every Monday from 1900.

Leko and Jangger Dance

Puri Anyar, Kerambitan, on request.

---

girls must be taught – literally physically manipulated – from an early age, so that 'the dance enters their innermost being'.

Topeng – the wayang topeng is a masked dance which, in Bali, recounts stories of former kings and princes. In its purest form, it is performed in silence by a single actor who portrays a series of characters changing his mask each time. Today, he is more likely to be accompanied by a narrator.

Jegog – a dance which originates from Jembrana. It is performed by young men and women accompanied by the music of the *jegog* – a bamboo xylophone not unlike the *angklung* of West Java.

Ramayana ballet – a portrayal of the great Hindu epic.

Wayang kulit – the famous shadow theatre of Java and Bali in which two-dimensional leather puppets are manipulated, their forms reflected onto a white cloth. In Bali, wayang kulit accords, it is thought, more closely with the original Majapahit form than does the Javanese equivalent. This can be seen in

Ramayana Ballet

Pura Dalem Puri, Ubud, every Monday from 2000.

Puri Saren Ubud, every Tuesday from 2000.

Grand Hyatt Bali, every Thursday from 1900.

Br Buni, Kuta, every Monday and Thursday from 2000.

Ubud Kelod, Ubud, every Wednesday, 1930-2100.

Mahabharata Ballet

Teges Village, Ubud, every Tuesday from 1830.

Gabor Dance

Puri Saren, Ubud, every Thursday from 1930.

Rajapala Dance

Puri Saren, Ubud, every Sunday from 1930.

Ubud Kelod, Ubud, every Tuesday, 1930-2000.

Calonarang Dance

Mawang Village, Ubud, every Thursday and Saturday from 1930.

Hotel Menara, Ubud, every Friday from 2000.

Classical Mask Dance and Legong Dance

Banjar Kalah, Peliatan, Ubud, every Thursday from 1930.

Women's Gamelan and Child Dancers

Peliatan Village, Ubud, every Sunday from 1930.

Sunda Upasunda

Puri Saren, Ubud, every Wednesday from 1930.

Baleganjur and Kecak dance

Baleganjur procession every afternoon around sunset at Galleria Nusa Dua, performed to cleanse the area. Bali's best Kecak dance every Monday, Wednesday and Friday at the Nusenglango Amphitheatre of Galleria Nusa Dua, only 7,500Rp, from 1900. Reservations and information: T771662, T771663, F771664.

Frog Dance

Sanur Beach Hotel from 1930.

Bebek Mas Restaurant, Kuta, every evening from 2000.

Penjor Restaurant, Sanur, every Sunday from 1900.

Innercourt Garden of Nusa Dua Beach Hotel, every Tuesday from 1900.

Gebyug Dance

'Gurnita Wreksa' Pura Dalem Puri, Peliatan every Monday.

Topeng Dance

Penjor Restaurant, Sanur, every Saturday from 2015.

Bali

the puppets with their elaborate headdresses and costumes, and in the carving of the faces which is similar in style to the low relief carvings on Majapahit temples in East Java. Many of the themes of Wayang Kulit have an educational or moral lesson, for example the story of Bima's search for holy water takes him to Heaven where he learns which actions merit rewards and which result in hideous punishment. As this is an effective and popular way for the public to absorb moral teachings, the government now uses Wayang Kulit to instil such secular duties as family planning, food hygiene and healthy living.

Gambuh – this is one of Bali's most ancient, and least known, dance dramas. Court tales are enacted in a highly stylized manner by actors dressed in rich costumes and accompanied by a traditional orchestra. Revived from near cultural extinction, *gambuh* is occasionally performed at Pura Desa Batuan in Batuan village, south of Ubud. There is also a Gambuh School in Padangaji village near Selat in Karagasem, see page 187.

Music Beryl de Zoete and Walter Spies, early foreign residents of Bali, wrote of its music in their paper of 1938 *Dance and drama in Bali*: "Music permeates their life to a degree which we can hardly imagine; a music of incomparable subtlety and intricacy, yet as simple as breathing. Like every other expression of Balinese life, it is easily accessible and at the same time inexhaustible in its interest and variety." It was Walter Spies, an American composer who was captivated when he first heard a recording of Balinese music in the late 1920s in New York, who played a crucial role in detailing and preserving the music of the island. He acted as a patron, wrote a brilliant, seminal book entitled *Music in Bali* (1966), and spread the gospel around the capitals of the world. He even wrote an orchestral work – *Tabuh-Tabuhan* – based on Balinese musical formulas, for which he won a Pulitzer prize in 1936. Such was his love of Bali and its music that what began as a short jaunt to the island turned into a life-long love affair.

Like Java, the basis of Balinese music is the gamelan orchestra. Sets of gamelan instruments – of which the gongs are regarded as the most important – are usually owned corporately, by the village or *banjar*. Making music is a tightly structured event; the notion of 'jamming' is simply not the Balinese way. Musicians learn their parts and the aim is for an orchestra to produce a perfect rendition of a composed piece. Reflecting this approach, the brilliance of Balinese music is in the whole, which is greater than its constituent parts. There are few superstars; it is the orchestra as a perfectly co-ordinated unit that determines success.

Experiencing Balinese music, dance & theatre Most visitors to Bali hear Balinese music or see local dances in the context of their hotels. Although people often assume that such performances cannot be 'authentic', all gamelan and dance groups are regulated by LISTIBIYA, the government arts council. This means that the quality is invariably high, and although pieces are usually condensed to make them more 'acceptable' to tourist audiences, the quality of the performance is rarely affected. However, for a more authentic environment, it is necessary to visit a temple anniversary festival or *odalan* (see page 238). Performances usually begin in the late afternoon or early evening with a gamelan recital and then continue after dark with dances and shadow plays. Note that visitors should dress and behave appropriately (see 'Rules, customs and etiquette', page 29). The two main music academies are STSI (Werdi Budaya Art Centre) on Jalan Nusa Indah in Denpasar; and Kokar/SMKI in Batubulan. There is also an annual Bali Arts Festival held from mid-June to mid-July in Denpasar. See the table for a listing of where to see dances.

Many villages have a gamelan orchestra; these can often be heard practising in the evenings on the 'bale banjar', the platform used as a meeting place in the centre of the village.

Modern Bali

Economy and tourism

Visitors to Bali may leave with the impression that the island's economy is founded on tourism. Certainly, tourism is a crucial element in Bali's economic growth and well-being. Yet over three-quarters of Bali's population still lives in rural areas, and the bulk of the inhabitants depend upon agriculture for their livelihoods. Since the mid-1960s, farmers have turned to the cultivation of high yielding varieties of rice and the use of large quantities of chemical fertilizers. Three-quarters of Bali's riceland now produces two or more crops of rice each year. There has also been a diversification of agricultural production into vegetables and fruit, cloves, vanilla, and livestock.

Outside agriculture, tourism is the next most important industry. The first tourists began to arrive just six years after the Klungkung *puputan* (see page 226). In 1914 the Dutch steamship line KPM was publishing brochures with lines like: "You leave this island with a sigh of regret and as long as you live you can never forget this Garden of Eden." Today about 300,000 tourists arrive each year by air, the same number again by sea from Java and Lombok. With a population of three million, this means a considerable influx of outsiders – both international and domestic. Given that approaching one half of visitors to Indonesia visit Bali alone, the significance of the island – which accounts for a mere 0.3% of the country's land area – in Indonesia's overall tourist industry is immense.

To serve this influx of visitors, a major building boom has been underway. By 1984, there were already over 9,000 hotel rooms on the island, and the boom continued through the 1980s so that now there are over 20,000. The government has tried to restrict development to buildings no taller than a coconut palm, and has encouraged construction in Balinese 'style'. Although there are not the crude, ungainly high-rise hotels of some other Asian resorts (the only such hotel is the *Bali Beach* on Sanur, constructed before the regulations came into force), the designs do rather stretch the notion of 'traditional' style (particularly those in Nusa Dua and Kuta).

At present, resorts are largely restricted to the south coast, but the government has plans to develop other parts of the island, in particular the north coast at Lovina and Pemuteran.

A projected new road around the island and tourist information centres in each of the island's districts are expected to help the dispersal of tourism to other areas. There is also a plan to develop 'special interest tourism' (or ecotourism), focusing on the island's marine and other natural resources. But although tourism has generated income, jobs and opportunities for Bali's inhabitants, there are those who point to the 'downside' of the industry: cultural erosion, environmental degradation, the undermining of traditional activities, inflation, the growth of crime and drug abuse. In the recent words of the director of the Bali Tourism Development Corporation: "If we do not reinvent Bali, it will not survive." By the year 2000 Bali will have consumed 81.5% of her potable water resources and by 2007 water supplies will be depleted. Now, more than ever before, Bali cries out for a master plan for tourism. On a more positive note, the Bupati (Regent) of Bandung (South Bali) has formally banned billboard advertising from certain areas of the island. At present these are in the main tourist areas of the south, but with luck the ban will be extended to cover the whole of Bali.

Perceptive visitors have been worrying about the impacts of tourism for over half a century. Miguel Covarrubias, who lived on Bali in the early 1930s,

Tourism and culture in Bali

One of the areas which has attracted attention among journalists, academics and many tourists who have been to Bali is the relationship between culture and tourism. Bali's tourist industry is unashamedly founded on culture. In a sense, it is the island's culture which is Bali's defining feature. In the 1970s the American anthropologist Philip McKean argued that far from destroying culture, tourism would support, nurture and reinforce culture. Indeed, partly as a result of his work, Bali became an exemplar of how tourism can be managed without undermining culture (see page 426 for a general discussion of the effects of tourism). Arts and crafts appeared to be revivified by the tourism experience, revenue earned was widely distributed through the banjar system of communal relations, and the Balinese appeared able to separate the sacred from the profane when it came to selling culture to tourists.

The tourism authorities in Bali embraced these views with alacrity. Cultural Tourism or Pariwisata Budaya was born in the 1970s. In 1986 the International Herald Tribune *published an article with the title "Bali: paradise preserved". The article stated:*

"If anything, tourism has pumped more life into the Balinese cultural Renaissance that began earlier this century. There are probably more superb artists and craftsmen in Bali today than at any time in its history."

Putting aside whether 'culture' can be reduced to just artists and craftsmen, this view is being challenged on a number of grounds. Most interesting perhaps is work which has tried to unravel what constitutes 'touristic culture', and what constitutes 'traditional culture' in Bali.

The sociologist Michel Picard wonders whether it is even possible to separate 'tourism' from 'culture' in the case of Bali. Many dances developed for tourists in the 1930s have, over time, become key markers of Balinese, and in some cases of Indonesian, culture. So making a distinction between what belongs to the world of 'tourism' and the world of 'tradition', is impossible. The two have merged. In short, 'cultural tourism' has become 'tourist culture'. As Adrian Vickers has written in his book Bali: a paradise created: *"This 'culture', expressed in art and religion, is what is promoted in tourist literature, what tourists come to see, and what is eventually accepted by the Balinese themselves as a definition of what is important in their own society." Michel Picard then takes this perspective that tourism is defining culture for the Balinese themselves, one step further when he writes that the Balinese have become "self-conscious spectators of their own culture – taking the growing touristification cum Indonesianization of their culture as the very proof of its 'renaissance'".*

wrote that the absence of beggars "is now threatened by tourists who lure boys and girls with dimes to take their pictures, and lately, in places frequented by tourists, people are beginning to ask for money as a return for a service".

There are some people – like Balinese anthropologist, Bangkal Kusuma – who see a subtle change in the nature of the tourist industry on the island. From being an industry which drew its life-blood from the maintenance of traditional Balinese culture (or at least what was perceived as 'traditional'), the emphasis is now very much on the McDonaldization of Balinese culture, driven often by investors in Jakarta. Kusuma also sees a reduction in the influence of regional tourist authorities and a related rise in that of the national authorities in Jakarta. The latter are now determining the path that tourist development should take on the island; they have perversely placed themselves in the position of identifying 'tradition' for the Balinese people. If this is so, then the challenge for those people who would wish to protect Bali is to carve out a distinctive niche for the island in the context of the nation. In other words to resist the attempts by the 'centre' to determine how tourism in Bali should develop. There is much debate as to who has benefited up to now from the 21% tax and service charge paid by tourists in the more upmarket hotels and restaurants. Some people say all the money has gone to Jakarta, while others insist it was pocketed by a former governor of Bali. However, there is unanimous agreement that Bali itself has not benefited, and that none of the money has been reinvested to improve tourist infrastructure.

Bali is becoming a Mecca for **refugees** from other parts of Indonesia as a result of the economic crisis. More than one million ethnic Chinese have arrived to set up new businesses on an island they see as a safe haven for their families. Most are very careful not to compete directly with established lines of business fearful of kindling the sort of backlash they have experienced in other parts of Indonesia (see page 418). Lower down the social ladder come refugees from Java hoping to scrape a living on the most prosperous island in the Indonesian Archipelago. The most recent refugees are East Timorese escaping from the brutal 'cleansing' and devastation wreaked on them by the militias and 'rogue' elements of the Indonesian military, including the élite and ruthless Kopassus section, formerly under the leadership of disgraced former President Suharto's son in law, Prabowo Subianto.

As Bali struggles to cope with a rising tide of waste and pollution and the demands made on its limited resources by tourism, there is a growing movement, fostered largely by the resident ex-pat population and a number of international hotels, to deal with the issues raised, in an environmentally friendly manner. It might come as a surprise to anyone who visits Bali during the rainy season to learn that there is a potential water shortage on Bali due to the lack of modern systems of water treatment and storage. The foremost of several environmental groups which have formed recently is the *Wisnu Foundation* (for information on their many projects contact them T0361-424758, greenbali@denpasar.wasantara.net.id). They have recently pioneered an 'Eco Rating for Hotels' to encourage and evaluate environmental management practices and each hotel, initially on Bali, will be graded. It was hoped that by the year 2000 the programme would have been implemented throughout Indonesia but the economic and political crisis put paid to that. The *Yayasan Yudistira Foundation* (for more information contact them at raenee@indosat.net.id) has set up a group to deal with the problem of Bali's many stray dogs. Although rabies is believed not to exist on Bali many of these dogs are in a sorry state and could pose a threat to tourism. Many of the volunteers are young trainee vets from Udayana University in Denpasar.

Belo, Jane (edit) (1970) *Traditional Balinese culture*, Columbia University Press: New York. Collection of academic papers, most focusing upon dance, music and drama.

Cook, Vern (1996) *Bali behind the seen: recent fiction from Bali*, Darlington, Australia: Darma Printing. Short stories by Balinese and translated by Vern – hard to obtain outside Australia.

Covarrubias, Miguel (1937) *Island of Bali*, Cassell: London (reprinted, OUP: Singapore, 1987). The original treatment of Bali's culture and still considered by many to be the best study of Balinese society despite being nearly 60 years old. It is an excellent background to the island and is highly entertaining.

Djelantik, AAM (1990) *Balinese paintings*, OUP: Singapore. Concise history of Balinese painting also covering the major contemporary schools of art.

Eiseman, Fred and Eiseman, Margaret (1988) *Woodcarvings of Bali*, Periplus: Berkeley.

Suggested reading

Cockfighting – Tajen

Cockfighting as entertainment was banned by the Indonesian government in 1981 but is still permitted as part of the ritual associated with all temple ceremonies including the odalan. *The spilling of blood,* tabuh rah, *is necessary as purification, to appease the evil spirits bhuta and kala, and to ensure a good harvest. The building of a new guest house or restaurant may also occasion a cockfight and the requisite blood offering, but in this instance the cockfight is not legal.*

Despite being illegal, cockfights still take place in secret throughout Bali purely as a betting medium, and may last for hours. They are usually staged in an arena or wantilan *(the traditional village meeting hall, open sided and two-tiered) with space for up to 100 people. The Dutch banned the sport, to no avail, in the 1920s because men would bet their life savings or even their wife. (For the record, the British government banned cockfighting in Great Britain in 1835). It was the national pastime and almost every male owned a fighting cock.*

Ritual fights usually take place outside the temple and follow an ancient and complex ritual as set out in the sacred lontar manuscripts. The cocks are categorized according to size, markings and colour, and rules pertain as to the choice of an auspicious day for the ceremony. Each male member of the local banjar is expected to bring a cock, and a percentage of the prize money goes to the banjar and towards the cost of the ceremony. The pemangku *(lay priest) consecrates the ground with rice wine and grains of rice. Prior to the first fight the owners of the fighting cocks walk around sizing up the opposition, discussing the sacred rules and arranging bouts. Specialists are hired to attach the razor sharp, 10-15 cm long blades or* taji *to the cocks' left leg; a system of handicapping is applied whereby the blade can be set at different less efficient angles to ensure an even match if one cock is deemed superior to its opponent. These taji are considered to have magic powers; whilst being forged by the* pande *(blacksmith) special rituals and precautions must be followed.*

There is a central bet decided by the juru dalem, *a local village leader of unblemished character, in agreement with the owners of the two cocks who each put up half the money, often with the help of backers and friends. This can amount to as much as a million rupiah and goes to the winning owner less 10-25% for the banjar. Following this, the spectators make their own bets, using a complex system of hand and facial signals. Nothing is written down,*

Eiseman, Fred B (1989 and 1990) *Bali: Sekala and Niskala*, Vol I Essays on Religion, Ritual and Art. Vol II Essays on Society, Tradition and Craft, Periplus: Berkeley. Informative collection of essays giving an insight into the Balinese way of life.

Hobart, Angela (1987) *Dancing shadows of Bali: theatre and myth*, KPI: London. Academic book examining the wayang theatre in Bali.

Kempers, AJ Bernet (1991) *Monumental Bali: introduction to Balinese archaeology and guide to the monuments*, Periplus: Berkeley and Singapore. New edition of Kempers's 1977 book, with photos and additional 'guide' section; best available.

Lansing, J Stephen (1991) *Priests and Programmers: technologies of power in the engineered landscape of Bali*, Princeton University Press: Princeton. An anthropological account of Bali's irrigation system; interesting for rice enthusiasts.

McPhee, Colin (1986), *A House in Bali*, OUP: Singapore. An amusing and informed account of Balinese society and the role of music in society by the American composer who visited Bali in 1929.

and while most bets are of small amounts, a village may put up a considerable sum on its chosen cock. The juru dalem also acts as judge, and adjudicator in any disputes.

Visitors may be surprised to see the priest assist one of the birds in the first bout of the ritual fight to ensure a speedy conclusion and a strong flow of blood. Two further fights are permitted by law although at Nyepi the fighting is allowed to go on all day. In practice most cockfights continue for most of the day and gambling takes place. Each fight is permitted to last for three rounds and may be timed by a ganji, a half coconut shell with a small round hole in the bottom about 1 cm in diameter, which is put in a bucket of water. Each round lasts for the time taken for the shell to fill with water and then sink. Most fights last only a few minutes and seldom go to three rounds. Any bird that runs out is disqualified. The defeated bird, if it survives, may become a family pet, but more likely it will die in battle and provide an especially tasty and auspicious meal.

Considerable prestige and financial gain may attach to the owner of a winning cock. Fighting cocks are prized by their owners, who pamper them, stroke, massage, wash them, give them names and train them. They are given special foods, including grains and jackfruit, to make them strong, to make their blood thick so that the cock does not bleed easily in combat, and to encourage an aggressive temperament. They lead a celibate life in order to save all their energy and spirit for the fight.

The cocks are kept in guwungan, bell shaped baskets made of bamboo, which allow for a very limited amount of movement. These baskets have a removable bottom which allows the cock to scratch and peck the soil. The guwungan are moved during the day so that they receive the right amount of light and shade, and are placed along the roadside so that the cocks can watch the passers-by and not become bored, and also to get them used to the noise and frenzy they will experience as part of the eventual fight. When being transported the cocks are carried in kisa, specially designed thatched coconut palm baskets, which restrict all movement but allow the head and tail feather to stick out ensuring that the latter are not damaged. The Balinese word for cock, sabung, can also mean hero or conqueror, as well as having the same double meaning that it does in English.

Cockfighting is very much an all-male event. Tourists of either sex are usually welcome, though this 'sport' is not for the fainthearted or for animal lovers.

Robinson, Geoffrey (1995) *The dark side of Paradise: political violence in Bali*, NY: Cornell University Press. This presents the Bali beneath the harmony and the beauty: an island with deep political and social divisions where Dutch and then Indonesian administrations have manipulated people for their own ends. It offers a particularly detailed account of the 1965 massacre. Certainly an alternative book to take on holiday.

Stuart Fox, David (1982) *Once a century: Pura Besakih and the Eka Dasa Rudra Festival*, Penerbit Citra Indonesia: Jakarta.

Tenzer, Michael (1991) *Balinese music*, Periplus: Berkeley and Singapore. Illustrated summary of Balinese music, drawing heavily on Spies's work, best introduction available.

Utrecht, E and Hering, B (1987) 'The temples of Bali', *Kabar Seberang Sulating Maphilindo* 18: 161-74.

Vickers, Adrian (1989) *Bali: a paradise created*, Periplus: Berkeley and Singapore. Excellent account of the evolution of Bali as a tourist paradise; good historical and cultural background, informed without being turgid.

West Nusa Tenggara: Lombok and Sumbawa

4

West Nusa Tenggara: Lombok and Sumbawa

258 Lombok

258 Ins and outs

263 Ampenan – Mataram – Cakranegara

270 Lombok's west coast

276 The Gilis

286 Northwest coast and Mount Rinjani

289 Central Lombok and the West

293 East Lombok

294 South Lombok and the south coast

300 Background

305 Sumbawa

306 Alas

307 Taliwang

307 Maluk

308 Sumbawa Besar

311 Moyo Island

312 Mount Tambora

313 Sumbawa Besar to Bima-Raba

313 Dompu

314 Hu'u

314 Bima-Raba

318 Sape

Lombok has been earmarked for tourist development for well over a decade, on the pretext that it is in a position to emulate Bali's success. Whether the development plans will ever come to fruition is another matter and for the time being it remains a relatively quiet alternative to Bali, although considerably busier and more developed than the islands to the east. While there are a number of first class hotels along the beaches (and several more under construction), away from these tourist areas, Lombok is still 'traditional' and foreigners are a comparative novelty. It is also a poor island; the famines of the Dutch period and the 1960s remain very much in the collective consciousness.

Most visitors to Lombok stay on Senggigi Beach, on the west coast and just north of the capital Mataram, or on the 'Gilis', a small group of islands north of Senggigi. However, the south coast, around Kuta, with its beautiful sandy bays set between rocky outcrops is more dramatic. There is now a surfaced road to Kuta and some good accommodation once you get there, including one international class hotel (but be aware that plans are afoot to continue this tourist development). There are also a handful of towns inland with accommodation. While Lombok has gradually expanded over the years it has not yet 'taken off' – which, of course, is why some people prefer it to Bali. Grand plans have been thwarted at every step, and the tourist industry is currently facing a serious downturn, related to Indonesia's political problems in general and, more particularly, the widely publicized communal violence on Lombok in January 2000.

West Nusa Tenggara

Lombok

Ins and outs

Getting there

Air **Selaparang Mataram Airport** lies north of Mataram and 20 mins south of Senggigi Beach. There are multiple daily connections on Merpati and Bouraq with **Denpasar** between 0800 and 1700 and regular connections (on *Merpati*) with destinations in Java, Sumatra and most towns in Nusa Tenggara, including **Sumbawa Besar** and **Bima-Raba** (Sumbawa); **Labuanbajo, Bajawa, Ende** and **Maumere** (Flores); **Waingapu** and **Waikabubak** (Sumba); and **Kupang** (West Timor). Talk of upgrading the airport to international status has still not come to anything. *Sempati* is no longer running as the assets of the Suharto régime remain frozen. *Garuda* is the only airline to offer direct connections with **Jakarta**. **Airport facilities**: a money changer (for US$ TCs only and cash), information office, and hotel booking counters. **Transport to town**: fixed-fare (non a/c) taxis to Senggigi Beach (12,000Rp), Mataram (7,000Rp), Kuta (36,000Rp) and Bangsal (22,000Rp). Bemos to Ampenan and Mandalika terminal in Sweta are available from the main road, 200 m from the airport (500Rp). For Bangsal, you need to take a public bus towards Tanjung, and ask to be dropped off at Pemenang. These are available 500 m from the airport, to the left. When you reach the first crossroads, turn left and wait for your bus connection. **International connections**: at present the only direct international connections are: a daily flight to **Singapore** with *Silk Air*. There were plans to build a new airport 40 mins' drive south of Mataram in the Praya area. The site has been fenced off, though it could be years before construction gets under way and locals believe it has been cancelled.

Route map of direct flights within Nusa Tenggara

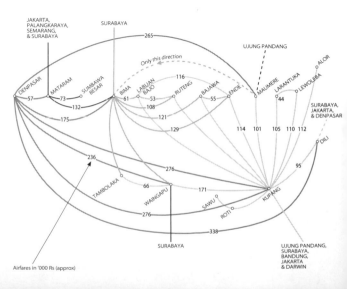

Airfares in '000 Rs (approx)

Lombok highlights

Temples The Mayura Water Palace and Gardens (page 263) is the largest temple complex on Lombok; other significant historical sights include **Taman Narmada** (page 289) and **Suranadi** (page 290).

Beaches The main beach resort area is **Senggigi** (page 270), while the **Gilis** (page 276) and **Kuta** (page 295) cater largely to budget travellers.

Natural sights Mount Rinjani dominates the island and can be climbed in 3-4 days (page 286).

Culture and performance Traditional villages in the centre (page 289) and south (page 294).

Sports Diving and snorkelling off the Gilis (page 276), **Kuta** for surfing (page 295).

Shopping Traditional **ikat textiles** from Pringgasela (page 291) and from workshops in Mataram (page 263) and basketry from Kota Raja (page 291).

West Nusa Tenggara

Bus *Perama*, 66 Jl Pejanggik 66, Mataram T635936 and 635928, and *Wannen* (also called *Nomad*), 4 Jl Erlangga Mataram, T631177, both operate shuttle buses geared to foreign requirements from Bali to Lombok. They both serve **Mataram**, **Senggigi Bangsal**, **Kuta**, **Lembar**. *Nomad* includes the boat trip to the Gilis, *Perama* goes to Tetebatu.

Road

There are shuttle buses from Bali, and buses to major destinations in Java, and also east to Sumbawa; *Damai Indah*, Jl Hasanuddin 17, Cakranegara (for Bali and Surabaya); *Karya Baru*, Jl Pejanggik, Mataram (for Surabaya, Bandung and Jakarta). A/c buses travel from Mataram to Bima (on Sumbawa) via Sumbawa Besar. Companies that operate this route include *Tirta Sari*, *Langsung Jaya* and *Mawar Indah*, all with offices on Jl Pejanggik. Prices for bus fares from Mataram are set by the government. There are bus connections with: **Jakarta**, **Bandung**, **Yogyakarta**, **Surabaya**, **Komodo**, **Labuhanbajo**, **Ruteng**, **Denpasar**, **Sumbawa Besar**, **Dompu**, **Bima**, and **Sape**. Price includes ferry tickets. The journey from Mataram to Sumbawa Besar is 6½ hrs, and to Bima, 12 hrs. Most buses leave from the Bertais terminal in Cakranegara. At your destination these buses will drop you off at the point along their route closest to your accommodation, you don't have to continue to the terminal. Likewise you can arrange to be picked up from your hotel.

Catamaran *Mabua Express* operate a round trip from Benoa (Bali) to **Lembar** on an a/c boat with aircraft seats and 'in-flight' video (2 daily from Dec to Jan and Jul to Aug, twice a week only in low season). The journey takes 2 hrs (US$20-30 depending on class). Departs Benoa 0800 and 1430, returns from Lembar 1130 and 1730. Booking advised T0361-672370, F672521 on Bali or Lembar T625895, F637224. Office at Jl Langko 11A, T621655, Mataram and on Senggigi Beach (opposite turning to *Senggigi Beach Hotel*). Bemos link Lembar with the Bertais bus terminal and with Mataram and Ampenan. The *Bounty Cruises* depart daily from Benoa, Bali at 0800 and return at 1600 from Lembar, offering similar service of videos and a/c.

Sea

Ferry Ferries sail every 2 hrs (on even hrs), linking **Lembar** (22 km south of Mataram on the west coast) with Padangbai, near Candi Dasa on Bali 4-4½ hrs (5,500-9,000Rp depending on class); arrive 30 mins early for a seat and expect to add on an hr here and there waiting to dock.

Accommodation at Lembar There are several losmen popular with backpackers offering basic accommodation near the port. **E** *Losmen Sri Wahyu*, Jl Pusri. Just over 1 km north of Lembar off the main road; follow the sign. Basic bungalows, squat toilets. Owners can arrange boat hire to some of the islands off the southwest peninsula including Gili Nanggu, Gili Genting, Gili Tangkong, all just to the west of Lembar, and Gili Gede and Gili Poh further to the west. **E** *Serumbung Indah*, 2 km north of the port on main road, T637153. Basic rooms with shared mandi.

Hang onto your luggage & bargain hard: the bemo drivers here are tough negotiators

From Lembar, bemos run to Mataram, Ampenan and the Bertais bus terminal, east of Mataram (for onward connections); for other destinations, it is easier to charter a bemo (for example, a large proportion of the people arriving at Lembar head straight for Bangsal, to catch a boat to the Gilis). There is a ferry linking Labuhan Lombok, on Lombok's east coast, with **Poto Tano** on Sumbawa's west coast. Boats leave Poto Tano hourly from 0330-1630 and at 1830. They leave Lombok on the hr from 0400-2100. This is a very pleasant 2 hr boat trip and boats are rarely crowded. The

Lombok Island

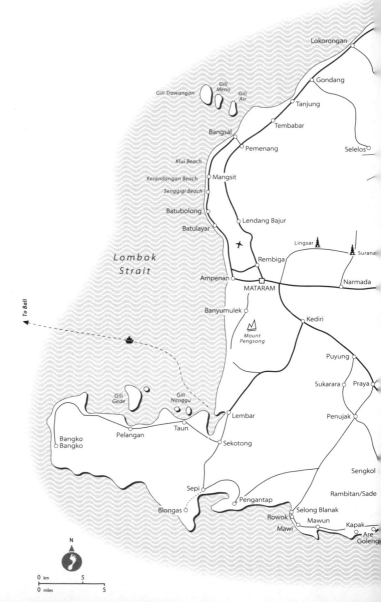

Pelni ship *Awu* docks at Lembar on its fortnightly circuit through Java, Kalimantan, Sumatra, Sulawesi and the islands of Nusa Tenggara. *Tilongkabila* also visits monthly *en route* for Sulawesi and the Philippines. The *Pelni* office is in Ampenan, Jl Industri 1, T37212.

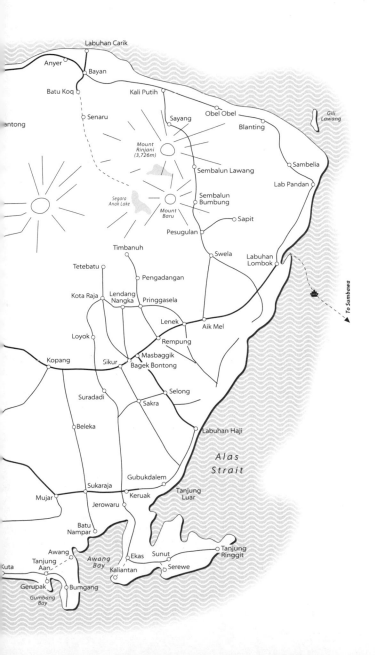

West Nusa Tenggara

Getting around

Lombok's main artery is the excellent road running east from Mataram to Labuhan Lombok. There is now a paved road to Lembar, Praya, Kuta and to Bangsal in the north. Most of Lombok's roads are paved, but the secondary roads are not well maintained and car travel can be slow and uncomfortable, not to mention the hazards of potholes and random rocks for motorcyclists. However, this is likely to change over the next few years as tourism expands.

Bus Minibuses (called bemos here) and colts are the main forms of inter-town and village transport. It is a good cheap way to get around the island and, unlike Bali, frequent changes of bemo are not necessary to get from A to B. However, they can be crowded and beware of being overcharged – check with losmen owners or other travellers before boarding. Foreigners may find it difficult to pay the local rate, particularly going to and from Lembar. The transport hub of Lombok is the Bertais terminal, 3 km east of Cakranegara (see page 269).

See also information on buses in 'Getting there' section above

Other land transport **Hiring** Greatest selection and availability at Senggigi Beach. Generally the cost of hiring transport is higher than on Bali and the vehicles are not as good. You may find it difficult to get insurance. Check everything works before you set off, including the windscreen wipers, and the spare tyre. **Cars**: from 50,000-60,000Rp/day; **Bicycles**: 5,000Rp/day; **Motorbikes**: 25,000Rp/day.

Cidomos These are the Lombok equivalent of the *dokar*, a two-wheeled horse-drawn cart. The word is said to be an amalgamation of *cikar* (a horse cart), *dokar* and automobile (because they now have pneumatic tyres). In the west cidomos are gradually being replaced by bemos, but in the less developed central and east they remain the main mode of local transport and are more elaborate, with brightly coloured carts and ponies decked out with pompoms and bells.

Safety

Riots and unrest broke out in Lombok in January 2000. Chinese-owned businesses were ransacked in Mataram and thousands of tourists, Chinese and Christians fled the island for Bali. The airport was inundated with people hoping to escape and some tourists even took to chartering helicopters. President Wahid accused army officers of fermenting the violence, trying to inflame latent communal and religious antagonisms to undermine his leadership and authority.

Inevitably, the tourist industry was significantly affected by this internationally reported outbreak of violence, and during our last visit in mid-2000 tourist numbers were down and hotel rates highly negotiable - that is if you feel comfortable with milking this misfortune. Many local people are quite clear that *agents provocateur* from elsewhere in the country precipitated the violence in defence of Muslims in Maluku (the Spice Islands). If this is so, then just as soon as these people leave the islands things should settle down to their formerly pretty amicable state of inter-communal affairs (and it seems, in mid-2000, that this was already the case). All locals, whether Muslim, Christian or Hindu were consciously trying to put foreigners at ease during mid-2000.

Ampenan – Mataram – Cakranegara

Mataram, the capital of Lombok, comprises the three towns of Ampenan, Mataram and Cakranegara (usually called Cakra). The boundaries between them have all but disappeared in an urban sprawl which stretches for almost 9 km, from west to east, ending at the bus terminal of Bertais.

Phone code: 0370
Population: 250,000
Colour map 1, grid B3

The port town of Ampenan in the west is of some interest. It has a characterful collection of small streets which include Malay, Arab and Chinese districts, a decaying collection of Dutch-era buildings, and considerable port activity. However, it does have a rather ramshackle, seedy feel. There are a few 'antique' shops, a market and towards the northern edge there is a Chinese cemetery. Mataram has a number of rather grand government buildings and is attractively laid out with broad, tree-lined streets and numerous gardens.

Cakranegara, the former royal capital, was the site of the battle between the Balinese king of Lombok and the Dutch in 1894, during which the palace was badly shelled (see below and page 300). These days, Cakra is the bustling, and in places rather ugly business district, but it also has the best selection of accommodation and shops. People here are very helpful and friendly, and will go out of their way to help you find what you are looking for.

West Nusa Tenggara

Ins and outs

See page 258.

Getting there

There is a one-way road system linking the 3 towns of the 'conurbation'. Bemos run across the city, travelling east down Jl Langko/Pejanggik and Selaparang to the bus terminal and west down Jl Pancawarga/Pendidikan and Jl Yos Sudarso to Ampenan.

Getting around
See also transport section page 269 for more details

Sights

The regional **tourist office** for West Nusa Tenggara, is on Jl Langko 70, T21866. They have maps and brochures and are friendly and helpful. ■ *0700-1400 Mon-Thu, 0700-1100 Fri, 0700-1200 Sat.*

Most of the conurbation's few sights are in Cakranegara, in the east of town. The description below runs from west to east

The **West Nusa Tenggara Provincial Museum** is in Ampenan on Jl Banjar Tilar Negara, at the west end of town. It houses a collection of assorted regional textiles and krisses. ■ *500Rp. 0800-1400 Tue-Thu, 0800-1100 Fri, 0800-1300 Sat-Sun.* Travelling east into Mataram, there are a number of **weaving factories** producing ikat cloth, although rarely in traditional designs. *Rinjani Hand Woven* on Jl Pejanggik was established in 1948 and tends to produce cotton textiles for the Balinese market, using motifs from Sulawesi, Bali and the other islands of Nusa Tenggara as well as Lombok. Behind the shop is a large weaving operation where the various processes can be seen. There is also a number of other factories in this area of town: *Slamet Riyadi Weaving* (which produces Balinese-style cloth) is on Jl Tenun, a narrow back street near the Mayura Water Palace (see below), while the well-known *Sari Kusuma* is at Jl Selaparang 45, in Cakranegara.

To the east, the **Mayura Water Palace and Gardens** and associated Pura Mayura just north of Jl Selaparang were built in 1744 by the Balinese king of Lombok. The Gardens contain a water lily-filled lake, with a floating pavilion – the *Bale Kembang* – set in the centre. The king would conduct audiences here, and originally there were tiers of wooden benches for officials of different grades. These were destroyed in 1894 during the Dutch assault on Cakranegara and have not been replaced, the *Bales Wedas* within the Palace was used to store weapons. ■ *500Rp. 0700-1700.* Across the road to the east of the Gardens is the Balinese **Pura Mayura**, also known as the **Pura Meru**. This temple was built in 1720 by Anak Agung Made Karang and is dedicated to the Hindu trinity – Siva, Vishnu and Brahma. It is composed of three courtyards symbolizing the cosmos. The innermost contains three symbolic Mount Merus, aligned north-south; the central court, two pavilions with raised platforms for displaying offerings; and the outermost, a hall containing a large ceremonial drum. The eleven-tiered meru is dedicated to Siva, and the nine-tiered merus to the south and north, Brahma and Vishnu respectively. ■ *Mon-Sun. Admission by donation.*

Right at the eastern edge of the town is Lombok's main **market** (see 'shopping'), next to the Bertais bus terminal on Jl Selaparang. Also here is the Cakranegara **bird market**. **Horse racing** takes place at the Selagalas track, on Jl Gora, north of the Water Palace, twice a week on Thursday and Sunday from 0800-1200 and at festivals. The ponies are ridden bare-back by young boys. During Ramadan, traditional **stick fighting** can be seen: a mix of graceful turns and harsh clashing of sticks against square shields of buffalo hide.

Excursions

Mount Pengsong Mount or Gunung Pengsong lies about 6 km south of Mataram. There is a small Hindu shrine at the summit and, on clear days, good views over to Bali and Mount Agung and to Mount Rinjani. Japanese solders hid here during the Second World War. Get there by chartered bemo or cidomo.

Mataram

Related map Mataram centre, page 266

N
0 metres 500
0 yards 500

■ Sleeping
1 Granada
2 Lombok Raya
3 Losmen Horas
4 Nitour (Wisma Melati)
5 Selaparang
6 Wisma Triguna

This rugged, arid region offers spectacular views and beautiful, deserted gold sand beaches to the few travellers who venture this way. It is an arduous drive over rough, potholed roads covering approximately 70 km. The sea here is covered with many *bagans* – fishing platforms made of bamboo which the local fishermen use for night fishing, attracting fish into their large nets with powerful lanterns. The area is sparsely inhabited, mostly scrubby with coconut and mangrove along the coast. The road ends at Bangko-Bangko.

The Southwest Peninsula

This sandy beach is 63 km from Mataram, past the harbour of **Lembar**, on the southwest tip of the island. It is a long drive on a poor road. There is sometimes surf here: this is a reef break. There is limited accommodation in bungalows and food. Hiring a jeep is the best way to get there, and in Kute the *Ocean Blue* surf shop, T/F0370-653911 and other helpful surf lovers will gladly arrange a trip out there and get provisions in. You might be able to get a lift on a truck heading down the coast. As the road improves bemos may begin to make the trip. On the way to Bangko-Bangko, the road passes **Taun**, with a good, white sandy beach (42 km from Mataram). **Pelangan** (47 km from Mataram) has a good beach and good snorkelling. From here you can catch a public boat to Gili Gede; **Labunan Poh** (55 km from Mataram) with a Japanese-run pearl farm nearby, is a coastal village from where it is possible to reach **Gili Poh** (good for snorkelling) and **Gili Gede** (a traditional Sasak island).

Bangko-Bangko

One hour by chartered fishing boat from Lembar (30,000Rp), Gili Nanggu is another tiny, but very attractive, island in this group which offers the perfect

Gili Nanggu

West Nusa Tenggara

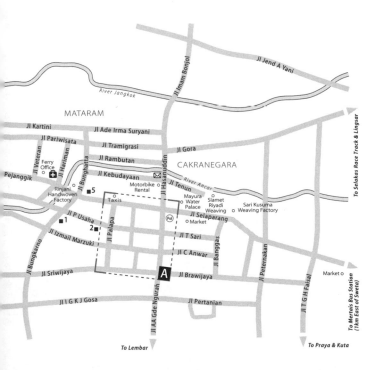

restful hideaway. (For boat hire to the islands ask around at Lembar harbour. Current rates are about 30,000Rp for 2 people, see also page 259. The owners of the Sri Wahyu Losmen can make arrangements for boat hire.) There is only one place to stay by the sea, **C** *Istana Cempaka*, Reservations: Jl Tumpang Sari, Cakranegara, Lombok, T622898. Very attractive bungalows on beach with private mandi, price includes breakfast, restaurant serves good freshly caught fish: very friendly Balinese owner who does not want to develop the island. It takes 30 minutes to walk around the island. Reasonable snorkelling. There is also basic losmen accommodation (**E**) in the village.

Essentials

Sleeping   The best selection of accommodation for travellers is in Cakra. Several small hotels and guesthouses are located in a pretty residential area of quiet lanes leading off Jl Pejanggik.

Ampenan **B** *Nitour (Wisma Melati)*, Jl Yos Sudarso 4, T623780, F636579. A/c, comfortable rooms, hot water and Western toilets, small garden, breakfast on verandah, rather overpriced, will offer substantial discount if they are not full. **C-E** *Hotel Zahir*, Jl Koperasi 32, T644485, variety of rooms nothing special, but has internet access. **E** *Wisma Triguna*, Jl Koperasi 76, T631705. Restaurant, basic large rooms with private bathrooms with Western toilet, could do with redecoration but good source of trekking information, set around large courtyard garden. **F** *Losmen Horas*, Jl Koperasi, a few doors down from *Hotel Zahir*, T631695, basic but decent, Eddy will arrange tours and treks. **D-E** *Wisata*, Jl Koperasi. Restaurant, a/c, smart grounds, good little on site shop. **F** *Angin Mamiri*, the last losmen on Jl Koperasi, T631713. A slightly bizarre, ramshackle place but a good chance to stay with an extended family who are very friendly. Not a word of English spoken, though.

Mataram centre

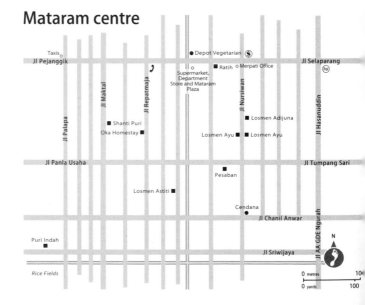

Mataram If you require a mini pool and/or meeting room there are a couple of upmarket hotels: **B** *Hotel Granada*, Jl Bung Karno, T622275 F623856. Small pool, meeting rooms and other business facilities. **B** *Hotel Sahid Legi*, Jl Sriwijaya, T636282, F632681. Small pool and reasonably comfortable business style hotel. **C** *Hotel Nitour*, Jl Yos Sudarso, T625328. Good coffee shop, poor pool. **C-E** *Paradiso*, Jl Angsoka 3, T632074. Just off the main drag of Mataram is this newly opened place with a leafy residential feel, spacious courtyard, TV, conference room, breakfast. Good value. There are several cheap losmen on Jl Pancawarga. **D** *Wisma Giri Putri*, Jl Pancawarga 29, T633222. Some a/c, attractive house, clean rooms, lofty stark restaurant.

Cakranegara **A** *Lombok Raya Hotel*, 11 Jl Panca Usaha, T632305, F636478. Attractive hotel with large pool set in tropical gardens, 135 rooms with private bath or shower, a/c, minibar, TV, telephone, balcony or verandah. Facilities include conference rooms, restaurant (mid-range to cheap) serving continental and Indonesian food, bar, coffee shop, 24-hr room service, car rental. The Garuda office is in the lobby. **B** *Granada*, Jl Bung Karno, T622275, F623856. A/c, restaurant, pool, best hotel in the area, attractive tropical gardens and aviary, good rooms with adequate services. **B-D** *Handika*, Jl Panca Usaha 3, T633578, F635049. Some a/c, reasonable restaurant, poor breakfast included in price, rooms are standard but clean, rates negotiable, central location, friendly staff, the hotel organizes car rental and tours. **B-D** *Hotel Pesaban*, 30 Jl Panca Usaha, T621378, 632936. Large, clean rooms with private bathrooms all with squat toilets, set in attractive gardens. Price includes tax and breakfast. Restaurant (cheap). **B-D** *Hotel Ratih*, 127 Jl Pejanggik, T631096, 626269, 626444, F624865. Mainly geared to Indonesian businessmen. 43 simple rooms with private bathrooms, Western toilet, a/c or fan, some with TV and telephone. Set in large gardens. **C** *Mataram*, Jl Pejanggik 105, T623411. Some a/c, price includes breakfast. **C-D** *Puri Indah*, 132 Jl Sriwijaya, T637633. Pleasant location on the outskirts of town, on the boundary between Mataram and Cakra, facing rice fields. Rooms are clean but a bit tatty and in need of redecoration, breakfast is not included. 30 simple rooms with private bathroom, shower, Western toilet, some rooms with a/c and TV. Decent sized pool and large gardens. Staff very friendly and speak good English. Restaurant (cheap). This hotel suffered fire damage in the violent demonstrations of 17 January 2000, and at the time of writing had not re-opened. **C-E** *Ayu*, Jl Nursiwan 20, T621761. Set around attractive courtyard, basic rooms with mandi, squat toilet, more expensive newer rooms across the road with Western toilet and fan or a/c, Balinese owner, price includes breakfast. **C-E** *Orinda*, close to Mertais Bus Terminal on Jl TLH Faisal, T624900. Friendly staff, clean rooms with showers, and a good restaurant. **C-E** *Shanti Puri*, Jl Maktal 15, T632649. Well run travellers' hotel with a range of rooms from basic with shared mandi and squat toilet, up to a/c or fan with Western toilet; rooms with balcony or verandah. Owner speaks good English and can help with travel information, airline/bus ticket bookings, bemo prices, motorbike or car hire, tours etc. Noticeboard with travel information, secondhand book exchange. Price includes breakfast and afternoon tea. Restaurant (cheap). Recommended. **D** *Selaparang*, Jl Pejanggik 40-42, T632670. Some a/c, clean, reasonable rooms. **E** *Adiguna Losmen*, 9 Jl Nursiwan, T625946 (behind BCA bank). 20 simple rooms with private mandi, squat toilet, set in small gardens. Price includes a good breakfast and afternoon tea/coffee. **E** *Oka Homestay*, 5 Jl Rapatmaja, T622406. A genuine homestay in the grounds of the family house, down a quiet side street off the main Cakra thoroughfare. 5 simple rooms with private mandi, squat toilet and fan. Set in large gardens full of birds and fruit trees. Price includes breakfast and tea/coffee all day. Run by a very friendly family whose son, Mut, speaks excellent English and has lived in Australia. They sometimes arrange BBQs and can help with information and travel advice. Often full even off-season. Highly recommended.

West Nusa Tenggara

Eating **Cheap** *Cirebon*, Jl Yos Sudarso 113. Ampenan, Chinese and seafood, very popular. *Aroma*, Jl Palapa 1. Good atmosphere, good food. *Timur Tengah* Jl Koperasi, T623073. Yummy, easy food and a good *nasi goreng*. *Flamboyant*, Jl Pejanggik 101. Seafood, with attractive ambience. *Depot Vegetarian*, Jl Pejanggik, opposite Mataram Plaza. Serves good, cheap Indonesian and Chinese food, includes meat. **Very cheap** *RM Cendana*, Jl Nurgiwan, Cakra. Clean, conveniently located near travellers' losmen. *Pondok Indah garden restaurant*, Jl Sriwijayah 2. Lovely berugas in neat garden, popular with courting Indonesians, does a tasty *es jampur* (multi coloured jelly in milk and ice, with palm fruit). *Warungs*, opposite *Astiti Guesthouse* in Cakranegara. *Café Inilah*, Jl Panca Usaha T641016. Popular with locals. Each warung has a different speciality and you sit inside a tent at a long wooden table. Friendly place, delicious food. Recommended. There are several warungs along Jl Yos Sudarso, in Ampenan, and scattered down side streets in Cakra and Mataram. You may have to look carefully to spot one as they often look like private homes: eg *Depot Sari* Jl Rapatmaja, which produces great *gado-gado*. **Kentucky Fried Chicken**, Cakra Plaza, Jl Pejanggik; *Selaparang*, Jl Pejanggik, next to *Rinjani's Weaving*.

Festivals **March/April** (7th): *Balinese Hindu New Year*, stone statues called *Ogoh Ogoh* are paraded through the streets to the Water Palace. Later they are burnt at the beach for purification, but some people can't resist taking them home instead. (16th): *Anniversary of Mataram* is marked by parades and performances. **May** (5th): *Hindu rice harvest festival*. **June** *Pura Meru festival*. **August** (17th): *Independence Day*. **October** (5th): *War memorial*. **November/December** (15th day of the 4th month of the Balinese lunar calendar): *Pujawali* held at Pura Meru in Cakranegara, at Pura Kalasa (Narmada) and at Pura Lingsar (north of Cakra). The Pujawali ceremony is followed 3 days later by the *ketupat war*, when participants throw *ketupat* (steamed rice wrapped in palm leaves) at one another. **December** (17th): *Anniversary of West Nusa Tenggara* is celebrated with dance and wayang kulit performances.

Shopping **Antiques**: there are a number of shops in Ampenan on the road north towards Senggigi, most with rather poor quality merchandise. Despite the layer of authentic dust, virtually none of the pieces on sale is antique. The original shop on this strip was *Sudirman*, Jl Yos Sudarso 88; close by is *Hary Antiques*, Jl Saleh Sungkar Gg Tengiri 2. *Renza Antique*, Jl Sudarso 29, for pottery and antiques. Antique kris spears and good information from knowledgeable family – contact Putu Mustika, Jl Tambanus 9, T633301. **Baskets**: the market next to the Mertais bus terminal (east of town) on Jl Selaparang sells local products, including baskets. **Handicrafts**: *Lombok Asli*, Jl Gunung Kerinci 36 (near the University); *Lombok Craft Project*, Jl Majapahit 7, T633804; *Pandawa*, Jl Ismail Marzuki; *Sidhu Putra*, Jl Gora 36, Cakranegara. **Markets**: Cakra market has everything from Calvin Klein's to bananas and counterfeit tapes. Sindu cheap crafts and blankets from all over Lombok. The (Sweta) Bertais market has everything including the kitchen sink. A real mix of aromas and sights, with a bird section to add some sound effects. **Pottery**: *Lombok Pottery Centre*, Jl Majapahit 7 (near the museum) T/F633804. This shop/showroom stocks some of the best earthenware goods produced in the village of Banyumulek, one of the main pottery centres on the island. *Sasak Pottery*, Jl Koperasi 102 (5 mins from airport), T631687, F31121. The largest pottery company on Lombok which also houses, so it is said, the largest earthenware showroom in Indonesia. The company also operates several hotel-based shops, and oversees the packing side of its business for shipment overseas. **Supermarket**: *Galael's*, Cakra Plaza Blok B, Jl Pejanggik. *Mataram Supermarket*, Jl Pejanggik 139B, well stocked, competitive prices. A huge megalith of a shopping mall is due to open near Bertais providing there is no more civil unrest. A number of investors, particularly in agricultural commodities, have pulled out of Lombok since January 2000. Remaining investors and entrepreneurs were just hanging in there, hoping for the best. **Textiles**: *Rinjani Hand Woven*, Jl Pejanggik 46, good value cotton and silk, ikat. Other weaving shops including *Sari Kusuma*, Jl Separang 45 and *Slamet Riyadi*, Jl Tenun 10, off Jl Hassanudin. Weaving demonstrations in the mornings.

Diving companies *Corona*, Jl Dr W Rambige, Mataram; *Rinjani*, Jl Pemuda, Mataram, T621402; *Satriavi*, Jl Pejanggik 17, Mataram, T621788; *Koperasi Wisata Rinjani*, Jl Pedidikan 25, Mataram, T635040; *CV Baronang Dive Centre*, Jl Mawar 13 T627793. *The Water Boom* waterpark, is now open in Mataram with slides and rapids, 10000Rp. **Horse racing** Every Sun at Selagalas village, 4 km from Mataram. **Golf** *Golong Golf Course* (east of Narmada), 9 holes, charmingly informal. Office: Jl Langko 27, Mataram, T22017. **Massage** *Subur Jaya*, (ask at Oka Homestay) is a good bet with guaranteed no wandering hands. **Pool and tennis** Available at Taman Mayura.

Sports

Bidy Tours, Jl Ragigenep 17, T632127. *Environmental Forum*, Jl Pejanggik 10B. *Mavista*, Jl Pejanggik Complek, Mataram, T622314. *Nominasi*, Jl Dr Wahidin 3, T621034. *Peramaswara*, Jl Pejanggik 66, T623368, 622764. *Putri Mandalika*, Jl Pejanggik 49, T622240. *Sakatours*, Jl Langko 7-8, T623114. *Satriavi*, Jl Pejanggik 17, T621788. *Setia*, Jl Pejanggik; *Wisma Triguna*, Jl Adisucipto 76, Ampenan, T621705 for 3 or 4 day hikes to the summit of Mount Rinjani.

Tour operators
The tourist information office at Ampenam has a comprehensive leaflet listing a further 26 tour & travel agents

Local Car hire: available from *Avis*, *Nitour Hotel*, Jl Yos Sudarso 4, T626579. *CV Metro*, Jl Yos Sudarso 79. *CV Rinjani*, Jl Bungkasno; *CV Surya*, Jl Raya Senggigi. **Dokars**: for short journeys around town. **Motorbike hire**: Several in town. Most travellers' guest-houses can rent cars/motorbikes but cannot supply insurance.

Transport

Bemo/bus The Terminal Induk Bertais, Lombok's transport hub, is on Jl Selaparang at the east edge of Cakranegara (2 km east of Mataram). Regular buses and bemos from here to **Labuhan Lombok** (and on to Sumbawa), **Bangsal** (for the Gilis), **Tanjung**, **Keruak** and **Bayan**. Bemos wait on Jl Salah Singkar to pick up passengers for *Senggigi Beach* (see 'Ins and outs' for bemo routes in town). Buses will drop you off at the point along their route nearest your destination if you ask. *Perama* run a bus service geared to tourists, see page 262. **Boat** *Pelni* office T637212, open: Mon-Sat 0900-1400.

Airline offices *Garuda*, T637950, 637951, in *Hotel Lombok Ralya*, Jl Panca Usaha. Open Mon-Fri 0730-1630. Sat and Sun 0900-1300. *Merpati*, Jl Pejanggik 69, T636745, 632226. There is also a *Merpati* office at Jl Yos Sudarso 4 (next to the *Nitour Hotel*). *Silk Air*, Pacific Supermarket, Jl Raya Senggigi, T693877, F693822. **Banks** *Bank Central Asia*, Jl Pejanggik 67, Cakra; *Bank Negara Indonesia*, Jl Langko 64. *Bank Rakyat Indonesia*, Jl Pejanggik 16; Money changers on road into Ampenan from Senggigi. More banks in smart high rise buildings opening along Jl Pejanggik including *Bank Exim*. They all change foreign currency and TCs. **Communications** General post office: Jl Majapahit Taman, Mataram T621345. **Post office**: Jl Langko 21, Ampenan. **Telephone office**: Jl Langko. Perumtel: Jl Pejanggik. **Internet**: at Post office; Laba_Laba_internet@hotmail.com, Jl Pejanggik 43, Mataram; fastest access at *Yan's Internet Café* round the corner, Jl Subak 2, T623828; and *Indo.net*, Cilinaya Plaza blok A17 Jl Panca Usaha, and next to the main Wartel is *E Computer*. **Medical services** Hospitals: *General Hospital*, Jl Pejanggik 6, Mataram, T621345. **Useful addresses** Immigration Office: Jl Udayana 2, T622520.

Directory

West Nusa Tenggara

Lombok's west coast

Most visitors to Lombok stay either at Senggigi Beach or on the 'Gilis'. Senggigi Beach stretches over 8 km from Batulayar to Mangsit. The road from Mataram to Bangsal winds through impressive tropical forest in the foothills of Mount Rinjani. A strategically placed 'coffee house' offers fabulous views of the surrounding countryside from the highest point on the road. Travelling further north along the coast from Mangsit, the road reaches Bangsal, the 'port' for boats to the Gilis. Senggigi is the most developed tourist area on Lombok with a range of budget and more expensive hotels. It is easy to see why this area was chosen by investors and local entrepreneurs. The beaches here – and they extend over several kilometres – are picturesque and the backdrop of mountains and fabulous sunsets adds to the ambience. While Senggigi village supports the main concentration of shops, bars, restaurants, tour companies and such like, hotels and bungalows stretch along the coast and the road for 8 km or so. The Gilis – three small islands off the coast north of Senggigi – are very different. While there are one or two more expensive places to stay, these islands are primarily geared to the backpacker market. There are no vehicles and there really isn't much more to do beyond sunbathing, swimming, snorkelling and generally relaxing. The size of the islands – minuscule – means that walking never becomes much more than a gentle stroll.

Senggigi

Phone code: 0364
Colour map 1, grid B3

Lombok's principle beach resort, Senggigi, lies 12 km north of Mataram on the island's west coast. The beach overlooks the famous Lombok Strait which the English naturalist Alfred Russel Wallace postulated divided the Asian and Australasian zoological realms (see box, page 302). The sacred Mount Agung on Bali can usually be seen shimmering in the distance. Hotels and bungalows are in fact found over an 8 km stretch of road and beach from Batulayar Beach in the south, to Batubolong, Senggigi, and Mangsit beaches, to the north. Mangsit is quieter and less developed, although there are a number of hotels under construction and land speculation is rife.

Many visitors express disappointment with Senggigi Beach itself which is rather tatty, overdeveloped and not very attractive. There are many hotels catering largely for the package tour trade, and they are not always particularly well-managed, or maintained. Their rates are highly negotiable off season. Many of the best guesthouses on Lombok are Balinese owned, and as prices on Bali rise inexorably, they no longer seem as overpriced as they once did.

Some regular visitors recommend avoiding Senggigi and staying at one of the beaches further north which are still quiet and undeveloped and offer beautiful, windswept beaches with lovely views across the Lombok Strait to Mount Agung on Bali and superb sunsets. They are also at present free of the hawkers that so mar a visit to Senggigi itself.

Sights In the mornings between 0800 and 1100, hundreds of brightly coloured fishing boats return to the beach. The fishermen leave at 0500 and use traditional methods of fishing eschewing nets for a length of string with 30 hooks; when the string feels heavy they know it is time to haul it in. If the wind is onshore they fish off Mangsit, if the wind is offshore they fish off Senggigi beach.

Two kilometres south of Senggigi, on a headland, is the **Batubolong Temple**. Unremarkable artistically (particularly when compared with the temples of Bali), it is named after a rock with a hole in it (*Batu Bolong* or 'Hollow Rock') found here. Tourists come to watch the sun set over Bali – devotees, to watch it set over the sacred Mount Agung.

Each evening an informal **beach market** sets-up on the beach in front of the Senggigi Beach Hotel; vendors lay out their wares (textiles, t-shirts, woodcarvings and 'antiques'); heavy bargaining is required – these people really know how to sell.

Senggigi Beach

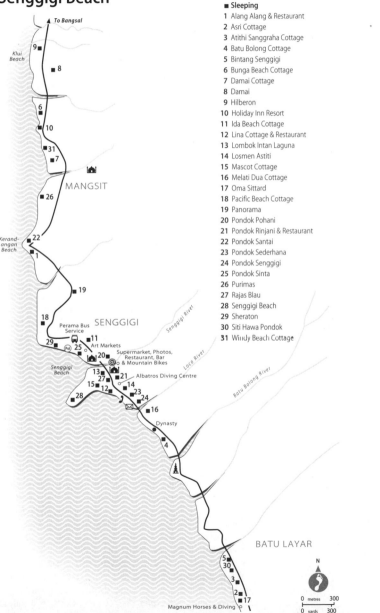

■ **Sleeping**
1 Alang Alang & Restaurant
2 Asri Cottage
3 Atithi Sanggraha Cottage
4 Batu Bolong Cottage
5 Bintang Senggigi
6 Bunga Beach Cottage
7 Damai Cottage
8 Damai
9 Hilberon
10 Holiday Inn Resort
11 Ida Beach Cottage
12 Lina Cottage & Restaurant
13 Lombok Intan Laguna
14 Losmen Astiti
15 Mascot Cottage
16 Melati Dua Cottage
17 Oma Sittard
18 Pacific Beach Cottage
19 Panorama
20 Pondok Pohani
21 Pondok Rinjani & Restaurant
22 Pondok Santai
23 Pondok Sederhana
24 Pondok Senggigi
25 Pondok Sinta
26 Purimas
27 Rajas Blau
28 Senggigi Beach
29 Sheraton
30 Siti Hawa Pondok
31 Windy Beach Cottage

●●

☞ *The plight of turtles on Bali and Lombok*

Although the Muslims of Lombok do not eat turtle meat they do eat the eggs. On neighbouring Bali, turtle meat is considered a great delicacy; it is made into satay and lawar (a Balinese speciality consisting of ground meat, blood and spices) and is an important ingredient in the ceremonial feasts that accompany religious festivals. Up to 25,000 green turtles a year used to be killed for their meat. In 1990, following appeals by the Worldwide Fund for Nature and with the green turtle facing extinction, a law was passed banning fishermen from catching them, except for ceremonial use. However, with a market value over 250,000Rp there is a great temptation to catch them illegally. Hornbill turtles were caught for their shells but since 1992 trade in tortoiseshell has been banned by CITES.

Turtles cover vast distances; some from Southeast Asia have been sighted as far away as Greece, verifiable because of tagging. Turtles return to the beach where they were born to breed; the magnetism of that beach is imprinted in their brains and they know where to return to decades later. Having laid her eggs the mother turtle will dig a second dummy nest in order to deceive predators. Turtle hatchlings will not emerge if the sun is too hot; they wait for the cool air of night. Some research suggests that temperature influences gender with more females being born when the temperature of the nest is hotter. Turtle eggs are softer at one end to allow the hatchlings to break out easily without damaging neighbouring eggs. Even with man's help, when the hatchlings are released into the sea only as few as six out of 200 may survive.

(See page 284 for information on turtle conservation.)

●●

Sleeping **Senggigi** The accommodation on 'Senggigi' is spread out for several kilometres along the main beach road and extends north to Kerandangan Beach, Klui Beach and Mangsit. All the hotels and guesthouses are easily accessible by bemo from Mataram. The better hotels have generators for when the mains power fails, which it does quite often. In the last two years over 10 new hotels have filled in the gaps between Batu Layar and Mangsit. There appears to be little separating them from the others in their respective price range. As noted earlier, the calamitous decline in Lombok's tourist fortunes has meant that hotel rates – at least in 2000 – were highly negotiable.

L-AL *Oberoi Lombok*, PO Box 1096, Mataram 833001, T638444, F632496, oberoil@ indosat.net.id, http://www.oberoihotels.com/lombm.htm New, luxury, 28 km from Mataram and north of Senggigi on Medana Beach. Just 50 individual bungalows. Facilities include beachside café, restaurant, cultural performances, pool, 18-hole golf course, tennis, business centre, good disabled access. **AL** *Sheraton*, Jl Raya Senggigi Km 8, PO Box 1154, T693333, F693140. A/c, restaurant, free-form pool, largest and newest addition to Senggigi, facilities include tennis courts, fitness centre and jacuzzi set into an attractive pool on beach-front. **A** *Ida Beach Cottages*, PO Box 51, T693013. A/c, restaurant, pool, situated above the beach, ornate rooms set on the side of the hill overlooking the sea, hot water. **A** *Lombok Intan Laguna*, PO Box 50, T693090, intan@ mataram.wasantara.net.id A/c, restaurant, attractive pool, most exclusive hotel on Senggigi until displaced by the *Sheraton*, good sports facilities. **A** *Puri Mas*, T/F693023, at the northern end of the beach. Pricey villas with beautiful ornate doors and balconies, and bungalows, expensive non-inventive restaurants. Further on is **A-C** *Alang Alang*, offering the same facilities, such as a good pool, and a restaurant which has a wide range of Indonesian food and concocts Western-style dishes with refreshing accuracy. **A** *Senggigi Beach*, PO Box 2, T693339, F693185. A/c, restaurant, pool, large, well-run hotel, in prime position, with extensive grounds, greater competition should improve it, overpriced. **A-B** *Graha*, T693400, central location, slightly to the south of the mass of hotels and places to eat. A/c, restaurant, watersports available, hot water, price includes breakfast.

B *Mascot Cottages*, PO Box 100, T693365, F693236. A/c, restaurant, large but rather dark rooms with hot water, no pool. **B** *Pacific Beach Cottages*, PO Box 36 (north of Senggigi), T693027. A/c, restaurant, shadeless pool, a bit tatty. Next door is the **B** *Panorama*, due for completion any minute, an excellent viewpoint for the sunset. **C** *Asri Beach Cottages*, Jl Senggigi, T693075. The rooms in the new block are reasonable, those in the older 2-storeyed bungalows are dirty and in poor condition. **C** *Batu Bolong Cottages*, Batubolong Beach, T693065, F693198. Restaurant, large, clean rooms but nothing special, rooms on the beach are more expensive. **C** *Pondok Senggigi*, T693273. Restaurant, traditional huts in garden compound, good value but wrong side of the road for the beach, loud music might disturb some. The **B-C** *Oma Sittard*, T693684, F693685, sittard@indo.net.id Leafy location, Lombok style luxury cottages with first floor balconies not facing the sea!

D *Atithi Sanggraha*, Jl Senggigi, Batu Layar (south of Senggigi), T693070. Average. **D** *Melati Dua*, Jl Raya Senggigi Km 13, T693288. Clean, popular. **C** *Bumi Aditya*, T693782, F693862, senggigi@indo.net.id High standards, great setting, set away from the beach down a track running inland, kids stay free, doctor on call, a/c, pool, bamboo walls inside, brick veneer exterior serious handicap. **D** *Pondok Rinjani*, PO Box 76, T693274, 693170. Basic accommodation in central Senggigi, set in large garden with 2 enormous live turkeys, private bathrooms with shower and Western toilet. Could do with a little redecoration, price does not include breakfast, restaurant (cheap), you might be disturbed by loud music from *Pondok Senggigi*. **E** *Astiti*, next to mosque, T693041. Ceiling fan, en suite mandi, price includes breakfast, some noise from mosque, otherwise quite peaceful. **E** *Pondok Shinta*, Senggigi, T693012. Probably the cheapest place to stay in Senggigi, catering for backpackers, basic rooms, some with private mandi, squat toilets, would benefit from redecoration, friendly, good value, price includes breakfast, tiny huts, near beach, central position. **E** *Siti Hawa Pondok*, Jl Raya Senggigi 999, Batu Layur, 4 km south of Senggigi, T695414. Budget accommodation by sea, price includes breakfast and tea all day. Bicycles for hire, Indonesian dinner with family. Siti Hawa's husband is a New Zealander and runs a programme to help 'poor village people' from the hostel, guests are welcome to become involved. **E** *Sonya*, behind *Kartika Restaurant*, T693447. Only really low budget place to stay on the whole beach, restaurant, fan, clean rooms with attached showers, terrace, good breakfast included, order meals in the morning if you want to eat in (good food).

Kerandangan Heading north from Senggigi the first beach is Kerandangan where the *Park Royal Group* is due to build a luxury hotel. In May 2000, however, the site was still not even showing a hint of construction, and with the proliferation of upmarket hotels along this stretch of beach, perhaps it would be better to not bother.

AL *Hilberon*, north of Klui Beach, Austrian owned, well-managed luxury hotel in attractive grounds beside quiet beach, restaurant. **AL** *Holiday Inn*, T693444, F693092. Mangsit, new, spacious and well designed, offering everything you would expect from this hotel chain including an arrow on the ceiling of each room to indicate the direction of Mecca. A/c, fabulous large bathrooms, satellite TV, tea and coffee making facilities in each room, minibar. Shopping arcade, water sports, tennis, fitness centre, children's playground, swimming pool, restaurants and outdoor cultural performance stage, set in 5 ha of tropical gardens, convention facilities. **A** *Bunga Beach Cottages* (at Klui Beach just north of Mangsit), PO Box 1118, T693035, F693036. 14 large, very attractive, a/c thatched cottages set in colourful, tropical

West Nusa Tenggara

gardens with swimming pool, beside the sea, excellent restaurant (mid-range). Helpful French co-owner, Anja, in residence, reservations essential at all times of the year for this very select, superbly run 'hotel'. Highly recommended. **A** *Lombok Dame Indah (Damai) Cottages*, Lendang Guar, Pemenang Barat, 12 km north of Senggigi 83352 (PO Box 1128), T693246, 693247, F693248. Cottages with bath, pool, restaurant. Tours, snorkelling and diving available. Set on opposite side of road to beach, on a hillside overlooking the Lombok Strait, traditional style Sasak bungalows, well furnished, quiet hotel. **A-C** *Santai Beach Bungalows*, Mangsit, T/F693038. Attractive, well-managed thatched bungalows built in the Sasak style, tastefully furnished with fan, private bathroom with Western toilet and shower. Set in a coconut grove beside the sea, restaurant (mid-range). **C** *Windy Beach Cottages*, Mangsit, PO Box 1116, T693191, 693192, F693193. 14 attractive traditional style thatched bungalows with fan, private bathroom with shower/bath, Western toilet, some with hot water. Set in large gardens amidst a coconut grove beside the sea, restaurant (cheap) offering good Indonesian, Chinese and Western food. Can arrange tours in their own vehicles, car hire available, well-managed, Windy's husband is a Scotsman from Lerwick in the Shetland Isles. They are also the local *Perama* shuttle bus agent. Recommended.

C-D *Pondok Damai*, Mangsit Beach Inn (reservations address: Jl Bangau 7, Cakranegara 83231), T693019. 15 attractive thatched bungalows set in beautiful gardens with assorted fruit trees, beside the sea. Private bathrooms featuring an indoor garden with shower and Western toilet, fan, TV, restaurant (cheap). Recommended. **E** *Pantai Inga*, southern end of Jl Raya, clean with shared showers, breakfast included. Fan rooms, thin walls, pool table, sometimes there is live music next door, so it can be noisy, 100 m from a quiet stretch of beach. Further on is **E-F** *Coconut Budi* with basic rooms, but cheaper than the rest if that is your criterion. **E** *Pondok Siti Hawa*, Batu Layar, 1½ km north of Senggigi. 3 chalets on the beach, each a different style, plus a few rooms near the road. Very friendly family, clean place, with breakfast included in price. Dinner with the family is also possible. Mr Hussein, the owner, donates all his profits to improving the lifestyle of the local villagers; he has initiated recycling programmes, built toilet facilities, provided money for schooling for the poorest children. 2 more chalets are planned for the future. Recommended.

Eating There are not many independent restaurants on Senggigi – most eating places are attached to hotels. However, with the recent and continuing rapid expansion in accommodation there has been an increase in the number of restaurants.

Cheap *Café Wayang*, on main road in Senggigi, T693098. A branch of the one in Ubud, Bali, building has character (complete with family of mice in the rafters!), but service not up to full speed. *Dynasty*, large open-air restaurant, overlooking the sea on the road to Senggigi, remains empty, except when there is some kind of local event. *Gossip*, Jl Lazoardi (near *Senggigi Beach Hotel*), live music, good food (particularly seafood) although limited menu. Recommended. *Rumah Makan Padang*, Jl Raya, 200 m south of the post office on the other side of the road, hidden in the corner, good typical spicy Lombok food, open 24 hrs. *Princess of Lombok*, T693011. Excellent Mexican food, steaks and seafood and live music. Free pick up from Senggigi. *Café Alberto*, does an unusual range of pizza and stages cultural shows. In the mall area is *Formula One Racing Café*, which shows Grand Prix on a large screen. Food and board (**C**) available. Nearby *Café Enak* has a European coffeeshop feel and shaded, al fresco tables and tasty food as the name indicates. **Very cheap** *Senang*, opposite the supermarket T693312 the place to be if garlic bread is your favourite, and with a decent *nasi goreng* to boot.

Club Rhinos after 1300 and *Jungle Bar*, which has cocktails sporting names such as Cosmic Colorada, relaxed live acoustic tunes in the day, more dance/disco in evenings.

Pacific supermarket on the main road has everything from food to t-shirts, film and gifts at reasonable prices. A few boutique-cum-craft shops have also popped up, less prone to haggling than the old school vendors, such as the Vrat Gallery.

The *Sasak Gardens* is the centre for watersports, with parasailing, waterskiing, windsurfing, sailing. Diving is very good value here; with two dives costing as little as US$30 off season. **Diving** *Baruna Watersports*, *Senggigi Beach Hotel*, T623430, 693210. *Rinjani* have a branch at the *Intan Laguna Hotel*, T636040, F633972. *Blue Coral Diving*, T693251, Blue_coral@mataram.wasantara.net.id *CV Albatross*, T693399. *Dream Divers*, T/F634547, Dreamdivers@mataram.wasantara.net.ID *Manta Diving*, T/F693239. **Snorkelling**: around Senggigi beach, masks for hire. **Rafting**: *Lombok Inter Rafting*, Perokoan Senggigi Square, T693202, also have branch in Bali. Offers good discount off season, guaranteed to take you off the beaten track, helpful staff, good English.

Anthea Wisata, Jl Lazoardi, T621572. *Bunga Tours* at *Bunga Beach Cottages*, T693035, F693036, guide Ayang has excellent English; *Mavista* at *Mascot Cottages*, T623865; *Nazareth Tours*, T621705 (in Ampenan); *Satriavi*, *Senggigi Beach Hotel*. Day trips to the Gilis; for example, on the *Studio 22 – Anthea Wisata* catamaran (US$20 per head), Jl Lazoardl. *Nazareth Tours* and *Satriavi* both organize treks up Mount Rinjani (see page 286). *Putri Lombok Wisata*, Jl Rasen, T693671, has competitive tour offers, good English and German.

Local Various forms of transport can be hired from travel agents along the main road. **Car hire**: 40,000-60,000Rp per day, both self-drive and with driver. *Kotasi*, Jl Raya Senggigi on main street near *Senggigi Beach Hotel* turning, T693058. **Bicycle hire**: 5,000Rp per day. **Motorbike hire**: 25,000Rp per day.

Road Bemo: bemos wait on Jl Salah Singkar in Ampenan to pick- up fares for Senggigi Beach and north to Mangsit. There are regular bemos linking Ampenan with Mataram, Cakranegara and the main Cakra bemo terminal between 0600-1800, 500Rp. *Perama* have an office here and run a bus service geared to travellers, see page 262.

Banks *Senggigi Beach Hotel* has a bank on site with exchange facilities for non-residents. Money changer at the Pacific Supermarket. **Communications** Post Office: centre of town, along Jl Raya. **Internet**: access on main street from: Bulam@mataram.wasantara.net.id; SenggigiPlanet@mataram.wasantara.net.id; *Millennium 2001*, Pluto@mataram.wasantara.net.id **Useful addresses** Police: opposite *Ida Cottages* (north end of beach).

Bangsal

The coast road north from Senggigi is slow, steeply switchbacking its way over headlands and past some attractive beaches. There is some surf on this part of the coast, mainly reef breaks, surfed by the locals on wooden boards.

Bangsal is just off the main road from Pemenang, and is little more than a tiny fishing village. However, as it is also the departure point for the Gilis, there are a couple of restaurants here which double up as tourist information centres, a ferry booking office, a money changer and a diving company. There is a charge of 2,500Rp per vehicle to drive down to Bangsal from Pemanang on the main road.

Sleeping E *Kontiki Bangsal Beach Inn*, traditional cottages near beach, with a peaceful atmosphere.

Transport
28 km from Mataram

Bemo Regular connections from Mataram or the Bertais terminal in Cakranegara; take a bemo heading for Tanjung or Bayan. Bemos stop at the junction at Pemenang, take a dokar the last 1 km to the coast. From Pelabuhan Lombok there are no direct bemos; either charter one (20,000Rp) or catch a bemo to the Bertais Terminal in Cakranegara and then another travelling to Bayan/Tanjung. From the port of Lembar, it is easiest to club together with other passengers and charter a bemo to Bangsal. **Bus**: regular connections with Lembar with *Perama Tour*, who have an office by the pier and sell all-in bus/ferry tickets to most destinations in Bali (Kuta, Sanur, Ubud, Lovina, Candi Dasa). **NB** it is not worth buying bus tickets on the Gilis; prices are considerably higher. **Sea Boat**: a new high speed boat service with Padangbai on Bali is supposed to be operating, but service is erratic. Regular ferries and boats to the Gilis (see 'Transport' in Gilis).

Directory Tourist offices *Kontiki Coffee Shop* is an informal information centre with a particularly helpful man who will advise on boat crossings; *Perama Tourist Service* (near the beach) provides bus and ferry connections with the Gilis, Senggigi and Lembar, and all towns on Bali. They also organize tours on Lombok as well as an excellent 7-day boat tour from Bangsal to Labuanbajo (Flores) via Moyo Island (Sumbawa) and Komodo. **NB** This tour is considerably cheaper in the opposite direction, ie Labuanbajo to Bangsal. The tour then returns to Bangsal from Labuanbajo along the same route. A worthwhile alternative to travelling overland; 8 people minimum.

The Gilis

Phone code: 0364
Malaria may exist on these islands so be sure to take precautions & be careful when swimming as there are strong currents between the islands

The three tropical island idylls that make up the 'Gilis' lie off Lombok's northwest coast, 20-45 minutes by boat from Bangsal. Known as the 'Gilis' or the 'Gili Islands' by many travellers, this only means 'the Islands' or 'the Island Islands' in Sasak. Most locals have accepted this Western corruption of their language and will understand where you want to go.

With the development of Bali into an international tourist resort, many backpackers have moved east and the Gilis are the most popular of the various alternatives. This is already straining the islands' limited sewerage and water infrastructures. During the peak months between June and August, Gili Trawangan becomes particularly crowded. (Although this was not the case in 2000.)

The attraction of the Gilis resides in their golden sand beaches and the best snorkelling and diving off Lombok – for the amateur the experience is breathtaking. However, the coral does not compare with locations such as Flores and Alor: large sections are dead or damaged (perhaps because of dynamite fishing). There is little to do on the islands except sunbathe, swim, snorkel or dive, or go for walks.

Ins and outs

Getting there Regular boats from Bangsal to the Gilis wait until about 16 people have congregated for the trip to the islands. Boats can also be chartered for the journey, ¾ hr to Gili Trawangan, 30 mins to Gili Meno, 20 mins to Gili Air. In the morning there is rarely a long wait but in the afternoon people have had to wait several hrs. An alternative is to buy a combined bus and boat ticket with one of the shuttle bus companies like *Nomad* or *Perama*. There are various alternatives. Within Lombok there are services from **Mataram** to the Gilis and from **Senggigi** to the Gilis. (From Senggigi, boats sail to the Gilis frequently throughout the day.) From Bali there are services from **Padangbai**, **Candi Dasa** and **Kuta** to the Gilis. Boats leave from 0700 onwards.

Seaweed farming

Seaweed farming is being encouraged off Gili Air as an alternative to fishing in order to protect the coral. Although laws against the use of dynamite fishing were passed in 1984, some fishermen still use it as well as stones to kill the fish, damaging the coral in the process. The waters round the island provide suitable conditions for seaweed farming: there is a good flow of water, but the reef protects the area from unwelcome strong currents; the considerable depth of the Lombok Strait keeps sea temperatures from becoming too high and keeps salinity at a constant level. These are all prerequisites for the successful cultivation of seaweed. From the fishermens' viewpoint seaweed farming has the added attraction of being less hard work than fishing. The green Kotoni variety is grown and is exported for use in the food industry.

The seaweed is farmed by fixing posts in the shallow seabed. Rope is attached to these posts making a frame about 2 m square. At roughly 30 cm intervals nodules of seaweed containing a seedhead are tied onto the rope using strips of shredded plastic bags. The seaweed must remain covered by water so the ropes are held afloat just under the surface using plastic bottles which are due to be replaced by more visually pleasing lengths of bamboo. After 40 days the seaweed is harvested and dried; 7 kg of wet seaweed producing 1 kg dry weight. This is then sold on Lombok for 800Rp a kilogram (or an equivalent value in rice and coffee), each family producing about 50 kg. Cuttings from the harvested seaweed are retained to grow on into the next crop.

West Nusa Tenggara

Getting around The islands themselves are small and compact enough to walk around. Even Gili Trawangan, the largest of the three, is little more than 2 km from end to end. Perama run a shuttle service between the islands which allows you to visit another island for the day, and then return. It is also possible to charter boats. Note that the downturn in tourism may have limited the frequency of departures.

The islands

Gili Trawangan The largest of the three islands – and the furthest west from Bangsal – is Gili Trawangan (Dragon Island). It is the most interesting island because of its hill in the centre; there are several trails to the summit and excellent views over to Mount Rinjani on Lombok from the top. **NB** Give the cows a wide berth. In the opposite direction, you can watch the sun set over Mount Agung on Bali. There is a coastal path around the island, which takes about 2½ hours to walk. Originally a penal colony, it now supports the greatest number of tourist bungalows. These are concentrated along its east coast, as are a number of restaurants (serving good seafood) and bars. For lone travellers seeking company, this is the best island. Snorkelling is good off the east shore, particularly at the point where the shelf drops away near *Blue Marlin Dive Centre* and at the north end of the beach near *Sudi Mampir Bungalows*. But, Gili Trawangan is in danger of ruining itself (like so many other tropical island idylls in the region). Indeed, for some, it already has. The most developed area is becoming brash, loud, and over-developed but the island is large enough to offer peace and tranquillity as well. Gili Air and Gili Meno are quieter, though they too have their noisy areas of discos and loud Western pop music in high season.

Over the years, rumours have abounded regarding Gili Trawangan and its future. A few years ago it was said that the island had been bought by a Japanese consortium who planned to develop it as a centre for upmarket tourism and build a golf course. Informed opinion is that the cost and scale of the infrastructure required to support this is sufficiently great that nothing will happen for a good few years. Other rumours concern a lack of planning permission for certain bungalows which has led to some being razed to the ground; as is usually the case, the reality is not as sensational as the rumours might lead one to believe and it is unlikely that travellers will be disadvantaged by any of the rumours currently doing the rounds.

There is concern on the part of local elders that Gili Trawangan might be becoming too 'Kuta-esque'. The mushrooming of stalls selling tourist items, sarongs etc, along the beach area near the boat landing, and restaurants featuring noisy, alcohol-ridden party nights, undermine the peace of this beautiful island and threaten local standards of morality.

Gili Islands

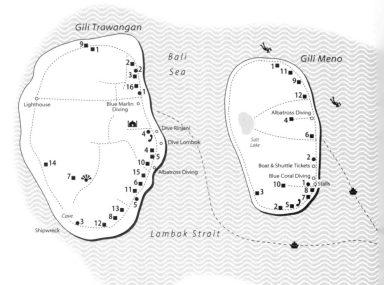

Gili Trawangan	15 Rudy's, Dua Sekawan	7 Kontiki
■ **Sleeping**	II & Damai Indah	8 Malia's Child
1 Cabya Bay	16 Sudi Mampir	9 Pondok Meno
2 Coral Cottages		10 Rawa Indah
3 Creative	● **Eating**	11 Santai
4 Danau Hijau	1 Excellent	12 Zoraya
5 Fantasi Beach	2 Good Heart	
6 Halim	3 Rumah Kita	● **Eating**
7 Iwan Homestay	4 Simple Food	1 Rust
8 Mawar	5 Villa Ombak	2 Wannen
9 Nusa Tiga		
10 Pak Majid, Dua	**Gili Meno**	**Gili Air**
Sekawan I & Sandy	■ **Sleeping**	■ **Sleeping**
Beach Bungalows	1 Blue Coral	1 Bupati's Place
11 Pasih Putih	2 Bougenvil	2 Coconut Cottages &
12 Pondok Santi	3 Bounty Lux Resort	Restaurant
13 Rainbow Cottages	4 Casablanca Cottages	3 Corner Cottage &
14 Rinjani Cottages,	5 Gazebo	Restaurant
Sunset & Mawar II	6 Janur Indah	4 Fantastic Bungalows

N

0 metres 500
0 yards 500

The most 'luxurious' accommodation is found in the developed area of the island behind the restaurants; locals already refer to it being like Kuta, although this is an exaggeration. Here you can find modern air-conditioned rooms with Western bathrooms; unfortunately you lose the peace and beauty associated with a small, relatively undeveloped island as the accommodation is hidden behind the noisy restaurants away from the beach. To find a tropical paradise visitors have to accept more basic facilities at the outer edges of the developed areas. Here guests can hear the waves lapping against the shore and the birds singing, watch truly inspirational sunrises and sunsets from the peace of their verandahs and believe they are in paradise. Room rates triple at some of the more upmarket places in the high season. Even off-peak rooms can become scarce so it is worth arriving on the island early. Gili Trawangan offers the best choice of restaurants of the three 'Gilis', and many people consider that it has the best snorkelling.

Inland from the tourist strip is the original village where life goes on almost as usual, a world apart from the tourists and therefore interesting to stroll through. Further inland there are scattered farms in amongst the coconut groves that dominate the interior, and some pleasant walks to be had.

Gili Meno (Snake Island), between Trawangan and Air, is the smallest of the islands, and also the quietest and least developed. The snorkelling off Gili Meno – especially off the northeast coast – is considered by some to be better than Trawangan, with growths of rare blue coral. There is a path running round the island; a walk of 1-1½ hours. The salt lake in the northeast of the island provides a breeding ground for mosquitoes. Accommodation on Gili Meno tends to be more expensive than on the other two islands and offers worse value for money at every price level. Some of the guesthouse owners live on Lombok and these bungalows are run by lads who are poorly paid and consequently have little motivation. However, the views from the many bungalows which face the sea are beautiful, especially towards the east and Mount Rinjani. Accommodation may be full as early as April, with the season running through September. However, with all the

Gili Meno

Perhaps unfairly, Gili Meno has a reputation as the 'Gili' island where you are at greatest risk of catching malaria. To counterbalance this, the locals insist there are no mosquitoes – none whatsoever!

5 Flying Dutchman on Safari & Restaurant
6 Gili Air & Internet
7 Gili Air Santay & Restaurant
8 Gili Indah, Restaurant, Internet & Reefseekers Dive Centre
9 Gita Gili
10 Gusung Indah Bungalows
11 Matahari
12 Nusa Tiga Bungalows
13 Pondok Gili Air Bungalows & Internet Café
14 Pondok Pantai

15 Salabose Bungalows & Restaurant
16 Sandi Bungalows
17 Yogi

● **Eating**
1 Bunga Tours
2 Haris Café
3 Pino
4 Sunrise

West Nusa Tenggara

recent problems this didn't apply during 2000, and might not do so in the future too – watch this space.

Gili Air

There are mice on the island, so shut food away

Gili Air (Turtle Island) is the easternmost island, lying closest to Bangsal. It has the largest local population, with a village in the centre of the island. The island takes about an hour to walk around. As the local population is Muslim, visitors should avoid topless sunbathing. The government is keen to develop the island sympathetically and to this end is donating 'useful' trees as part of its plan to keep the island green and beautiful. Last year young mango trees were dispatched to Gili Air; the year before, coconut seedlings were being planted all over the island. Despite the number of bungalows, it remains a peaceful place to stay. Snorkelling is quite good off the island. Look out for Imek, the pet deer. She belongs to the owner of the *Gili Indah* but tends to hang out further west near the *Flying Dutchman* and *Salabose* bungalows. Imek follows the island's travelling guitar to the beach parties in search of nightlife, and will knock over your beer and slurp it up if you turn your back! She and her twin brother came from Sumbawa over 10 years ago. Her brother had to be put down as he became increasingly aggressive with age but Imek will stand for hours being petted.

With the downturn in tourism since the 'troubles' of January 2000 the people of Gili Air have formed a grass roots association. The objective is to create a sustainable foundation to preserve their lifestyle and to address the growing environmental distress of the island. Before tourism washed ashore here, Gili Trawangan happily traded rice with Gili Meno for salt from the lake and with Gili Air for nuts and tapioca. It is relatively recently that these idylls have become involved in the cash economy and outside world and some locals at least believe that it might be possible to return to the good ol' days.

Essentials

Security

When leaving your accommodation take sensible precautions and make sure you lock both the door to the bathroom and the front door. As most bathrooms have no roofs, a favoured way for thieves to gain entry is over the bathroom wall and into your room via the bathroom door. **NB** There are no police on the islands, so if you want to make a report, expect the extra hassle of contacting the station at Ampenan or Tanjung.

Sleeping

During the peak months between Jun & Aug it can be difficult to get a room, so arrive early in the day

Many bungalows are upgrading the standard of their rooms; of the more basic ones there is often little difference – they tend to charge the same rates, and the huts are similar in design and size, attractively built out of local materials, in a local style, mostly raised on stilts. Mosquitoes can be a problem at certain times of year and mosquito nets are routinely provided. Rates tend to be in our **E** and **F** categories for the simpler bungalows with either attached or shared mandi, often also including breakfast. The most luxurious bungalows fall into our **A** category. Very few places offer all meals these days. Free tea and coffee are sometimes available all day. Friendliness and the cleanliness of the mandis tends to be the deciding factor at the basic bungalows. The higher the price, the more likely tax and service charge will be extra, and the less likely breakfast will be included. If a/c is important to you, check that it is available during the day and all night. At some accommodations the a/c works off a generator which is only switched on for a few hours at night. There are two upmarket hotels on Gili Meno, one on Gili Air and new modern bungalows with a/c and Western bathrooms on Gili Trawangan.

Gili Trawangan (25 bungalows and rising, mostly along the east coast): **NB** Tips on where to stay from travellers are probably your best bet. Unless otherwise stated all bungalows have private mandis with squat toilets. **A-B** *Blue Marlin*, T632424,

F693043, bmdc@mataram.wasantara.net.id 8 bungalows behind the Blue Marlin dive centre (see the entry below under diving) with a/c, attached hot water showers, and private balconies. **B-D** *Danau Hijau*, modern bungalows with Western bathrooms in built-up area. **B-D** *Fantasi Beach*, perhaps the most upmarket of the bungalows with spring beds, modern rooms and bathrooms, though in the built-up area away from the sea, good breakfast, reports of theft here. **C-D** *Dua Sekawan I* and *Sandy Beach Bungalows*, both offer modern rooms with Western bathrooms, good breakfast, can be noisy as it is situated in the built-up area. **C-D** *Pak Majid* has just been rebuilt to provide modern, attractive rooms with private bathrooms, Western toilet and fan, in the built-up area of the island. **C-E** *Dua Sekawan II*, en suite mandi, toilet and shower, avoid old building, new bungalows are noisy – disco next door. **D** *Creative*, one bungalow has a Western toilet, others with private or shared mandis. **D** *Halim*, on beach, nice bungalows, friendly. Recommended. **D** *Pasih Putih*, price includes breakfast, which is brought to your room every morning, hammocks on the balconies. **D** *Santigi Bungalows*, on beach, outside mandi. Popular. **D** *Trawangan Beach Cottages*, T623582, on beach, outside mandi, noisy. **D** *Wisma Mountain View*, on beach, attached mandi. **D-E** *Coral Cottages*, at the quieter northern edge of bungalow development near to good snorkelling, if you are looking for a Western toilet, two of the bungalows have squat toilets raised on concrete to seat height! – not a huge success but perhaps better than nothing. **D-E** *Nusa Tiga*, one of the best locations on its own at the north end of the island set in large gardens with three colourful 'tame' parrots. Clean and quiet, excellent breakfast included, private mandi with squat toilet, the water here is very saline. Good restaurant, serving cheap food and large portions, good value; 15-min walk from the bars, owner organizes 'all you can eat' Indonesian buffets. **D-E** Next door is new Chinese losmen **C-D** *Caby Bay*. **D-E** *Pondok Santi*, set in a peaceful coconut grove at the southern end of the island, well made bungalows with western toilets. During the rainy season the coconut palms block out some light so the bungalows are damper with more mosquitoes, 20-min walk to the best snorkelling, joint owner is from Australia. **D-E** *Rainbow Cottages*, in a quieter area to the south, joint owner is from Holland. **D-E** *Rudy's Bungalows*, off beach, some attached mandis. **D-E** *Sudi Mampir*, one of the best locations with each bungalow facing the sea and memorable views of the sunrise over Mount Rinjani, situated in a quiet corner of the island. **D-E** *Mawar II* (4 bungalows), **D-E** *Rinjani Cottages* (4 bungalows), **E** *Simple Bungalows*, off beach, simple. **E** *Sunset* (10 bungalows with 2 beds, mosquito nets, oil lamps, hammocks on balconies and a large breakfast). All 3 of these establishments are situated on the western side of the island, taking advantage of the splendid sunsets featuring Mount Agung on Bali as a breathtaking backdrop. Very peaceful, all offer similar accommodation and have their own small restaurants, it's about a 40 min walk into 'town' for other restaurants and shopping, or take a dokar. Just inland from here is the **D-E** *Iwan Homestay*, which has a good ambience and there is a popular restaurant next door, the *Rumah Kita*, which will do boiled eggs and soldiers on request.

Gili Meno A *Bougenvil Resort*, T635295, T/F627435. The most expensive place on the island set in a secluded position at the southern end of the island, large attractive rooms. A little overpriced. Rooms with a/c, bathroom with Western toilet and hot water, minibar, satellite TV, pool, restaurant (mid-range). **A** *Gazebo Meno*, PO Box 1122, T/F635795 or Gazebo Hotels, PO Box 3134, Bali, T0361-286927, F288300. 10 bungalows set in large coconut grove. Attractively furnished large rooms with separate seating area, wooden floors, bathrooms with Western toilet, bath (no hot water), a/c, verandah. Restaurant (mid-range to cheap). **A-C** *Bounty*, new and luxurious resource-gulping hotel. Comfortable but rather out of place in resource-starved Lombok. **B-D** *Angkasa Biru*, *Casablanca Cottages*, PO Box 1163, Mataram, T0370-633847, F693482. Not the best location set a short distance inland near small

Meno has a reputation as a mosquito haven, so choose your accommodation carefully

West Nusa Tenggara

pools of stagnant water in the wet season. Attractively furnished rooms amidst pretty gardens except for the cheapest rooms, which are at the back facing inland with no breeze. All bathrooms with Western toilet, some with hot water. A/c or fan. Tiny but inviting pool. Somewhat overpriced. Restaurant (cheap). **B** *Casablanca*, T/F633847. Pool and cosy garden, away from beach. **B-E** *Zoraya*, T633801. 6 attractive bungalows with private bathroom, some with Western toilet. A/c or fan. Electricity only runs from 1800-0100 so there is no a/c during the heat of the day. 4 bungalows with shared mandi at the back facing inland with no views. Diving is available but standards may not be high. Good snorkelling at this location. **C** *Janur Indah*. Attractive bungalows, bathrooms with Western toilet. **D-E** *Blue Coral*, basic bungalows in need of repair in good location at north end of island. Private mandi, squat toilets and internet access. Worth investigating to see if they have been renovated and cleaned! **D-E** *Kontiki*, simple, with private mandi and Western toilets. **D-E** *Malia's Child*, T622007. Basic accommodation, mostly with shared mandi, squat toilet, 2 with Western toilet. Very average. **D-E** *Pondok Meno*, one of the best of these basic bungalows. Good location, set in pretty gardens. Shared mandi (1 private mandi), squat toilet. **D-E** *Pondok Santai*, next door to the Pondok Meno is very similar. **D-E** *Rawa Indah*, basic bungalows a short distance inland. Squat toilets, some with private mandi. **D-E** *Santai*, 2 bungalows. Basic with private mandi, squat toilets, good location.

Gili Air To make the most of this 'paradise' island it is best to stay in one of the bungalows dotted around the coast within sound and sight of the sea. There is also accommodation inland from the point where the boats land on the south coast but this location does not offer sea views. Several of the bungalows are owned by Europeans married to Indonesians and these tend to be the better run and more attractive. In the village there are several small shops which sell basic provisions and fruit. The price of accommodation doubles or more in the high season; some greedy and unscrupulous owners turn travellers away in the morning knowing that by late afternoon accommodation seekers will be so desperate that they will pay quite outrageous prices. However due to the decrease in tourists since early 2000 this has all been put on hold. With so few visitors in 2000, room occupancy rates were very low and rates correspondingly weak. **B** *Hotel Gili Air*, formerly *Hans Cottages*, T/F634435, giliair@mataram.wasantara.net.id The most upmarket accommodation on the island, 24 rooms, private bathrooms with western toilets and attractive indoor gardens. Fan or a/c, some with hot water, the deluxe rooms are built of brick which does not breathe as well in this tropical climate as the more attractive, cheaper thatched rooms. Well sited beside the beach with gardens and a fine view of Mount Rinjani. Restaurant (mid-range), many European dishes, the giant clams that sometimes appear on the menu are a protected species and should not have been caught, let alone eaten, *Reefseekers* (see under Diving) try to buy these clams from the fishermen and release them back into the sea. **B** *Hotel Gili Indah*, PO Box 1120, T636341, F637328. The next most upmarket accommodation consisting of bungalows with private bathrooms and Western toilets. Some rather dark, set in rather shaded and gloomy grounds. Restaurant, though quite pricey, is very average. The owner, Pak Aji, is Kepala Desa of the 'Gilis' which are now self-governing, and is a keen conservationist which bodes well for future development on the islands. **C-D** *Hans Cottage & Restaurant*, formerly *Bulan Madu* and once owned by a German, about whom rumours abound, this once luxurious house offers curious accommodation today. There are 3 rooms which can be let separately. The 2 downstairs rooms are large with nice verandahs and private bathrooms. The upstairs room, also large with private bathroom has good views and access to a 3rd floor lookout. All rooms have fans, and the house has great potential but needs to be redecorated. The bathrooms in particular need a good clean and new tubs, the existing ones are badly scarred. If the restaurant is in use, it could be noisy. Prices are reasonable. Large garden. **C-D** *Coconut Cottages*

& Restaurant (*Pondok Kelapa*), T635365, coconuts@indo.net.id 7 attractive bunga-lows with private bathrooms all enclosed, 4 with Western toilet, fan, mosquito nets, internet access, but bedbug problem. Very well run, set in flower-filled gardens amidst a coconut grove 30 m from the beach where you can watch the sun rise over Mount Rinjani on Lombok. Near the best area for snorkelling, offers a book exchange, Elaine, the owner's wife, is from Scotland, restaurant (mid-range to cheap), good food, will organize special Sasak dinners by prior arrangement. Recommended. **D** *Fantastic Bungalows*, on east side of island (best swimming and snorkelling here), 6 well-run bungalows with own (clean) mandi, price includes good breakfast, tuna and mayonnaise baguettes top the menu. Recommended. **D** *The Flying Dutchman on Safari*, 5 well-run bungalows, built by the friendly Dutch owners, Jan and Vincent, offering super, new bathrooms with squat toilets, mosquito nets, hammock on veran-dah and gardens with banana trees. The restaurant serves a good value Indonesian buffet every night at 2000 (book by 1800) and bar. The bungalows are particularly well made, using expensive *alang alang* grass for the roofs (as was traditional before many people switched to cheaper grasses), coconut wood and bamboo. Good sunset views. Highly recommended. **D** *Pino's Cottages & Corner Cottage*, one of the first places you come to going up the east coast. Run by German woman, bungalows face each other away from beach. Own mandi, 4 with Western toilet, electricity (occa-sional) in some bungalows, restaurant on the beach with reasonable food. **D** *Pondok Gili Air Bungalows and Café*, sasaksavage@hotmail.com Attractive, clean bungalows with private mandis and squat toilets and cookie jars. In attractive garden, well run by very friendly and helpful Australian woman, Dee. The place has its own generator, internet access and uses bottled water for making tea. Can arrange deli-cious Sasak dinners with one day's notice, offers a book exchange. Recommended. **D-E** *Sandi Bungalows*, simple and clean with attached mandi and squat toilet. Quiet location. **F** *Bamboo Cottages*, hammock on the balcony, choice of breakfast included in the price, very friendly owners.

The best of the remaining bungalows (all in the **D-E** price category) are: *Gusung Indah Bungalows; Salabose Bungalows* (one of which has a Western toilet), good sunset views; *Pena; Gita Gili*, good breakfast; *Gili Air Santay*, good bungalows with and without attached showers, all with electricity, excellent food, 500 m east of the boat 'dock' and situated inland; *Bupati's Place*; *Nusa Tiga*, inland from the east coast, German owner.

The choice of food is better on Gili Trawangan. A number of restaurants serving excel-lent seafood, particularly fish; 'specials' or the 'chalk-boards', will tell you what is the fresh catch.

Eating
Many restaurants show videos in the evenings

Gili Trawangan *Excellent Restaurant*, good, cheap food. Recommended. **Very cheap** *Simple Food*, limited menu but large helpings, friendly and enthusiastic own-ers. Recommended. Many of the accommodations in the built-up area feature restau-rants, some with barbecue facilities, the number of customers should indicate which are best. The new, 2-storey *Villa Ombak* constitutes the most sophisticated way to dine here, with an outdoor terrace near the water, and a balcony on the first floor. Good value.

Gili Meno *Bougenvil* and *Gazebo* both have restaurants (mid-range to cheap). *Malia's Child & Rust* offer simpler and cheaper food with good views across to Lombok. *Janur Indah* has been recommended. *Rusty's* warung does big portions of *nasi goreng* and similar dishes, for that after-swimming hunger. *Café Lumblumba*, the closest thing to a party zone, and does Padong style food.

West Nusa Tenggara

Gili Air Many of the restaurants cater primarily to Western tastes and the 'Indonesian' food is often disappointingly bland. There have been some cases of food poisoning caused by eating fish which was not gutted prior to being stored. Restaurants and bungalows with the best food are: *Pondok Gili Air* which also has good vegetarian food, fish and yoghurt, has a rotating specialized menu and rare delicacies such as lemon cake with caramel sauce and double chocolate cake. Recommended; *Corner Restaurant and Bungalows*, *Coconut Cottages* (Pondok Kelapa); *Nusa Tiga Bungalows* and *Flying Dutchman*, a good nightly buffet dinners – all cheap. *Hotel Gili Air*, formerly *Hans Cottages*, and *Il Pirata* (both mid-range), run by an Italian couple in a thatched building designed in the shape of a boat, good, though pricey, Italian food.

Nightclubs *Go Go Bar* on Saturdays and *Legends* on Friday, both on Gili Air.

Sports

Warning: it is advisable not to dive if taking Larium as a malaria prophylactic

Diving Whilst the diving here may not be quite as good as that in some other parts of Indonesia, it is ideal for less experienced divers as many of the dives are no deeper than 18 m and the waters are calm. Best diving conditions are late Apr through Aug. *Reefseekers*, now located in the *Gili Indah Hotel* at the Harbour, PO Box 1097, Mataram, c/o *Gili Indah*, T0370-636341. This is the outstanding dive centre on Lombok. Members of PADI International Resort Association No 2979, they offer a full range of courses to PADI Divemaster. Run by Ernie and Kath from England who have over 23 years experience, they operate to the highest safety standards and welcome inspections of the equipment and compressors by prospective divers. Experienced divers must bring their certificates and preferably their log books. *Reefseekers* are also very involved in conservation and are members of the Cousteau Society doing research into local ecosystems. Through their conservation survey work they have discovered new and exciting dive sites. All dives are guided. Because of their strict adherence to the highest safety standards this is an ideal place for nervous divers and beginners. Ernie is also working with Newcastle University researching local growing conditions, soil analyses etc, to determine the best crops and plants for the island. *Reefseekers* are starting a 'Turtle Hatchery Project' to increase numbers of hornbill and green turtles, both of which are under threat in their natural habitats. They plan to bring turtle eggs from breeding grounds on the east coast of Java. These will be placed in a sandpit measuring 2½ sq m where the eggs can incubate in safety. After this they will be transferred to a pen until they are ready for release at 3 months old. Visitors will be offered the opportunity to adopt a turtle to help fund the project, or make a donation once they have viewed the baby turtles. See tinted box, page 272. *Blue Marlin Dive Centre*, head office: Gili Trawangan, T632424, F642286, bmdc@mataram.wasantara.net.id, www.diveindo.com Counters on Gili Air, Jl Raya Senggigi Beach, *Senggigi Palace Hotel*, Jl Koperasi 81, Ampenan, Lombok. PADI courses up to Divemaster Course, courses start at US$25 for an introduction to scuba diving with 1 dive, up to US$299 for the PADI Open Water Course. Resident English instructor, Simon Liddiard. This is the best dive centre on Gili Trawangan. *Albatross Dive Center*, Jl Raya Senggigi, Km 8, PO Box 1066, Mataram 83010, T693399, F693388. Also at the *Sheraton Hotel*, Senggigi Beach, PADI courses up to Open Water (US$350) and Advanced Diver (US$240). Also operates on Gili Trawangan and Gili Meno. *Blue Coral Dive Centre*, T634496, operates on all 3 Gili islands and offers PADI courses and night dives. Expect to pay about US$50 for 2 dives. There are also many other dive shops. If taking an introductory dive course check that the instructor speaks acceptable English (or Dutch, German etc). **Snorkelling**: snorkels and fins can be hired for 3,000-5,000Rp from many of the losmen. The snorkelling off Gili Trawangan is marginally the best; be careful off Gili Meno, as the tide is strong and the water is shallow, and it is easy to get swept onto the coral.

Fishing Deep sea and night fishing available from tour companies and *Albatross Dive Center* (see under 'Diving' for address), approximate costs US$200-300. A popular glass-bottomed boat does the rounds between the three islands, and indeed is the only way to go between Air and Meno in the low season short of chartering your own boat. It costs US$25 and stops off at a few good spots, and you have lunch on Trawangan.

Massage Sometimes available at *Rudi's*, a restaurant set back from the beach, near where the ferry docks on Gili Trewangan. *Abar* is the best masseur on Gili Air; ask at *Pondok Gili Air*, for the rare pleasure of a masseur who is suitable for women – ie no misplaced rubbing!

Boat Public boats from the islands to **Bangsal** leave at 0800 and 1200 approximately. For onward connections to Bali arrive at the ticket booth by 0730. At Bangsal you can also book through to Bali with one of the shuttle bus companies. **Gili Air** boats are blue, **Gili Meno** are yellow, and **Gili Trawangan** are red and white. The 'Island Hopping' boat makes 2 round trips a day connecting the islands. Currently, the boat leaves Gili Air at 0800 and 1400 to Gili Meno. It leaves Gili Meno to Gili Trawangan at 0845 and 1515. It leaves Gili Trawangan to return to Gili Meno at 0915 and 1445 and leaves Gili Meno to return to Gili Air at 0945 and 1545. It takes approximately 20-30 mins for each leg of the journey. **NB** There are reports that with the downturn in tourist arrivals the frequency of departures has decreased. Check on arrival. Be prepared to be whisked in to the air by a bevy of men carrying you over the foot of water to your boat, for a small fee.

Transport

Don't purchase bus tickets on the islands, as they are more expensive

Banks It is best to change money before leaving the 'mainland' as rates are more expensive on the islands. There are money changers on Gili Trawangan. On Gili Air, the *Gili Indah* will change money. Some of the losmen on each of the islands will also change money. **Communications** Post office: There is a post box at the *Gili Indah Hotel* on Gili Air, where the boat docks. Letters *do* get through, but there are no stamps available on the island. Each of the islands has a *Wartel*. On Gili Air you can make phone calls at *Pondok Kelapa* (*Coconut Cottages*). The owner does not require a minimum of 3 mins, which the Wartel does. **Internet**: a number of places offer internet access on the islands, more to follow.

Directory

West Nusa Tenggara

Northwest coast and MountRinjani

Following the coast north from Pemenang and Bangsal, the road passes the turn off for Sir Beach (about 2 km north of Pemenang). This northwest coast is little touched by tourism and there are several 'traditional villages' where the more adventurous tour companies take visitors. The best-known of these is Bayan at the foot of Mount Rinjani's northern slopes and about 50 km from Pemenang. Mount Rinjani, rising to 3,726 m, dominates north Lombok.

Siri Beach Siri Beach is down a dirt track, to the left are coconut plantations, and reaches the deserted long, narrow strip of soft, white sand on a headland looking across to Gili Air. Take all food and drink: no facilities here. This is worth a visit to get away from the crowds. To get there, take a bemo running north from Pemanang – the walk to the beach is about 2 km from the road.

Bayan

This is a traditional Sasak village and the birthplace of Lombok's unique Muslim 'schism' – *Islam Waktu Telu* (see page 303). There is a mosque here which is believed to be 300 years old. Some authorities postulate that when the Muslim 'saint' Sunan Giri (or possibly Senopati) arrived on Lombok he landed here, and so Bayan was the first village to be converted to Islam. The village is the jumping-off point for climbs up Mount Rinjani (see below). No accommodation.

Transport **Bemo** Connections with the Bertais terminal in Cakranegara, 2,000Rp. From Bayan
50 km from Pemenang bemos run up to Batu Koq. Bemos also run east from here along the very scenic coastal road to Labuan Lombok. From the looks of surprise it is clear that few *orang putih* make this (long) journey.

Mount Rinjani

Visitors who have made the effort invariably say that the highlight of their stay on Lombok was climbing Mount Rinjani. It is certainly the most memorable thing to do on the island. The views from the summit on a clear day are simply breathtaking. The problem is that the ascent requires three days (although some keen climbers try to do it in two) and few tourists are willing to sacrifice so much time. There is the additional problem that not only is the summit often wreathed in cloud, but views down to the blue-green lake within the caldera are also often obscured by a layer of cloud which lies trapped in the enormous crater.

Mount Rinjani is the second highest mountain in Indonesia outside Irian Jaya – rising to an altitude of 3,726 m. The volcano is still active but last erupted some time ago – in 1901, although in 1997, rumblings left dust raining for a week. The mountain, and a considerable area of land surrounding the mountain totalling some 400 sq km, has been gazetted as a national park. Beyond this there is a further 760 sq km of forest and scrub which is also protected to varying degrees. The location of Lombok between the Asian and Australasian zoo geographic realms is reflected in the presence of a number of birds of Australian origin – including the highly distinctive sulphur-crested cockatoo. Mount Rinjani is believed by locals to be the seat of the gods, in particular Batara, and although Lombok is ostensibly Islamic, each year during the *Pakelem* ceremony gold offerings are carried up to the mountain and tossed into the lake. There are also regular pilgrimages of local Sasak (Waktu Telu) priests to the summit each full moon.

West Nusa Tenggara

There are two routes up Mount Rinjani. The easier and more convenient begins about 2 km to the west of the village of Bayan, on the way to Anyer. The track leads upwards from the road to the small settlement of **Batu Koq** and from there, 1 km on, to another village, **Senaru**. Tents, equipment and guides or porters can be hired in either of these two settlements (ask at the losmen); accommodation is available (see below). It is recommended that trekkers check in at the conservation office in Senaru before beginning the ascent. A guide is not essential as the trail is wellmarked from Senaru to the crater rim; however, suitable climbing gear is required (see below). From Senaru, the trek to the summit takes about two days, or 10 hours solid climbing. On the trek up, the path passes through stands of teak and mahogany, then into pine forest and lichin. There are stunning views from the lip of the crater down to the beautiful blue-green and mineral rich lake, **Segara Anak** (Child of the Sea), below. A third day is needed to walk down into the caldera. The caldera is 8 km long by 5 km wide.

On the east side of the lake is **Mount Baru** (New Mountain), an active cone within a cone that rose out of the lake in 1942. It can be reached by boat and the climb to Mount Baru's summit, through a wasteland of volcanic debris, is rewarded with a view into this secondary crater. Along the base of the main crater are numerous hot springs – like **Goa Susu** (Milk Cave – so called because of its colour) – which are reputed to have spectacular healing powers; bathing in them is a good way to round-off a tiring descent.

West Nusa Tenggara

Around Mount Rinjani

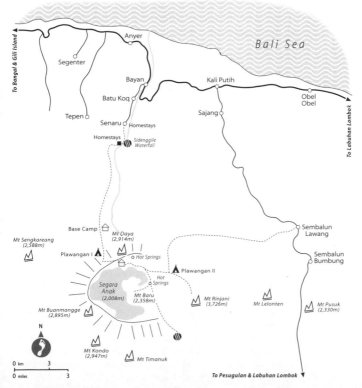

This alternative route is less well marked. A guide is recommended to show climbers the route to the second rim

An alternative and more difficult route up the mountain – but some climbers who have done both claim this is the more interesting – is via **Sembalun Lawang**, **Sembalun Bumbung** or **Sapit** on the mountain's eastern slopes. There is accommodation here (see below) and guides are also available but there is a shortage of equipment for hire. There is food available to buy for the trek but the range of victuals is not as good as in Senaru. To get to Sembalun Bumbung, take a bus from Labuhan Lombok. For details on Sapit, see page 292. The climb to the crater takes about 9 hours. For ambitious climbers who intend to reach the true summit of Mount Rinjani – rather than just the caldera – this is the better of the two routes. **NB** In early 2000 the Australian Embassy in Jakarta was advising visitors not to to climb Mount Rinjani because of fears of violent theft. However no one going up, nor the guides, seemed concerned or particularly aware of any great problems. Nonetheless, check before beginning the climb.

Round trip taking in both sides of the mountain: because each side of Rinjani offers its own character a recommended alternative is to climb up the eastern flank and down the western. To do this, go to Senaru to rent equipment and buy supplies (the choice is best here), return to Anyer or Bayan and take a bemo or ojek to Sembalun Lawang. (Start early, bemos to Sembalun Lawang are rare after 1600.) Hire a guide and porter in Sembalun Lawang and stay the night. The next day the guide can show the route to the second rim (6-7 hours); from here the climb to the summit (3-4 hours) and then down into the caldera (3 hours), and from there up to the first rim and back down to Senaru (6-7 hours) is well marked and the guide is not needed.

Best time to climb
The climb, though not technically difficult, is arduous & climbers should be in reasonable physical condition

Climb from May to November, during the dry season when it is less likely to be cloudy. Do not attempt the climb during the rainy season as the trail can be treacherous. **Recommended equipment**: water, sweater and coat, foam camping roll, sleeping bag, tough walking shoes, food/supplies, firewood (there is increasing evidence of climbers chopping down trees within this National Park in order to light a fire). *Please* take all your litter with you. **NB** Some climbers have complained of the poor quality of some of the equipment hired in Senaru; check it carefully. **Guides**: cost about 80,000Rp per day and porters 40,000Rp per day. A tent and/or sleeping bag hired for the guide would be greatly appreciated; it's cold on the mountain.

Sleeping
It is possible to stay at Batu Koq and Senaru, as well as at Sembalun Lawang if making the climb from the east. Senaru has the best selection of (basic, all **E**) losmen and new ones seem to open almost every month. **Senaru**: *Bale Bayan Guesthouse*, near the mountain, clean and friendly, the owner speaks reasonable English and German. Recommended. *Pondok Senaru*, clean, well run, big restaurant, ice cold mandi. **Batu Koq**: *Segara Anak Homestay* has been recommended. Price includes breakfast and supper; some exquisite views. *Guru Bakti*, good bungalows especially those at the rear which offer superb views down the valley, price includes breakfast. **E** *Cemari Siu*, just as good. On the southeast slopes of Rinjani at the village of **Sapit** is the **D-E** *Hati Suci Homestay*, peaceful. Highly recommended. A good base for climbing the mountain. **E** *Balelangga*, 300 m down the road run by the brother of Hati Suci is also excellent. Your house on the hill with breathtaking views. He will bring tea to your hammock on the porch for sunrise and then you can tumble back into a brand new Western bed. **Sembalun Lawang**: **E** *Diriam Guesthouse*, very helpful and friendly place, the owner speaks some English and can help arrange the trek although equipment is in short supply and may not be availabler. Recommended. **Camping**: there are trekkers' camp sites at various positions up the mountain – the corrugated shelters are rather dilapidated and the litter is bad.

December (2nd week): *Pakelem*, offering feast on Segara Anak to ask for God's blessings. **Festivals**

The most convenient way to climb Rinjani is by booking a place on a 'tour'. Several **Tours**
tour operators in Mataram (see page 269), Senggigi (page 275) and on the Gilis organize climbs, (about US$180 all-in). Tours are also available from losmen at various vil-
lages, such as Sapit.

Bemo For the more usual north route, take a bemo from the Bertais terminal to **Transport**
Bayan, and then a second bemo from Bayan to Senaru. Alternatively, walk from Bayan.
For the east route, take a bemo from Labuhan Lombok to Sembalun Bumbung; for
transport to Sapit, see page 292. **Taxi** A taxi from Bangsal to Senaru should cost
about 10,000Rp per hr of journey time.

Central Lombok and the West

Lombok's excellent main road runs for 74 km, east to west; from Mataram to
Labuhan Lombok – the small port where ferries leave for Sumbawa. Most of the
destinations in central and west Lombok can be visited on a day trip from
Senggigi Beach; there is little accommodation available. East of Mataram (and
10 km from Cakranegara) is the town of Narmada with its rather down-at-heel
'pleasure garden'. A little way northwest of here is Lingsar, the site of the Waktu
Telu Temple. The cool hill town of Suranadi, 7 km to the north of Narmada, is set
at 400 m above sea-level (where there is a hotel). About 25 km east of Narmada, a
road to the north (just after Sikur) leads up the lower slopes of Mount Rinjani,
through Kota Raja, to a second hill resort, Tetebatu.

Narmada

The **Taman Narmada**, or terraced 'pleasure garden' opposite the bemo station, was built in 1805. There are various spring-fed pools here, one of which is
open to the public for swimming (admission to pool 500Rp). The gardens are
supposed to be a scale model of the upper slopes of Mount Rinjani, including a
replica of the holy crater lake, *Segara Anak*. The whole ensemble was laid out
by King Anak Gede Karangasem of Mataram when he was too old to climb the
real thing. A Hindu Balinese temple is situated above the bathing pools. The
gardens are a popular picnic spot for Indonesians, but sadly are poorly maintained and rather dirty. There are, however, good bargains available within the
grounds for t-shirts. Dance performances are held here (2,000Rp). ■ *Admis-*
sion to garden 200Rp. 0700-1800 Mon-Sun.

November/December. *Pujawali*, an annual festival held in conjunction with the **Festivals**
Pekalem festival on Mount Rinjani (when pieces of gold are thrown into the crater
lake). Once a year there is a 'duck-chasing' festival at Taman Narmada. Ducks are
released onto the lake and at a signal from the leader of the ceremony boys plunge in
to collect the birds. They are allowed to keep any ducks they catch.

Bemo Regular connections with the Bertais terminal in **Cakranegara**. **Transport**
11 km east of Mataram

West Nusa Tenggara

West Nusa Tenggara

Lingsar

The **Waktu Telu Temple**, also known as the Lingsar Temple, was originally built in 1714, and then rebuilt in 1878. Both Hindu Balinese and Muslim Sasaks come to worship here, and there are compounds dedicated to each religion. It is particularly favoured by adherents of Lombok's unique Islam Waktu Telu religion – although their numbers are rapidly dwindling (see page 303). A lake here is said to contain holy fish, but seems rather too dirty to sustain any kind of marine life. ■ *0700-1800. Admission by donation. Dress modest, sash required.*

Festivals November/December. *Pujawali*, a seven-day festival, culminating in the two religions, the Muslims and Hindus, staging mock battles in the lower courtyard where they throw rice cakes (or *ketupat*) at one another.

Transport **Bemo** Take a bemo from the Bertais terminal in Cakranegara to Narmada, and change here for Lingsar. If driving oneself, there is a more direct back route along a minor road from Cakranegara to Lingsar.

Suranadi

Phone code: 0370
Colour map 1, grid B4

Set at an altitude of 400 m, this is the site of one of Lombok's holiest temples – **Pura Suranadi**. The site was chosen by a Hindu saint who led settlers here while in a trance. Suranadi is the name of a celestial river in Hindu mythology and the temple is situated at the source of a mountain spring. Ornate Balinese carvings decorate the shrine. In the courtyards of the temple are several holy springs; the large black eels living in the pools fed by the springs are sacred and catching them is forbidden. For a small donation, the keepers will bang on the walls of the pools and throw hard-boiled eggs into the water to attract the eels from their dark lairs.

The small village of **Sesoat** is 5 km away with good warungs, an ice cold river to swim in, and a thriving market. It has been drawn into the global economy through logging, and at present is not treeless and scarred like so many other places in Asia, but it probably will be before too long.

Sleeping **B-C** *Suranadi*, Jl Raya Suranadi, PO Box 10, T633686, F635630. A/c, restaurant, tennis, hot water, Lombok's original colonial hotel, now refurbished and with a new wing, friendly, with a slightly murky, spring-fed, swimming pool also used by many local people. **B-D** *Teratai Cottage and Restaurant*, T633829, F633826. Pleasant cottages both standard and luxury, with swimming pool set amongst the tiered padis that create a dramatic verdant vista from the restaurant, which serves a mix of Western and local food. Very courteous staff.

Eating Recently 3 restaurants have sprung up on the road near a few 100 m from these hotels offering a variety of food from cheese burgers to noodle concoctions of numerous types.

Transport **Bemo** From the Bertais terminal in Cakranegara to Narmada, and then change to
7 km north of Narmada, another travelling north to Suranadi (500Rp for each leg of the trip).
18 km from Mataram

Tetebatu

Tetebatu is a tiny village on the slopes of Mount Rinjani. There is very little to do here, except enjoy the beautiful scenery and visit the surrounding villages. The presence of the *Wisma Soedjono* here at the end of the road has made Tetebatu into something of a mountain 'retreat' for Westerners. There are good walks in the surrounding countryside, a number of which start from the *Wisma Soedjono*, ranging from short ambles to half or full day trips. For the longer walks you need to arrange a guide. Even a short walk can be most rewarding. Walking down towards the rice paddies, is like entering a different world. The maze of narrow paths which connect the paddies provides a fascinating, yet discreet, insight into rural life in central Lombok. There is a good vantage point on a low hill for watching the people and their animals at work and play in the fields.

Colour map 1, grid B4
Tours to Telebatu are advertised in Senggigi & the Gilis

Excursions The villages in this part of Lombok are well worth exploring, and this is best done by hiring a car or motorcycle. **Kota Raja** is a market town 7 km south of Tetebatu noted for its handicrafts, particularly basketwork. Tours to Tetebatu are advertised in places such as Senggigi and the Gilis. **Loyok**, just off the road to Tetebatu, is known for its bamboo crafts and palm leaf boxes while **Pringgasela**, east of Kota Raja, is a centre for ikat weaving (see below). **Lendang Nangka** is a traditional Sasak village 7 km east of Kota Raja; while **Masbaggik**, on the main road just to the east of the turn-off for Kota Raja and Tetebatu is a pottery-making town. There are other craft villages in the central highlands area.

Sleeping Several new guesthouses have recently opened in this area. **C-D** *Wisma Soedjono*, some a/c, restaurant (**1-2**) slow service, large pool, occupies a lovely position looking out over paddy and pineapple fields and the south slopes of Mount Rinjani, the owners speak English and hire out motorbikes for visiting the surrounding countryside. There is a variety of accommodation, including some 'traditional' Sasak houses along the side of the hill. **D** *Lentera*, east side of the village, sparklingly clean bungalows with large beds, clean showers and a restaurant (breakfast included). **B-E** *Hotel Melati* or the *Green Orry Inn*, T683662. Private mandi, tourist information, good portions in the restaurant, although Phil Collins may have to be endured *ad nauseam*. **E** *Pondok Bulan*, bamboo-and-thatch or concrete-and-tile bungalows, near the rice paddies and offering bicycle hire (4,000Rp). **E** *Mentariku Bungalows*, Benteng Village, 5 km on the road from Lendang Nangka to Tetebatu, F622298. Traditional Sasak style accommodation, in beautiful valley looking towards Mount Rinjani. Price includes breakfast, a stunning retreat. **E** *Wisma Dewi Enjeni*, 2 km south of Tetebatu, lovely views, price includes breakfast.

Transport 11 km north of the main road linking Mataram with Labuhan Lombok. **Bemo** From the Mertais terminal in Cakranegara to Paok Motong and then another bemo to Tetebatu (2,500Rp).

Pringgasela

East of Kota Raja is this small weaving village, where traditional back-strap looms have not yet been displaced by more advanced technology, and where natural rather than artificial (chemical aniline) dyes are still in use. As there is accommodation available in Pringgasela, this is a good place to experience the 'real' Lombok.

Sleeping Family-run homestay. Suhaidi (better known as 'Eddie') can arrange tours and trekking. **D** *Sasak House Homestay*, friendly, shared mandi.

Transport **Bemo**: from the Bertais terminal in Cakranegara to Rempung and then a dokar to Pringgasela or from Labuhan Lombok.

Sapit

Sapit is a small Sasak village on the southeast slopes of Mount Rinjani, with views west towards the mountain and east over the sea to Sumbawa. Set amidst rice paddies, it is one of the most relaxing places to unwind and also makes a good base for climbing Mount Rinjani. There are also grimy hot springs, cascading waterfalls, canyons and the forest of the green and black monkeys all within walking distance, and can be incorporated into the treks arranged by the homestays listed below. For the truly adventurous, it is also possible to arrange an all-in trip to Kalimantan, where these homestay families are originally from, with the Wild Man from Borneo himself, Gilang. Guaranteed to show you the 'authentic' way of life and most beautiful areas of interest. http://members.tripod.com/orangs or Gilang98@hotmail.com

Excursions **Mount Rinjani** is a 3-5 day excursion from Sapit (see page 286); guides are available in the village and charge about 80,000Rp per day.

Sleeping **D-E** *Hati Suci Homestay*, F622160, http://sites.netscape.net/hatisuci/info Restaurant, bungalow and dorm accommodation, clean and professionally run, stunning views, peaceful, breakfast included, tours/treks organized, Canadian partner. Highly recommended. *Balelangga* is 300 m along the road, and is similarly situated and laid out with well kept gardens. However you get a better sunrise from here and Adi will bring tea to your hammock and wake you up for it. Sprung mattresses, a large range of good books and an open walled restaurant with cushions on the ground and low tables. Highly recommended Both *Hati Suci* and *Balelangga* can be booked through Noor Family, Jl Kesra VII Perumnas, Mataram, T0370-636545, F635753, Hatisuci@mataram.wasantara.net.id; Balelangga@mataram.wasantara.net.id

Tours From here you can arrange an all in trip to **Kalimantan** where these homestay families are originally from, with the Wild Man from Borneo himself, Gilang. Guaranteed to show you an authentic way of life and the most beautiful areas of interest. http://members.tripod.com/orangs or Gilang98@hotmail.com

Transport **Bus**: regular buses from the Bertais terminal in Cakranegara to Pringgabaya; from Pringgabaya catch a bemo to Sapit. Total journey time 2½ to 3 hrs. From Labuhan Lombok, take a bus to Pringgabaya and then a **bemo** to Sapit. The same applies from Kute, catch bemo to Praya and on. **NB** to catch the last bemo to the door of these homestays you must reach the bottom of the mountain by 1500.

Labuhan Lombok

Labuhan Lombok is the small ferry port for Sumbawa. It is little more than a fishing village and most tourists are only too happy to catch the first ferry out.

Sleeping **E** *Losmen Muanawar*, basic. **E-F** *Lima Tiga*, new losmen, very clean and well-run when it opened, shared mandi, price includes breakfast, the best place to stay here. Recommended.

Cheap: *Warung Kelayu*, close to the *Lima Tiga* losmen, good value local food.

Bemo: from the Bertais terminal in Cakranegara, 2 hrs along an excellent road, with only the dokars to delay your progress. There is now a good road running up the north coast from Labuhan Lombok right round to Bayan. Bemos do this journey. To make a round trip back to Mataram change bemos at Bayan. **Sea Boat**: there is a ferry linking Labuhan Lombok, with Poto Tano on Sumbawa's west coast. Departures on the hr 0300-1600 and 1800, return hourly on the half hr 0330-1630 and 1830. A very pleasant 1½ hrs crossing with spectacular views of Rinjani and the off-shore islands (4,000Rp).

East Lombok

Few people visit the east which is drier, poorer and more sparsely inhabited than the west. However, there is now a sealed road running round the north coast of the island from Labuhan Lombok which links up with the west coast road at Bayan. On the way you encounter superb sea views and stunning glimpses of Mount Rinjani. To the south of Labuhan Lombok is the fishing port of Labuhan Haji with some basic accommodation, and a rugged route to Tanjung Ringgit at the end of the mystical southeast peninsula (see page299).

Northeast Coast

Travelling north from Labuhan Lombok you reach Labuhan Pandan after about 12 km. Here there are deserted, black sand beaches and fabulous views of uninhabited islands and the west coast of Sumbawa. You can hire boats to take you to these islands with their gold sand beaches for about 40,000Rp a day; bring all the food and water you need as there is nothing on these islands.

E *Siola Homestay* is a good bet if you want to escape from the tourist shuttle brigade. *Perama* runs a camp on one of the islands, though we heard complaints from travellers who had been stranded there when the *Perama* boat broke down. They then ran out of drinking water, and the final indignity was when *Perama* tried to charge them for the extra nights they were forced to endure on the Island. There is a Japanese conservation project on **Gili Luwang** and **Sulat**, where you can camp. Also you could try **Air Manis** village with a losmen of the same name, Jl Raya Sambela. It's cheap, clean and comfy and provides an insight into local life. There are a number of pristine beaches along the east coast, such as Obel Obel, with good surf.

Continuing north from Labuhan Pandan, you pass through the fishing village of **Sambelia** with some traditional style bugis' houses on stilts, then on to **Blanting**, with enchanting seaviews *en route*. The landscape here is mostly very arid, though as you approach Obel Obel, about 50 km from Labuhan Lombok, it becomes more luxuriant, and there are a number of pristine beaches, with good surf. At Kali Putih you can either head south up into the foothills of Mount Rinjani along a poor road to the villages of **Sembalun Lawang** and **Sambalun Bumbung** or continue west to Bayan.

Transport It is possible to do this trip from Labuhan Lombok by bemo, however, having your own transport would be preferable.

South Lombok and the south coast

From Cakranegara, a good road runs 26 km southeast to the market town of Praya. Three kilometres before Praya is the small village of Puyung, and 2 km south of here the popular weaving village of Sukarara. Turning south from Praya, the road reaches the pottery-making village of Penujak after 5 km and continues south to Sengkol. This area is one of the centres of Sasak culture with a number of traditional villages. It is a poor part of the island, with low grade agricultural land and abandoned paddies. The road ends at the quiet beach and fishing village of Kuta, 32 km from Praya and 58 km from Mataram.

Sukarara Sukarara is a small **weaving village** southeast of Mataram. The weavers here still use traditional backstrap looms but the workshops along the main road are now geared to tourists and the quality is indifferent, with artificial dyes in widespread use. Traditional Lombok designs are still produced – in particular cloth inter-woven with gold and silver thread – but it is becoming increasingly difficult to find finely worked, quality cloth.

Transport *25 km from Mataram* **Bemo**: from the Mertais terminal in Cakranegara bound for Praya; get off at Puyung, 3 km north of Praya. From here either walk or hire a dokar for the 2-km ride to the village.

Penujak Penujak is a **pottery-making village** 5 km south of Praya on the road to Kuta. The New Zealand government has been providing aid to support and develop the craft since 1988, in particular through improving design, technology and marketing. Both traditional pottery forms such as the *gentong* (storage jar), *kaling* (water jar) and *periuk* (cooking vessel) along with designs produced purely for the tourist market are on sale. A major problem the industry has faced is adapting to a market where size/weight and fragility are both serious impediments to increased sales. Other important pottery-making villages include **Rungkang** and **Masbaggik** in East Lombok, and **Banyumulek** to the south of Mataram. The latter two villages also receive support from the New Zealand project.

The road splits at Penujak. One branch leads on to the south coast of Silungblanak where there is a good sandy beach. The other road goes on to Kuta.

Transport **Bemo**: from the Bertais terminal in Cakranegara to Praya; change in Praya and catch another travelling south to Penujak.

Sade The area south of the town of Sengkol to Kuta Beach is one of the centres of Sasak culture and there are a number of 'traditional' Sasak villages here. The best known is Sade where women, realizing their potential as a tourist attraction, still wear traditional Sasak dress. Also here, there are some of the few remaining examples of Sasak architecture, including the tall-roofed, thatched, *lumbungs* (rice barns). But, Sade is firmly on the tour bus circuit and although the villagers have made a conscious effort to maintain 'tradition' for the foreign visitors, the economy is geared as much to tourism as to agriculture. Women frantically sell textiles while the children hustle.

Transport **Bemo**: from the Bertais terminal in Cakranegara to Praya; change here and catch another travelling south towards Kuta.

Kuta Beach

Kuta Beach, also sometimes known as Putri Nyale Beach, is situated amongst the most spectacular coastal scenery on Lombok; rocky outcrops and cliff faces give way to sheltered sandy bays, ideal for swimming and surfing.

Phone code: 0370
Colour map 1, grid B4

Kuta itself has a stretch of sand on Lombok's south coast in a bay with a little fishing village at its head. There is a substantial fishing fleet of sailing boats with brightly decorated dugout hulls and outriggers. There are no 'sights' other than the Sasak villages about 20 minutes' drive inland beside the main Mataram to Kuta road.

Until very recently the only accommodation was in simple bungalows offering only the most basic facilities. This is starting to change, with a **3** *Novotel* open on the coast 3 km past Kuta to the east, and several new upmarket bungalows have been built.

The beach is the focal point of a strange annual festival, called the ***Bau Nyale*** (see Sumba, page 378 for similar event), when thousands of seaworms come to the surface of the sea. Local people flock here to witness the event, and it is becoming quite a popular tourist attraction. See below for details.

Still a quiet place to stay, there is a good road linking it to Mataram with regular shuttle bus connections. To book shuttle tickets, the Perama office (open 0600-2100) is located a few doors down from the Segara Anak Bungalows.

Kuta has been earmarked for future development. A plan for a '*Putri Nyale Resort*' has been published (of which the *Novotel* is part of the first phase), envisaging the construction of multiple luxury hotels, two golf courses, lagoons, craft villages and an international size airport. Estimates vary, from 2-10 years, as to when the new airport will be built. However, the land has already been fenced off which is an encouraging start. The site lies to the east of the main road about 20 minutes' drive from Kuta (about 40 minutes to 1 hour from Mataram). When the airport is built Kuta may well become the premier resort on Lombok, taking over from Senggigi. Kuta has the advantage of lower rainfall, better beaches, a spectacular and undeveloped coastline and only a 20-minute drive as against 1½ hours or so to Senggigi. Thirty minutes walk from Kuta beside the main Mataram road is a large billboard mapping out the proposed developments, it makes for interesting speculation. Some years ago,

West Nusa Tenggara

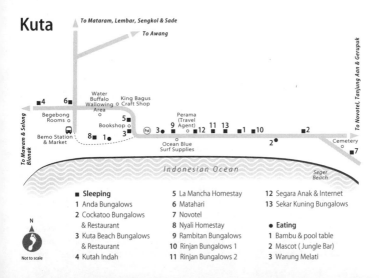

Kuta

To Mataram, Lembar, Sengkol & Sade
To Awang
To Novotel, Tanjung Aan & Gerupuk
To Mawam & Selong Blanak

Water Buffalo Wallowing Area
King Bagus Craft Shop
Begebong Rooms
Bookshop
Perama (Travel Agent)
Bemo Station & Market
Ocean Blue Surf Supplies
Cemetery
Indonesian Ocean
Seger Beach

N
Not to scale

■ **Sleeping**	5 La Mancha Homestay	12 Segara Anak & Internet
1 Anda Bungalows	6 Matahari	13 Sekar Kuning Bungalows
2 Cockatoo Bungalows	7 Novotel	
& Restaurant	8 Nyali Homestay	● **Eating**
3 Kuta Beach Bungalows	9 Rambitan Bungalows	1 Bambu & pool table
& Restaurant	10 Rinjan Bungalows 1	2 Mascot (Jungle Bar)
4 Kutah Indah	11 Rinjan Bungalows 2	3 Warung Melati

wealthy property developers from Java bought up the best beaches along this eastern coastal strip. In time, luxury class hotels will sprout up changing forever this beautiful landscape. For the independent traveller now is the time to enjoy it before development takes over.

On this note the young people of Kute have formed an excellent organization, Kute Youth Association Forum. They are negotiating with the *Novotel* to train the legions of barefoot pineapple/sarong children, and provide transport for them from their villages and a fixed market spot on the main drag. Their project will establish an integrated tourism plan whilst benefiting the social, cultural and ecological integrity of this beautiful area. All aspects of development and change have section leaders with relevant expertise, posing a comprehensive, sensitive and earnest approach to the hurdles of modernization.

Animal lovers can enjoy watching the water buffaloes, of which there are many herds in this area, wallowing in their mud pools on the outskirts of the village. As part of their grooming the buffaloes have their hair shaved. The steep rock 10 m high on the beach at Kuta provides hours of entertainment for the baby goats who leap with amazing agility up its vertical sides playing games, while the rest of the flock grazes on the rock's sparse vegetation. But, most people come here not to ogle at the animals but to surf.

Excursions At present the roads beyond Kuta are poor but this could change rapidly. Some impressive new side roads have been built leading off the main coast road but with no bridges over the rivers! The coast road continues east from Kuta past some magnificent, white sandy bays (no shade from the sun, and currently without any facilities). After 2 km a potholed tarmac road turns off to Seger Beach, one of the beaches where the Nyale fish come ashore. The smart new offices of the Lombok Tourism Development Group are on the right just before Tanjung Aan.

Four kilometres further on again, past low-lying swampy land is the fine gold sand beach at **Tanjung Aan**, set in a horseshoe shaped bay, it is good for swimming, though there are stones and coral about 10 m out. Despite its distance from any development there are stalls, and hawkers materialize as soon as any foreigners appear. **NB** There is no shade on any of these beaches, just basic scrub. The track bends round to the south and ends at **Gepupak (Desert) Point**.

There are many **walks** in the area: climb the hill immediately to the west of Kuta for spectacular views over the south coast. The hills to the west of Kuta have deposits of gold, nickel and tin, due to be mined in a joint venture with a Canadian mining outfit. The **Seger hills**, 2 km to the east, have numerous farm trails and a small cemetery; near Seger beach is a rocky promontory with more superb views, especially at sunset.

Surfing beaches The best are: **Are Guling**, **Mawi**, **Mawun** and **Selong Blanak**. **Gerupak (Desert Point)** is rated as one of the best surf spots in the world outside Hawaii. Kuta was originally 'discovered' by surfers.

Traditional villages Sade and **Rembitan**, 9 km north of Kuta just off the main Mataram road, 20 minutes' drive.

Sleeping Accommodation has improved recently with one luxury class hotel and some smart new bungalows. More will surely be built now that Kuta is beginning to be developed – although Indonesia's political problems may put some of these plans back a few years. The older bungalows are rather unattractive, made of clapboard with linoleum floors, squashed together and facing away from the sea. Rooms are usually small (and bedbugs can be a problem), up on stilts. They are mostly of similar standard and in our **D-E** categories, although cheaper rooms do come down in price to our **F** category.

Most of the bungalows are strung out along the beach road a short distance from the village but two of the best, *Kuta Indah* and *Matahari* are in the village itself, a 10 min walk from the beach: 29 luxury class hotels are scheduled to be built over the next few years including a *Sheraton*.

A *Novotel*, Mandalika Resort, Pantai Putri Nyotle, Pujut, T653333, F653555. 3 km east of Kuta village, beside the sea. The most luxurious hotel in the Kuta area, though others will soon follow. This new 3-star hotel offers the usual luxuries including a swimming pool. Built in traditional style with thatched roofs crowned with animated carvings of ducks and other animals. The hotel is attractively furnished using locally produced handicrafts and a decadent, overflowing raised pool that is at eye level with the sea.

B-D *Kuta Indah Hotel*, T653781, F653628, kutaindah@indo.net.id Attractive, new accommodation on the western edge of Kuta village, 8 mins walk from the beach. 50 rooms in bungalows overlooking large central gardens shaded by coconut palms. Superior rooms with a/c, hot water, telephone, TV (satellite includes CNN), bathrooms with Western toilets. Standard rooms with fan and cold water; rooms are large, bright with white tiled floors and verandahs with seating. A good sized pool. Restaurant has some of the best food in town at reasonable prices (mid-range to cheap). Hotel offers free transport to Tanjung Aan and Mawan beaches. Safety deposit box, car hire, airport transfer. Recommended. **B-E** *Matahari*, T654832, F654909. Inland, in the centre of the village, set in lovely, flower filled gardens; rooms range from fairly basic, older rooms with private bathroom, to fairly luxurious new rooms with a/c, hot water and marble bathrooms. Be prepared to bargain. Lending library and book exchange, safety deposit box, car/motorbike rental, tours. Free transport to Tanjung Aan and Mawan beaches. Restaurant (mid-range to cheap).

D-E *Anda*, T654836. Several new, attractive bungalows with private mandi and western toilet, let down by their location facing the family quarters away from the beach. Run by a friendly family. Offers the only internet access apart from the Novotel. **D-E** *Cockatoo*, T654830/1. A peaceful location at the end of the road running along the beach east of Kuta. The newer bungalows are clean and attractive with private mandi and Western toilets, the older rooms are basic with squat toilet; bungalows face each other across a large garden. Restaurant (mid-range to cheap). **D-E** *Rinjani 2*, T654849. A mixture of rooms and bungalows with private mandi (some with western toilet), the newer bungalows are better value. Set in pretty gardens. The 2-storey bungalow at the front with an upstairs balcony overlooking the beach has the best view in Kuta. *Rinjani 1*, same ownership as *Rinjani 2* but these are older, rather basic bungalows in need of maintenance, though set in pretty gardens with a pond. Most have private mandis, some with Western toilets. **D-E** *Segara Anak*, T654834, F654835. Very lively and popular with budget travellers. Convenient location on the beach, next to the *Perama* office. 30 fairly basic rooms with private bathroom (Western toilets, some without toilet seats). Rooms set close together; the best rooms are the newer ones at the back overlooking the papaya grove and the hills. Very helpful staff, can provide a local map with a cycling route. Safety deposit box, money changer, small bookstore and book exchange, mountain bike and motorbike hire, snorkelling equipment, postal and fax service. Popular restaurant (mid-range to cheap).

At present the other accommodation along the beach road are older, very basic, and some are in need of renovation, this will probably change rapidly in the next few years. Most offer private mandis with squat or Western toilets, and face each other rather than the beach. There are also several homestays offering basic accommodation (with shared use of squat toilets) which could be of interest if you wanted the opportunity to live with a local family, or if all the other accommodation is full. High season, when accommodation may be full, is Aug and during the Nyale festival in Mar.

West Nusa Tenggara

Eating The best food is at the restaurant of the *Kuta Indah Hotel*. Seafood features prominently on many menus. But it is often overpriced and over-rated. Restaurants are attached to several of the above places to stay including *Rinjani Agung Beach*; *Florida*; *Anda*; *Cockatoo Inn*, good spring rolls, popular with tour buses; *Segara Anak*, popular; next door is the *Golden Flower*, which does excellent local food and huge portions of chips and omelette. *Bamboo*, near the village.

Bars & clubs Night life is pretty thin on the ground, but three times a week the local lads at the informal Jungle Bar knock out classic Marley tunes and this brings in a range of different types of tourists. Low key, very good atmosphere, even for single females (a rarity in Lombok's tourist centres). Cultural shows of discordant music and stick fighting are put on from time to time at the hotels. Be prepared to be hauled on stage to participate. The instruments have their origins in Bali, but the style and sound has evolved completely differently over the years.

Festivals **February/March** (on the 19th day of the 10th month of the Sasak lunar calendar): *Nyale ceremony*, several days before the ceremony "the rain comes down cats and dogs with lightning and thundering thunder bolts". Calm weather follows and thousands of mysterious sea worms called Nyale fish (*Eunice viridis*), 'hatch' on the reef and rise to the surface of the sea off Kuta. According to the legend of Putri Nyale, the episode is linked to the beautiful Princess Nyale who drowned herself here after failing to choose between a bevy of eligible men. The worms are supposed to represent her hair, and celebrations are held each year to mark her death. Traditionally, this was a time for young people to find a partner for marriage and it is still an occasion when the usual strictures controlling contact between the sexes are eased. The worms are scooped from the sea and eaten.

Shopping The local shops along the beachfront sell basics including fruit at reasonable prices. An endless stream of young children offer locally woven sarongs of variable quality, t-shirts and fruit. The pineapples here are delicious, as are the green bananas (to tell green bananas from unripe yellow bananas just squeeze; the ripe green bananas will feel soft). Kuta has its own market on Sat, selling all manner of fruit, vegetables, roosters, raw tobacco and the odd plastic gadget. Sengkol and Praya market days are Sat, Mon and Thu. Surf equipment, lessons, boat travel, adrenalin inducing surf videos from *Ocean Blue Surf Shop*, see below.

Sports **Surfing** Most people come here to Kuta to surf. Boards, lessons, other equipment, boat travel, repairs and adrenalin busting nightly videos of the biggest tubes and breaks in the world are shown at the *Ocean Blue Surf Shop*, Kuta T/F653911.

Transport **Bus**: Daily *Perama* shuttle buses at 0930, also an afternoon service if there is sufficient demand; the *Perama* office is adjacent to *Segara Anak*. Public bemo to Praya from the bemo stop several times a day, about 2,000Rp, 1 hr, from there you can catch a bemo to Bertais, 30 mins. 32 km from Praya, 54 km from Mataram. **Bemo**: from the Bertais terminal in Cakranegara (Mataram) to Praya and then a second from Praya to Kuta. Nomad also run a shuttle bus to Mataram. Public bemos also connect Kuta with Lahbuan Lombok (for ferries to Sumbawa). **Motorbikes**: are available to hire, often at very reasonable prices, eg 25,000Rp per day. Ask at your accommodation. Bemo services are increasing and more villages are coming on line, especially along the coast roads east and west of Kuta. Best to hire your own transport, though be aware that roads are bumpy and anyone prone to car sickness may not want to plan long drives. You can hire a car with driver but self-drive is recommended here; the local drivers have limited skills for the most part and can be ferocious in their use of accelerator and brakes. Mataram to Kuta is just over 1 hr, depending on traffic.

Useful information **Security:** there is an 'honoured' tradition of inter-village theft in these parts. A thief from one village gained prestige by successfully stealing from other villages. We were warned to be very careful if out walking after dark. Take extra precautions to safeguard money and valuables. However, all over Lombok local neighbourhood watch style groups have formed, HQ Praya, and will get your stolen goods back within the day! Hence crime has decreased considerably.

West of Kuta

There is now a sealed road running west of Kuta as far as Selong Blanak. Along the way there are several good beaches, all fairly deserted. Twenty minutes' drive (10 km) west of Kuta is **Mawan Beach**. A perfect horseshoe shaped bay with a golden sand beach, a large tree and two bamboo shelters (called *garuga*) and several coconut palms offering some protection from the sun. Good for swimming, very protected though the sea bed slopes steeply near the shore. The road west climbs steeply out of Kuta with spectacular views of the south coast, and mist covered hills in the rainy season. Further west near Selong Blanak are more good gold sand beaches at **Mawi** and **Rowok**. Mawi in particular offers good surfing. The road continues to the fishing village of **Selong Blanak** with its wide, sandy bay and accommodation a little inland. Few travellers make the trip further west to **Pengantap**, **Sepi** and **Blongas**; the last of which has good surfing, snorkelling and diving, though be wary of sharks. From Sepi the poor road heads inland via Sekatong to the port of **Lembar**. All roads deteriorate west of Pengantap and should probably be avoided in the wet season. There are some bemos, though most people get here by private or chartered transport. The better accommodations offer free transport to Tanjung Aan Beach to the east and Mawan Beach to the west.

D-E *Selong Blanak Cottages*, clean and well run, rooms with private mandi, restaurant (cheap), the deserted beach is about 2 km away and free transport is provided (the same applies for Sepi and Blongas nearby).

The occasional bemo runs to Selong Blanak from Praya.

East of Kuta

Shortly before Tanjung Aan the road forks; taking the left fork, northeast, the road passes through Sereneng *en route* to Awang, 18 km from Kuta. The right fork goes to Gerupak about 9 km east of Kuta. From here there are boats across Gumbang Bay to Bumgang for about 10,000Rp. From Bumgang there is a path north which connects with the road to Awang. The villagers in this area make their living from fishing and seaweed farming and will hire out boats for about 40,000Rp a day.

From Awang boats can be chartered across the bay to Ekas for about 30,000Rp return. **Ekas** has accommodation and good surfing and snorkelling. There are spectacular views from the cliffs overlooking Awang Bay on both sides, particularly from Ekas. It is possible but time-consuming to reach Ekas by public bemo: from Praya catch a bemo bound for Tanjung Luar and Gubukdalem, get off just before Keruak at the turning south to Jerowaru and wait for a bemo going to Ekas, which is *en route* to Kaliantan in the southwest corner of the peninsula.

Tanjung Ringgit on the southeastern tip of Lombok is difficult to reach and for the most part, the scenery is unexceptional. This place is shrouded in magic and mystery with tales of spirits and demons living in the caves. (If a young woman goes there the tale goes that she will fall in love and never return.) It has connections with the Waktu Telu religion. To get here the choice is an arduous overland journey ending in a rough dirt track or chartering a boat from the fishing town of Tanjung Luar, 55,000Rp approximately.

Sleeping **Ekas D** *Laut Surga Cottages*, F0364-693122. Restaurant, popular with surfers, this remote place several kilometres south of Ekas is set on a pretty, secluded beach. However, due to financial pressures, it may close after the next high season (ie it will be closed by early 2001).

Transport **Bemo** A few bemos travel these routes and their numbers are slowly increasing, but the best way to see the area is with your own transport. **Boat** From Awang. In the dry season it is possible to drive there via Jerowaru.

Background

History

It seems that the Sasak population of Lombok converted to Islam during the 16th century when either Sunan Giri or possibly Senopati, two of Java's famous nine Muslim saints, arrived from Java. Local legend has it that epidemics only began to afflict Lombok after the introduction of Islam and that it was by turning to Islam Waktu Telu that further epidemics were prevented. At this time – although the history is sketchy to say the least – it seems that Lombok was ruled by a series of Sasak princes who spent their time fending off successive invasions from Sumbawanese, Makassarese and Balinese attackers.

In the 17th century, the Balinese king of Karangasem invaded West Lombok and attempted to annex the island. He failed, and it was not until 1740 that the Balinese established a stronghold in the west. Even then, the independently minded Sasaks of the east managed to maintain their autonomy until the 19th century. Nonetheless, the Balinese – as the dominant group – imposed their culture on the Sasaks. They became the ruling caste, occupied all the positions of authority, and stipulated for example, that while a Balinese man could marry a Sasak woman, a Balinese woman was prohibited from marrying a Sasak man. The Balinese overlords also attempted to control the economy of the island: if a Sasak man died without leaving any male children, all his lands were automatically confiscated. Given the harshness with which the Sasaks were treated by their rulers, it is no wonder that they rebelled on a number of occasions, and when the chance offered itself, asked the Dutch to come to their rescue.

The Dutch In 1894, the Dutch resident of North Bali succeeded in persuading his superiors in Batavia to mount an invasion of Lombok as a prelude to an invasion of South Bali. The pretext for the invasion was that the local Sasaks had requested Dutch assistance in ridding themselves of their Balinese overlords. General Vetter was put in charge of the invasion force and he landed his troops on the south coast. Negotiations with the Balinese and the Sasaks broke down, and the former attacked the bivouacked Dutch. General Van Ham, the second in command, along with 100 other soldiers was killed and the Dutch withdrew to the coast where they built further fortifications. Reinforcements were sent to bolster Vetter's force, which in the Dutch view had been a victim of 'sinister treachery' on the part of the Balinese. With their Sasak allies, the Dutch set about attacking and looting every town and village in South Lombok. Mataram was taken apart, literally stone by stone – even the trees were cut down. On the 18 November 1894 Vetter shelled and destroyed the palace at Cakranegara. The Crown Prince Ktut and several thousand Balinese defenders were killed in the attack, while the Dutch lost only 460 men – 246 of whom died of disease. As was later to be the case during the Dutch campaigns in Bali, rather than surrender, the Balinese chose to die in a *pupatan* or 'fight to the death' (see page 72). The King of

Lombok's crafts

Banyu Mulek *(6 km from Mataram):
earthenware products.*
Beleka *(10 km east of Praya): baskets,
bags, cases and other goods made from
reeds and rotan (rattan).*
Getap *(1 km east of Cakranegara): a
village of blacksmiths where swords,
knives and other objects are cast.*
Loyok Kutaraja *(40 km east of
Mataram): furniture and woven goods.*
Masbaggik *(44 km east of Mataram, see
page 291): earthenware bowls and pots,
now produced with the marketing and
technological help of a New Zealand NGO.*
Penjanggik *(4 km east of Praya): a
weaving village producing hand-woven
cloth distinct from that at Sukarara.*

Penujak *(5 km south of Praya, see page
294): earthenware bowls and pots, now
produced, as at Masbaggik, with the
marketing and technological help of a
New Zealand NGO.*
Pringgasela *(50 km from Mataram, see
page 291): a weaving village, although
many of the hand-woven cloths are no
longer made to traditional designs.*
Sayang-Sayang *(1 km north of
Cakranegara): lacquered boxes made
from palm leaves.*
Senanti *(73 km from Mataram): wood
carvings.*
Sukarara *(25 km from Mataram, see
page 294): traditional, and some not so
traditional, hand-woven textiles.*

West Nusa Tenggara

Cakranegara was sent into exile, where he died six months later, and when the treasure house of the palace was opened it yielded, to the delight of the Dutch, 230 kg of gold, 7,299 kg of silver and three caskets of jewels.

For the Sasaks and the remnant Balinese population of Lombok, the years of Dutch rule from 1900 to 1940 were not happy ones. Indeed, the Dutch period on Lombok represents, in the eyes of many historians, an object lesson in the excesses and inequities of colonial rule. The Dutch taxed everyone heavily, not just the peasants, but also the landlords and the aristocracy. The latter passed the costs of their taxation on to their tenants, who therefore had a double burden to bear. It has been estimated that over a quarter of a farmer's rice harvest – which was already barely sufficient to ensure subsistence – was forfeited in taxes. There was a consequent sharp deterioration in conditions in the countryside and by the 1920s a class of marginalized paupers had been created where previously there was none. Meat and rice consumption fell, malnutrition became widespread, and when harvests failed, famine ensued. Farmers were forced to eat their seed grain and an island which should have produced a surplus of food was afflicted with endemic famine. Historians believe Lombok's condition was rooted in the nature of the colonial system itself.

Even after the Dutch had withdrawn and Indonesia had achieved independence, life on Lombok remained difficult. Famines became almost a way of life, and in 1966 many thousands died of starvation after a particularly poor harvest. The inhabitants of Lombok, and of the other islands of Nusa Tenggara, talk of *lapar biasa*, literally 'normal hunger' (akin to the 'hungry season' in Africa). Even the introduction of new rice technology in the early 1970s helped little – the rice was devastated by the brown plant hopper (known by entomologists as the BPH). To try and ease these pressures, the government has been settling people elsewhere in the archipelago as part of the transmigration scheme – 42,000 were moved between 1973 and 1983. But, this out-migration of Lombok's inhabitants has not stemmed the growth of the island's population. Unlike many other areas of Indonesia, the country's family planning programme has had only a marginal effect on Lombok. Analysts maintain that the strong Muslim beliefs of the majority of Sasaks has prevented the adoption of family planning methods, and fertility rates remain high, as does infant mortality.

Wallace's line

In his book The Malay Archipelago, published in 1869, the great Victorian naturalist Alfred Russel Wallace wrote: "If we look at a map of the Archipelago, nothing seems more unlikely than that the closely related chain of islands from Java to Timor should differ materially in their natural productions". During his travels he noted the "remarkable change...which occurs at the Straits of Lombock, separating the island of that name from Bali; and which is at once so large in amount and of so fundamental a character, as to form an important feature in the zoological geography of our globe". Wallace was struck by the change in the faunal composition of Bali and Lombok – two islands separated by a strait only a few kilometres wide. The former was dominated by animals of Asian origin, and the latter of Australasian – Wallace's Indo-Malayan and Austro-Malayan regions respectively.

The first reference to Wallace's 'line', as it became known, is contained in a letter he wrote to Henry Bates who had just returned to London from his South American travels, in January 1858. Since then, numerous zoogeographers and naturalists have offered their own interpretations, all highlighting the change in fauna but postulating various different 'lines'. Even Wallace changed his mind: his original line had Sulawesi in the Austro-Malayan region, but by 1880 he had decided the island to be anomalous, and then in 1910 he drew his line to the east of Sulawesi, placing it in the Indo-Malayan region. The other lines proposed include Weber's line (1894), Lydekker's line (1896) and an updated Weber's line (1904), of which the last has received the greatest recognition.

The validity of Wallace's line rests on the distribution of animals through the island arc of the Lesser Sundas. Botanists have found little to lead them to similar conclusions. For example, the majority of East Asian mammals – like the elephant and rhinoceros – do not extend beyond Bali. Likewise, over 80% of reptiles, amphibians and butterflies in Sulawesi are of western origin. But some naturalists have stressed the importance of ecology in determining the faunal composition of the islands of the Lesser Sundas. The Oxford zoologist W George has summed up this view by writing that Wallace's line "marks the division between a rich continental fauna associated with high rainfall, forests and varied habitats and an impoverished fauna associated with low rainfall, thorn scrub and restricted habitats".

However, perhaps most remarkably, Wallace 'predicted' the theory of plate tectonics and continental drift when he wrote that the distribution of animals "can only be explained by a bold acceptance of vast changes in the surface of the earth".

Geography

Lombok is divided into three *kabupaten* or districts – West, East and Central. The capital Mataram has become fused with the former royal city of Cakranegara, forming a rather sprawling town along the main east-west road. At the last census in 1991 the population of Lombok was 2½ million, the majority of whom are Muslim Sasaks. The population at the beginning of 2000 had reached close to three million.

Covering 4,700 sq km, Lombok is dominated by the magnificent volcano Mount Rinjani which rises to 3,726 m – making it the highest peak in Indonesia outside Irian Jaya. A hard, three-day climb to the crater can be organized. The island's main crop is rice, which is primarily cultivated in irrigated paddy fields on the fertile central plain. Like Bali, irrigation is regulated through a supra-village organization, the *subak* (see page 229). Other crops include cassava, cotton, tobacco, soyabean, areca nuts, chilli peppers (the name Lombok

Islam Waktu Telu

On Lombok, it is thought that there are still a handful of adherents of Islam Waktu Telu. A figure of 1% of the population (25,000 people) is quoted, but this seems unlikely. Waktu Telu is a mixture of Islam and ancestor and spirit worship. Because the religion is not considered one of the five 'official' religions of Indonesia (they are Islam, Hinduism, Buddhism, Catholicism and Protestantism), the adherents of Islam Waktu Telu have been ignored and – at times – even persecuted. In 1919-20 the Waktu Telu rebelled against what they saw to be an unholy coalition between the Dutch and members of the rival religion, Islam Waktu Lima. Orthodox Muslims regard Waktu Telu as a travesty of the teachings of the Prophet and between 1927 and 1933 one fervent Islam Waktu Lima missionary travelled the island breaking-up idols and

converting the population to orthodox Islam. Now that many Sasaks are almost embarrassed to admit they are believers of Waktu Telu, it is likely that before long, the religion will have been consigned to the history books. This is not just because the religion is unpopular, but also because while it is possible for a Sasak to convert to orthodox Islam, a Sasak is only a Waktu Telu by birth, and cannot convert from orthodox Islam to Waktu Telu. Like the giant panda, Islam Waktu Telu is on an evolutionary dead-end.

The ceremonies and festivals of the religion focus upon the stages of a person's life, and upon the natural world – particularly that connected with agricultural production. Adherents to Waktu Telu only obey the central tenets of Islam – namely, belief in Allah and Mohammad as his prophet.

is Javanese for 'chilli pepper'), cinnamon, cloves, vanilla and coffee. Lombok is also an important exporter of frogs' legs. Because of the rapid increase in the population of Lombok, there has been an associated increase in the pressure on the environment. Forests are now reduced to degraded secondary growth, over-grazing is commonplace, and erosion serious. To try to offset the decline in the fortunes of agriculture, there has been some attempt to diversify the economy. The island's main export is now pumice, although seaweed and sea cucumber are harvested for the Asian market and tourism is rapidly becoming a major source of revenue.

Climate Lombok is drier than Bali, but wetter than the islands to the east, and receives an annual rainfall of 1,500-2,000 mm. The dry season spans the months from May to July, the hot rainy season from November to March when downpours can be quite severe and prolonged. The west is considerably wetter than the rest of the island, receiving rain even during the dry season. The east, north and south are noticeably more arid.

Culture

People The largest ethnic group are the Muslim Sasaks, the original inhabitants of Lombok, who maintain their unique language, dress and customs. There is also a significant population of Hindu Balinese who survived the Dutch invasion of 1894 (see below), along with smaller groups of Chinese, Sumbawanese, Buginese and Makassarese. Most of the Balinese and the other 'immigrant' groups are concentrated in the west, and it is in this area that Balinese *pura* are interspersed with Islamic mosques.

The Sasaks embrace two forms of Islam: the traditional – and now virtually 'extinct' – *Islam Waktu Telu* (see page 303) and the more orthodox, and more popular, *Islam Waktu Lima*. The 'traditional' marriage ceremony in Lombok

West Nusa Tenggara

is very similar to that of Bali where the bride-to-be is kidnapped by the groom and his accomplices. The *kawin-lari* or runaway marriage is known in Sasak as *merari*.

Arts & crafts In comparison to neighbouring Bali, Lombok is not nearly as rich in terms of artistic achievement. Distinctive ikat cloth is still produced on the island, although even this is suffering from a decline in quality as weavers turn out material at an ever-faster rate to satisfy burgeoning tourist demand. Traditionally, Sasak women were expected to weave a trousseau of about 40 pieces of cloth. Some of these are believed to be imbued with magical powers and they are important in ceremonies during the life cycle, for example during circumcision and tooth-filing. Such *kain umbak* are unremarkable, coarse weave cloths, often striped. Lombok's basketwork is, however, highly regarded and finely worked baskets are probably one of the best, and most distinctive, products of the island.

Tourist development: the next decade From the late 1980s through to the late 1990s, Lombok underwent considerable change and the plan was to further promote the island as an alternative to Bali. The Indonesian government continues to view Lombok as a nascent Bali, and the Lombok Tourism Development Corporation has been established to oversee an expansion in hotels and other facilities. In 1995, 308,200 tourists visited Lombok, of whom 167,250 were foreigners. This latter figure is up from a mere 44,850 in 1988. Like so many other areas of Indonesia, the political and economic problems of 1997, 1998, 1999 and 2000 brought Lombok's upward tourism trajectory to an end. Arrivals were down and hotels half full. The riots of January 2000 saw tourists chartering helicopters out of Lombok, whilst even those Indonesians not involved with the issues at hand took up weapons in Mataram in case any marauding herds passed by. Consequently, tourist numbers are down and rates highly negotiable if you feel comfortable with milking this misfortune. On the up-side, many people are quite clear that *agents provocateur* from elsewhere precipitated the violence in defence of Muslims in Melaku. This would imply that no actual acute conflict is present in Lombok itself. Indeed, Muslims, Christians and Hindus alike are consciously trying to put foreigners at ease.

Virtually all the developments – built and planned – are along the coast, particularly on the west side of the island. A large proportion of the coastline from Senggigi to Bangsal has already been bought by speculators or hotel groups and has been fenced-off.

One constraint to these plans is Lombok's limited infrastructure. Rural roads are paved but generally poor, the airport can only accommodate small planes, and telecommunications capacity is limited. Nonetheless, several international hotel chains including *Sheraton, Heritage, Oberoi* and *Holiday Inn* have opened hotels on the island over the last decade or so. Several more are under consideration, although doubtless many have been put on the back burner while investors decide what the future of tourism in Lombok and, more widely in Indonesia is likely to be. Kuta, on the south coast, has been the focus of plans which will change this quiet stretch of coastline into an international resort with marinas, golf courses and several luxury hotels. Needless to say, old Lombok hands view the changes with horror and trepidation.

West Nusa Tenggara

Sumbawa

Most people do not linger in Sumbawa. They use the island as a route between the apparently more enticing islands of Lombok to the west and Flores to the east. This is a shame, not least because Sumbawa is singularly different from the rest of Nusa Tenggara.

Sumbawa's landscape is harsh and dry with rugged, boulder-strewn hills, scrubby vegetation and a bright searing light. When the mist hangs over the land in the early mornings, the island looks almost like a moonscape. There is a handful of oases of cultivation – for example, around Dompu, to the east of the island – but generally Sumbawa is infertile and population densities here are markedly lower than the richer islands of Lombok and Bali to the west. The people of Sumbawa are largely Muslim but, even so, there is a significant division between the Sumbawanese to the west (with their capital at Sumbawa Besar) and the Bimanese to the east (with their capital at Bima). Sumbawa's attractions are largely natural: the surfing beaches at Hu'u, the coral and snorkelling off Moyo Island, and hiking to the summit of Mount Tambora, an imposing volcano which erupted in the early 19th century and devastated large swathes of Nusa Tenggara.

West Nusa Tenggara

Background

Even though Sumbawa covers nearly 16,000 sq km its population remains just one million. The island is divided into three districts: Sumbawa, Dompu and Bima. In fact, Sumbawa is really two islands – joined by a thin isthmus – in one. Locals refer only to the western half as 'Sumbawa'; the east is Bima. It is said that when the first ever marriage occurred between the royal houses of Sumbawa and Bima in 1929, the bride and groom could only communicate with one another in Dutch, such had been the degree of mutual ignorance. Sumbawa Besar has been influenced by its neighbours to the west, with a language reminiscent of Sasak, whilst Bima looks to the east, with a language more akin to that spoken in Flores.

Islam was introduced to Sumbawa in the early 17th century when the King of Bima became a Muslim, and thus a Sultan. The Dutch did not exercise control over the island until the early part of the 20th century, and this lasted barely a single generation before the Japanese invaded. Today, the royal court of Bima still survives, but in an impoverished state. The two main towns on Sumbawa are Sumbawa Besar, to the west, and Bima-Raba in the east.

There are a number of cultural traditions specific to Sumbawa, not least that of horsemanship. 'Small but cute' as one locally-produced tourist brochure puts it, horses are displayed by 5-10 year old boys during the months of August and September to celebrate the anniversary of West Nusa Tenggara's independence. This event is celebrated particularly enthusiastically at Lapfadi and Sera Ala Kempo.

Dance forms specific to Sumabawa include: Da'ha hira where the movements are reminiscent of weaving. Bongi Monca (yellow rice), which is a welcome dance formerly reserved for VIPs, performed and sung by women, the custodians of hospitality. Hadrah is an Islamic tradition of the island. Known as *tambour* or *rebana*, the songs are devoted to Allah.

The fiery Sumbawanese spirit can be seen in the following ritualized forms of self defence. Guntao combines flute, tambourine and gongs in a martial style and is usually performed at weddings, circumcision ceremonies and at paddy harvest time. Mpaa Sila is very similar but performed with swords as opposed to bare fists. Lanja, another ritual dance demonstrating the strength of the performer is used by young men to woo potential wives. Rawa Mbojo (Bimanese music and song) recounts a complex love tale in verse sung to a local type of violin.

The island runs east-west for 280 km but varies in width from as little as 15 km, to 90 km at its widest point. Like the rest of Nusa Tenggara, Sumbawa is volcanic in origin, most clearly illustrated when Mount Tambora erupted in 1815 to devastating effect, killing an estimated 12,000 people (see page 312).

Ins & outs

Getting there There are flights to Sumbawa Besar and Bima Raba towards the western and eastern ends of the island respectively. But most people arrive by ferry either from Lombok to the west or from Flores (via Komodo) to the east. The port for Lombok is Poto Tano on the western end of the island; for Flores via Komodo it is Sape on the eastern tip. Regular ferries ply these 2 routes. *Pelni* ships dock at Sumbawa Besar's port of Badas and at Bima-Raba's port, but few people arrive or leave the island this way. There is also a high-speed ferry linking Bima with Bali and Kupang (Timor).

Getting around The Trans-Sumbawa highway is excellent, and made-up all the way from Poto Tano (the port on the west coast, serving Lombok) to Sape (on the east coast, serving Komodo and Flores). It is 250 km from Sumbawa Besar to Bima-Raba. There are no large towns on Sumbawa; bemos provide the main means of local transport with larger buses and minibuses providing links across the island. There are also horse-drawn carts for a more sedate form of short-distance travel.

Alas

Alas was once the main port for Lombok; now ferries leave from Poto Tano, 22 km to the south and 10 km off the main road. There is little reason to stay here, but there are losmen available if travellers get stranded (Poto Tano has no accommodation).

Sumbawa Island

Highlights, Sumbawa

Surfing at Hu'u and Maluk
Snorkelling off Moyo Island
Hiking to the summit of Mount Tambora

D *Hotel Telagga*, Jl Pahlawan, is the first
option coming in to Alas, some a/c and
attached Indonesian restaurant. **E** *Anda*, Jl
Pahlawan 14, T169. **E** *Selamat*, Jl
Pahlawan 7, T26.

Sleeping

Road Bus: connections with Sumbawa
Besar, Poto Tano and Taliwang.

Transport
22 km from Poto Tano

Taliwang

Taliwang lies to the south of Alas and Poto Tano; people travelling further south
to the surfing beach at Maluk may have to stay overnight here, but there is little
reason to extend a stay – although it is friendly enough. **Beware**: There are lots of
dogs in this part of Sumbawa and many would not seem to make ideal pets.

Phone code: 0372

A 15 minute walk out of Taliwang is a 856-ha lake, **Lebuk Taliwang**. Noted as
an ideal place to relax, swim and fish; boats can be hired at the lakeside if you
feel like cutting adrift.

Excursions

E *Hamba*, Jl Sudirman 64, T8. **E** *Taliwang*, Jl Sudirman, T81014, some rooms with
shower, English speaking management, the best place in town – but still basic.
E-F *Tubalong*, Jl Sudirman 11, T81018. **F-E** *Losmen Azhar*, Jl Pasar Baru, close to the
market, basic but welcoming.

Sleeping

Cheap *Taliwang Indah*, good value dishes. The following restaurants have all been
recommended: *Coffee House Casanova*, *Sinar Remaja*, Jl Sudirman 113; *Anda*, Depot
Dewi and *Kediri* at Komplek Terminal Taliwang.

Eating

40 km from Alas, 40 km from Maluk. **Road Bus**: bus connections with Poto Tano and
Alas and onward to Sumbawa Besar. **Bemo**: to Sumbawa Besar. **Trucks**: take travellers further south to Maluk.

Transport

Maluk

Maluk is a beach, with good surf, on
Sumbawa's west coast, south of
Taliwang. **NB** The coral is just below
the surface and surfing can be hazardous – this is only for the most adventurous of surfers. The beach is
fantastic and the swimming good.

Phone code: 0372

The district capital of Jereweh, also
known as 'Super Shark', is 30 km away
and because there is a large mine here,
accommodation is now said to be readily
available. There is just one official place
to stay in Maluk, although there are a
number of homestays. **C-D** *Hotel Trophy*, a new place to stay and the best run
and most comfortable accommodation
in Maluk, managed by an Australian –
although he may have moved on with

Sleeping

West Nusa Tenggara

176

anti-Aussie sentiment. **E** *Maluk Beach Bungalows*, Jl Pasir Putih, newer place than the *Surya* so the bungalows are in better nick. **E** *Surya Bungalow*, Jl Pasir Putih, bungalows on the edge of town.

Transport
95 km south of Poto Tano, 40 km from Taliwang

Road Bus: from Poto Tano, catch a bus south to Taliwang 45 km, and from here a truck to Maluk 40 km. From Sumbawa Besar, catch a bus from the Bawah terminal to Taliwang 114 km and then a truck onwards. **Sea Boat**: a more direct route to Maluk is from Labuhan Haji on Lombok's east coast, 1½ hrs.

Poto Tano to Sumbawa Besar

The road from Poto Tano to Sumbawa Besar follows the coast and offers views of beautiful, deserted beaches, and brightly painted stilted wooden houses. Grapes and mangoes are grown in this area, and you will pass mats of rice laid out to dry by the roadside, and fields of sturdy, Sumbawan horses. The bus conductor, sitting on the left front side of the bus, acts as a second pair of eyes to the driver, giving signals on right hand bends to tell the driver about oncoming traffic and whether the road bends left or right next. You'll notice clay water urns perched in the clefts of trees outside houses.

Sumbawa Besar

Phone code: 0371
Colour map 1, grid B5

This dusty, quiet but tree-filled town on the north coast of the island is really only a stop-over on the way east to Bima-Raba and the island of Komodo, or west to Lombok. But while Sumbawa Besar may be little more than a village it is the capital of the district of Sumbawa and a former royal capital to boot. It is small enough to walk around, and is very friendly – the locals are inclined to invite visitors back to their houses. Certainly the Hello Missus/Mister phenomenon is alive and well. Women may find they have an ojek/moped or two gallantly trailing their route for company!

Ins and outs

Getting there
Sumbawa Besar's small airport is 2 km from town and there are links with Bali, Sulawesi, Java and other destinations in Nusa Tenggara. Most people, however, arrive by bus. There are connections all the way through to Lombok and east to Sape, for Komodo and Flores. Badas is Sumbawa Besar's port, 9 km west of town. The Pelni ship *Tatamailau* docks here.

Getting around
Sumbawa Besar is a small town and not a struggle to come to terms with. Bemos and dokars (known here as *cidomos*) provide local transport but it doesn't take long from one end of town to the other. The **tourist Office** is on Jl Garuda, T21932, T21581.

Sights

Sumbawa Besar's main sight is a large wooden palace on Jalan Sudirman, at the east side of town. The **Istana Tua**, known locally as *Dalam Loka* ('Old Palace') is a fabulous old wooden building looking impressive in its forlorn, picturesque, decrepid state. It is raised off the ground on 99 wooden pillars, with a massive wooden entrance ramp, it was extensively renovated in 1985 but without further renovation its days must be numbered. Built a century earlier in 1885 by Sultan Mohammad Jalaluddin III, it is now an empty shell, but is impressive nonetheless. It is due to metamorphose into a museum, although the pieces to stock the museum have yet to materialize. ■ *Admission by donation. 0900-1600 Mon-Sun.*

Just opposite the entrance are some picturesque old stilted houses. An abandoned **Dutch fort** is visible from the palace, situated on the hill overlooking the town. Next to the palace is the modern and uninspired **Mesjid Nurul Huda**.

Not far from the post office on Jalan Yos Sudarso is a poorly maintained Balinese temple, **Pura Agung Girinatha**. A short walk east of here, on Jalan Cipto, is the very ordinary **Seketeng Market**. On the road out of town to the northwest, the overlooking hillside is covered with tombstones, once brightly adorned with coloured glass and pottery, now considerably faded. Most definitely a peaceful retreat despite (or because of?) the morbid associations.

Kencana Beach 10 km west of town, offers snorkelling.

Excursions

Sleeping at Kencana Beach A-B *Kencana Beach Inn*, Jalan Raya Tano, Km 11, Teruna Beach, 10 km west of town, 20 mins' drive from town and airport (book through *Tambora Hotel* in town), T22555, F22439. Once popular with backpackers this seaside accommodation owned by the *Tambora Hotel* has gone way upmarket and now offers attractive but pricey bamboo bungalows set in landscaped gardens overlooking the sea. (But note that in early 2000, due to the appalling state of the tourist industry, rates were way down from the rack rate.) Rooms are a/c or fan with western toilets. Good pool, 'private' beach. Watersports: snorkelling and diving equipment sometimes available for hire, pool and a stage where traditional Balinese and Sumbawan dances are performed. Restaurant (mid-range to cheap), serves local specialities and a special Sumbawan buffet service is a little unpredictable. A quiet spot to rest. Transfer from *Tambora Hotel*. *Getting there*: by bemo.

Essentials

B-D *Dewi Hotel*, 60 Jl Hasanuddin, T21170/23360. Recently modernized, clean, bright and airy, probably the most attractive place to stay in town. Some rooms with a/c, hot water, TV and phone, all with private mandi. All but the cheapest rooms have western toilets, and balconies or verandahs. If you want a fan room with western toilet this is the place to stay. Friendly staff. There is a wooden replica of the Istana Tua in the reception

Sleeping
Accommodation is primarily geared to Indonesian visitors

West Nusa Tenggara

Sumbawa Besar

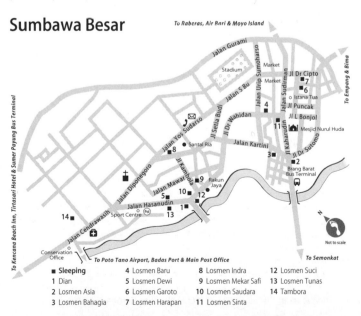

■ **Sleeping**	4 Losmen Baru	8 Losmen Indra	12 Losmen Suci
1 Dian	5 Losmen Dewi	9 Losmen Mekar Safi	13 Losmen Tunas
2 Losmen Asia	6 Losmen Garoto	10 Losmen Saudara	14 Tambora
3 Losmen Bahagia	7 Losmen Harapan	11 Losmen Sinta	

West Nusa Tenggara

hall. Recommended. **B-D** *Tambora Hotel*, 2 Jl Kebayan, T21555, 22111, 22444, F22624. The best hotel in town, well run, clean and quiet, but rooms are drab, could do with redecoration, and are pricey for what they offer; the clientele is largely Indonesian businessmen and foreign tour groups. Some rooms with a/c, hot water, western toilets, bath, TV, phone, fridge and mosquitoes, though staff will spray with insecticide. Fan rooms do not have western toilets. Impressive entrance hall, large grounds, good but fairly pricey restaurant (mid-range) In early 2000 the only items on the menu were *nasi goreng* and *mie goreng*, so be prepared to get gastronically bored. Staff are very helpful and can help with air and bus tickets; they will make bookings and arrange for long distance buses to pick you up from the hotel. Only limited English spoken. Price includes bread and coffee for breakfast. Less than 1 km from airport, 15 mins' walk from bus station. Recommended. **B-E** *Tirtasari*, Jl Garuda Labunan, T21987. Attractive location right on the beach, 15 mins from the centre of town. Some rooms with a/c and hot water, private mandis with western toilet. Tropical gardens. Restaurant (mid-range to cheap). Pool. **D-E** *Hotel Cendrawasih*, Jl Cendrawasih, some a/c, situated in a residential area, has clean and homely rooms. **D-E** *Hotel Dian*, Jl Hasanuddin, T21708/22297, a/c, central, spotless. **D-E** *Losmen Saudara*, Jl Hasanuddin 50, T21528. Rather dark rooms, attached mandi, some rooms with a/c, fan rooms are basic with squat toilets, mainly Indonesian clientele. **D-E** *Losmen Suci*, Jl Hasanuddin 57, T21589. Restaurant, courtyard with open air restaurant, rooms with private mandi and squat toilet, some rooms rather dirty, friendly staff. **E** *Losmen Garoto*, Jl Batu Pasak 48, T22062. Fabulous views overlooking the Istana Tua from the balconies of the upstairs rooms. Rooms, however, are very basic and small with fan and private mandi, squat toilet, located in a quiet residential area, 10 mins walk from the bustle of the centre of town. **E-F** *Losmen Baru*, Jl Dokter Wahidin, see the comments for Losmen Harapan - reasonable place to stay, good rates. **E-F** *Losmen Harapan*, Jl Dokter Cipto 5, T 21629, this place and the Losmen Baru are really much of a muchness, cheap and reasonable rooms for the price. **E-F** *Losmen Indra*, Jl Diponegoro 48A, T21878. Next to bus station, extremely basic, grimey, some rooms with private mandi, squat toilets, only stay here if you are desperate.

Eating   Stalls and warungs around the Bawah bus terminal on Jl Diponegoro and at the Pasar Seketeng on Jl Dr Cipto. At night warungs open by the stadium on Jl Yos Sudarso selling the usual bakso (soup with unidentifiable balls floating in it), sate and so on. The main concentrations of restaurants are on Jl Hasanuddin and Jl Kartini; lots of locals can be seen eating here, which is a good a sign as any.

Mid-range   *Tambora Restaurant* (at hotel of same name), Jl Kebayan 2, good but fairly pricey food. Recommended. **Cheap**   *Putra Jogya*, Jl Hasanuddin, on the opposite side of the road from Kristal and specialises in seafood. Next door to Putra Jogya is the muralled *Pondok Bamboo* where the gigantic sound system takes up much of this small café. **Very cheap**   *Cirebon* Jl Kebayan 14. *Rakun Jaya*, Jl Hasanuddin 53, Indonesian. *Kristal*, Jl Hasanuddin, offers all the usual but with a large range of pigeon dishes, *burung dara*. *Usfa Warna*, Jl Kartini 16, Chinese and seafood.

Shopping   Market stalls set up every morning adjacent to Jl Sudirman, selling the usual fare of fruit and vegetables. Birds and chickens proliferate. Around town there is a good range of open fronted shops.

  Dynasty Art Shop, Jl Garuda, T21644, has a range of local paintings, depicting a combination of religious and cultural themes. Supermarket and chemist adjacent to *Tambora Hotel*, open 0730-2100. Apotik Dinasti, Jl Garuda; Apotik Medika, Jl Diponegoro.

Sports   **Diving & snorkelling**   Snorkelling and diving equipment used to be available from the *Kencana Beach Inn*, but does not seem to be at the market.

Tour operators   *Tarindo Wisata*, Jl Kebayan 2, T21416/22275. *Tirta Martan*, Jl Garuda 88.

Local Bemos: the station is in front of the Seketeng Market on Jl Dr Cipto. Bemo rides in town cost 500Rp, to Badas Port (the port for Sumbawa Besar) 3,000 Rp. There are also bemos to Kencana Beach. **Dokars** (known as *cidomos*): 500Rp.

Air The airport is only 2 km west of the town centre across the bridge south of the *Tambora Hotel*. There are 'taxis', but it is easy to walk, or catch a bemo. Regular connections on *Garuda/Merpati* with **Denpasar, Jakarta, Mataram, Surabaya, Ujung Pandang** and **Yogyakarta**.

Road Bus: in the last edition of the *Indonesia Handbook* we reported on some confusion regarding bus terminals: how many there were, and which were open or closed. Things haven't got much clearer in the intervening couple of years! Even the tourist office and hotels seemed unclear. But to the best of our knowledge the following applies: Terminal Bawah has closed. **Terminal Brang Barat** on Jl Kaharuddin operates as a hub for bemos going to surrounding villages. It no longer has many long-distance buses running east, as was formerly the case although there are occasional morning departures for Bima-Raba. The main bus terminal is the **Terminal Sumer Payung** on Jl Garuda/Jl Labuhan Sumbawa around 5 km north of town where buses depart for destinations east such as **Bima-Raba** and **Dompu** and west to **Utan, Alas, Taliwang** and to **Poto Tano** port (for Lombok). *Perama* has closed its local operation but do still run shuttle buses from Lombok and Bali to the main destinations in Sumbawa. There are direct buses from **Mataram** (Lombok) to Sumbawa Besar and onward to Bima-Raba. A/c buses to Mataram, leave at 0700, 0800, 0900, 1300 and 1500, and will pick you up from your hotel. The price includes ferry. There is no a/c day bus to Bima-Raba, though you might get seats on an a/c bus coming through from Mataram. Buses to Dompu and Bima-Rabu leave roughly hourly from 0600-1000 and from 1300-1600. There are a/c night buses leaving at approximately 2000 and midnight. Buses will drop you off near your hotel. Bus times approximately are: Bima 6-7 hrs, Sape 7½ hrs, Dompu 4 hrs, Taliwang 3 hrs, Poto Tano 2 hrs, Mataram 6 hrs. The buses are non smoking. **NB** Buying a ticket from the hotels will cost extra, the advantage is that you will be picked up from your hotel. Buses will also drop you off at the point along their route nearest your accommodation.

Sea Boat: there are regular buses from Poto Tano to Alas, and then onward to Sumbawa Besar and Bima-Raba. Badas is the main port for West Sumbawa and is where the *Pelni* ships dock. Pelni office, Badas Harbour, T22344, 9 km west of town, accessible by bemo.

Airline offices *Merpati*, 117 Jl Diponegoro, T21416. Located just west of bus station. Open 0800-1300, 7 days a week. **Banks** *BNI*, Jl Kartini 10, open 0800-1600 Mon-Fri. Will change major currencies and TCs (good rates). **Communications General Post Office:** Jl Garuda, west of town on the road to the airport; Post Office on Jl Yos Sudarso 6A. Open 0800-1500 Mon-Fri, 0800-1100 Sat. **Telephone office:** (international telephone, telex, telegram & fax): Jl Yos Sudarso (opposite Post Office). **Medical services Hospitals:** *General Hospital*, Jl Garuda, T217087 (west edge of town). **Useful addresses** PHPA Office: Jl Candrawasih 1A, T21446 (west, just past the *General Hospital*).

Transport
70 km from Alas,
92 km from Poto Tano,
250 km from Bima-Raba

Directory

West Nusa Tenggara

Moyo Island

Moyo Island is just accessible as a day trip (the *Kencana Beach Inn*, see above, organizes day trips to the island), although it is best to stay overnight. The south area of the island is a national park and lies just to the north of Sumbawa Besar. Rich in wildlife, with particularly good snorkelling off the south coast, it is being considered for 'hunting safaris'. Pigs, buffaloes and deer live here in the wild. Moyo is home to the rare bird, gosong, (megapodius) is now under protection. The **Mata Jitu Waterfall** is notable on this idyllic island. ■ *Contact the PHPA office in Sumbawa Besar (see below) before visiting the island. Best time to visit: Jun-Aug. No snorkelling equipment available for hire on Moyo.*

Phone code: 0371
Colour map 1, grid B6

Sleeping L *Amanwana*, Moyo Island, T2333, F22288. Reservations c/o *Amanusa*, Nusa Dua, Bali, T71267, F71260. A remarkably luxurious 'tent' hotel. The first so-called 'Aman Hideaway', 'tents' are large chalets with canvas roofs, a/c, king-size beds, divans and large bathrooms. The hotel has a restaurant, bar, lounge and library and rates include all food and drink and most activities, surely one of the most civilized ways to camp on this pristine island. If you mention Moyo, Princess Diana is the oft-spoken reply.This indicates that privacy is given the upmost respect here, and many celebrities have chosen this resort. Alternatively there is much cheaper accommodation (**F**) available in PHPA bungalows.

Transport There are three ways to reach the island. From **Labuhan Sumbawa**, sailing boats can be chartered for the 3-4 hr journey. Alternatively, go to **Labuhan Sawo**, much closer to Moyo, and charter a local boat for considerably less. Get to both Labuhan Sawo and Sumbawa by bemo from the Seketeng market in Sumbawa Besar. It is also possible to reach Moyo from **Kencana Beach**, 10 km west of Sumbawa Besar. The *Kencana Beach Inn* has a speedboat which can be chartered, 1½ hrs and a slower launch, 3 hrs. Bemos run to Kencana Beach from Sumbawa Besar.

Mount Tambora

Mount Tambora is 2,800 m high and is best known for the eruption of 5-15 July 1815, which killed tens of thousands and made the following summer one of the coldest ever. It is said that the paintings of JMW Turner (1775-1851) reflect the magnificent fiery sunsets that the eruption brought on. *The Fighting Téméraire* is one such painting, of which Thackeray wrote: "The old Téméraire [the second ship of the line after Nelson's Victory at Trafalgar] is dragged to her last home by a little, spiteful, diabolical steamer. A mighty red sun, amidst a host of flaring clouds, sinks to rest on one side of the picture, and illumines a river that seems interminable, and a countless navy that fades away into such a wonderful distance as never was painted before." Unfortunately, however, *The Fighting Téméraire* was painted in 1839, 14 years after Mount Tambora erupted. Still, it makes a pleasing story.

Climbing the mountain There are two coloured lakes in the caldera. To climb the mountain really requires a 2-3 day excursion. A guide is essential – they can be hired at Pancasila; the police also recommend that trekkers register at their station in Calabai before setting out. The track is often difficult to follow, through thick forest. Wear trousers and long-sleeved shirts (to avoid leeches) and a sturdy pair of walking boots. There are freshwater streams en route, but they are not always easy to find, so take a supply of water and some food. Thick vegetation gives way to pine forest and then a volcanic landscape on the approach to the rim of the volcano. Cloud cover is often bad, making for disappointing views from the summit. It is possible to climb down a precipitous slope into the caldera, where there is a lake. ■ *Getting there: charter an early morning boat from the harbour in Sumbawa Besar to Calabai, where there is accommodation; then take an ojek or dokar the 15 km to Pancasila; this is the start of the climb.*

Tours Tours can be organized to surrounding villages for buffalo races, to off-shore islands (including Moyo), and to trek to the summit of Mount Tambora (2,820 m) (see above). The *Tambora Hotel* will organize three-day treks to the summit of Mount Tambora, and Abdul Muis and Stephen Annas are recommended as guides (both contactable through the hotel). The *Kencana Beach Inn* (see excursions page 309) organize trips to Moyo.

South of Sumbawa Besar

Near **Batu Tering village**, about 25 km south of Sumbawa Besar off the main road to Lunyuk, are some **megalithic remains** at **Airenung**. Also in the area are some **caves**, Liang Petang and Liang Bukal with stalactites and stalagmites. As with caves the world over, imaginative locals have decided that the cave formations look like assorted people, beds and weaving looms! You will need a torch. The caves are also said to harbour strong magic. The nearby bat caves are also worth a visit – be prepared for a rather pungent experience. The area around **Lunyuk** on the south coast, about 75 km from Sumbawa Besar, is the site of a transmigrasi programme with settlers from Java, Bali and Lombok. The village of **Sukamaju** was settled in 1972 by migrants from Nusa Penida and today is one of the most successful farming communities on Sumbawa. Set in a beautiful area isolated by mountains, the farmers grow rice, corn, coconuts and peanuts. A new dam has been built providing an irrigation system so the farmers are no longer dependent on the rains. One of the villagers is a 100-year-old man who has written poems in Balinese recounting his experiences and the journey from Nusa Penida at the age of 70. The community gather wild plants for their healing properties and continue to practice their religion celebrating traditional Balinese ceremonies with gamelan music and dancing. Burial ceremonies are expensive so cremations are a rare event, only three have been held in the past 25 years. The Kepala Desa, Dewa Budiasa, studied economics in Bali and can arrange accommodation with local families for visitors with a genuine interest in learning about the lifestyle of the community. You will need to speak some Indonesian. Nearby there are white sand **beaches**, and this area of the south coast is a turtle spawning area, particularly the beach at Lampui. ■ *Getting there: by bus from Sumbawa Besar to Lunyuk, 3 hours; bemo connection to the village.*

Sumbawa Besar to Bima-Raba

The road east from Sumbawa Besar runs through a boulder-strewn, arid landscape and after just over 100 km reaches the coast, passing the picturesque fishing village of Labuhan Jambu. Wood and tile houses are elevated on stilts, with traditional boats hauled up on the beach or moored along the shore. Tour parties sometimes stop here. The regular bus will stop, but it won't wait. From here the road follows the coast before cutting inland to Dompu. Sit on the left of the bus for spectacular views as the road descends and rises through volcanic peaks and folds, densely vegetated with palms and bamboo. If you were wondering what the cluster of plastic bags are hanging in the bus are there for, the sounds and smells of heaving stomachs soon explains all! The surfing beach of Hu'u lies 40 km to the south of Dompu. From Dompu the road continues east to Sumbawa's main town, Bima-Raba.

Dompu

Dompu is the capital of Dompu district and en route between Sumbawa's two principal towns, Sumbawa Besar and Bima-Raba. Surfers making their way south to the beach at Hu'u (see below) may have to change buses here and possibly stop-over for the night.

Phone code: 0373
Colour map 2, grid A1

The road into Dompu branches right until it reaches a large roundabout. Dompu's streets spread outwards from here like spokes in a loose grid formation. Broad, leafy streets run to an epicentre that sports a statue of a surfer. The road then leads off to the western corner of town and the main mosque. Unmistakable with its chrome garlic bulb-like top and slightly ominous, black tiled minaret.

Sleeping **D-E** *Wisma Samada*, Jl Gajah Mada 18, T21417. Clean, courteous, smart communal area with CNN. A well run place. **D-F** *Wisma Praja*, Jl Soekarno Hatta 6, T215177, a/c, en suite mandi, hotel with good ambience, nestled in the heart of town. **E** *Anda*, Jl Jend A Yani, T195. **E** *Bala Kemar Cottages*, Jl Merdeka 82, Empang, only accommodation on the main road, half way between Sumbawa Besar and Dompu, just west of Empang, restaurant, big rooms but no fans, en suite mandi. **E** *Karijawa*, Jl Sudirman T230. **E** *Manura Kupang*, attractive garden location.

Transport 40 km from Hu'u. **Road** **Bus**: regular connections with **Bima-Raba** and **Sumbawa Besar** (approximately 2,000Rp, journey time widely variable according to passenger demand). Onward buses to **Hu'u** (2,000Rp). You will probably find it quite difficult to catch a normal bemo from Hu'u down the 6km of road to **Lakey Beach** as the majority of surfers come by chartered taxi, paying in the region of 100,000Rp from Dompu or Bima.

Hu'u

Phone code: 0373
Colour map 2, grid B1

A surfing beach popular with Australians since the late 1980s who come here on 'package tours' and stay in surf camps. The surf is best in April, although the resort is most crowded during July and August. A relatively hassle-free location for tourists, especially lone women travellers, with a peaceful beach and nothing else. That's if you are not including the possible trek up the nearest volcanic mound to yet another abandoned Japanese canon from the Second World War.

Sleeping **B** *Hotel Awan Gati*, the most upmarket establishment on Pantai Lakey, two storey with internet facilities, the first in Sumbawa. Good choice of food in restaurant, cappucinos to Hungarian goulash, chronically slow service, Awangati@indo.net.id **B-C** *Primadona Lakey Cottages and Restaurant*, Lakey Beach, Jl Nanga Doro, Dompu, Sumbawa Hu'u, T21168/21384/21585. One of the newest places in Hu'u, set right on the beach, private bathrooms with western toilet, **D** *Balumba Cottages*. **D-E** *Lakey Peak Cottages*, excellent atmosphere, towering tempe, fish, and chicken sandwiches served with chips and salad. Recommended. **D** *Mona Lisa Bungalows*, some with attached mandi, and a popular restaurant. **E** *Lestari*, some with attached mandi, not so well kept as the others and now looking a little down-at-heel. **D-E** *Fatima's*, good rooms, heaving and popular restaurant. Spaghetti marinara, nasi jampur, garlic bread and king prawns plus a lot more.

Transport 40 km from Dompu. **Road** **Bus**: direct morning buses to Hu'u from Terminal Bima in **Bima**. Otherwise catch a bus from either Bima or **Sumbawa Besar** to Dompu, and from here a connection south to Hu'u.

Bima-Raba

Phone code: 0371
Colour map 2, grid A2

Bima-Raba, also known as Raba-Bima, are twin towns (Raba and Bima or, if you like, Bima and Raba) separated by about 3 km. Most of the activity is centred on Bima. This is where the hotels and losmen are to be found, where the port is located, and from where buses leave for Sumbawa Besar and Lombok/Bali. The bus terminal for Sape (and from there to Flores) is in Raba, as well as the central post office. Constant bemos link the two towns. *Dokars* here are called *ben hurs* – and it really is due to the film (it must have made quite an impact on the population of Bima-Raba). The half-starved, large dog-sized animals that masquerade as horses would not have passed muster in Roman days. On the *ben hurs* 'don't eat too much' is often written in Bimanese (an Austronesian language), reflecting the desolate nature of the island, the formerly frequent famines and the concern of its inhabitants for food security.

Salt is an important export from this region and during the dry season you can see the salt-pans in use along parts of Bima Bay. The salt is then put in blue plastic sacks and shipped from Bima port. Horses are another important export and you might see them being loaded onto ships down at the harbour, or squashed together sideways while waiting for the boat to depart.

The inhabitants of the town refer to themselves as Dou Mbojo, or 'People of Mbojo', and the name Bima is thought to be taken from the Hindu epic poem the Mahabharata in which one of the heroes is named Bhima. Traditionally, society was stratified into four classes: the royal family, nobles, commoners, and slaves. Today, though, Bima-Raba is a multi-ethnic place with settlers from Flores and Timor, Chinese including Cantonese and Hokkien, Arabs from southern Arabia, Makassarese and Bugis from Sulawesi, and Javanese – along with some Europeans called '*Dou Turi*'. (Although this means tourist it is also used for expatriates.)

Sights

Bima's principal sight is the **Sultan's Palace** which faces onto the main square, at the east edge of the town centre. Built in 1927, it has been converted into a museum and houses a dismal collection of weapons, baskets, farm implements and other assorted paraphernalia. Traditional dances are irregularly performed here. The Bimanese Sultanate was swept to one side after the Revolution, and almost disappeared from sight. However, the predilections of tourists, as well as a government policy to promote regional cultures as part of an attempt to strengthen national culture, has led to a resurgence in interest in Bima's royal roots. ■ *Admission by donation. 0700-1800 Mon-Sun.*

The **central market** is in the heart of town between Jl Sultan Kharuddin and Jl Sulawesi. Stall food is available here. Climb up the hills behind the Terminal

West Nusa Tenggara

Bima

To Tolobali (Graves) & Golf Course

To Port

Jl Maradinata
Jl Mongonsici
Jl Sarae
Ben Hur Stop
Jl Pompa   2■ $ 7■   Jl Hasanuddin   Jl Diponegoro
Night Market
Jl Kaharuddin
Jl Sultan Ibrahim   ■3
To Post Office
Jl Sumbawa   Ben Hur Stop   Sultan's Palace
Restaurants $ 5■ ■1
Jl Lombok   Jl Sulawesi
Merpati Office
■8   4■   To Wavo & Sape
Jl Karantina   ■6   Jl Soekarno Hatta
Racetrack
To Wavo & Sape
Jl Terminal Baru   Sultan's Grave
Bima Bus Terminal

N
Not to scale

To Airport, Dompu & Sumbawa Besar

■ **Sleeping**
1 Lila Graha   3 Losmen Komodo   5 Pelangi   7 Sangyang Bima
2 Losmen Kartini   4 Parewa   6 Putera Sari   8 Viva

Bima, or to the south of Jl Soekarno-Hatta for views over the town and bay. One of the Sultans has his grave here (ask for *makam sultan*).

Excursions **Lawata Beach** 3 km south of town on the road to Dompu and Sumbawa Besar, hardly deserves to be called a beach. Locals come here for the sunsets. ■ *Getting there: by ben hur or walk*. **Sleeping**: **B-C** *Lawata Beach Hotel*. Scenic location overlooking Bima Bay with views of the Donggo mountains to the west. The beach is disappointing and the sea uninviting, but the hotel has a good swimming pool. Simple accomdation in cottages with private bathroom, shower, western toilet, a/c. Open sided restaurant serving good, reasonably priced food. Hotel in need of redecoration but makes a pleasant alternative to staying in town.

Kolo on Bima Bay to the north of town is visited for its snorkelling. ■ *Getting there: boats can be chartered from Bima port, or cadge a lift on one of the regular boats, 1 hr.*

Maria lies 30 minutes outside Bima-Raba, on the road to Sape and is notable for its traditional wood and tile rice barns (*lengge*) massed on the overlooking hill. The local residents are often characterized – wrongly – as belonging to some unspecified hill 'tribe'. They are, in fact, lowland Bimanese although their hillside residence means that they do, reportedly, speak some of the Wawo language. (They live quite close to the upland Dou Wawo.) Anthropologist Michael Hitchcock, who has worked in Bima, wonders what the people of Maria make of the pejorative 'hill tribe' label. Given that it brings tourists and money, possibly with gratitude. ■ *Getting there: by bus from Kumbe terminal in Raba.*

Sambori Lama, a traditional village high in the hills south of Bima, makes an interesting day trip. The road is rough and the final track leading down into the valley where the village lies has to be taken on foot. The houses, with steep sided thatched or corrugated iron roofs, are built on stilts with the livestock living below. You might see young women pounding rice in tall bamboo containers, and betel nuts laid out to dry. The ingredients for siri/pinang (betel nut, the stalk or leaf of the siri vine and small packets of lime) are on sale in the markets of most villages in these parts.

Sangeang Volcano lies off the north-east coast of Sumbawa. This island volcano last erupted in 1986. Following the eruption the inhabitants of the island were resettled in the newly created town of Sangeang Darat from where they continue to fish and cultivate their fields on the slopes of the volcano; it is considered too risky to let them return to live on the island. It is possible to climb the 2,000 m high volcano; hire a boat from the villagers to make the crossing. Locals believe these former inhabitants of Sangeang island practice black magic.

Climbing Mount Tambora to the northwest of Bima-Raba is a three-day excursion (see page 312). ■ *Getting there: there is usually one bus a day to Calabai from the Bima station.*

Tours *Grand Komodo* run recommended tours from Bali to Komodo (see page 324), but it is possible to sign on in Bima-Raba. They also arrange tours to sights around the town. Their office in Bima is at Jalan Soekarno-Hatta, T2812, F2018. *Komodo Tours*, as well as the *Parewa Hotel* (which also has a boat for charter to Komodo) have minibuses for charter to explore the surrounding countryside.

On arrival in Bima do not be discouraged by the presence of the army. During our last visit here in mid-2000 some 50 soldiers had been sent from Lombok after a wedding had got out of hand. Locals said that 4 people had been killed by the police as they attempted to quieten the rowdy party-goers and a mini riot had ensued outside the police station. It seems that the riot was little more than a local affair but the quick reaction to send troops is indicative of the uneasy socio-political atmosphere in this area. A few days before the wedding debacle travellers reported their bus reversing for one mile as it was surrounded by angry sword-wielding locals disputing an issue of personal honour.

B *Sangyang Bima*, Jl Sultan Hasanuddin 11, T41438. A/c, pool in new extension, well-run, but rooms only average for the price. The owner was having financial problems and it may currently be shut. **C-D** *Lila Graha*, Jl Lombok 20, T42740. Some a/c, central, noisy, with poor rooms, pricey but good restaurant, includes breakfast. **C-D** *Parewa*, Jl Soekarno-Hatta 40, T42652. Some a/c, this building was to be a cinema but the owner couldn't get the licence. En suite mandi, top rooms have hot water, no outside windows. Restaurant mainly Chinese/Indonesian food. **D** *Sonco Tengge Beach Hotel*, Jl Sultan Salahuddin, T42987. 1½ km from town on road to Dompu, alternative to being in town, rooms are clean, beach is nothing to speak of, get there by *ben hur*. **E** *Losmen Kartini*, Jl Pasar 11, T42072. Shared mandi, upstairs rooms are more airy, a little grubby, central, near market. **E** *Losmen Komodo*, Jl Sultan Ibrahim (next to Sultan's Palace), T42070. Shared mandi, simple but friendly and fine, recommended. **E** *Putera Sari*, Jl Soekarno-Hatta 7 (near intersection with Jl Sultan Hasanuddin), T42825. Acceptable rooms, shared mandi. **E** *Viva*, Jl Soekarno-Hatta (near intersection with Jl Sultan Hasanuddin), T42411. Reasonable rooms, shared mandi, cheap, often full. **E** *Losmen Pelangi*, Jl Lombok 8, T42878. Stuck in the not so appealing centre of Bima, but clean, cheap and close to the warungs.

Sleeping

Cheap *Lila Graha*, Jl Lombok 20, Chinese, Indonesian, seafood. *Ariana*, Jl Martadinata (on road to harbour). *Parewa Modern Bakery and Ice Cream*, Jl Lombok. **Very cheap** *Anda*, Jl Pahlawan and the nearby *Kurnia* offer rock bottom nasi jampur etc in big portions.

Eating

There is a considerable sized **market** selling the usual fare in Bima. **Antiques and handicrafts**: There are a couple of specialised artshops in town. For hand woven textiles try *Mutmainah*, Jl Hasannudin 46. *Waspada*, Jl Sulawesi 2 has a large range of bamboo, pottery and wood carvings from all over Sumbawa. *Rinjani Antiques*, Jl Soekarno Hatta stocks carvings from wood, gold, silver and even ivory (the latter, of course, is currently outlawed under CITES).

Shopping

Local Bemos: run between the two bus terminals and through both Bima and Raba.

Air Mohammad Salahuddin airport is 20 km south of town, outside Tente and on the Trans-Sumbawa highway. Regular connections by Garuda/Merpati with Bali, Lombok and other destinations in Nusa Tenggara. You can catch a Bemo taxi into town, although it is easy to walk out onto the main road and wait for a bus.

Transport
250 km from Sumbawa Besar, 45 km from Bima-Raba

Road Bus: Bima-Raba has two bus stations. Terminal Bima is at the southwest edge of Bima town on Jl Terminal Baru (south along Jl Kaharuddin). Buses from here for all points west – **Dompu**, **Hu'u**, **Sumbawa Besar**, **Lombok**, **Bali** and **Surabaya**. The Kumbe terminal for Sape (the port for Komodo and Flores) is in Raba town, 5 km from Bima. Regular minibuses to **Sape**. Bemos run constantly between the two terminals through Bima and Raba. Bus companies such as *Jawa Baru*, *Bima Indah* and *Surya Kencana* have their offices on or near Jl Kharuddin, between the market and Terminal Bima.

Sea Boat: Bima's harbour is walking distance from Bima town. The *Pelni* ships *Tatamailau* and *Tilongkabila* dock here on their 2-week circuits through Java, Kalimantan, Sulawesi and Nusa Tenggara. However in mid-2000 only 1 of these 2 ships was running due to lack of custom. The *Pelni* office is at Jl Martadinata (also known as Jl Pelabuhan) 103, near the docks. A new fast ferry service was inaugurated from Bali's Benoa Harbour to Bima and Kupang (Timor) in mid-2000. The 70 m, 925 passenger ship

West Nusa Tenggara

Barito with a top speed of 36 knots leaves Bali every Fri afternoon at 1800 on its 16 hour voyage to Bima and Kupang. For more information contact *Gama Dewata Bali Tours* (in Bali) at T62-(0)361-263568 or T62-(0)361-232704, F62-(0)361-263569.

Directory **Airline offices** *Merpati*, Jl Soekarno-Hatta 60, T42697. **Banks** *BNI*, Jl Sultan Hasanuddin, US$ cash only. Bank Rakyat Indonesia, Jl Soekarno-Hatta, T43352, ATM available. **Communications** General Post Office: Raba (get there by minibus from Bima). **Medical services** Hospital on Jl Langsat.

Sape

Phone code: 0374
Colour map 2, grid A2

Sape is the usual place to stay, while waiting for the ferry to Komodo Island and Flores. The port itself – Labuhan Sape – is about 4 km from Sape town. Most of the population are not Bimanese at all, but Bugis – the famed seafarers from Sulawesi. Nothing happens in Sape, but staying here does make it easier catching the 0800 ferry. The accommodation is some of the poorest in Indonesia. The **Komodo Tourist Centre**, between Labuhan Sape and Sape town, is of marginal use only, but some they do have information on Komodo.

Excursions **Labuhan Sape** (Sape Port) is 4 km from town and can be reached on foot or by *ben hur*. There is boat building along the road, fishing boats landing their catch in the morning, and a mosque with a lighthouse-style minaret.

Sleeping Basic and of uniformly poor quality, losmen are all found on Jl Pelabuhan, on the seaward side of town. Because it is usually necessary to stay the night in Sape to catch the ferry, the town is a 'choke point' and accommodation is sometimes in short supply between the peak months from Jul-Sep. An alternative is to stay in Bima and catch an early bus to Sape. New losmen are opening here and the hope is that the challenge of some competition may improve standards. **F** *Friendship*, dirty, small rooms, dark with uncomfortable beds. **F** *Give*, dirty. **F** *Ratnasari*, cleanish (for Sape), the best of a very bad bunch. **E-F** *Mutiara*, right by the dock, one of the newer losmen, reasonably clean, pleasant and well-stocked with biscuits and sanitary towels, and at the last count amongst the best of this very poor bunch.

Eating *Hovita*, Jl Pelabuhan, friendly, cold beer, good fish (if asked in advance). Recommended. *Surabaya*, next to *Losmen Give*. *Sape Cafe*, one of the few reasonable choices available. **Very cheap** *Arema* next to *Mutiara* good range of dishes and large portions, but reputed to give maggot ridden fish to tourists! Extremely low ceilings, expect hostility and confrontation at first if assumed to be Australian, (a legacy of the East Timor debacle).

Transport
45 km from Bima Raba

Road **Bus**: the station is on the seaward side of town, although buses will drop passengers off near the losmen. Regular connections with Raba's Kumbe terminal, 1½ hrs. From Kumbe, bemos run to Bima town and then on to the Bima terminal for buses west (see page 317). **Sea** **Boat**: the ferry for Komodo 6½ hrs (12,000Rp) and Labuanbajo 10 hrs (15,000Rp), leaves from the port 4 km east of town every day except Fri at 0800. *Ben hurs* whisk passengers from Sape town to the port (price inflated on morning of ferry departure). The ferry also takes motorcycles, cars, goats and buffalo; buying tickets the night before means you miss the scrum on the morning of departure. The boat ride between Sape and Komodo is uneventful; but between Komodo and Labuanbajo the ferry weaves between barren, mangrove wreathed islands. At certain times of year, the currents which converge here cause impressive up-wellings and depressions in the sea.

Directory **Communications** Post Office: Jl Pelabuhan 34. **Wartel:** Jl Pelabuhan (between *Losmens Give* and *Ratnasari*).

East Nusa Tenggara

5

East Nusa Tenggara

322 Ins and outs

324 Komodo

329 Flores

332 Labuanbajo to Ende

347 Ende to Larantuka

358 Lembata

361 Alor

365 Sumba

383 West Timor

395 Roti (Rote)

398 Savu (Sabu, Sawu)

East Nusa Tenggara is considerably drier than the islands to the west, and the further east you go, the more arid it becomes, more like Australia than the jungle-clad tropics. The lack of rain is compounded by the geography of the islands. They are long and thin, and rivers tend to be short and fast-flowing. This makes it difficult to utilize the water for agriculture. East Nusa Tenggara is not one of Indonesia's industrial powerhouses. The province's main exports are coffee, fish and sandalwood.

Christianity has made greater inroads into the provinces of Nusa Tenggara than anywhere else in Indonesia. Islam had scarcely penetrated these remote islands before the Portuguese arrived in the 16th century, and the population were therefore more amenable to conversion. Today, 90% of the population is Christian, and Christianity is one of the few forces which binds together a geographically dispersed population, made up of no less than 37 ethnic groups with different histories and cultural traditions.

For the visitor, East Nusa Tenggara offers a mosaic of cultures from Christian Flores, including the Catholics of Larantuka – a legacy of Portugal's short-lived 16th century sojourn here – to Muslim West Timor and Sumba where pre-Christian and pre-Muslim religious influences remain strong. Geographically East Nusa Tenggara is equally varied, from the mountains and volcanoes of Flores to the rolling grasslands of Sumba. Finally, there are East Nusa Tenggara's most famous inhabitants: the giant dragons of Komodo.

Ins and outs

Getting around
For information on getting to each island, see individual islands' 'Ins and outs' sections

Travelling through the islands of East Nusa Tenggara, particularly Flores (see page 329 for more information), used to be difficult enough to deter all but the most adventurous visitor. Now the islands are readily accessible, and surfaced all-weather roads link the main towns of the province. This has meant that in the peak tourist months from July to September, accommodation may become stretched in smaller towns – or at least it was until the communal violence and associated bad press of 1998, 1999 and 2000. As a result, since 1998, the number of tourists visiting Nusa Tenggara has been significantly below normal. There is essentially only one road through Flores, so visitors travel along a very tightly defined route and there are choke points at Labuanbajo (the port for the ferry to Komodo and Sumbawa) and Bajawa, both on Flores.

Air The two 'ends' of Nusa Tenggara – Mataram in Lombok and Kupang in West Timor – are well provided for in terms of air connections. **Kupang** is an international gateway and there are regular flights to/from Darwin, Australia. These two cities also provide a reasonably efficient domestic service. *Merpati* does operate services to many of the smaller towns through the islands of Nusa Tenggara, but with the exception of **Maumere** on Flores these are intermittent and limited. In addition, flights to these towns are often over-booked and because the planes are usually small there is not much 'give' in the system. It is best to build a reasonable degree of flexibility into your schedule. To get to other areas of Indonesia from Nusa Tenggara, it is usually necessary to fly to Bali first, and then catch a connection.

Bus As noted above, overland transport has improved considerably. The main road through the islands of Nusa Tenggara is all-weather and public transport is reasonably efficient and timely, though it might not be comfortable. There are no a/c services east of Sumbawa (before getting to West Timor) and most departures are early morning. Expect to average about 30-50 km per hour.

Bicycle and motor bike A fair number of people work their way through Nusa Tenggara by bicycle or motorbike. The roads are much quieter than on Java and Sumatra, and other road users tend to drive more slowly – although pot holes and livestock provide hazards. Spare parts for unusual bikes and motorbikes may be impossible to obtain so either travel well prepared or buy an Indonesian-assembled

East Nusa Tenggara

East Nusa Tenggara highlights

Komodo: giant 3 m-long 'dragons', the largest reptiles in the world.

Flores: snorkelling and diving near Maumere and in the Seventeen Islands National Park; **climbing** to see the 3-coloured crater lakes of Mount Kelimutu at sunrise; **trekking** to traditional villages; historical Larantuka; and fabulous textiles.

Solor and Alor archipelagoes: Lamalera and its **traditional whaling communities**; **diving and snorkelling** on Alor.

Sumba: megalithic tombs, traditional villages; surfing; the **pasola festival**; and traditional ikat textiles.

West Timor: traditional villages and textiles; **surfing** on Roti.

machine on arrival. See the section on page 37 for more information on bicycling.

Sea   Because of the fragmented geography of this region boats remain an important form of transport. There are daily ferries linking Lombok with Sumbawa, and Sumbawa with **Flores** via **Komodo**. East of Flores ferries become more intermittent, with connections just once or twice a week. However note that these schedules have become even more variable and subject to change than usual. Remain flexible, patient and double check all information at the relevant terminal.

When to go   Rainfall averages only 800-900 mm in East Flores, Alor and East Sumba, and the dry season stretches over seven months, from April to October.

Money in Nusa Tenggara   Money changing facilities in a handful of major towns and in particular in Kupang, West Timor are reasonable, but in many smaller towns travellers' cheques denominated in US$ or US$ cash are the best option. Other currencies are often either not accepted or exchange rates are poor. Note that travellers' cheques should be from one of the major companies – *Amex, CitiBank, Bank of America, Thomas Cook*. Credit cards are only rarely accepted.

Language   Bahasa Indonesia is useful in Nusa Tenggara, but not essential if travellers stick to the main route through the islands. You will find that just a few words go a long way in communication and in making a good impression. Indonesians are proud of their language and honoured to find Westerners trying to learn. They will also be eager to help you to improve it still further!

Health warning   Malaria is a serious problem in parts of Nusa Tenggara with the recent emergence of the potentially fatal *P falciparum* as the dominant strain. Areas affected include Komodo, along the north coast of Flores, including Riung, Maumere, Labuhanbajo, the island of Roti and Timor. Larium (Melfoquine), the most effective anti-malarial drug believed to be 95% effective, causes side effects in 22% of people who take it. Of these a very small minority (the manufacturers claim 1 person in 10,000) suffer serious problems including fits, manic depression and panic attacks. However, many more travellers die from malaria than from Larium. Citronella, an essential oil used in a base for moisturisers and in candles is highly effective as a deterrent to mosquitos and a natural alternative to DEET. Also B12 tablets (B12 is found in high concentrations in beer and garlic) similarly appears to ward off the little beasts.

Safety warning   Following East Timor's resounding vote in favour of independence in 1999, the pro-Jakarta militias fled to the camps of West Timor. In 2000 there was a destinctly anti-Western sentiment in some areas of West Timor and in September three UN workers were murdered near Atambra.

East Nusa Tenggara

Komodo

Colour map 2, grid A3   *The principal reason people come to Komodo is to see the illustrious Komodo dragon. But there is more to the reserve than giant lizards – there is also good trekking, swimming and snorkelling. The park covers 59,000 ha, and is made up not just of Komodo Island, but also Rinca and a number of other surrounding islets. The highest peak on this rugged spot is Mount Satalibo (735m).*

Ins and outs

Getting there   *Merpati* flies to both Labuanbajo (see page 335) and to Bima (page 317); the former is closer to Komodo. From either town it is then necessary to catch the ferry (see below). The rich and famous arrive direct by helicopter.

    There are now two ferries a week between Flores and Sumbawa via Komodo, leaving both Sape and Labuanbajo daily at 0800. The journey from Sape takes 6½ hrs; from Labuanbajo, 3½ hrs. The ferry cannot dock at Komodo as the water is too shallow so small boats come alongside to take passengers to the *PHPA* office to register. It is possible to charter a boat for a 2-day trip to Komodo from Sape. But some of the boats are said to be unreliable and currents in the Sape Strait are strong. Locals recommend going through

Komodo National Park

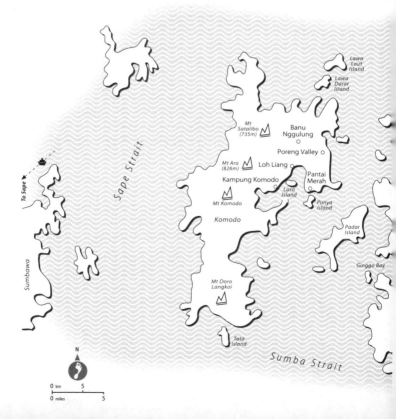

one of the tour companies in Bima for safety's sake (see page 316) or from Labuanbajo (see page 333). It is cheaper to hire a boat from the nearer port of Labuanbajo. Before chartering a boat, visit the Komodo Park offices in Sape or Labuanbajo for advice.

Kampung Komodo is the only village on the island; Loh Liang – the PHPA-run camp for tourists – is about a 30 min walk away. The only way of getting around the island is on foot and the national park office maintains paths to various parts of Komodo.

Getting around

The National Park

After the luxuriant vegetation of Bali, Komodo can come as a bit of a shock – at least during the dry season. The islands of the Komodo archipelago are dry and rainfall is highly seasonal. For much of the year, therefore, the grasslands are burnt to dust and interspersed with drought resistant savanna trees such as the distinctive lontar palm (*Borassus flabellifera*). In contrast the seas are highly productive, so there is good **snorkelling**, particularly off **Pantai Merah** and **Pulau Lasa** – a small island near Komodo village. The irridescent blue of the water, set against the dull brown of the islands, provides a striking backdrop. However, this image of Komodo as barren is transformed during the short wet season when rainfall encourages rapid growth and the formerly parched landscape becomes green and lush.

Despite the other attractions of Komodo, it is still the **dragons** which steal the show. They are easily seen, with Timor deer (their chief natural prey) wandering amongst them. Other wildlife includes land crabs, wild pigs, black drongos, white-bellied sea eagles – and cockatoos, evidence that this is part of the Australasian faunal world. Monkeys, by contrast, are absent. ■ *The island is a national park and visitors must register and buy an entrance ticket (27,000Rp) on arrival at Loh Liang on Komodo or Loh Buaya on Rinca. Note that between 1 August and the end of September the cost of an entrance ticket rockets. The ticket is valid for seven days. The park HQ at Loh Liang consists of an office, information centre, four bungalows, a souvenir shop, church and mosque, and a restaurant.*

Flores Sea

Siaba Besar Island

Sebayur Besar Island

Labuanbajo

Berloka

Loh Buaya

Rinca

Kima Bay

Mount Doro Raja

Lenteng

Flores

Baru Bay

Rinca

Mt Doro Ora

Motang Island

The most accessible viewing spot is the dry river bed at **Banu Nggulung**, 30 minutes' walk (2 km) from the accommodation at Loh Liang. Guides can take you there for a small fee, depending on the size of your group (5,000Rp per person). **NB** Visitors are only allowed to walk alone along marked trails. Those wishing to hike off the trails and see the dragons in a more natural setting, must hire a guide. This is not just to generate income for the wardens: there have been fatalities (see

Walks

East Nusa Tenggara

👉 *Indonesia's living dinosaur: the Komodo dragon*

The Komodo dragon (Varanus komodoensis), a massive monitor lizard, is the largest lizard in the world and can grow to 3 m and weigh over 150 kg. They are locally called ora *and were not discovered by the West until 1911. In 1990 the Komodo National Park authorities estimated the number of dragons to be 3,336, although it is probably smaller today as the population is thought to be in slow decline. The dragon is found on only four islands; about 2,000 live on Komodo Island, with significant numbers also on Rinca (700), Pulau Motang and on the northern coast of Flores. Of all the large carnivore species, the ora has the most restricted range. They are strictly protected and cannot be exported live to zoos or, for that matter, dead to museums.*

The dragons living on Rinca and Flores are rather more reddish in colour than those found on Komodo which are blacker, suggesting there has been little interbreeding between the populations for some considerable time. However, the dragons do swim between islands in search of food despite these being treacherous waters with strong tides. There are also dangers for the dragon associated with losing body heat on their journey (they are, of course, cold blooded). The best time to see the dragons is shortly after sunrise when they have just woken up and lie out in the sun to warm their bodies in readiness to go hunting. There is little water on these islands and in order to avoid the danger of dehydration the dragons must avoid spending too long in the sun.

Like other animals, the size of the Komodo dragon has been grossly exaggerated. Major PA Ouwens, the curator of the Botanical Gardens at Buitenzorg (Bogor), Java, who first scientifically

described the animal and collected the type specimen in 1912, was informed by the Governor of Flores that specimens of over 7 m existed; these were almost certainly over-estimates or mis-identified estuarine crocodiles. Even the celebrated British television zoologist David Attenborough, during his 1957 visit to the island succumbed to exaggeration, claiming to have seen a dragon "a full 12 feet" in length. The largest accurately measured dragon was one exhibited at the St Louis Zoological Gardens in 1937 reported as measuring 10 ft 2 ins and weighing 365lbs. The extreme size of the Komodo dragon is thought to be due to it having evolved on these isolated islands, insulated from competition by other carnivores. The same is true of other reptiles – for example, the Galapagos iguana.

The reptile is essentially a solitary creature, hunting and scavenging by day. An opportunist, it feeds largely on carrion but will also kill its own prey which can include animals as large as a water buffalo, or even the young of its own species. Prey is usually killed by first biting the animal and then patiently following it for several days. The wound becomes infected and turns septic and the animal becomes increasingly weak. When it is unable to escape the dragon moves in for the kill. Flesh is torn from the carcass with teeth and claws and swallowed whole.

With other dragons competing for carrion it is important to consume the carcass as quickly as possible and they are voracious eaters, devouring almost their own body weight within 30 minutes, taking a further five days to digest the prey. The dragons have a superb sense of smell; this allows them to pick up the scent of death more than 10 km away and several metres underground. Despite their

box). Group walks are at 0700 and 1600. It seems that the morning is better for sightings. For around 25,000Rp per person (but highly negotiable) a guide can take you to **Poreng Valley**, a 7-km walk from the PHPA office. There is a reasonably good chance of spotting a dragon and even if you don't, you will see plenty of other wildlife. There is a short 30 minute walk along the beach from Loh Liang bungalows to the stilt village of **Kampung Komodo**, which can be done without a guide. **Mount Ara** can be climbed in less than 2 hours (8.5 km to reputation as man-eaters, dragons rarely kill people, and often wander through the village on Komodo island more interested in eating the fishermen's catch or untended domestic animals. They can often be seen scavenging along the beach and will eat anything, even tiny crabs. Fewer than ten people are said to have been killed this century. A Swiss baron – admittedly a frail 80-year old – was killed in 1979 and there has been another reported fatality since.

Recent research has focussed on the dragon's lethal saliva which contains virulent bacteria. Toxicologists have been fascinated by their findings which suggest the bacteria originate in the decaying carrion scavenged by the dragon. The dragon's supremely sharp teeth cut into its own gums while it is chewing, and this combination of toxic saliva and blood provide an ideal breeding ground for the bacteria to survive for days, even weeks, until the dragon attacks its next prey. Of interest is how the dragon remains immune to the toxicity of its own saliva and whether it has an antidote which might prove of medical use.

A female dragon will only mate with a male who is strong enough to pin her down. He then wins her over in a rather touching manner, flicking his tongue over her and rubbing her back with his chin. Mating usually takes place in June and July. A month or more later, usually at night, the eggs – a clutch will number about 25 eggs – are laid about 2 m underground after the female has built an extensive burrow which may take up to a week to excavate. She includes many false entrances and dead-end tunnels as the eggs will be under constant threat from hungry male dragons and females in search of a ready-made nest. The female assiduously guards her nest for the first three months, never even leaving it to eat, and living off the fat stored in her tail.

The eggs hatch after eight to nine months at the end of the rainy season (March to May) when food is plentiful. The dragons hatch fully formed and able to fend for themselves, and make straight for the trees where they spend the first two years of their life safe from the cannibalistic tendencies of the adults which are too big to climb trees. They continue to spend much of the time in trees until they are seven or eight years old and large enough to defend themselves. Their only defence is speed and young lizards, less than 4 years old, are remarkably fast moving ; they are said to be able to outrun a dog over short distances. Dragons are thought to live for up to 50 years.

Male dragons frequently fight, often over females. Like many lizards they inflate their bodies to intimidate the enemy. The loser will then lie in a submissive posture and endure 'claw raking' whereby the victor rakes the body of the loser with his claws in a sign of victory.

Research is underway to determine the origins of the dragon. Study of the chromosomes indicate they are more closely related to the Australian goanna than to other monitor lizards in Asia and Africa. There is little fossil evidence in Indonesia but in Australia the reconstructed bones of Megalania prisca, which died out millions of years ago, show remarkable similarities to the Komodo dragon. However, at 6-7 m in length and 10 times the weight, Megalania prisca was even bigger than the Komodo dragon.

East Nusa Tenggara

the summit) and the cost is 35,000Rp per group; from the summit there are fantastic views over the reserve. At the start of the treks you may see an attractive stick rack; beware for guides only! Tourists report being rapped smartly over the knuckles when trying to borrow staffs which are reserved for the sole purpose of prodding the dragons into action.

Excursions

Rinca Island Rinca Island can be reached from Komodo and has a wider range of wildlife including wild horses and water buffaloes, as well as dragons, and has the added advantage of fewer tourists. **Sleeping E** *PHPA bungalows* at Loh Buaya, 25,000Rp per night for a single, 40,000Rp double. Basic accommodation, these stilted wooden cabins are the haunts of various rodent and insect populations, so be prepared. Similarly, no food available, so take your own. It is more likely that you will go as part of an organized tour (arranged in Labuhanbajo or Lombok) and therefore you will be catered for. Rinca is fast gaining popularity over Komodo and recent visitors have been highly complimentary about trips there. ■ *Getting there: there is not yet a ferry service to Loh Buaya. Private tours run from Labuanbajo on Flores or from Komodo. Some boats travelling from Lombok to Flores stop off here. Ask about chartering a boat at the Sinbad shuttle office opposite Dewata Ayu Restaurant.*

Essentials

Sleeping The only accommodation on Komodo is in the **E** *PHPA bungalows* at Loh Liang which has a capacity of about 40. They are simple but clean bungalows in a beautiful bay. Electricity from 1800-2200. Bedding consists of mattresses on the floor. During the peak season of Jul-Sep, visitors must resort to sleeping in the dining room, some rooms have their own mandi, for no extra cost. The quality of the rooms is not great, but if you have the time, it is well worth staying on the island. The cafeteria provides basic and rather overpriced food. **Camping**: there is a camp ground at Loh Liang.

Shopping There is a souvenir shop at Loh Liang and hawkers sell carved wooden dragons of various sizes as well as pearls, bone carvings and necklaces.

Sports **Boats** Speedboats are available. **Diving and snorkelling** There is good diving and excellent snorkelling over the reef off Pantai Merah and around Pulau Lasa offshore from Kampung Komodo. It is best to bring your own mask although there is a dive shop (*Binga Corner*) just by the jetty which hires out masks, fins and diving equipment.

Komodo Island

Flores

Flores stretches over 350 km from east to west, but at most only 70 km from north to south. It is one of the most beautiful islands in the Lesser Sundas. Mountainous, with steep-sided valleys cut through by fast-flowing rivers, dense forests and open savanna landscapes, Flores embraces a wide range of ecological zones. One of the local names for the island is Nusa Nipa *or 'Serpent Island', because of its shape.*

Ins & outs

There are **air** connections with Labuanbajo, Bajawa, Ruteng, Ende, Maumere and Larantuka, but services can be unreliable. **NB** There seems to be some problem with booking *Merpati* flights out of Ende, either back to Denpasar or on to Kupang. To get around this difficulty, it is advisable to fly out of Maumere, where the office seems to be more switched on and they are contactable by telephone. Regular **ferries** link **Labuanbajo**, on Flores' west coast with Sape on Sumbawa, sailing via Komodo. Less frequent ferries connect **Ende** with Waingapu on Sumba, Kupang on Timor, and Ujung Pandang (Makassar) on Sulawesi. There are also vessels from **Larantuka** to Kupang and Lewoleba. *Pelni* vessels dock at **Labuanbajo**, **Ende**, **Maumere** and **Larantuka**.

Getting there

East Nusa Tenggara

Overland transport on Flores – a 375 km-long island – is neither quick nor comfortable but visitors can at least luxuriate with the thought that it used to be much worse! The Trans-Flores Highway is now almost complete and though hardly comfortable, travel is quite bearable. The road twists and turns, and rises and falls, through at times breathtaking scenery, stretching over more than 700 km to cover the 375 km-length of the island. It is these contortions that the road must endure to cross Flores' rugged landscape which makes travel slow – expect to average 25-30 km per hr, less in the wet season. The Highway is made up almost all the way from Labuanbajo in the east to Larantuka in the west with the exception of one section over the mountains between Ruteng and Bajawa, which is in the process of being rebuilt. **Buses** are the main form of transport between centres; expect to spend a good deal of time covering even modest distances. On minor roads, open trucks (known as *bis kayu*) with bench seats are still used. In towns like Ende and Maumere, bemos are the main form of local transport.

Getting around

Despite improvements in communications, overland travel is still exhausting. It is best to overnight in at least 3 towns on the journey across the island. Flooding & earthquakes have also stalled efforts to make travel quicker

Flores is a conservative island – short skirts and vests are not appropriate; dressing in such a manner is considered impolite.

Conduct

Lone women travellers may find more harassment on Flores than on Lombok or Sumbawa. It is advisable only to engage in short conversations with men. Make sure you lock your door and windows at night. Some losmen have cavities between bathrooms with manholes big enough to let in an intruder. Try to discover who is inhabiting the adjacent rooms.

Security

Following the earthquake of December 1992 there was something of a shortage of accommodation on Flores and at peak times hotels and guesthouses would be crammed to over-flowing. This is no longer the case and visitors should have little

Accommodation

difficulty finding a room at most times of year. Indeed, outside only the most touristed towns, expect to be the only foreigner around. This may change as Indonesia's tourist industry recovers, but it was true as of mid-2000.

Background

On 12 December 1992 at 1330 an **earthquake** measuring 7.2 on the Richter scale struck eastern Flores. Over 1,500 people were killed by the quake and associated *tsunami* (tidal wave), many in the districts of Sikka, Ende and East Flores and their respective capitals of Maumere, Ende and Larantuka. Islands off the north coast where the wave struck were devastated – particularly Pulau Babi where 700 out of a total population of 1,000, died. One fisherman was quoted as saying: "The second [tidal] wave was as high as a coconut tree. The waves were hot, like lava." Low-lying islands were literally swamped as the *tsunami* washed over them, destroying everything in their paths. In Maumere it is thought that over 40% of the town was destroyed by the quake and similar levels of devastation have been reported for Ende. However, reconstruction has been rapid and most hotels in the two district capitals survived relatively unscathed.

History Flores' history is sketchy. It appears that Chinese mariners first made contact with the island – perhaps as early as the 12th century – to trade in sandalwood. As Flores lay on the trading route to Timor (sandalwood) and the Moluccas (spices), Portuguese chroniclers also noted the existence of the island in the 16th century. Dominican missionaries built a stone fort and church on Solor, just off Flores' east coast, in 1561, and later one at Larantuka. So enthusiastic were the Dominican friars in their proselytizing that by 1599 there were thought to be 100,000 Roman Catholics in East Flores, laying the foundations for Flores' Roman Catholic complexion. The sandalwood traders from Melaka and Macao who based themselves here also began inter-marrying with local women, creating a group of *mestizos.*

By the time the Portuguese were in decline as a power in the archipelago at the beginning of the 17th century, they had established settlements at Solor, Ende and Sikka. The Dutch, seeing little of value on Flores, concentrated their attentions elsewhere. As a result, although they established a mission at Ende in 1670, Portuguese religious influence over Flores continued to remain strong (see box, page 357). It was not until 1859 that Portugal officially ceded all its claims to Flores to the Dutch. And this was only agreed on the understanding that Flores would remain Roman Catholic.

Flores

The textiles of Flores

Because Flores' geography has made contact between the island's peoples difficult, a number of distinct textile traditions have evolved. Three broad types stand out: the textiles of Manggarai to the west, those of Ngada in the centre, and the cloths of Ende, Sikka, Lio and Larantuka to the east.

***Manggarai** textiles show stylistic links with both Bima (Sumbawa) and south Sulawesi. Predominant colours are red, blue and green, and designs may be either bold and simple, or complex and minutely worked. Geometric motifs are the norm, and it is unusual for these to be interlinked. The best cloths have a tapestry weave border design along the edge. Unlike other areas of Flores, the designs of Manggarai are produced by weaving, not by dyeing the warp (ikat).*

***Ngada** textiles from central Flores can be found on sale at the market in Bajawa. Women's sarongs and men's shawls are made from rough home-grown and home-spun cotton, dyed red and blue, with an elementary ikat design. The more expensive and harder to find weft ikat kain kudu have horse motifs and are traditionally part of a woman's dowry.*

*The textiles of the east are the richest and show a range of influences, from Sumba, Solor, and even Europe and India. They are made using the warp ikat technique (see page 181) and feature geometric, animal and floral motifs. If weavers are Muslim, the animal designs have been reduced to geometric shapes. Cloths from **Lio** villages (eg Nggela and Jopu, see pages 349 and 349) are finely patterned, with yellowish-brown designs on a dark red or blue ground. The motifs, often floral, are contained within parallel bands. It is also possible today to find cloth decorated with aeroplanes, cars, ships, and even teapots. The warp ikat from **Sikka** (see page 352) is probably the most immediately attractive of Flores' textiles to the Westerner. Cloth is made from thick, handspun cotton, and the ikat designs are bolder. Sikka ikat is a grey weave on a dark blue, almost black, background, although reddish hues are also common. Motifs are usually natural – flowers, chickens, crabs.*

Across the island, it is increasingly difficult to find quality cloth made using natural dyes and handspun cotton. It is more usual to see cloth coloured using synthetic dyes and made from commercially-spun cotton.

Unlike neighbouring Sumbawa, the deep volcanic soils here are fertile; the **Geography** problem is that in most areas the unreliable and highly seasonal rainfall makes agriculture difficult. Strangely, the area of the island with the highest density of population is also among the driest: the district of Sikka (Maumere). Here population densities can exceed 600 people per sq km, and even the 1930 census recorded a population of over 100,000. Because of the population pressure, farmers have cleared forested slopes right up to the watersheds, causing severe problems of erosion and land degradation. Conservation measures such as terracing were introduced by the Dutch, but in general these have proved ineffective. It has only been when farmers have owned their land that they have seen the economic sense of investing time and money protecting the land and soil.

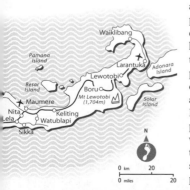

People In total, the island covers an area of 14,300 sq km, and supports a population of 1.5 million. The majority of the population is Roman Catholic, but pre-Christian animist beliefs still exert a considerable influence even among those who are nominally Christian. There are five major ethnic groups on the island: the Manggarai, Ngada, Sikka, Ende and Larantuka. In general, while the inhabitants in east and central Flores are Papuan-Melanesian, those in the west are Malay. The mountainous terrain and the difficulties of communication have effectively isolated these various groups from one another until fairly recently.

Labuanbajo to Ende

Labuanbajo at the western tip of Flores is the ferry port for Komodo Island and Sape (Sumbawa). From here the Trans-Flores Highway works its way eastwards through a fragmented and mountainous landscape to the hill town of Ruteng, 125 km away. Nearly 40 km north of Ruteng is the small port of Reo. Continuing on the Trans-Flores Highway from Ruteng, the road runs east and then turns south towards the coast, before climbing again to another hill town – Bajawa – a distance of 130 km. The district of Bajawa is best known for the strange thatched cult 'houses' which can be found in the surrounding villages. With a good range of accommodation, Bajawa is one of the best places to stop off on a journey through Flores. From Bajawa, the road deteriorates, although it is in the process of being improved. The route passes through a rock-strewn, almost African savanna-like landscape, before reaching the coast after about 100 km, which the road follows for the final 30 km to the port of Ende.

Labuanbajo

Phone code: 0385
Colour map 2, grid A4

Labuanbajo, or Bajo, is really just an overgrown fishing village. Like Sape on Sumbawa, the town is little more than a transit point for catching or disembarking from the ferry. But there the comparison ends. There is good accommodation here, some excellent restaurants, and reasonable beaches, with offshore snorkelling. It is also an excellent base from which to explore Komodo and Rinca, or to join a boat tour via the reserve and other islands on the way to Lombok (see 'Tours', below). The town is stretched out along one road which runs from the dock, along the seashore, and then south towards Ruteng. **Pramuka Hill**, behind the town, offers good views over the bay, especially at sunset.

Tourist information is available from the *PHPA* information booth, on the main street opposite *Gardena Hotel*. They can provide information on Komodo and Rinca islands. There is also a rather under-funded but enthusiastic tourist office, *Dinas Pariwisata*, behind the *Telekom* Office. ■ *Mon-Thu 0700-1500, Fri 0700-1430.*

Excursions **Waicicu Beach** lies 15 minutes by boat north of town. It offers good snorkelling and diving (snorkel equipment is for hire from the *Bajo Beach Hotel*). See below for details of accommodation, under 'Beach accommodation'.

Komodo It is possible to charter a boat for the day to see the dragons; shouldn't be more than about 80,000Rp-100,000Rp (see Rinca, below for details).

Rinca Island is part of the Komodo National Park and even closer to Labuanbajo. See page 328 for details. It also has a small population of Komodo dragons and thousands of fruit bats, which fly from the mangrove swamps inland at dusk. PHPA accommodation available. ■ *Getting there: boat charter, day trip (1½ hrs each way). Ask at the PHPA booth in town about boat charter;*

the Bajo Beach and Mutiara Beach Hotels both have vessels for charter. **NB** *Not all the boat charterers are reliable. Check before paying by insisting on seeing the vessel and by talking to other visitors to confirm the itinerary.*

One day trips to the islands **Bidadari** and **Sabobo** can be arranged through hotels or tour operators (on main road), 55,000Rp for return boat ride. Good snorkelling in clear water and, potentially, the island to yourself.

Kanawa Island Overnight stays on this island sleeping in bungalows on stilts can be arranged through *Kanawa Tours* (on main road below *Garden Restaurant*), 25,000-35,000Rp for boat and accommodation. This tranquil island, lying barely a metre above sea level, is perfect for those seeking an escape from resorts with their beach hawkers and gawpers. Dropping in for lunch is entirely possible. However, all water and products are shipped in from the harbour making this a resource-decadent experience. Get there before global warming and rising sea levels makes it a submarine experience.

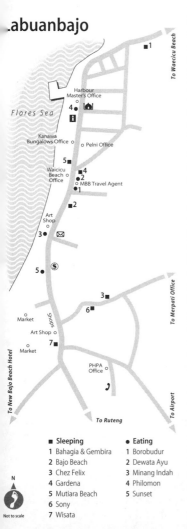

.abuanbajo

Flores Sea

Harbour
Master's Office
4
Kanawa
Bungalows Office
Pelni Office
5
Waicicu
Beach
Office
4
2
MBB Travel Agent
1
2
Art
Shop
3
5
Market
Shops
Art Shop
Market
7
PHPA
Office

To Waecicu Beach
To Merpati Office
To New Bajo Beach Hotel
To Ruteng
To Airport

N
Not to scale

■ Sleeping
1 Bahagia & Gembira
2 Bajo Beach
3 Chez Felix
4 Gardena
5 Mutiara Beach
6 Sony
7 Wisata

● Eating
1 Borobudur
2 Dewata Ayu
3 Minang Indah
4 Philomon
5 Sunset

Tours *Perama Tours* have boats for charter to Komodo and Rinca. They provide snorkelling equipment but it is poor quality. *Perama* also offer 4 day/3 night boat tours from Labuanbajo to Bangsal (Lombok) stopping at Komodo and Moyo Island (Sumbawa) en route and with one day in Lombok and a night 'camping' on the coral island of Perama, sleeping on bamboo beds beneath rudimentary shelters. The other nights are spent sleeping on deck. The tour then returns from Bangsal to Labuanbajo along the same route. Ten people maximum and eight staff; good, if a little repetitive, fresh food, expensive at around 200,000Rp. **NB** Check out the boat before agreeing to a tour; some boats are overloaded and pretty uncomfortable – we have received reports that *Perama* have been overloading their boats, picking up passengers along the way. There are various other people operating these tours, but confirm that they go to the places agreed upon: *Mutiara Beach Hotel* organize a four-night tour; *Waicicu Beach Hotel* organize a two-day boat trip to Sape, via Rinca Island and Komodo (with snorkelling stops) and a visit to 'Flying Fox Island'. *Chez Felix Hotel* put on a very similar deal. Average eight people per boat, good service and food. More expensive if stopping at Sape. Disappointments abound regarding these trips. Be sure to check that enough provisions are on board, and that a cool box is available if cold

East Nusa Tenggara

Bintang beer is your priority. On most boats guests sleep on deck and, even in the dry season, bad weather can make the journey difficult to bear. After two nights of rain and no dry clothes tempers quickly become frayed!

Sleeping Hotels and losmen stretch out along the main street running south (to the right as the ferry docks from Sape). **D-E** *Bajo Beach*, T41009. Central, clean, well run, car, boat and snorkelling equipment for hire, price includes breakfast, tends to get booked up by tour groups. Currently under haphazard reconstruction. **D-E** *Wisata*, past bridge on road to Ruteng, T41020. Restaurant with rather lacklustre service, rooms are clean with showers attached, pretty garden, well run by friendly and helpful staff and well maintained, good value. **D-E** *Gardena*, on the main street perched on a hill with good views (from some rooms) over towards Komodo, simple bungalows arranged around a courtyard with attached showers but basic toilets, food is good but portions small, tours arranged to Komodo and Rinca, and through Flores, good source of information. **E** *Mutiara Beach*, Jl Pelabuan 31 (opposite *Bajo Beach*), T41039. Decent restaurant, very basic rooms, though the upstairs rooms are rather less small and dark than those below and have a view of the harbour, attached mandi. **E** *Chez Felix*, south end of town, up a hill, T41032. Good views of the harbour from the porch some with attached bathrooms, good clean, light rooms, popular family-run establishment, tours available, English spoken. Recommended. **F** *Sony Homestay*, opposite *Chez Felix* south of town on a hill with good views, good food, basic but clean rooms have attached bathrooms and views. **F** *Bahagia Homestay*, to the north of the harbour, next to the mosque, very basic. **F** *Gembira Homestay*, very basic and pretty dingy. **Beach accommodation**: there are a number of excellent beach bungalow resorts which are reached by boat, laid on 'free' of charge by the owners. All the resorts have offices in Labuanbajo itself. They can advise on where the various boats dock. Prices usually include all meals. **B-C** *New Bajo Beach*, on the coast 2.5 km to the south of town, T41047. The smartest hotel in the area with a/c in the more expensive rooms. **D** *Cendana Beach Hotel*, 4 km south of Labuanbajo, T41125. On a rather grey beach. Free bus service to the hotel from town. Large clean rooms, bathrooms with showers and WC. **D-E** *Waecicu Beach Resort*, booking office in town is opposite *Dewata Ayu Restaurant*. Three boats leave Labuanbajo daily for the 20 min journey to this beautiful resort. Fairly good beach and snorkelling. Relaxed atmosphere, helpful management. Pleasant cottages ranging from the very basic to the reasonably basic, meals included. Bus tickets for sale at competitive prices and tours organized to traditional villages and to Rinca Island. **D-E** *Kanawa Island Bungalows*, booking office in town near *Gardena Hotel*. Boats leave from Labuanbajo at 1100 daily and the journey takes 1 hr to an otherwise uninhabited island. Beautiful beach and good snorkelling. **E** *Pungu Island Hotel*, booking office is near *Sunset Restaurant*. 1-hr journey by boat to reach the island. The newest of the beach resorts, provides free snorkelling equipment, karaoke and organizes tours. Prices negotiable depending on length of stay.

Eating **Mid-range** *Puri Komodo*, upmarket ambience, open in the evening only, opposite the tour operators. **Cheap** *Dewata Ayu*, next door to the *Borobudur Restaurant*, good views of the bay and a tasty range of seafood; *Borobudur*, almost opposite the *Mutiara Hotel*, serves a wide range of delicious innovative food, popular, recommended. *Gardena*, huge fish platters, swiss roti and quality guacomole, a good little restaurant. **Very cheap** *Sunset*, south on Jl Yos Sudarso, on the harbour side of the road, simple Indonesian dishes.

Shopping Between 0630 and 0900 multiple stalls set up along the main road selling vegetables. The usual shops can be found, with a particularly large range of flipflops. There is a small choice of sarongs and woven cloth; and a good shop for wooden carvings, including some rather gruesome masks.

To build in pairs: the Ngadhu and Bhaga

Much of the art of the Lesser Sundas is based upon maintaining balance between opposites: between male and female, old and young, living and dead, white and black. This concern for harmony is reflected in the cult altars of **Bajawa** where ngadhu represent the male ancestors of the clan, and bhaga the female ancestors.

Ngadhu are known in some areas of Flores as ndaru and elsewhere as peo. The bhaga is also known as sao heda. Ngadhu consist of a carved wooden post surmounted by a conical thatched roof, usually about 2-3 m in height. The bhaga is built to resemble a miniature house with dimensions of around 3-4 m, again with a thatched roof and usually standing on a raised platform. The bhaga is often used as the cooking site during important rituals and the two are constructed as a pair, usually positioned close together outside the house of the prominent clan that commissioned their erection. Clans undertake this task as an indicator of their position in society, and also usually after a sign has been received from the ancestors of that clan.

There seems to be some disagreement among specialists as to the timing of construction. Some authorities maintain that the female bhaga must always be built before its male counterpart. The explanation for this is said to relate to the pattern of courtship: men court women, not the other way around, so that the female must be in place ready for the male to make his advance. Other specialists argue quite the reverse, and state that only when the ngadhu post has been planted in the ground can the construction of the bhaga begin. It is possible that both groups are correct, and that there are regional differences across this part of Flores.

The male post is carved from the wood of a particularly hard tree (the sebu or hebu tree) which is dug out of the ground, roots and all. Should any sprouts later appear from roots left in the ground, then danger beckons for the clan. Various rites are observed before a tree is selected. For example, a spear plunged into the ground must remain upright as it would be demeaning for a man to fall over in public. Having selected a tree, it must be dug in the afternoon between three and four o'clock. The tree is then carried back to the village by four men, to great celebration. These festivities exclude women of child-bearing age and young girls, as it is believed that they might be in danger of being raped by the tree. The tree is placed close to its female companion and buffaloes and pigs are slaughtered. The post is then carved over a three day period – from the top down (face, body and then legs). During the construction of the ngadhu those men involved must have no contact with women and observe various sexual and bathing prohibitions. At the end of the carving period, the post is 'planted' in the ground and yet further fesitivities and sacrifices ensue. The end of the work is marked by the naming of bhaga and the ngadhu. The names chosen are usually those of the ancestors of the clan that commissioned the construction.

Conversion to Christianity, inevitably, is changing these traditions and many clans no longer bother with bhaga and ngadhu, although weathered examples can be found in many villages. Presumably, in a few decades, they will have become objects of veneration in the museums of Indonesia, their cultural function and role lost.

East Nusa Tenggara

Varanus, Waerana Beach Resort. *Mega Buana Tour and Travel.*

Tour operators

Local The *Bajo Beach* and *Mutiara Beach Hotels* both have vehicles for hire to explore the surrounding countryside. **Air** The airport is 2 km from town. Airport tax: 11,000Rp. Flights are met by bemos. Daily connections on *Merpati* with **Denpasar**, **Kupang** and other destinations in Nusa Tenggara including **Ende**, **Ruteng** and **Bima**.

Transport
125 km from Ruteng,
255 km from Bajawa,
380 km from Ende,
528 km from Maumere

Flights are often booked well ahead during the peak season (Jul-Sep) and so double booking seems particularly common here. **Bus** There is no bus station; buses cruise the hotels and losmen picking up passengers. Connections with **Ruteng** (4 hrs) and **Bajawa** (13 hrs). It is even possible to make the exhausting journey all the way to **Ende** on a bus that meets the ferry from Sape. *Sinar 99* run a packed, but relatively efficient service; *Komodo* run buses to Ruteng. **Boat** Sat-Thu ferries leave at 0800 for **Sape**, Sumbawa, (10 hrs) via **Komodo** (3½ hrs). Buses meet the ferry from Sape/Komodo and take passengers straight on to Ruteng. Boats travel frequently between Labuanbajo and the **Gilis** (Lombok) (see page 276), via Komodo (beware of being overcharged for entrance fee to Komodo). The *Pelni* vessels *Tatamailau*, *Tilongkabila* and *Pangrango* dock at Labuanbajo on their fortnightly circuit through the islands of Nusa Tenggara.

Directory **Airline offices** *Merpati*, east of town, towards airport. **Banks** *BNI*, main road (150 m towards Ruteng from *Bajo Beach Hotel*), will change US$ cash and TCs from major companies (*Amex*, *Thomas Cook*, *BankAmerica*, *Citibank*), though the rates are poor. Money changer on the same road. **Communications** Post Office: in the centre of town. Telephone: *Telkom* office, south of town, near the *PHPA* office. Several *Wartel* offices around town: one near the *Wisata Hotel*, another on the main road. Internet: *Komodo Internet Café*, run by a young lady entrepreneur, WAECICU@hotmail.com, T41344.

Ruteng

Phone code: 0385
Colour map 2, grid A4

Ruteng is a market town at the head of a fertile valley. It is a peaceful, pleasant spot to stop en route through Flores. This upland area – the town is 1,100 m above sea level – is chilly at night. It is a centre of coffee cultivation cultivation and is also home to Flores' bakery, which appears to supply the rest of the island. Despite being predominantly Catholic, the practice of **whip fighting** or *caci* is still practiced, particularly during wedding festivities. Opponents flail each other, the scars being regarded as honourable and, apparently, beautiful by local women. The practice has long been part of the rituals surrounding ancestor worship in the Manggarai district and is seen as a blood offering to the spirits of the ancestors. The Manggarai are a secretive people and elders who retain knowledge of their traditions are generally unwilling to discuss these matters with outsiders. Most weddings are held during the peak tourist months from June to September. Displays of *caci* can be arranged by most hotels.

Ruteng

To Reo

Merpati Office

To Labuanbajo

To Airport

Jl Bhayangkan
Jl Komodo
Market
Shops
Jl Waeces
Jl Adi Sucipto
Jl Kartini
Jl Niaga
Sports Field
Jl A Yani
Jl Motang Rua
Jl Kabupaten
Jl Yos Sudarso
Market
Rumah Adat
Jl Baruk
Jl S Riyadi
Jl Diponegoro

N

0 metres   200
0 yards   200

■ **Sleeping**
1 Agung I & III
2 Agung II
3 Dahlia
4 Manggarai
5 Pondok Wisata
6 Ranaka
7 Rima
8 Sidha

● **Eating**
1 Bambooden
2 Dunia Baru
3 Merlin
4 Pade Doang I
5 Pade Doang II
6 Sari Bundo

The best view of town is from **Golo Curu** (Welcome Mountain). Walk north **Walks** along the road to Reo past hotels *Agung 1* and *111*, then cross the small bridge. A path bears off left leading past stations of the cross to a shrine to the virgin at the summit. The round trip takes about 1½ hours.

Mount Ranaka, which reaches a height of 2,140 m, is one of the highest points **Excursions** on Flores. The volcano last erupted the late 1980s. It is a 7 km walk to the top from Robo village which can be reached by bemo from Ruteng; alternatively it is possible to charter a bemo to take you to within 2 km or so of the summit.

Ranamese Crater Lake is surrounded by forest but has a good path round its shore. Popular with the locals at weekends, as it is a good spot for fishing. The lake is best explored in the early morning when the bird-life is most active. **NB** It is probably best not to go alone if female. ■ *Getting there: take a bemo from Ruteng to Borong village; the path to the lake begins near here.*

Pongkor, 45 km southwest of Ruteng and **Lambaleda**, 50 km to the north-west are two traditional villages worth visiting. Lambaleda is a weaving centre. ■ *Getting there: trucks (bis kayu) run from Ruteng to Pongkor (2 hrs) and to Lambaleda via Benteng Jawa. Alternatively, explore the route north to Reo – regular trucks make the journey, through spectacular scenery (see below).*

B-E *Sindha*, Jl Yos Sudarso 26, T21197. Close to *Manggarai*, reasonably priced restau- **Sleeping** rant, some recently added VIP rooms provide bathrooms, TV and a balcony, helpful management, clean and well variety of maintained rooms. **C-D** *Agung 111*, behind *Agung 1*, T21180. Favoured by tour groups, light, spacious and clean. Rooms on the upper floor have good views over town. **C-E** *Rima* Jl A Yani 14, T22195/6. Very attractive wooden chalet-style hotel, with decent restaurant, beautiful views, and close to the centre of town, some rooms with own mandi, clean and comfortable and even the outside mandi has a shower (though it only operates in the mornings). Rather lethargic service and expensive tours on offer, but economy rooms are recommended. **D** *Dahlia*, Jl Bhayangkan 18, just off Jl Motang Rua (main road), T21377, F21441. This large, quiet hotel is set back from the main road. It is clean and efficiently run. Buckets of water can be heated up for a warm mandi for those staying in more expensive rooms; a luxury well worth requesting after the water has been chilled by the cold Ruteng nights. Recommended. **E** *Agung II*, Jl Motang Rua 10, T21835. In centre of town, set back from the road, large clean rooms, some with own mandi, basic facilities. **E** *Agung I*, T21080. North of town on road to Reo, T21180. Quiet with big rooms, some with western loos and showers. **E** *Manggarai*, Jl Adisucipto, T21008. The more expensive rooms are large and with own mandi, simple but clean. **F** *Pondok Wisata* Jl Slamet Riyadi 9, opposite Agogo bus agency, T21753. Dorm accomodation with communal mand, clean but basic. **F** *Ranaka* Jl Yos Sudarso 2, T21353. Rather dingy, small rooms have own mandi, cheap.

Ruteng is not renowned for the quality of its food. There are several warungs in the **Eating** bus station and market area, where dog, known as 'RW', is available. Don't be surprised if 'RW to be' is swinging alongside your bus window in Flores. **Mid-range** *Dunia Baru* Jl Yos Sudarso 10, T21690. Serves a wide range of Indoensian and Chinese food, the locals come here to watch TV. **Cheap** *Merlin*, near *Hotel Dahlia*, good Chinese food. **Very cheap** *Bambooden*, Jl Motang Rua 30, T21589. Attractive bamboo-walled restaurant offering good cheap Indonesian dishes but the entire menu is not always available. *Depot Pade Doang 1*, Jl Lalamentik 5, T21216. Indonesian food. *Pade Doang 11*, Jl Motang Rua 34, T22057. Tasty Chinese and Indonesian food. **Bakeries**: *Flores Bakery*, a wide range of cakes and breads. It is possible to go round the back to watch the production process, if requested.

East Nusa Tenggara

Shopping Ruteng's bustling market on the east side of town sells a variety of goods including Manggari sarongs which are predominantly black with brightly coloured embroidered motifs.

Transport **Air** The airport is on the outskirts of town; bemos meet flights. Daily connections on
125 km from *Merpati* with **Denpasar**, **Kupang** and other destinations in Nusa Tenggara. **Bus** The
Labuanbajo, station is on the west side of town, a short walk downhill from the centre. Regular con-
130 km from Bajawa, nections with **Labuanbajo** (4 hrs), **Bajawa** (6 hrs), **Ende** (10 hrs) and along the scenic
255 km from Ende route north to **Reo** (2 hrs – see Reo transport section). Also buses to other local destinations. Long-distance departures are in the morning. *Komodo Bus* and *Nusa Indah*
(for Labuanbajo) both have their offices on Jl Amenhung; *Agogo* (for buses to Ende) is
at Jl Yos Sudarso 4.

Directory **Airline offices** *Merpati* agent, Jl Kancil 5, T21197, F217465, open 0700-1700 daily. **Banks** *Bank*
Rakyat Indonesia, Jl Yos Sudarso, for TCs. Open: Mon-Fri 0730-1300, Sat 0730-1100.
Communications **Post office**: Jl Baruk 6 (south side of town), opens daily at 0900, closes
weekdays at 1500, Fri 1130, Sat 1300, and Sun 1200. **Telephone**: *Telekom* Office, Jl Kartini, open
24 hrs. *Wartel* Office, Jl Bhayangkara, open 0700-2300; Jl Pertiwi, open 24 hrs.

Reo

A small town on the north coast, Reo is off the Trans-Flores Highway and
therefore rarely visited by tourists. The central focus of the town is the Roman
Catholic church.

Reo

Sleeping **E** *Losmen Nisang Nai*, Jl Pelabuhan,
opposite the police station on the northern edge of Reo, some rooms with own
mandi; **F** *Telukbayar*, Jl Mesjit 8, small
dark and rather grubby rooms.

Eating There are a couple of very cheap, small and
simple places to eat in Reo. *Selera Anda*, Jl
Pelabuhan, Javanese food. *Mekar Sari*, Jl
Pelabuhan, Padang food.

Transport **Bus** The views along the road from
38 km from Ruteng Ruteng are the main reason to come to
Reo. The route takes you past spectacular
cascades of padi fields which stretch as far
at the eye can see. Rather precarious route,
with precipitous drops. Regular connections with **Ruteng**. **Boat** There are said to
be infrequent boats from Reo to
Labuanbajo and also to **Riung**. It might be
possible to hitch a lift to other ports in
Flores, and mixed cargo boats bound for
Surabaya also sometimes stop here.

Bajawa

Bajawa makes a pleasant and logical stop on the Trans-Flores route. This hill town is the capital of the Ngada District. It lies 1,100 m above sea level and is encircled by three volcanoes, the largest of which is **Mount Inerie**, which reaches 2,245 m, making it the highest peak on Flores. The town has a pleasant climate, with fresh days and chilly nights. The bustling **Inpres market** sells traditional textiles – embroidered blankets from Bajawa and ikat from Ende and Kelimutu. It is well worth a visit. But Bajawa's main attractions lie outside the town itself. The traditional houses of the area are some of the most striking on Flores, and despite being a predominantly Christian area, the Ngada District is best known for its thatched cult altars known as *ngadhu* and *bhaga* (see 'Excursions' and box). There is a **tourist information** office, *Dinas Pariwisata*, on Jl Sugio Pranata that still seems to be trying to establish what it is there for. The *Camellia Restaurant* has plenty of information for travellers and usually (although none were available on our last visit) several good maps of the area.

Phone code: 0384
Colour map 2, grid B5

Excursions

Bajawa is an excellent base from which to explore this interesting upland area

Langa, a village 6 km south of town, is home to 64 different clans and despite having a few modern houses, has a fine collection of *ngadhu* and *bhaga* (see box). There is a hot spring where the locals bathe and do their washing 30 minutes away, as well as a couple of waterfalls and the traditional villages of **Bela** and **Borado** within walking distance. **Sleeping** It may be possible to stay overnight with local villagers. ■ *Getting there: the village lies 2½ km off the main Trans-Flores highway towards Ende; bemos are sometimes available for the short trip from the turn off. It is also possible to do the easy 6 km journey from Bajawa on foot.*

Bena is a village 19 km south of town, past the turn off to Langa and en route to Monas, with spectacular views down to the sea. It is probably architecturally one of the best preserved villages in the Ngada District and is the ceremonial centre of the area. The synthesis of Catholic and Animist beliefs is more marked here than anywhere else on the island and is neatly captured by the image of the chapel alongside a megalithic grave site. There are lively New Year celebrations between the 15th and 21st of January. ■ *Small entry fee to village. Getting there: buses leave from the market in Bajawa, 1½ hrs.*

Wogo Lama or **Old Wogo** lies about 20 km east of Bajawa and has a collection of rather neglected megaliths just beyond the village. **Sleeping** There is a Christian mission at nearby Mataloko which will provide accommodation for visitors. ■ *Getting there: take a bemo from the market in Bajawa to Mataloko which is on the main road to Ende (45 mins) and then walk the penultimate kilometre or so to New Wogo (a village which has been converted to the joys of electricity and television), and then the final kilometre to Wogo Lama.*

Bongedu, **Watu** and **Maghilewa** are a group of villages on the far slopes of Mount Inerie. Getting here requires a long walk which has its positive side: few people make it here. There are beautiful groups of traditional houses, *ngadhu*, *bhaga* and megalith graves as well as spectacular views of the volcano. Ask Lucas (see 'Tours') to take you there.

Throughout June **Soa** hosts events where you can watch *sagi*, a form of traditional boxing. There is a **market** every Thursday. There are some wonderful hot springs outside the village (small entrance fee). Again, it is advisable for lone women to be cautious. Even wearing clothes into the springs like the local women, does not ensure that low intensity harassment and wandering hands will not occur. **Sleeping** D bungalows have recently been built next to the hot springs. ■ *Getting there: take a bus or bemo from Naru bus station in Bajawa to Soa village, from where it is a short walk to the springs.*

East Nusa Tenggara

Tours Lucas, who lives in Langa, occasionally runs tours from hotels in Bajawa. He is now in the logging business (shame!), but has over nine years of experience and is a wealth of information. He speaks good English (and adequate German, French, Dutch and Japanese) and is very knowledgeable about the co-existence of animism and Christianity in the Ngada region. He also provides his guests with delicious home cooked meals, made by his wife. Damianus, who is based in the *Virgo Hotel* runs daily 8 hour tours to the hot springs in Soa and a number of the surrounding villages. He can also be contacted at the *Kambera Hotel*. There are a number of other guides who can take you around the Ngada villages and explain the meanings of the objects you are seeing, but try and talk with them first, in order to establish their language skills. Generally guides hire themselves out for 50,000Rp per day, and expect lunch and refreshments on top.

Sleeping Bajawa has an impressive range of places to stay from mid-range down to budget. This was because just about everyone travelling through Flores broke their journey here. However, during our last visit in mid-2000 we were the only foreigners in town – save for a lone Dutch man who was only staying because he had blood poisoning and couldn't move. All prices below include a simple breakfast. **C** *Kembang*, Jl Martadinata 18, T21072. Fairly recently renovated, all rooms have a/c, own mandis with showers, spring beds. Featureless building but good large rooms with big windows. The verandah faces a pretty central garden. **D-E** *Ariesta*, Jl Diponegoro, T21292, light, clean rooms arranged around an attractive courtyard. **D-E** *Elizabeth*, Jl Inerie, opposite *Telecom* office, T21223. Sparklingly clean rooms, some of which have showers, good mosquito nets, but it's on the outskirts of town. **E** *Anggrek*, Jl Letjend Haryono 9, T21172. Own mandi with toilet, popular restaurant which serves tasty Indonesian and travellers' food, good source of information, and friendly manager named Leonard. Unfortunately this place was closed in mid-2000 due to the downturn in the tourist industry but it may open if things improve. **E** *Dagalos*, Jl A Yani 70, rooms have private mandi, good food but dark and dingy rooms. **E** *Dam*, Jl WZ Yohanes, T21145. Rooms have private mandis. Small hotel with basic facilities but very friendly management. **E** *Edel Way*, Jl Ahmad Yani. Very similar to the Korina (see below) – attached mandis and a reasonable level of cleanliness. **E** *Losmen Melati Johny*, Jl Gajah Mada, T21079. Small, dark rooms, but clean. Car available for hire and a restaurant serving very cheap Chinese and Indonesian food. **E** *Melati Korina*, Jl Ahmad Yani, T21162. Some rooms with own mandi, western toilets and showers, free tea and coffee all day. **E** *Stela Sasandy*, Jl Ahmad Yani. Again, a place on a par with the Korina and Edel Way. Attached facilities, showers, reasonable. **E** *Melati Virgo*, Jl Mayjend D Panjaitan, T21061. Clean rooms with own mandi, arranged around a central courtyard. Free tea and coffee available on request and there is a tour guide who is based in the hotel (see 'Tours', above), well organized staff. Recommended. **E** *Sunflower*, off Jl Jend A Yani, T21230. Rooms at the front of the building with a little porch area are clean with a view over town and a private mandi, but the rooms inside are rather dark and unappealing. Usefully, this is a popular meeting place for guides. **E-F** *Kambera*, Jl Eltari 9, T21166. Restaurant on 1st floor serving very cheap Indonesian food for more basic rooms (**F**) with a communal mandi. Small rooms with private mandis. Amusingly decorated with murals on the walls of the communal areas. Helpful, if a little (and charmingly) disorganized. **E-F** *Nusantara*, Jl Eltari 10, T21357. More expensive rooms are big and bright with own mandi, basic facilities, clean sheets.

Eating **Very cheap** *Anggrek*, Jl Letjend Haryono 9, popular restaurant serving good Indonesian and traveller's food. *Camellia*, Jl A Yani 74, Chinese, Indonesian and travellers' food, if ordered in advance. Great guacamole. *Kasih Bahagia*, Jl Basuki Rahmat, Chinese and Indonesian food. *Wisata*, Jl Gajah Mada, next to the market. Wisata Fried Rice is the house speciality. There is a *foodstall* every evening from 1830 serving martabak (Indonesian meat pancake); many warungs near the market. Dark, chewy RW (dog) in large supply sauteed with chillis – ***Warung Jakarta***, near Toko Korniawan, does very good 'beef' (dog in disguise?) sate.

Textiles Bajawa blankets and ikat from Ende and Kelimutu are available from the Inpres market (see box, page 331). The shops in the centre sell everything from Islamic hair ties, counterfeit Manchester United goods, to new CD players, karaoke machines and Chinese potions of dodgy provenance.

Shopping

Air The airport lies 28 km north of town, around 5 km from Soa. Merpati-operated minibuses bring passengers into Bajawa. There is also a *Merpati* service out to the airport; alternatively catch a bemo to Soa and then travel from there. Connections on *Merpati* with **Denpasar**, **Kupang** and other destinations in Nusa Tenggara. **Road Bemos**: run from the terminal on Jl Basuki Rahmat to the surrounding villages. **Bus**: for buses going long distance you have to go to the Watujaji Terminal 3 km to the southeast of town which can be reached by bemo. Buses to **Riung** (3 hrs), **Labuanbajo** (12 hrs, 15,000Rp), **Ruteng** (6 hrs, 7,500Rp, and keep eyes peeled for Ranamese crater lake on the right), **Ende** (5 hrs, 7,500Rp), and **Maumere**. Note that most buses leave early morning. **Boat** Bajawa's nearest port is Aimere on the south coast. There is a boat to **Kupang** at 1800 on Mon, returning to Aimere on Wed from Kupang. There are also occasional boats to **Maumere** and **Labuanbajo**.

Transport
68 km from Riung,
130 km from Ruteng,
255 km from
Labuanbajo,
125 km from Ende

Airline offices *Merpati*, Jl Budi Utomo/Pasar Rahmat (by market), T21051. **Banks** *BNI and Bank Rakyat Indonesia*, both on Jl Soekarno-Hatta, the former has an ATM, both will change TCs and cash in most major currencies. **Communications** General Post Office: Jl Soekarno-Hatta. **Telephone & telegraph** *Perumtel*, Jl Soekarno-Hatta (near *Bank Rakyat Indonesia*).

Directory

East Nusa Tenggara

Riung (Nangamese)

Riung

Flores Sea

Stilt Village

To Watujapi Hill

& Guide Centre
4■

Dragon Cage

PHPA Office

6■

○ PHPA Office

■5

●1
●2 Market

3■ ■2

■1

To Mbay & Ende

N

0 metres 200
0 yards 200

■ **Sleeping**
1 Florida
2 Liberty

● **Eating**
1 Cilegon
2 Suluwesi

3 Madona
4 Nur Ichlas
5 Pondok SVD
6 Tamari Beach

Most people refer to Nangamese (a small town on Flores' north coast) as Riung. For the pedantically inclined, Riung is actually the name of the surrounding sub-district, and not the town. The locals are mainly Muslim fishermen and Catholic farmers who dwell further inland cultivating rice and corn.

Phone code: 0384
Colour map 2, grid A5

The **tourist information** office is a blue bamboo shack in the harbour and serves as a base for Riung's six licenced guides who run tours to the reserve for 30-40,000Rp per person (minimum of five in a group). **NB** Lunch and cost of snorkel hire is not included. Good local information.

There is a pleasant walk to the top of **Watujape Hill** (3 km) from where there are spectacular views over the reserve.

The **Seventeen Island National Park** – is named in honour of Indonesia's Day of Independence – the 17

Excursions

August. This ignores the fact that there are, actually, 24 islands. The largest of the islands, Pulau Ontoloe, sometimes known as Bat Island, has a huge population of flying foxes. It offers superb snorkelling in extensive coral gardens (but no diving facilities – yet) and the islands have a number of idyllic white sand beaches. Tourists returning from Maumere report that the standard of snorkelling is much better here. There is also a small population of monitor lizards known as *mbou*, closely related to the famous Komodo dragon, but rather smaller (see page 326). These beasts require considerable patience to see in the wild so for a more reliable sighting, there is a captive specimen near the *PHPA* office, from where tickets to the reserve must be purchased.

Sleeping

Electricity in Riung runs from 1800-0600; all prices include a simple breakfast

D-E *Pondok SVD*, large rooms, very clean, fan, excellent bathroom with western loo and shower. Recommended. **D** *Florida*, very clean and good mosquito nets. Sylvester, the brother of the manager, is a licenced guide. **E** *Homestay Liberty*, pleasant verandah, though rooms are a bit dark, communal mandi. **E** *Madona*, cheapest place in town, communal mandi. **E** *Nur Ichlas*, closest accommodation to the sea with good views of the harbour and stilt village, communal mandi. Recommended. **E** *Tamari Beach*, rooms decked out in shocking pink, attractive garden, communal mandi.

Eating

All accommodation also offers food, though most of it is pretty basic. **Cheap** *Pondok SVD* offers the widest range. **Very cheap** There are also two warungs *Cilegon* and *Suluwesi*, near the entrance to the market. Next door is *Anda*, only gado gado and mie/nasi, but large portions.

Shopping

Textiles Local textiles can be bought for about 80,000Rp for a reasonable quality piece. Fine examples will cost considerably more, while there are always 'tourist' pieces available for somewhat less.

Tour operators

The *PHPA* office, near *Tamari Beach Homestay*, has posters displaying the variety of fauna you are likely to see on the reserve.

Transport

120 km from Bajawa

Road Bus: three buses run to and from **Bajawa** every day, but check that they are direct as those doing the detour via **Aegela** and **Mbay** take twice as long as the newer 3 hr direct route. One depature daily to **Ende** (5-7 hrs). **Trucks**: trucks go along the north coast to **Pota**. Change here for another truck to **Reo** (total journey time 6 hrs). **Sea Boat**: occasional boats from **Reo** and **Maumere**.

Seventeen Isles National Park

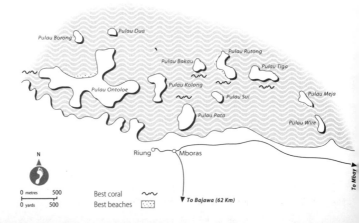

Pulau Borong · *Pulau Dua* · *Pulau Rutong* · *Pulau Bakau* · *Pulau Tiga* · *Pulau Kolong* · *Pulau Ontoloe* · *Pulau Sui* · *Pulau Meja* · *Pulau Pata* · *Pulau Wire*

Riung · Mboras

N

0 metres 500
0 yards 500

Best coral ~~~
Best beaches ▓▓▓

▼ *To Bajawa (62 Km)*

To Mbay

Much ado about adat

Commentators on things Indonesian probably use the Indonesian word *adat* more than almost any other. The word is taken from the arabic word 'ada, meaning custom, and it refers to any locally accepted code of norms, behaviour, laws, customs or regulations. Often a society's adat is the totality of all these, and there is therefore not just one adat, but many adats, both within and between societies. It has enormous breadth of coverage including, for example, the accepted duties of husband and wife, customary practices in village wood lot use, the correct procedure in rituals, the accepted allocation of duties between different ranks, and rules on inheritance.

Adat is often viewed as the glue which helps Indonesian people to function and interact without conflict – or at least with a minimum of conflict. Any local leader was expected to be conversant with the accepted adat, and this was traditionally passed down the generations through verse, proverb, adage and aphorism. An intimate awareness of adat was akin to wisdom. The Dutch quickly grasped the importance of adat, and they codified it and used the resultant laws to help govern and administer at the local level.

Today, adat is in decline. Success and wisdom is less likely to be measured in terms of an intimate awareness of adat than in terms of academic achievement and economic power. Increasingly, the core of modern adat is the state 'ideology' of pancasila (see page 410), not the inherited layers of customary behaviour enshrined in the traditional meaning of the word, adat.

East Nusa Tenggara

Ende

Ende is the largest town on Flores with 60-80,000 inhabitants, and is the capital of the district of Ende. The town is sited in a spectacular position on the neck of a peninsula, surrounded by mountains. To the south is the distinctive flat topped Mount Meja (Table Mountain), and on the other side of town is Mount Ia, a dormant volcano that last erupted in 1969. The Portuguese had established a settlement here as early as the 17th century and it then became a popular posting with the Dutch. In Dec 1992 the town was devastated by an earthquake, with an estimated 40% of buildings destroyed (see page 330). A large number of haphazard corrugated iron roofs seem to have appeared, precariously attached to unfinished plaster and wood interiors. However, it is still an attractive place to visit, with a friendly atmosphere. In the evenings, groups of local youths collect on street corners to play guitars and sing.

Phone code: 0381
Colour map 2, grid B6

Sights Ende is best known in Indonesia as the spot to which Soekarno was exiled by the Dutch between 1934 and 1938. **Soekarno's house** and **museum**, is on Jl Perwira. It has a poor collection of photographs, and little else. The museum is only likely to be of interest to Soekarno acolytes and students of modern Indonesian history. ■ *Mornings (0700-1200, but variable).*

In town, the **Mbongawani market** on Jl Pelabuhan is colourful with traditional healers selling local cures, and a good range of textiles also on sale (see 'Shopping', below). There is a night market, **Pasar Potulando**, on Jl Kelimutu.

A stroll along the sea front is pleasant with the brightly coloured houses of the Muslim fishermen lining the landward side of the route. You will pass **Museum Bahari**, run by Fr Gabrielle Goran, which exhibits shells and marine life around Flores; there are 744 different species on display. ■ *0700-1900 daily. Entrance by donation; profits support the local orphanage.*

For good views of the town and bay, climb **Mount Meja**, about 45 minutes walk to the top, starting from the market; walk south on Jl Gajah Mada and turn left towards Waniwona village.

There is a **tourist office** in the *Kantor Bupati*, Jl Eltari (near intersection with Jl Nangka), where you can ask for a pamphlet and map of the sights around Ende. ■ *0800-1400 Mon-Sat.*

Excursions   **Mount Ia**   To climb to the crater of this dormant volcano takes about 2 hours, and affords good views of the town and bay. ■ *Getting there: catch a bemo to Rate village from the central market and ask for directions.*

Mount Kelimutu is too far to reach in a single day except by chartered vehicle; it is better to spend the night in Moni (see page 349). However, the *Wisata* and *Dewi Putra* and *Ikhlas* hotels have vehicles for charter (100,000Rp) for a day trip to Kelimutu with a *very* early departure.

Nangalala Beach lies 13 km west of Ende. The beach has reasonable swimming and is popular at weekends with locals. ■ *Getting there: catch a bemo from the central market bound for Nangapanda or Nangaroro and get off at the Km 13 marker.*

Nuabosi, 9 km northwest of Ende, offers wonderful views of the town; there is also a *rumah adat* (traditional clan house) here. ■ *Getting there: catch a bemo from the central market.*

There is a pleasant **walk** along the coast from the Wolowona bus terminal

Ende

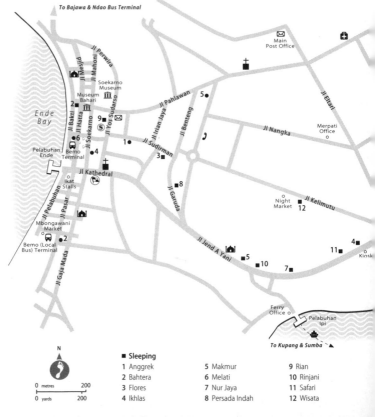

N

0 metres 200
0 yards 200

■ **Sleeping**		
1 Anggrek	5 Makmur	9 Rian
2 Bahtera	6 Melati	10 Rinjani
3 Flores	7 Nur Jaya	11 Safari
4 Ikhlas	8 Persada Indah	12 Wisata

on the edge of town (constant bemos travel there from the town centre) east to **Wolotopo**, about 6 km. Wolotopo has some *rumah adat* (traditional houses) and weaving. It is beautifully positioned.

Ngalupolo is a village a further 7 km east of Wolotopo (see above). It has some *rumah adat*, ikat weaving, ivory tusks and gold jewellery on show (donation required for display). One of the traditional houses is said to be 200 years old. ■ *Getting there: there should be a daily boat at 0700 (except Fri) from Pelabuhan Ipi in Ende to Ngalupolo, which then returns in the afternoon. It is possible to walk from town to the port, or catch a bemo heading east.*

Nggela is a coastal weaving village east of Ende (see page 349). There are homestays here. ■ *Getting there: 4 to 5 hrs from Ende by bis kayu (truck) from the Wolowona terminal (one departure per day). Boats leave from Pelabuhan Ipi (outside Ende) every morning roughly between 0600 and 0700. To get to Pelabuhan Ipi, enter the airport and walk across the runway. Continue through the village (an interesting visit in itself) to the beach and harbour. It is not possible to return the same day by boat, as the boat only waits 15 mins and it is an hour's walk from the coast to Nggela. To return the same day, take a bus via Moni.*

Tours There are as yet no good tour agents in Ende, but the *Dewi Putra*, *IKhlas* and *Wisata* hotels have cars for charter to Kelimutu, and surrounding villages. The Dewi Putra tour visits local villages, beaches and the surrounding countryside – bargain hard.

● **Eating**
1 Depot Ende
2 Istana Bambu
3 Merlin
4 Minang Baru
5 Saiyo
6 Terminal

Nangonasa Bay

To Wolowana Bus Terminal, Moni & Maumere

Sleeping

Lock your door at night – the maze of linked corrugated iron roofs provide a convenient vantage point for intruders! All losmen & hotels include a simple breakfast in the room rate; most are out of the centre of town

C-D *Dwi Putra*, Jl Dewantara, T21465, some a/c, all rooms with private mandi, restaurant, noisy downstairs, quieter upstairs, clean, and unlike most other hotels, it is central, the manager's brother organizes tours (see above). Recommended. **C-D** *Wisata*, Jl Kelimutu 68, T21368. Some a/c, clean, attached mandi, range of rooms – the most expensive are extensive. Helpful friendly staff, restaurant (mid-range) serves Indonesian and Chinese food. **C-E** *Safari*, Jl Jend A Yani, T21499. All rooms with private mandi with a shower, some a/c, villa with large light, clean rooms and attractive garden and a (formerly) very good, very cheap restaurant. But in mid-2000, with all the economic troubles and lack of visitors, only chap chay and mie/nasi goreng ayam were available. **D-E** *Flores*, Jl Sudirman 28, T21075. Some a/c, reasonably spacious rooms, the more expensive ones with showers. The cheap restaurant serves a wide range of food including Chinese and western dishes. **D-E** *Rian/Wisma Dwi Putra*, Jl Yos Sudarso 23, T21223. Some a/c, western toilet, shower and fan. Recently changed its name, so as not to be confused with *Dwi Putra*. **E** *Anggrek*, Jl Gatot

East Nusa Tenggara

Subroto, T22538. WC and showers in the mandi. Clean, large, light rooms. Very cheap restaurant serving Indonesian and Chinese food. **E** *Bahtera*, Jl Bakti 5, T21414. Good location right on the sea front, rooms are a bit dark and there is a basic, grimey communal mandi. No English spoken. **E** *Melati*, Jl Gatot Subroto 12, not far from airport, T21311. Reasonably clean with attached mandi, and a raised area for sipping tea and coffee. **E-F** *Ikhlas*, Jl Jend A Yani, T21695. Choice of rooms from small and dark to light and roomy, some with attached mandi. Satellite TV on the verandah (constant CNN and MTV – when electricity supply allows). Avoid rooms right next to TV. Good very cheap restaurant, large choice of western and Indonesian dishes (the toasted sandwiches are recommended), breakfast not included, good source of information, cheap laundry service, popular with travellers, this is the best of the budget range and offers good value. Recommended. **E-F** *Nur Jaya*, Jl A Yani, T21252. Clean, good communal mandi with shower and a restaurant selling very cheap Indonesian food. Unfortunately the bamboo under the mattresses is falling apart from damp. **F** *Persada Indah* (formerly *Amica*), Jl Garuda 17, T21683. Quiet, very basic accommodation. **F** *Losmen Liana*, Jl Kelimutu 15, T21078. This was closed at the time of our last visit in mid-2000, the other hotel owners seemed vague about whether it would reopen or where the owner had disappeared to. **F** *Makmar*, Jl A Yani 17, basic and dingy, but cheap. **F** *Rinjani*, Jl A Yani 18, like the *Makmar*, basic and dingy but cheap. These last two places are largely frequented by local prostitutes and their clients.

Eating
There are lots of good places to eat in Ende; this is a selection of the best

Mid-range *Istana Bambu*, Jl Pasar 39, T21480. Excellent mie goreng and a wide range of tasty seafood (though item 45 'craps in oyster sauce' sounds less appetising). Recommended, although if you order fish you may have to wait while they run out and get it. *Terminal Restaurant*, Jl Hatta 70 (by the old terminal kota), good fish and lobsters plus usual Indonesian favourites. **Cheap** *Merlin*, Jl Jend A Yani 6, Chinese restaurant, recently revamped and is now flashy and rather overpriced. *Depot Ende*, Jl Sudirman 6, good cheap Indonesian and Chinese. **Very cheap** *Minang Baru*, Jl Soekarno (near Cathedral), excellent Padang food, also sells textiles, has an unusual aquarium – there are fish swimming about in the mandi tank (apparently to eat the mosquito larvae). *Saiyo*, Jl Benteng 7, very good Padang food. The cheapest cold beer in Ende is available from the kiosk opposite *Ikhlas Hotel*. The **night market** (open 1800-2030) sells fruit and snack foods.

Bakeries & coffee shops Jl Kemakmuran (near *Flores Theatre*).

Entertainment **Cinemas** *Flores Theatre*, Jl Kemakmuran 1 – occasionally shows western movies.

Shopping **Books** *Toko Nusa Indah*, Jl Kathedral 5 (just up the hill from the Cathedral). **Tailors** Making-up new clothes and mending, Jl Soekarno, near Cathedral. **Textiles** Good, reasonably priced, ikat from Ende, Kelimutu, Moni and elsewhere (see box, page 331) fairly widely available in town. Salesmen and women visit the losmen, and congregate at the end of Jl Pelabuhan (near Jl Hatta and the port). For a sarong, expect to pay pay 60,000-80,000Rp, depending on the quality. There is also a good range on sale at the *Minang Baru Restaurant*, includes Sumba blankets.

Transport
54 km from Moni,
147 km from Maumere,
284 km from Larantuka,
125 km from Bajawa,
255 km from Ruteng

Local Bemos: ply the main roads, routes are marked over the roof. Most link the town bus terminals, Ndao and Wolowona. The bemo terminal is by the Pasar Mbongawani, near the centre of town.

Air Ende's **Ipi airport** is on the southeast edge of town; bemos to the centre cost about 2,500Rp, although it's only a 50 m walk to the main road where the frequent public bemos are a third of the price. It is a 5-10 min walk from the airport to the closest of the losmen. Daily connections on *Merpati* with **Denpasar**, **Kupang** and other destinations in Nusa Tenggara.

Bus Ende has 2 bus terminals. Ndao terminal is situated on the northwest side of town, off Jl Imam Bonjol, 1 km from the centre. From it buses head for **Riung** (4 hrs), **Bajawa** (5 hrs), **Ruteng** (10 hrs) and other destinations to the west. For destinations to the east, the Wolowana terminal is at the end of Jl Gatot Subroto, 4 km from the town centre. Buses to **Wolowaru** (2¼ hrs), **Moni/Kelimutu** (2½ hrs), between 0600 and 1400, frequent buses to **Maumere** (6 hrs), 1 early morning bus to **Larantuka** (10 hrs). Constant bemos link both terminals and the town centre. Buses from Bajawa and Maumere drop passengers off at losmen if requested. A minibus leaves the *Ikhlas Losmen* every night at 1700, going all the way to Labuanbajo. *Agogo* bus company runs a service to **Ruteng** and **Maumere** and has its offices at Jl Pelabuhan 28.

Sea Boat: Ende's main port is Pelabuhan Ipi, to the southeast of town. Some smaller vessels also dock at Pelabuhan Ende, Jl Hatta 1, in the heart of town. A *Pelni* ship leaves at 1200 on Wed or 0600 on Thu for **Sabu**, **Rote** and **Kupang** (on Timor). The *Pelni* ships *Awu* and *Pangrango* dock here. Every Saturday at 1500 a boat heads for **Waingapu** on Sumba, before turning back towards **Labuanbajo**, **Badas** and **Surabaya**. And every other Wed at 0900 another vessel also leaves for **Waingapu**, and continues on to **Labuanbaojo**, **Bima** and **Ujung Pandang** (Makassar). There is also a boat to **Kupang** at 1700 on Thu and Sat. The *Pelni* office is at Jl Kathedral 2, T21043. Finally there is a bi-weekly ferry service to **Waingapu** (Sumba) on Wed afternoon continuing on to **Sape**, and currently arriving there at 1600 on Friday.

Airline offices *Merpati*, Jl Nangka, T21355, open 0800-1300 and 1600-1700 Mon-Sat (closed Wed), open 1000-1200 Sun. **Banks** *BNI*, Jl Sudirman, up the hill from *Depot Ende Restaurant*, will change cash and TCs in major currencies; *BRI*, Jl Yos Sudarso, will change TCs; *Bank Danoman*, Jl Pasar Ende, allows users to withdraw money on Visa or Mastercard, and will also change US$. **Communcations** General Post Office: the main post office is on Jl Eltari on the northernmost edge of town; there is a more central and smaller branch office on Jl Yos Sudarso, only open in the mornings. Telephone, telegraph & fax: *Perumtel*, Jl Kelimutu 5 (international). **Medical services** Hospitals: Jl Mesjid.

Directory

East Nusa Tenggara

Ende to Larantuka

For the first 45 minutes out of Ende the road rises spectacularly up through a limestone gorge, with worryingly precipitous drops. After 50 km the road reaches the town of Moni, the logical base for trips to the stunning crater lakes of Mount Kelimutu. From Moni the road descends to the coast and the town of Maumere, a distance of 93 km. The coral gardens near Maumere offer some of the best snorkelling and diving in Indonesia. Continuing east from Maumere, the last leg of the Trans-Flores Highway runs 137 km to the port of Larantuka. This was one of the centres of Portuguese missionary activity in Flores, and remains among the most obviously Christian towns on the island.

Kelimutu and Moni

Mount Kelimutu, with its three-coloured crater lakes, is one of the highlights of Flores. The first foreigners to climb the volcano were the Dutchmen Le Roux and Van Suchtelen in 1915. The lakes, at an altitude of 1,640 m, are said to have changed colour 37 times in the last 50 years (though it is not clear who counted), presumably as the chemicals and minerals in the water react, though the exact chemistry behind the transformations remains a mystery. In the 1970s they were red, white and blue, this gradually gave way to the less spectacular maroon (almost black), iridescent green, and yellow-green. In

Mount Kelimutu

1997 they underwent another transformation and are currently brown black, cafe au lait and milky blue. Local villagers believe that the lakes are the resting places for souls called by Mutu (Kelimutu). When mists lie over the lake someone is thought to be passing over: young people are destined for one lake, the old for another, while witches and evil people go to the third. On a clear morning, the view of the crater lakes and the surrounding mountains is simply unforgettable.

Ascending and descending the mountain Reaching the summit used to require an early morning/late night trek of 12 km; today there is a truck which takes people up to the summit at about 0400, in time for the sunrise, it takes about one hour (but is overpriced at at 15,000Rp). At the time of writing the bridge across to the base of the craters had collapsed due to heavy rains, and trucks were charging 100,000Rp per load of tourists. *Ojeks* (motorcycle taxis) will also take people to the top of Kelimutu for around 5,000Rp. Make it known at your losmen that you wish to be picked up. The truck descends at about 0700 but it is often worth staying longer to see the lakes in full sunlight. Everyone waits on the viewing platform at the summit for dawn, hoping that it will be clear – it is often cloudy, so it may be necessary to wait a few days in Moni but this is no real hardship as there are some pleasant walks nearby (see 'Excursions'). **NB** It is cold, both at the summit and on the open truck; take a sweater, or use an ikat sarong, which will serve as a handy alternative to a sleeping bag (sold all over Moni for 30,000-45,000Rp). Remember to bring food and drink because although refreshments are available, they are limited and relatively expensive – on disembarking from the bus you will probably be offered tea or coffee at 10,000Rp for a small cup. The walk down the mountain is easy enough in daylight and very worthwhile. The road to the summit is 12 km, but the well marked path – Jl Potong (Jl Shortcut) – only 8 km, note that the shortcut is by the toll station, not before. Only the foolhardy would attempt the shortcut by starlight. The main path is through stunning countryside and takes you past hot springs (where a bath is very refreshing, but it may create some interest from the locals) and a waterfall – good for a dip. There is also a further turning off this path which takes you through a number of villages in which it is possible to watch ikat being woven, to drink tea and coffee and buy

Around Ende

sarongs. At the end of the trail through the villages is the quirky *rumah makan Agnes*, which serves basic and very cheap noodles and rice dishes, though service is slow. ■ *Entrance fee to volcano: 2,500Rp.*

The friendly nearby village of Moni (altitude 600 m) is in the heart of Lio District which has a rich weaving tradition with blues and reds being the most common colours. It is a good base from which to make walks in the beautiful surrounding area and excursions to local villages (see below). The **market** on Tuesday mornings on the playing field is worth seeing: there is a good range of ikat for sale; traditional herbalists also set up their stalls. The village has become the main tourist base from which to visit the mountain. There are also beautiful walks in the surrounding area and a couple of **hotsprings** and a **waterfall** just a few hundred metres along the road to Ende, which gives you the option of a warm mandi. Next to *Daniel's Homestay* is a **high thatched traditional house** in front of which daily traditional dance displays are held (around 5,000Rp).

Wolowaru is situated on the main Ende-Maumere road, 11 km from Moni. This is a bigger town than Moni but has not developed into such a tourist base for climbing Mount Kelimutu. It is worth visiting on market days (Mon, Wed and Sat) when there is a reasonable range of ikat on sale (see page 331). It is also possible to use the town to visit the ikat-weaving villages in the surrounding countryside, including Nggela and Jopu (see below). **Sleeping** Includes: **E** *Losmen Kelimutu*, clean, some attached mandis. The *Jawa Timur* next door, is a popular restaurant stop for buses travelling through the town; it has good food. ■ *Getting there: 15 mins by bemo from Moni, or on a bus from Ende or Maumere.*

Jopu is a weaving village 4 km from Wolowaru, producing weft ikat (see page 331). The various processes involved in producing ikat are on view to visitors (see page 181). ■ *Getting there: take a bemo directly there or go to Wolowaru, from where bemos go to Jopu more frequently.*

Nggela, 15 km from Wolowaru on the same road as Jopu, is a weaving village has become over-touristed. However, ikat is on sale and production processes are on view (see page 181). The locals employ rather pushy sales tactics. There are hot springs and a couple of homestays here. ■ *Getting there: take a bis kayu to Wolowaru, and a bemo to Nggela; there is also a daily boat (except Friday) to Ende from the beach, which is a steep 2-km descent from Nggela, 2½ hrs, only recommended for the hardy, as it is easy to fall out of the small canoe, which transports you from shore to boat. Alternatively, the 19 km walk from Wolowaru is very beautiful, through paddy fields and along the beach (take a short cut from Wolojita and take plenty of water to drink).*

D *Bungalow Hotel* (10 mins walk from Moni village on road to Ende), clean and attractive. Recommended. **D** *Arwanty's Homestay*, brand new and right in the centre of Moni, the owner has just sent us details about her 3 new and 2 improved bungalows, each with spacious living rooms, good bathroom facilities, verandah, and a restaurant serving traditional cuisine. **D-E** *Sao Ria Wisata*, the more expensive rooms are clean and attractive with good views over the valley. The cheaper rooms on the other hand are rather dark and very basic and look out onto the back of the pricier accommodation. **E** *Hidayah Bungalows*, some with private mandi. The hot springs are just 3 mins walk away in the direction of Ende. Clean bamboo bungalows on stilts, helpful management can provide mosquito nets on request and can organize bus tickets at the right price. Free tea and coffee throughout the day. Recommended. **E** *Homestay Wisata*, a little way out of town on the road to Maumere; good for those who want to escape the crowd. Large bamboo rooms on stilts, very cheap restaurant

The number of losmen in Moni reflects how heavily the village has become reliant on the tourist trade. However, like so many other towns in Flores, in mid-2000 during our last visit there were scarcely any tourists about

serving Chinese and Indonesian food. **E** *Losmen Maria*, clean rooms for up to 3 people, private mandi with showers, further bungalows are under construction. **E** *Palm Homestay*, out of town, the first hotel you pass on the road from Maumere towards Wolowaru, situated in the middle of a fruit garden and very peaceful compared with places in town, single and double bungalows with and without attached mandi, good transport information, excellent buffet dinner, breakfast included. **E** *Watugana Bungalows*, this little gem of a place is set back from the road just opposite the *Mountain View*. Attractive bungalows on stilts arranged around a lovely little garden. Simple facilities but very clean, a small breakfast is included in the cost but for a little extra, a huge breakfast can be laid on. Central location, best of the budget accommodation. Recommended. **E** *Wisma Kelimutu*, shower in the mandi but otherwise very basic and rather dirty though the staff are very friendly. A new block should soon be completed. **F** *Amina Moe*, cheapest rooms in town. Basic outside mandi, simple rooms, comfortable communal sitting-room. Excellent huge and cheap buffet laid on every night: price includes breakfast and tea/coffee, a real favourite. Recommended. **F** *Daniel*, cold water, shared mandi, friendly and popular, rats in the rafters. **F** *Pondok Wisata Lestari*, 40 m off the main road, clean communal mandi, thin bamboo walled rooms. **F** *Pondok Wisata Regal Jaya*, communal mandi, small but clean rooms with good mattresses.

Eating **Cheap** *Amina Moe* best buffets of the homestays; tasty and a big choice, place order before 1730, always more than you can eat. *Mountain View Restaurant* good view, great food and big helpings. Indonesian and travellers' food, serves Moni cake. *Nusa Bunga* serves curry as well as Indonesian and travellers' food. *Rona* Indonesian and Western food including eight Italian dishes which are surprisingly good. Rona cake, a version of Moni cake, is tasty and filling and makes a welcome change from the standard nasi and mie fare. Pricey drinks though you can bring your own. **Very cheap** *Kelimutu*, down road from *Sao Ria Wisata Hotel*, Indonesian and Western food. *Rumah Makan Sarti* serves Indonesian and Western food, weavers often work next to the restaurant. *Wisata*, on the right hand side of the road heading towards Maumere, about 400 m from the market. Lovely view and very good food, friendly owners; a good place to sit and relax.

Transport **Road** **Bus**: regular connections with Ende 2 hrs, and Maumere 3 hrs; there is also a daily bus doing the 9 hr journey through to Bajawa. **NB** It can be difficult to get out of Moni in the high season; you may have to hitch a lift on a truck travelling to Nggela on market day. The buses passing through the town are often full; it may be necessary to catch a *bis kayu* to Wolowaru and wait for the bus there.

11 km from Wolowaru,
54 km from Ende,
93 km from Maumere

Directory **Communications** The *Kelimutu Restaurant* 1 km along the road to Ende from Moni, has the only telephone in the area. It is generally only possible to make domestic calls and seems rather temperamental.

Maumere

Phone code: 0382
Colour map 3, grid A2

Most people come to this region to dive and snorkel in some of the best sea gardens in Indonesia and explore the surrounding villages. Maumere itself, with a population of about 70,000, is a rather featureless, disorganized town that still seems to be coming to terms with being (comparatively) large. The tourist office, *Kantor Pariwisata*, is on Jl Wairklau, T21562. To get there, walk along Jl Gajah Mada towards Ende, turn right after the Perusahaan Umum Listrik, and walk 400 m – the office is just past the *Kantor Statistik*, 10-15 minutes in total from town centre. They provide a useful booklet, but little English is spoken.

It is possible to walk around Maumere in a morning. The central market is just that – central – with a good selection of ikat cloth on sale (see 'Shopping').

The port (Pelabuhan Maumere), usually quiet, is five minutes walk to the northwest; on the way there the road passes **Maumere Cathedral**. If you are staying in town, the nightlife makes for a surprising diversion. Maumere is the 'Las Vegas of Flores'. During August there is a nightly night market; it is not actually a market, more like a fair where you can risk your rupiah on the roulette wheels and bingo boards, buy snacks and sample the local alcoholic brews from street sellers. In September there is also bareback horse racing.

Excursions

Waiara and **Sao Wisata Beaches** lie 12-13 km east of Maumere. There is good swimming and the sea off the coast is a marine park and offers superb snorkelling and diving – or at least it did until the December 1992 earthquake. The coral has been badly damaged, especially off Sao Wisata Beach. The most seriously affected coral gardens are those in shallow waters, some of the deeper dive sites escaped relatively unscathed. Two dive clubs are based here and run dive boats out to the reefs (see 'Diving Clubs'). It is easiest to reach the reef by booking a place on one of their dive boats. **Sleeping** Homestays available on Permaan Island, as are local guides (but limited English spoken). ■ *Getting there: by bemo from the Terminal Timur. It is also possible to reach the marine park by chartering a boat from Keliting (9 km east, take a bemo from Terminal Timur) for about 65,000Rp per day. There are regular boats crossing between the islands out on the reef and Keliting on market days (Wed and Fri).*

Ladalero is home to the biggest museum on Flores, the **Blikan Blewut Museum**. It is situated 9 km from town, on the road to Ende. A cluttered, mixed, yet interesting display of ethnographic exhibits, textiles and ceramics assembled by the local Seminary (Societas Verbi Divini). ■ *Admission to*

East Nusa Tenggara

Maumere

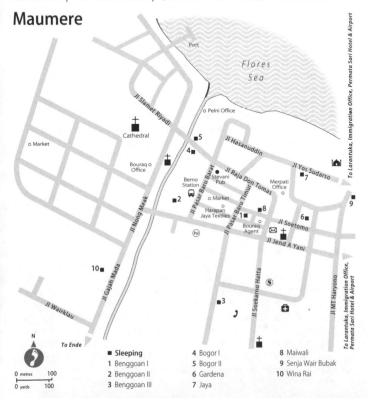

Flores Sea

Port

o Pelni Office

Jl Slamet Riyadi

✝ Cathedral

o Market

Bouraq o Office

✝

Bemo Station

Stevani Pub

Jl Pasar Baru Barat

Jl Raja Don Tomas

Jl Hasanuddin

Jl Yos Sudarso

Merpati Office o

■5

■4

o Market

Harapan Jaya Textiles

Bouraq Agent

Jl Pasar Baru Timur

■1 ■

■8

Jl Soetomo

✝

Jl Jend A Yani

■2

Jl Nong Meak

(Pol)

Jl Gajah Mada

10■

Jl Wairklau

Jl Soekarno Hatta

Ⓢ

♪

■3

✝

N

To Ende

To Larantuka, Immigration Office, Permata Sari Hotel & Airport

To Larantuka, Immigration Office, Permata Sari Hotel & Airport

Jl MT Haryono

Jl Sudarso

■7

9■

■6

0 metres 100
0 yards 100

■ Sleeping	4 Bogor I	8 Maiwali
1 Benggoan I	5 Bogor II	9 Senja Wair Bubak
2 Benggoan II	6 Gardena	10 Wina Rai
3 Benggoan III	7 Jaya	

museum by donation. 0730-1400 Mon-Sat, 1000-1400 Sun. Getting there: take a bemo from Terminal Barat.

Nita is about 2 km from Ladalero and 11 km from Maumere. The 'Rajah' here has a collection of old elephant tusks and other memorabilia. There is a worthwhile weekly market held here each Thursday. ■ *Getting there: take a bus from Terminal Barat.*

Sikka is a weaving village from which the entire region around Maumere takes its name. It is possible to buy ikat here at reasonable prices (check at the craft shops for comparison – see 'Shopping' below) and see some of the multiple stages of the ikat process – something like 35 in all (see page 181). If on a tour, all the stages may be demonstrated. There is also an attractive **Portuguese church** at Sikka, white with green fretwork, built in 1800. ■ *Getting there: take a bus from Terminal Barat.*

Watublapi is another, less frequently visited, weaving village, 11 km south from Geliting (which lies just east of Maumere, on the main trans-Flores road). Nearby is Bliran Sina Hill from where there are views north to the Flores Sea and south to the Sawu (Sabu) Sea. There is a large Catholic seminary here and it is sometimes possible to stay overnight. ■ *Getting there: take a bus from Terminal Timur.*

Wodong lies 27 km east of Maumere. See page 355 for details. ■ *Getting there: take a bus or bemo from the Lokaria terminal to Wodong.*

Nuabari is a village where animist beliefs continue to play an important role. Indeed Nuabari is unusual in a number of respects. To start with, the language of the inhabitants and the cloth that they weave have much more in common with the area around Moni than with Maumere. There are also numerous examples of megalithic graves sites. Holes are dug into solid rock and the bodies placed in a foetal position within the excavated cavities. If a couple wishes to be buried together, the one who dies first will be exhumed on the death of his/her partner and the bodies arranged face to face, placed back in their resting place, and the grave resealed. Bodies must be embalmed as they generally lie for at least a week while the graves are prepared to receive them. Visitors may also be able to see inside the chief's house which is decorated with masks and carvings. The chief is the functional and spiritual leader of Nuabari and two other nearby villages. Elaborate rituals must be carried out so that this power can pass from father to son. It is said that the chief can sense his impending death and calls for a period of fasting. He then cuts his son's skin along the forearms, thighs and on either side of his back. He proceeds to rub a mixture of his bile and herbs into the wounds which completes the transfer of authority. Donations of 1,000Rp to an education fund for local children. Bring your own water as there is none available here. ■ *Getting there: the village can be reached on tours arranged from the Gardena Hotel.*

Tours Day tours from Maumere to Sikka weaving village, the Ladalero museum and Nita; or to Geliting Market and Watublapi weaving village or to Sea World can be arranged by many of the hotels. Some also have cars and drivers for charter. For example the *Hotel Maiwali*'s minibus can be chartered to Wairara Beach, Sikka weaving village, Ladalero, Kelimutu (either in one day leaving at 0300; or over two days with a night in Moni). *Harapan Jaya*, a textile shop on Jl Moa Toda also has a car for hire. Expect to pay about 140,000Rp for a day's hire to out-of-town destinations, 95,000Rp for around town. *Wina Ria Hotel* can arrange boats for snorkelling. Alternatively, enquire at the tourist information office.

A-D *Permata Sari Inn*, Jl Jend Sudirman 1, 2 km from town, T21171. On the beach, attractive clean rooms all with attached bathrooms, quite nice bungalows but overpriced. **C-E** *Senja Wair Bubak*, Jl Yos Sudarso, T21498. Some a/c, becoming the most popular of the budget places, range of rooms from simple with shared facilities to rather more comfortable a/c rooms. Good facilities including tours and motorbike and car hire. **C-E** *Wini Rai*, Jl Dr Soetorno, T21362 (about 5-10 mins walk out of town on road to Ende). Some a/c, shared mandi in cheaper rooms but more expensive are large and clean with attached facilities, garden, can arrange tours around Flores and book tickets, economy rooms come recommended. **D** *Gardena*, Jl Pattirangga 28, 5 mins from town centre on quiet side street, T21489, F23404. Some a/c, all rooms with inside mandi, comfortable atmosphere. Hires out cars and motorbikes (see 'Transport'). Good source of information and popular with travellers. Best place to get hold of tour guides. **D-E** *Bogor*, Jl Slamet Riyadi 2, T21191. An extensive hotel complex with a car for rent, a good little shop and a restaurant with cheap Indonesian and Chinese food. **D-E** *Maiwali*, Jl Raja Don Tomas 40, T21220. Some a/c, the more expensive rooms are comfortable, quiet and clean but the fan-cooled rooms are expensive and cheaper hotels offer a better deal. Some very active midnight karaoke enthusiasts! **D-E** *Jaya*, Jl Sultan Hasannudin, T21292. Some rooms with a/c, prices includes breakfast and afternoon tea. Friendly but near the mosque so wake up calls come around 0430. **E** *Lareska*, Jl S Pranoto 3, T21137. The economy rooms are upstairs and far more attractive than the more expensive rooms below. There is a good view from the upstairs balcony area. Don't be put off by the ground floor room, the cheaper rooms come recommended. **E** *Losmen Bogor II*, Jl Slamet Riyadi 4, T21137. Edge of town, recently renovated, the rooms are bright and clean, with big windows looking on to the waterside (ask for a room with a window as some don't have one), the upstairs rooms (shared mandi) are nicer than the downstairs rooms (own mandi but dark). **E** *Naga Beach*, 10 km west of town (take bemo 5 from *Losmen Bogor II* or from Pasar Baru), T21605. 50 m from the beach, clean bungalows with shared mandi, very friendly, good value, price includes breakfast. **E-F** *Benggoan III*, Jl Ahmad Yani, T21284. Some a/c, this featureless hollow building was badly damaged during the 1992 earthquake and repair work seemed to take years to get started, economy rooms are rather grubby, no food is provided for breakfast. **F** *Homestay Varanus*, Jl Nong Meak, T21464. Friendly place with a nice garden, good value but the earthquake damage is taking some time to repair. Recommended.

Dive Clubs at Waiara (12 km from town) **B-C** *Pondok Dunia Laut (Sea World Club)*, Jl Nai Roa, Km 13, PO Box 3, T21570, F21102. Some a/c, attractive cottages, and better value for money than the *Flores Sao Wisata*, although the diving equipment and support is reportedly not as good, price includes breakfast (see 'Diving' below). **B** *Flores Sao Wisata*, Waiara Beach, T21555, F21666. Better of the 2 dive centres, good equipment, **A** per day if diving, at this price the rooms are rather under-equipped (see 'Diving' below).

At beaches near Maumere **E** *Paga Beach*, on coast south of Maumere (go to Terminal Ende and take an hourly bemo running to *Paga Beach Hotel*, 1 hr drive). Very clean and attractive bamboo huts, white sand swimming beach, decorated by weird and wonderful plants and imaginative use of concrete. Has a little craft shop. **E-F** *Nogo Beach*, fan optional for additional charge. Price includes breakfast, can arrange snorkelling trips and hire out equipment.

Cheap *Golden Fish*, Jl Hasan Nudu, fresh seafood and Chinese food. *Stevani's Pub and Restaurant*, Jl Raya Centis (near intersection with Jl Raja Don Tomas), open air thatched pavilions in garden, travellers', Chinese and Indonesian food and karaoke from 2100 most evenings. **Very cheap** *Bambu Den*, Jl Gajah Mada 46, Chinese and Indonesian food. *Rumah Makan Sumber Indah*, Jl Raja Centis, Javanese, Chinese and seafood. *Sarinah*, Jl Raya Centis, Chinese, excellent seafood.

Sleeping
All prices include morning tea but no breakfast unless stated. Because Maumere is a popular diving area, it features on many tour itineraries & consequently hotel prices tend to be somewhat steeper than normal

East Nusa Tenggara

Eating
It is generally acceptable to bring your own drinks to a restaurant. For the widest choice of places try the main street down to the harbour

Bars *Toko Go*, Jl Dr Soetorno 14, sells cheap cold beer and soft drinks. **Evening Market**, behind *Stevani's Pub*, sells cheap *arrack* (local brew) and fruit. Beruga style huts in a pleasant garden.

Entertainment **Karaoke** *Stevanis* and *Sinta Pubs* both do nightly karaoke sessions, the first geared more to western the latter to local tastes.

Shopping **Textiles** Excellent range of ikat from all over Nusa Tenggara on sale at *Harapan Jaya*, Jl Moa Toda, reasonable prices (though not bargains): ikat from Roti and Sabu, Ende (80,000Rp), Sumba (265-315,000Rp), Larantuka and Lembata (115-265,000Rp), Manggarai (near Ruteng) (55-80,000Rp), West Timor (150-200,000Rp), Sikka (25-35,000Rp). Also textiles next door at Subur Jaya; *Kota Pena Art Shop*, Jl Gaja Mada, T21032, a fantastic range of arts and crafts from all over East Nusa Tenggara. An education even if you are not buying, though some of the smaller pieces are very tempting and quite affordable, bargaining possible.

Sports **Diving** Although the earthquake of December 1992 is now history, the effect of the earthquake on the area's sea life is still evident. Large stands of coral were destroyed and these will take years to recover. Although other sections of reef, remarkably, appear to have survived intact, regular visitors report that the diving is still not back to its pre-earthquake best. *Flores Sao Wisata* on Waiara Beach (see 'Sleeping' above) offer package deals, which include airport pick up. *Pondok Dunia Laut (Sea World Club)* (see Sleeping) offer an all-in package, which includes 2 dives per day, boat trip, tank and weights, accommodation and all meals for 2 people, they also have diving equipment and windsurf boards for hire to non-residents. **Snorkelling**: it is possible to book a place on *Sao Wisata's* dive boat, with equipment, lunch and drinks provided.

Tour operators *Astura*, Jl Yos Sudarso, T21498. *Floressa Wisata*, Jl Jend A Yani, T21242. *Sikka Permai*, Jl Pasar Lama, T21236. Watch out for tour agents selling tickets with someone else's name on them for full price. Check tickets with the airline office.

Transport

82 km from Wolowaru, 93 km from Moni, 147 km from Ende, 137 km from Larantuka. Travelling east from Maumere to Larantuka the road is good & the countryside particularly beautiful

Local Bemos: the bemo station is by the old market on Jl Jend A Yani in the centre of town. Local journeys cost 500Rp, 1,000Rp if they go right off their route. Bemos criss-cross the town linking the 2 bus terminals, Barat and Timur (or Lokaria). **Cars**: can be chartered for around 130,000Rp per day (see 'Tours', above), motorcycles for 25,000Rp per day (both *Gardena* and *Wini Rai II* arrange hire).

Air Maumere's **Waioti Airport** is 2 km east of the town centre, off the road towards Larantuka. Transport to town: taxis to the town centre or walk the 750 m to the main road and catch a bemo. Regular connections by *Merpati* and *Bouraq* with **Jakarta**, **Denpasar**, **Bima** and **Kupang**, and towns in Kalimantan and Sulawesi.

Bus Maumere has 2 bus terminals; Terminal Barat on Jl Gajah Mada for destinations to the west, including **Wolowaru** (3 hrs), **Moni** (3½ hrs) and **Ende** (5 hrs); and Terminal Timur (also known as Terminal Lokaria) east of town on Jl Larantuka for eastern destinations including **Larantuka** (4 hrs) and **Wodong**. It is now possible to travel straight through to **Bajawa**, though this requires a gruelling 10-hr journey. Buses link the 2 terminals and the town centre (500Rp). Buses arriving in Maumere drop passengers off at their losmen/hotels and those leaving will cruise town for aeons and also pick up from losmen/hotels. *Agogo* (for Ende, Moni and Wolowaru) has its offices on Jl Jend A Yani; *Sinar Remaja* on Jl Pattirangga, and *Sinar Agung* (for Larantuka and Ende) on Jl Gajah Mada by the Terminal Barat. Losmen/hotels will also usually book tickets.

Boat The Pelabuhan Maumere is a 5-10 mins walk northwest from the town centre. The *Pelni* ship *Awu* docks here on its 2 week circuit between calling at ports in Java, Sulawesi and Nusa Tenggara. The *Pelni* office is next to *Losmen Bogor II* on Jl S Pranoto (aka Jl Slamet Riyadi), just over the bridge on the road to the port. Irregular mixed cargo vessels leave here for **Ende**, **Reo**, **Riung**, **Kupang**, **Larantuka** and **Surabaya**.

Airline offices *Bouraq*, Jl Nong Meak, T21467 (also agent on Jl Moa Toda, next to *Benggoan I losmen*). **Merpati**, Jl Raja Don Tomas, T21342, open 0800-1400 and 1900-2100. **Banks** *BNI*, Jl Soekarno-Hatta (behind and to the side of the Kantor Bupati), will change TCs and cash in major currencies. *BRI*, Jl Raja Centis, open 0730-1430 Mon-Fri, 0730-1130 Sat. *Bank Danamon*, Jl Raja Centis, will change banknotes and can withdraw money from Visa or Mastercard. **Communications** General Post Office: Jl Jend A Yani (on the square near the Kantor Bupati). **Telephone & telegram**: *Telekom*, Jl Soekarno-Hatta (200 m from Jl Jend A Yani) (international). The *Wartel* office is next door to *Gardena Hotel* on Jl Patirangga and is open 24 hrs every day. **Medical services** Hospitals: *General Hospital*, Jl Kesehatan, T21118. **Useful addresses** Immigration office: Jl Kom A Sucipto, T21151 (slip road to airport). **Police**: Jl Jend A Yani, T21110.

Directory

Waiterang Bay and Wodong

Wodong is a small village 25 km east of Maumere, en route to Larantuka. There are five excellent, though basic, places to stay along the beach outside Wodong village (see 'Sleeping', below). There is good snorkelling here, and Wodong is also convenient as a base from which to trek to Mount Egon (see 'Excursions', below). The two losmen hire out masks and flippers and can arrange fishing trips and excursions to offshore islands. For those looking for a place to enjoy the landscape of Flores away from the masses, this is a good place to stay for a few days.

There is a good walk up the hill behind the bay, 1½ hours. The route is marked by white signs erected by staff from *Flores Froggies*. From the top of the hill are some great views out across the bay. If you take a bemo to Blidit village, there is a 45 minute walk to some hot springs at the base of Mount Egon (ask for *mata air panas*).

Excursions

    Mount Egon (1,703 m) is an active volcano, visible from Wodong. The trek to the summit takes 3½-4½ hours and is well worthwhile. From Blitit (see below, for information on reaching Blitit), follow the gravel track until it reaches a roadside, concrete water culvet and a rocky ford. Here is the first of a series of stone cairns marking the way to the summit. The route passes from scree into dry grassland, and from grassland into savanna scrub forest, with eucalyptus predominating. The path through the forest is clear enough; it emerges into more open landscape after about 2 hours. From here the summit is visible, and it is about another hour's walk to the top. Near the peak, old tubes – now lying in disuse – laid by the Japanese during their occupation of Indonesia for sulphur extraction – are visible. A path leads around the crater edge, and another snakes its way into the caldera. The caldera lake, though, has dried out. From the crater lip there are superb views – on a clear day – over the sea towards Pulau Besar. **NB** Take ample water and some food for the trek. ■ *Getting there: take a bemo to Blitit, at the end of the surfaced road (it is also possible to arrange a pickup after descending from Mount Egon). Ask the owners of the Wodong Homestay or Flores Froggies if they will make the necessary arrangements.*

    Boat trips can be arranged to the white sand beaches of **Pulau Indah**, where there is good snorkelling. There used to be a village on the island but it was destroyed in the 1992 earthquake. **Pulau Besar** is the largest of the three offshore islands and has three traditional villages. **Pulau Pondok** is reportedly good for shell collecting – although live shells should not be taken.

Sleeping   All the accommodation is in simple bungalows except at *Pondok Praja*. All prices include a simple breakfast but there is no pressure to eat other meals at the same place that you are staying. All places are within a few mins walk from each other so it is easy enough to look around and weigh up the competition. **D** *Pondok Praja*, substantial bungalows, with negotiable prices. Rice, noodles and the odd bit of chicken and fish available at warung prices. As a novel attraction, there is a Second World War bomb crater in the back garden. **D-E** *Ankermis*, some rooms with own mandi, bungalows are set slightly back from the beach, behind some freshwater pools, excellent restaurant (see below). **E-F** *Flores Froggies*, run by a French couple, as one might expect, old but attractive bungalows on the beachfront, the travellers' and Indonesian food comes recommended, friendly, the bungalows have attached mandis, dormitory accommodation also available. Recommended. **E-F** *Wodong Bungalows*, some rooms with own mandi, mosquito net, good and very cheap restaurant, friendly, good source of information (check the visitors' book), popular, with free use of bikes, canoes and snorkles. **F** *Waiterang Beach*, this relatively new place is the cheapest in Waiterang Bay. The bungalows look directly on to the sea. Inexpensive simple restaurant.

Eating   **Cheap** *Ankermis*, this restaurant is a bit pricier than the others, but there is a definite correlation between what you pay and what you get, try *hot gossip nasi campur*.

Sports   **Diving**, **snorkelling** and **fishing**: the 2 losmen can arrange diving with the *Sea World Club* outside Maumere; they also hire out masks and flippers and can arrange fishing trips.

Transport   **Bus**: regular connections with **Larantuka** and **Maumere**. From Maumere, take a
25 km from Maumere   bemo or bus from Terminal Lokaria to Wodong.

Larantuka

Phone code: 0383   The small town of Larantuka is the district capital of east Flores, with a popula-
Colour map 3, grid A3   tion of 30,000. It is strongly Christian – though there is also a significant Muslim population – with a remarkable Easter celebration showing Portuguese origins (16th century). Particular devotion is shown to the Virgin Mary, a statue of whom was reportedly miraculously washed-up on the shore here. On 8 September 1887, Don Lorenzo Diaz Viera de Godinho II consecrated the entire town to the Virgin. The town's name means 'on the way', and its strategic position made it a locally important port – Magellan's chronicler Francesco Antonio Pigafetta records passing here in 1522 on the expedition's voyage home from the Spice Islands (Maluku).

The **Chapel of the Virgin Mary**, in the centre of town, houses the sacred statue of the Virgin (see 'Festivals'). On Saturday, the Mama Muji pray in ancient Latin and Portuguese, distorted to such a degree that it is unintelligible even to students of the language (see box). There are also prayers said each evening. There are a number of other churches in town including the century-old **Cathedral of Larantuka** and the **Chapel of Christ** (Tuan Ana Chapel). The old **docks** are also worth visiting. Larantuka was fortunate to survive the earthquake, which devastated much of Eastern Flores, relatively unscathed.

Sleeping   **B-D** *Fortuna II*, Jl Basuki Rachmat 168, out of town, T21383. Some a/c, the best hotel
The rooms in   in town and, as the name suggests, the up-market sister hotel to the *Fortuna I* which is
Larantuka tend to be   across the road. It also shares an inconvenient location but the rooms are spacious
rather overpriced. All   and comfortable and certainly the plushest in town. **B-E** *Fortuna I*, Jl Basuki Rachmat
hotels except Rulies   171, 2 km northeast of town, T21140. Private bathroom, the more expensive rooms
include a simple   have a/c and are not particularly attractive, the cheaper rooms are small but clean.
breakfast in the price   **B-E** *Tresna*, Jl Yos Sudarso 8, T21072. Some private mandis, food served. This was the

The old Catholics of Larantuka

In 1613 a Dutch ship, the Half Moon, anchored off Solor and bombarded the Portuguese fort there, forcing the 1,000 strong population to surrender. Two of the Dominican friars – Caspar de Spiritu Santo and Augustino de Magdalena – asked that rather than withdraw to Melaka with the rest of the population, they be landed at Larantuka. Here they set about building another mission and by 1618 they had established more than 20 missions in the area. However, as the Portuguese lost influence so the Roman Catholics of Larantuka became isolated. The raja of the area took the title 'Servant of the Queen of the Rosary' and the church's devotional objects – chalice, cross, statues and so on – became part of local adat or tradition. Christianity became fossilized: the few Dutch Protestant ministers were sent smartly packing when they unsatisfactorily answered questions about Mary, Mother of Jesus, and visits by Portuguese Roman Catholic priests were few and far between.

Even so, the Roman Catholic rites and beliefs inculcated by the original Dominican friars were handed down through the generations. Devotees were taught to say their prayers in Latin and old Portuguese, and to wear robes like those of 17th-century penitentes, with pointed hoods. When the Roman Catholics of Larantuka were finally 'rediscovered' by the Dutch priest, Father C de Hesselle in 1853 he was amazed to see the population keeping to a tradition over two centuries old. The most remarkable of these ceremonies is the Easter parade, replete with a rudely-hewn cross carried in procession (see 'Festivals' below).

place where visiting officials holed up – they have now moved on to the *Fortuna II* – but the rooms are quite reasonable and it has a more central location next to the Chapel of the Virgin Mary, quaint garden and friendly management. **F** *Rulies*, Jl Yos Sudarso 40, T21198. A friendly, if rather scruffy, hotel with dorm accommodation and communal mandi, the place which attracts most of the backpacker business. Good source of information.

Cheap The *Rumah Makan Nirwana* is one of the few restaurants in Larantuka and serves good, Chinese/Indonesian dishes. **Very cheap** *Rumah Makan Sri Solo*, near *Hotel Rulies*, basic Indonesian food. There are also a number of warung along Jl Niaga, the main coast road. *Jagung Titi* is a local speciality, a snack food which is best described as squashed popcorn.

Eating
Larantuka is not noted for its gastronomic prowess & the choice of places to eat is limited

Easter (movable), the sacred statue of the Virgin is washed and dressed on Maundy Thursday (the water, in the process, becoming Holy Water with healing powers). In the afternoon the statue is kissed (the *Cio Tuan* ceremony) by the townspeople and other pilgrims, while the streets are cleaned and prepared for Good Friday. On the afternoon of Good Friday, the statue is taken to the Cathedral, where a statue of Jesus from the Chapel of Christ joins it. Following the service at about 1900, the statues are paraded through the town in a candle-lit procession. There are numerous other festivities during Holy Week.

Festivals

Local Bemos provide transport around town.

Transport
137 km from Maumere

Air Gewayan Tana airport is 12 km north of town. One flight per week on *Merpati* from Kupang and on to **Lewoleba** and **Lembata**. It is not very reliable so don't count on making the journey.

Bus The bus terminal is 5 km west of town, but many will pick-up from hotel/losmen if arranged beforehand. Regular connections with **Maumere's** Terminal Timur, (4½ hrs), it is possible to be dropped off in **Wodong**.

East Nusa Tenggara

Boat A ferry leaves Larantuka port of Waibalun (5 km from town on road to Maumere) on Mon and Fri at 1400 for **Kupang**. It is usually packed, although the captain sometimes allows tourists to sleep behind the wheelhouse or on the roof; making for a wonderful panorama of the stars and far more comfortable than on deck. Ferries from Kupang to Larantuka departs Wed and Sun. A twice-daily ferry (well, that's the theory – in mid-2000 it didn't always run) connects Larantuka with **Lewoleba** (4 hrs). On Friday at 0800 there is a direct ferry to the whaling village of **Lamalera**. It is also possible to sail to **Wairwarang** on Adonara. A ferry also runs from Larantuka to **Solor** and **Lembata** on Tue, Thu and Sun. The *Pelni* ships *Tatamailau* and *Sirimau* also dock here on their fortnightly circuit.

Directory **Airline offices** *Merpati* agent, Jl Diponegoro 64 (opposite the Cathedral). **Banks** *BNI and BRI* will both change US$ bills.

Lembata

Colour map 3, grid A4   *Lembata is a small island to the east of Flores, famous for its traditional whaling communities. The village of Lamalera is particularly renowned in this respect. The largest town on the island is Lewoleba, situated on the west coast. This part of Nusa Tenggara has a very long dry season and agriculture is limited to dryland crops like maize. In some areas, slash-and-burn agriculture is still practised, and fires can be seen at night burning on the mountain slopes.*

Ins and outs

Getting there *Merpati* has one **flight** per week from Kupang to Lewoleba via Larantuka, returning the same day to Kupang. It is often cancelled. The *Hotel Rejeki I* operates as the local Merpati agent. **Lewoleba airport** is 3 km from town. There are 2 **ferries** per day from Larantuka to Lewoleba, leaving early morning and early afternoon, (4 hrs). Ferries also do the route twice every 3 days but the boat is faster and cheaper. A large car/passenger ferry also calls at Lewoleba on Tue, Thu and Sun on its drawn-out journey between Larantuka and Kalabahi on Alor, 15 hrs, the same schedule applies in the opposite direction. The Kupang-Larantuka ferry calls at Lewoleba on Mon and Fri, returning to Larantuka before continuing on to Kupang on Tue and Sat. **NB** These schedules seem to change rather frequently, so check first. If your travelling morale is low at this point, the boat passage in and out of these islands, as it weaves between volcanoes, is worth the wait.

Getting around **Trucks** run daily from Lewoleba to Puor, a 6 km walk from the whaling village of Lamalera. The harbour is 1 km from town and **becaks** are available. There are 2 return **ferries** to Larantuka daily except on Mon when there is only one and a boat runs to Lamalera every Mon morning, 4 hrs, returning the same evening. This boat is scheduled to allow villagers to get to the weekly market at Lewoleba. There is also a direct boat from Lamalera to Larantuka every Wed (6 hrs).

Lewoleba

Lewoleba is Lembata's main town and the capital of Solor regency. There is a spectacular **weekly market** held in Lewoleba each Monday; Lembata ikat featuring fish and whale motifs is available.

About 1 km west of Lewoleba harbour is a quiet swimming **beach**. Ask at the stilt village to be taken to the sand island, **Pulau Siput**, by boat – though you may have to bargain hard.

Ile Ape is a volcano accessible from Lewoleba. The rumbling noise and sulphurous odours as you approach the steaming crater is evidence enough that Ile Ape remains active. Although the last eruption was some 40 years ago it is still worth checking at your hotel that it is safe to climb before embarking. It is just about possible to climb the volcano in a day, but it is better to arrange to spend a night en route. ■ *Getting there: take a bemo to Jontana (30 mins). Ask in Stefano's Homestay here for a 'guide'. The first stop on the route up is at Kampung Lama, 3 hrs from Jontana – a traditional village well worth visiting in its own right. It is possible to stay here overnight (the cost is usually included in the guiding fee). From Kampung Lama it is 4½ hrs to the summit.*

Excursions

Lerahinga Beach, 18 km from Lewoleba, offers good snorkelling as well as excellent views of the imposing Mount Ile Ape. ■ *Getting there: by bemo from the market in Lewoleba; most bemos travel all the way to the beach, otherwise it is a 1 km walk from Lerahinga village.* **NB** *The last bemo back to Lewoleba departs at 1530.*

C-E *Hotel Lewoleba*, Jl Avalong 15, T41012. The ekonomi rooms with shared mandi are small, but the VIP rooms are spacious and they are the only ones in town with a/c (and attached mandi). The restaurant here serves cheap Chinese and Indonesian food. **E** *Rejeki Hotel*, Jl Trans Lembata, good central location, helpful staff, well maintained rooms (newer ones with attached mandi), and a reasonably priced shop. The somewhat eccentric exterior decoration makes this place easy to find – the attached restaurant is good, cheap, and the speciality is venison (*daging rusa*). **E** *Pondok Wisata Lile Ile*, (also known as 'Mr Jim's' to the locals), Jl Trans Lembata, fantastic views of two volcanoes and onto the nearby stilt village, basic rooms with shared mandi, can provide meals if requested. **E-F** *Losmen Rejeki II*, the cheaper sister establishment to the *Sumber Rejeki* and not so well located, simple rooms with shared mandi.

Sleeping
All losmen/hotels include breakfast & afternoon tea in the room rate. It is usually possible to leave luggage if trekking

Very cheap *Bandung*, Jl Trans Lembata, excellent cheap Indonesian restaurant, near *Rejeki Hotel*. *Warung Ojalali*, Pasar Inpres, set menu of fish, rice and vegetables – good value. *Warung Surabaya*, Pasar Inpres, range of Indonesian dishes, advantage is that this place is open until late.

Eating

Textiles Lembata ikat (see page 331) is produced in villages across the island; available from Lewoleba market.

Shopping

Cinema A rather impromptu cinema, made of canvas, sometimes sets up on the outskirts showing Bollywood movies. An interesting trans-cultural experience.

Entertainment

Banks The *Sumber Rejeki Hotel* will change US$ cash, as will the *Flores Jaya* shop opposite the post office, at poor rates, but otherwise there are no places to exchange money so bring enough for your stay. **Communications** Post office: Jl Trans Lembata (opposite the *Sumber Rejeki Hotel*). **Telephone:** *Telekom* office, 1 km east of town along the main road; open until 2300.

Directory

Lamalera

The traditional whaling village of Lamalera is on Lembata's south coast. The population trace their origins to Lapan Batan, an island between Lembata and Pantar. Unlike many of the other villages on Lembata which are land-based and rely on maize, rice and sweet potatoes, the population of Lamalera relies on fishing, and particularly whaling (see box). Until the late 1980s, Lamalera was so far off the beaten track that virtually no one ventured there; the village has now become part of the travellers' itinerary. Even the tour company

East Nusa Tenggara

👆 *Lamalera's whaling*

There has been subsistence whaling in Lamelera for at least 200 years. As the local people do not grow crops, they rely on bartering whale products at the markets in order to obtain agricultural goods. They hunt whales all year round but there are two main seasons – Lefa and Baleo. Lefa runs from April to November corresponding with the south-east monsoon, when the great whales migrate through the area to the rich southern oceans. During this period it is traditional for whale hunts to occur daily, except on Sundays when Catholicism takes precedence over the local adat. During Baleo, which spans the months from November to March, the whale boats only go out if a whale is sighted and the weather conditions are favourable.

The whalers of Lamelera specialize in catching manta rays and sperm whales (known as ikan paus, 'pope fish'). But they also occasionally take sharks, whale sharks, pilot whales, killer whales and dolphins. They are hunted from open rowing boats known as peledang. Each boat belongs to a particular village clan and they are constantly repaired and rebuilt over the centuries. They are said to be modelled on the ships that brought the original

inhabitants from Lapan Batar. When the hunt is underway, the men shout hilibe – 'give chase'. The hunters use hand thrown harpoons or tempuling which have blades attached to poles up to 8 m long. The harpooner, perched on the boat's bow, literally launches himself off the vessel to plunge the iron as deeply into his prey as possible. On occasions, having harpooned a whale, the boat is towed for hours – in one instance all the way into Australian waters. The day's catch is then processed on the beach. The meat is divided traditionally among families in the village. All parts of the whale are used, the meat being dried in the sun, the oil boiled off and used for lighting despite the arrival of electricity.

Because, like the Eskimos and a handful of other people, the hunters of Lamalera are traditional and non-commercial, they have been exempted from the worldwide ban on whaling. There is some debate over when whaling in the area started: 1566 seems to be a popular date; the year the Portuguese arrived. It is thought that they only kill 20-30 whales a year, and this number is declining as young men are migrating to larger towns, leading to an increasingly aged whaling crew.

Natrabu runs a tour to Lamalera from Kupang. To go along with the whalers as a paying passenger will cost about 40,000-50,000Rp.

As dusk approaches, an alternative hunt can be seen in progress around the rock pools on the beach. Local children scour the pools searching for small fish and mud-skippers which they harpoon with sharpened, painted sticks that are shot unerringly to their targets using rubber bands.

There is a **barter market** – Pasar Wolandoni – on Wednesdays and Saturdays where local women swop goods. It is also possible to use money but fascinating just to spectate. ■ *Walk for 25 mins towards the football field then bear right and walk along the beach for another hr and a half – quite a distance but a pleasant and easy walk.*

It is possible to swim on **Lamalera Beach** though the waves are quite strong and it's necessary to dress modestly (women in shorts and a T-shirt, men in shorts). Alternatively, ask directions to **Walinama Beach** which is outside the village so you can wear what you like.

Sleeping
Prices include all meals

E-F *Homestay Josef (The White House)* 2 small dorms, inside mandi with western toilets. It is the closest homestay to the beach. Run by the local English teacher, a good source of information. Situated on the top of the hill, so superb views of Lamalera (especially from the mandi). **E-F** *Homestay Maria*, simple, clean accommodation, motherly management and better food than most. **E-F** *Homestay Abil*, basic accommodation but friendly staff.

No restaurants or food shops, so visitors must eat in their homestay. Food tends to be **Eating**
very simple, so it might be worth bringing provisions such as biscuits and fruit.

Local textiles made from handspun and dyed cotton are available for between **Shopping**
200,000Rp and 350,000Rp. Some people have also begun to make carefully constructed miniatures of the whaling boats – which sell more cheaply.

Road Trucks run daily from Lewoleba to **Puor**, a 6 km walk from Lamalera. For the **Transport**
return journey leave early to walk during the cool of the early morning and to be in
Puor in good time for the 1000 truck departure.

Alor

The rugged island of Alor, east of Lembata, is 100 km long and 35 km wide at its Phone code: 0386
widest point. Although most of the population are nominally Christian, the Colour map 3, grid A6
island illustrates, in mircrocosm, Indonesia's enormous cultural diversity.
Because of Alor's fragmented and rugged environment its people have remained
isolated from one another until comparatively recently. A population of just
150,000 can count between them seven major linguistic sub-groups and 50 dis-
tinct languages – which amounts to a language for every 3,000 people. The vari-
ous tribes of the island – such as the Nedebang, Dieng, Kaka and Mauta –
practice shifting cultivation, although as land becomes scarcer, so they are being
forced to become settled agriculturalists.

    Alor is reputed to have the best dive sites in Nusa Tenggara, although as the
currents here are strong it is most suited to more experienced divers. The Adi
Dharma Hotel is a good source of information on diving although most people
pre-book through agents in Kupang (Timor). Even if your pocket is not deep
enough for diving the snorkelling is said to be fabulous.

    A little piece of historical ephemera: Sir Francis Drake sailed past Alor in the
Golden Hind, having been blown off course towards Wetar, east of Alor.

Ins and outs

Alor's **Mali airport** is 28 km from Kalabahi. There are connections on *Merpati* from **Getting there**
Kupang daily, except Fri, and also flights from Larantuka, Lewoleba, Rote and
Denpasar. There is a *Merpati-operated* minibus that meets flights and also takes passengers out to the airport. The ferry dock is about 1 km south of town. Ferries link
Kalabahi with **Kupang** (West Timor), **Atapupu**, **Lewoleba** and **Larantuka**, as well as
a number of smaller ports in the islands of eastern Nusa Tenggara. From Kupang the
ferry leaves on Tue and Thu and arrives in Kalabahi the following day, returning to
Kupang on Mon and Wed. On Sun the same boat does a leg from Kalabahi to Atapupu
(on Timor), returning to Kalabahi the following day. **NB** These schedules are subject to
frequent change. The *Pelni* vessel *Awu* calls here twice on its fortnightly circuit
through Nusa Tenggara. However in mid-2000, for a range of economic reasons, the
ship was not calling and local people offered conflicting information as to whether it
would resume its normal schedule.

The *Adi Dharma Hotel* can arrange motorbike hire. Local bemos are 500Rp and they stop **Getting around**
operating at 1900. It is possible to charter bemos on an hourly rate to visit local villages.

East Nusa Tenggara

Kalabahi

The capital of Alor, Kalabahi, is on the west coast. The football field in the centre of town, and clearly also in the centre of men's hearts, pulsates with life and action on Sunday afternoons when half the town seemingly congregates here to watch matches between local teams. There is also a statue of a local hero at the football field, in traditional Alor battledress. The statue was erected to commemorate the 28 local residents who lost their lives during an earthquake on 4 July 1991. Kalabahi, as one might expect, has the greatest concentration of facilities on Alor and is the best base from which to explore the island.

Excursions **Takpala**, 12 km east of Kalabahi, is the principal village of the Abui tribe and there are breathtaking views of Benelang Bay from the entrance. Because Takpala is relatively accessible it is also relatively touristed. However, this doesn't seem, on surface impressions at least, to have dented the Abui's determination to maintain their culture and ways. Pak Timatius is the caretaker chief as his nephew is considered too young and inexperienced (at 28 years old, in 2000) to take on the role. It could be a long wait: Pak Timatius believes 50 to be an appropriate age to become chief. Local custom dictates that the Abui marry within their tribe, and as there are only 250 members this doesn't allow a lot of scope for playing the field. When a man has found the woman of his dreams, he then pays a 'bride price' in moko drums (see box). The houses of Takpala are divided into three levels. The open first floor is used as a meeting and living area. The enclosed second floor is used for cooking and sleeping. And the roof space is used for storage – the smoke from the cooking fire helping to ward off vermin and protect food stocks. (See 'Shopping', below, for information on market day – Monday – in Takpala.) **NB** It is considered polite to bring small gifts such as betel nut, coffee and sugar. ■ *Getting there: take a bemo from the market bound for Mabu; the bemo drops off within 1 km of the settlement.*

Atimelang is less frequently visited and therefore, reportedly, more traditional. It is possible to stay overnight here and then walk back to Mabu the following day. ■ *Getting there: catch a bemo from the market to Mabu; it is a 5 km walk from here.*

Mali Beach, 12 km east of Kalabahi, has wonderful white sand and is a good snorkelling spot. The reef lies 300 m off-shore. There are plans underway to build some accommodation here.

Alor Kecil has some excellent snorkelling, although there are also dangerously vicious cold water currents. Local fishermen will sometimes take people out to the west side of **Pulau Kepa** which is protected from the currents and reputedly has even better snorkelling. Sharks are said to be numerous. **Sleeping** E *La P'tite Kepa homestay*, new, 500 m from the shore, and built traditionally, price includes three meals a day and journeys between the island and Alor Kecil. There are motorbikes for hire, and excursions can be arranged.

Dulolong is a coastal village en route to Kokar. Ask to see the grave of King Nampira and his family.

Ampera is a coastal village between Dulolong and Alor Kecil. The people here have a dialect and culture distinct from that of surrounding communities. They are prolific potters.

There is a good **walk** from Kalabahi to **Monbang** (a traditional village), on to **Otvai** (where there are fantastic views of Kalabahi Bay), and then back to Kalabahi. The round trip takes about 7 hours – ask at hotel/losmen for directions.

The Moko drum currency debâcle

Before the 19th century, bronze moko drums were traded and used as bride price. They are related to the Dongson drums of northern Vietnam, although no exact equivalent has ever been found there. The older examples of moko also show similar decoration to their presumed Vietnamese prototypes, although newer examples have Chinese and Indian inspired floral motifs. How these drums came to Alor is not known, but they have also been discovered elsewhere in the Indonesian archipelago (see Bali, page 134).

Around 1900, imitation brass moko began to be made in large quantities in Gresik, Java and exported to Alor. They created chaos in a monetary system which owed its stability to there always being a limited number of moko in circulation. In 1914, in an attempt to stabilize the moko, the Dutch introduced coinage and forbad all use of the drums in transactions, except in tax payments. This exemption was designed to take moko out of circulation; some 1,660 drums were acquired, and then melted down.

Bride price in Alor is still sometimes paid using moko. The cheapest drum, and thus presumably the cheapest wife, is said to cost about 150,000-200,000Rp. The oldest drums are the most valuable, and through time their association with powerful people, drums are thought to acquire powers of their own. Such drums are rarely traded, but remain within the family.

Sleeping *All hotels include a simple breakfast & afternoon tea or coffee in the room rate. All also have some more pricey rooms with a/c*

C-D *Pelangi Indah*, Jl Diponegoro 100, T21251. Some a/c, the more expensive rooms have a/c and excellent western bathrooms, the cheaper rooms are pretty basic by contrast, the attached restaurant serves good Indonesian and Chinese dishes and cheap, cold beer, a good little hotel. **D** *Adi Dharma*, Jl Martadinata 12/26, T21280. On the waterfront, the owner, Pak Enga, speaks English and is helpful and knowledgeable. The rooms are well maintained and very clean and there are great views of Kalabahi Harbour from the verandah. It is also fairly central, with good meals (if ordered in advance), and tours are available (but rather expensive). **D-E** *Melati*, Jl Dr Sutomo 1, T21075. Some a/c, view of the harbour, simple accommodation, recently refurbished, clean, but cheapest rooms are still rather dingy. **D-E** *Nusa Kenari Indah*, Jl Diponegoro 11, T21119. Some a/c, set back from the road and with a small garden, rooms here are spacious and fine, the more expensive with a/c and attached mandi.

Eating

People in Kalabahi evidently don't seem to eat out much and there isn't the flow of tourists to create the demand for imaginative restaurants and food. The best places are the hotels, although there are the usual (mediocre) foodstalls which set up from early evening in the market area. **Cheap** The best hotel restaurant is that attached to the *Pelangi Indah* which also serves good value and cold beer. **Very cheap** Of the dedicated restaurants the best is the *Rumah Makan Jember*, Jl Panglima Polim 2, which serves the usual range of Indonesian favourites but with better quality ingredients and in a more hygienic setting than other places. The *Warung Kediri*, next to the *Adi Dharma Hotel*, serves reasonable Javanese food. It's also worth sampling the various food stalls that spring up at night, east of the BNI bank.

Shopping

Textiles Alor ikat; some are rather inferior, but there are villages on Alor still producing high quality cloth. The best place to sample a range of textiles is in Takpala (see 'Excursions') on Mon when a cruise ship visits and every textile agent worth his/her salt descends on the village. There is also a market at Moru on Sat, 30 mins by bemo from Kalabahi.

East Nusa Tenggara

Sports **Diving and snorkelling** Alor is gaining a reputation for having some of the best dive sites in Indonesia, with an enormous variety of marine life. Strong currents make this, though, a destination for the experienced diver. Most people pre-book through companies in Kupang.

Transport **Boat** Ferries leave for **Larantuka** from Kalabahi on Sun, Tue and Thu in the early evening arriving the following morning after mooring for the night in **Balauring** and stopping, among other places, at **Lewoleba**. The length of the trip depends on where the passengers want to stop.

Directory **Banks** *BNI*, Jl Dr Sutomo; *Bank Rakyat Indonesia*. Both banks with change cash and travellers' cheques from major companies denominated in US$.**Communications** Post office: Jl Dr Sutomo, open Mon to Sat 0700-1600. **Telephone office:** *Telekom* office behind the market.

Pulau Pantar

Pantar is the next largest island in the Alor group, after Alor itself. Very few people make it here and little English is spoken. Boats dock at **Baranusa**, where there is one homestay. From here trucks run to **Kakamauta**, the nearest village to the volcano **Mount Sirong**. It is possible to climb the volcano – which is still active – in about 2-3 hours.

Sleeping **E** *Homestay Burhan*, Baranusa, room rate includes all meals. It is also possible to stay in Kakamauta with the kepala desa (**E**).

Transport **Boat** Boats leave Kalabahi for Baranusa every Tue, Thu and Sun (4½ hrs, 9,000Rp).

Sumba

The oval island of Sumba is noted for its megalithic tombs (mainly in the west), fine ikat cloth (mainly in the east) and horseback-fighting festivals. Lying outside the volcanic arc that runs through Java and the other islands of Nusa Tenggara, the generally subdued relief of Sumba presents a startling contrast to Java, Bali and Flores. Because Sumba lies off the usual overland route through the Lesser Sundas – which runs through Flores and Sumbawa to Lombok and Bali – the island is relatively untourbsted.

Sumba is a real treasure house for the visitor interested in art and culture. Unlike the other islands of East Nusa Tenggara, Sumba never came under the early influence of either Muslim or Christian missionaries and as a result, traditional beliefs are much stronger here. The same goes for the island's material culture. Megalithic tombs and ancestral, thatched houses remain easily accessible and Sumba's distinctive traditional ikat blankets continue to be made in large number (in part because of demand from outsiders). Finally there is Sumba's energetic pasola festival when massed ranks of horsemen engage in mock combat – a 'game' which frequently results in serious injury and sometimes in death. There is also, for those less enamoured with culture and art, excellent surfing on the west coast and long, deserted sandy beaches.

Ins and outs

Getting there There are **flights** to Waingapu and Waikabubak and *Pelni* ships also dock at the ports of both towns (but note that Waikabubak airport is 42 km from town, while the port is 60 km away). A weekly **ferry** links Waingapu with Ende on Flores and the island of Savu. From Waikabubak's Waikelo harbour there is a ferry to Larantuka, also on Flores, calling at Sape on Sumbawa twice weekly.

Getting around As in the other islands of Nusa Tenggara, the government has invested considerable sums upgrading the road infrastructure. Moreover, because the terrain is less demanding than Flores the roads are in better condition. There are bus services to all major settlements. New roads are being built and minibuses are also new, making travel to many places easy and painless. You are less likely to be hassled on Sumba than almost any other part of Indonesia. As Sumba prospers, more villages will become easily accessible by public minibus. Look out for the 'names' of individual minibuses and trucks brandished across their front windscreens, some unprintable!

NB The two luxury developments on Sumba's south coast, one 5 km from Baing in the southeast and the *Sumba Reef Lodge* south of Waikabubak near Rua Beachare now open. The owner admits spreading rumours in his book 'Surfing Indonesia' that locals often killed tourists for attending festivals! This was intended to deter more surfers coming and finding the 'secret spots'.

Background

Geography Though Sumba is only 300 km long and 80 km wide, the two regencies of East and West Sumba are environmentally very different. While the east of the

East Nusa Tenggara

island is generally dry (annual rainfall 674 mm) and barren, the west is considerably wetter (1,826 mm), and consequently much greener. The dry season stretches over seven to eight months from April to October. During these months, the rolling landscape is dry and desolate; but during the rainy season the green grasslands of the west are not unlike those of Ireland. Rice can be cultivated only in the valleys where perennial rivers flow, and in the dry season these – like the Lewa Valley, mid-way between Waingapu and Waikabubak – are small oases of green in an otherwise parched landscape. In times past Sumba was known as the 'Sandalwood Isle' but destruction of these forests for commercial gain has left much of the island, especially in the east, fit only for extensive cattle grazing and horse raising. The island's population is about 425,000: 280,000 in the agriculturally richer west, the remainder in the east. These days Sumba's wealth is based on the export of horses and buffaloes; every year about 40,000 of each are exported to Java.

History Historically, Sumba was known as a source of horses, slaves and sandalwood, but lying as it does to the south of the island arc of Nusa Tenggara, it managed to escape the successive streams of Hindu, Muslim and Christian interlopers who influenced the area. Although the island did come under the influence of the Majapahit Kingdom of Java from the fifth century, and rather later from the Sultanate of Bima in Flores, it was never directly ruled from the outside. The first Europeans to note the existence of the island were the crew of the Portuguese vessel the *Victoria* in the 16th century, part of Magellan's expedition. Although marked on maps following this original sighting, it was not until the Dutch arrived in the 17th century that western contact intensified. Even then, it was not until the early 20th century that a colonial administrator was installed.

Sumba Island

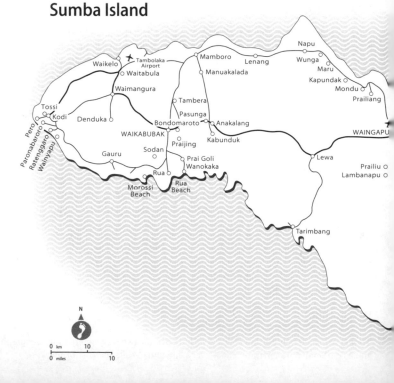

Sumba has nine mutually unintelligable languagea, eight of which are concentrated in the more ecologically fertile west. This is probably due to conditions that did not force much co-dependence for survival. In addition, each tribe has a highly sophisticated ritual linguistic form. In a ceremonial setting, male participants call out reinforcing couplets, reminiscent of haiku. This can go on throughout the night and following day, spontaneously improvised, getting more complex as the calls build up. An example: The horse's tail is high (meaning the person in question has a noble spirit), the reply call, the dog has a black tongue. This refers to a glib talker that has kept his integrity. And so on. The symbolism and related couplets are complex representations of their socio-cultural interrelationships and cosmology.

Culture

Today, it is thought that over 50% of the population, predominantly in the west, still adhere to the traditional, animist, religion of ancestor worship *agama merapu*. The merapu are the original ancestors of each patrilineal clan. Another 35% are Protestant and the remainder, Catholic, Muslim, Hindu and Buddhist. The government has been trying – much as they have in the Toraja area of Sulawesi – to stamp out the slaughter of pigs, chickens and buffalo in 'wasteful' traditional ceremonies. Those who flout the ban and are caught are fined – even detained for a while. Success is patchy and many people have taken to clandestine slaughtering at night. Funerals and the ceremonies associated with blessing a new house 'demand' that guests be fed and animals killed – perhaps 25 pigs for a house ceremony, up to 100 buffalo for the funeral of an important personage.

At the time of our last visit in mid-2000 there was only one Westerner in evidence outside the costly surf resort. The economic crisis has hit Sumba even more severely than the rest of the country. There is a sense that local people blame the West for their economic plight, and hence their rather less-than-welcoming looks. Commerical agriculture and the cattle export trade drew this previously self sufficient island into the cash economy, but provided no safety net for hard times. In particular the area around Waingapu is very depressed. To those familiar with the island the effects are said to be devastating. In view of the circumstances that people are facing in Sumba, you may feel that it is probably inappropriate to bargain aggressively. For example, the cost of a skein of yarn doubled between 1998 and 2000, with no corresponding rise in incomes. Indeed, tourism is virtually moribund. The double whammy has been the gift of financial autonomy by the central government. This may look good in the international press: local control for local people! But central government has merely used it as an excuse to cut of support for basic services and administration. The Sumba government may now be able to tax local businesses, and use the proceeds for local use, but with so little economic activity there is scant scope.

East Nusa Tenggara

Kawangu

Lailuru

Melolo

Umabara

Pau

Rende

Kananggar

Baing

Nggongi

Kaliuda

Kalala

●●●

The ikat hinggi blankets of Sumba

Sumba produces perhaps the most distinctive warp ikat in Indonesia. Traditionally, the weaving of cloth was the preserve of aristocratic women who, free from agricultural and household chores, had the time to produce finely woven cloth. Ikat is still woven on backstrap looms, although natural indigo and red morinda dyes are being replaced by chemical substitutes. The most commonly produced cloth is the hinggi, a large blanket worn by men. Characteristic motifs include animals such as horses, dogs, snakes, monkeys, crocodiles, fish and lizards. Each has its own symbolism – dogs with warriors, snakes with rebirth and long life, crocodiles with the afterlife. Another common motif is the skull tree or andung, which draws upon the former practice of hanging the heads of vanquished enemies from a tree in the centre of a village to scare away evil spirits.

The quality of Sumba ikat is declining, and most lengths of cloth can only be described as 'tourist' material: large and simple motifs, often without the important border strip or kabakil, woven with machine spun yarn, coloured with chemical dyes, and showing 'bleeding' of dye across the borders between design elements. First-class cloth is almost exclusively reserved for burial, and no local, quite literally, would be seen dead in the blankets sold to visitors. Wrapping the body in fine ikat ensures that the spirit of the dead man or woman will reach Parai Merapu – Merapu heaven. The transition from the physical world to that of the spirits is critical, and the various elements of the death rite must be strictly adhered to.

Some people maintain that it is cheaper to buy cloth in Bali where shop owners purchase in bulk from villages with which they have special relations. Tour groups visiting villages like Rende have pushed prices up considerably.

●●●

Sumbanese villages & houses The layout of a *paraingu* – or village – in Sumba should conform to traditional rules. The village symbolizes a ship, with a bow (*tunda kambata*), deck (*kani padua*) and stern (*kiku kemudi*). The houses are arranged around the ancestors' burial place.

Important villages of clan chiefs are built on hills while less important villages surround them at lower elevations. Similarly, ancestral houses *uma merapu* have high peaked roofs whilst houses not associated with the ancestors have lower roofs and are called *uma kamudungu* 'bald houses'. Buffalo horns on the outside of houses are indicative of past sacrifices and denote wealth and prestige; they also protect the house and ward off evil spirits. Through their part in sacrifices buffaloes act as a link with the spirit world.

In the open space in the centre of the more warlike villages can be found the 'skull tree' *andung*, a dead tree on which in earlier headhunting times the skulls of enemy taken in battle were hung. The life force believed to emanate from these heads was considered to be a source of fertility, and the tree acted as a symbol of strength and security for the village as well as the focal point for rites of war.

The striking, traditional, thatched houses – low-sided, yet high-peaked – are built around a fireplace which is positioned between the four main pillars. There are two doors: a front door for men, and a rear entrance for women. Due to poor ventilation, the smoke from the open fire tends to fill the houses, making them dirty and suffocating. Each consists of three 'floors': cattle are kept at ground level and most weaving takes place here. The first floor is the main living area, with various rooms for sleeping (divided according to sex, age and rank), grain storage, cooking and eating. The upper section, known as the *uma deta* or *hindi merapu*, is for the spirits; here, sacred objects are stored. In West Sumba, some of the finest traditional houses can be seen at Anakalang, Tarung and Prai Goli; in East Sumba, at Prailiu and Pau. The dwellings in West Sumba tend to have higher roofs.

The right side of the house is symbolically male, the left side female. The four central posts supporting the house are also either male or female and must be placed following strict ritual customs. The front right corner post of the house is considered sacred; this is where the priest makes offerings, speaks to the ancestors in their language, and channels the power of the ancestors stored in the heirlooms in the high peaked roof to the living. The right back corner post is the site of animal sacrifices. The left back corner post is the domain of women and is the place where domestic animals are fed. The left front corner post is where the sacred rice is cooked and served by the women who then pass it to the priest by the front right post.

Sumba Ikat motifs

A design based on the mamuli, a gold ear ornament & traditional marriage gift.

East Nusa Tenggara

Cockatoos

Man with skull tree (andung), & cockatoos

Roosters

Horses

☞ Sumba's megalithic tombs

The construction of megalithic graves is characteristic of both East and West Sumba. However, in East Sumba the grave construction cannot begin until after the intended occupant is dead. This means that some families have to keep the corpse of their relative in a kind of limbo until enough funds and time have been found to build the monument. In West Sumba people help to build their own tombs. Here the socially ambitious seek enhanced prestige while they are still alive by having large gravestones hauled to their village; a feat which requires the expenditure of large sums of money for the many kinsmen needed to help, and for ceremonial feasting.

Limestone boulders weighing anywhere up to 30 tonnes are dragged on wooden rafts (tena) to the site of the grave. Tena means ship, and a textile sail is raised to help the stone on its journey. The graves are not spatially separated from the village houses, and many are used for more mundane purposes like drying corn or dyed textiles, or for lounging on during evening village events. There are four main types of megalithic tomb in Sumba: the first is a simple dolmen, with four stone pillars supporting a rectangular stone slab. The second, is similar to the first, but carved and ornamented. The third has stone walls enclosing the four pillars. And the fourth, the added feature of stone stairs leading up to the covering slab.

The purpose behind the many rituals and ceremonies, at which offerings of food and valuables are made, is to ensure good relations between the living and the ancestors to guarantee the former's well-being. (These days the government limits the number of buffalo which can be sacrificed to prevent families going into penury.) Even numbers, in particular four and eight, are considered auspicious.

The highest parts of the house are considered sacred and are connected with the ancestors; the house having become sacred as a result of the heirlooms being stored in its roof since the heirlooms represent the spirit of the founding ancestor residing in the house. The heirlooms are powerful objects used in rituals as a medium through which contact with the ancestors can be made; some heirlooms, particularly those that are very old and made of gold, silver or other metal are believed to be so powerful that disasters may result if they are mishandled. The most powerful are not even allowed to be looked at and are housed in sealed boxes or inside many different containers.

Some clan origin-houses in Sumba have accumulated so much sacred power leading to a wealth of taboos and prohibitions that living in them has become too dangerous for their owners who fear they might inadvertently break a taboo and incur the wrath and retribution of their ancestral spirits. They prefer to install more expendable family slaves as caretakers. This is the case with the ancestral house in Rende.

Visiting Sumbanese villages Part of the attraction of Sumba lies in the ease with which a traveller can witness traditional ceremonies and festivals which are genuine, entirely for the benefit of local clans and not part of a tourist charade. Having maintained its autonomy over the centuries, and lying off the main tourist routes, Sumba's age old traditions and beliefs remain largely intact, particularly in West Sumba. If you want to explore new territory there are countless traditional villages rarely, if ever, visited by travellers; ask at hotels as someone working there may come from just such a village worth visiting, this is particularly likely in West Sumba. Some travellers consider that the people in West Sumba are even friendlier than East Sumba's villagers as they are not so concerned with tourism and making money from selling ikat. Hotels are only full during high

The Sumbanese slave trade

Sumba's role as a source of slaves dates from as early as historical accounts exist. The Sultan of Bima on Sumbawa, and the sultans and kings of South Sulawesi, Flores, Lombok and Bali all obtained slaves from the island. At Ende, in Flores, it was said by the Dutch visitor Goronvius in 1855 that "there is hardly a man to be found, of moderate or even limited means, who is not the owner of some 20 slaves, all of them from Sumba". Dutch interest in Sumba as a source of slaves dates from the mid-18th century, and the island quickly became the major supplier to the colonial power.

Why Sumba should have filled this role is linked to the nature of society and the absence of a strong, central power. The structure of Sumbanese society was rigidly divided into an aristocratic (maramba) class, and a slave (ata) class. This social stratification was more prominent in the

east and even today wealth and power lie in the hands of 4 or 5 men. The west is more diverse ethnically and culturally with seven different languages spoken and more opportunity for advancement based on merit rather than heredity. The latter could be freely bought and sold, and even denied the right to marry, own property or to have a funeral – the essential qualities of human existence. When the first colonial administrator was dispatched to Sumba in 1866, he reported the island to be lawless and politically fragmented. By this time, the northwest coast was effectively depopulated, such were the numbers of slaves plucked from the island by raiders. The trade was officially abolished in 1860, but continued until the early 20th century. The first Resident was even given a slave girl as a welcome gift when he first arrived on the island.

season (July/August) and at the time of the Pasola (February/March). At other times of the year surprisingly few visitors come to Sumba and you may well find yourself the only foreigner in town, even in Waikabubak.

Important When visiting local villages it is courteous and advisable to observe local etiquette and take a gift of betel nut to share with your hosts; it would be polite also to stop and chat or, bearing in mind any language restrictions, at least to partake of some betel nut with the headman. It can cause offence if visitors treat these villages as a zoo, you are after all invading their territory uninvited. If offered betel nut, it is impolite not to take some. It's fairly tasteless and even after half an hour of chewing you are unlikely to have swallowed any as it does not readily dissolve; without the lime it will not stain your mouth and you can remove it later. Alternatively, hide it to dispose of later. Betel is easily bought in the market where you will see stalls selling piles of 'betel' (in fact areca) nut (*pinang*) together with the catkin (*sirih*) for 1,000Rp-5,000Rp for a double sized quantity, and in separate piles, lime (*kapur*) in the form of a white powder in little plastic packets for 100Rp. Alternatively, you could take coffee, sugar and cigarettes or simply make a donation of 1,000Rp at each village you visit. Don't expect just to wander in and look around. You will probably be asked for 1,000Rp for photographs.

Conduct and dress Women should avoid wearing short shorts and skimpy skirts, and men and women should avoid wearing singlets. Even conservative dress does not ensure your physical integrity will necessarily be respected. Roving hands should be slapped off!

Waingapu

Phone code: 0387
Colour map 2, grid B2

Waingapu is the capital of the regency of East Sumba, and the island's largest town with a population of 25,000. A hot dusty place spread out over a large area in two concentrations, one by the harbour, and the other about 1 km inland, convenient for the bus station and market and where many of the hotels are found. Waingapu suffers from having little attractive accommodation, and few restaurants serving appetizing food. It is a base from which to explore the far more interesting surrounding countryside. The **tourist office** *Kantor Cabang Dinas Pariwisata*, on Jl Suharto T791, has no useful maps or pamphlets, but helpful staff.

Sights The **Old Docks** area (*Pelabuhan Lama*) can be entertaining: fishing boats, and the occasional inter-island mixed cargo boat, dock here. Watch Sumba's famous horses and buffaloes being loaded onto small inter-island boats and new Japanese minibuses being precariously unloaded. There is a pleasant walk along a street bordering the shore with views of the sea and harbour; follow one of the sidestreets off Jl Yos Sudarso to reach the sea. At night look out for the amazing neon lit decorations on minibuses. Overlooking the dock on Jl Kartini are some picturesque colonial-era buildings dating back to the first half of the century. Nearby, just off Jl Yos Sudarso, is a small **market**, with a larger market next to the bus station on the outskirts of town. Neither is particularly notable.

Excursions Although Waingapu and East Sumba do not have the megaliths of West Sumba, it is the centre of fine ikat production (see page 368) and there are a number of weaving villages within easy reach of the town.

Prailiu is an ikat weaving village only 2 km southeast of town. Stages in the ikat weaving process can usually be seen, or make arrangements in advance with the weavers. There is cloth for sale – it is even sometimes possible to buy good, finely-worked ikat here. The village has a small number of inferior 'megalithic'

Waingapu

Sleeping
1 Elim
2 Kaliuda
3 Losmen Lima Saudara
4 Losmen Permata
5 Merlin
6 Sandlewood

Eating
1 Mini Indah
2 Rajawali

East Nusa Tenggara

tombs, both modern and traditional in design. ■ *Getting there: walk or take one of the constant bemos that run from the bemo stop near the bus terminal.*

Kawangu is another weaving village, 11 km east of Waingapu. Like Prailiu, stages in the ikat process can often be witnessed and there is cloth for sale. ■ *Getting there: regular bemos run from the bemo stop next to the bus station.* For those who still haven't had their fill, **Lambanapu** is yet another ikat weaving village worth a visit, 7 km from Prailiu.

Melolo is a lovely town 60 km southeast of Waingapu (see page 375). It is a good base from which to visit the area southeast of Waingapu including the ikat-weaving villages of **Rende**, **Pau** and **Umabara** (see the Melolo entry for information of these villages).

Kaliuda is an ikat weaving village, 50 km past Melolo and 110 km from Waingapu, just off the road to Baing (see page 376). **Kalala** surfing beach is close by (see page 376).

Prailiang, reached down a rough road off the main road shortly before Mondu which has a Friday market. This is a good example of a traditional fortified hilltop village where ancient customs and rituals are still strong. The remnants of the encircling wall can be seen. The villagers work the land surrounding the hill. ■ *Getting there: by bus to Mondu; ask the driver to let you off at the turn off to Prailiang.*

Maru, on the coast 60 km northwest of Waingapu, is a traditional village with important rituals and ceremonies. Market day is Monday. ■ *Getting there: buses run daily.*

Kapundak This traditional area is difficult to reach though there are plans to upgrade the road. Local legend has it that this is the place where the ancestors landed when they first came to Sumba. In consequence it is an area of great significance to all Sumbanese; the village of **Wunga** is the religious focus where important ceremonies take place. ■ *Getting there: you can take the bus to Maru, but it is best to hire your own transport.*

Northwest of Waingapu

The *Elim/Elvin*, *Merlin*, *Permata*, and *Sandle Wood Hotels* can arrange cars and guides to take tourists around the main sights. Ali Fa'daq at the *Permata* speaks excellent English and has the best background knowledge of Sumba. He has films of some traditional ceremonies. Zaid Bachmid (with some English) at the Tourist Office is also willing to guide tourists. Prices for the day, including car and guide, range from 120,000Rp to 140,000Rp.

Tours

C-D *Elim/Elvin*, Jl Jend A Yani 73, T61323. Friendly owners are a good source of information, reasonable rooms, every type of room available from dorm beds to rooms with fan or a/c and private mandi, tours, guides and car/motorbike hire, cheap restaurant. **C-D** *Merlin Hotel*, Jl DI Panjaitan 25, T61300, F61333. Quite new with attractive décor, the best hotel in town and very reasonably priced, most rooms with modern private bathrooms, more expensive rooms have a/c, the stairs might pose a problem for old people and for the vertically challenged, as the treads are almost 1 ft high, cheap restaurant on 3rd floor. At the time of our last visit here only a limited menu was available, and there were complementary rats and cockroaches even in the VIP room. **C-D** *Sandle Wood*, Jl DI Panjaitan, T61887. The second best place to stay but original rooms are badly in need of redecoration, especially the bathrooms. There are rooms with shared and private mandis, and the kapok filled beds have compressed over the years and are now rock hard. The newer wing with a/c rooms is better, breakfast included (the restaurant is cheap but not recommended), unfortunately the Chinese owner always seems to be asleep and the staff have no authority so obviously complaints fail to filter back to him. **D** *Lima Saudara*, Jl Wanggameti 2, T61083. Rooms

Sleeping
Most of Waingapu's hotels & losmen are found around the bus station, about 1½ km south of the town centre or in the harbour area

rather dirty, attached bathrooms, average, price includes breakfast. **E** *Kaliuda*, Jl Dl Panjaitan 3, T61264. Behind bus station, clean, well run, best of the budget places, some rooms with private mandi, all squat toilets, some dirty. **E** *Losmen Permata* (aka *Ali's Place*), Jl Kartini 10, T61516. Overlooking the old docks near the centre of town. Basic rooms with private mandi, squat toilets, the owner Ali is very knowledgeable about local culture, and is himself well-known, being big in politics, nice position on grassed square. Popular.

Eating **Cheap** *Hotel Merlin* restaurant with a book exchange, good place to sip a cold beer overlooking the town. Recommended. *RM Restu Ibu*, Jl IR Juanda, T21218. Recommended. **Very cheap** *Mini Indah*, Jl A Yani (between the two halves of town), very variable, you might have an excellent meal or an inedible one. The same applies to *RM Siang Malam* down the road from the Merlin. *Rajawali*, Jl Sutomo 96, good Chinese, seafood, pleasant atmosphere. Recommended.

Shopping The best place to buy Sumba's **ikat** is on Bali where prices are more reasonable and dealers are prepared to negotiate. The ikat-producing villages tend to have only a limited selection of pieces as most, including the best pieces, are swiftly purchased by dealers, and the villagers rarely bargain. In town *LA 'Louis' Art Shop* has two branches: at Toko Kupang, Jl WJ Lalamentik 15 (just pass the *Sandle Wood Hotel*) and on Jl Yos Sudarso near the port area, T61536, 61132 (home); open 0800-2200 or by appointment, good selection, bargaining recommended. Recommended. The *Sandle Wood Hotel* has a large selection of mostly rather average ikat; they seem strangely reluctant to show any quality. Sumba **blankets** vary a great deal in quality and a reasonable piece cannot be bought for less than 150,000Rp; good lengths are 400,000Rp or more.

Tour operators *Eben Haezer*, Jl Jend A Yani 73, T323, by the *Elim Hotel*.

Transport **Local** **Bemos**: ply the main routes around town; the central bemo stop is near the bus terminal. **Car/minibus hire**: from the *Losmen Surabaya* (hourly rate); or the *Sandle Wood Hotel* (slightly cheaper); for longer journeys, charges are roughly 60,000Rp return to Melolo, 70,000Rp to Paun and Rende, and 90,000-120,000Rp to Waikabubak and Baing. The *Merlin* and *Permata* will also hire out cars for the day (it is worth comparing prices). **Motorcycle hire**: available from most hotels, about 20,000Rp per day.

173 km from Waikabubak,
178 km from Melolo,
185 km from Rende,
220 km from Baing

Air Waingapu's **Mau Hau Airport** is 6 km southeast of town. Free transport to town provided by hotels. Drivers congregate in the arrivals hall. Taxi available, or catch one of the regular bemos that run along the road just outside the terminal to the bus station in town. The *Merpati* minibus takes passengers from the *Merpati* Office (*Hotel Elim*) to the airport. Daily flights by *Merpati* and/or *Bouraq* to **Kupang**. Also daily flights on *Merpati* to **Bima**, 3 times a week via **Tambolaka** (Waikabubak). Other destinations include **Surabaya**, via Bima and Denpasar, and direct to **Denpasar** on *Bouraq*.

Bus The station is 1½ km south of town, near most of the hotels, on Jl El Tari. Regular bemos link it with town. Several buses each day at approximately 0700, 0800, 1200 and 1500 to **Waikabubak** (4 hrs – sometimes with over an hr cruising for fares). Also several departures each day to **Melolo** (for Rende), (1½ to 2 hrs), **Lewa** (2 hrs), and **Baing** (4 hrs). Buses will pick passengers up from hotels and losmen with advance warning. The best seats are up front next to the driver. These usually need to be reserved in advance either through your hotel or at the bus company headquarters. Buses to Waikabubak stop half way at Langa Leru for about 20 mins. There are stalls and warungs where you can get excellent strong coffee and something to eat. **Taxi**: for groups of 4 or more it can make sense to hire a car; public transport, though cheap, is slow (see 'Local' transport above).

Boat The *Pelni* ships *Awu* and *Pangrango* dock at the new harbour – Pelabuhan Baru; other vessels, including pioneer vessels *(Perintis)*, dock at the old harbour or Pelabuhan Lama. Though only 200 m from the old harbour by water, the Pelabuhan Baru is a circuitous 7-km ride by bemo. The *Awi* and *Pangrango* dock twice a fortnight on their circuit through Nusa Tenggara. *Pelni* ships sail to **Ende** and **Kupang** via **Sawu** and **Roti**; ask at the *Pelni* office for details. There is also a weekly ferry linking Waingapu with Ende (Flores) and Savu (Sawu). At the time of writing, it docks on Wed am, leaves for Savu on Wed pm, returns to Waingapu on Thu am, and leaves for Ende on Fri pm, 10-12 hrs. There are also other, smaller boats heading out of Waingapu for other islands in Nusa Tenggara. Ask at the harbour. A *Perintis* ship currently sails from Waikelo Harbour to **Larantuka** on Eastern Flores, 8-12 hrs. The *Pelni* office is near the harbour (see map), T21265, F21027, staff are very helpful and some speak good English. Don't necessarily be put off if *Pelni* say there are no cabins available when you make a booking. Cabins frequently materialize on the day, if you have cash to spare.

Airline offices *Bouraq*, Jl Yos Sudarso 57, T21363, 21906, Yanca is very helpful, speaks excellent English and will bring tickets to your hotel in the evening, a former tour guide in West Sumba he is very knowlegeable about the island. *Merpati*, Jl Jend A Yani 73 (at the *Elim Hotel*), T323462, open Mon-Fri 0700-1700, Sat 0700-1400, Sun and holidays 0900-1300. **Banks** *Bank Rakyat Indonesia*, Jl Jend A Yani 36, changes cash and TCs, open 0800-1200, except Fri when it closes at 1100. **Communications** General Post Office: Jl Sutomo 21, open 0800-1400, except Fri 0800-1100. **Perumtel:** Jl Cut Nyak Din 19 (international telephone, telex & fax). **Medical facilities** Hospitals: *General Hospital*, Jl Adam Malik, Hambala. | **Directory**

Melolo

Melolo is a lovely, overgrown (with vegetation), little town 60 km southeast of Waingapu. Melolo itself has few traditional houses but Rende and Pau (see below) are easily reached from here by bus or on foot. Market day is Friday. | *Colour map 2, grid B5*

Rende is 7 km on along the road south from Melolo to Baing. It not only produces good ikat, but also has some of the most impressive megalithic tombs in East Sumba, with carvings featuring animals, sea creatures and humans. There are traditional houses here, though many now have tin roofs. The largest of these is the recently rebuilt home of the Raja. It may be possible to stay with a family here. The inhabitants believe that the earth is built on five house posts like their own homes; earthquakes happen when a mouse chews the central post destabilizing the earth and causing it to shake. Wednesday is market day (see page 370). Unfortunately, because Rende is firmly on the tour group itinerary, prices of cloth are high and rising. Good pieces made with home-grown cotton and using natural dyes are around 1,000,000Rp. The best weaver in the village sells cloth from the house close to the *kepala desa's* (headman's) residence. ■ *Getting there: by bemo from Melolo.* | **Excursions**

From Melolo, there is a pleasant 4 km walk past rice paddys to another traditional village: **Pau**. There are more megalithic tombs, peaked traditional houses and ikat at the village of **Umabara**, about 5 km west of Melolo. Alternatively take a bemo from Melolo and ask to be dropped off at the turning for the village. Both Pau and Umabara are about a 30 minute walk from the main road; follow the road until you reach a stone horse, take the right fork to reach Umabara and take the left for Pau. The Raja of Pau has a fine collection of ikat. At both these villages expect to sign the visitors book and give a small donation. **Lailuru** to the north of Melolo is another ikat weaving village. **Sleeping** There is a *homestay* in Rende (at the *kepala desa's*).

Sumba death rites

A notable aspect of Sumbanese society is the very close association of the living with the dead. Graves are constructed on the doorstep of houses in the open space in the centre of each village. Death is viewed as the beginning of eternal life; life itself being merely a stage which is passed through en route to the attainment of eternal life. The transition from the physical world to the world of the spirits is critical to the Sumbanese and is ensured by strict adherence to the burial rite. Following a person's death, a close relative calls his or her name four times; should there be no answer, he or she is pronounced dead. No crying is allowed for three days following the death. The body is bathed, coated in coconut oil (in East Sumba the body is also coated with the blue dye used in ikat which protects the corpse) and dressed in ikat sarongs. The number, and quality, of the sarongs is indicative of status. The arms and legs of the body are broken, and the dead person placed in the foetal position, either in a wooden coffin, or wrapped in buffalo hide. The body is placed over a hole so that the blood can drain down a bamboo pole into the ground. The body, except if the dead person was of lowly status, is guarded by four men. During this period, the spirit of the deceased is still regarded as roaming the village.

The second stage of the burial ceremony involves the preparation of the tomb. A stone is dragged into the village by large numbers of people. Relatives bring cattle, horses or pigs to be sacrificed, the size of the sacrificial gift being dictated by the status and closeness of relationship with the deceased. The corpse is then taken to the tomb and buried with many valuable objects. In the past, if the person was of royal blood, a slave was buried alive along with the corpse.

The wealth consumed at funeral ceremonies was deemed necessary to ensure a safe passage to the world of the ancestors where the deceased could bring benefit to his clan. The greater the display of wealth at his funeral the higher the status he would merit in the spirit world. There is great wealth buried in the soil of Sumba and there have been cases of unscrupulous dealers, allegedly from Java, going out into likely areas of the countryside with metal detectors in search of buried treasure.

Sleeping **E** *Losmen Hermindo*, Melolo, owned by the local Chinese shop owner, clean, 5 rooms with shared mandi, squat toilet and fan. 2 new rooms with attached bathroom and western toilet, price includes breakfast, meals available, or eat at the warungs which serve good cheap food.

Transport **Bus** Several direct buses from **Waingapu** starting from 0700 (2 hrs). **Bemos** run all
60 km from Waingapu day from Melolo to Waingapu until about 1600.

Kaliuda Kaliuda is an ikat weaving village, 50 km past Melolo and 110 km from Waingapu, just off the road to Baing. The ikat produced here features, predominantly, chicken and horse motifs. Weavers from other villages make fun of the local artists saying – 'Oh, all they can do are chickens and horses'. Much of the ikat is unfinished (that is, without the border strip) and clearly, therefore, for tourist rather than local consumption.

Sleeping The *kepala desa* takes in visitors, but the rooms are very basic and rather dirty. **Transport** 50 km from Melolo and 110 km from Waingapu. **Bus**: 2 or 3 buses each day from the terminal in **Waingapu**.

Kalala Kalala is on Sumba's southeast coast, 5 km from Baing and also close to Kaliuda. It has a good beach and is one of the best places to surf.

Sleeping The upmarket resort built here is currently closed; there are no plans to re-open it. **Transport Bus**: from **Waingapu**, 4 hrs, or from **Melolo**, 2 hrs.

Waikabubak

Waikabubak is the regency capital and the largest town in West Sumba. Even so, it is really little more than a village, with a population of only around 15,000. Situated at 800 m above sea-level, the town is cooler than Waingapu and during the coldest months of June and July can be chilly at night.

Phone code: 0387
Colour map 2, grid B3

Almost 70% of the population of this region are nominal Christians; unwilling converts, they still follow and attach much more importance to their animist religious practices. One of the unfortunate consequences of their conversion is that many of the old ancestral heirlooms have been sold and some of the important ceremonies are no longer performed.

Nonetheless, Waikabubak is a very pleasant town with trees, parks and four traditional hilltop 'kampungs' within its boundaries. It is a good base from which to see the fine megalithic tombs in this area of Sumba and at the appropriate time of year it is also possible to see the *Pasola*. This spectacular festival takes place in four different districts of West Sumba after the full moon; in February at Tossi Village in Kodi district (see 'Excursions', below) and Sodan village in Lamboya, and in March in Wanokaka and Gaura districts. Verify exact dates and location with your hotel or the tourist office. Alternatively, if when you are out walking you notice an endless stream of people converging on a village join them, they will probably be delighted to invite you along and will indicate appropriate behaviour which will include giving a gift or donation. Homestays are available in nearby villages (see 'Festivals', below). The **tourist office** is out of town on Jl Teratai 1, T21240, and is moderately helpful.

The village of **Tarung** is only 500 m west of town, set on a small hill. Being so close to Waikabubak, it has inevitably been influenced by the large number of tourists who walk up here. Nevertheless, it has several – rather plain – tombs and 33 traditional, thatched houses (see box, page 370). Tarung is the centre of the Marapu religion where many important rituals take place including the Wula Podhu New Year festival. Admission to village is by donation.

Another village that can be reached on foot from Waikabubak is **Bondomaroto**. This is an ikat-producing village with some rather inferior

East Nusa Tenggara

Waikabubak

To Mamboro
To Mona Lisa Cottages, Waitabula, Tambolaka Airport & Racetrack

Kampung Belakiku Kampung Tarung Stables Jl Adiaksa
Graves
Kampung Ende Football Pitch Jl El Tari Jl Veteran 5
Kampung Prai Kalembung Graves 3 Merpati Office Jl Sudirman Graves
Bus Ticket Agent 2 Jl Malada 1
Market Jl A Yani 4 Jl Gajah Mada Jl Teretal
Art Shop Jl Basuki Rahmat
Jl Palapa

To Anakalang, Waingapu & Bondomaroto Praijing

To Wanokaka Rua & Morossi Beaches

N
Not to scale

■ **Sleeping**
1 Artha   3 Losmen Pelita   5 Rakuta
2 Losmen Aloha   4 Manandang

☞ *Pasola: of worms and warriors*

This fertility rite involves a battle between massed ranks of horsemen representing two villages. They use (these days blunted by Government order) spears, and the battle can last from morning until nightfall. It not unusually results in serious injury, even death. The pasola is also a ritual 'cleansing'. Anyone injured or killed is deemed to have transgressed against the gods; their injury is believed to be divine retribution, a price that must be paid by the individual to ensure the gods will not wreak revenge on the whole village or its harvest in the coming year. Human blood is the price of atonement. The battle is preceded by other traditional pursuits and ceremonies – traditional boxing (pajura), purification rituals, and the nyale ceremony (see below). The date of the pasola is determined by the appearance of the Nyale worms (see page 295) on the shores of the sea a few days after the full moon; their appearance is part of the worms' annual reproductive cycle in which their tails, filled with sperm or eggs, are deposited and are carried to the shore where they are much

sought after as ritual food. Prior to the coming of the Wua Nyale, the combatants and supporting villagers go to the sacred beach. As the moon rises traditional boxing pajura commences; the blood that is spilled also acts as a blood offering to the gods. As dawn breaks, priests from the ancestral village inspect the nyale in order to foretell the coming harvest, the larger the number, the more abundant the crop. Following this the 'pasola' begins and continues for much of the day. The pasola is particularly popular in the districts of Wanokaka (18 km south of Waikabubak), Lamboya and Kodi. The combat itself symbolizes the contest between the upper and lower worlds – between Merapu, the gods of heaven, and Nyale, the goddess of the sea. The duality of male and female, the sky and the earth mirrors the duality so common in the rites and rituals of Nusa Tenggara. *NB* The timing of the festival is decided at the last moment; although the Jakarta-based national tourist office may decide the festival will occur on a certain day, if it does it is pure serendipity.

tombs and traditional high roofed dwellings. You may be lucky and witness a festival taking place – ask in town. On the last day of Tarungs' celebration of Wula Podhu the villagers have a day long celebration. Admission to the village is by donation. Bondomaroto, 2 km from Waikabubak, is just off the main road to Waingapu. Follow the dirt track south and take the left hand path. To the right lies the beautiful village of **Praijing**. Weaving can be seen in both villages.

Excursions **Anakalang District**, 20 km east of Waikabubak, is easily accessible as a day excursion from town (see page 381). The district is particularly rich in megalithic tombs and significant villages include **Pasunga**, **Kabunduk**, **Lai Tarung**, **Matakakeri** and **Galubakul** (details on these places are included in the Anakalang entry). There are many other traditional villages worthy of a visit. The *Artha Hotel* has details of some of these.

Some 40 km to the north of Waikabubak about 7 km inland from Mamboro is one of the oldest traditional hilltop villages, **Manuakalada**. **Mamboro** (market day Saturday), on the coast 46 km north of Waikabubak, was a centre of the slave trade which made the local rajas some of the richest in Sumba.

Wanokaka lies 18 km south of Waikabubak and features several traditional villages. The main road south passes through a scenic, hilly landscape with brilliant green ricefields. This is one of the districts where the spectacular annual *Pasola festival* is held (see 'Festivals' below). Nearby, the village of **Prai Goli** or **Paigoli** has one of the finest, best carved, tombs in Sumba. **Sodan**, 25 km southwest of Waikabubak where an important New Year festival takes place at the time of the full moon in October, is a traditional hilltop village and

East Nusa Tenggara

another important centre of the Merapu religion. This is an area steeped in magic and taboos. Each evening at sunset the sacred drums are struck to call the spirits of the ancestors. One drum was made of human skin but eight years ago a fire destroyed many of the traditional houses in the village and the drum; this village is being rebuilt. **Waigalli**, **Pulli** and **Waiwuang** are other traditional villages in the area with carved tombs. ■ *Getting there: by hire car or motorcycle (see 'Transport').*

Kodi District, west of Waikabubak offers superb coastal scenery and many beautiful beaches as well as traditional villages and megaliths (see page 382). Villages worth exploring her include **Waimangura**, **Kodi**, **Pero** (where there is accommodation), **Ratenggaro**, **Wainyapu**, **Paronabaroro**, **Tossi**, **Bondokawango** and **Bukarani**. Although it is possible to explore the area using Waikabubak as a base, and particularly if you charter your own transport, it is obviously easier staying in Pero. ■ *Getting there: to catch the direct bus from Waingapu to Kodi aim to be at the bus station by 0600, 2½ hrs; alternatively you can catch a bus to Waitabula 1½ hrs, then change to a connecting bemo.*

Pantai Rua and **Pantai Morossi** are two good surfing beaches south of Waikabubak (see page 382). ■ *Getting there: it is easiest to hire a motorcycle, or charter a car, 1-2 hrs (see Local transport in Waikabubak entry). It is possible to can by public bus to Pantai Morossi, with a 20 min walk to the beach.*

Hotels can provide guides and transport. Traditional dances can be arranged in Wanokaka (roughly 150,000Rp, performance lasts 45 minutes), and at Kodi. An entire Pasola with a hundred horses can be arranged for around 3,500,000Rp, inclusive of the cost of police for security and health insurance for the Pasola team! **Tours**

B *Mona Lisa*, Jl Adyaksa 30, T21364. Roughly 3 km from the centre of town on the road to Waitabula. Attractive bungalows with private bathrooms, shower, western toilet, hot water, restaurant (mid-range) the hotel provides a bus to the airport, prices highly negotiable off-season, usually well-booked peak season. **B-E** *Manandang*, Jl Pemuda 4, T21197, 21292. 17 rooms, the largest hotel in town, includes a 'new' wing and there are plans to build a swimming pool. Clean, rooms with private bathrooms, shower and western toilet, first class rooms have hot water, fan and satellite TV, economy rooms with shared mandi, price includes breakfast and tax. Restaurant (cheap) offers an extensive and reasonably priced menu, satellite TV in lobby, car hire available. Recommended. **D** *Artha*, Jl Veteran No 11, T21112, 21676. 16 rooms, 10 mins walk from town centre, this small hotel is well-run, clean with very friendly and helpful staff, set around an attractive garden, price includes breakfast and tea all day. Restaurant serves cheap, good, simple food. The three cheapest rooms are the best value in town, all rooms with private bathroom, shower, western toilet. VIP rooms have fan and fridge. Jack, the manager, and Meno both speak English and are extremely helpful. They can arrange a visit to a local festival, advise on etiquette and explain what is happening: you might become the guest of the headman of the village of Tarung for one of that village's festivals, or you might be invited to a wedding, no fee will be asked but a gift would be in order. Photographs of the more interesting villages, beaches and rituals are displayed at the reception desk, satellite TV in lobby, parking, car hire and guides available. Highly recommended. **D** *Rakuta*, Jl Veteran, T21075. Shared mandi, rather run down, all meals included. **D-E** *Pelita*, Jl A Yani 2, T21104, 21392. The dirty standard rooms with shared mandi are basic, rather depressing, and overpriced, the newer, more expensive rooms with private mandi (shower and western toilet) are fine once you are inside, very cheap restaurant, only stay here if everywhere else is full. **E-F** *Aloha*, Jl Gajah Mada, T21024. 8 rooms, very popular with budget travellers, clean, four cheaper rooms with shared mandi, four better rooms **Sleeping**
It's essential to book during pasola

East Nusa Tenggara

with private mandi, all squat toilets, restaurant good, simple, cheap food, cars and motorbikes for hire, guide available. Recommended.

In addition to the above it is possible to stay in almost every village by making arrangements with the *kepala desa*, and thus gain a fascinating insight into local life and customs. Expect to pay in the **E** category.

Eating   Most visitors eat in their hotels or losmen; the *Manandang* has the best food in town (see the 'Sleeping', above). Alternatively, there are a selection of good, cheap warungs on Jl Jend A Yani.

Festivals   **Full moon** (movable) **Wula Podhu**, a period of fasting, and a festival, held in the village of Tarung just outside Waikabubak. Traditional dances, musical celebrations and sacrifices, ending with an extravagant night of dance and song. The combat itself or *pasola* symbolizes the contest between the upper and lower worlds – between Merapu, the gods of heaven, and Nyale, the goddess of the sea. The duality of male and female, the sky and the earth mirrors the duality so common in the rites and rituals of Nusa Tenggara. For more background to the festival see the box. **Porung Takadonga** festival takes place every two years in Lai Tarung village (see village entry).

April/May (moveable) **'Pajura'**, traditional boxing, sometimes takes place during these months, where the hands are bound with straw and the winner is the first to draw blood, held to commemorate the harvest.

August (17th, public holiday) **Horse racing** takes place once a year to commemorate Independence and lasts a week. The spirited Sumba horses are broken in and ridden for the first time in a muddy 'field'. The mud serves as an anchor and prevents them from bucking wildly. Depending on size, a horse is worth 250,000Rp to 700,000Rp with stallions being worth more than mares. A large buffalo is worth 1-2 million Rp, the price being indicative of its symbolic and ceremonial role in the Merapu religion.

Shopping   Like Waingapu, door-to-door salesmen and women camp outside hotels selling bits-and-pieces and, in particular, Sumba ikat blankets. As the centre of production is East Sumba these are better purchased there.

Art Shop, Jl A Yani 99, has photocopies of a book by two Swedish anthropologists describing local customs. Many pieces and jewellery carved in West Sumba's villages from horn, bone, wood and stone, containers for betel nut, religious objects and stone statues. Many of these objects show examples of local symbolism. Beads and fertility carvings, with outsized phalluses attached, are on offer.

Textiles Ikat is best bought in East Sumba.

Transport   **Local** Public transport is irregular but improving all the time. **Car hire**: hiring a car to
137 km from Waingapu,   visit out-of-town sights makes good sense for groups of 4 or more. Most losmen and
47 km from Waikelo   hotels have vehicles for charter and they display rates for different destinations – **Waikelosawa**, **Wanokaka**, **Lamboya/Sodan**, **Waitabuta**, **Waikelo**, **Memboro** and **Kodi**. A cheaper and equally flexible way to get around is by **motorcycle taxi**; alternatively, some losmen/hotels are willing to rent out motorbikes by the day (25,000-40,000Rp).

Air The airport is 42 km northwest of town at Tambolaka. *Merpati* operate 3 flights per week to **Kupang** (2½ hrs), via **Waingapu**, and to **Bima** (40 mins). There are share minibuses into town. Note that it can be difficult to get a seat.

East Nusa Tenggara

Bus: the terminal is on the southwest edge of town, off Jl Jend A Yani. 3 departures daily for **Waingapu**, the first at about 0700-0800, 4 hrs. Connections with regional market towns generally through the day until early afternoon. From Waingapu, passengers are dropped-off at their losmen or hotel; those travelling to Waingapu will be picked-up at their hotel or losmen if given advance warning. There are several bus agents along Jl A Yani where you can buy tickets, arrange hotel pick up and reserve seats; *Sumba Mas*, *Bumi*, *Indah* and *Tambora Indah* all have newish buses.

Sea Boat: Perentis ships operate out of Waikelo harbour, bound for **Larantuka** on Flores. The trip takes 8-12 hrs. 60 km from Waikabubak on Sumba's north coast and near the airport. It is also sometimes possible to hitch a ride on one of the inter-island mixed cargo boats that stop here

Airline offices *Merpati*, 1st floor of building, corner Jl Malada and Jl Jend A Yani. **Banks** *Bank Rakyat Indonesia*, Jl Gajah Mada; *BNI*, Jl Jl Jend A Yani. **Communications** Post Office: corner Jl Jend A Yani and Jl Sudirman. Closed Sun, open every other day 0900-1400, except Fri, 0900-1130. **Directory**

Anakalang District

Anakalang is a district 20 km east of Waikabubak and, conveniently, close to the main road to Waingapu. This district has the greatest concentration of megalithic tombs to be found in Sumba: a mass marriage ceremony is held here every two years in the summer to coincide with the full moon. *Colour map 2, grid B3*

At **Pasunga**, on the main road, there is one of the largest tombs in Sumba. It features a man and woman, and was carved over a period of six months in 1926. Over 150 buffalo were reportedly sacrificed as part of the funeral ceremonies. The tomb is for the clan elders.

The nearby village of **Kabunduk** is the important 'origin village' of the local clan and also has some well-carved graves. It is the site of the largest tomb in Anakalang District, named 'Resi Mona', where the rajas of the district were buried. The layout of this village is typical: in the central space there are graves, a supplementary altar for crops, a village altar and a skull tree; some flat stones indicate the spot where a supplementary altar is placed to serve as the focus at rituals and ceremonies.

Lai Tarung – walking distance from Kabunduk – is regarded as an important ceremonial and spiritual centre. There are 10 carved stone pillars on which sits a 'traditional' house. Reach this hilltop village of the ancestors by following the track uphill at the end of Kabunduk village and on past some houses and tombs. The *Porung Takadonga* ceremony is held here every two years to communicate with and honour the spirits of the ancestors of the Merapu religion and commemorate their arrival on Sumba. The priest speaks in the language of the ancestors for several hours; this is followed by dancing, some warlike, as clansmen wave their spears menacingly. From Kabunduk, it is a 20 minute walk to **Matakakeri**, where there is what is touted as being the heaviest megalith in Sumba – weighing 70 tonnes – and erected in 1939 following the death of the King of Anakalang. It is said (these figures are often quoted, but have not been substantiated) that 2,000 men were required to quarry the stone and then move it here, and that three people died in the process, 250 buffalo were slaughtered and 10 tonnes of rice consumed during the burial ritual.

Continue on the main road south of Kabunkuk for about 3 km to reach the village of **Galubakul**, site of Sumba's largest tomb (there seems to be considerable competition between the various claimants of the 'largest tomb in Sumba' title) where Umbu Sawola, one of the island's most important rajas, and his wife are buried. Another 1½ hours' walk along this road south of Anakalang is the **Mata Yangu waterfall** with a pool at the base of the 60 m drop.

East Nusa Tenggara

Sleeping It is possible to stay in one of the traditional houses by the altars which has been converted into a homestay. First see the kepala desa who has an interesting collection of old photographs taken by a Swiss anthropologist, and some ritual heirlooms.

Transport **Bus** Take a bus heading for Lewa/Waingapu or for Anakalang. Most depart in the morning, although there are departures later in the day.

Kodi District

Kodi District offers superb coastal scenery and many beautiful beaches as well as traditional villages and megaliths. En route to Kodi district look out for the rice paddies near **Waimangura** (market day Wednesday) about 28 km west of Waikabubak. Kodi is the main town and market day is also Wednesday.

Pero near Kodi on the west coast offers some basic accommodation on a spectacular stretch of coast, though the waves can be powerful and swimming is not always for the faint hearted.

There are good walks in the area around Kodi passing traditional villages and megalithic tombs. Follow the beach south from Pero to **Ratenggaro**, approximately 5 km, with superb sea views. From this raised village there are more grand views with the picturesque traditional village of **Wainyapu** just across the mouth of the river, easily reached at low tide. **Paronabaroro** is slightly inland enroute to Ratenggaro; here you will find the highest roofs in Sumba, as well as stone tombs and possibly even some women weaving.

Going north from Pero follow the path along the coast for about 5 km to reach **Tossi**, the most traditional village in Kodi and one of the sites of the annual Pasola festival (see 'Festivals', below). Other traditional villages include **Bondokawango** and **Bukarani**. All these villages can be reached by road from Kodi if you have your own transport.

Sleeping **E** *Losmen Stori*, Pero on the only street in this village, basic rooms with shared mandi
Come prepared and squat toilet, price includes 3 meals (there is nowhere else to eat in town). Best to
for mosquitos arrive on Wed, market day in Kodi, when there is an abundance of food; by the following Tue meals in the losmen offer little more than rice and noodles. It is possible to stay with the *kepala desa* in Ratenggaro.

Transport **Bus** To catch the direct bus from Waingapu aim to be at the bus station by 0600, 2½ hrs; alternatively you can catch a bus to Waitabula 1½ hrs, then change to a connecting bemo.

Pantai Rua & The two surfing beaches of Pantai Rua and Pantai Morossi are on the coast south
Pantai Morossi of Waikabubak. Pantai Rua is good for surfing, but Pantai Morossi is reputedly even better – the south coastline of Sumba is exposed to the onslaught of the Southern Seas. Both, though, are considered safe for swimming.

Sleeping **Pantai Morossi**: the **B** *Sumba Reefs Hotel* very upmarket, and catering largely for the package tourists from Bali. **B-C** *Palm Resort*, surfer destination, large rooms, TV, air con, reasonable quality place, expensive restaurant. **E** *Homestay Mete Bulu*, about a 15-min walk from the beach, up a steep hill, rather mosquito-ridden. **Pantai Rua**: **E** *Homestay Ahong* basic, but very friendly, and provides 3 decent meals daily. Under construction on the island south of the beach is a luxury resort aimed at package tourists. **Transport** **Road**: it is easiest to hire a motorcycle, or charter a car, 1-2 hrs (see Local transport in Waikabubak entry). It is possible to can by public bus to Pantai Morossi, with a 20-min walk to the beach.

West Timor

Timor is one of the driest islands in the Indonesian Archipelago. The terrain is beautiful but often bleak with rock strewn hills, isolated communities, and poor soils. In the west it is probably most often associated with the Indonesian invasion and annexation of the former Portuguese colony of East Timor in 1975.

West Timor has become a popular place to visit for tourists largely because it lies at the beginning or end of a journey through the islands of Nusa Tenggara. There are reasonable beaches and some snorkelling, but nothing spectacular. The refreshing hill towns of Soe and Kefamenanu, both with traditional villages in their vicinities, are worth the journey, as are the rarely visited islands of Roti and Savu. Note, however, that following the debacle in East Timor, West Timor is not the happiest of places and in some areas Westerners are not welcome.

Ins and outs

Getting there Kupang is the largest town in this part of Indonesia. There are international air connections with Darwin, Australia and also good links with domestic destinations. Get a taxi into the centre of town. **NB** Taxi drivers encourage tourists to go to hotels of their choice (where they receive a commission), saying others are full. Try to ask at reception without the taxi driver in company. Airport taxi service T33824. Bemos running between Penfui/Baumata and town pass the airport turn off. It is a 1½-km walk from the airport buildings to this spot. Connections by *Merpati* and *Bouraq* with Jakarta, Dili and Bali, and other destination in Java, Sulawesi, Nusa Tenggara, Irian Jaya and Kalimantan. Kupang's Tenau harbour is visited by a number of *Pelni* vessels and there are also more frequent ferry links with Ende and Larantuka (both on Flores), and with Savu and Alor.

West Timor

Getting around Buses travel to all major settlements in West Timor. Bemos are the main form of town and local transport.

Safety warning Following East Timor's resounding vote in favour of independence in 1999, the militias fighting to maintain the territory's link with Jakarta fled to West Timor where they are still based as this book goes to press. At the beginning of September they attacked and killed three UN staff working in the town of Atambua, not far from the border between West and East Timor. Foreigners are viewed with suspicion in some areas and not a little hostility – especially if they are Australian (or thought to be so) – Australian forces led the UN force into East Timor.

NB: In the last edition of this book we included a section on East Timor. This edition has no such section for two reasons. First, East Timor appears to be heading for full independence and will be a sovereign state after a period of UN tutelage. Second, Dili and many other towns in the region were razed to the ground during the violence following the vote for independence in mid-1999.

Background

Administratively, Timor Island is slightly confusing. **West Timor** or **Timor Barat** consists of three districts which constitute part of the province of East Nusa Tenggara: Kupang (centred on the city of Kupang which is also the capital of East Nusa Tenggara), Timor Tengah Selatan and Timor Tengah Utara. The east section of Timor, and a small coastal enclave in West Timor known as Ambeno, is known as **East Timor** or **Timor Timur**. This was formerly Portuguese East Timor, annexed in 1975 by Indonesia, and then granted independence under UN tutelage in 1999.

The districts of West Timor cover a total of 16,500 sq km and have a population of 1.25 million. The island's long dry season stretches from April to October, with annual rainfall of 1,200 mm – 2,000 mm being concentrated in the months from November to March. Soils are generally thin and unproductive. Most of the population is concentrated in the slightly wetter interior where cattle raising is the principal occupation. Because of the Portuguese and Dutch influences, the bulk of the population is Christian: 58% are classified as Protestant, 35% Roman Catholic.

History Timor became a focus of European interest because of the valuable aromatic sandalwood that grows here. Formerly an important export of Sumba and Solor as well as Timor, the earliest reference to trade in perfumed sandalwood is contained in the chronicles of the Chanyu Kua Dynasty, written in 1225. The Chinese, sometimes using Javanese intermediaries, probably began buying the wood in the 10th century, perhaps even as early as the third century. Their accounts describe Timor as being covered with sandalwood trees – something that is difficult to believe today.

European contact with the island dates from the early 16th century. The Portuguese may have sighted Timor in 1512 when an expedition was sent from Melaka to seek the famed and fabulously wealthy Spice Islands. However, the earliest confirmed European reference to the island is contained in a letter from the Commander of Melaka, dated 6 January 1514. Physical contact with the island dates from 1561 when a Portuguese settlement was established on neighbouring Solor and Dominican friars began to evangelize on Timor. Though much of their time was spent on missionary activity, they also became involved in the sandalwood trade. Other important exports of the period were horses and slaves. It was at this time that the inter-marriage between Portuguese sailors, soldiers and traders from Melaka and Macao with local women laid the foundations for Timor's influential *mestizos* community – locally known as the *Topasses*, from the Dravidian word *tupassi*, meaning 'interpreter'.

The Portuguese began to lose influence to the Dutch at the beginning of the 17th century and the important harbour of Kupang was wrested from the Portuguese in 1637. However, the Dutch showed only a marginal interest in securing this distant colonial possession and the day-to-day administration of the island was left to 62 petty kingdoms, ruled by Catholic princes. Indeed, it was not until 1859 that a treaty was finally ratified determining the boundary between the Dutch and Portuguese territories. Even this agreement was unsatisfactory as it left the status of the Portuguese enclave of Ocussi (now Ambeno), ambiguous. This was not to be resolved until 1905. The friction between the Dutch and the Portuguese provided the basis for the later conflict between Indonesia and East Timor. This resulted in East Timor's annexation by Indonesia in 1975 and nearly 25 years of occupation.

Kupang

The origins of Kupang are not known, although the name is Timorese for 'Lord', probably referring to the ruler of the area. The Dutch first landed here in 1613, and received a warm welcome from the Kupang. He apparently even expressed an interest in being converted to Christianity. This was not pursued by the Dutch who left, not to return for another 40 years. In 1647 the Portuguese began construction of a fort, which was abandoned before it was completed. Six years later, the headquarters of the Dutch in Solor were damaged by an earthquake, and they moved their operations to Kupang, building upon the fortifications left by the Portuguese. Kupang was to remain the centre of Dutch influence in the area until independence.

Phone code: 0380
Colour map 3, grid C4

East Nusa Tenggara

The town was initially focused on Jl Siliwangi, but quickly spread inland from the coast. Today, the city is the capital of the province of East Nusa Tenggara with a population of 120,000, most of them Protestants, and the University of Nusa Cendana, (12 km outside town). There are three **tourist offices**. *Kantor Pariwisata Parpostel*, is on Jl Soekarno 29 (next to Post Office). A central location but next to useless. The *Provincial Tourist Office*, on Jl Basuki Rakhmat 1, T21540, is 5 km from town off Jl Soeharto. Catch a bemo travelling towards Baun and ask for Kantor Gubernor Lama, the turning is just past the Pentecostal Chapel. They can provide some useful handouts. ■ *0700-1400 Mon-Thu, 0700-1100 Fri, 0700-1230 Sat*. The *Tourist Information Desk*, on Jl Soekarno 25 (next to church), is a helpful and convenient source of information, especially for independent travellers.

Kupang is not well-endowed with sights. Despite its history, there are virtually no pre-Second World War buildings. Jl Siliwangi, the seafront road (although the sea is usually out of sight), is the bustling heart of the city, as it has been since the Dutch settled here in 1637. Street salesmen and women hawk traditional herbal and spiritual cures, and there is a **market** at the east end of the street (where it becomes Jl Garuda). To the west of Jl Siliwangi, the coast road crosses **Air Mata**. This is the small river where Captain Bligh landed after his extraordinary 7,000 km, 41-day voyage in an open boat from the spot near Tonga in the Pacific where the mutineers on his ship *HMS Bounty* set him and his supporters adrift. Walking further west along the road, past the army barracks and church, are good views of the coast and the islands beyond. This was the site of the Dutch **Fort Concordia** built in 1653. Back in town and close to the Kota Kupang bemo terminal at Jl Soekarno 23, is a fine and

Sights

well-maintained **Dutch church**, orginally constructed in 1873. It is simple and pure in conception, barring the ornate porchway.

About 4 km out of town, 300 m from the long-distance bus terminal, is the **Museum of Nusa Tenggara Timur**. The exhibits are well displayed, but less well explained. The collection includes textiles, ceramics, traditional weapons and ethnographic pieces. Notable is the fine bronze Dongson (Vietnamese) drum (see page 144), collected on Alor, with its frogs symbolizing and promoting rain, along with the bronze *moko* dowry vessels, also from Alor (see box, page 363). The ikat process is illustrated with the use of a series of models and sets. ■ *Admission by donation. 0800-1500 Mon-Thu, 0800-1100 Fri, 0800-1230 Sat. Getting there: take bemo No 10 from the city centre to Walikota.*

Excursions **Lasiana Beach** lies 12 km east of Kupang, and is quiet during weekdays. At weekends it becomes popular as a picnic spot for locals. *Warungs* and drinks vendors operate on the beach and at the west end of the beach there is a small plateau where there are good views over Kupang Bay. **Sleeping D** *Lasiana Beach Cottage*, not always open, attached bathrooms, rather grubby. ■ *There is an admission charge to beach. Getting there: take bemo No 17 heading for Tarus and ask to be let off at the entrance to the beach.*

Baun lies 30 km from Kupang and is a weaving town; the processes of ikat can be seen, although the quality of the work produced is variable. Visitors have recommended *Ibu Raja* as producing the best cloth. There is a **market** in Baun on

Kupang

■ Sleeping
1 Backpackers
2 Cendana
3 Eden
4 Fatuleu Homestay
5 Flobamor II
6 Laguna Inn, Kelimutu & Adian
7 L'Avalon Backpackers
8 Maliana
9 Marina
10 New Orchid
11 Safariah
12 Timor Beach

● Eating
1 Garnda Tomor
2 Happy Café
3 Karang Mas (Bar)
4 GI Modern Bakeri
5 Palembang
6 Teddy's Bar

East Nusa Tenggara

Saturday (from 0700). ■ *Getting there: take a bemo from the Kota Kupang terminal in town to Sikumana terminal and from there another bemo to Baun.*

Semau Island is good for swimming and snorkelling but is best reached on a tour (see 'Tours' below) as there are no regular ferries. There is talk of running game-fishing boats (marlin) from the island, the season stretching from March-September. **Sleeping C** *Uiasa Beach Cottages*, attached mandi, price includes three meals; and *Flobamor II Cottages* (book through *Flobamor II Hotel* in Kupang, see below). ■ *Getting there: if not on a tour, catch a bemo bound for Bolok or Tenau from the Kota Kupang terminal and get off at Pantai (Beach) Namosain, southwest of town. Boats can sometimes be hired from here for the trip to Semau (45 min).*

A **sandalwood factory** lying 3 km north of town at Bakunase is open to visitors. ■ *Getting there: direct bemos to Bakunase from Terminal Kota.*

Tours There are a number of well-organized tour and travel companies in Kupang. They offer city tours, tours to the weaving village of Baun, Lesiana Beach tours and a number of other day trips (all these are prices for three people). They also arrange longer tours to destinations on Timor and the other islands of East Nusa Tenggara (Flores, Alor, Komodo, Sumba etc). *Teddy's Bar and Restaurant*, also run a less formal tour service, with day snorkelling tours to Semau Island departing 1000, Rote Island surfing safaris, city tours, fishing and camping expeditions.

Sleeping **A** *New Orchid* (aka *Orchid Garden*), Jl Fatuleu 2 (facing the *Fatuleu Homestay*), T33707, F33669. A/c, restaurant, pool, central location, clean bungalows and attractive garden, best place near the centre of town. **A** *Sasando*, Jl Perintis Kemerdekaan 1, T33334, F33338. A/c, restaurant, pool, tennis, good views, but out of town near bus terminal so not convenient for anyone intending to explore on foot. **B** *Flobamor II*, Jl Jend Sudirman 21, T33476. A/c, hot water, comfortable but over-priced and now rather down-at-heel. Accommodates the main *Merpati* office, and a dive centre. **B-D** *Marina*, Jl Jend A Yani 79, T22566. Some a/c, small, friendly, central, price includes breakfast, cheaper rooms without attached bathrooms, rather gloomy.

C *Kelimutu*, Jl Gunung Kelimutu 38 (close to *Laguna Hotel*), T31179. Some a/c, clean and quiet, price includes breakfast and lunch or dinner. **C-D** *Cendana*, Jl Raya El Tari 23, T21541. Some a/c, some distance out of town near the Kantor Gubernor, but regular bemos into city centre, nice garden atmosphere, popular, price includes breakfast. Recommended. **C-D** *Laguna*, Jl Gunung Kelimutu 36, T21559. Some a/c, painted entirely in a wonderful green, on a quiet side street but central, clean with good bathrooms. Recommended. **C-D** *Maliana*, Jl Sumatra 35, T21879. Clean, spacious rooms with fans, with mandi and western toilet en suite, friendly management. Recommended. **C-D** *Maya*, Jl Sumatra 31, T32169. Some a/c, good rooms and good value, garden, on sea front but still central, more expensive rooms with hot water and TV, popular so often full, price includes breakfast. Recommended. **C-D** *Susi*, Jl Sumatra 37, T22172. Some a/c and TV, on seafront but still central, clean and quiet. **C-D** *Timor Beach*, Jl Sumatra (near *Maya Hotel*), T31651. Some a/c, on seafront but still central, rooms are dirty and the hotel is poorly maintained, but position is some recompense. Has an OK restaurant. **D** *Adian*, Jl Kelimutu 40, T21913. Popular with Indonesians, good position. **D** *Fatuleu Homestay*, Jl Fatuleu 1, T31374. Quiet street in garden atmosphere, clean, and central. Recommended.

E *Losmen Safariah*, Jl Moh Hatta 34, T21595. Rooms only average, attached mandi, reasonable location. **F** *Backpackers*, Jl Kancil 37B, Airnona (about 7 km from town centre but there are regular (No 3) bemos), T31291. Dirty but cheap, near swimming pool, good for information, price includes breakfast, of sorts. **F** *Eden*, Jl Kancil, Airnona, 7 km from town centre, regular bemos, T21931. Thatched bungalows in peaceful location by swimming pool, wonderful trees, but rooms shabby and poorly maintained, price includes breakfast. **F** *Losmen Isabella*, Jl Gunung Mutis 21, T21407. Central (just off Jl Siliwangi), but dirty. **F** *L'Avalon Backpackers*, Jl Sumatra 1 No 8, T32278. Quiet, friendly place, with lots of travellers' information, but basic. Price includes breakfast, tea and coffee.

Eating

Local specialities include daging s'ei (smoked beef)

Indonesian Cheap: *Hemaliki*, Jl Soekarno, attractive garden and restaurant serving Indonesian, Chinese, seafood and Japanese. *Lumintu*, Jl Garuda 1 (by the market square), Indonesian, good and cheap *ikan bakar* (barbecue fish). *Palembang*, Jl Mohammed Hatta 54 (near the general hospital on bemo route 2), serves a wide range of excellent Chinese and Indonesian dishes, very popular and very good. **Very cheap**: *Bundo Kanduang*, Jl Jend Sudirman 49, Padang. *Garuda Timor*, good food, clean restaurant, good value. *Happy Café*, Jl Ikan Paus 3 (near the bemo terminal), large portions of freshly cooked Indonesian and Chinese dishes, excellent value. *Ibu Soekardjo*, Jl Moh Hatta 23, Indonesian. *Tunggal Dara*, Jl Siliwangi (facing the market square), Indonesian dishes, hardly refined but one of the cheapest places to eat.

Chinese Cheap: *Lima Jaya Raya*, Jl Soekarno 15, clean, reasonably priced, good range of dishes, Chinese, crab specialities. Nightclub upstairs. *Mandarin*, Jl Jend Sudirman 148 (next to *Astiti Hotel* and intersection with Jl Harimau), good, simple, Chinese. Recommended. *Hemaliki*, Jl Soekarno good, cheap Chinese and seafood.

International Cheap: *Teddy*'s Bar & Restaurant, Jl Ikan Tongkol 1-3, western, seafood, lobsters, steak, live music.

Seafood Ceap: *Timor Beach*, Jl Sumatra, seafood, overlooking beach.

Bars *Teddy*'s Bar, Jl Ikan Tongkol 1-3, live music, popular with westerners, pricey. Good place to network if looking for yacht work. *Karang Mas*, Jl Siliwangi 84/88, 1 of the best places to watch the sunset clutching a cold beer, the bar has a terrace overlooking a small beach, small menu of mediocre food. *Pantai Bar*, *Timor Beach Hotel*, Jl Sumatra, bar overlooking the sea, another place to watch the sunset over Kupang Bay.

Shopping **Books** *Istana Beta Bookshop* on Jl Jend A Yani 58 (past the *Marina Hotel*) has town maps.

Crafts *Loka Binkra Crafts Centre* is on the road to the airport, just before the 8 km marker. Catch a bemo bound for Tarus or Penfui.

Textiles Kupang is a centre for the sale of Nusa Tenggara Timur ikat, but it is highly variable in quality. For *tenunan asli* (cloth woven from home-grown and spun cotton and coloured with natural dyes) expect to pay 150,000Rp upwards. Wrap-around sarong blankets or *selimut* worn by men are decorated with bright, bold geometric and stylized animal and bird motifs. Try: *Toko Dharma Bakti*, Jl Sumba, or the house (21D) on the side street off Jl Soekarno near the *5 Jaya Raya Restaurant*.

Tour operators *Natrabu*, Jl Gunung Mutis 18, T21095. *Pitoby Tours*, Jl Jend Sudirman 118, T21443, F31044, branch at Jl Siliwangi 75, T21222. *Varanus*, Jl Perintis Kemerdekaan.

Transport

110 km from Soe, 283 km from Atambua

Local Bemos: there are a huge number of bemos, which must be among the noisiest and most ostentatious in Indonesia with names like James Bond and Givenchy. Routes are marked over the roof, and most ply between the city bemo terminal

(Terminal Kota Kupang) at the end of Jl Soekarno near the intersection with Jl Siliwangi, and the out-of-town bus terminal, Walikota. A board at Terminal Kota Kupang gives all routes and fares.

Air Kupang's **El Tari international airport** is 14 km northeast of town. There are taxis into the centre of town (airport taxi service T33824). **NB** Taxi drivers encourage tourists to go to hotels of their choice, saying others are full – they receive a commission. Try to ask at reception without the taxi driver in company. Bemos running between Penfui/Baumata and town pass the airport turn off – it is a 1½ km walk from the airport buildings to this spot. Connections by *Merpati* and *Bouraq* with **Jakarta**, **Dili** and **Bali**, and other destinations in **Java**, **Sulawesi**, **Nusa Tenggara**, **Irian Jaya** and **Kalimantan**. International connections with **Darwin**, Australia on Merpati. No visa required for entering Timor as it is a 'gateway' port (this applies to nationals of those countries permitted visa-free entry), but you must have an onward ticket out of Indonesia. Flights from Darwin are usually not too booked up.

Road **Bus**: the long-distance Oebobo bus terminal, better known as Walikota, is some way east of town. Regular bemos run between it, along different routes, and the central bemo terminal at the end of Jl Siliwangi. Buses from Oebobo to **Baun**, **Bolok**, **Baumata**, **Tarus Kejamenanu** (5 hrs), **Soe** (2½ hrs), **Niki Niki** (3 hrs), **Atambua** (7 hrs) and **Dili** (13 hrs), with change of bus at Atambua. *Natrans*, who run buses to Dili via Atambua have a counter at the terminal; *Tunas Mekar*, who run night buses to Dili sell tickets at Jl Siliwangi 94 (near the Terminal Kota bemo station).

Sea **Boat**: Kupang's Tenau harbour is southwest of town. Catch a bemo bound for Tenau or Bolok. The *Pelni* ships *Sirimau*, *Awu*, *Dobonsolo* and *Pangrango* visit Kupang on their 2 week circuits. The *Pelni* office is at Jl Pahlawan 3, T21944 (5 min walk west of Jl Siliwangi; a new building off, but visible from, the road). There are also a number of ferries serving surrounding ports and islands; these leave from the Bolok ferry terminal, a few km further on from Tenau. Catch a bemo bound for Bolok. The ferry office (Perum Angkutan Sungai, Danau dan Penyeberangan) is at Jl Cak Doko 20, T21140. Ferry services are as follows: **Kupang-Ba'a** (Rote) daily at 0900 (returning same day); **Kupang-Ende** (Flores) 1400 Mon and 1300 Tue (returning Wed) (about 18 hrs, ventilation in economy reportedly better than 1st class); **Kupang-Larantuka** (Flores) 1500 Sun and Wed (returning Tue and Sat); **Kupang-Savu** 1600 Wed (returning Thu); **Kupang-Kalabahi** (Alor) 1400 Tue and Sat.

Airline offices *Bouraq*, Jl Jend Sudirman 20A, T21421. *Garuda/Merpati*, Jl Kosasih 13, T21205. **Directory**
Banks Kupang is the best place to change money before Lombok/Bali. It is also possible to obtain cash advances on Visa and Mastercard. *Bank Dagang Negara*, Jl Soekarno 10, change most TCs and currencies; *Bank Rakyat Indonesia*, Jl Soekarno, *Danamon*, Jl Jend Sudirman 21, change most TCs in US$ and A$, plus major currencies cash. **Communications** General Post Office: Jl Palapa (out of centre, for poste restante). Post Office: Jl Soekarno 29 (more convenient), open Mon-Sat 0700-1600. **Telephone Offices:** Jl Urip Sumohardjoll. Perumtel, Jl Palapa. **Medical facilities** Hospitals: *General Hospital*, Jl Moh Hatta. **Useful addresses** Immigration Office: Jl Soekarno 16, T21077.

Soe

Soe is the cool, spread out capital of the regency of Timor Tengah Selatan, lying 800 m above sea-level. During the coldest months of June and July it can be chilly and a sweater is needed during the day – it is always cool at night. Soe's cooler climate means that it used to be a good apple growing area. But a few years ago the crop was devastated by a pest infestation, and it still hasn't recovered. The town is best-known for the large regional market held here every day

Phone code: 0391
Colour map 3, grid B5

of the week but it is not the most characterful of places. The *Kantor Pariwisata* **tourist office** is on Jl Kakatua. It is open from 0700-1200, some useful leaflets and a few of the staff speak some English.

Excursions The countryside around Soe represents the heartland of West Timorese culture. Typical villages can be found along the **Soe-Kefamenanu road**. There are also beautiful, traditional villages on the **Soe-Kupang road**, 20 km from Soe. ■ *Getting there: it is possible simply to hop on and off public buses. A better, though more expensive alternative, is to hire a car (about 50,000Rp per day) – see 'Local transport' below.*

Niki Niki, 30 km from Soe on the road to Kefamenanu, contains the graves of the Amanuban kings of the Nope Kingdom and also holds a good market on Wednesdays. ■ *Getting there: by bus or bemo running towards Kefa.*

Oinlasi, 50 km southeast of Niki Niki, has a fabulous market every Tuesday (0700-1400); ikat is sold here as well as various handicrafts. In the middle of the market is the *Rumah Makan Sudmampir* which does an excellent nasi goreng. ■ *Getting there: frequent buses from Soe to Oinlasi, especially on market day, 1½ hours.*

Boti is an animist village 13 km from Oinlasi, which is worth visiting for its traditional buildings (see box) and to watch lively displays of traditional dance. One dance depicts a young man coming back from a head hunting raid which used to be an initiation right and a prerequisite for marriage. The men make whooping calls to their ancestors thanking them for their assistance in battle. The participants wear a dazzling array of the local *kain* cloth. Gongs and a goat skin drum provide a musical beat. This may be followed by harmonized singing accompanied by a *lecu* (a type of guitar made from a large gourd). All the houses in the village are built in the traditional style except the Raja's house which is a wood and corrugated iron construction decorated with western

East Nusa Tenggara

Soe

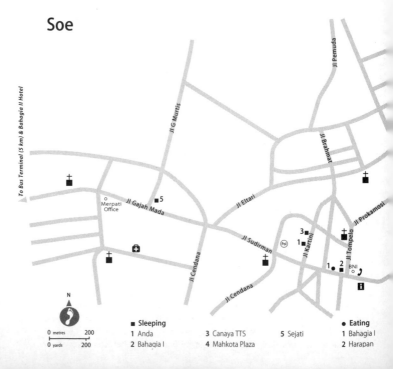

■ Sleeping			● Eating
1 Anda	3 Canaya TTS	5 Sejati	1 Bahagia I
2 Bahagia I	4 Mahkota Plaza		2 Harapan

Traditional buildings in Boti village

Ume Kbubu *is the name given to the houses so characteristic of this part of West Timor. In the area around Soe they tend to be domed, oval in shape and, with their low entrances, look rather like thatched igloos. They are used for sleeping and eating.*

Lopo – *every house has a lopo – it has an attic storage section and lower sheltered area where friends and family congregate out of the hot sun. Discs of wood on the supporting poles serve to prevent vermin from ascending into the grain storage area. A lot of time and effort obviously goes into the construction of these buildings. They are*

beautifully made and once inside you can see how ornately and neatly bound together they are in a lace work of bamboo weave and grasses. The lopo next to to the Raja's house in Boti deserves particular attention. On its pinnacle is a stylized carving of three perched birds. Birds are the Raja's 'totem'. It is believed in the village that the bloodlines of the birds and the Raja have crossed and he is therefore obliged to protect and preserve them. For this reason small birds are not hunted in the village and there are noticeably greater numbers of them about than in other areas of West Timor.

artefacts. The Raja is unusual in being monogomous. Most other leaders of Kingdoms have at least two or three wives. Married men are distinguished by their hair which is left to grow long after the marriage ceremony. **Sleeping** In the Raja's house (**E**), price includes all meals, a display of traditional dancing and a full demonstration of weaving techniques. ■ *Getting there: bus to Oinlasi and then walk 10 km from Oinlasi to Boti. Bring plenty of water. Alternatively, charter a bemo in Soe. A guide is really essential if you want to make the most of your visit, as few of the villagers speak any Bahasa.*

Oehala Waterfall is around 10 km from Soe, on route to Kapan. From the main Soe-Kapan road it is a pleasant 2 km stroll down a shady path to the cascade at the base of which is a pool where it is possible to swim. The best viewing spot from where you can see the largest number of 'steps' of the waterfall is around halfway down – the local tourist board have enterprisingly built a bench here. ■ *Getting there: take a bemo to Kapan.*

B-C *Bahagia 11*, Jl Gajah Mada, T21095. **Sleeping** The price variation reflects a variation in room size more than quality. Pricey restaurant, Merpati agent here. **C-D** *Bahagia 1*, Jl Diponegoro 72, T21015. Good restaurant (cheap) very clean rooms, some with their own mandi. **D** *Mahkota Plaza*, Jl Suharto 11 (near the bus station), T21168. Restaurant, wide range of food, very clean, light and spacious with attached bathrooms. Sometimes closed in low season. **D** *Sejati*, Jl Gajah Mada 18, T21101. Some

3 Mahkota Plaza
4 Sri Solo

East Nusa Tenggara

rooms with attached inside mandi. **E-F** *Wisma Gahaya TTS*, Jl Kartini 7, T21087. Next door to *Anda*, large clean rooms. **F** *Anda*, Jl Kartini 5, T21323. Pak Yohannes, who speaks good English and Dutch, has gone wild with the decoration of his hotel. Every surface is covered with concrete or plaster of Paris models or reliefs. There is a model helicopter on the roof and a model ship with rooms you can stay in around the back of the hotel. The facilities are rather basic but you can't say the place doesn't have character.

Eating **Cheap** *Harapan*, Jl Suharto, tasty Indonesian, Chinese and seafood; there are a few good restaurants near the market such as **Very cheap** *Sri Solo*, which serves good reasonably priced Indonesian food and *Sari Bondo*, which serves Padang food.

Transport **Local** **Car hire**: (around 50,000Rp/day). Ask at the *Mahkota Plaza Hotel*. **Road** **Bus**:
111 km from Kupang, the terminal is a little way out of town, so catch a bemo. Regular connections with
86 km from **Kupang** (2½ hrs), **Kefamenanu** (2 hrs), and **Atambua** (4 hrs). For **Dili** it is necessary to
Kefamenanu, go via Atambua.
172 km from Atambua

Directory **Airline offices** The *Merpati* agent is in the *Bahagia 11 Hotel* on Jl Gajah Mada, open 0800-1700 Mon-Sat. **Banks** It is possible to change TCs at the *BNI* near to the tourist office on Jl Diponegoro.

Kefamenanu

Phone code: 0391 Kefamenanu, known as 'Kefa' to the local people, is the capital of the regency
Colour map 3, grid B5 of Timor Tengah Utara. It lies between Timor's northern and southern mountain ranges and, like Soe, is a highland town. It lies at an altitude of 400 m, and
experiences chilly nights. During June and July, the coldest months, a sweater
may be needed in the evenings. The town has simple accommodation and can
be used as a base to explore the surrounding countryside. There is a **tourist
office** with some interesting leaflets on Jl Sudirman.

Excursions The area around Kefamenanu is rarely visited by tourists. There are numerous
traditional villages and towns including **Maslete** (4 km south) and the hill
village of **Nilulat**.

However, possibly the most memorable village is **Tamkesi**– situated at the
heart of the Biboki Kingdom. Over seventy thousand people are members of
the Kingdom but only 12 families are able to inhabit this central village.
Despite the abolition of Kingdoms in 1958 by the central Indonesian government, two men still dominate the village – the King (the administrative leader)
and the Kaiser (the spiritual leader). They can no longer sentence men to
death, as was previously the case, but the respect they command is undimin-
ished. It is polite to bring gifts to the villagers such as betel nut and tobacco.
Biboki textiles are famous for their combination of embroidery and ikat (resist
dyed thread). Producing these traditional textiles is highly skilled work and
they are consequently expensive (expect to pay over 30,000Rp for a scarf and
more than 300,000Rp for a good quality piece). ■ *Getting there: catch a bus the
42 km to Manafui from the main Kefa terminal. From Manafui it is a tough 8 km
walk to Tamakesi. A guide who can speak Dawanese is needed, as very few villagers can speak Bahasa.*

Kua Popnam or Popnam cave, is filled with stalagmites and stalagtites.
■ *Getting there: take a bemo from the market to Tua Mese from where it is a 4 km
walk along a good path.* The nearby **Taekas** village has some excellent examples of *lopo* (see box) and traditional Timorese houses.

Oelolok village has a good Tuesday market and is 25 km from Kefa.
■ *Getting there: take a bemo from the market place.*

B-D *Ariesta*, Jl Basuki Rakhmat 29, good clean rooms, some with a/c, an amusing version of a *lopo* with coloured lights is in the back garden, friendly staff. Recommended. **C-D** *Cendana*, Jl Sonbai, T31168. Some a/c, attractive rooms arranged around a small garden. Restaurant in complex or the staff will take you free of charge to a restaurant in town. **E** *Setankai*, Jl Sonbai, T21217. Communal mandi, basic and rather dirty. **E** *Sokowindu*, Jl Pattimura, T31122. Central place, communal mandi, basic but clean rooms.

Sleeping

Cheap *Rumah Makan Padang*, the best restaurant in town. **Very cheap** *Rumah Makan Ayam Kalasan*, Jl Basuki Rachmat 9, T21212. Chicken dishes. *Rumah Makan Sari Bondo*, Jl Sonbai, Padang food. *Stella Maris*, Jl Kartini, Indonesian food. *Warung Pojok*, Jl Kartini, Indonesian food.

Eating

November 30: **Culture and Art Festival**. Traditional dances, music, food and handicrafts on show and on sale.

Festivals

There is a NGO-run ikat shop on the northern edge of town which buys cloth at a fair price from villagers and sells it on without a huge mark up. It is part of the OXFAM fair trading initiative.

Shopping

Road **Bus**: regular connections with Soe 2 hrs, Kupang 4½ hrs Atambua 1½ hrs, and Dili. To get to Oecussi catch the bus from the market place in the centre of town. For other destinations it is necessary to go to the main bus terminal whcih is 1 km south of town. Bemos run to and from here.

Transport
197 km from Kupang, 86 km from Soe, 86 km from Atambua, 60 km from Oecussi

Banks The *Bank Danomon* on the corner of Jl Keniri and Jl Kartini can only change US$ banknotes and does so at a poor rate. **Communications** Post Office: Jl Imam Bonjol. Telkom Office: near *Hotel Ariesta*.

Directory

Atambua and the Belu Region

The Belu Region borders East Timor; the area around Atambua itself shares a common language with the East Timorese – *tetun* – the main variations of which are the highland and lowland versions rather than a sharp east/west distinction. The cloth woven in the part of the Belu region bordering East Timor is predominantly striped red with sections of ikat. They are often a combination of hand dyed and shop dyed thread. In the *bunak* speaking region around Weluli the cloth is predominantly black.

Phone code: 0389
Colour map 3, grid B6

The Belu Region

The capital of the Belu Region, **Atambua**, is the second largest town in West Timor, after Kupang. It is set at an altitude of 350 m and is the last significant settlement before crossing from West Timor into East Timor. The majority of the population is Catholic. The heart of the town is just 200 m from the bus terminal. The market area is close to the terminal, and there is also a good range of restaurants, hotels, shops and supermarkets. Atambua's port of Atapupu is 24 km north of town. Travellers going by bus between Kupang and Dili have to change here.

Safety warning In September 2000 three UN staff were killed in Atambra. UN forces in East Timor airlifted other UN personnel out of the area. When this book went to press, travel in this part of West Timor was not recommended.

Excursions **Atapupu**, Atambua's port 24 km north of town is little more than a fishing village and is worth visiting if there is time to kill. The coast here is protected by mangroves. In **Mota Ain** village, reached by bemo from Atapupu travelling towards East Timor, the local people extract salt from seawater using ancient brick ovens. Around 15 km west of Atapupu is **Octopus Bay** or *Kolam Gurita*. This is reportedly home to a wide range of fauna including crocodiles. ■ *Getting there: regular buses head for Atapupu from the terminal.*

Betun is an attractively located town 60 km from Atambua. On the approach to Betun from Atambua the road passes through beautiful scenery including through a protected forest. Eight kilometres from Betun is **Masinlulik** where there are bubbling mud pools or *lumpur yang mindialih*. There is a small hotel here, **D** *Sesawi*, which serves a simple breakfast and has a little shop attached. Kingdoms persisted in the Belu region until 1958 when they were officially dissolved by the government in Jakarta. Wehali, the mother kingdom, was very extensive

Atambua

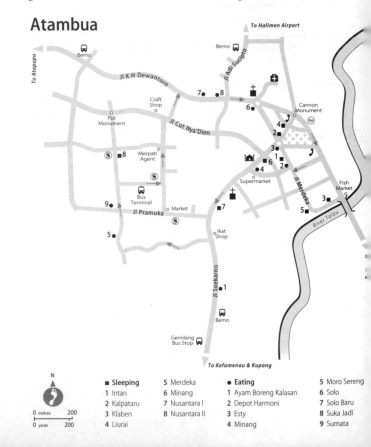

■ Sleeping	5 Merdeka	● Eating	5 Moro Sereng
1 Intan	6 Minang	1 Ayam Boreng Kalasan	6 Solo
2 Kalpataru	7 Nusantara I	2 Depot Harmoni	7 Solo Baru
3 Klaben	8 Nusantara II	3 Esty	8 Suka Jadi
4 Liurai		4 Minang	9 Sumata

East Nusa Tenggara

stretching over the entire area of Timor and (at least in the eyes of the local people) including all the islands as far west as Flores. Laran just south of Betun was the centre of the kingdom. ■ *Getting there: buses to Betun run from the bus terminal.*

C-D *Intan*, Jl Merdeka 12A, T21343. Some a/c, very attractive clean rooms, morning and afternoon snacks included. The staff speak some English. **C-D** *Nusantara 11*, Jl IJ Kasimo, T21773. Some a/c, very clean arranged around a garden, the hotel is near the market. **D** *Kalpataru*, Jl Jend Subroto 3. Very clean and attractive hotel, good clean communal mandi. Pak Blaas, the owner, is a mine of information and speaks good English, good value. Recommended. **D** *Minang*, Jl Sukarno 12A, T21379. Communal mandi, simple but clean, restaurant attached. **D** *Nusantara 1*, Jl Sukarno 42, T21377. Small, rather run-down looking rooms and on the main road so quite noisy. **D-E** *Liurai*, Jl Sudirman 4, T21804. Simple but fairly clean rooms, building work appears to be in progress. **E** *Klaben*, Jl Dubesianau 4, T21079. Rather dingy.

Cheap *Esty*, next to *Intan Hotel*, serves good seafood. **Very cheap** *Depot Harmoni*, Chinese and Indonesian food. *Padang*, best Indonesian food in town. *Minang*, Jl Sukarno, serves a reange of basic Padang food. *Solo Baru*, Jl Kihagar Dewantoro, good cheap Indonesian food, popular with locals. *Suka Jadi*, Jl Kihagar Dewantoro, good Indonesian food, popular with locals.

Eating

There is a **craft shop** on Jl Cut Nya'Dien and a shop specializing in *ikat* on Jl Sukarno. **Local Bemos**: follow the routes shown on the street map.

Shopping
Transport
279 km from Kupang, 169 km from Soe, 121 km from Oecussi, 86 km from Kefamenanu

Air Atambua has an airstrip but unfortunately no flights. **Bus** Regular connections with **Atapupu** (45 mins), **Kupang** (7 hrs), **Soe** (4½ hrs), **Kefamenanu** (2 hrs), and **Dili** (4 hrs). **Boat** *Pelni* operate a ship which circuits between **Kupang** and **Dili** via Atapupu (Atambua's port), 24 km north of town. On Mon a ferry arrives from **Kalabahi** on Alor, returning to Kalabahi the same day. **NB** This schedule is subject to frequent change.

Airline offices *Merpati* agent near the market. **Banks** It is only possible to change US$ banknotes at the *BRI* and *BNI* branches in town – there is nowhere on Timor outside Kupang or Dili which can change TCs. **Communications** Telephone offices: there is a 24 hr *Wartel* telephone office on Jl Gatot Subroto and a Telkom office on the east side of town.

Directory

Roti (Rote)

*Roti Island, or Rote, just off the southwest tip of Timor, is administered as part of the regency of Kupang. It covers 1,214 sq km and has a population of nearly 100,000. The capital is the town of **Ba'a**, situated almost midway up the north coast of the island. The villages both northeast and southwest from Ba'a are worth visiting for their markets and traditional architecture. Oeseli Beach, 58 km southwest from Ba'a is good for swimming.*

Colour map 3, grid C3

Ins and outs

The airport is 8 km from Ba'a. There are 2 flights/week on *Merpati* from Kupang (30 mins) but the service is unreliable. The ferry dock is at Pante Baru, about 30 km northeast of Ba'a; bemos wait to take passengers to the capital. The *Pelni* vessel *Pangrango* leaves from Kupang's Bolok harbour every day at 0900, returning the same day in the early afternoon, 4 hrs.

Getting there

Getting around There is a direct bus from Pante Baru (the port) to Nembrala on Tue and Fri, or hire a car or motorcycle for the day.

Background

As on Savu, the lontar palm is the traditional subsistence crop here (see page 398). The tradition of making working clothes from the fibres of the lontar palm has now died out, but some people still continue to make shrouds for the dead from the fibres. At birth, each Rotinese baby is given, when it cries, a drop of Roti sugar – presumably indicating the former importance of the lontar palm to the islanders' collective livelihoods. The Rotinese supplement their income by fishing and jewellery making.

The western tip of the island is currently reasonably untouched as a result of its relative inaccessibility. To get there is is necessary to make an arduous four hour bus journey along a poor road. The beach itself stretches as far as the eye can see and the sea is crystal clear. The area is also very popular with surfers. Locals already say that Rote today is akin to the Kuta of the 1960s, though it would be a pity to see this remote region so aggressively commercialized.

Rotinese locals customarily gather in the late afternoon, avoiding the intense heat of the day to make their habitual evening stroll around the town centre which follows the mandatory afternoon siesta.

Around the island

Nemberala Nemberala (or Dela) village, on the west coast, about 35 km from Ba'a, is close to the main surfing beach and there are a handful of homestays here for the really adventurous surfer. The best months for surfing are reputed to be from April to September. Nemberala village itself is centred around a football pitch and a volley ball court both of which spring to life every evening as the more active residents get involved in matches. ■ *Getting there: a bus meets the ferry from Kupang at Pante Baru (the port) and takes passengers direct to Namberala. Alternatively hire a motorbike in Ba'a.*

Excursions **Ndana Island** is a tiny island just south of Roti, reportedly home to a wide range of wildlife including a population of turtles. There is also a red lake which according to legend is stained by the blood of the people of Ndana who were massacred by a neighbouring tribe. ■ *Getting there: there is not yet a regular ferry service but a boat can be chartered in Nemberala for about 100,000Rp for up to 6 people.*

Sleeping **At Ba'a**: **E** *Kesia*, Jl Pabean, restaurant, attached mandi. **E** *Ricky's*, Jl Gereja, near the mosque, some fans, some a/c, attached mandi. **E-F** *Hotel Wisata Karya*, Jl Kartini 1, clean rooms with shared facilities, well priced.

At Nemberala: **B** *Nemberala Beach*, just outside the village on the beach, comfortable place with a/c and satellite TV. **E** *Anugara*, includes all meals which are of an excellent standard, good mosquito nets. The nearest place to the best surf and very popular with surfers. **E** *Mr Thomas Homestay*, room rate includes all meals (and good ones) as well as tea, coffee and drinking water. **E** *Tirosa*, includes all meals, communal mandi, operated by the village headman.

Shopping **Textiles** The Rotinese produce a distinctive ikat, which is strongly influenced by *patola* cloth – Gujarati cloth from India which was imported in large quantities from the 16th century. Patola motifs – floral designs, diagonal crosses – were incorporated into the traditional textiles of the island, as they were through much of Nusa Tenggara. Cloth is often decorated with flower motifs using red, white, brown and black hues. Unfortunately, there are few weavers left on Roti now – many of the local people have left the island, seeking work in Kupang – and it is becoming hard to find good cloth.

Airline offices *Merpati* agent on Jl Pabean in Ba'a. **Banks** Not possible to change TCs on Roti, only US$. **Directory**

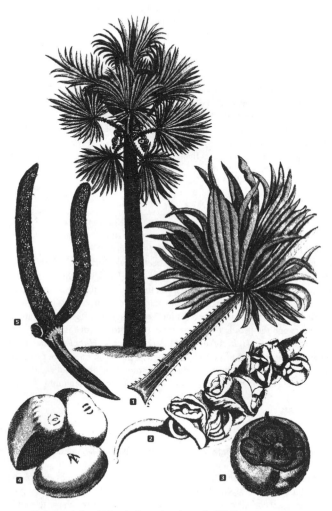

East Nusa Tenggara

The lontar palm from G E Rumphius' *Het Amboinsche Kruydboek* (1741)

1 Leafstalk
2 Female inflorescence with young fruit
3 The fruit
4 Three seeds
5 Male inflorescence with tiny flowers

Savu (Sabu, Sawu)

Colour map 3, grid C1   *Savu Island, also spelt Sabu and Sawu, lies over 250 km west of Kupang, but is still part of the regency of Kupang. The island covers 460 sq km and supports a population of about 50,000 people, predominantly Protestants. The 'capital' of the island is the town of **Seba**, which has an airport and a dock. The dry season here extends over 7 months (April-October), sometimes longer, and the rains are intermittant. It is a dry, barren and unproductive island. Its geographical isolation means that few tourists get here and it is relatively untouched.*

Ins and outs

Getting there   There is 1 (perhaps 2), flights/week on *Merpati* from Kupang to Seba town (via Roti); the service is unreliable, enquire at *Merpati* office. Boats dock at Seba on the north coast. The *Pelni* vessel *Pangrango* leaves Kupang's Bolok harbour twice a week for Savu, on Tue and Fri (at 1600), returning to Kupang the following day, 8 hrs. Once a week, on Fri, a ferry docks from Waingapu (Sumba), returning to Waingapu and then continuing on to Ende (Flores). There are also other, irregular, departures from Kupang's Tenau harbour.

Background

Traditionally, the slow-growing lontar palm (*Borassus sundaicus*) has met the subsistence needs of the population. The sape from this tree, known as *tuak*, is drunk fresh, made into cakes of red sugar (*gulu merah*), boiled into a sugary syrup (*gula air*) or fermented into palm beer (*iaru*) which can be further distilled to produce a kind of sweet gin known as *sopi*. The fruit of the tree is eaten, its wood is used for boats and houses, and the leaves for thatching. In the past leaves were also spun to make cloth and pulped for paper.

    The women of Savu produce a distinct warp ikat cloth. It is said that about 300 years ago the people of Savu were divided into two distinct clans – the Greater Blossoms (*Hubi' Ae*) and the Lesser Blossoms (*Hubi' Ike*) – based on female blood lines. Within each clan there were several sub-groups called Seeds (*Wini*). Each group wove distinctive motifs on their cloth and even today, local people can recognize cloth and its origin by its clan motif.

Essentials

Sleeping   Basic, friendly accommodation in Seba, with little to choose between them. **E** *Makarim Homestay.* **E** *Ongko Da'i Homestay.* **E** *Petykuswan Homestay.*

Shopping   **Textiles**: a distinctive warp ikat cloth is hand-woven on Savu, in bands of floral and geometric designs, set against a dark indigo and rust ground. The Savunese sarung is known as the *si hawu*, while the *higi huri* is a blanket. Men's clothing has tended to keep more faithfully to traditional designs, while women have been happy to incorporate western-inspired motifs such as vases of flowers, birds and rampant lions.

Background

6

400

Background

402   History

410   Modern Indonesia

Indonesia was created more by historical accident than by design. The East Indies – as it was then – was haphazardly pieced together by the Dutch over a period of three centuries: from 1610 when they gained their first toehold in the Spice Islands of Maluku, an area of magical wealth in the eyes of contemporary Europeans, through to the early decades of the 20th century when West Irian (Irian Jaya/West Papua) was finally incorporated. The result, by the outbreak of the Second World War, was a vast, sprawling territory of diverse people cemented by little more than the colonial glue of the Dutch. That this artificial creation should have survived intact is one of the greatest achievements of Indonesian independence – and, to some, one of its greatest surprises. (Indonesia's motto is Bhinneka Tunggal Ika, *officially – and rather loosely – translated as 'Unity in Diversity'.) The fact that now, after half a century of independence, Indonesia is at risk of disintegrating is a source of delight for some, and horror for many.*

While Bali and the Eastern Isles are just a very small slice of Greater Indonesia, their history, economy, society and politics are tied up with those of the wider country. This background section on the history and politics of Indonesia is designed to provide the bigger picture, complementing the more detailed island-specific information in each of the book's 'travelling' chapters.

History

Prehistory

After Thailand and East Malaysia, Indonesia – and particularly Java – has probably revealed more of Southeast Asia's prehistory than any other country in the region. Most significant was the discovery of **hominid fossils** in Central Java in 1890, when Eugene Dubois uncovered the bones of so-called 'Java Man' near the village of Trinil. He named his ape-man *Pithecanthropus erectus*, since changed to *Homo erectus erectus*. These, and other discoveries – particularly at Sangiran, also in Central Java and Mojokerto – indicate that Indonesia was inhabited by hominids as long as 1.8 million years ago. Excavations in Central Java have also revealed other fossils of early Man – *Pithecanthropus soloensis* and *P modjokertensis*. Among the skulls of *P soloensis* a number has been found to have had their cranial bases removed, leading scientists to postulate that the species practised anthropophagy – less politely known as cannibalism – which involved gouging the brains out through the base. Alternatively, the surgery might have been part of a post mortem ritual.

Following the end of the last Ice Age 15,000 years ago, there began a movement of Mongoloid peoples from the Asian mainland, south and east, and into the Southeast Asian archipelago. As this occurred, the immigrants displaced the existing Austro-melanesian inhabitants, pushing them further east or into remote mountain areas.

The practice of **settled agriculture** seems to have filtered into the islands of Indonesia from mainland Southeast Asia about 2,500 BC, along with these Mongoloid migrants. Settled life is associated with the production of primitive earthenware pottery, examples of which have been found in Java, Sulawesi and Flores. Later, **ancestor cults** evolved, echoes of which are to be seen in the megaliths of Sumatra, Java, Sulawesi, Bali, Sumbawa and Sumba. These cultures reached their height about 500 BC. Among the various discoveries has been evidence of the mutilation of corpses – presumably to prevent the deceased from returning to the world of the living. In some cases, ritual elements of these megalithic cultures still exist – for example on the island of Sumba in Nusa Tenggara, among the inhabitants of Nias Island off West Sumatra, and among the Batak of North Sumatra.

The technology of **bronze casting** was also known to prehistoric Indonesians. Socketed axes have been discovered in Java, several islands of Nusa Tenggara (eg Roti) and in Sulawesi. But the finest bronze artefacts are the magnificent kettledrums of East Indonesia (see page 144). It is thought these were made in Vietnam, not in Indonesia, and arrived in the archipelago when traders used them as barter goods. Later, locally made equivalents such as the *moko* of Alor (see page 363) were produced, but they never achieved the refinement of the originals.

Pre-colonial history

Unlike the states of mainland Southeast Asia which did enjoy a certain geographical legitimacy prior to the colonial period, Indonesia was a fragmented assemblage of kingdoms, sultanates, principalities and villages. It is true that there was a far greater degree of communication and intercourse than many assume, so that no part of the archipelago can be treated in isolation but nonetheless, it is still difficult to talk of 'Indonesian' history prior to the 19th century.

The great empires of the pre-colonial period did range beyond their centres of power, but none came close to controlling all the area now encompassed by the modern Indonesian state. Among these empires, the most powerful were the

Major pre-colonial powers

Srivijaya	7th–14th	Palembang
Sailendra	8th–10th	Central Java
Sanjaya	8th–11th	Central & East Java
Kediri	11th–13th	Kediri, East Java
Banten	12th–17th	Banten, West Java
Singasari	13th	East Java
Majapahit	3th–15th	East Java
Gowa	16th–17th	Makassar, South Sulawesi
Mataram	16th–18th	Central Java
Aceh	16th–19th	Aceh, North Sumatra
Karangkasem	18th–19th	Bali & Lombok

Srivijayan Kingdom based at Palembang in South Sumatra; and the great Javanese Dynasties of Sailendra, Majapahit and Mataram. There was also a string of less powerful, but nonetheless influential, kingdoms: for example, the sultanate of Aceh in North Sumatra, the Gowa Kingdom of South Sulawesi, the trading sultanates of the Spice Islands of Maluku, and the Hindu kingdoms of Bali. The history of each of these powers is dealt with in the appropriate regional introduction.

Even after the European powers arrived in the archipelago, their influence was often superficial. They were concerned only with controlling the valuable spice trade, and were not inclined to feats of territorial expansion. To get around this lack of a common history, historians tend to talk instead in terms of common processes of change. The main ones affecting the archipelago were the 'Indianization' of the region from the 1st century AD and the introduction of Hinduism and Buddhism; the arrival of Islam in North Sumatra in the 13th century and then its spread east and south during the 15th century; and the contrast between inwardly focused agricultural kingdoms and outwardly orientated trading states.

Colonial history

During the course of the 15th century, the two great European maritime powers of the time, Spain and Portugal, were exploring sea routes to the East. Two forces were driving this search: the desire for profits, and the drive to evangelize. At the time, even the wealthy in Europe had to exist on pickled and salted fish and meat during the winter months (fodder crops for winter feed were not grown until the 18th century). Spices to flavour what would otherwise be a very monotonous diet were greatly sought after and commanded a high price. This was not just a passing European fad. An Indian Hindu wrote that: "When the palate revolts against the insipidness of rice boiled with no other ingredients, we dream of fat, salt and spices".

Of the spices, cloves and nutmeg originated from just one location, the Moluccas (Maluku) – the Spice Islands of eastern Indonesia. Perhaps because of their value, spices and their places of origin were accorded mythical status in Europe. The 14th century French friar Catalani Jordanus claimed, for example, that the clove flowers of Java produced an odour so strong it killed "every man who cometh among them, unless he shut his mouth and nostrils".

It was in order to break the monopoly on the spice trade held by Venetian and Muslim Arab traders that the Portuguese began to extend their possessions eastwards. This finally culminated in the capture of the port of Melaka by the Portuguese seafarer Alfonso de Albuquerque in June 1511. The additional desire to spread the Word of God is clear in the speech that Albuquerque made before the battle with the Muslim sultan of Melaka, when he exhorted his men, stressing:

"... the great service which we shall perform to our Lord in casting the Moors out of this country and of quenching the fire of the sect of Mohammet so that it may never burst out again hereafter".

From their base in Melaka, the Portuguese established trading relations with the Moluccas, and built a series of forts across the region: at Bantam (Banten), Flores, Ternate, Tidore, Timor and Ambon (Amboyna).

Many accounts of Indonesian history treat the arrival of the Portuguese Admiral Alfonso de Albuquerque off Malacca (Melaka) in 1511, and the dispatch of a small fleet to the Spice Islands, as a watershed in Indonesian history. As the historian MC Ricklefs argues, this view is untenable, writing that "... in the early years of the Europeans' presence, their influence was sharply limited in both area and depth".

The Portuguese only made a significant impact in the Spice Islands, leaving their mark in a number of Indonesian words of Portuguese origin – for example, *sabun* (soap), *meja* (table) and *Minggu* (Sun). They also introduced Christianity to East Indonesia and disrupted the islands' prime export – spices. But it was the Dutch, in the guise of the *Vereenigde Oost-Indische Compagnie* or *VOC* (the Dutch East India Company), who began the process of Western intrusion. They established a toehold in Java – which the Portuguese had never done – a precursor to later territorial expansion (see box). But this was a slow process and it was not until the early 20th century – barely a generation before the Japanese occupation – that the Dutch could legitimately claim they held administrative authority over the whole country.

The idea of Indonesia, 1900-42

The beginning of the 20th century marks a turning point in Indonesian history. As Raden Kartini, a young educated Javanese woman, wrote in a letter dated 12 January 1900: "Oh, it is splendid just to live in this age; the transition of the old into the new!" It was in 1899 that the Dutch lawyer C Th van Deventer published a ground-breaking paper entitled *Een eereschuld* or 'A debt of honour'. This article argued that having exploited the East Indies for so long, and having extracted so much wealth from the colony, it was time for the Dutch government to restructure their policies and focus instead on improving conditions for Indonesians. In 1901, the Ethical Policy – as it became known – was officially embraced. Van Deventer was commissioned to propose ways to further such a policy and suggested a formulation of "education, irrigation and emigration". The Ethical Policy represented a remarkable change in perspective, but scholars point out that it was very much a creation of the European mind and made little sense in Indonesian terms.

Locals bringing nutmeg to sell to Dutch factors in Banda, the Moluccas, 1599.

The VOC – the world's first multinational

The Dutch East India Company was a unique enterprise at the time of its creation in 1601. Not only was the company based on long-term investment at a time when most trading investment lasted only as long as the voyage, but it also linked together a series of forts and factories across the globe manned by employees from many different countries. This global reach and the cosmopolitan nature of its employees has led some historians to pronounce the VOC to be the world's first multinational company.

Although the VOC was a private enterprise – a joint stock company with founding capital of 6.5 million guilders – the Dutch Republic also saw it as an agent of national policy and provided cannon and arms free of charge for the defence of its ships. The company reached the peak of its powers at the end of the 17th century, when it had 22 factories scattered across Asia, and 11,500 employees. In the decade between 1700 and 1710, 280 VOC ships sailed from Holland eastwards.

It is usually said that sloppy management led to the demise of the VOC but this was undoubtedly amplified by the effects of the Fourth Anglo-Dutch War (1780-1784) when English men-of-war seized most VOC vessels sailing for home. In 1795 the Company was nationalized and at the end of the century it had accumulated debts of 219 million guilders.

The Indonesian economy was also changing in character. The diffusion of the cash economy through the islands and the growing importance of export crops like rubber and coffee, and minerals such as tin and oil, were transforming the country. Christianity, too, became a powerful force for change, particularly in the islands beyond Muslim Java. There was large-scale conversion in central and North Sulawesi, Flores, among the Batak of Sumatra, in Kalimantan, and Timor. In response to the inroads that Christianity was making in the Outer Islands, Islam in Java became more orthodox and reformist. The 'corrupt' *abangan* who adhered to what has become known as the 'Javanese religion' – a mixture of Muslim, Hindu, Buddhist and animist beliefs – were gradually displaced by the stricter *santris*.

At about the same time, there was an influx of *trekkers*, or Dutch expatriates, who came to the East Indies with their wives and Dutch cultural perspectives, with the intention of going 'home' after completing their contracts. They overwhelmed the older group of *blijvers* or 'stayers', and there emerged a more racist European culture, one that denigrated *Indische* culture and extolled the life-style of the Dutch. The Chinese community, like the Dutch, was also divided into two groups: the older immigrants or *peranakan* who had assimilated into Indies culture, and the more recent *totok* arrivals who zealously maintained their culture, clinging to their Chinese roots (see box, page 418).

So, the opening years of the 20th century presented a series of paradoxes. On the one hand, Dutch policy was more sensitive to the needs of the 'natives'; yet many Dutch were becoming less understanding of Indonesian culture and more bigoted. At the same time, while the Chinese and Dutch communities were drawing apart from the native Indonesians and into distinct communities based upon Chinese and European cultural norms; so the economy was becoming increasingly integrated and international. Perhaps inevitably, tensions arose and these began to mould the social and political landscape of confrontation between the colonialists and the natives.

A number of political parties and pressure groups emerged from this maelstrom of forces. In 1912, a Eurasian – one of those who found himself ostracized from European-colonial culture – EFE Douwes Dekker founded the Indies Party. This was a revolutionary grouping with the slogan 'the Indies for those who make their home there'. In the same year, a batik merchant from Surakarta established the Sarekat Islam or 'Islamic Union', which quickly became a mass organization under the leadership of the charismatic orator HOS Cokroaminoto. Seven years later it had over 2 million members. In 1914, a small group of *totok* Dutch immigrants founded the Indies Social-Democratic Association in Semarang. Finally, in 1920 the Perserikatan Komunis di India (PKI) or the Indies Communist Party was established.

In 1919, the Dutch colonial authorities decided to clamp down on all dissent. The flexibility that had characterized Dutch policy until then was abandoned in favour of an increasingly tough approach. But despite the rounding-up of large numbers of subversives, and the demise of the PKI and emasculation of the Sarekat Islam, it was at this time that the notion of 'Indonesia' first emerged. In July 1927, Sukarno founded the Partai Nasional Indonesia or PNI. In October 1928 a Congress of Indonesian Youth coined the phrase "one nation – Indonesia, one people – Indonesian, one language – Indonesian". At the same congress the Indonesian flag was designed and the Indonesian national anthem sung for the first time – *Indonesia Raya*. As John Smail writes in the book *In Search of Southeast Asia*:

"The idea of Indonesia spread so easily, once launched, that it seemed to later historians as if it had always existed, if not actually explicitly then inchoate in the hearts of the people. But it was, in fact, a new creation, the product of a great and difficult leap of the imagination. The idea of Indonesia required the denial of the political meaning of the societies into which the first Indonesians had been born".

In spite of Dutch attempts to stifle the nationalist spirit, it spread through Indonesian, and particularly Javanese, society. By 1942 when the Japanese occupied the country, the idea of Indonesia as an independent nation was firmly rooted.

The Japanese occupation, 1942-45 Although the Japanese occupation lasted less than four years, it fundamentally altered the forces driving the country towards independence. Prior to 1942, the Dutch faced no real challenge to their authority; after 1945 it was only a question of time before independence. The stunning victory of the Japanese in the Dutch East Indies destroyed the image of colonial invincibility, undermined the prestige of the Dutch among many Indonesians, and – when the Dutch returned to power after 1945 – created an entirely new psychological relationship between rulers and ruled.

But the Japanese were not liberators. Their intention of creating a Greater East Asia Co-Prosperity Sphere did not include offering Indonesians independence. They wished to control Indonesia for their own interests. The Japanese did give a certain latitude to nationalist politicians in Java, but only as a means of mobilizing Indonesian support for their war effort. Sukarno and Muhammad Hatta were flown to Tokyo in November 1943 and decorated by Emperor Hirohito. For the Dutch and their allies, the war meant incarceration. There were 170,000 internees, including 60,000 women and children. About a quarter died in captivity.

One particularly sordid side of the occupation which has come to light in recent years is the role of 'comfort women'. This euphemism should be more accurately translated as 'sex slaves' – women who were forced to satisfy the needs of Japanese soldiers to aid the war effort. For years the Japanese government denied such comfort stations existed, but documents unearthed in Japan have indicated beyond doubt that they were very much part of the war infrastructure. Much of the attention has focused upon comfort women from Korea, China and the Philippines, but there were also stations in Indonesia. These women, so long cowed and humiliated into silence, are now talking about their experiences to force the Japanese government to accept responsibility. Dutch-Australian Jan Ruff is one of these brave women. A young girl living in Java before the war, she was interned in Camp Ambarawa with her mother and two sisters. In February 1944 she was taken, along with nine other girls, to a brothel in Semarang for the sexual pleasure of Japanese officers. In her testimony at a public meeting in Tokyo in December 1992 she recounted: "During that time [at the brothel] the Japanese had abused me and humiliated me. They had ruined my young life. They had stripped me of everything, my self-esteem, my dignity, my freedom, my possessions, my family." Belatedly, the Japanese government offered its "sincere apologies and remorse" in August 1993, 48 years afterwards. The fact that the apology came on the last day of the Liberal Democratic Party's period of government detracted from the honesty of the remarks. Many still feel that Japanese leaders find it difficult to be sincere about events almost half a century old.

As the Japanese military lost ground in the Pacific to the advancing Americans, so their rule over Indonesia became increasingly harsh. Peasants were forcibly recruited as 'economic soldiers' to help the war effort – about 75,000 died – and the Japanese were even firmer in their suppression of dissent than the Dutch had been

Expansion of Dutch influence and control

Establishment	Date of of Control*
Maluku	1610
Java	1811
Kalimantan	1863
Lombok	1894
Sumatra	1903
Sulawesi	1905
Nusa Tenggara	1907
Bali	1908
Irian Jaya	1928

Marking the approximate date when the Dutch achieved effective control over the area. Note that, even so, many areas remained isolated from Dutch administration.

Background

before them. But as the military situation deteriorated, the Japanese gradually came to realize the necessity of allowing nationalist sentiments greater rein. On 7 September 1944, Prime Minister Koiso promised independence, and in March 1945 the creation of an Investigating Committee for Preparatory Work for Indonesian Independence was announced. Among its members were Sukarno, Hatta and Muhammad Yamin. On 1 June Sukarno mapped out his philosophy of Pancasila or Five Principles which were to become central tenets of independent Indonesia. On 15 August, after the second atomic bomb was dropped on Nagasaki, the Japanese unconditionally surrendered. Sukarno, Hatta, and the other independence leaders now had to act quickly before the Allies helped the Dutch re-establish control. On 17 August 1945 Sukarno read out the Declaration of Independence, Indonesia's red and white flag was raised and a small group of onlookers sang the national anthem, Indonesia Raya.

In September 1945, the first units of the British Army landed at Jakarta to re-impose Dutch rule. They arrived to find an Indonesian administration already in operation. Confrontation was inevitable. Young Indonesians responded by joining the revolutionary struggle, which became known as the Pemuda Movement (*pemuda* means youth). This reached its height between 1945 and mid-1946, and brought together young men and women of all classes, binding them together in a common cause. The older nationalists found themselves marginalized in this increasingly violent and fanatical response. Men like Sukarno and Hatta adopted a policy of *diplomasi* – negotiating with the Dutch. The supporters of the Pemuda Movement embraced *perjuangan* – the armed struggle. Not only the Dutch, but also minorities like the Chinese, Eurasians and Ambonese suffered from atrocities at the hands of the Pemuda supporters. The climax of the Pemuda Movement came in November 1945 with the battle for Surabaya.

Revolutionary struggle, 1945-50

In 1947, the Dutch were militarily strong enough to regain control of Java, and East and South Sumatra. At the end of 1948, a second thrust of this 'Police Action', re-established control over much of the rest of the country. Ironically, these military successes played an important role in the final 'defeat' of the Dutch in Indonesia. They turned the United Nations against Holland, forcing the Dutch government to

● ●

☞ A stroll along Jalan history

Many important figures in Indonesia's independence movement, as well as heroes from history, have lent their names to thoroughfares throughout the archipelago.

Abdul Muis – Sumatran independence writer.

Jend A Yani, Brig Jend Sutoyo, Lets Jend Haryono, Panjaitan, South Parman, and **Suprapto** – were the six generals (along with one captain) killed on 30 September 1965 in the attempted PKI coup (see page 409).

Cik di Tiro (1836-91) – most famous of the ulamas or religious leaders who led the resistance against the Dutch in Aceh.

Cokroaminoto (1882-1934) – a leader of the Sareket Islam (Islamic Union), the first mass organization to be established in Indonesia in 1912. He was a forceful orator and highlighted numerous grievances against the Dutch.

Diponegoro, Prince (1785-1855) – led the Java War of 1825-30 against the Dutch, was captured in 1830 and then exiled to Manado and Ujung Pandang in Sulawesi where he died.

Gajah Mada – famous Prime Minister of the Majapahit Kingdom who served from 1331-64 during the first 14 years of Hayam Wuruk's reign. Gajah Mada University in Yogya is one of the country's premier universities.

Haji Agus Salim – leader of the political Reform Islam movement, and right-hand man to Cokroaminoto.

Hang Tuah – naval hero who's exploits are immortalized and glorified in the Sejarah Malayu (Malay History), the literary mastalay world. Hang is an honorific equivalent of 'Sir'.

Hasanuddin (r.1653-69) – Sultan of Gowa in South Sulawesi who resisted the Dutch.

Hayam Wuruk (r.1350-89) – less well known as King Rajasanagara, he presided over Majapahit's golden age.

Imam Bonjol (1772-1864) – the most influential leader of the religious Padri movement in West Sumatra. He was captured by the Dutch in 1837 and exiled to Priangan, then to Ambon and finally to Manado where he died in 1864.

Jendral Sudirman (1915-50) – Islamic teacher who became an officer in the Japanese volunteer army Peta (Pembela Tanah Air, Protectors of the Fatherland) and later a leading force in the revolution.

Kartini, Raden Ajeng (1879-1904) – the daughter of a noble bupati, educated at a European lower school in Jepara, Kartini is seen as an early Indonesian suffragette. She tragically died in childbirth at the age of 25. Her moving letters have been published in Dutch (Door duisternis tot licht – 'Through Darkness into Light') and in English (Letters of a Javanese Princess).

Majapahit – the Java-based empire.

Pattimura (1783-1817) – a Christian Ambonese soldier whose proper name was Thomas Matulesia and who led a rebellion against the Dutch from Saparua, near Ambon in Maluku.

Srivijaya – the Palembang-based empire.

Teuku Umar – Acehnese leader who helped lead the ulama movement against the Dutch in the late 19th century.

● ●

give way over negotiations. On 2 November the Hague Agreement was signed paving the way for full political independence of all former territories of the Dutch East Indies (with the exception of West Irian), on 27 December 1949.

From independence to Guided Democracy to coup: 1950-1965

In 1950, Indonesia was an economic shambles and in political chaos. Initially, there was an attempt to create a political system based on the Western European model of parliamentary democracy. By 1952 the futility of expecting a relatively painless progression to this democratic ideal were becoming obvious, despite the holding of a parliamentary general election in 1955 with a voter turnout of over 90%. Conflicts between Communists, radical Muslims, traditional Muslims, regional groups and minorities led to a series of coups, rebel governments and violent confrontations.

Indonesia was unravelling and in the middle of 1959, President Sukarno cancelled the provisional constitution and introduced his period of Guided Democracy.

This period of relative political stability rested on an alliance between the army, the Communist PKI, and Sukarno himself. It was characterized by extreme economic nationalism with assets controlled by Dutch, British and Indian companies and individuals being expropriated. The **Konfrontasi** with the Dutch over the 'recovery' of West Irian from 1960-62, and with Malaysia over Borneo beginning in 1963, forced Sukarno to rely on Soviet arms shipments and Indonesia moved increasingly into the Soviet sphere of influence. Cracks between the odd alliance of PKI and the army widened and even Sukarno's popular support and force of character could not stop the dam from bursting. On 1 October 1965, six senior generals were assassinated by a group of middle-ranking officers, thus ending the period of Guided Democracy. MC Ricklefs writes:

"... on that night the balance of hostile forces which underlay guided democracy came to an end. Many observers have seen tragedy in the period, especially in the tragedy of Sukarno, the man who outlived his time and used his popular support to maintain a regime of extravagant corruption and hypocrisy."

The coup was defeated by the quick-thinking of General Suharto whose forces overcame those of the coup's leaders. However, it undermined both Sukarno and the PKI as both were linked with the plot – the former by allowing the PKI to gain such influence, and the latter by allegedly master-minding the coup. Most Indonesians, although not all Western academics, see the coup as a Communist plot hatched by the PKI with the support of Mao Zedong and the People's Republic of China. It led to massacres on a huge scale as bands of youths set about exterminating those who were thought to be PKI supporters. This was supported, implicitly, by the army and there were news reports of 'streams choked with bodies'. The reaction was most extreme in Java and Bali, but there were murders across the archipelago. The number killed is not certain; estimates vary from 100,000 to one million and the true figure probably lies somewhere between the two (500,000 is widely quoted). In Bali alone some scholars believe that 80,000 people died – around 5% of the population. The difficulty is that the body count kept by the military is widely regarded as a gross under-estimate. Oei Tjoe Tat, a cabinet minister under Sukarno, was sent on a fact-finding mission to discover the scale of the massacres. He calculated that by January 1966 half a million people had died. The military's figure at that time was 80,000. As it was an anti-Communist purge, and as China had been blamed for fomenting the coup, many of those killed were Chinese who were felt, by their mere ethnicity, to have leftist-inclinations and Communist sympathies. Few doubt that the majority were innocent traders and middlemen, whose economic success and ethnic origin made them scapegoats. Islamic clerics and members of youth groups seem to have been particularly instrumental in singling out people for extermination. While these uncontrolled massacres were occurring, power was transferred to General Suharto (although he was not elected president until 1968). This marked the shift from what has become known as the Old Order, to the New Order.

That the events of 1965 remain contentious is reflected in the government's attempts to re-write, and in places to erase, this small slice of history. In 1995, three decades after the events of 1965-66, the authorities banned Oei Tjoe Tat's autobiography *Oei Tjoe Tat: assistant to President Sukarno*. It seems that the account of the anti-Communist purge diverged too much from the official history. The fact that banned novelist and former political prisoner Pramoedya Ananta Toer had a hand in the book also can not have endeared it to the authorities. By the time it was banned, however, around 15,000 copies had already been sold. Documents relating to the 1965-66 upheaval are restricted, and instead the government produces its own sanitized version of events. This has it that the Communists were behind the

Background

attempted coup, that President Sukarno was misguided in allowing the Communists to gain so much power, and that only the quick-thinking and courageous military, with Suharto at the fore, thwarted the attempt and saved Indonesia from turmoil.

Political & economic developments under the New Order, 1965-present
When Suharto took power in 1965 he had to deal with an economy in disarray. There was hyper-inflation, virtually no inward investment and declining productivity. To put the economy back on the rails he turned to a group of US-trained economists who have become known as the Berkeley Mafia. They recommended economic reform, the return of expropriated assets, and a more welcoming political and economic climate for foreign investment. In terms of international relations, Suharto abandoned the policy of support for China and the Soviet Union and moved towards the Western fold. Diplomatic relations with China were severed (and only renewed in 1990), and the policy of confrontation against Malaysia brought to an end.

The 33 years from 1965 through to 1998 was one of political stability. Suharto stayed in power for over three decades, and he presided over a political system which in a number of respects had more in common with the Dutch era than with that of former President Sukarno. Suharto eschewed ideology as a motivating force, kept a tight control of administration, and attempted to justify his leadership by offering his people economic well-being. He was known – until the 1997-98 economic crisis – as the 'Father of Development'.

Pancasila: Sukarno's five principles

- *Belief in the One Supreme God*
- *Just and Civilized Humanity*
- *Unity of Indonesia*
- *Democracy guided by the inner wisdom of unanimity*
- *Social Justice for all the people of*

Indonesia
Indonesia's national symbol is the mythical bird, the Garuda which, in Indonesia's national symbol is modelled on the Javan hawk-eagle, a bird endemic to Java and of which there are probably 200-300 pairs in the wild. On its chest is emblazoned the pacasila while its claws clasp the legend Bhinneka tungal ika –

Modern Indonesia

The last few years has seen a transformation in Indonesia's economic and political landscape. No commentator was sufficiently prescient to foresee these changes and no one knows where, ultimately, they will lead. For the first time since the attempted coup of 1965, Indonesia is entering truly uncharted territory. The chronically pessimistic see Indonesia fragmenting and the economy continuing to bump along the bottom as political instability prevents investor confidence returning. Optimists see stability returning in a brighter post-East Timor/post Suharto era and economic and investor confidence with it. With Aceh seemingly on the road to quasi or full independence, Irian Jaya - now renamed West Papua - clamouring for more autonomy, and resource-rich provinces like Riau and East Kalimantan demanding a larger slice of the pie, the central government in Jakarta is finding it almost impossible to keep people happy.

Politics

From 1965 through to 1998 Indonesia was under the control of a military-bureaucratic élite led by President Suharto. Power was exercised through Sekber Golkar, better known as just Golkar, the state's very own political party. In political terms at least, Indonesia was one of the world's most stable countries. It might not have been rich or powerful, but at least there was continuity of leadership. But in 1998 all that changed. Suharto was forced to resign after bitter riots in Jakarta brought on by the collapse of the Indonesian economy, but fuelled by decades of nepotism and corruption. What began as student protests escalated into communal violence and some 1,200 people were killed. The critical Chinese community – central to the operation of the economy – fled the country (for the interim at least) and an already dire economic situation became catastrophic. Suharto's vice-president, B.J. Habibie took over the helm but with scarcely a great deal of enthusiasm from the general populace, or from the military. Elections were held on 7 June 1999, the first free elections for 44 years, and they were contested by scores of parties. Megawati Sukarnoputri, former president Sukarno's daughter, won the largest share of the vote through her party PDI-Perjuangan (PDI-Struggle). Even with PDI-P's victory, however, some feared that B.J. Habibie would call on the political muscle of Golkar to secure him victory in the presidential elections. But the tragedy of East Timor put paid to that and he had to face the humiliation, in October 1999, of a vote of censure and no confidence in the newly muscular and independent People's Consultative Assembly (Indonesia's parliament).

Politics in the post-Suharto era

On 7 June 1999, Indonesians enjoyed their first truly democratic elections since 1955. Despite dire predictions to the contrary, they were largely peaceful. About 112 million votes were cast – 90% of eligible voters – at 250,000 polling stations around the country. A total of 48 parties contested the poll, 45 of them new, and Megawati Sukarnoputri's Democratic Party of Struggle (PDI-P) won the largest share of the vote, attracting 34% of the total. In second place came Golkar with 22%. This was a surprise to some foreign observers given the bad press Golkar had received, but reflected the party's links with the bureaucracy and a strong showing in the Outer Islands where 'reformasi' had had less of an impact. The three other parties to attract significant numbers of votes were the National Awakening Party (12%), the National Mandate Party (7%) and the United Development Party (10%).

Indonesia's first taste of democracy since 1955 has led to profound changes in the character of both politics and politicians. In the past, MPs had no constituency as such and so were rarely bothered about the need to represent real people. They merely had to make sure they pleased the party bosses. Members of the new parliament, however, not only have responsibilities to their electorates but are also likely to be much more outspoken. Because presidents will now have term-limits (Suharto was in power for 32 years) this will confer greater power on parliament. As Dan Murphy said in mid-1999 and before the presidential elections, "The next president…will confront populist and legislative challenges like no one has faced since Megawati's father and Indonesia's first president, Sukarno, dispensed with democracy 40 years ago" (FEER, 19.8.99).

Under former President Suharto, **Golkar** was, in effect, the state's own party. All state employees were automatically members of Golkar, and during election campaigns the state controlled the activities of other parties. Not surprisingly therefore, Golkar was able consistently to win over 60% of the votes cast in parliamentary elections, and controlled the Parliament (DPR) and the People's Consultative Assembly. Even before Suharto's resignation in 1998 there was the enduring sense that the tide of history was running against Golkar. The provinces where Golkar did least well were in the country's heartland – like Jakarta and East

Background

Java. It was here, in Java, that Indonesia's middle classes and 'new rich' were beginning to clamour for more of a say in how the country was run, and by whom. With Golkar's loss of the elections of 1999 to the PDI-P, the party has come to accept a new and less central role in the country. In the past all bureaucrats were automatically members of Golkar and were expected to support and represent Golkar. This is no longer the case.

But despite the fact that the PDI-P won the 1999 parliamentary elections, there were commentators who did not think that Megawati, the party's leader, would become president. Prior to the East Timor débâcle, some feared that B.J. Habibie would ally himself with one or two other parties and use Golkar to gain the presidency against the run of votes. That assumption was shattered when it became clear that the people of East Timor would vote for independence. But Habibie's mistake was not that he failed to control the army and the militias, but that he was foolish enough to offer the East Timorese a referendum on independence in the first place.

In October 1999 the People's Consultative Assembly voted for **Indonesia's new president** – and it was a cliffhanger. Indonesians could watch – another first for the country – democracy in progress as their representatives lodged their preferences. It was a close contest between Megawati Sukarnoputri, the people's favourite, and the respected **Abdurrahman Wahid**, an almost blind cleric and leader of the country's largest Muslim association, the Nahdlatul Ulama (NU), who is a master of the politics of appeasement; a quality which in the President of such a diverse nation can stymie progress and blunt his (or her) effectiveness. As it turned out, Wahid won by 373 votes to 313 as he garnered the support of Golkar members and many of those linked to Muslim parties. Initially, Megawati's vociferous and easily agitated supporters rioted when they realized that their leader had been, as they saw it, robbed of her democratic entitlement. Wisely, Wahid asked Megawati to be his vice-president and she asked her supporters to calm down and return home. The election of Wahid and Megawati was, arguably, the best combination that could have been hoped for. It allied a moderate with a populist, and it kept army commander-in-chief General Wiranto out of the two leadership spots (although he was asked to join the cabinet). Wahid's cabinet, announced a few days after the election, showed a desire to calm tensions and promote pragmatic leadership. Significantly, he included two Chinese in his cabinet (one, the critical finance minister), as well as one politician from Aceh and another from West Papua – the two provinces with the greatest secessionist inclinations. On his election to the presidency, four critical questions faced Indonesia's new president. First, how to mend the economy; second, how to keep the country from disintegrating; third how to promote reconciliation between the different racial and religious groups; and fourth, how to invent a role for the army appropriate for a democratic country entering the 21st century.

Indonesia has changed in other ways – although these changes could be reversed should the move towards democratization begin to falter. For a start, the **judiciary** and the **press** are increasingly independent. During the last few years of the Suharto era, hesitant steps towards greater press freedom were often followed by a crackdown on publications deemed to have crossed some ill-defined line in the sand. The independence of the judiciary was, if anything, an even more vexed issue. Political opponents of Suharto and his cronies could not expect a fair trial and foreign businessmen found using the courts to extract payments from errant Indonesian businessmen and companies a waste of time. In 1997 a clerk at the Supreme Court was heard explaining to a litigant how Indonesia's legal system worked: "If you give us 50 million rupiah but your opponent gives us more, then the case will be won by your opponent" 'quoted in *The Economist*, 2000'. This approach to legal contests may have the advantage of simplicity, but it hardly instilled a great deal of confidence that a case would be judged on its merits.

• •

Indonesian political parties (1999)

Indonesian Democratic Party of Struggle (PDI-P, Partai Demokrasi Indonesia Perjuangan), leader Megawati Sukarnoputri
Golongan Karya (Golkar), leader Akbar Tanjung
National Awakening Party (PKB, Partai Kebangkitan Bangsa), leader Matori Abdul Djalil
National Mandate Party (PAN, Partai Amanat Nasional), leader Amien Rais
United Development Party (PPP, Partai Persatuan Pembangunan), leader Hamzah Haz

• •

In the six months following Suharto's resignation nearly 200 new publications were registered. The government under Habibie was rather more thick-skinned than its predecessor, and in June 1998 a law permitting the Information Ministry to ban any publication for criticizing the government was scrapped. This move towards greater press freedom in the post-Suharto era has meant a much more active, campaigning and, occasionally, sensationalist press – something that President Wahid sometimes finds rather harder to stomach than did Habibie.

It has always been recognized that a critical ingredient – indeed a central element – in Indonesian political life is the army. For many years the army has been viewed as the only group in the country (beyond Golkar) with the necessary cohesion and unity of purpose to influence political events at a broad level. This wider role was enshrined in the constitutional principle of *dwifungsi*, or dual function, which gave the army the right to engage in politics and administration as well as defend the nation from external aggressors and internal insurrection. (This was amply illustrated in the army response to events in East Timor.) Around two-thirds of army personnel, according to political scientist Harold Crouch, were under this system, assigned to territorial rather than combat duties. As such they engaged in such things as "overseeing the activities of political parties and non-governmental organizations, intervening in land disputes, [and] dealing with striking workers or demonstrating students..." In the countryside the army was seen as a stabilizing force and the guarantor of ethnic and religious peace. The army has traditionally regarded itself as the protector of the nation, and more particularly the protector of ordinary Indonesians against potentially venal civilian politicians and their business associates. The key role that the military played in Indonesia's independence movement – after the civilian revolutionary government had capitulated to the returning Dutch after the end of World War Two – gave it further credibility to speak not just for itself, but also for the country as a whole.

The army in Indonesian politics

Like so much in Indonesia, these assumptions must be re-examined in the light of Suharto's fall from power, the army's response to the riots of 1998, its role in East Timor, and the democratic elections of 1999. In 1999 the army changed its name from Abri to **TNI**. This, though, does not detract from the fact that the army has lost credibility particularly as a result of the way it has dealt with, some would say fermented, sectarian and secessionist conflicts from Jakarta to Aceh, East Timor and Maluku. Moreover, it has become clear that a new generation of officers is in charge. These men, importantly, cannot call on their revolutionary credentials to justify and legitimate their positions and their actions. Moreover, the great unifying message of the 1970s and 1980s – the need to fight communism – no longer carries much influence. (That said, the code ET is still attached to some people's ID cards, designating that they are former political prisoners, and in mid-1999 the Indonesian parliament debated a bill that would have banned the teaching of Marxist-Leninism outside universities.)

Through some nifty footwork on his part, President Wahid managed to sideline the army (see below). However, while the army may have a smaller role to play in

Background

political and civilian affairs, the police are hardly ready to fill the void created by the retreating army. With just 200,000 poorly trained and paid officers, the police are barely able to keep the peace and in many cases stand idly by while civilian vigilantes mete out justice.

Disintegration? It has long been said that Indonesia is one of the world's most unlikely countries, a patchwork of cultures and languages pieced together by little more than the industriousness of the Dutch. In early 1999 President B.J. Habibie, as a sop to the international community, surprisingly offered the people of **East Timor** a referendum on independence. The UN was called in to supervise the vote on 30 August but, against UN advice and pleading, he refused even a small international peacekeeping force. The vote itself proceeded smoothly and with little in timidation. On 4 September the results of the vote were announced: 78.5% of a turnout of well over 90% chose independence. It seems, and this might seem incredible to anyone who has followed the East Timor story, that the Indonesian military were expecting to 'win' the vote and were piqued that the population were so patently ungrateful for all their hard work. So, with the announcement of the results, mayhem broke out. Militias, formed, encouraged, armed and orchestrated by the Indonesian military murdered, raped and terrorized the population of the tiny province. Tens of thousands fled to the hills and into neighbouring West Timor. (On 13 September one UN official suggested that just 200,000 out of East Timor's 800,000 population were still living in their homes.) Dili was virtually razed to the ground. The UN compound was besieged. Only the most intense international pressure, and vociferously negative international press coverage, forced Habibie to allow the UN to authorize an Australian-led force to enter the province.

The reluctance of the military to allow East Timor's independence can be linked to two key factors. First, between the annexation of East Timor in 1975 and the referendum of 1999, the army lost perhaps as many as 20,000 men trying to quell the independence movement there. To give up was to admit that it was all a waste of time and blood. And second, and much more importantly, there was the fear that East Timor's independence might herald the break-up of Indonesia. Aceh and West Papua (formerly Irian Jaya) were the most obvious provinces that could break away. Legally speaking, there is a clear difference between East Timor and anywhere else in Indonesia. East Timor's annexation by Indonesia was never recognized by the UN. (UN maps always indicated the territory as a separate country.) But the fear was that this nuance would be lost on people with desires for independence.

The 7,500-strong Australian-led UN force landed in Dili in late September 1999 and control of the territory passed from the Indonesians to the UN. Alongside the Aussie troops, there were British Gurkhas, New Zealanders, and even contingents from the region, including Thai and Malaysian troops. (Asean came out of the crisis poorly, yet again showing an inability to act in a timely and forceful manner.) Even as UNIFET (the UN International Force for East Timor) strengthened its hold on Dili the withdrawing Indonesian troops destroyed the town they had called their own for nearly 25 years. As one soldier told *The Economist*, "We built this place up. Now we've torn it all down again" (2.10.99). During October, UNIFET extended its control east and west from Dili, as far as the border with West Timor where the militias were holed up. Rumours of a militia build-up and possible major incursion did not materialize, although there were some firefights between UNIFET and militia gangs. At the end of October Xanana Gusmao, jailed for 20 years by Indonesia and the most likely person to become East Timor's first president, returned home. Before leaving Australia he said: "We will start from zero to reconstruct not only our country, but ourselves as human beings" (*The Economist*, 16.10.99).

A complication – and another reason why the Indonesian army were so reluctant to give up their hold on this dry and poverty-stricken land – was the decision taken

Two years of living dangerously

August-December 1997	The rupiah and economic collapse
January 1998	Suharto agrees to conditions of S$43 billion IMF bail out
May 1998	Jakarta erupts as students protest and riots spread; 1,200 die
May 1998	Suharto resigns; B.J. Habibie steps in as interim president
August 1998	Food riots in Jakarta
November 1998	Student riots in Jakarta
January-March 1999	Communal chaos in Ambon, Maluku
February 1999	Heightened tensions in East Timor
September 1999	Massacres in East Timor following pro-independence vote Student and nationalist demonstrations in Jakarta
October 1999	Student and nationalist demonstrations in Jakarta Abdurrahman Wahid and Megawati Sukarnoputri elected President and Vice President
December 1999	Communal violence in the Spice Islands escalates
January 2000	Riots in Lombok; tourists and Christians flee to Bali
June 2000	Communal violence spreads to Central Sulawesi

by the UN on 27 September 1999 to investigate human rights abuses in the province. And they were right to be worried. When the UN and Indonesian reports were published at the beginning of 2000, 6 generals were mentioned by name, including General Wiranto (see below).

It was not just East Timor and Aceh that have been wracked by violence. Indeed, the spread of unrest to other areas of the country would seem to bear out the army's fears: that taking the lid off more than three decades of top-down control would lead to an upsurge of violence right across the country. Conspiracy theories abound as to which interested party is seeding this violence. Some believe that much of the unrest is being orchestrated by the military – anxious to prove that without their control the country will disintegrate. Influential individuals from the Suharto era may be trying to destabilize the country in order to regain power. As criminologist Yohanes Sutoyo explained to Dini Djalal of the *Far Eastern Economic Review*, "The New Order [of former President Suharto] taught us that the only way to solve a problem is with violence", adding, "It is difficult to undo this" (FEER 13.7.2000). At the beginning of 2000, communal violence in the Spice Islands of Maluku escalated and by mid year an estimated 3,000 people had been killed. In Central Sulawesi, murderous groups were killing villagers. In central Kalimantan deadly clashes broke out between indigenous Dayaks and migrants from Madura Island who came as part of the Suharto government's *transmigrasi* programme. Bali and Lombok were also the scenes of unprecedented violence at the beginning of 2000, some of it aimed at the Chinese community, many of whom are Christians. In Jakarta, and in some other cities on Java, vigilante groups have taken it upon themselves to mete out retribution on small-time criminals. Reports of people stealing bicycles being lynched, beaten, doused with kerosene, and set alight were common during 2000. The police, in such cases, have stood by, powerless to intervene.

While disintegration, partial or otherwise, is a possibility, the government is in the process of introducing laws that will lead to far-reaching **decentralization** to try and head off those who would prefer even greater autonomy. But there are worries that this attempt to devolve power to the provinces will permit local power-brokers to dominate affairs and make corruption even worse. It will also mean that poor provinces such as East and West Nusa Tenggara will no longer be able to rely on

Background

cross-subsidization by richer provinces such as Riau and Aceh. Furthermore, it is far from clear that there are sufficient numbers of competent people in the provinces to handle such an increase in the power and role of local level government.

Gus Dur tries to put it back together President Abdurrahman Wahid, better known as Gus (a term of respect) Dur (from his name), did not have an easy task when he assumed the presidency at the end of 1999. And as this book went to press it was not clear when and if Indonesia's economy would recover (see the next section), or whether Indonesia would survive as a country roughly corresponding to the one he took over. Nor was it clear whether he would survive as president to the end of his term.

Gus Dur has always been renowned for his cunning and wily ways – and his fondness for obtuseness. When he was leader of Nahdlatul Ulama (NU), the world's largest Muslim organization, he was one of President Suharto's very few critics. And he was also able to present himself as a moderate Muslim: one who would protect the interests of Indonesia's non-Muslim population while remaining a respected Muslim cleric, leader and thinker. In January 2000 he travelled to Saudi Arabia to court the Arab world and then flew to Davos in Switzerland for the World Economic Forum. Here he met with Prime Minister Barak of Israel and George Soros. He explained: "We need investments and, you know, the Jewish community everywhere are very active in the commercial side…" (FEER 10.2.2000). His critics say he undermines Indonesia's stability and economic recovery by his impulsiveness; he frequently makes statements without consulting his cabinet (as happened when he said, while on an overseas trip, that General Wiranto should resign), and people also complain of his readiness to blame conspirators for the country's problems. His supporters believe he is a great master who disarms his opponents by his seeming foolishness before bringing them down. With few political cards to play, now that many in his coalition government have turned against him, his defenders believe that speaking out is his only weapon. Without the backing of a fully functioning bureaucracy, or the military power used by his predecessor, his force of personality and ability to bluff are the only tools at his disposal.

His greatest victory (or so it seemed at the time – see below) so far has been to **sideline the army** and emasculate its leadership as a political force. This also showed him at his wily best. Initially Wahid included General Wiranto, the army's powerful chief of staff, in his cabinet but not, significantly, as defence minister. Instead he appointed him as security minister. This helped to separate the general from his power base. Then the president said that he would sack anyone implicated in human rights abuses in East Timor. Reports commissioned by the Indonesian government and by the UN into just this issue were released on 31 January 2000. Moreover, both came to the same conclusion: that members of the Indonesian army had assisted the militias in East Timor to murder, rape and pillage. More to the point, the Indonesian report mentioned six generals by name, including General Wiranto. The president was abroad at the time but in an interview said he thought that Wiranto should resign. Instead the general pointedly turned up at a cabinet meeting. However in the middle of February, having initially said that the general could stay, he changed his mind once more and, in the middle of the night, sacked the general from his post as security minister (although he remained an 'inactive' member of the cabinet). Cut off from the army and in a government post with no significance, General Wiranto was successfully trapped in a no man's land of Gus Dur's making.

But Wahid did not just get rid of Wiranto. He appointed a civilian as minister of defence and promoted officers in the navy and airforce to influential positions, thus downgrading the traditionally highly dominant army. This culminated in a major reshuffle at the end of February 2000. Now it is moderate reformers who fill most of the influential posts in the armed forces. Furthermore Wahid insisted that military men in the cabinet would have to resign from their military posts before taking up their political appointments.

While Gus Dur might have sidelined the army, he hadn't counted on the public (probably orchestrated from above – possibly by factions of the army) taking up arms to deal with the problems of the nation. At the beginning of 2000, as Muslim-Christian violence in Maluku escalated, radical Muslims in Java began to prepare for a *jihad* (holy war) in this far-flung province. White-robed warriors in their thousands, some wielding swords, congregated in Jakarta to make their feelings clear – and then began to train for battle. Despite Gus Dur's attempts to stop them leaving for Maluku, they began to arrive in the region by the end of May 2000. As the year wore on it became increasingly clear that Wahid's victory over the generals was a Pyrrhic one. Infuriated by the president's actions the army began to undermine his leadership. In particular, a series of bombings in Jakarta seemed to involve the army, or groups in the army.

During the course of 2000, many people who initially welcomed Wahid's accession to the presidency became increasingly disenchanted with his leadership – and with his methods. In an attempt to address this mounting criticism, in a speech to the annual meeting of the People's Consultative Assembly (MPR) on 9th August (at which he faced the risk of a vote of censure) he proposed far-reaching changes to the management of state affairs. In effect he proposed a more equal, four-way sharing of power between his to-date marginalized Vice President Megawati Sukarnoputri, two new 'Co-ordinating' ministers, and himself. The two co-ordinating ministers were later announced as being Sulsilo Bambang Yudhoyono, a retired general, and Rizal Ramli. Significantly, neither of these two men had prior links with any political party. Under this system Wahid would become, in effect, Indonesia's face to the wider world: a sort of roving ambassador for the country. Wahid claimed in the speech that he was ceding 'duties and not authority', but the distinction is a fine one.

Wahid's proposed changes were a tacit acceptance on his part that he had lost his way. It sometimes seemed, in the months leading up to the August 2000 meeting, that Wahid lacked the clarity of mind to address key issues, and especially those of an economic flavour. His woolly pronouncements and tendency to prevaricate exasperated many businessmen and foreign investors.

As this book went to press towards the end of 2000, Indonesia was continuing to lurch from crisis to crisis, both economic and political. President Abdurrahman Wahid's government was becoming increasingly embattled as his problems mounted. In particular he seemed to have lost control of the army and the police who were, apparently, ignoring or going against his orders. This extended from his order for the army and police to crack down on the militias in West Timor (following the murder of three UN personnel there in September); to his demand that Tommy Suharto, one of former President Suharto's sons be arrested in connection with a spate of bombings in Jakarta (the police released him saying there was not sufficient evidence to hold him); to a ceasefire in the northern Sumatran province of Aceh, which the army also apparently chose to ignore. Some commentators were wondering whether the army was once more out of control and it was even being suggested that Wahid might be toppled by an army-inspired coup.

Suharto may have gone, but he and his family have kept much of their wealth. In the 1997 listing of the world's richest, *Forbes Magazine* put Suharto's fortune at US$16 billion. While this was indicative of the sums of money the former president managed to squeeze out of the nation and its people, far more corrosive was the wealth that his children managed to amass. Nepotism may be a way of life in Southeast Asia, but there are limits to what is deemed acceptable. Suharto's six children (three sons and three daughters) built up vast business empires on the basis of their family connections. The two biggest non-Chinese conglomerates – Bimantara and Humpuss – were both run by sons of the president, Bambang

The (former) first family: what to do with them & their fortunes?

Background

The politics of envy: the Chinese in Indonesia

The Chinese make up about 4-5% of Indonesia's population and, as the communal violence of 1998 amply proved, are still treated with suspicion. There are still 300,000 Chinese living in Indonesia who have yet to choose whether they are Indonesians by nationality, or Chinese. The community adopts a low profile – in Glodok (Jakarta's Chinatown), for example, there are few Chinese signs on the shopfronts. Indeed, until recently there was a ban on displaying Chinese characters. The so-called masalah Cina – or 'Chinese problem' – continues to be hotly discussed, much of the debate centering on whether the Chinese should be assimilated or integrated into Indonesian culture.

The animosity between the 'Indonesian' and Chinese communities is based upon the latter's economic success, and their role as middlemen, shopkeepers and moneylenders. Most of the country's largest firms are Chinese-owned – known as cukong – and the richest families are also Chinese. It has been estimated that the 4% or 5% of the population who are Chinese control 70-80% of private capital (although this is probably an over-estimate). Such evident success has given rise to envy. Some indigenous businessmen, known as pribumi, have called for the implementation of an

explicit economic policy of positive discrimination in favour of native Indonesians modelled on the New Economic Policy in Malaysia.

Former President Suharto might have scorned such an idea but when he invited 30 of the country's top Chinese businessmen to his palace in 1990 he was seen, on television, explaining to them that if inequalities were not reduced, "social gap, social envy and even social disturbance will happen". This barely concealed warning of a possible repeat of the events of 1965 was not lost on the Chinese community and was tragically realized during the riots of May 1998. These started as student-led pro-democracy and anti-Suharto demonstrations, but quickly became anti-Chinese. Gangs of men, it was reported, systematically targeted Chinese businesses and families. In total, 1,200 people were killed (to be sure, not all Chinese) and more than 150 Chinese women were raped. Wealthier families escaped to the airport, and from there to Singapore. Poorer ethnic Chinese hunkered down to escape the mobs. "We expected protection", one computer shop owner told The Economist, "but it never came" (22.08.98). This was a tragedy not just for the Chinese, but also for Indonesia. In the first half of 1998 US$16 billion left the country, much of it belonging to ethnic Chinese convinced that they no longer belonged.

Trihatmodjo and Hutomo 'Tommy' Mandala Putra. They managed to do this by drawing on their ties with their father to secure lucrative contracts and licences. One Asian ambassador in Jakarta was quoted in the *Far Eastern Economic Review* back in April 1992 as saying: "The central question is whether the avarice of the children will ultimately undermine 25 years of pretty good leadership". An *Economist* survey of the country in 1993 reflected similar sentiments, when – likening him to former Javanese kings – it described Suharto as having: "A paternal style, a professed lack of interest in power, a circle of deferential courtiers and the ability to dispense seemingly unlimited patronage...". In 1998 the Indonesian Business Data Centre put Suharto family's fortune (Suharto plus his children) at 200 trillion rupiah. At the pre-crisis exchange rate this amounted to US$80 billion.

The economic crisis undermined the finances of the children's business empires and Suharto's resignation removed their ultimate guardian and patron. The business empires of Suharto's children are now struggling to survive. The family as a whole has seen the value of its assets decline from US$80 billion to under US$20 billion. This does not mean, of course, that the children themselves are on the breadline –

like many millions of ordinary Indonesians during the economic meltdown. Perhaps most surprising is the fact that the Suharto children have been allowed to continue to run their businesses, not all of which are moribund.

But while his children may have come under intense scrutiny and criticism, Suharto himself is not quite the hate figure that most foreigners would expect him to be, given the corruption and repression of his years in power. The Suharto era was one of stability and economic dynamism and many Indonesians look back on it as a golden period which brought better living standards to most people. Even so, Habibie, Suharto's protégé, was forced by events to set up a commission to investigate whether Suharto had acquired his wealth through illegal means. In October 1999, incredibly, the commission decided that there was insufficient evidence to bring the former president to court.

Under Gus Dur's presidency there has been a more concerted effort to bring Suharto to book, and in 2000 the Attorney General Marzuki Darusman began proceedings leading to a possible trial for corruption. At the end of May 2000 the former president was placed under house arrest at his palatial home in Menteng, a suburb of Jakarta, and police were stationed around his home – as much to protect him from the periodic mob attacks on his home than to keep him from escaping. In August it was formally announced by state prosecutors that President Suharto, more than two years after his resignation, would stand trial for embezzling more than US$571 million from the state. The trial began in August with his lawyers arguing that the former president was not fit to stand trial. Mr Assegaf, one of his lawyers, said that: "It is impossible for him to stand trial. Suharto is incapable of comprehending questions and of responding to them immediately". President Wahid promised to pardon Suharto, but insisted that he stands trial first. However, on 28 September the Jakarta court dropped all charges against the former president declaring, on the advice of a panel of doctors, that he was, indeed, mentally and physically unfit to stand trial. This infuriated activists who believe that Suharto embezzled not US$571 million, but a truly stupendous US$45 billion. A few days before the announcement another court sentenced Suharto's youngest son Tommy to an 18 month prison sentence for corruption. At least this was something, but scarcely sufficient to assuage the desire for retribution held by many people.

Indonesia's acceptance into the international fold has been hampered for years by numerous small and large stumbling blocks. The 'occupation' of East Timor, government policy in West Papua, corruption, the nature of the political system, the failure to respect labour rights, and the human and environmental impacts of the transmigration programme, to name just a few. Just when Indonesia is on the verge of expunging the stain on its credibility one or more of these issues jumps out and progress is stymied.

There can be no doubt that the major stumbling block was **East Timor**. Even before the tragic events which followed the vote for independence in mid-1999, East Timor was a thorn in Indonesia's attempts to punch its weight. (For a country of over 200 million people, the fourth most populous on earth, it has a remarkably low international profile.) For the foreseeable future it is hard to imagine that Indonesia will be able to look much beyond its own manifold challenges, from creating a democratic and robust civil society to rebuilding its economy. So, for the next five years, expect Indonesia to be on people's television screens, only if there is sufficient televisual bloodshed, except, perhaps, to defend its policies in various secession-minded outer provinces. Nationalist sentiment was stoked by the presence of UN forces in East Timor (widely seen to be Australian forces in East Timor) and Indonesia's failure to come to terms with its misguided imperialist spree has raised the stakes still further. At the end of September 1999, US Secretary of Defense William Cohen warned that Indonesia could face 'political isolation' and the

Domestic hangovers & international relations

Background

ensuing 'economic consequences' if it did not control its military. This, of course, begs the question: Are the generals listening (only one of the leading generals, General Wiranto, actually spoke any English)?

Marking out the path to the future

In the last edition of this book, the summary of politics in the country concluded with the paragraph:

"All in all, it would be a brave person who would predict the path of change over the next five years. The Western obsession with the 'natural' evolution towards greater political pluralism and a market economy makes it hard to imagine that things might go 'backwards'; the experience of China following the Tiananmen Square massacre illustrates the dangers of such blithe assumptions. Nor does the pressure from the West for progress on human rights take into account Indonesia's unique set of conditions. The country's middle classes were estimated in 1995 to number just 14 million people – about 7% of the total population – and the evolution of civil society is still in its infancy. It is unlikely that the army will give up its influence and the sheer geographical, social and cultural complexity would make the country extremely hard to hold together in the event of free-for-all democracy."

The events of the last two years make predicting the future even more perilous. It may be that democratization continues, that political power is increasingly devolved to the provinces, that East Timor is given its independence, that the legal system is made more accountable and transparent, that the press is given its head, that secessionist tendencies in Aceh and West Papua are quelled peacefully, and that the Parliament becomes more active. Or it may not.

Economy

In their influential publication *The East Asian Miracle* (1992), the World Bank counted Indonesia one of Asia's 'miracle' economies. It was on this basis that grand predictions were made about Asia – and about Indonesia. The 21st century was to be the era of the Pacific with the Asian tigers, Indonesia included, in the vanguard. Just as the resignation of Suharto has changed Indonesia's political landscape beyond all recognition, so the economic crisis which began with the fall of the Thai baht in mid-1997, has led to a profound transformation in Indonesia's economic and developmental prospects. (The two, clearly, are linked: Suharto's loss of political legitimacy was intimately associated with the fall of the economy. He was, after all, Bapak Pembangunan or the Father of Development.) Of all the countries of Asia, Indonesia has been most severely hit by the crisis. Never has a country fallen from economic grace so far and so fast. In the space of 18 months the economy contracted by 20%. At one point virtually all the companies listed on the Jakarta stock exchange were technically bankrupt and the rupiah had lost 85% of its value against the US$.

To understand what has happened to Indonesia's economy over the last few years it is first necessary to reflect on the 'miracle', because there is little doubt that the years of Suharto's presidency led to unparalleled rates of economic growth and improving standards of living for most people in most places.

The making of a miracle?

"The road that was sealed for the first time in living memory, the new school, the new health clinic, the improved irrigation system, all these were convincing evidence that *pembangunan* (economic development) meant improved access to public amenities, which in turn could lead to increasing earning opportunities, and higher family incomes and living standards. By the latter part of the 1970s, it was impossible to doubt that incomes and living standards were improving, especially in Java, where the great majority of the rural population were concentrated. These were remarkable achievements for a country as backward as Indonesia was in the mid-1960s" (Anne Booth 1995: 109).

••

Political and Economic Risk Consultancy (PERC) put Indonesia
at the top of the list of Asian countries (ie worst) in terms of
corruption in 2000

	2000
Singapore	0.71
Hong Kong	2.49
Japan	3.90
Malaysia	5.50
Taiwan	6.89
Philippines	8.67
Thailand	8.20
South Korea	8.33
China	9.11
Vietnam	9.20
India	9.50

••

From 1965 through to 1997 the Indonesian economy gradually recovered from the extreme mismanagement that characterized the period from independence in 1950. With the advice of the so-called Berkeley Mafia – a group of reform-minded, US-trained economists – there was an attempt to increase efficiency, reduce corruption and entice foreign investment. Like the other countries of the region, export-orientated development became the name of the game. In 1996 Dennis de Tray, the World Bank's country manager heaped praise on Indonesia's economic performance. "We give Indonesians a very good report card", he said, adding that in 1995 "few countries [in the world] have had better economic performance".

On 17th August 1995, at the celebrations marking the 50th anniversary of Indonesia's proclamation of Independence, President Suharto squinted into the skies as the N-250, a home-built and home-designed 70-seat commuter aircraft, made its maiden flight. The plane, named *Gatot Kaca* after one of the characters in a Hindu epic, illustrates Indonesia's technological 'coming of age'. While critics may have wondered about the excessive concentration of financial and human resources in a single product of such dubious commercial value, the N-250 instilled an intense sense of pride and self-confidence in the Indonesian people, though not perhaps the low-paid Golkar party members who were forced to make a donation towards the plane's development. Moreover, as the plane left the tarmac Suharto gave the go-ahead for Habibie to produce a jet airliner – codenamed the N-2130 – by 2003. (These grand plans are now, it would seem, history. The IMF insisted, as part of its aid package to revive the ailing economy in 1997, that government money could not be used to fund the project. Instead ITPN continues forlornly to look for private sector funding for this lame-duck project. Since then both the N-250 and the N-2130 have been put on hold and the workforce halved.)

Development has been based upon a series of 5-year plans known as *Repelitas* (standing for *Rencana Pembangunan Lima Tahun*), the first beginning in 1969. Indonesia's GDP per person was about US$1,300 in 1996; in 1967 it was only US$70. At the beginning of 1995 Indonesia made the transition from being a 'low income' to becoming a 'middle income' country according to World Bank criteria.

Indonesia is the only Asian member of OPEC and has benefited from its **oil wealth**. This has enabled the government to pursue ambitious programmes of social, agricultural and regional development. After the first oil price rise in 1973 following in the wake of the Arab-Israeli Yom Kippur War, when the cost of a barrel of oil quadrupled in less than a year, the government was awash with funds. These were

From oil to non-oil

Background

used to build 6,000 primary schools a year, expand roads into the less accessible parts of the Outer Islands, and subsidize rice cultivation so that the country attained self-sufficiency by 1985. But the oil boom also promoted **corruption** on a scale that was remarkable even by Southeast Asian standards. It was said, for example, that importers were having to pay US$200 million a year in bribes to the notoriously corrupt Customs Department, and that even the lowliest coffee boy had to pass US$1,000 under the table to buy himself a job. This investment would, of course, be repaid in a few months, as the coffee boy's share of the bribes trickled down through the system. Such was the degree of corruption that in 1985 Suharto was forced to take the unprecedented step of calling in a Swiss firm, Société Générale de Surveillance, to oversee import procedures.

The decline in oil prices since the early 1980s forced the government to become rather more hard-headed in its approach to economic management. This led to a conscious attempt to promote **non-oil industries** and from the early 1980s these were the principal source of growth. By 1997, over 20% of Indonesia's GDP was produced by the manufacturing sector and oil and gas accounted for less than a quarter of total exports. Foreign investors were attracted by Indonesia's low wage rates when compared with Malaysia and Thailand, its political stability when compared with China, and its comparatively investor-friendly environment when compared with Vietnam.

The human costs of rapid growth

While there is little doubt that Indonesia achieved a great deal between 1965 and 1997, there was also little doubt that the country's strategy of fast-track industrialization had its **human costs**. People were being displaced from the countryside to swell the ranks of the urban labour force, causing social tensions to escalate. Many of the jobs in industry were non-formal, and non-contractual, so few workers felt they had much security. Union representation was through the tame, institutionalized, All-Indonesia Workers Union or SPSI. When independent unions were established (which Indonesian law allows) their leaders were hounded by the internal security agency Bakorstanas and sometimes eliminated. In July 1993, for example, the East Java labour activist, Marsinah was murdered. As John McBeth in the *Far Eastern Economic Review* recorded: "Marsinah was tortured for 3 days and then sexually violated with a sharp instrument before being dumped on a roadside and left to bleed to death". There were also many examples of **child labour** and of poor workplace safety. Before the crisis there were, officially, 2.4 million child workers in the country, although some NGOs believed the real figure to be four times larger. The difficulty of determining whether child work is exploitative is reflected in the term that the government used to describe underage labourers: *anak yang terpaksa bekerja* or 'children who are compelled to work'. If children worked below a certain minimum number of hours a day and if their labour was crucial to household survival then it was, officially, permitted.

Another major cause for concern in the country during the period of rapid growth was the uneven nature of development. This had both a spatial and a human component. To begin with, the great bulk of investment was concentrated in Java – some 64% of total foreign investment. Over vast swathes of the archipelago, the export-driven boom was just hot air. '**Social justice** for all Indonesians' is one of the principles enshrined in *pancasila*, the state ideology, and the glaring inequalities between the rich and the poor, and between different regions of the country, became an issue of driving concern.

This was reflected in the initiation of a **poverty alleviation** programme at the beginning of April 1994, *Inpres Desa Tertinggal* or the Presidential Instruction Programme for Less Developed Villages. This aimed to reduce poverty from roughly 15% to 6% by 1998 by specifically targeting those for whom wealth had not 'trickled down'. In preparing for the programme, the National Development Planning board drew up a map of 20,633 villages where poverty was endemic and by 1996 some 2.3 million families had been accepted on to the scheme.

In mid-1996 President Suharto tried another tack to narrow the glaring **inequalities** within the country. He made a personal plea for rich individuals and companies to hand over 250 billion rupiah to finance a poverty alleviation programme. 11,000 people and firms, selected on the basis that each had an income after tax of over 100 million rupiah – were sent a booklet asking them to share their wealth with the needy. The booklet asked these favoured few to "carry out the noble task of poverty alleviation together with the government".

Although Indonesia's population of poor and near-poor were the most evident sources of concern even during the period of rapid economic growth, there was also growing discontent among those groups who had gained most from the country's progress. High school leavers and even university graduates were finding that jobs in private business or the public sector, previously virtually guaranteed by dint of their having a degree or secondary school certificate, increasingly hard to find. With expectations growing as the consumer culture bit, so these individuals were finding their aspirations thwarted. A disgruntled, educated, largely urban-based mass of young men and women was the last thing Suharto wanted as he tried to stem the desire for greater political pluralism. His fears were borne out in the civil disturbances which led to his resignation in 1998.

Even before the economic crisis swept all before it, there were commentators highlighting the problems that Indonesia faced maintaining rapid economic growth. To begin with, levels of **corruption** have always been quite horrendous. Journalist John McBeth has written of the "army of 4 million underpaid bureaucrats [who] lurk in ambush in thickets of red tape" waiting to pounce on unsuspecting businessmen. Indonesia comes close to the top in the World Corruption Stakes: in 1996 it was thought to be running close behind China and Vietnam, while Transparency International put Indonesia at the top of a field of 41 countries. But it was not just corruption which worried businessmen. The way in which the politically well-connected gained access to lucrative contracts and licences, the burgeoning business empires of the various Suharto children, and the lack of transparency in the system were all also sources of concern. (For those who might be interested in the semantics of corruption, *pungli* are 'hidden taxes' while the colloquial term for a bribe is *uang licin* or *wang liken*, 'slippery' or 'greasy' money.)

The poisonous nature of corruption is widely recognized in Indonesia. There is even an acronym for the conjuncture of corruption, graft and favouritism – KKN, standing for Korrupsi, Kollusi and Nepotise. Nor has it gone away just because Suharto has been ejected from the presidency. The Bali Bank scandal engulfed the country in September 1999 when auditors PriceWaterhouseCoopers reported that US$70 million had been diverted from the Bank to Golkar, former President Habibie's party.

The individual charged with the monumental task of eradicating corruption from the system is Teten Masduki, head of Indonesia Corruption Watch (ICW), which was established in June 1998. (In one of the first statements after his election as Indonesia's new president in October 1999, Mr Wahid promised to stamp out corruption and stated that any cabinet minister found to be involved in such practices would be forced to resign.) Mr Teten, formerly a labour activist, argues that more insidious than the major corruption scandals which garner the headlines is the day-to-day petty corruption which is such a part of Indonesian life. It is this which, in his view, corrodes and corrupts Indonesian people and society. The problem for Mr Teten is a shortage of funds and people, and a legal system which is chronically unable to deal with complicated corruption cases and prone to capitulate in the face of powerful, rich and influential people.

In addition to corruption, foreign investors and local businessmen highlighted poor infrastructure, a lack of skilled workers, a cumbersome bureaucracy and high interest rates as major constraints to growth. Perhaps most critical of all was – and is

Constraints to growth

Background

– the need to upgrade **education and skills**. In 1996 just 4% of the workforce had a university education and 60% of those aged between 15 and 29 were educated to primary level only. Thus, even while Indonesia was enjoying some of the fastest rates of economic growth in the world, there were those who wondered whether the country would be able to make the critical transition from sweat shop to industrial power house.

The 1997 economic crisis: falling tigers

Like the rest of Southeast Asia, Indonesia was buffeted – some might say torn limb-from-limb – by the collapse of the Thai economy in July 1997. Initially it looked like Indonesia might come out of the crisis in better shape than Malaysia and the Philippines, not to mention Thailand. But as the year wore on the economic outlook became grimmer and grimmer. Forest fires clouded the economic skies in September; continued pressure on the rupiah pushed it to record lows against the US$ in October; and foreign analysts continued to peg back their estimates of economic growth. As the economy sank further, the government, like the Thai government before it, called in the IMF on 8 October 1997. The size of corporate Indonesia's short term US$ debts grew by the day as the rupiah sank, and the number of banks believed to be insolvent reached almost a score by the end of the month. Initially it appeared as though Suharto was so upset by the IMF's dire assessment of Indonesia's economy, and the corruption and rent seeking that is so much a part of the system, that it seemed he might go elsewhere for money rather than bite the IMF bullet. As John McBeth vividly put it in an article in the *Far Eastern Economic Review* in October 1997: "When the forces of reform hit up against the immovable object of political interests, reform makes a detour." The Indonesian economist Djisman Simandjuntak summed up the lack of readiness and understanding in many quarters of government, the bureaucracy and academia:

"The chaotic nature of globalization is not well understood by our top officials, by the business elite, even by people in academia. Our founding fathers fought against colonialism and liberalism, and there was always this dream of big government and enough natural resources to make Indonesia self-sufficient."

Finally, right at the end of October, a US$43 billion package was approved with sizeable pledges from Japan and Singapore (US$5 billion each), the World Bank (US$4.5 billion) and Asian Development Bank (US$3.5 billion), the USA (US$3 billion), and Malaysia and Australia (US$1 billion each). The IMF itself promised US$10 billion.

Of course, the money did not come without strings and these became clearer when Finance Minister Mar'ie Muhammad announced a series of reforms in November. These included the dismantling of some monopolies, the liquidation of 16 smaller banks, and plans to cut some of the links that bestow advantages on well connected companies.

While the emphasis in the media was on the big picture, it became evident by the end of 1997 that Indonesia's crisis was also affecting the *wong cilik* – the little people. Taxi drivers were finding fares harder to come by as the middle class switched from taxi to bus, rice prices rose, and cleaners and office boys in the banks threatened with closure were turfed onto the street.

Not soon after the ink was dry on the IMF agreement, student-led riots broke out in Jakarta, culminating in President Suharto's resignation in May 1998 (see above). Political uncertainty turned an economic crisis into an economic massacre. GDP shrank by 14% in 1998; the cost of recapitalizing Indonesia's banks was put at US$80 billion, equal to over 80% of GDP; the rupiah sunk so far that by June 1998 it had lost over 80% of its value; and virtually all the companies listed on the Jakarta stock exchange were technically bankrupt. As *The Economist* put it, by this time "Indonesia's economy, and the economies in it, [had] entered the twilight zone" (31.1.98).

Again, there was a tendency to gloss over the impacts of the crisis on the 'real' economy. In 1999 it was thought that 20% of the country's population or 40 million people were living in poverty. Beggars, prostitutes and children were all noticeably present on the streets of Jakarta and other large cities. What began as an economic crisis had, by 1998, become a social and a political crisis too.

Touching bottom

Just when it seems that Indonesia's economy can't fall any further, and is on the mend, something happens to undermine confidence. While other crisis-hit Asian economies like Thailand, South Korea and Malaysia are on the mend, Indonesia is stuck in the doldrums.

Indonesia's economic prospects, as has been true for the last three years, are critically linked to political stability. A March 2000 Asian Development Bank report on the prospects for the Asian economies warned of the fragility of Indonesia's economic 'recovery'. The ADB report described the situation in Indonesia as "highly problematic", noting that most banks are insolvent and operating only with the Indonesian central bank's support. The report continued: "Speeding up and sustaining the recovery process depends crucially on the rejuvenation of the moribund banking system."

The key challenge – and this sounds dull and tedious - is to initiate systematic and effective restructuring of the corporate sector, and particularly the banking sector. The difficulty is that business culture and nationalist sentiment is hampering progress in debt settlement. This has made it more difficult for the government to implement tough policies, especially if 'vulture' foreign investors are buying up businesses on the cheap.

Background

The agency which is central to restructuring efforts is IBRA – the Indonesian Bank Restructuring Agency – which, by mid-2000, controlled a huge chunk of the country's corporate wealth. The Agency is empowered with the job of selling off these assets and thus recouping some of the US$80 billion that the government (and the IMF) have spent trying to put the banking sector back together again. But local business interests and many politicians are loath to see foreigners doing-down Indonesians, however incompetent their business management may have been. Thus, while there are important economic considerations slowing down the process, much more important is the political climate and the role that vested interests are having in hampering progress. At the end of 1999, for example, Standard Chartered Bank's plans to buy Bank Bali failed because of a nationalist backlash (as well as pressure from within the company). President Wahid's appointment of his younger brother Hasyim Wahid as an 'expert' adviser to IBRA in April 2000, when he scarcely has the qualifications to be paraded as such, raised fears of Suharto-style nepotism and cronyism. (Wahid's brother turned down the post following public disquiet.)

It also seems that President Wahid has not helped. While he may have been skilful in his handling of the army, his critics say he hasn't a clue about economics – and they are not very much more complimentary about the president's first Finance Minister Kwik Kian Gie. Perhaps Kwik's most stunning piece of economic diplomacy occurred in May 2000 when he told Dow Jones that "if I were a foreign investor, I wouldn't come to Indonesia". So much for raising confidence. Ministers in his government have been fighting over key portfolios and Wahid hasn't been able (or willing) to take the lead and impose his will. The failure of Wahid to convince investors that he has the political strength to resist nationalist pressures is scaring off foreign companies. In March the IMF delayed the release of US$400 million in loans (part of a US$5 billion agreement signed in January) because the country was failing to meet its obligations and, in particular, its corporate restructuring obligations. (This US$400 million tranche was later released on 17 May.)

In 1999 the economy expanded by 0.2%. But although economic growth is picking up it is not growing fast enough to improve livelihoods. Economists have calculated that with so many people entering the workforce each year, the economy has to grow by 4-5% a year just to absorb these new workers. For tangible improvements, 7% is probably necessary and Indonesia is some way off that. People are looking to 2004 or 2005 for real improvements to start filtering through.

The tourist industry

Tourism is Indonesia's third largest foreign exchange earner: it generated US$6.1 billion in 1996. In the previous three years the figures were, working back from 1995 to 1993, US$5.2 billion, US$4.8 billion and US$3.6 billion. President Suharto tipped the sector to become the country's largest foreign exchange earner by the end of the century. In 1996 the number of visitors arriving in the country topped the 5 million mark for the first time (the reported figures was 5,034,472). This was up from 4.3 million in 1995, 4 million in 1994 and 3.4 million in 1993. The tourist authorities in Indonesia were predicting, at that time, that 8 million tourists would be visiting the country by 2000, and 11 million by 2005.

Ha! Even before the calamitous last few years, some analysts doubted that these targets would be met, and pointed to the slowdown in tourist arrivals since the spurt of the late 1980s and early 1990s. In comparison to fellow Asean members Singapore, Malaysia and Thailand, the Indonesian Tourist Promotion Board is wonderfully amateur. This situation was not helped by the removal of virtually their entire budget by the government as a result of the economic crisis and many overseas tourist information offices have been closed down. The rotund rhino that became the symbol of the 1991 Visit Indonesia Year is still propped up outside hotels across the country, indicating that while neighbouring countries fine tune their PR campaigns month-by-month, Indonesia stumbles along with Stalinist-style Five Year Plans. Nor is it just a question of marketing; there is a real shortage of facilities and tourist infrastructure beyond a few key destinations like Bali. Lombok, for example, has been waiting to explode now for close to a decade and the upgrading of the island's Selaparang Airport to international status – which has been imminent for years – is still set at some indeterminate date in the future. Tourist arrival figures are low compared with Thailand, Singapore or Malaysia. In terms of tourists per square kilometre, Thailand receives around 10 tourists per year, Indonesia around 1.

The last few years are ones that Indonesia's tourist supremos would prefer to forget. In no particular order: widespread forest fires and associated haze in 1997 and 1999; riots in 1998, 1999 and 2000; murderous communal conflict in 1998, 1999 and 2000; secessionist violence in 1997, 1998, 1999 and 2000; political instability; economic meltdown… With all this bad news being reported in the international media there is little wonder that the Indonesian Tourist Promotion Board has found it hard to stop arrivals plummeting.

Footnotes

7

Footnotes

429 Indonesian words and phrases

432 Glossary

435 Index

440 Maps

438 Shorts

Indonesian words and phrases

The Indonesian language – Bahasa Indonesia

There are more than 500 languages and dialects spoken across the archipelago, but it was Malay that was embraced as the national language – the language of unity – at the All Indonesia Youth Congress in 1928. Republicans had recognized for some time the important role that a common language might play in binding together the different religions and ethnic groups that comprised the East Indies. Malay had long been the *lingua franca* of traders in the archipelago, and, importantly, it was not identified with any particular group. Most importantly of all though, it was not a Javanese language. This muted any criticism that Java was imposing its culture on the rest of the country. Before long, Malay was being referred to as *Bahasa Indonesia* – the Indonesian language.

As visitors to Indonesia will quickly notice, the written language uses the Roman script. Through history, three scripts have been used in the country: 'Indian', Arabic and Roman. Indian-derived scripts include Old Javanese or Kawi, and Balinese. Arabic was associated with the spread of Islam and has tended to be confined to religious works. It proved to be particularly unsuited to use with Javanese. At the beginning of the 20th century, the Dutch assigned Ch A van Ophuysen to devise a system for Romanizing the Malay language. The Roman script gained popularity during the 1920s when the Indonesian nationalist movement associated its use with political change and modernity. In 1947 a number of spelling reforms were introduced of which the most important was the change from using 'oe' to 'u', so that 'Soekarno' and 'Soeharto' became, respectively, 'Sukarno' and 'Suharto'. Another series of spelling changes were introduced in 1972 to bring Bahasa Indonesia in line with Bahasa Melayu (Bahasa Malay). Nonetheless, as Bahasa Indonesia gained acceptance as a 'national' language, so it began to diverge from the Malay spoken in Malaysia. Today, although the two are mutually intelligible, there are noticeable differences between them in terms of both vocabulary and structure. The two countries' respective colonial legacy can be seen reflected in such loan words as *nomor*, from the Dutch for number in Indonesia, and *nombor* from the English in Malaysia.

The government has avidly promoted Bahasa Indonesia as the language of unity and it is now spoken in all but the most remote areas of the archipelago. Children are schooled in the national language, and television, radio and newspapers and magazines all help to propagate its use. But although most Indonesians are able to speak 'Bahasa', as it is known, they are likely to converse in their own language or dialect. Of the 500 other languages and dialects spoken in the country, the dominant ones are Sundanese, Javanese and Madurese (all three spoken on Java or Madura), Minang and Batak (on Sumatra), and Balinese.

In Indonesian, there are no tenses, genders or articles and sentence structure is relatively simple. Pronunciation is not difficult as there is a close relationship between the letter as it is written and the sound. Stress is usually placed on the second syllable of a word. For example, *restoran* (restaurant) is pronounced res-TO-ran.

Vowels

a is pronounced as *ah* in an open syllable, or as in *but* for a closed syllable.
e is pronounced as in *open* or *bed*.
i is pronounced as in *feel*.
o is pronounced as in *all*.
u is pronounced as in *foot*.
The letter *c* is pronounced as *ch* as in *change* or *chat*.
The *r*'s are rolled.
Plural is indicated by repetition, *bapak-bapak*.

Footnotes

Learning Indonesian

The list of words and phrases below is very rudimentary. For anyone serious about learning Indonesian it is best to buy a dedicated Indonesian language textbook or to enrol on a course. In Indonesia, there are courses on offer in Jakarta, Bali and Yogyakarta. A phrase book and/or some knowledge of the Indonesian language comes in very handy away from tourist sites.

Useful phrases

You will be asked constantly "Where you are going?" ("Wake Mana?"). To the Indonesians it is the common form of address. Most travellers reply "jalan, jalan" which means "walking, walking". Indonesians do not always seem very happy with this response. Instead try saying "cuci mata" which literally translates as "washing my eye"; ie relaxing. This brings a smile of real pleasure to Indonesians: they will feel you understand their customs. As an alternative you can say "makan angin" (literally) "eating the air".

Yes/no	*Ya/tidak*
Thank you [very much]	*Terima kasi h [banyak]*
Good morning (until 1100)	*Selamat pagi*
Good day (until 1500)	*Selamat siang*
Good afternoon (until dusk)	*Selamat sore*
Good evening	*Selamat malam*
Welcome	*Selamat datang*
Goodbye	
(said by the person leaving)	*Selamat tinggal*
Goodbye (said by the person staying)	*Selamat jalan*
Excuse me, sorry!	*Ma'af*
Where's the ...?	*... dimana?*
How much is ...?	*... berapa harganya?*
You're welcome, don't mention it	*Kembali*
I [don't] understand	*Saya [tidak] mengerti*
Sweet dreams (said as you take leave to people last thing at night)	*Mimpi Indan*

The hotel

How much is a room?	*Kamar berapa harga?*
Does the room have air-conditioning?	*Ada kamar yang ada AC-nya?*
I want to see the room first please	*Saya mau lihat kamar dulu*
Does the room have hot water?	*Ada kamar yang ada air panas?*
Does the room have a bathroom?	*Ada kamar yang ada kamar mandi?*

Travel

Where is the train station?	*Dimana stasiun kereta api?*
Where is the bus station?	*Dimana stasiun bis?*
How much to go to ...?	*Berapa harga ke ...?*
I want to go to ...	*Saya mau pergi ke ...*
I want to buy a ticket to ...	*Saya mau beli karcis ke ...*
Is it far?	*Ada jauh?*
Turn left/turn right	*Belok kiri/belok kanan*
Go straight on	*Terus saja*

				Days
Monday	*Hari Senin*	Saturday	*Hari Sabtu*	
Tuesday	*Hari Selasa*	Sunday	*Hari Minggu*	
Wednesday	*Hari Rabu*	today	*hari ini*	
Thursday	*Hari Kamis*	tomorrow	*hari besok*	
Friday	*Hari Jumat*			

				Numbers
1	*satu*	20	*dua puluh*	
2	*dua*	21–	*dua puluh*	
3	*tiga*		*satu ... etc*	
4	*empat*	30–	*tiga puluh ... etc*	
5	*lima*	100	*se-ratus*	
6	*enam*	101	*se-ratus satu ... etc*	
7	*tujuh*	150	*se-ratus l*	
8	*delapan*		*ima puluh*	
9	*sembilan*	200–	*dua ratus ... etc*	
10	*sepuluh*	1,000	*se-ribu*	
11	*se-belas*	2,000	*dua ribu*	
12	*dua-belas ... etc*	100,000	*se-ratus ribu*	
		1,000,000	*se-juta*	

				Basic Vocabulary
airletters	*surat udara, aerogram*	hot (temperature)	*panas*	
airmail	*pos udara*	hot (spicy)	*pedas*	
all right/good	*baik*	I/me	*saya*	
bank	*bank*	immigration office	*kantor imigrasi*	
bathroom	*kamar mandi/ kamar kecil*	island	*pulau*	
		letter	*surat*	
beach	*pantai*	market	*pasa*	
beautiful	*cantik*	medicine	*obat*	
big	*besar*	open	*masuk*	
boat	*prahu*	parcel	*paket*	
bus	*bis*	police	*polisi*	
bus station	*stasiun bis*	police station	*stasiun polisi*	
buy	*beli*	post card	*kartu pos*	
can	*boleh*	post office	*kantor pos*	
chemist	*apotek*	restaurant	*rumah makan*	
clean	*bersih*	room	*kamar*	
closed	*tutup*	ship	*kapal*	
day	*hari*	shop	*toko*	
delicious	*enak*	sick	*sakit*	
dentist	*doktor gigi*	small	*kecil*	
dirty	*kotor*	stamps	*perangko*	
doctor	*doktor*	stop	*berhenti*	
eat	*makan*	taxi	*taksi*	
envelope	*amplop*	ticket	*karcis*	
excellent	*bagus*	that	*itu*	
express	*ekspres*	they	*mereka*	
expensive	*mahal*	this	*ini*	
food	*makan*	toilet	*WC ("way say")*	
fruit	*buah*	town	*kota*	
hospital	*rumah sakit*	train station	*stasiun kereta api*	
hotel	*hotel/losmen/ penginapan/ wisma*	very	*sekali*	
		water	*air*	
		what	*apa*	

Footnotes

Glossary

A

Abdi dalem court servants of Java

Adat custom or tradition

Alang Torajan rice barn

Amitabha the Buddha of the Past (see Avalokitsvara)

Andesite volcanic building stone

Andong horse-drawn carriage

Angklung traditional Javanese bamboo musical instrument

Arhat statues of former Buddhist monks

Atavaka flesh-eating ogre

Avadana Buddhist narrative, telling of the deeds of saintly souls

Avalokitsvara also known as Amitabha and Lokeshvara, the name literally means "World Lord"; he is the compassionate male Bodhisattva, the saviour of Mahayana Buddhism and represents the central force of creation in the universe; usually portrayed with a lotus and water flask

B

Bahasa language, as in Bahasa Malaysia and Bahasa Indonesia

Bajaj three-wheeled motorized taxi

Banaspati East Javan term for kala makara (see kala)

Banjar Balinese village organization

Banua Torajan house

Batik a form of resist dyeing common in Malay areas)

Becak three-wheeled bicycle rickshaw

Bendi 2-wheeled, horse-drawn cart

Bhaga cult altar of Flores

Bodhi the tree under which the Buddha achieved enlightenment (*Ficus religiosa*)

Bodhisattva a future Buddha. In Mahayana Buddhism, someone who has attained enlightenment, but who postpones nirvana in order to help others reach the same state

Brahma the Creator, one of the gods of the Hindu trinity, usually represented with four faces, and often mounted on a hamsa

Brahmin a Hindu priest

Budaya cultural (as in Muzium Budaya)

Bupati regent

C

Candi sepulchral monument

Candi bentar split gate, characteristic of Balinese pura

Cap batik stamp

Chedi from the Sanskrit *cetiya* (Pali, *caitya*) meaning memorial. Usually a religious monument (often bell-shaped) containing relics of the Buddha or other holy remains. Used interchangeably with stupa

Cidomo Lombok's two-wheeled, pony carts

Cukong Chinese-owned corporations

Cultuurstelsel the Dutch `culture system' introduced in Java in the 19th century

Cunda see Tara

Cutch see Gambier

D

Dalang wayang puppet master

Dayak/Dyak collective term for the tribal peoples of Borneo

Delman horse-drawn carriage

Dharma the Buddhist law

Dipterocarp family of trees (Dipterocarpaceae) characteristic of Southeast Asia's forests

Dokar horse-drawn carriage

Durga the female goddess who slays the demon Mahisa, from an Indian epic story

Dvarapala temple door guardian

E

Epiphyte plant which grows on another plant (but usually not parasitic)

F

Fahombe stone-jumping of Nias Island

Feng shui the Chinese art of geomancy

G

Gambier also known as cutch, a dye derived from the bark of the bakau mangrove and used in leather tanning

Gamelan Javanese and Balinese orchestra of percussion instruments

Ganesh elephant-headed son of Siva

Garuda mythical divine bird, with predatory beak and claws, and human body; the king of birds, enemy of naga and mount of Vishnu

Gautama the historic Buddha

Golkar ruling party in Indonesia

Gopura crowned or covered gate; entrance to a religious area

Gunung mountain

H

Hamsa sacred goose, Brahma's mount; in Buddhism it represents the flight of the doctrine

Hariti child-eating demon who is converted to Buddhism

Hinayana 'Lesser Vehicle', major Buddhist sect in Southeast

Asia, usually termed Theravada Buddhism

I

Ikat tie-dyeing method of patterning cloth
Indra the Vedic god of the heavens, weather and war; usually mounted on a 3 headed elephant
Islam Waktu Telu Islam of Lombok

J

Jaba front court of Balinese temple **Jaba tengah** central court of Balinese temple
Janur Balinese bamboo `pennants'
Jataka(s) birth stories of the Buddha, of which there are 547; the last ten are the most important
Jeroan back court of Balinese temple

K

Kabupaten regency, Indonesian unit of administration
Kala (makara) literally, `death' or `black'; a demon ordered to consume itself; often sculpted over entranceways to act as a door guardian, also known as kirtamukha
Kalanaga same as the kalamakara but incorporating the mythical naga (serpent)
Kepala desa village headman
Kerangas from an Iban word meaning `land on which rice will not grow'
Kerapan sapi bull races of East Java and Madura
Keraton see kraton
Kinaree half-human, half-bird, usually depicted as a heavenly musician
Kirtamukha see kala
Klotok motorized gondolas of Banjarmasin
Kraton Javanese royal palace

Kris traditional Malay sword
Krishna an incarnation of Vishnu
Kulkul Balinese drum
Kuti living quarters of Buddhist monks

L

Lapar biasa `normal hunger'
Laterite bright red tropical soil/stone sometimes used as a building material
Linga phallic symbol and one of the forms of Siva. Embedded in a pedestal shaped to allow drainage of lustral water poured over it, the linga typically has a succession of cross sections: from square at the base through octagonal to round. These symbolize, in order, the trinity of Brahma, Vishnu and Siva
Lintel a load-bearing stone spanning a doorway; often heavily carved
Lokeshvara see Avalokitsvara
Lontar multi-purpose palm tree; the fronds were used for manuscript sheets
Losmen guesthouse

M

Mahabharata a Hindu epic text written about 2,000 years ago
Mahayana `Greater Vehicle', major Buddhist sect
Mandi Indonesian/Malay bathroom with water tub and dipper
Maitreya the future Buddha
Makara a mythological aquatic reptile, somewhat like a crocodile and sometimes with an elephant's trunk; often found, along with the kala, framing doorways
Mandala a focus for meditation; a representation of the cosmos
Meru name given to the tapered shrines of Bali
Meru the mountain residence of the gods; the centre of the universe, the cosmic mountain

Moko bronze dowry `drums' of Nusa Tenggara
Mudra symbolic gesture of the hands of the Buddha

N

Naga benevolent mythical water serpent, enemy of Garuda
Naga makara fusion of naga and makara
Nalagiri the elephant let loose to attack the Buddha, who calmed him
Nandi/Nandin bull, mount of Siva
Negara kingdom and capital, from the Sanskrit
Negeri also negri, state
Ngadhu cult altar of Flores
Nirvana `enlightenment', the Buddhist ideal
Nyi Loro Kidul Goddess of the South Seas

O

Odalan festival celebrating a Balinese temple's anniversary
Ojek motorcycle `taxi'
Ondel-ondel paired human figures given to newly-weds in Java

P

Paddy/padi unhulled rice
Padmasana stone throne
Padu-raksa ceremonial gate
Paliwijaya/Palawija a second crop, planted after rice
Pamedal Agung main gate
Pancasila Sukarno's five guiding principles
Pantai beach
Pasar market, from the Arabic `bazaar'
Pasisir Javanese coastal trading states
Pelni Indonesian state shipping line
Pemuda literally `youth', but historically refers to the Pemuda Movement against the Dutch
Pendopo open-sided pavilion of Java

Perahu/prau boat

Peranakan 'half caste', usually applied to part Chinese and part Malay people

Perintis 'pioneer' ships which ply minor routes between Indonesia's islands

PKI Perserikatan Komunis di Indonesia, the Indonesian Communist Party

Pradaksina pilgrims' clockwise circumambulation of a holy structure

Prajnaparamita the goddess of transcendental wisdom

Prang form of stupa built in the Khmer style, shaped rather like a corncob

Prasada see prasat

Prasat residence of a king or of the gods (sanctuary tower), from the Indian prasada

Pribumi indigenous (as opposed to Chinese) businessmen

Priyayi Javanese aristocracy

Pulau island

Puputan 'fight to the death')

Pura Balinese temple

Pusaka heirloom

R

Raja/rajah ruler

Raksasa temple guardian statues

Ramayana the Indian epic tale

Rumah adat customary or traditional house

S

Sago multi-purpose palm

Sal the Indian sal tree (*Shorea robusta*), under which the historic Buddha was born

Saka Hindu calendar used in Bali

Sakyamuni the historic Buddha

Sawah wet rice

Silat or bersilat, traditional Malay martial art

Singha mythical guardian lion

Siti Inggil literally `High Place' in a kraton; used for enthronements

Siva one of the Hindu triumvirate, the god of destruction and rebirth

Songket Malay textile interwoven with supplementary gold and silver yarn

Sravasti the miracle at Sravasti when the Buddha subdues the heretics in front of a mango tree

Sri Laksmi the goddess of good fortune and Vishnu's wife

Stele inscribed stone panel or slab

Stucco plaster, often heavily moulded

Stupa see chedi

Subak Balinese irrigation society

Susuhunan Hindu king or sultan

T

tamu market

Tara also known as Cunda; the four-armed consort of the Bodhisattva Avalokitsvara

Tau tau Torajan effigies of the deceased

Tavatimsa heaven of the 33 gods at the summit of Mount Meru

Theravada 'Way of the Elders'; major Buddhism sect also known as Hinayana Buddhism (`Lesser Vehicle')

Tirta holy water

Tongkonan Torajan ancestral house

Totok 'full blooded'; usually applied to Chinese of pure blood

Transmigration the Indonesian government sponsored resettlement of people from the Inner Islands to the Outer Islands

U

Ulama Muslim priest

Ulu jungle

Urna the dot or curl on the Buddha's forehead, one of the distinctive physical marks of the Enlightened One

Usnisa the Buddha's top knot or `wisdom bump', one of the physical marks of the

Enlightened One

V

Vishnu the Protector, one of the gods of the Hindu trinity, generally with four arms holding the disc, the conch shell, the ball and the club

VOC the Dutch East India Company or Vereenigde Oost-Indische Compagnie

W

Wali the nine Muslim saints of Java

Wallace's Line division between the Asian and Australasian zoological realms

Waringin banyan tree

Warung foodstall or small restaurant

Wayang traditional Malay shadow plays

Wayang Topeng masked dance of Java

Wuku Hindu-Javanese calendar, now primarily in use only in Bali

Index

A

Abadi 179
Abian Soan 177
accommodation 31
adat 343
Agung Gianyar Palace 150
Agung Girinatha, Pura 309
Agung, Mount 158
AIDS 54
Air Sanih 214
Air Terjun Gitgit 192, 194, 212
air travel 24
   domestic 34
airport information 25
airport tax 25
Al Miraj 51
Alas 306
Alor 361
Alor Kecil 362
Amed 181
Amlapura 176
Ampenan 263
Ampera 362
Anakalang District 378, 381
antiques 48
Anturan 204
architecture
   Bali 231
   Sasak 294
Armed Forces Day 50
art
   Bali 231
Asak 163
Atambua 393
Atapupu 394
Atimelang 362

B

Ba'a 395
background 427
Bahari Museum 343
Bahasa Indonesia 18
   See also 'language'
Bajawa 339
Bale Kambang 164
Bali 69
   background 224
Bali Barat National Park 218
Bali Museum 73
Balian Beach 222

Balina Beach 167
Balinese dancing course 213
Balinese names 236
Balinese painting 234
Balinese pura 231
Bangli 150
Bangsal 275
Banjar 209
Banjar Hot Springs 209
banks 23
Banu Nggulung 325
Banyualit 205
Banyumulek 294
Baranusa 364
Barong Ket 114
Baru, Mount 287
batik 49
Batu Koq 287
Batuan 128
Batubelig 92,95
Batubolong Temple 270
Batubulan 128
Batur, Lake 155
Batur, Mount 155
Batur, Pura 156
Baun 386
Bayan 286
beaches 14
Bebandem 163, 177
becaks 39
Bedugul 192
Bedulu 147
Bela 339
Belimbingsari 219
Belu 393
bemos 39
Bena 339
Benoa 117
Beratan 212
Berewa Beach 96
Besakih, Pura 158
Betun 394
bicycles 37,39
Bidadari 333
Bima-Raba 314
bird watching 134
bis kayu 39
bites, insects and snakes 57
Blanco, Antonio 131
Blanjong, Pura 98
   Inscription 98
Blanting 293
Blikan Blewut Museum 351
Blongas 299
boats 40
Bondokawango 382
Bondomaroto 377

Bongedu 339
Bongol 123
Bonnet, Rudolf 233
books 60
Borado 339
Botanical gardens
   Bali 192
Boti 390
Brahma Vlhara Asrama 209
Bratan, Lake 191
Brayut family planning 214
Budakling 179
Bugbug 163
Buitan 167
Bukarani 382
Bukit Demulih 153
Bukit Jati 153
Bukit Kusambi 177
Bukit Peninsula 113
Bukit Sari 131, 190
Buleleng Regency 195
bull racing
   Lovina Beach 202
   Negara 220
Bungaya 163
buses 35
business hours 26
Buyan, Ke 192
Buyan, Lake 191

C

Cakranegara 263
camping 33
Candi Dasa 169
Candikuning 193
Canggu 96
Canggu Beach 96
car hire 38
cargo ships 25
catamaran 259
Cecil Pantai 165
Cekik 217
Celuk 128
checklist 21
Chinese, Indonesia 418
Christianity 29, 243
climate 16
   Bali 230
   Lombok 303
clothing 20, 28, 49
communications 42
Communist puputan 228
Concordia Fort 385
conduct 27
consulates 20

corruption 422
cost of living 23
crafts
   Bali 235
   Lombok 304
credit cards 22
cremation 241
culture
   Bali 235
   Lombok 303
currency 22
customs 22

D

Dalem, Pura 213
dance
   Bali 244
   Jegog 246
   Kecak 244
   Kris 244
   Legong 245
   Sanghyang dedari 245
   Topeng 246
Dencarik 209
Denpasar 72
Desa Lembongan 110
diarrhoea 56
disabled travellers 26
diving 14
   Amed 181
   Benoa 117
   Gilis 284
   Maumere 354
   Menjangan, Pulau 212
   Nusa Lembongan 109
dolphins 201
Dompu 313
drama
   Bali 244
   Gambuh 247
dress 20, 28
drink 43
driving 38
drugs 27
Duda 186
Dulolong 362
Dutch colonization 225
Dutch fort 308
duty-free allowance 22

E

Egon, Mount 355
Eka Dasa Rudra 238
Ekas 299
electricity 26
email 42
embassies 20
Ende 343

F

ferries 40
festivals 50
   Bali 238
fish 56
Flores 329
   transport 329
food 43, 48
forts
   Concordia 385
   Dutch 308
fossils 402

G

Galubakul 381
Garebeg Maulad 51
gay travellers 26
Gedong Kirtya 200
geography
   Bali 228
   Flores 331
   Lombok 302
   Sumba 365
Gepupak (Desert) Point 296
geringsing 170
Gianyar 149
gifts 29
Gili Air 280
Gili Gede 265
Gili Meno 279
Gili Nanggu 265
Gili Poh 265
Gili Trawangan 277
Gilimanuk 217
Gilis, The 276
Goa Gajah 131
Goa Lawah 164,171
Goa Susu 287
Golo Curu 337
Green Turtle 99
Gunung Agung 182
Gunung Ara 326
Gunung Ranaka 337
Gunung Sirong 364

East Lombok 293
East Nusa Tenggara 319
   transport 322
economy
   Bali 249

Footnotes

H

handicrafts 15
Hari Pancasila 50
health 52
hill stations 14
 Ubud 130
Hinduism 29
history
 Bali 224
 Flores 330
 Lombok 300
 Sumba 366
 West Timor 384
holidays 50
horsecarts 39
hot springs
 Penatahan 190
hotels 31, 32
Hu'u 314

I

Ia, Mount 344
Idhul Adha 51
Idul Fitri 51
ikat 49
 double 170
 geringsing 170
Ile Ape 359
Imlek 50
immunisation 52
Independence Day 50
Indonesia Decade Pass 35
Inerie, Mount 339
inoculations 19
Inpres market 339
insects 55
internet access 42
Iseh 187
Islam Waktu Telu 303
Islamic holidays 51
Istana Tua 308

J

Jaganatha, Pura 73
Jagaraga 213
Japanese occupation 406
Jasi 163
java man 402
Jayaprana, Pura 212
Jembrana 221
jewellery 49
Jimbaran 114
Jontana 359
Jopu 349
Julah 215
Jungut Batu 110
Jungutan 186

K

Kabunduk 381
Kakamauta 364
Kalabahi 362
Kalala 376
Kalibukbuk 205
Kaliuda 373,376
Kamasan village 164
Kambing, Nusa
 (Goat Island) 171
Kampung Komodo 326
Kampung Lama 359
Kanawa Island 333
Kapal 189
Kapundak 373
Karangasem 176
Karangasem
 Regency 161
Kartini Day 50
Kawangu 373
Kawi, Gunung 147
Kebo Edan, Pura 134
Kediri 190
Kedisan 156
Kefamenanu 392
Kelimutu 347
Kelimutu, Mount
 344, 347
Kemenuh 128
Kenaikan Isa Al-Masih 50
Kencana Beach 309
Kerambitan 223
Kerandangan 273
Kherta Ghosa 163
Kintamani 156, 157
Klungkung 163
Kodi District 382
Kolo 316
Komodo 324, 332
Kota Raja 291
Kua Popnam 392
Kupang 385
Kuta (Bali) 79
Kuta (Lombok) 295

L

Labuan Lalang 212
Labuanbajo 332
Labuhan Haji 209, 293
Labuhan Lombok 292, 293
Labuhan Pandan 293
Labuhan Sape 318
Labunan Poh 265
Ladalero 351
Lai Tarung 381
Lailuru 375
Lamalera 359
Lambaleda 337
Langa 339

language 18, 430
 Bali 236
 East Nusa Tenggara 323
language courses 18
Larantuka 356
Lasiana Beach 386
Lawata Beach 316
Le Mayeur Museum 98
Legian 85
Lembar 259,265,299
Lembata 358
Lembongan, Nusa
 109,164
Lendang Nangka 291
Lerahinga Beach 359
Les waterfall 216
lesbian travellers 26
Lewoleba 358
Lingsar, Lombok 290
Lipah Beach 183
Loloan Timur 221
Lombok 270
Lovina Beach 201
Loyok 291
Luhur, Pura 190

M

Maduwe Karang, Pura
 213
magazines 60
Maghilewa 339
Malaria 55
Mali Beach 362
Maluk 307
Mamboro 378
Manggis 167
Manggis Beach 167
Manuakalada 378
maps 64
Maria 316
marriage
 Bali 241
Maru 373
Mas 128
Masbaggik 291,294
Masinlulik 394
Maslete 392
Masopahit, Pura 74
Mata Yangu
 waterfall 381
Matakakeri 381
Mataram 263
Maumere 350
Maumere Cathedral 351
Mawan Beach 299
Mawi 299
Mayura Water Palace
 and Gardens,
 Cakranegara 263
Mayura, Pura 264
Mbongawani
 market 343
Medewi Beach 222
medical care 52
Meja, Mount 344

Melolo 373, 375
Mengwi, Bali 190
Menjangan, Pulau 212
Mesjid Nurul Huda 309
metalwork 49
Monbang 362
money 22
 Nusa Tenggara 323
Moni 347, 349
Moon of Pejeng 134
Mota Ain 394
motorbike hire 39
Moyo Island 311
Muharram 51
Muncan 186
Munduk 194
museums 15
music 244, 248

N

Nangalala Beach 344
Narmada 289
national parks 14
Ndana Island 396
Negara 220
Nemberala 396
newspapers 42
Ngalupolo 345
Nggela 345, 349
Ngis 163
Niki Niki 390
Nilulat 392
Nita 352
Nuabari 352
Nuabosi 344
Nusa Ceningan 110
Nusa Dua 113, 123
Nusa Lembongan 109
Nusa Penida 109, 110
Nusa Tenggara Timur
 Museum 386
Nyepi 50

O

Octopus Bay 394
odalan 248
Odalan 238
Oehala Waterfall 391
Oelolok 392
oil 421
Oinlasi 390
ojeks 39
Old Wogo 339
oplets 39
Otvai 362

P

Pacung 215
Padang cuisine 46
Padangaji 187
Padangbai 165
Paigoli 378
painting 49

palaces 15
Palasari 219, 220
Panca Walikrama 238
Pancasari 193
Pancasila 29, 410
Pantai Cecil 165
Pantai Morossi 379, 382
Pantai Rua 379, 382
Pantar Island 364
Paronabaroro 382
Pasar Agung, Pura 187
Pasar Potulando 343
passports 19
Pasunga 381
Pau 373, 375
Pejeng 133
Pelangan 265
Pelni 40
Pemaron 204
Pemuteran 210, 219
Penatahan 190
Penataran Agung, Pura
 153, 158
Penelokan 156, 157
Pengantap 299
Pengsong, Mount 264
Pengubengan, Pura
 160
Penida, Nusa 109,164
Penujak 294
people
 Flores 332 Lombok
 303
 Bali 235
Perasi 163
Pererean Beach 96
Pero 382
Perumtel 42
Petitenget 92
Pondok Batu, Pura 215
Pongkor 337
Poreng Valley 326
ports 25
Portuguese church,
 Sikka 352
postal services 42
Potulando Pasar 343
Prai Goli 378
Praijing 378
Prailiang 373
Prailiu 372
Pramuka Hill 332
Pringgasela 291
prohibitions 22
Pujung 157
Pulaki 210
Pulau Besar 355
Pulau Indah 355
Pulau Pantar 364
Pulau Pondok 355
Pulli 379
Puputan 228
Puputan Square 72
Pura 231
Purajati 155

Purbakala
  Archaeological
  Museum 134
Puri Agung 176
Puri Saren 131
Puri Semarapura 163
Putung 167, 186, 187

Q

quinine 53

R

rabies 58
radio 43, 68
rafting 15
  Telaga Waja River 76
Ramadan 51
Ramayana ballet 246
Rambut Siwi Temple 221
Ranamese Crater, Lake
  337
Ratenggaro 382
religion 29
  Bali 236
Rende 373, 375
Reo 337, 338
restaurant price guide
  44
rice 43
Rinca Island 328, 332
Rinjani Mount 286
Rinjani, Mount 286, 292,
  302
Riung (Nangamese) 341
Rote (Roti) 395
Rowok 299
Rungkang 294
Rupiah 22
Ruteng 336

S

Sabobo 333
Sabu Island 398
Sade 294
safety 30
  Lombok 262
  West Timor 384
Sakenan, Pura 99
Sambalun Bumbung 293
Sambelia 293
Sambiranteng 216
Sambori Lama 316
Sampalan 110
Sangeang Volcano 316
Sangeh 131, 190
Sangsit 212
Sanur 97
Sao Wisata beach 351
Sape 318
Sapit 288, 292
Savu 398
Sawan 213
seaweed 277

Seba 398
Sebatu 157
security 30
Segara Anak 287
Seketeng Market 309
Selat 187, 188
Selong Blanak 299
Semau Island 387
Sembalun Bumbung
  288
Sembalun Lawang
  288, 293
Sembiran 215
Seminyak 92
Senaru 287
Senggigi 270
Sengkidu 167
Sengkidu Village 168
Sepi 299
Serangan Island 99
Seririt 210
Sesajen 238
Sesoat 290
Seventeen Island
  National Park 341
shopping 15, 48
Sibembunut 153
Sibetan 186
Sidan 153
Sideman 187, 188
Sikka 352
Singaraja 198
Singsing Air Terjun 209
Siri Beach 286
sleeping 31
snake bites 57
Soa 339
Sodan 378
Soe 389
Soekarno's house 343
Spies, Walter 233
student travellers 27
Sukamaju 313
Sukarara 294
Sultan's Palace 315
Sumba 365
Sumbanese villages and
  houses 368
Sumbawa 305
Sumbawa Besar 308
sunburn 57
Suranadi 290
Suranadi, Pura 290
surfing 15
  Bukit Peninsula 113
  Canggu 96
  Hu'u 314
  Kalala 376
  Maluk 307
  Medewi Beach 222
  Namberala 396
  Nusa Lembongan 109
  Pantai Rua 382

T

Taekas 392
Tahun Baru 50
Takpala 362
Taliwang 307
Taman Ayun, Pura 190
Taman Burung Bali Bird
  Park 128
Taman Gili 164
Taman Narmada 289
Taman Nasional Bali
  Barat 211
Tamblingan, Lake 194
Tambora, Mount 312
Tamkesi 392
Tanah Lingis 179
Tanah Lot 189
Tanaharon 179
Tanjung Aan 296
Tanjung Ringgit 299
Tarung 377
Taun 265
taxis 39
Tegalgundul 97
Tegen Koripan, Pura 157
Tejakula 215
telephones 42
television 43
temples 15
Temukus 206
Tenganan 170
Tetebatu 291
Tibubiyu 223
Timbrah 163
time 26
Timor, West 383
tipping 29, 47
Tirta Pura 160
Tirta Empul 149
Tirta Telaga Tista 186
Tirtagangga 178
tooth-filing 243
Tossi 382
tour operators 16
tourism
  Bali 249
  Lombok 304
tourist offices
  in Indonesia 25
  overseas 17
tours 16
Toya Bungkah 155, 157
Toyapakeh 111
transport 24
  domestic 34
  planning 13
travellers' cheques 23
trekking 14
  Komodo 325
  Lake Batur 155
  Mount Egon 355
  Mount Kelimutu 347
  Mount Rinjani 286
  Mount Tambora 312
Trunyan 156

Trunyon 216
Tuban 88
Tukad Mungga 204
Tulamben 185, 216
turtles 272

U

Ubud 130
Ujung 177
Ulun Danau Bratan Pura
  191
Ulun Siwi Temple 114
Uluwatu Temple
  114, 121
Umabara 373, 375
Umelas 97

V

vaccinations 19, 52
visas 19
voltage 26

W

Wafat Isa Al-Masih 50
Waiara beach 351
Waicicu Beach 332
Waigalli 379
Waikabubak 377
Waingapu 372
Wainyapu 382
Waisak Day 50
Waiterang Bay 355
Waiwuang 379
Waktu Telu Temple 290
Wallace,
  Alfred Russel 302
Wanokaka 378
Warpostel 42
Wartel 42
water 47
Watu 339
Watubilapi 352
Wayang kulit 246
Wayang puppets 50
weaving 50
weaving factories 263
websites 18, 65
weights and measures
  26
Werdi Budaya Art Centre
  74
West Nusa Tenggara
  255
West Nusa Tenggara
  Provincial Museum 263
white river rafting
  See 'rafting'
wildlife 14
Wodong 352, 355
Wogo Lama 339
Wolotopo 345
Wolowaru 349
women travellers 27

woodcarving 50
words and phrases 429,
  430, 431
working in Bali 27
Wunga 373

Y

Yeh Gangga 223
  Pura 191
Yeh Pulu 132

Z

Zaid Bachmid 373

Shorts

53	A miracle of nature: the devil's powder
408	A stroll along Jalan history
73	Bali highlights
23	Banks, credit card cash withdrawals
214	Brayut family planning
144	Bronze kettledrums of Vietnam
36	Bus prices
241	Caru
243	Christianity on Bali
181	Cloth as art: Ikat in Southeast Asia
252	Cockfighting - Tajen
246	Dance performances on Bali
38	Driving in Indonesia
323	East Nusa Tenggara highlights
20	Embassies and consulates overseas
407	Expansion of Dutch influence and control
32	Hotel price guide
326	Indonesia's living dinosaur: the Komodo dragon
48	Indonesian food glossary
413	Indonesian political parties
17	Indonesian Tourist Promotion offices overseas
303	Islam Waktu Telu
52	Islamic festivals for 2002
360	Lamalera's whaling
259	Lombok highlights
301	Lombok's crafts
403	Major pre-colonial powers
182	Mount Agung
28	MTV has a lot to answer for!
237	Orientation and directions
410	Pancasila: Sukarno's five principles
378	Pasola: of worms and warriors
240	Penjor and janur
421	PERC put Indonesia top in terms of corruption
44	Restaurant price guide
277	Seaweed farming
242	Self-immolation and human sacrifice in 1633
376	Sumba death rites
370	Sumba's megalithic tombs
160	The 1979 festival of Eka Dasa Rudra at Pura Besakih
178	The Bali Aga: the original Balinese
239	The Balinese calendars: saka and wuku
191	The Balinese pagoda: the meru
238	The banjar
229	The gift of water: rice and water in Bali
99	The Green Turtle
368	The ikat hinggi blankets of Sumba
363	The Moko drum currency debâcle
357	The old Catholics of Larantuka
272	The plight of turtles on Bali and Lombok
418	The politics of envy: the Chinese in Indonesia
227	The sign of the swastika
371	The Sumbanese slave trade
331	The textiles of Flores
405	The VOC - the world's first multinational
335	To build in pairs: the Ngadhu and Bhaga
26	Touching down, Bali
250	Tourism and culture in Bali
391	Traditional buildings in Boti village
163	Traditional villages and festivals of Karangasem
415	Two years of living dangerously
302	Wallace's line

Maps

183 Amed area & Tulamben	**260** Lombok Island
287 Around Mount Rinjani	**203** Lovina Beach
394 Atambua	**205** Kalibukbuk
226 Bali, Eight regencies of	**264** Mataram
196 Bali, North	**266** Mataram centre
148 Bali, North and east	**351** Maumere
232 Bali Pura	**124** Nusa Dua
78 Bali, South	**109** Nusa Lembongan
218 Bali, West coast	**110** Nusa Penida
151 Bangli	**165** Padangbai
393 Belu Region, The	**40** Pelni ports
177 Bemo stops from Amlapura	**159** Pura Besakih
118 Benoa	**338** Reo
315 Bima	**341** Riung
172 Candi Dasa East	**258** Route map of direct flights
171 Candi Dasa West	within Nusa Tenggara
75 Denpasar	**336** Ruteng
322 East Nusa Tenggara	**102** Sanur
344 Ende	**271** Senggigi beach
348 Around Ende	**342** Seventeen Isles National Park
330 Flores	**199** Singaraja
278 Gili Islands	**390** Soe
132 Goa Gajah	**366** Sumba Island
147 Gunung Kawi	**309** Sumbawa Besar
115 Jimbaran Bay	**306** Sumbawa Island
162 Karangasem	**89** Tuban
328 Komodo Island	**136** Ubud
324 Komodo National Park	**129** Around Ubud
386 Kupang	**138** Central Ubud
80 Kuta (Bali)	**122** Uluwatu
295 Kuta (Lombok)	**377** Waikabubak
333 Labuanbajo	**372** Waingapu
86 Legian	**383** West Timor

Footnotes

Will you help us?

We try as hard as we can to make each Footprint Handbook as up-to-date and accurate as possible but, of course, things always change. Many people write to us – with corrections, new information, or simply comments. If you want to let us know about an experience or adventure – hair-raising or mundane, good or bad, exciting or boring or simply something rather special – we would be delighted to hear from you. Please give us as precise information as possible, quoting the edition number (you'll find it on the front cover) and page number of the Handbook you are using. Your help will be greatly appreciated, especially by other travellers. In return we will send you details about our special guidebook offer.

email Footprint at:
BAL1_online@footprintbooks.com
or write to:

Elizabeth Taylor
Footprint Handbooks
6 Riverside Court
Lower Bristol Road
Bath
BA2 3DZ
UK

Advertisers

84 AquaMarine Diving, Bali
16, 441 Bali Barong Tours, USA
441 Bali Hotels, Indonesia
17 Exodus Travels Ltd, UK
206 Krisna Enterprises, UK
139 Villa Kerti Yasa, Indonesia

A

Indonesian Ocean

Boat to Ujungpandang,
Selatan

Tengah Islands

Map 2

NUSA TENGGARA BARAT

LOMBOK

Flores Sea

Medang Island

Sebaru

Mintaunae

Pancasila

Calabai

Ketupa

Moyo Island

▲ *Mount Tambora*

B

Saleh Bay

Labuhan
Carik

Anyer

Kali Putah

Blanting

Gili Lawang

Santong

Batu Koq

Bayan

Sayang

Sembalun

Sambelia

Lab Pandan

Utan

Mount Rinjani
(3,726m)

Lawang

Mount Baru

Labuan

Sumbawa Besal

Semongkat

Selelos

Segara Anak Lake

Labuan

Lape

Labuhan
Jambu

Timbanuh

Poto
Tano

Alas

Semanung

Batu
Tering

Suranadi

Tetebatu

Lombok

Aik Mel

Narmada

Kopang

Masbaggik

Lenanguar

Plampang

Empang

Sakra

Labuhan
Haji

Taliwang

Beleka

Praya

Keruak

Mujur

Jerowaru

Jereweh

Lunyuk

Ropang

▲ *Mount Takan*

Batu

Nampar

Jerowaru

Alas Strait

Awang Bay

Ikas

Tanjung
Ringgit

Kuta

Sunut

Maluk

Sekongkang

SUMBAWA

Gumbang Bay

Bumgang

Savu Sea

C

4   5   6

Map 2

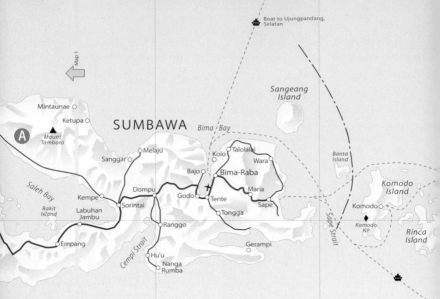

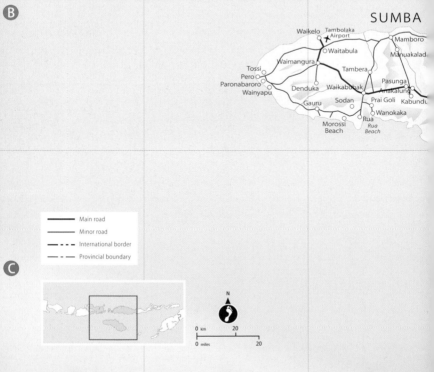

SUMBAWA

Mintaunae
Ketupa
Mount Tambora
Melaju
Sanggar
SUMBAWA
Bima Bay
Kolo
Talolalai
Wara
Bajo
Bima-Raba
Saleh Bay
Kempe
Dompu
Godo
Maria
Rakit Island
Labuhan Jambu
Sorintai
Tente
Sape
Ranggo
Tongga
Empang
Gerampi
Cempi Strait
Hu'u
Nanga Rumba

Sangeang Island
Banta Island
Komodo Island
Sape Strait
Komodo
Komodo NP
Rinca Island

Boat to Ujungpandang, Selatan

NUSA TENGGARA TIMOR *Sumba Strait*

SUMBA

Waikelo
Tambolaka Airport
Waitabula
Mamboro
Manuakalad
Waimangura
Tambera
Tossi
Pero
Paronabaroro
Wainyapu
Denduka
Waikabubak
Pasunga
Anakalung
Kabundu
Gauru
Sodan
Prai Goli
Wanokaka
Morossi Beach
Rua
Rua Beach

Main road
Minor road
International border
Provincial boundary

N

0 km 20
0 miles 20

Map 3

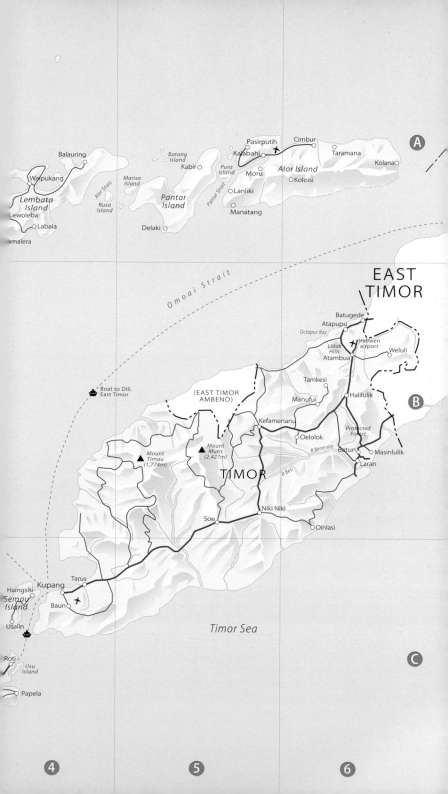

What the papers say

"If 'the essence of real travel' is what you have been secretly yearning for all these years, then Footprint are the guides for you."
Under 26

"Footprint can be depended on for accurate travel information and for imparting a deep sense of respect for the lands and people they cover."
World News

"Footprint Handbooks, the best of the best."
Le Monde, Paris

"Intelligently written, amazingly accurate and bang up-to-date. Footprint has combined nearly 80 years' experience with a stunning new format to bring us guidebooks that leave the competition standing."
John Pilkington, writer and broadcaster

Mail order
Available worldwide in bookshops and on-line. Footprint travel guides can also be ordered directly from us in Bath, via our website **www.footprintbooks.com** or from the address on the imprint page of this book.

Liz Capaldi

Liz Capaldi is a freelance writer with a long-standing interest in the East having grown up in Japan. She began as a researcher and writer in the art world and her articles have appeared in such publications as The International Herald Tribune, The Chicago Tribune, Collector's Guide and Arts Review. More recently she was editor and joint organizer of a festival of Japanese culture and art in Britain. Her great love, though, is Bali and she has spent many months exploring the island and travelling more widely through the Indonesian archipelago.

Joshua Eliot

Joshua has a long-standing interest in Asia. He was born in Calcutta, grew up in Hong Kong, has worked in rural Thailand, and teaches about Southeast Asia. He is the author and editor of several books on the region and has conducted research in Thailand, Sumatra and Laos. Joshua has been travelling in the region for over 20 years and he speaks Thai, and some Lao and Indonesian.

Jane Bickersteth

Jane has worked on the Southeast Asia series of the Footprint guides since the first edition in 1992. She has been visiting the region for over 15 years, including a year there whilst she researched the first edition of the Footprint Indonesia Handbook. Jane is associate editor of TravelMole, the on-line community for travel professionals.

Jasmine Saville

Jasmine's interest in Indonesia stems from her academic background in political economy and environmental issues. As a writer, the kaleidoscope of cultures, the rich ecology and the beautiful landscapes of the Eastern Islands are an inspiration and an education. She researched this portion of the guide while Indonesia was in the midst of profound political, social and economic change.

Acknowledgements

Thanks to the following readers who have written to us with comments and updates for this new edition: Aprianto, Indonesia; Jana Baard, The Netherlands; Andrea Bindel & Jens Zimmermann, Germany; Richard Boustead, Indonesia; Roy and Audrey Bradford, Spain; Morten Burmeister, Germany; P.A. Degens, Australia; E. Dunkerley, UK; Carl Gay, UK; Rt Reverend Richard Harries, UK; Tracey Hughes, UK; Hengky Kondoy, Indonesia; Marcel Lootens, Belgium; Selwyn McVean, Singapore; Elizabeth Morrell; Mike Napier, UK; M.G.Nicholson, UK; Eckehard Quin, Austria; Alan Reeve, UK; Peter Rendle, UK; Kim Saunders, UK; Marilyn Staib, UK; Markus Steinberg; Christian Strombeck, Germany; Juliane Thiessen, Germany; Simon Tonge, Indonesia; Anwar Wahyudi; Peter York, Ireland; Indonesia; Dirk Zeiler, Germany.

And a special mention to Richard Boustead in Sanur, Indonesia, for all his help, information and kindness.

The health section was compiled by Dr David Snashall, Senior Lecturer in Occupational Health, United Medical Schools of Guy's and St Thomas' Hospitals and Chief Medical Adviser, Foreign and Commonwealth Office, London.